# THE CLASSICS OF WESTERN SPIRITUALITY
## A Library of the Great Spiritual Masters

President and Publisher
Kevin A. Lynch, C.S.P.

## EDITORIAL BOARD

Bernard McGinn—Professor of Historical
Theology and History of Christianity, University of Chicago
Divinity School, Chicago, Ill.

John Meyendorff—Professor of Church History, Fordham
University, Bronx, N.Y., and Professor of Patristics and Church
History, St. Vladimir's Seminary, Tuckahoe, N.Y.

Seyyed Hossein Nasr—Professor of Islamics, Department of
Religion, Temple University, Philadelphia, Pa., and Visiting Professor,
Harvard University, Cambridge, Mass.

Heiko A. Oberman—Director, Institute fuer
Spaetmittelalter und Reformation, Universitaet Tuebingen, West
Germany.

Alfonso Ortiz—Professor of Anthropology, University of
New Mexico, Albuquerque, N. Mex.; Fellow, The Center for
Advanced Study, Stanford, Calif.,

Raimundo Panikkar—Professor, Department of Religious
Studies, University of California at Santa Barbara, Calif.

Jaroslav Pelikan—Sterling Professor of History and Religious
Studies, Yale University, New Haven, Conn.

Fazlar Rahman—Professor of Islamic Thought, Department of Near
Eastern Languages and Civilization, University of
Chicago, Chicago, Ill.

Annemarie B. Schimmel—Professor of Hindu Muslim Culture,
Harvard University, Cambridge, Mass.

Sandra M. Schneiders—Assistant Professor of New
Testament Studies and Spirituality, Jesuit School of Theology,
Berkeley, Calif.

Huston Smith—Thomas J. Watson Professor of Religion,
Adjunct Professor of Philosophy, Syracuse University, Syracuse, N.Y.

John R. Sommerfeldt—Professor of History, University of
Dallas, Irving, Texas.

David Steindl Rast—Monk of Mount Savior Monastery,
Pine City, N.Y.

William C. Sturtevant—General Editor, Handbook of North
American Indians, Smithsonian Institution, Washington, D.C.

David Tracy—Professor of Theology, University of Chicago
Divinity School, Chicago, Ill.

Victor Turner—William B. Kenan Professor in
Anthropology, The Center for Advanced Study, University of
Virginia, Charlottesville, Va.

Kallistos Ware—Fellow of Pembroke College, Oxford;
Spalding Lecturer in Eastern Orthodox Studies, Oxford
University, England.

# EARLY DOMINICANS

## Selected Writings

EDITED WITH AN INTRODUCTION BY
SIMON TUGWELL, O.P.

PREFACE BY
FATHER VINCENT DE COUESNONGLE, O.P.

PAULIST PRESS
NEW YORK • RAMSEY • TORONTO

Cover Art
*Saint Dominic* by Guido da Siena, Italian mid-thirteenth century Sienese School. Courtesy of the Fogg Art Museum, Harvard University.

Library of Congress
Catalog Card Number: 82-81686

ISBN: 0-8091-2414-9 (paper)
0-8091-0325-7 (cloth)

Published by Paulist Press
545 Island Road, Ramsey, N.J. 07446

Printed and bound in the
United States of America

# Contents

# CONTENTS

### Section II
### WILLIAM PERALDUS'
### SERMON ON PRAYER
### 163

### Section III
### HUMBERT OF ROMANS'
### TREATISE ON THE
### FORMATION OF PREACHERS
### 179

### Appendix to Humbert
### A SELECTION FROM
### "THE GIFT OF FEAR"
### 371

# CONTENTS

## Section IV
## THE DOMINICAN
## FAMILY
## 385

## Appendix
## THE EARLY DOMINICAN
## CONSTITUTIONS
## 453

## Bibliography
## NOTES ON TEXTS
## AND AUTHORS
## 471

ix

### Editor of this Volume

SIMON TUGWELL, O.P., has been teaching Dominican spirituality since 1971 at the Dominican study house in Oxford. Since 1976 he has been Regent of Studies there. He also lectures in spiritual theology, patristics and ancient philosophy. For a part of each year he lectures for the Institute of Spirituality at the Pontifical University of St. Thomas in Rome (the Angelicum), and at the Study House for Dominican Sisters in Rome.

He has published numerous articles in a wide variety of journals, both scholarly and popular. His books include *Prayer: Keeping Company with God, Prayer in Practice, Reflections on the Beatitudes* and, most important for readers of this present volume, *The Way of the Preacher.* He has lectured and preached in many different countries and continents.

He was educated at Lancing College, Sussex, England and at Corpus Christi College, Oxford, where he read classics and English, before entering the Dominican Order.

### Author of the Preface

FATHER VINCENT DE COUESNONGLE, O.P., has been Master of the Order of Preachers—82nd successor of Saint Dominic—since 1974. Born in Quimper, Brittany in 1916, he taught moral theology in France, then became responsible for education in his Province of Lyons, and finally was in Rome as an Assistant General to the former Master of the Order before being elected to lead the Dominicans. He is a member of the Vatican's Congregation for Religious, is Vice-President of the Union of Superiors General, and was a representative of the religious orders at the last two Synods of Bishops. A collection of his letters to the Order, *The Courage of the Future,* was recently published in English (Dominican Publications, Dublin).

# Preface

For the last fifty years, studies on the origin of the Order of Preachers and critical editions of texts have been multiplying. In many countries, there has been a desire to make this research available to the larger public, lest it remain the sole domain of specialists.

Father Simon Tugwell, of the English Province, Regent of Studies of the Dominican convent in Oxford, who also teaches a course at the Pontifical University of St. Thomas Aquinas in Rome, is well known for his writings on Dominican life. He allies with a meticulous historical scholarship the wish to read the sources afresh, bearing in mind the circumstances of our own time—an approach not lacking in originality. This explains the interest aroused in me by this volume, *Early Dominicans*, which is part of the series Classics of Western Spirituality.

It is not simply from brotherly affection for the author that I am introducing this work today. It happens that he is touching on one of my deepest convictions: the discovery of the origins of the Order is ever to be revived, and all members of the Dominican Family need translations of texts similar to this one, in order to be able to live out our distinctive charism more intensely in today's world and today's church, without losing anything of its original vitality.

I note with pleasure the richness of the Introduction and the notes. The author has opened to us a vast panorama, yet he does not disdain to grapple at times with points of scholarship still discussed by the best specialists.

In several places, Father Tugwell has recourse to manuscript sources not yet published. His work, thus, brings new light for a better understanding of Humbert of Romans, the fifth Master of the Order, whose influence on Dominican institutions and the development of the Order is well known.

This return to the thought of St. Dominic and to the insights of

# PREFACE

the first generations of Dominicans, which is manifest in this book, is in harmony with the last Vatican Council in its orientation towards an "aggiornamento" of the religious life. Far from burying us in the past, the selection of readings and the presentation of them offered to us by Father Tugwell opens to us the future.

For anyone who knows how to read the history of the Order with an ear to the cry of the contemporary world, the charism of St. Dominic has an astonishing youthfulness. We are deeply grateful to Father Simon Tugwell for helping us in this rediscovery of what is essential and what is permanent.

Vincent de Couesnongle, O.P.
*Master of the Order of Friars Preachers*

Given at Santa Sabina, Rome
*April 25, 1981*

# Foreword

This volume contains a selection of thirteenth-century texts illustrating the life and spirituality of the early Dominicans. It is natural that the central text should be about preaching and what it means to be a preacher, since the Dominicans were founded specifically to be an Order of Preachers. The treatise *On the Formation of Preachers* by Humbert of Romans, the fifth Master of the Dominican Order, is the most authoritative document from the period on the spirituality and attitudes that are appropriate to those whose vocation it is to be preachers.

St. Dominic himself wrote almost nothing; the only surviving personal letter of his is reproduced here. Otherwise, to gain a picture of the founder of the Order, it is necessary to look at a variety of historical sources, and so there is a selection here of texts about St. Dominic.

Since Dominic very deliberately created a structure for his Order that would remain flexible and adaptable to new personalities and new situations, we need also to look at some of his companions and followers if we are to grasp the mood and vitality of his Order. Accordingly, there is also a selection of texts by and about some of the more interesting thirteenth-century Dominicans apart from the founder and in addition to Humbert of Romans. Pride of place must go to St. Dominic's congenial successor, Blessed Jordan of Saxony, who is well represented here.

St. Dominic established not only the Order of Friars Preachers, but also several convents of nuns; then, in the course of the thirteenth century, various organisations of lay people also became attached to the Order. So a final section in this book deals with what is now known as "the Dominican family," consisting of nuns and sisters and laity, as well as the friars.

For reasons of space, St. Thomas Aquinas and St. Albert the

# FOREWORD

Great are not included here; it is hoped that a separate volume in this series will be devoted to these two great masters.

And, since this volume confines itself to the thirteenth century, several interesting developments that occurred later on in the Order are not represented here. The German mystical movement, for instance, in which Dominicans such as Meister Eckhart, Blessed Henry Suso and John Tauler played an important part, belongs, at least as far as Dominicans are concerned, to the fourteenth century. Luis of Granada, who was influential amongst others on St. Francis of Sales, and Domingo Bañez, who was one of St. Teresa's favourite spiritual advisers, belong to the sixteenth century. St. Catherine of Siena (fourteenth century) and Savonarola (fifteenth century) have already featured in other volumes in this series.

But, however important later developments may be, they cannot be understood without reference to the beginnings of the Order. This volume provides the reader with a wide range of material concerning these beginnings. It aims to communicate something of the first excitement and originality of the early Preachers. And, through St. Dominic and his companions, we are invited to contemplate, from a particular point of view, the example of our Lord himself, who went about tirelessly proclaiming the gospel of the Kingdom of God, and who still calls his church to follow him and to proclaim to all the nations of the world the liberating truth that he himself proclaimed, and that he himself is.

# Introduction

## I. The Problem of Dominican Spirituality

Some religious Orders in the Middle Ages produced unmistakable and obviously important "spiritual writers". No librarian would have any hesitation about classifying most of the works of the great Cistercian fathers as spiritual,[1] and it would not be difficult to identify the spiritual writings of a man like Hugh of St. Victor († 1142).[2] In the thirteenth century, the Franciscans are evidently engaged in producing spiritual works;[3] some of the works of St. Bonaventure (c. 1217–1274) have already appeared in this series.[4] And in due course the Dominicans too began to write books that have found their way into the spirituality sections of our libraries. In the critical edition of the works of Savonarola (1452–1498) there are two volumes of *Operette Spirituali*,[5] and, before that, there are the *Spiritual Letters* of Bl. John Dominic (c. 1355–1419),[6] not to mention the works of the famous German Dominican mystics, Meister Eckhart (c. 1260–1328), Bl. Henry Suso (c. 1295–1366) and John Tauler († 1361),[7] or the *Treatise on the Spiritual Life* by St. Vincent Ferrer (c. 1350–1419),[8] or the writings of St. Catherine of Siena (c. 1347–1380).[9] But in the thirteenth century, the century of the Dominican Order's birth, one is hard pressed to find any spiritual books at all, let alone "spiritual classics". There are the letters of Bl. Jordan of Saxony, which fill a slim volume and which have a modest claim to be regarded as a classic (some of them are included in this volume); there is an unpublished treatise from the end of the century, written by the novice master of Toulouse for the encouragement of his novices, but, though it enjoyed a certain success in the Order, it is certainly no classic.[10] There are the German writings of Mechtild of Magdeburg (c. 1207–c. 1282), who was for a time associated with the Dominicans; but she was not actually a Dominican, and, in fact, ended her days as a Cistercian nun.[11] As we

1

should expect from an Order of Preachers, there is a large quantity of more or (generally) less inspiring sermons, but most of these have long been forgotten. From St. Dominic himself, apart from a couple of official documents, we have only one very short letter, which is included in this volume. In fact, the seeker after works from the formative period of Dominican history that could count as spiritual and as classics, let alone as classically Dominican spiritual classics, finds himself disappointed.

There is one work, however, that does perhaps deserve the title "Dominican spiritual classic." It does not seem to have been enormously successful in the Middle Ages and it is not very well known in our own time, but it can be argued that it deserved and deserves a better fate: the treatise *On the Formation of Preachers* by the fifth Master of the Order, Humbert of Romans. In this work, Humbert unfolds his vision of what it means to be, precisely, a preacher; not, that is to say, to be someone who, amongst his other occupations, sometimes preaches, but to be someone defined, totally and simply, as a preacher, someone whose whole life is, in principle, structured around his vocation as a preacher. So far as I know, Humbert's was the only attempt made in the Middle Ages to present preaching like this as a focus for a person's whole life and spirituality, and its failure, as a book, is one symptom of the originality (eccentricity, some would say) and difficulty of the whole notion of a religious order defined as an Order of Preachers.

Since one of the obvious requirements for a preacher is that he should be ready to preach, a considerable part of Humbert's book consisted of suggestions for sermons, and this was something the Middle Ages could understand. Nearly all the surviving manuscripts, therefore, contain only the material for sermons, which made up the second part of the book, reducing Humbert's work to being no more than one among several collections of model sermons, comparable, for example, to that of Jacques de Vitry from slightly earlier in the century.[12] But when, at the beginning of the seventeenth century, Jerónimo Xavierre, the Master of the Order,[13] ordered a massive search throughout the convents of every Dominican province for early Dominican material, including specifically Humbert's *Formation of Preachers* (of whose importance he had apparently been persuaded by Cardinal Paolo Camillo Sfondrati[14]), only one manuscript was, eventually, found, in Portugal. On the basis of this manuscript the provincial of Aragon, Simon Bauça,[15] produced the first printed edition to include the essential first section of the work (Barcelona, 1607). The modern editor is not in a much better position. Bauça's manuscript is, seemingly, lost, his edition has become extremely hard to find, and only four other manuscripts of the first section are known, three of them in Spain.[16]

But, in spite of this lack of popularity, an exposition of what it means to be a preacher, from the pen of so authoritative a writer as Humbert, must surely count as, at least, classically Dominican; and, granted the modern interest in apostolic spirituality, and the renewed emphasis, canonised by Vatican II, on the apostolic nature of the church's life, maybe Humbert's message can be heard now with less difficulty than it was in his own day.

But even so, his book is plainly not in the same literary genre as the spiritual writings of a St. Bernard or a St. Bonaventure, and the reasons for this indicate something very basic about the temper of Dominican spirituality

First of all, we find in Humbert none of the dramatic fervour or emotional intensity that is characteristic of the Cistercian writers. Though he, like them, no doubt wishes to encourage the zeal and enthusiasm of his brethren, he sets about it, not by composing fervorinos, but by presenting his exposition as clearly as he can; he appeals to the emotions strictly by way of the mind. And this is typical of the Dominicans, at least in their writings; if, in their preaching, they sometimes spoke in more emotive ways, as St. Dominic is said to have done,[17] they did not, in general, allow much of this into their literary style. Typically they present us with pertinent facts, points of theoretical or practical doctrine, relevant texts of scripture and so on, and clarify the implications of these to the utmost of their ability, and then leave us to react in whatever way we like. The vast majority of early Dominican writings, therefore, are not immediately exciting to read; they become exciting only if we are prepared to undertake the intellectual work they expect of us.

Secondly, and even more importantly, the early Dominicans were not particularly concerned, either for themselves or for others, with what has come to be called the "interior life". Some of them, certainly, were great men of prayer, but their prayer was simple, devotional and largely petitionary.[18] They retained the monastic practice of spending some time in private prayer after Compline and Matins, though this was not put into any constitutional text as an obligation, and Humbert several times exhorts the brethren to make use of this opportunity; by the end of the century it is a custom well enough established to be insisted on by some superiors.[19] But there is no hint of any methodical "mental prayer," such as we find in later centuries, nor is there any sign of any theory of mystical progress attached to these simple prayers. When thirteenth-century Dominicans do comment on the ascent of the soul to God, it is in intellectualist terms that belong more within the domain of speculative theology than in the kind of mystical theology we have since become accustomed to.[20] What we know of the prayer of St. Dominic shows that it was habitually intercessory, and his meditations and contemplations are shown as resulting typically in preaching of one kind or another. This suggests that even the prayers and devotions of the Dominicans have an apostolic quality, and this impression is reinforced by the discovery that Jordan of Saxony, who was regarded by his brethren as a powerful man of prayer, says of himself, "I hardly ever pray," a complaint echoed in other early Dominican writings.[21] The all-absorbing ambition of the friars was to be "useful to the souls of others."[22] Their own spiritual exercises were designed to make them better preachers, and their own spiritual progress was not sought as a goal in its own right, but rather as a kind of spin-off from their service of others.[23]

This service of others was determined by the needs of others. And in the thirteenth century what was needed most was, first, basic catechesis, doctrinal and, especially, moral, and, secondly, the development of a new Catholic theology to cope with recent intellectual advances, particularly in the Universities. It was only in the fourteenth century that the Dominicans began, in any serious way, to develop a more "mystical" doctrine, and this was prompted, typically, by the needs of the German nuns who claimed so much of the attention of the brethren in that country.[24]

It is an interesting sign of the Dominicans' earlier lack of interest in mysticism that, after saying that all religious are specially "contemplative," Humbert should go on to explain that this means that they should be full of eyes, like the strange beings in Ezekiel's vision: "They should have eyes to the rear, to see whether they are being enticed back to the things they have abandoned, and eyes in front, to see whether they are, like the apostle, surpassing themselves in what lies ahead of them, namely spiritual things, and eyes to the left, to see that they do not lose heart when things are difficult, and eyes to the right, to see that they do not become proud when things are going well."[25] We shall later on meet other Dominican uses of the word "contemplative," and each time we shall find ourselves, not only a long way from the world of the later Carmelite doctors, but also from the kind of teaching St. Bonaventure gives about the soul's journey towards God.

Are we to conclude, then, that the early Dominicans did not really have a spirituality? Such a conclusion would be possible only if we insist on a very narrow definition of "spirituality." Certainly the Dominicans may oblige us to redefine our terms somewhat, and their lack of manifestly "spiritual" literature may make our quest more difficult; but maybe the very elusiveness of their spirituality is itself a lesson. After all, if we look back to the Desert Fathers, we find one of the most respected of their "old men," abba Poemen, refusing to converse with a distinguished visitor precisely because the visitor wanted to talk "about spiritual things."[26] And if we look ahead to that great Jesuit spiritual director, Jean Pierre de Caussade, we find him too warning his nuns not to be concerned about how "supernatural" their life is, and insisting that it is in the ordinary, everyday things that perfection is forged, with no need to "decorate" life with "irrelevant marvels."[27]

Be that as it may, there is in any case one important theological point to be made. Whatever else we may mean by spirituality, it is surely indisputable that our spiritual life must mean a life motivated and led by the Holy Spirit. And the two major New Testament accounts of the sending of the Holy Spirit (John 20:21–2, Acts 1:8ff) both make it clear that the Holy Spirit is given to the church in the first place to empower her to fulfill the task that Christ gave her, of bearing witness to him. In St. John's account, our Lord says to his disciples, "As the Father has sent me, so I send you. . . . Receive the Holy Spirit." Hugh of St. Cher, the first Dominican to become a cardinal, is surely not too wide of the mark in interpreting this to mean that the disciples are being sent out to do the same job as Christ, namely, to preach.[28]

St. Catherine understood very precisely the nature of the Dominicans' participation in the supernatural life. Several sources inform us of a vision she had, in which she saw the Son of God proceeding from the Father, followed by St. Dominic; she realised that, just as the Divine Word comes from the Father and makes him known to the world, so preachers come from God to share in that same divine mission and to be the bearers of that same Word.[29]

# INTRODUCTION

The claim that is implicit in the very idea of a religious Order of Preachers, and that is made explicit by Humbert, is that, for those who are called to be preachers, it is precisely the *gratia praedicationis*, the "grace to be a preacher," that must be the nucleus of their whole supernatural life. There can be no separating their spirituality from their mission.[30] It is precisely as preachers that they are called to be filled with and led by the Spirit.

And of course this means that their spirituality must be sought, not only in their writings, but also in their actual exercise of their mission. This is why a study of Dominican spirituality inevitably turns, to some extent, into a study of Dominican history. We need to know what Dominic and his followers did as preachers, and how they did it; we need to know what stories later Dominicans told about their founding fathers. That is why there is a substantial first section in this book devoted to Dominican history and historiography. In my selection of texts and in my notes, I have tried to give a reasonably generous amount of this kind of evidence and information, while bearing in mind that it would be inappropriate in a contribution to this series simply to present biographical material. In the notes I have also tried, briefly, to put a little flesh, or at least a name and a date, to most of the people who are mentioned in the course of the text.


## II. Monks, Heretics and Preachers

The High Middle Ages was, in many ways, a restless period. There were a lot of people milling about in the towns, and a lot of people on the move, such as merchants, pilgrims, students, whether they were serious students in pursuit of learning or just the rowdy clerics whom ecclesiastical authority was constantly trying to curb, and marauding soldiers, often no better than bandits. But amid all this seething mass of humanity, there was one class of people that was expected to remain tranquil and aloof: the religious. For centuries it had been an integral element in the Western notion of monasticism that monks should stay put in their cloisters,[31] and already the Egyptian monks had begun to reinterpret the primitive Christian ideals of "exile for God" and "pilgrimage" in such a way that they could be harnessed to a stable way of life.[32] The Cistercians had similarly and more recently re-affirmed the same conviction, that the best way to be a pilgrim and sojourner upon the earth was to be

6

enclosed in a monastery.[33] As a result of renewed emphasis on poverty and the common life, the canons too had increasingly become enclosed and withdrawn, like the monks.[34] It is quite natural that Jacques de Vitry, surveying the scene in Europe at the beginning of the thirteenth century and not liking very much of what he saw, should refer to "the tranquil haven of the Cistercian Order" and call the abbey of St. Victor "an utterly tranquil haven" for those "desiring to escape from the shipwreck of this world."[35] So powerful had this model become that it had begun almost to look as if the only recognised hope for those who wished to be fully serious about their conversion to Christ was for them to become monks or canons and largely to hide themselves away from the turmoil of life in the world.

The other side of the picture, which reinforced the same conclusion, was the general worldliness of the secular clergy, including the higher clergy, of which so many contemporary writers complain.[36] Even when the active clergy are not being accused of any extreme of wickedness, there is still a clear suspicion that they cannot be expected to be all that good. When St. Bernard offers a kind of apologia for the active clergy, it is in terms of the text from Ecclesiasticus 42:14, "Better the iniquity of a man than the blessing of a woman." The monks, identified with the "woman" of the text, are told not to be too critical of the iniquity of the "man," that is, the active clergy, because, granted their situation, such active clergy are bound to be imperfect.[37] Similarly Jacques de Vitry, in his account of the parish priest of Neuilly, Fulk, who became a famous and influential preacher (a kind of twelfth-century Curé d'Ars, as he has been called[38]), does not fail to let us see his proneness to anger,[39] one of the imperfections mentioned by St. Bernard as likely to arise in any active ministry.

Long before the Middle Ages, in fact, St. Jerome had suggested that there was a fundamental choice to be made between looking after your own spiritual interests by withdrawing into monastic seclusion, and taking the risk of looking after other people's interests as an active priest.[40] Although his own position changed, or at least became more subtle,[41] he was remembered in the Middle Ages chiefly as the exponent of the view that active ministry was a temptation for a monk: it is a monk's business to weep, not to teach.[42]

Against this background, it is not surprising that the friars, both Dominican and Franciscan, were greeted with incredulity and alarm, because of their habit of wandering round and frequenting public places. Even someone as sympathetic as Jacques de Vitry regarded

Franciscan life as dangerous, because of its lack of enclosure and stability.[43]

However, as Jacques de Vitry himself realised, the friars were not really as much of an innovation as they appeared to be.[44] As Pope Paul VI remarked on one occasion, there is a certain affinity between the church and the gypsies.[45] Our Lord himself was a wandering teacher, in the best (or worst, as some thought) tradition of Galilee,[46] and he sent his disciples out to be itinerant preachers. In the early centuries of christian history we find evidence of this tradition continuing, and even hardening into a *rule* of itinerancy, *obliging* some people never to settle down anywhere. It is probable that this is the true beginning of christian monasticism, long before the more settled monasticism of Egypt.[47]

Even in the period of Benedictine supremacy there had always been an undercurrent of something more primitive and less structured, and in the twelfth century this broke out afresh with renewed vigour. At least partly in reaction against the feudal solidity of the established modes of monastic life, people began looking for something more simply evangelical, more penitential, more expressive of the notion that we are pilgrims on the earth.[48] In particular, the model of the "apostolic life," as found in Luke 10, began to exercise a new fascination.[49]

Typical of this new spirit is the movement of the "Poor Men of Lyons," founded by Waldes in the mid-twelfth century. He was a prosperous merchant who felt a call to abandon everything for Christ. He procured translations of the New Testament and began to study these, and came to the conclusion that he should abandon home and security and wander round, like the apostles, preaching and accepting whatever hospitality he was given. It was evidently an attractive formula, and, in spite of official opposition, he succeeded in retaining quite a few followers. There has been considerable controversy about whether their fundamental inspiration was a desire to preach or whether their basic purpose was simply to imitate the poverty of the apostles; but this is probably an unnecessary debate: what they wanted was the whole "apostolic life," and preaching was necessarily a part of this.

Their ministry, however, although it was evidently successful in some quarters, was not appreciated by the hierarchy, and they were ordered to stop it. Waldes therefore went to the Pope, and received qualified approval of his programme, on condition that he and his followers did not presume to preach anywhere unless they were invited to do so by the local clergy. At this stage there is no doubt that their intention was to operate within the official church.

Unfortunately they soon found that, in spite of the Pope's blessing, they were not receiving invitations to preach, and this precipitated a crisis for them. They concluded that they should "obey God rather than men," and so resumed preaching, uninvited, and this led to their condemnation. Finding themselves thus forced out of the church, they inevitably began to drift towards less orthodox circles, and, in due course, some of them adopted positions that were incompatible with Catholic belief. But at least some of them retained a deep desire to be accepted within the Catholic church.[50]

One of the factors that helped the success of the Waldensians was a widespread disillusionment with the official church. The Gregorian reform had made the laity much more sensitive to the shortcomings of the clergy, and had also, in attempting to rescue the church from secular interference, succeeded in concentrating rather too much power in the hands of the clergy, thereby fostering the impression, all too often, that the clergy were more interested in power and wealth than in preaching the gospel. Particularly in the South of France this had led to considerable disaffection with the clergy among the aristocracy and gentry, and this disaffection made them inclined to be sympathetic towards preachers who denounced the worldliness of the clergy and who abandoned their claims on tithes and other such revenues.[51]

This situation left the way wide open for the incursion of preachers who were far more seriously heretical than the Waldensians. By the beginning of the thirteenth century there was already a strong and organized counter-church in the South of France, committed to dualist doctrines imported from the East. The Catharists, or Albigensians, had infiltrated nearly all the leading families in the area, and were able to hold their own against successive Catholic counter-offensives largely because of the shortcomings of the official clergy, who were, on the whole, neither setting an inspiring example of evangelical living nor building up the faith of their people by preaching solid doctrine.[52]

The tragedy of the church was that a real movement of evangelical fervour, which should have been revitalising the church from inside, was being pushed to and beyond the fringe by a combination of lack of effective understanding and leadership on the part of the official clergy and a serious lack of doctrinal formation on the part of the people. After a dispute at Pamiers in 1207, at which St. Dominic's bishop, Diego, took a leading part, one of the knights who was present said, "We should never have thought that the Catholics had so many powerful arguments."[53] It is to be supposed that a fair number of the followers of the heretics were not so much abandoning Catholicism as almost entirely ignorant of it.

There was therefore a twofold need, if the church was to hold her own. She had to show convincingly that the new evangelical spirit could find its true home within the church, and she had to remedy the appalling ignorance of her people by providing a more effective and more informed body of preachers.

So far, little had been achieved to meet either need. There had indeed been individuals who had embodied the new evangelical spirit without falling foul of ecclesiastical authority, but they had been no more than isolated individuals. St. Stephen Muretus had refused to identify himself with any of the official forms of religious life, preferring, more humbly and simply, to work out the implications of radical conversion to Christ for himself;[54] but his followers had soon become only another, fairly traditional, religious Order. Men like St. Robert of Arbrissel († 1117) and St. Bernard of Tiron († 1117) had been remarkably successful itinerant preachers, but their followers, both men and women, were not encouraged to imitate them in this, but were shut up instead in monasteries. St. Norbert of Xanten († 1134) had likewise been an itinerant preacher, but his followers, except for the very earliest, were soon formed into an Order of singularly withdrawn reformed canons, the Praemonstratensians.[55] Fulk of Neuilly had, for a time, been a supremely successful preacher, but the only institutional consequence of his monastery was a new monastery of Cistercian nuns.[56]

Innocent III had clearly recognised the demands of the situation and had encouraged devotees of the "apostolic life" as far as he could; two groups of Waldensians who returned to the fold were allowed to continue their preaching and were not obliged to conform to any monastic norms,[57] and the Humiliati had similarly been given their place in the official church.[58] But these were only small movements, insufficient to meet the need. He had also tried with all the means at his disposal to encourage preaching and to foster the better education of the clergy.[59] He had set up a special preaching mission in the South of France, staffed by Cistercians. But they met with little success, and, by 1206, they were fed up and were thinking of abandoning their mission as hopeless.

It is at this juncture, at last, that St. Dominic comes into our story.[60]

He was born in Castile in about 1170, in a rugged, mountainous region only fairly recently won back from the Moors; it is perhaps significant for his later career that he was born and bred in an area like this, which was still very much on the frontier of christendom. From his earliest years he was reared as a cleric, being sent to do his first studies under the auspices of an uncle of his who was an archpriest somewhere in the neighbourhood. As a student in Palencia a few years later, he attracted attention by his generous response to the plight of the poor during a time of famine, which shows already his eagerness to meet the needs of others. As a result of his reputation for charity, he was recruited by the prior of the canons of Osma, Diego. Under the leadership of the bishop, Martin Bazán, the cathedral chapter of Osma had returned to full common life, and ardent young men were needed to fill its ranks. Dominic was just such a one, and he evidently impressed his fellow canons with his piety and zeal. Even then he had a great desire to devote himself to the salvation of souls, though as yet this desire could find little practical outlet except prayer.

In 1201 Dominic became subprior of the cathedral chapter, and, later in the same year, Diego became bishop of Osma. The two men were evidently much in sympathy with each other, and it was probably as a friend, not just as part of his retinue, that Diego took Dominic with him in 1203 when he was sent off to Denmark on an embassy for the king.

In fact, they had to make the journey twice, and these two trips proved decisive for the development of Dominic's vocation. On the way to Denmark the first time, they stopped at Toulouse, and here Dominic was confronted immediately with the fact of heresy in the diocese. He discovered that the landlord with whom they were lodging was an Albigensian, so he sat up all night arguing with him, and finally persuaded him to return to the church.

Then in Denmark, on the second trip, he found himself in a church that was buzzing with missionary enthusiasm. The archbishop of Lund was planning a mission to Livonia and Estonia, and almost certainly Diego and Dominic were caught up in his enthusiasm. At any rate, when they left Denmark, instead of returning to

Osma, they went to Rome, bearing a letter from the archbishop of Lund; and there Diego asked to be relieved of his diocese, so that he could go and preach to the pagans. The natural conclusion is that he wanted to join the missionary expedition in the North, and surely Dominic would have wanted to go with him.

Diego was not allowed to resign his see. So he and his party set off for home. For some reason, which we can only guess, they went first to Cîteaux, where Diego, out of devotion, took the Cistercian habit. (Such a gesture, on the part of an active bishop, did not, of course, mean that he became a monk; it expressed only a kind of spiritual affiliation.[61]) Then they set off for Osma.

On their way they came to Montpellier. There, in late March or early April, 1206, they found the three papal legates responsible for the preaching mission against the heretics in the *Midi*, discussing gloomily what they ought to do. Their efforts, as we have seen, had met with almost no success. They were wondering whether they should not just go back home to their monasteries.

But Diego, who had possibly discussed the situation in Languedoc with the Pope, was not in favour of giving up. He suggested rather that they ought to change their tactics. Instead of travelling round in the impressive style expected of church dignitaries, they should imitate the style of the original preaching of the apostles— which would, of course, also mean imitating the style of the heretics. Diego evidently grasped at once the immense advantage that their evangelical and austere manner gave to the heretics. The only real hope of restoring the balance was for the Catholics to show that they could be equally evangelical and austere. A combination of solid, well-argued, Catholic doctrine and an apostolic life-style, modelled on the formula of Luke 10, stood more chance than anything else of winning back the heretics to the true faith.

The Cistercians were rather taken aback by Diego's suggestion. After all, it was generally considered unseemly for senior ecclesiastics to beg, and the Cistercians disapproved heartily of the idea of their own monks begging. Only the very next year the Cistercian General Chapter was to order a Swiss monastery to be closed if the monks there could find no way of supporting themselves without begging.[62] However, the legates said they would be willing to try the new method, provided someone respectable led the way. Diego at once volunteered, and, without further ado, he sent his retinue home with all his baggage and, keeping only Dominic with him, he set off to preach, barefooted, begging his bread from door to door.[63] And so began the Preaching of Jesus Christ in Languedoc. And so, indirectly, began the Order of Friars Preachers.

In 1207 Diego died, and so did one of the original three legates. But others came, for a time, and the Pope gave emphatic support, so for several years there were Catholic preachers systematically covering the ground, imitating, as Diego had recommended, the humble methods of the apostles.

But in 1208 one of the legates was assassinated, and so the whole situation was inevitably changed. The Pope could not overlook the murder of his own representative, particularly as there was reason to suspect that the Count of Toulouse was implicated in the crime. He decided that the time had come to use more forcible methods to restore order in the region. Since the local authorities had manifestly failed in what was considered their duty, neither curbing the activities of marauding mercenary soldiers, who had been terrorizing the district, nor driving out the heretics from their territories, the Pope appealed to the higher suzerain, the King of France, and called for a crusade. The result was a long and cruel war, in which genuinely religious motives became entangled with territorial ambitions, and the loyalty of the southern Catholics to their church was painfully forced into conflict with their loyalty to their own country and rulers.[64] For a time it looked as if Simon de Montfort, who was put in charge of the crusading army, was going to be able to achieve a swift victory, but this hope was soon shattered. When he was killed in battle in 1218 his son and heir, Amaury, withdrew almost entirely from the fray, leaving it to the King himself, far too late, to intervene.

But while all this was going on, the preaching was not abandoned. Dominic, with or without assistants, continued doing what he had been doing since 1206. And, during a lull in the storm, he was invited, with the strong support of Fulk, the bishop, to establish himself in Toulouse itself. There, with a few companions, he formed a religious community of diocesan preachers. Their mandate was to assist the bishop in every way to fulfil his obligation as teacher and preacher in his diocese. Though the conversion of heretics remained an important goal, the instruction of the faithful was just as important. From the very first, it is the whole doctrinal mission of the church that was entrusted to the incipient Order of Preachers.

In 1215 Dominic accompanied Fulk to the Lateran Council, at which, among other measures, strong statements were promulgated about the need for auxiliary preachers and for the proper training of the clergy. But Dominic, in addition, had a special purpose of his own: he wanted to get his community recognised by the Holy See as an Order of Preachers.

The oddity of this is captured vividly in an early fourteenth-century sermon, preached by Bl. Jordan of Pisa (c. 1260–1311). When Dominic, he tells us, proposed to the Pope the foundation of an Order of Preachers, the Pope wondered to himself, "Who is this man, who wants to found an Order consisting entirely of bishops?"[65] Though the term *Ordo Praedicatorum* had, in fact, already acquired a broader sense[66] (Jacques de Vitry applies it to the Franciscans[67]), it was still generally assumed that only the bishops were the ordinary *ex officio* preachers. As late as 1270 a Franciscan writer could still dispute the right of the Dominicans to the title, on the grounds that no one except a bishop could claim to be more than an auxiliary preacher, a preacher *per accidens,* that is, not a preacher by definition.[68]

But this was not in fact the problem raised by the Pope. In accordance with the recent decree of the Council, he could not authorise the foundation of any new religious establishment unless it adopted one of the recognised religious Rules. He therefore sent Dominic back to his brethren, promising him that once they had agreed on a Rule, he would do all that they wanted.

The brethren unanimously voted to adopt the Rule of St. Augustine, together with the austere customs of the reformed canons in such matters as food and clothing.

St. Dominic then went back to Rome. In the meantime Innocent III had died, but his successor, Honorius III, was eager to continue the policies of his predecessor, and he does not seem to have made any difficulty about granting Dominic the recognition that he wanted. Like Innocent III, he must have realised that this was just what the church needed. If an Order of Preachers could really come into existence like this, not only would it provide at least some of the men needed to bring to fruition the hopes the Council had expressed in its canon on preachers, but its apostolic way of life would also help to harness for the church the evangelical yearnings that had in the past so easily become disillusioned and disaffected with the official church.

The scope of this task, of course, far transcended the limits of a single diocese, and, while he was in Rome this time, Dominic progressively realised that his Order could not go on being merely a diocesan institute. At first he seems to have been concerned only to consolidate his position in Toulouse. He got the Pope to confirm the revenues that had been granted to his brethren there; and, showing how well he realised the need for a proper intellectual formation for the clergy, including his own preaching brethren, he secured another Bull from the Pope, commanding the University of Paris to send Masters and students to Toulouse to establish a proper faculty of theology there.[69] But further reflection, in the international milieu of the papal curia, suggested a wider vision. It was quite possibly now that Dominic began to think that, rather than fetch theologians to Toulouse, he might just as well send his brethren to the theologians in Paris (he never did use the Bull to fetch the theologians, anyhow). He evidently rediscovered his own personal desire to go off and preach to the pagans, and he began to entertain the vision (according to the thirteenth-century source, he literally had a vision[70]) of his brethren going out, two by two, into the whole world to preach the gospel. To facilitate the realisation of this vision, he secured a new Bull of confirmation with slightly different wording, eliminating the suggestion that the new community of preachers was essentially tied to one location.

With this enlarged vision, St. Dominic finally came into his own as, not just a preacher, not just the father of preachers, but the instigator of a preaching mission reaching out into the whole world.

To the end of his life, St. Dominic remained an indefatigable preacher, spending long hours on the road, talking to anyone who was prepared to listen to him, whether or not he knew their languages.[71] St. Dominic the preacher was never sacrificed to St. Dominic the founder and organiser.

But he was also very conscious of his role as the father of those who attached themselves to him. His brethren were gratefully aware of the support he gave them by his prayers for them and by his warm affection and cheerful companionship, and, not least, by his persistence in encouraging them never to settle for less than the demanding standards they had set themselves.[72] To this day Dominicans all over the world turn to St. Dominic as their loving father (*pie pater Dominice*[73]) for help and support.

But, preacher that he was, father that he was, he was also an organiser of missions. Before his death, he had sent out Dominican missions in all directions. But he also knew that the needs of men could not wait for there to be Dominicans to satisfy them. For a mission in the North of Italy, in which he was involved with his friend Cardinal Ugolino (later Pope Gregory IX), he asked the Pope to recruit hand-picked missioners from several other Orders, men whom he knew to be endowed with a "grace of preaching."[74]

When St. Dominic returned to Toulouse in 1217, he did not at first do anything to disrupt the little community he had assembled there. But at Whitsun he surprised them all (and a great many other people too) by announcing that he was going to disband them and send little groups of them elsewhere, leaving only a few behind in Toulouse. As an early chronicler remarks, he appreciated that "hoarded grain goes bad, but it fructifies if it is scattered."[75] Resisting all objections, he merely replied that he knew what he was doing.

And so the Order began to spread, first to Paris and Spain, then to all the countries of Europe and even beyond. By the time he died in 1221, there were five Dominican provinces, with six more in the making. Today there are forty-one provinces, and a considerable number of vicariates, especially in the Third World.

### III. The Apostolic Life

St. Dominic, as we have seen, following in the footsteps of his bishop, Diego, adopted the apostolic life, modelled on Luke 10, as the most promising way of combating the heretical "evangelical" preachers. It is time now for us to consider more closely the significance of this.

It has been suggested that this adoption of a style of life calculated to appeal precisely to those people who were impressed by the heretics was essentially an apostolic "gimmick."[76]

It has also been suggested, particularly by Franciscan writers, that the full evolution of Dominican poverty into conventual mendicancy was due to the influence of St. Francis.

Neither of these suggestions has found much favour with recent Dominican historians,[77] but the first, at least, deserves closer scrutiny, and a comparison with the Franciscans helps to highlight the specificity of the Dominicans.

Of St. Dominic's own devotion to poverty of an extreme kind there can be no doubt.[78] And, as Régamey has pointed out recently, if you want to convert a heretic, you need a sympathetic understanding of what makes him a heretic.[79] Only someone who genuinely shared the evangelical aspirations of those who were disaffected with the official church could have hoped to make much impression on them. When Durandus of Huesca and several other Waldensians submitted themselves to Diego at the conclusion of the debate at Pamiers in 1207, it was presumably at least in part because they recognised in the bishop a Catholic version of the ideals to which they were themselves drawn.[80] There can be no question of a mere posture of poverty adopted for strategic reasons.

And there seems little reason to suppose that any external influence was at work in the development of the conventual mendicancy finally adopted by the Dominicans in 1220. At first, Dominic was content that his communities should enjoy certain guaranteed revenues, but between 1216 and 1220 he engaged in a determined campaign to persuade his brethren to adopt a more extreme form of poverty.[81] This was surely the natural outcome of his desire that they should, like the apostles, be dependent on the generosity of spontaneous benefactors, rather than on even the most modest financial rights.

This concern can be connected with other ideas that seem to be fundamental to Dominic's understanding of his task. In the first place, it is clear that he understood Diego's formula for preaching in humility to mean preaching with no other authority than that of the word of God. He refused several bishoprics that he was offered and left his Order, at least at first, with a definite instinct against any acceptance of positions involving official cure of souls.[82] The preaching of the brethren was to be kept distinct from any exercise of authority, even ecclesiastical authority. One of the problems the Order posed, in fact, was precisely whether this kind of separation was legitimate between the ministry of preaching and the official cure of souls.[83] The Dominicans wanted a kind of ministry that was quite different from that exercised by clergy who had an official claim on their flocks. And, granted the close link between the spiritual claims of the clergy and their financial claims on their people, the repudiation of one kind of claim would naturally lead to the repudiation of the other kind too.[84]

But it is also characteristic of St. Dominic to prefer to appeal to people's spontaneous generosity rather than to rely on the pressure of institutionalised routine. As we shall see shortly, the machinery of Dominican obedience differs from that of the monks in precisely the same way.

The development of Dominican poverty can thus be understood simply in terms of basic Dominican ideas, without reference to any external factors. It was no more than an extension to their communities of the principle of total trust in Providence, which was expected of individual preachers in accordance with Luke 10, and a way of making more thorough their renunciation of rights over other people.

In any case, Franciscan influence seems unlikely for at least two reasons. First of all, there are considerable historical difficulties about the occasion suggested for the alleged meeting between Dominic and Francis that is supposed to have prompted Dominic to opt for a more radical poverty than he had previously envisaged.[85] In the second place, Dominican poverty is significantly different from that of the Franciscans. Whereas the Dominicans were from the outset committed at least to individual mendicancy and never made any attempt to earn their living by manual or any other kind of labour, St. Francis wanted his followers, on the whole, to earn their keep by doing lowly jobs, and they were to beg only if all else failed, or, occasionally, as an exercise in humility.[86]

Rather than explaining the development of Dominican poverty, the Franciscans can serve to highlight the grain of truth that there is in the theory that it was essentially only an apostolic gimmick.

The Waldensians, as we have seen, in all probability, were inspired by the whole programme of imitation of the apostles and took up preaching as part of that programme. This is even more clearly the case with St. Francis. Almost exactly two years after the fateful meeting took place in Montpellier, which launched Diego and Dominic on their way as preachers, Francis also took a decisive step towards the realisation of his vocation. He had already adopted the austere life of a penitent, but in 1208 one day he was suddenly overwhelmed by hearing the gospel read in church about the sending out of the apostles. After getting the priest to explain it to him after Mass, he exclaimed, "That's what I want!". And at once he took off his shoes, abandoned his staff, got rid of his spare tunic, and began to preach penance in the neighbourhood.[87]

It is quite clear that the initial motivation of his preaching is basically the recognition that it is part of the whole programme of Luke 10. It is taken up, then, as part of an ascetic way of life. Even years later, when the Franciscans have become much more clerical and far more seriously involved in preaching and teaching, their characteristic bias is still towards an ascetic view of their life.

Diego and Dominic, by contrast, start preaching because preaching is needed. They are responding to an external need, not just following the impulses of their own spirituality. It is because they see a need that they want to be preachers, and it is because they want to be preachers, in this particular situation, that they find that they also want to adopt the apostolic style of life.

It is revealing to see how differently the two Orders develop their appropriation of the same fundamental text. The Dominicans rapidly lose interest in the details of Luke 10, concentrating their claim to be apostolic on the claim that they are doing the job of the apostles. The rest is reduced to the simple formula of "preaching in poverty,"[88] and this poverty is seen largely in function of the job: They claim that their poverty gives them the best economic system for the work they want to do.[89]

The Franciscans, by contrast, remain fascinated by all the details. We find later Franciscans expatiating interminably on the propriety of not wearing shoes,[90] and wondering whether it is contrary to the principle of not having two tunics to sew two tunics together in the winter.[91]

The two Orders can thus be seen to grow out of two different options. Both respond to the same notion of *vita apostolica*, based on the same New Testament texts, but for Francis the emphasis is on *vita* (this is the term he uses for his Rule), and apostolate is envisaged at first only as a potential part of the whole way of life, on a par with any other occupation, and later, after the victory of the clerics, it is envisaged as growing out of and being validated by the whole way of life,[92] whereas for Dominic the emphasis is rather on *apostolica*, and his followers are fired more by the ideal of the apostolic job, defining the apostolic life more in pragmatic terms, justifying the way of life by reference to the apostolate rather than the other way about; literal adherence to the details of the text hardly comes into their view at all.

It is quite contrary to the original thrust of the Dominican Order for Dominicans to adopt a way of life simply to satisfy ideological needs of their own. The Dominican Order exists in order to be useful to other people, and it has always had to be prepared to adapt its own style and behaviour to fit the requirements of those it seeks to serve.

*IV. Dominican Obedience*

A similar playing down of ascetic details is found also in the way in which the Dominicans appropriated their monastic and canonical inheritance. St. Dominic himself had been a Canon Regular, and he and his followers adopted the Rule of the canons, the Rule of St. Augustine, together with some of the austerities of the various congregations of reformed canons. From the outset, unlike the Franciscans,[93] a disciplined cenobitic life was part of their conception of what their Order should be. But a comparison with canonical and monastic texts shows at once that their understanding of the role of regular observance is quite different from that of the monks or the reformed canons.

The predominant influence in the preceding century had been that of the Cistercians, whose constitutions had left a deep imprint on those of many new congregations of canons, including those of the Praemonstratensians, which, in turn, influenced those of the Dominicans. This means that a comparison between the Dominican constitutions and those of the Praemonstratensians will reveal, not only the ways in which the Dominicans distanced themselves from the legislative ideals of the reformed canons, but also something of how they reacted to the whole Cistercian vision of regular life. This provides a valuable context for the story told by Salagnac of a dispute between St. Dominic and some Cistercians.[94]

The Cistercians dreamed of an ideal of perfect regular observance. The founders of Cîteaux were Benedictine monks of Molesme who were dissatisfied with the observance there; eventually they received permission to found their own monastery, where they could follow the Rule of St. Benedict to the full. Over the years they then developed a body of law of their own, but one of the main purposes of such law was to safeguard and standardise their observance of the Rule.[95]

How far the Dominicans were from sharing this ideal is suggested by a comparison of the role of laybrothers in the two Orders. The Cistercians realised that there were some jobs that needed to be done in the monastery and its farmlands, which would interfere with the regular observance of the monks; they therefore recruited laybrothers to do such jobs, so that the monks would be able to retain the perfection of their observance.[96] St. Dominic, by contrast, wanted the Dominican laybrothers to have full responsibility for all the temporal affairs of the Order so that the clerics would be free to concentrate on study and preaching.[97] The difference in primary focus between the two Orders could hardly be demonstrated more clearly.

At least one of the reasons for the Cistercian insistence on observance was the somewhat pessimistic view of human motivation that had been traditional in Western monasticism for centuries. It was assumed that people left to their own devices were intolerably liable to go astray. The immense apparatus of monastic observance was a shield against human frailty. We can see this anxiety at work in the way in which some "religious gentlemen," almost certainly Cistercians, interfered with a group of free-lance hermits who had established themselves at Oigny, not far from Cîteaux. In about 1216 these "religious gentlemen" arrived and harangued the poor hermits about the dangers of their way of life, and persuaded them to adopt a more formal structure with a rule and an abbot. They meekly succumbed to this pressure and composed some constitutions, which are marked by a profound Cistercian influence.[98]

This Cistercian anxiety explains very well why the Cistercians were so worried by St. Dominic's carefree way of sending even his young men out all over the place, and why they were so confident that, if they watched these young men, they would find them getting into mischief.

St. Dominic, we are told, retorted by accusing the Cistercians of being "disciples of the Pharisees." This is a very precise accusation. Hugh of St. Cher can help us to see what it means: " 'Pharisee' means 'divided.' The Pharisees were divided from others by their own peculiar traditions and by their stricter way of life, by a certain religious discipline which they practised. . . . They signify hypocrites . . . who appear outwardly to be holy, but are inwardly unclean."[99] The Dominican anxiety is evidently that the perfection of observance can become an end in itself, bypassing the need for genuine inner conversion and becoming a substitute for charity. It is the same anxiety that led some Dominicans to resist the introduction of more detailed regulations into their own constitutions on the grounds that it was "superstitious" to want this kind of legislation.[100]

In the Appendix to this book I have presented a selection from the early Dominican constitutions side by side with the corresponding texts from the Praemonstratensians, and even a casual comparison shows how thoroughly the Dominicans are out of sympathy with the Cistercian ideal as reproduced by the Praemonstratensians.

The Dominicans take over the Praemonstratensian Prologue, in which this ideal is expressed; but they make no attempt to provide the detailed legislation that is required if the programme announced there is to be realised. And this is surely deliberate, because the Praemonstratensians had provided just such detailed legislation, and there was nothing to prevent the Dominicans adopting as much of it as they wanted.

In 1220 they further sabotaged the programme by inserting their principle of dispensation, which is something quite new in religious law. Previously dispensations had been used only as a concession to human weakness, but the Dominicans use them as a concession to the job that their members have to do. Their over-riding aim is to be useful to the souls of others; observance must never be allowed to stand in the way of that.

But then, in any case, they did not share the traditional pessimism about people's motivation. They presupposed generosity and were prepared to take the risk of not providing too many safeguards against human frailty and wickedness. They contented themselves with providing a broad outline of how the community's day was to be shaped, leaving plenty of room within this for individual and collective initiative.

It is very striking how far Dominic trusted his young men, and our early sources reveal the basis for this trust: the security of the wandering, unprotected, friars is located, not in the Order's prudential measures, but in the Providence of God, expressed particularly in the loving care of the Mother of God. And so the main protection Dominic offers his friars is to pray for them, not to shut them up.

He is also most insistent that the Dominican constitutions are only human law and are enforced therefore only by human sanctions. The Dominicans are the first religious to state explicitly that breaking their laws does not constitute a sin.[101] Religious rules had tended to acquire an air of divine authority, which suggested that any breach of them would automatically mean a contravention of the will of God. Thus the author of the Rule of the Master explicitly claims divine authority for his teaching, prefacing each section with the heading, "The Lord's answer through the Master." St. Francis too claims the authority of divine revelation for his Rule, which, in any case, he presents as being no other than the rule of the gospel.[102] But it becomes a hallmark of Dominican legislation, for the nuns, the Order of Penance and the lay confraternities as well as for the friars, that breaking Dominican law, as such, involves no sin at all.[103] Where Franciscan confraternities are warned that it is at least a venial sin to break their rules,[104] the Dominicans are quite explicit that not even venial sin is involved.

# INTRODUCTION

In several Dominican texts this is connected with the conviction that what matters is the generosity with which people serve God, and the fear that this would be diminished if too much pressure were brought to bear on them.[105] This is why St. Thomas maintains that every act of obedience must always be a free, deliberate, rational act,[106] and that no superior can ever claim authority over his subjects' consciences.[107] According to St. Thomas, even if your conscience is in fact wrong, it is still less sinful to obey it against the commands of your superior than it is to obey your superior against the commands of your conscience.[108]

In connexion specifically with religious obedience St. Thomas proposes that it should be seen in educational terms: it is a way of helping the aspirant towards perfection.[109] And, in St. Thomas' view, no human educator can strictly do more than assist a process that depends principally on the individual's own God-given abilities. What is more, the disciple has no right to make over all responsibility to any human instructor: whatever any other human being tells him must be referred to that higher authority which comes from God himself, namely, his own mind, which carries the imprint of divine truth in its own rational powers.[110] Thus the whole apparatus of regular life can never properly be seen as an absolute value in itself, to be pursued with fussy precision; what it does do is structure a context within which a person can attempt to realise the particular kind of perfection to which he aspires.

The nature and shape of Dominican obedience is reflected very accurately in the formula of Dominican profession: "I, N., make profession and promise obedience to God and to blessed Mary and to you, N., Master of the Order of Preachers and to your successors, according to the Rule of blessed Augustine and the constitutions of the friars of the Order of Preachers, that I will be obedient to you and to your successors until death."[111] Since 1256 obedience has also been promised to St. Dominic, after our Lady.[112]

This is a highly unusual formula, and it contains two essential elements: the promise of obedience to God, and the promise of obedience to Dominic or whoever the Master of the Order may be. These two promises enshrine the generosity with which a man or woman gives himself or herself to God (compare the story in *Lives of the Brethren* IV 10 iv, below, p. 131) and the generosity with which he or she turns himself or herself over to Dominic and his successors.

(The clause about the Rule and constitutions is not meant to be a promise to obey the constitutions; it is a safeguard against unwarranted claims on the subject's obedience on the part of a superior.[113])

The promise of obedience to God is quite extraordinary in such a context. Although, no doubt, all religious would have conceded the importance of being obedient to God, in fact "obedience to God" was all too frequently invoked to support a more or less anarchical position of rebellion against human authority.[114] In face of this, the Catholic response was generally to make obedience to church authority the criterion of obedience to God.[115] But the Dominicans prefer to formulate their profession in such a way that obedience to God is recognised as a distinct value. The danger that obedience to God will be invoked simply to sanction self-will is mitigated by the promise of obedience to the Master, but obedience to the superior is at the same time relativised by the explicit recognition of the independent claims of God.

This is very necessary in an Order of Preachers. The early Dominicans were well aware that it is God who makes preachers. The mandate from the church is important, but in the last analysis it is the charismatic "grace of preaching" that determines whether or not a man is a preacher. The Order does not make preachers, it can only recognise them.[116] A preacher is therefore answerable to God in a way that cannot be reduced to his answerability to the Order.

A Dominican preacher is, then, not typically a man seeking the security of an ordered way of life, which will protect him from his own unreliable instincts, nor is he a man desiring to have his every move governed by the will of another; he is a man eager to throw himself into the task given him by God, in the context of a world-wide mission held together by the generous loyalty that has inspired its members to put themselves at the disposal of its leader and Master. And he cannot afford to allow his initial generosity to be swamped by too much prudence or fussiness.

### V. The Intellectual Life

There is, however, one observance that is a matter of life and death for the preacher: study.[117] Even if it is not true that training and intellectual expertise actually create the ability to preach, it is nevertheless vital that the preacher should be concerned to give of his very best, in the service of his charism. If he fails to train his mind in the discipline of study, he will be less than generous in his pursuit of his calling.

As we have seen, St. Dominic procured from the Pope a Bull summoning theologians to come and teach in Toulouse. But even before this, probably in 1215 or 1216, he had been taking his brethren to the theology lectures being given in Toulouse by an Englishman, Alexander Stavensby.[118] Shortly afterwards, in 1217, he sent some of them to Paris, the centre of theological learning. Early the next year he took the first steps towards establishing a house in Bologna, the other great University centre in Europe.

Rapidly the friars themselves became teachers as well as students. According to Jacques de Vitry's account of the Dominicans in Bologna, which probably derives from information he received about their very earliest years there, they met every day for instruction from one of their number on the bible,[119] and as early as 1220 they decreed that no new foundation was to be made without a conventual lecturer.[120] And their lectures were not just for the benefit of their own members. When the bishop of Metz wanted to have a convent of Dominicans founded in his diocese in 1221, one of the reasons he gave was the value of their theological lectures.[121]

Above all, the Dominicans took their place in the Universities. From 1229 onwards they held a chair of theology in Paris; soon they had two. There such men as Albert and Thomas taught and wrote.

The involvement of the Order in the academic world and the immense growth of its own academic structures was by no means accidental to the Order's purpose. As we have seen, one of the needs felt by the church in this time was for a more informed, better educated, clergy. The Order of Preachers tried to respond to this need as part of its whole programme of proclaiming and expounding the truth of the Catholic faith wherever it was required.

The Dominican academics were by no means simply leisurely scholars, pursuing their own intellectual interests. They were, above all else, pedagogues. The amazing bulk of their writings was inspired by the needs of their students and of the church at large. Albert's undertaking to comment on the whole Aristotelian corpus was called forth by the need to show exactly what Aristotle had taught, at a time when some intellectuals were using Aristotle to support plainly heretical positions, and by the demands of his students. St. Thomas wrote his great *Summa Theologiae* as an aid to beginners in theology. It was in response to the needs of the mission field that the Dominicans, particularly in Spain, began to undertake the study of Arabic; from 1250 onwards we find the Order officially setting up houses for the study of oriental languages and of Greek.

A considerable amount of thirteenth-century Dominican literature emanates from academic circles, including the most famous, the writings of St. Albert and St. Thomas. At least indirectly, some of these writings have important implications for spirituality. For instance, the espousal by Albert and Thomas of an intellectualist interpretation of the works of the pseudo-Dionysius, against the prevailing anti-intellectual interpretations (made famous, finally, by the *Cloud of Unknowing*), indicates a distinctive Dominican contribution to medieval spiritual theology. Also, St. Thomas's thesis of the "unicity of form," which led to furious controversy after his death,[122] prompted the late Gervase Mathew, in an article on Dominican spirituality published in 1936, to declare that what struck their contemporaries most about the early Dominicans was their belief that man has to be seen as a whole, body and soul, vivified by a single vital principle.[123] This has obvious significance for spirituality, and sets the Dominicans apart at once from the Franciscans, their chief opponents in this controversy. St. Francis referred to the body as "brother body," as if it were quite external to himself, and said that the soul "lives in the body like a hermit in his cell."[124] This kind of dualistic imagery has no place in the Thomist view.

Also the Thomist doctrine of grace, sharpened to a fine point in the sixteenth and seventeenth centuries by a protracted controversy with the Jesuits, inevitably leads to a view of spirituality quite different from that associated with the Jesuits. (Consciously or unconsciously, one of the greatest exponents of "Thomistic" spirituality was the English anchoress, Julian of Norwich.) The Jesuit theory of grace went with their Society's concern to stress the importance of human effort and responsibility, a stance deliberately adopted in face of the emphasis on grace and on trusting faith in God's love, characteristic or taken to be characteristic of the Alumbrados and, later, the Protestants.[125] But the Dominicans refused to accept the view that God merely makes it *possible* for me to do good, leaving it to me actually to do it; they retained the much stronger doctrine, derived from St. Paul by way of St. Augustine, that my good deeds, while being genuinely mine, are also entirely due to God.[126] This makes for a much less anxious, much less uptight, kind of spirituality.

These are all important elements in Dominican spirituality, and they have roots, at least, in the thirteenth century. Space unfortunately prevented the inclusion in this volume of any works by Albert or Thomas, but this deficiency will, it is hoped, be remedied in a separate volume devoted exclusively to these two great theologians.


### VI. Dominican Nuns and Laity

So far we have been concerning ourselves only with the Dominican friars, but by the end of the thirteenth century the Order already consisted of far more than friars. The enclosed nuns, after considerable debate, had won their right to be recognised as part of the Order, and, since 1285, there was a Dominican Order of Penance (the Order to which, later, St. Catherine of Siena was to belong), officially part of the Order, under the jurisdiction of the Master. There was also a number of lay confraternities associated with the Order.

Though none of the Dominicans except the friars were, technically, preachers, all the different kinds of Dominican had a part to play in the Order's enterprise of upholding the truth and values of Catholicism.

The nuns, initially, were founded simply because there was a need. Convents of heretical women played quite an important part in the economy of southern France, which meant that converts to Catholicism were sometimes left in a very precarious position. It was to provide for some of these that Diego established a community of religious women at Prouille. It is not quite clear what future was envisaged for them; it is quite possible that, at first, the intention was that they should become affiliated with the Cistercians, and it may have been the Cistercians' growing reluctance to take on any more convents of women that obliged the nuns of Prouille to consolidate their position on their own.[127]

St. Dominic also made another foundation for women in Toulouse, but little is known about it, and it does not seem to have lasted very long.[128]

The next major development towards the establishment of an Order of Dominican nuns occurred in Rome. Once again, it was a recognised need that evoked the response. The general laxity of religious life for women evidently left some of them desirous of a more serious (and, at the time, that meant more strictly enclosed) form of religious life.[129] In Rome in particular there was a need to provide something better for the women, and Honorius III tried to get the Gilbertines to found a reformed monastery for them at San Sisto. After much dithering, they finally declined, and the site was given to St. Dominic instead. It may be suggested, quite plausibly, that he asked for the site, thinking that it would give him a useful location in Rome for his brethren,[130] but it is clear that, having assumed responsibility for the scheme of providing a decent monastery for women, he threw himself into it with his characteristic energy.

This time there can be no doubt that a convent of women is being founded quite specifically under Dominican auspices.

St. Dominic also received the religious profession of an aristocratic young lady in Bologna, Diana d'Andalò, and let her commit herself to founding a Dominican nunnery there. Because of various problems, this nunnery was not in fact founded until after Dominic's death.

Another convent was founded in Madrid, and St. Dominic put his own half-brother, Mames, in charge of it.

In succeeding years a great many convents of women were founded or incorporated into the Order, and, though the brethren were reluctant to take on too much responsibility for looking after nuns, for fear that it would prevent them from doing their primary work of preaching, the nuns held their own and were recognised as a full part of the Dominican Order.

Since strict enclosure was evidently one of the things these women wanted, there could be no question of their playing an active role in the apostolate of the Order. But it is clear that they were expected to be interested in the work of the Order,[131] and, from the time of Bl. Jordan onwards, there can be no doubt that they are regarded as having a special responsibility to support this work with their prayers.[132]

At Prouille, in the beginning, they also provided a domestic base for the itinerant preachers, rather on the model of the Albigensian convents. This formula was not followed thereafter (by the time the nuns were installed in San Sisto the brethren had already moved to their new home at Santa Sabina). The domestic basis for the preaching was rather to be maintained by the laybrothers. But nevertheless the friendship of the nuns was highly valued by at least some of the brethren, as we learn particularly from the letters of Bl. Jordan, and must be seen as an important part of the human support that enabled them to do their work.

# INTRODUCTION

However, as the Order expanded, groups of women who had been living more or less informally as religious now began to seek affiliation with the Dominicans (as they had previously sought to attach themselves to the Cistercians). This means that some of the monasteries of Dominican nuns were not initially inspired by any specifically Dominican vision, and it is sometimes difficult to see what difference it really made to them that they were Dominican.[133] The only typically Dominican characteristic they all had, at least after they were all put under the same constitutions, was the principle that the constitutions do not bind on pain of sin. But they do not seem to have been encouraged to develop any serious intellectual life of their own, and, except where their foundation was directly inspired by the Order, they do not seem to have been particularly interested in the apostolate. Their most obvious enthusiasm is for bodily penance. In Germany, where there was an exceptionally lush pullulation of Dominican nunneries, it is in almost every case clear that the basic impulse that led to their formation was quite independent of the life and spirit of the Dominican Order, and they are related to the Order, at first, far more as an area of enthusiasm needing doctrinal instruction (which the German brethren provided devotedly) than as an integral part of the movement inspired by the apostolic zeal of St. Dominic.

There is therefore an ambiguity about many of the houses of Dominican nuns, and in all of them there is a certain incompleteness about their Dominican identity, and this makes the early sources concerning the nuns frequently disappointing and sometimes disconcerting.

The Order of Penance, the ancestor of the present-day Third Order Regular, was not originally attached to any particular Order. In the thirteenth century there was a move to gather the men and women who wanted to adopt the status of penitent (which carried certain civic privileges as well as religious obligations) into more organised fraternities, and these gravitated especially towards the Mendicant Orders. But the lack of clarity about their canonical position led to innumerable problems and quarrels, and eventually the Master of the Dominican Order, Munio of Zamora, decided to establish an Order of Penance which would be legally subject to his jurisdiction, and promulgated a Rule to give effect to this in 1285.

The members of the Order of Penance had a social rather than a doctrinal apostolate; they typically ran hospitals and hospices and organised assistance for the poor. The doctrinal apostolate of St. Catherine of Siena in the fourteenth century was quite exceptional, though suggestive of possibilities that have begun to be more widely realised in our own time.

Once again, the most obviously Dominican feature of the Dominican Order of Penance is the declaration that the Rule does not bind on pain of sin.[134]

In addition to the Order of Penance, there were a lot of confraternities attached to the Dominicans, and the statutes of some of these bear eloquent witness to the Dominican desire not to bully people into being holy. Like the Order of Penance, the confraternities were generally concerned with social work of one kind or another, as well as providing an occasion for their members to receive regular instruction and preaching. They also typically had a devotional purpose, often localised in a particular shrine or chapel.[135]

But some at least of the Dominican confraternities had a more explicitly doctrinal significance, even if they did not, strictly, share in the doctrinal mission of the Order. For example, St. Peter Martyr established the Society of the Faith to assist in the struggle against heresy, and there was also a confraternity of our Lady, whose foundation is similarly associated with St. Peter Martyr, intended to bolster the orthodox belief in Christ as true God and true man by focusing devotion on the Mother of God.[136] This confraternity was revived in the fifteenth century as the Confraternity of the Rosary,[137] and this link between the rosary and the thirteenth-century campaign to safeguard orthodoxy against anti-Incarnational heresy is the small kernel of historical truth lurking in the legend that St. Dominic received the rosary from our Lady as a weapon against heresy.

In many different ways, then, we can see how the impetus of St. Dominic's missionary vision attracted men and women to put themselves under his leadership and patronage. In our own age, when the church is less nervous about ascribing a real apostolic role to laymen as well as to clergy, to women as well as to men, we may expect to see a richer flowering of some of the potentialities only dimly foreshadowed in the thirteenth century. From our modern vantage point, we may regret that the early Dominicans did not make more of the apostolic potential of all these men and women they attracted, and we may wish that they had followed the Waldensian example in allowing lay men and women to share in their preaching mandate.[138] But the evident risk of false doctrine led the official church, rightly or wrongly, to insist that only the clergy could be allowed to engage in doctrinal preaching, though permitting laymen on occasion to offer moral exhortation. (We should also remember that the level of education for the laity was, on the whole, lower in the Middle Ages; many of our present-day educated laymen would probably have been clerics in the thirteenth century.) And the authoritativeness of St. Paul's ban on women's teaching was far too strong for the church to allow any apostolic function to women, though in fact the influence of some women, like Mary of Oignies, Douceline and Mechtild of Magdeburg in the thirteenth century,[139] was recognised and appreciated by many people, including prominent churchmen.

### VII. Humbert of Romans

We come, finally, to Humbert of Romans. He was elected Master of the Order in 1254, at a General Chapter held in Budapest at the special invitation of King Bela IV of Hungary.[140] During the chapter the King's young daughter, Margaret, made her profession in the hands of the new Master, in view of the King's projected foundation of a Dominican nunnery there.

By this time, the Order had grown considerably in numbers, without a corresponding development of its structures and institutions. Jordan of Saxony, who succeeded St. Dominic in 1222, whose character is revealed in the stories and letters contained in this volume, had been a magnetic figure, who attracted many young men into the Order, particularly in the Universities. His successor, the distinguished canonist Raymund of Peñafort, had re-organised the constitutions into rather more logical shape. But for some decades the Order had basically been allowed to develop in all directions, simply following its own momentum. The results, if lively, were a bit chaotic. There was such diversity among the brethren that people did not always realise that all these men in fact belonged to the same Order,[141] and the constitutions and customaries by which the nuns lived varied riotously from convent to convent.[142] In addition, the rather undiscriminating recruiting policy followed by some houses had filled the Order with what several Chapters politely referred to as "useless persons."[143] The time was clearly ripe for a major attempt to draw together the various threads and consolidate the essential structures of the Order.

Humbert was just the man for such a job. By temperament he

was an efficient and thorough organiser, a compulsive dotter of *I*'s, but he was also scrupulously faithful to the whole varied inheritance of the Order and never allowed his liking for regularity and conformity to make him forget the demands of the Order's apostolate.

Born round about 1200[144] at Romans, near Valence in France, he went as a young man to study in Paris, and, after taking his Master of Arts there, he stayed on to study Canon Law for a time. Towards the end of 1224 he entered the Order in Paris. Two years later he was put to work as lecturer in theology at Lyons. By 1237 he was prior of Lyons, and round about 1238 he was elected provincial of the Roman province. He must have made his mark in Rome, because we are told that several people voted for him at a papal election, probably in 1241. In 1244 or 1245 he was elected provincial of France, to succeed Hugh of St. Cher, who had been made a cardinal in 1244. As provincial of France, Humbert was charged with producing a standard Dominican lectionary.[145] In 1254 he became Master of the Order.

As Master, he immediately took in hand the revision and standardisation of the whole Dominican liturgy. The magnificent Prototype that was produced as a result is once again in the Order's possession, at Santa Sabina in Rome. He also united all the Dominican nuns under a single set of constitutions, based on those he had himself drawn up for the nuns of Montargis, while he was provincial of France. He also had a new edition of the constitutions of the brethren prepared, as well as a statute to govern the academic life of the Order. Under his rule, measures were taken to improve discipline in Dominican houses (which was probably very necessary in view of the number of "useless persons" in some of them), and a new missionary drive was launched, supported by centres of oriental studies. Humbert also attempted to make a systematic collection of historical and hagiographical material about the Order and its two saints, Dominic and Peter Martyr, one major result of which was the publication of Gerald de Frachet's *Lives of the Brethren*. He also wrote a *Letter on Regular Observance* (generally, though misleadingly, known under the title of *The Three Vows*). It was also probably while he was Master that he wrote his commentary on the Rule of St. Augustine, and a letter dealing with various problems that had arisen about Dominican law.

In addition to all this, Humbert was also involved in some of the public affairs of church and state. For example, in 1255 he was asked to help resolve a problem about the constitutions of the Carthusians, an Order he had himself wanted to join as a young man, and which his brother had in fact joined. In 1258 he was asked by King Louis IX of France (whose son had become Humbert's godchild two years earlier) to advise him about the settlement of a dispute between the houses of Clermont, Poitiers and Anjou.

One of the first and most serious problems facing the new Master in 1254 was a savage attack on the mendicants in the University of Paris.[146] The smouldering resentment felt by many of the traditional clergy against the mendicant incursion into their pastoral and academic territory (in which Humbert had already been involved in 1235, when he was sent to resolve a quarrel between the Dominicans and the canons of Besançon over pastoral responsibility) now flared up so powerfully that by the end of November 1254 there was considerable doubt whether the mendicants would be allowed to go on doing their work at all. In that month the ailing Pope Innocent IV was persuaded to rescind all the privileges that had been granted to the medicants, thereby undermining their position completely. He died less than three weeks later, and a supporter of the friars was elected with remarkable speed to replace him. The first public act of the new Pope, Alexander IV, was to restore the mendicants to their previous position. But this only led the opponents of the friars to make even more sensational accusations against them. In 1256 William of St. Amour published an apocalyptic call to the leaders of the church, in which he suggested that the friars were the harbingers of Antichrist. The mendicants succeeded in procuring the condemnation of this work, which won them a few years of relative peace, but the quarrel broke out again with a new wave of pamphleteering in 1269, and went on, in fact, until the Council of Trent, though after the Council of Lyons in 1274 the Dominicans and Franciscans, at least, were well enough established not to be seriously endangered.

Humbert was, naturally, intimately involved in these battles, and, among other measures that he took, he tried to patch up relations with the Franciscans, which had been bad for some time, by issuing a joint encyclical with the Franciscan Minister General, urging the two Orders to cooperate in the struggle for their survival.

One way or another, Humbert had had ample opportunity to get to know his Order and to reflect on its life and work and its significance for the church by the time he resigned, probably on grounds of ill health, at the General Chapter in London in 1263. All of this experience he now put to good use, devoting his remaining years chiefly to writing. Declining the patriarchate of Jerusalem, which he was offered, he settled down at Lyons, and there he composed the treatise *On the Officials of the Order*, a commentary on the constitutions (which he did not complete), a book for the use of preachers of the Crusade, and, not least, his book *On the Formation of Preachers*. Finally, in preparation for the Council of Lyons, probably at the request of the Master of the Order, he wrote a very competent document, known as the *Opus Tripartitum*, in which he analysed the state of the Western church, relations between the Greeks and the Latins, and the condition of the Holy Land.

He died on July 14, 1277, and was buried at Valence. In the following year the General Chapter had his name inscribed in the Order's Martyrology. He has been venerated as Blessed within the Order, but was never officially beatified.

The quality that emerges with peculiar clarity in all Humbert's works is his colossal common sense and good judgment. It is a sign of this that much of what he did and wrote remained effective in and beyond the Order for centuries after his death. The Dominican liturgy was still essentially the same as his when it was, unfortunately, suppressed in 1968. His commentary on the Rule enjoyed considerable success. His manual for preachers of the Crusade long outlived its original purpose. His book *On the Officials of the Order* was included in the first printed edition of the Dominican constitutions in 1505, and was dropped only in 1872.[147] From there it was pillaged by the Jesuit Polanco, and so came to influence the first Jesuit constitutions.[148]

But what is perhaps even more impressive is the way in which Humbert, in spite of his own instinctive bias, succeeds in doing justice to all the different facets of Dominican life. It is clear that he longed for greater discipline and uniformity in the Order, but he recognised that an Order of Preachers could not expect to have the same kind of uniformity that other Orders have. In spite of his deep appreciation of the regularity of conventual life, he insists that conventual observances and conventual jobs must be subordinated to the needs of the apostolate.[149] For all his concern to ensure the proper training of his men, he states as strongly as anyone the charismatic nature of the office of preaching.

When all is said and done, it is about preaching that he waxes as nearly lyrical as a man of his temperament ever does. In his treatise *On the Formation of Preachers* he ascribes even a cosmic significance to preaching, and culls from the traditional Gloss on the bible innumerable ingenious symbolic applications of scriptural texts to preachers, to fire the imagination of disheartened or shy preachers with new enthusiasm for their job. The problem that preaching sometimes seems to interfere with the spiritual progress of the preacher he grasps by the horns, displaying in all kinds of ways that the risk is worth taking. Yet at the same time he does not forget the cautionary tales of men who had gone overboard through being too confident in their own charism and talents.[150] "Obedience to God" and "obedience to man" balance and protect each other; the intoxicating prospect of sharing in the work of God himself and of having cosmic significance is, in true Christian style, forced to keep its feet on the ground by a healthy pragmatic realism.

It is in the work of Humbert that the complex, yet coherent, vision that St. Dominic had followed in practice finds its fullest and most balanced theoretical exposition. In the words of the epitaph in which his brethren expressed their appreciation of him, he was indeed "sure and reliable in his counsel, and never defeated by any decision he had to make."[151]

## NOTE ON THE EDITING OF THE TEXTS

With few exceptions, there is a remarkable lack of serious critical editions of early Dominican texts. The printed editions do not always make very good sense, and, when they do make sense, there is always the risk that this is due more to the ingenuity of the editors than to the original authors. I have preferred, therefore, to go to the manuscripts for myself. But, in the time available, it was obviously not possible for me to do anything like enough work to produce critical texts of all the pieces to be included here, and in no case can I claim that I have resolved all the problems, even to my own satisfaction. This volume of translations must therefore be regarded as a kind of progress report. Because of this, it seemed necessary, to be fair to the reader, to provide rather more in the way of textual notes than is normal in this series. These notes can, of course, be ignored by those who have no use for them. Where there is any serious doubt about the text, I have presented the evidence I have. In the Notes on the Texts at the back of the book, I have indicated what manuscripts and printed editions I have used, and the reader can calculate, if he cares to do so, the varying degrees of thoroughness this represents. In the case of the *Nine Ways of Prayer of St. Dominic* and the first part of Humbert's *Formation of Preachers* I have used almost all known sources, and hope shortly to be in a position to publish critical editions of the Latin texts. I am also about a third of the way towards a critical text of the collection of sermons that forms the second part of Humbert's book. In the meantime, and with regard to the remaining texts, I shall be willing to do my best to answer any queries about the Latin texts that interested readers may care to send me.

## NOTE ON THE TRANSLATION

In the translation I have aimed, naturally, to be as accurate as possible, even about such details as the proper form of people's names, though this is often uncertain. Where scriptural references are given in the text, I have included them in the translation, though following the modern method of indicating chapter and verse. In a few cases, where a few words of scripture are quoted for no other reason than to indicate a precise reference, I have simply substituted a reference and omitted the quotation. References are given in accordance with current editions of the traditional Latin Vulgate (not the revised Vulgate published recently). Since quite often the content of modern versions, based on the original Hebrew or Greek, is substantially different from the Vulgate, more confusion than benefit would have resulted from giving references to such modern versions. In the interests of greater clarity, however, I have adopted the rather solecistic practice of referring to I & II Samuel and III & IV Kings. Scriptural, patristic and other references not given in the original texts, I have identified, where possible, in the notes. In the identification of such references I have often been helped by the work of previous editors; in the case of Humbert, I have been particularly helped by Mosca's Italian translation. However, I have nowhere simply reproduced references given by previous editors without verifying them for myself, and in quite a few cases I have ventured to disagree with the identifications proposed by my predecessors. I hope that future scholars will similarly subject my references to critical scrutiny.

No translator, I suppose, can entirely avoid idiosyncrasies in his interpretation of his material. In a few places where I am particularly conscious of this hazard, I have added a note to alert the reader.

Finally I must record my gratitude for and amazement at the generous and patient way in which innumerable people have endured and answered my persistent requests for help and information. My brethren and other colleagues in Oxford and in Rome have allowed me to pester them over and over again, and their knowledge and wisdom have helped me enormously. I must particularly mention Fr. Miguel Itza, O.P., of Salamanca, who procured copies for me of the three Spanish manuscripts of Humbert, and Fr. Ulrich Horst, O.P., of Walberberg, who kindly sent me a copy of some German material that I could not find in England. I am also indebted to the various libraries whose manuscripts I have been allowed to use. And, not least, I am grateful to the Master of the Dominican Order, Fr. Vincent de Couesnongle, for his encouragement in this work and for agreeing to write a Preface to it.

## Notes

1. For translations of many of these, including several of the works of St. Bernard, William of St. Thierry and St. Aelred of Rievaulx, from the twelfth century, see the series *Cistercian Fathers* (Kalamazoo, 1970ff).

2. Cf. Hugh of St. Victor, *Selected Spiritual Writings*, trans. A religious of C.S.M.V. (London, 1962).

3. Most of the works published in the series *Bibliotheca Franciscana Ascetica Medii Aevi* (Quaracchi-Grottaferrata) derive from the thirteenth century.

4. St. Bonaventure, *The Soul's Journey into God, The Tree of Life, The Life of St. Francis*, trans. E. Cousins (New York, 1978). The best edition of the spiritual works is still that in vol. VIII of *Opera Omnia* (Quaracchi, 1898).

5. Savonarola, *Operette Spirituali*, ed. M. Ferrara (Rome, 1976).

6. B. Giovanni Dominici, *Lettere Spirituali*, ed. M. T. Casella and G. Pozzi (Fribourg, 1969).

7. Four volumes of the critical edition of the *Deutschen Werke* of Eckhart by J. Quint have so far been published (Stuttgart, 1936ff); two volumes of the projected complete English translation by M. O'C. Walshe have been published (London, 1979). Matthew Fox has published a selection in *Breakthrough* (New York, 1980). The only serious edition of Suso is still K. Bihlmeyer, *Heinrich Seuse: Deutsche Schriften* (Stuttgart, 1907), apart from the critical edition of *Horologium Sapientiae* by P. Künzle (Fribourg, 1975). For an

# INTRODUCTION

English translation, see Sr. Ann Edward, *The Exemplar: Life and Writings of Bl. Henry Suso* (Dubuque, 1962). For editions of Tauler, see Kaeppeli, *Scriptores* III p. 21. There is a selection of texts in English translation in Elizabeth Strakosch, *Johann Tauler: Signposts to Perfection* (London, 1958) and Sr. Mary Jane and E. Colledge, *Spiritual Conferences by John Tauler* (St. Louis–London, 1961).

    8. The Latin text is included in P. Fages, *Oeuvres de S. Vincent Ferrier* (Paris, 1909). English translation by the Californian Dominican nuns (London, 1957).

    9. A new edition of the *Dialogue* was published by G. Cavallini (Rome, 1968); the first volume of a critical edition of the Letters was published by E. Dupré-Theseider (Rome, 1940). There is a translation of the *Dialogue* by S. Noffke in the Paulist Press Classics of Western Spirituality (New York, 1980), and of selected Letters in M. J. Ronayne and K. Foster, *I, Catherine* (London, 1980).

    10. MS Toulouse 418. Extracts were published by R. Creytens, AFP 20 (1950) pp. 114–193. The text was an important source for H. M. Cormier, *L'Instruction des Novices à l'usage des Frères Prêcheurs* (Paris, 1882).

    11. Mechtild's book, *Das fliessende Licht der Gottheit*, was composed at the request of her Dominican confessor, Heinrich von Halle (about whom nothing much else seems to be known). On the question of whether or not she was technically a Dominican, see Grundmann, *Religiöse Bewegungen*, p. 329[22]. In any case, there is no doubt that she eventually entered the Cistercian monastery of Helfta. There is an English translation of her book, with Introduction, by L. Menzies (London, 1953).

    12. On Jacques de Vitry, see p. 381[7]. For a bibliography of printed texts of some of his sermons, see J. F. Hinnebusch, *The Historia Occidentalis of Jacques de Vitry*, p. x.

    13. Master of the Order 1601–1607, made a cardinal 1607, died 1608. See Mortier, *Histoire des Maîtres Généraux* VI (Paris, 1913) pp. 52–121. For his energetic support for historical research in the Order, see A. Papillon, AFP 6 (1936): 6–8.

    14. See the Preface to Bauça's edition (Barcelona, 1607), reprinted in *Maxima Bibliotheca* XXV p. 420. Sfondrati (1561–1618) was the nephew of Pope Gregory XIV, who made him a cardinal in 1590. In spite of being one of the most influential men in the church of his time, he preferred a simple, austere way of life, and was a friend and admirer of St. Philip Neri. In 1608 he made over to the Dominicans his titular church, Santa Cecilia, a gift confirmed in 1613 by the Pope (ACG 1608; BOP V 695).

    15. Simon Bauça was born in Majorca, where he entered the Order. After a fairly routine academic career in the Order (lecturer in Arts in Majorca in 1584, lecturer in Theology in Puigcerdá in 1588, senior lecturer in

# INTRODUCTION

Theology in Majorca in 1594, Master of Theology in 1600), he became titular provincial of the Holy Land and socius of the Master General, a position he held in 1605; by 1607 he was provincial of Aragon, and in 1608 he was made bishop of Majorca. In that capacity he preached at the Jesuit celebrations in Majorca in honour of the beatification of Ignatius of Loyola in 1610. See F. G. M. Pio, *Delle Vite de gli Huomini Illustri di S. Domenico* II (Pavia, 1613) p. 316; Provincial Chapters of Aragon, MS Barcelona, Bibl. Univ. 241 (I am grateful to Fr. Stephen Forte, O.P., for allowing me to use his transcript); AGC 1600, 1605; Eubel; J. S. Diaz, *Dominicos de los siglos XVI y XVII: Escritos localizados* (Madrid, 1977) pp. 77–8.

16. See below, pp. 477–478.

17. *Acta Canon.* 33.

18. Cf. A. Lemonnyer, *L'Année Dominicaine* 63 (1927) p. 275.

19. Humbert I 165–6, II 91–8; cf. P. Philippe, *La Vie Spirituelle*, Suppl., Feb. 1948, pp. 426–30.

20. Cf. especially the commentaries of St. Albert on Ps. Dionysius in vol. XXXVII of the Cologne edition, on which there is an excellent article by E. H. Wéber in G. Meyer and A. Zimmermann, *Albertus Magnus—Doctor Universalis* (Mainz, 1980) pp. 409–39.

21. Cf. Jordan, *Libellus* 13; *The Nine Ways of Prayer; Lives of the Brethren* III 6; Jordan, Letter 12; letters of Peter Martyr and Raymund of Peñafort.

22. Prim. Const., Prologue.

23. Humbert writes at some length on the various benefits to be derived from meditations and private prayers (II 87–98), and he regards it as being part of the novice master's job to instruct his novices in meditation, though clearly this does not mean anything like the later methods of formal meditation (II 231); but *On the Formation of Preachers* 236 and 264 shows how all of this is, in the case of a preacher, subordinated to his task of preaching; 33ff shows how the preacher's own benefit is a consequence of his preaching.

24. Cf. H. Denifle, *Archiv für Litteratur- und Kirchengeschichte des Mittelalters* II (Berlin, 1886) pp. 641–52.

25. *Formation of Preachers*, part II, I iv. Cf. Ezek. 1:18, Phil. 3:13.

26. *Sayings of the Desert Fathers*, Poemen 8.

27. J. P. de Caussade, *Lettres Spirituelles*, ed. M. Olphe-Galliard, I (Paris, 1962) p. 97; *L'Abandon à la Providence Divine*, ed. M. Olphe-Galliard (Paris, 1966) p. 130.

28. *Postillae in Bibliam* VI 397.

29. Raymund of Capua, *Life of St. Catherine of Siena* 204–5; T. Caffarini, *Libellus de Supplemento*, ed. G. Cavallini and I. Foralosso (Rome, 1974) pp. 38–9.

30. Humbert, *Formation of Preachers* 260ff. There has been considerable controversy on this point during this century. Dominican historians rightly

stressed the evidence for the primacy of preaching in early Dominican sources (e.g., Mandonnet-Vicaire I pp. 76–9), but writers on Dominican spirituality, basing themselves on St. Thomas, have tended to stress the primacy of contemplation (some references are given in Tugwell, pp. 22–3). But there is now a greater readiness all round to accept that the specific purpose of the Order is its apostolate, and that the urge to preach the gospel to those who need it most ought to be the driving force in Dominican life, and that the contemplative element in Dominican life is neither a higher goal than apostolate nor an autonomous goal somehow juxtaposed beside apostolate, but an integral part in the apostolate itself. See, for example, A. D'Amato, *Il Progetto di S. Domenico* (Rome, c. 1979); V. de Couesnongle, *Le Courage du Futur* (Paris, 1980).

31. E.g., Jerome, PL 22:514; Augustine, PL 40:575; Rule of St. Benedict, 1.

32. Cf. P.Rousseau, *Ascetics, Authority and the Church* (Oxford, 1978) pp. 48–9.

33. Cf. J. Leclercq, *L'Érémitisme et les Cisterciens* (Misc. del Centro di Studi Medioevali IV, Milan, 1965) pp. 573–6; id., *Studia Monastica* 3 (1961) pp. 46–9; G. Constable, *Opposition to Pilgrimage in the Middle Ages, Studia Gratiana* 19 (1976) pp. 125–46.

34. Cf. Meersseman, *Ordo Fraternitatis* pp. 248–50; C. Dereine, RHE 42 (1947) pp. 370–8.

35. *Hist. Occid.* XV, XXIV. The image is traditional: cf. Gregory, PL 75:511A.

36. See below, p. 115[101].

37. *Sermons on the Canticle* 12:9.

38. Mandonnet-Vicaire II p. 39.

39. *Hist. Occid.* VIII.

40. Letters 14:6, 58:5.

41. Cf. Letter 52; Rousseau, op. cit. p. 126.

42. PL 23:351B. On medieval use of this text, see M. Peuchmaurd, *Recherches de Théologie Ancienne et Médiévale* 29 (1962) p. 74.

43. *Hist. Occid.* XXXII. The tone is much sharper and more critical in Letter VI, in a passage sometimes regarded as an interpolation; but its authenticity is plausibly defended by the latest editor, R. B. C. Huygens, *Lettres de Jacques de Vitry* (Leiden, 1960) pp. 131–2, and by K. Esser, *Anfänge und ursprüngliche Zielsetzungen des Ordens der Minderbrüder* (Leiden, 1966) p. 141. Cf. also Sermon 34, to the Friars Minor, in Pitra, p. 401.

44. *Hist. Occid.* XXXII; Letters, ed. cit., I p. 75.

45. Allocution to a party of gypsies, August 28, 1975.

46. For Galilaean itinerant teachers, see W. D. Davies, *The Setting of the Sermon on the Mount* (Cambridge, 1966) p. 422; Babylonian Talmud, *Hullin*

# INTRODUCTION

(Soncino translation) p. 141. And cf. *Aspects du Judéo-Christianisme* (Paris, 1965) p. 42.

47. E.g., Didache 11:5–6; Ps. Clement, *Letters on Virginity* II 3. See G. Kretschmar, *Zeitschrift für Theologie und Kirche* 61 (1964) pp. 32–41.

48. Cf. J. Leclercq, *Studia Monastica* 3 (1961) pp. 33–46; E. Delaruelle, *Les Ermites et la Spiritualité Populaire* (Misc. del Centro di Studi Medioevali IV, Milan, 1965) pp. 212–41.

49. Cf. M. D. Chenu, *RHE* 49 (1954) p. 70; Tugwell, pp. 111–6.

50. On the Waldensians see K. V. Selge; CF 2; C. Thouzellier, *Catharisme et Valdéisme en Languedoc à la fin du XII^e siècle* (Paris, 1966); Tugwell, pp. 112–29; M. Lambert, *Medieval Heresy* (London, 1977) pp. 67–91, 151–164. For some references to the controversy about their original motivation, see Renard, p. 251[57].

51. Cf. Griffe I p. 197 (against Vicaire's view in *SDHT* pp. 66–7 that it is rather the penchant for heresy that explains the anti-clericalism). On the role of the Gregorian reform, see Vicaire, *SDHT* pp. 70–76.

52. On the Albigensians, see Borst; CF 3; Thouzellier, op. cit.; Lambert, op. cit., pp. 7–23, 49–66, 108–150. On the name "Albigensian" see C. Thouzellier, *Hérésie et Hérétiques* (Rome, 1969), pp. 223–262. On the unreliability of most popular writings on the subject and the unusual level of fantasy which has characterised them, see CF 14.

53. Puylaurens 8. On the lack of education in the church at this time, see Mandonnet-Vicaire II pp. 19–21. The complaint that preaching is being totally neglected is found a century earlier in the famous letter of gratitude from the devil to the clergy, as found in William of Malmesbury, PL 179:1222C.

54. *Vita S. Stephani* 32 (SOG p. 122).

55. On the twelfth-century itinerant preachers, see Mandonnet-Vicaire II pp. 33–40; Meersseman, *Ordo Fraternitatis* pp. 246–64; Vicaire, CF 15 pp. 31–5. On the religious foundations they left behind them, see Jacques de Vitry, *Hist. Occid.* XX, XXII, and Hinnebusch's bibliography under Fontevrault, Premonstratensian Nuns, and Thiron. Cf. also J. Châtillon, *Revue d'Histoire de la Spiritualité* 53 (1977) pp. 3–46. On the motivation of the earliest Praemonstratensians, see H. Kroll, *Analecta Praemonstratensia* 56 (1980) pp. 21–38; the only clearly "apostolic" follower of St. Norbert is Bl. Hugh of Fosse († c. 1161), who joined him before the Order was established. See also F. Petit, *Nobert et l'Origine des Prémontrés* (Paris, 1981).

56. Jacques de Vitry, *Hist. Occid.* VIII.

57. PL 215:1510–3; PL 216:289–93. See Mandonnet-Vicaire II pp. 43–5; CF 2.

58. On the Humiliati, see Jacques de Vitry, *Hist. Occid.* XXVIII, with Hinnebusch's bibliography; SCH 8 pp. 73–82.

# INTRODUCTION

59. Mandonnet-Vicaire II pp. 85–92.

60. I basically follow the account given in Vicaire's magisterial *St. Dominic and His Times*. References to original sources can be found there.

61. Mandonnet-Vicaire I p. 40[14]. For the suggestion that Diego was already planning to join the Cistercian mission in the *Midi* and that he took their habit for missionary reasons, see Vicaire, *SDHT* p. 59; *Dominique et ses Prêcheurs* pp. 180–97. However, this would surely have required that Diego actually appeared publicly as a Cistercian during his preaching mission, and Cernai, himself a Cistercian, would surely have mentioned it if he had. In general, the arguments of C. Thouzellier, *Hérésie et Hérétiques* (Rome, 1969) pp. 196–203, against such a suggestion seem overwhelming. Thouzellier even doubts whether the alleged visit to Cîteaux on this trip took place at all (ibid. p. 194).

62. *Statuta Capit. Gen. O.Cist.*, ed. J. M. Canivez (Louvain, 1933) I p. 340. For other Cistercian references, ibid. pp. 193–4, 385; *Analecta S. Ord. Cist.* 6 (1950) p. 28. For bishops, see PL 215:682.

63. The story as told by Cernai (21ff), Jordan (*Libellus* 20ff) and Puy-laurens (8) is evidently oversimplified. Diego cannot have stayed long as a preacher in the *Midi*, as he was back in Spain by April 29. (This, incidentally, resolves the problem felt by many historians, why Diego failed to obey the Pope's injunction to return to his diocese: the solution is that he *did* return to his diocese.) After that he seems to have commuted between the two countries, as his presence is attested from time to time in both of them. See J. Gallén, *Les Voyages*, pp. 80–4.

64. Cf. CF 4 pp. 234–259; CF 7 pp. 419–37.

65. Sermon on St. Dominic's day, preached in Santa Maria Novella, Florence, in 1303 (*Prediche* I [Florence, 1831] p. 235). On Jordan of Pisa, see C. Delcorno, *Giordano da Pisa* (Florence, 1975). For the historical uncertainty of the common designation "Jordan of Rivalto" see Delcorno pp. 5–7. In his heyday in Florence Jordan often preached four or five times a day, we are told (ibid. p. 17), and his sermons were probably taken down, in the first place, by members of the various lay confraternities attached to the Dominicans there (ibid. pp. 70–77).

66. Mandonnet-Vicaire II pp. 49–64.

67. *Hist. Occid.* XXXII (on which see below, note 92).

68. Pecham, *Tractatus Tres*, pp. 126–7.

69. MOPH XXV pp. 76–8; Vicaire, *Dominique et ses Prêcheurs*, pp. 66–74.

70. Constantine 25 (MOPH XVI p. 304).

71. Cf. Constantine 44 (MOPH XVI p. 316); *Lives of the Brethren* II 10 (MOPH I pp. 74–5).

72. Cf. *Acta Canon.* 6, 8, 32; Jordan, *Libellus* 104–5; Salagnac, *De Quatuor* I 8.

73. The verse *Pie pater Dominice* is first found in an early correction in

the Prototype of the Dominican liturgy (f. 353$^v$, 415$^r$, 493$^r$), which suggests a date not much later than 1256.

74. MOPH XXV p. 125.

75. Ferrandus 31 (MOPH XVI pp. 231–2).

76. R. F. Bennett, *The Early Dominicans* (Cambridge, 1937) p. 46.

77. For the whole debate about Franciscan influence, see Hinnebusch, *History* I pp. 155–6; Vicaire, *Dominique et ses Prêcheurs,* pp. 237–41.

78. E.g., *Acta Canon.* 32.

79. P. R. Régamey, *Ce que croyait Dominique* (Paris, 1978) pp. 29–30.

80. Notice, however, Vicaire's warning against supposing that the events of 1207 reflect a change only in the Catholics, with no real change on the part of Durandus and his companions (CF 2 pp. 183–5).

81. *Acta Canon.* 26.

82. Prim. Const. II 27; MOPH XX 1249 and 1254; and especially the letter Humbert sent to Albert to dissuade him from becoming a bishop (QF 27 pp. 154–6). See also *Formation of Preachers* 515 on the need for preachers to avoid jobs that put them in a position of power.

83. On the Dominicans' separation of their preaching ministry from *cura animarum* and the opposition it aroused, see Y. Congar, *Archives d'Histoire Doctrinale et Littéraire du Moyen Age* 1961, pp. 35–151.

84. Cf. the distinction made by St. Thomas, *Contra Impugnantes* 7:12, 4, between parochial clergy who have a *right* to financial support, and mendicants who do not have such a right.

85. Apart from the chronological difficulties indicated by the historians, it is important to notice the literary purpose of all the early stories we have about alleged meetings between Dominic and Francis. Our earliest source, Bartholomew of Trent, simply says that they were friends, with no further details (ASOP 22 p. 41). Next comes a Franciscan story (2 Celano 148–50) that makes St. Dominic remark publicly that everybody ought to follow St. Francis. Then there is a Dominican story (MOPH I pp. 9–11) that turns Francis into Dominic's assistant. Finally there is a Franciscan story about Dominic's attending a Franciscan General Chapter and being so impressed that he resolved to adopt their total mendicancy for his own Order (the earliest source is Olivi's *Lectura super Lucam;* for bibliography and textual comment, see Vicaire, *Dominique et ses Prêcheurs,* p. 239). The salient feature of all three stories is that they are clearly part of the propaganda put out by each Order to demonstrate its own right to recruit for itself people who have joined the other Order. Cf. Matthew Paris, *Chron. Mai.* (Rolls Series 57) IV 279; BOP I 141, 284, 303, 491; Eccleston, *De Adventu,* pp. 101–2; Provincial Chapter of Provence 1264.

86. St. Francis, *Regula non Bullata* 7:8, 9; *Testamentum* 22. *Scripta Leonis* 3, 59–63.

87. 1 Celano 22–23; *Legenda Trium Sociorum* 25.

88. Cf. *De Approbatione Ordinis*, ed. T. Kaeppeli, AFP 6 (1936) pp. 145–6. Kaeppeli dates this text to 1260–1270, but it probably belongs to the earlier round of the controversy with the Franciscans, reported by Matthew Paris, *Chron. Mai.* IV 279, under the year 1243.

89. Kilwardby, in Pecham, *Tractatus Tres*, pp. 129ff; St. Thomas, IIa IIae q.188 a.7.

90. Pecham, *Canticum Pauperis*, pp. 160–8; *Tractatus Pauperis* 4, ed. A. van den Wyngaert (Paris, 1925) pp. 41–3. Bonaventure, *Opera Omnia* VIII pp. 306–7, 386–90, 402–5.

91. See Bonaventure, *Opera Omnia* VIII p. 451[3].

92. Preaching is mentioned simply as one possibility in *Regula non Bullata* 17:1–5, where the essential thing is said to be that the friars should all preach by their example. For the position of preaching in the early years of the Order, see J. F. Godet, *Franziskanische Studien* 59 (1977) pp. 53–64. David Flood (ibid. p. 313 and 60 [1978] p. 317) argues that Jacques de Vitry missed the point entirely in describing the early Franciscans as an "order of preachers" (cf. above, note 67). It was as a result of the clerical take-over of the Order, officially pronounced victorious when Faversham became Minister General in 1240, that preaching came to be regarded as a normal task of the Order. The claim then begins to be made that the friars' apostolic way of life gives them a privileged right to the exercise of the apostolic office of preaching (e.g., Pecham, *Tractatus Tres*, p. 128; *Canticum Pauperis*, p. 188).

93. See especially Jacques de Vitry, *Hist. Occid.* XXXII.

94. See below, p. 91.

95. Important texts in *Analecta S. Ord. Cist.* 6 (1950) pp. 8, 14–15, 17, 23.

96. Ibid. pp.14–15.

97. *Acta Canon.* 26.

98. *Le Coutumier de l'Abbaye d'Oigny*, ed. Pl. F. Lefèvre and A. H. Thomas (Louvain, 1976) pp. xxxvi, 43.

99. *Postillae in Bibliam* VI 239.

100. See below, p. 142.

101. Cf. Meersseman, *Ordo Fraternitatis*, pp. 1290–1314.

102. *Regula non Bullata*, Prol. 2, 24:4; *Regula Bullata* 1:1. This is why Francis attempted in his *Testamentum*, 38–9, to prevent the brethren from adding glosses to his Rule: it is, as it stands, inspired by the Lord (*Test.* 14–15, 39). Cf. also *Scripta Leonis* 113; Angelo Clareno, in H. Boehmer, *Analekten zur Geschichte des Franciscus von Assisi* (Tübingen-Leipzig, 1904) p. 87.

103. Nuns: ASOP 3 p. 338. Order of Penance: Meersseman, *Dossier*, p. 156. Confraternities: see below, pp. 434, 449–50.

104. E.g., explicitly the 1295 statutes of the Confraternity of our Lady and St. Francis, Parma (Meersseman, *Ordo Fraternitatis*, p. 1300). Cf. also Hugh of Digne, *Expos. Reg.* p. 107:30.

105. Humbert II p. 48; Statute of the Bologna Congregation of St. Dominic, 10.

106. IIa IIae q.104 a.1 ad 1.

107. IIa IIae q.104 a.5.

108. *De Veritate* q.17 a.5.

109. IIa IIae q.186 a.5.

110. *De Veritate* q.11 a.1 corpus and ad 1.

111. Prim. Const., I 16.

112. ACG 1254–6.

113. Cf. St. Thomas, IIa IIae q.104 a.5 corpus and ad 3.

114. E.g., PL 216:292BC; Bernard Gui, *Manuel de l'Inquisiteur*, ed. G. Mollat (Paris, 1926–7) I p. 86, II pp. 40, 68; Thomas of Cantimpré, *De Apibus* I xxii 1.

115. E.g., Bernard of Foncaude, PL 204:818CD.

116. Prim. Const., II 20.

117. Jordan, Encyclical of 1233 (below, pp. 123–4).

118. On Alexander Stavensby, later bishop of Lichfield and Coventry, see Vicaire, *Dominique et ses Prêcheurs*, pp. 60–5.

119. *Hist. Occid.* XXVII.

120. Prim. Const., II 23.

121. MOPH XXV pp. 157–8. On the teaching role of the Dominicans, see Hinnebusch, *History* II pp. 10–14; Meersseman, AFP 19 (1949) pp. 157–9.

122. See F. J. Roensch, *Early Thomistic School* (Dubuque, 1964).

123. *Blackfriars* 17 (1936) pp. 650–7.

124. *Scripta Leonis* 96, 80.

125. St. Ignatius of Loyola, *Spiritual Exercises:* Rules for thinking with the church, 15–17.

126. The controversy between the Thomist Dominicans and the Jesuits generated an enormous amount of literature. For some of the basic documents in the early stages of the debate, see L. de Molina, *Concordia*, ed. J. Rabeneck (Madrid, 1953); B. de Heredia, *Domingo Bañez y las Controversias sobre la Gracia* (Madrid, 1968). For a brief account of the whole dispute, see New Catholic Encyclopaedia under *Congregatio de Auxiliis.*

127. Mandonnet-Vicaire I pp. 106–7; Vicaire, *SDHT* p. 128

128. MOPH XXV pp. 58, 80; Vicaire, *SDHT* pp. 166–7.

129. Cf. Jacques de Vitry, *Hist. Occid.* XV.

130. V. J. Koudelka, AFP 31 (1961) pp. 49–50.

131. Cf. Cecilia, *Miracula* 6.

132. Cf. the letters of Jordan of Saxony, Raymund of Peñafort and Peter Martyr contained in this volume.

133. Cf. H. Grundmann, *Religiöse Bewegungen*, pp. 223–8; SCH 10 pp. 90–2. C. Champion (*L'Année Dominicaine* 63 [1927] p. 165) claims that the first

prioress of Unterlinden actually asked the Benedictine nuns of Steinbach to train the Dominican nuns in religious life, but this does not seem to be true. Hedwig left Steinbach to become a Dominican because she felt that Steinbach had become too lax (QF 2 p. 19). Such a recruit was obviously a Godsend to the new community, and they certainly made use of her expertise, especially in the liturgical chant (*Lives of the Sisters*, ed. cit., pp. 364–6), but that is not quite the same thing. A similar case occurred at Engeltal (QF 11 p. 29).

134. On the Order of Penance, see Meersseman, *Dossier;* id., *Ordo Fraternitatis*, pp. 355–409. On Munio of Zamora, Master of the Order 1285–1291, see Mortier, *Histoire des Maîtres Généraux* II pp. 171–293; Hinnebusch, *History* I pp. 225–29.

135. The fullest study of Dominican confraternities is Meersseman, *Ordo Fraternitatis.*

136. Meersseman, *Ordo Fraternitatis*, pp. 760ff, 927–9.

137. Ibid. pp. 1144ff.

138. For the Waldensians, see PL 204:805A. On lay preaching in general in this period, see R. Zerfass, *Der Streit um die Laienpredigt* (Fribourg, Bâle, Vienne, 1974). Meersseman (*Dossier*, p. 24; *Ordo Fraternitatis*, p. 379) and, even more strongly, Vicaire (*Dominique et ses Prêcheurs*, p. 405) claim that the Dominican Order of Penance did share in the apostolic work of the friars, and even in their canonical mandate, according to Vicaire; but this does not seem to be the case. See Tugwell, pp. 132–3; id., *New Blackfriars* 59 (1978) pp. 571–2.

139. On Mary of Oignies, see below, p. 383[26]; on Douceline, see CF 11 pp. 251–267; on Mechtild, see above, note 11.

140. MOPH I p. 337.

141. Humbert II pp. 7, 39.

142. R. Creytens, AFP 21 (1951) p. 215.

143. Cf. ACG 1240, 1245; Provincial Chapter of Provence 1245, 1250. Cf. also Hugh of St. Cher, in Humbert II 508.

144. In General I follow Heintke, *Humbert von Romans*, corrected by reference to M. H. Vicaire, *Humbert de Romans*, in *Dictionnaire de Spiritualité* VII (Paris, 1969) 1108–13. References to sources can be found there. E. T. Brett, *The Life and Works of Humbert of Romans* (University Microfilms, 1981) came into my hands too late for me to be able to make use of it here.

145. ACG 1246, 1247. Heintke, p. 72, is wrong to suggest that Humbert was a member of the commission of four brethren charged with revising and standardising the Dominican liturgy as a whole; it is quite clear from the Chapter Acts that these were two separate responsibilities. Heintke, pp. 48–51, is also wrong to identify our Humbert with the Humbert "de Panzano" commissioned by the Roman Province in 1244 (MOPH XX p. 4) to revise the lectionary for their province (see A. Walz, MOPH XVI p. 357).

146. On this controversy, see above, note 83; M. M. Dufeil, *Guillaume de Saint-Amour et la Polémique Universitaire Parisienne* (Paris, 1972).

147. R. M. Louis, AFP 6 (1936) pp. 337–344.

148. A. Hsü, *Dominican Presence in the Constitutions of the Society of Jesus* (Rome, 1971); M. R. Jurado, *Origenes del Noviciado en la Compañia de Jesus* (Rome, 1980) pp. 51, 77–80.

149. Humbert II pp. 33ff.

150. E.g., MOPH I p. 293.

151. Printed in Berthier's edition of Humbert, I p. xv.

# Section I

## ST. DOMINIC & HIS FRIARS

# A. St. Dominic

*Saint Dominic is an unusually retiring kind of founder. He deliberately tried not to impose his own views too much on his associates, and he did not leave his followers either a Rule of his own devising (as St. Francis did) or a corpus of writings to guide and inspire them. All the same, it is clearly appropriate to begin any outline of Dominican spirituality with some attempt to portray the founder of the Order. In the almost total absence of writings of his own, such a portrait has to be built up from a variety of sources. In this section, we begin with two early hagiographical writings from within the Order. The first is a Life of St. Dominic included by Jean de Mailly in the second edition of his collection of saints' lives (which was a forerunner of the more famous Golden Legend by another Dominican, James of Varagine). This dates from about 1243. The second, very different in style and, it must be admitted, decidedly less attractive, is a sermon (or sermon notes) by Thomas Agni of Lentini, a Sicilian Dominican who, as the first prior of Naples, clothed Thomas Aquinas in the Dominican habit. In its dry, schematic way, this sermon, presumably preached some time before 1255 when Agni became a bishop, is interesting because of its exclusive concentration on St. Dominic as a preacher. While Franciscan hagiography from the very beginning strove to present St. Francis as a kind of "second Christ", the Dominicans never forgot that what was most important about their founder was the job that he did and that he bequeathed to them to do. After this, we turn to one of the major sources for the biography of St. Dominic, the evidence submitted by nine Dominicans who knew him to the commission set up by the Pope to investigate his sanctity with a view to his Canonization. After this, I have put together a miscellany of texts from a variety of sources, which illustrate different facets of St. Dominic's life and character. Finally,*

51

*we have a very precious little document, the* Nine Ways of Prayer of St. Dominic, *of unknown authorship, but evidently based on material collected in Bologna and put together between 1260 and 1288, probably nearer the earlier date than the later.*

# The Life of St. Dominic
## by Jean de Mailly

St. Dominic, the first father of the Order of Preachers, originated in Spain in the town called Caleruega in the diocese of Osma. Before conceiving him, his mother had a dream in which she saw a puppy emerge from her womb carrying a blazing torch in its mouth; it appeared to be setting the whole world on fire. This dream signified what kind of man he was going to be: an outstanding preacher, who would rekindle with the fiery word of his preaching the charity which was growing cold in many people,[1] and chase the wolves away from the flocks with his timely barking and rouse to the watchfulness of virtue those who were asleep in their sins. Also a certain lady who lifted him from the font dreamed that he carried a kind of star on his forehead, filling the whole earth with its light.[2]

His father, who was called Felix, and his mother, Jane, brought the boy up religiously and were careful to have him instructed in how to read the Divine Office. After he had finished studying the liberal arts, he applied himself seriously to theology for four years, almost always staying up at night or sleeping on the ground, as his custom had been from early childhood. While he was a student at Palencia, there was a severe famine in Spain, and he sold all that he had in the way of books and other equipment, to help those who were dying of hunger.

Because of his reputation, Diego,[3] the bishop of Osma, made him a canon regular in his church. And the canons too were so impressed by his outstanding virtues that they made him their subprior, against his will. He became a model of life for everyone and an exemplary religious, and amongst all the other virtues with which he was endowed he had a special gift of weeping for the afflicted and for people in distress and for souls that were perishing, whose salvation he longed for jealously. He often used to spend the night in prayer, asking the Lord to give him the grace to help the salvation of those who were perishing.

Meanwhile the king of Castile asked bishop Diego to go to the Marches[4] to arrange a marriage between the king's son and a certain noble girl there. The bishop took Dominic with him on this journey.

When they came to Toulouse, St. Dominic converted to the faith a heretic who gave them hospitality. They returned to the king and told him gladly that the girl had accepted his proposal; then the king sent Diego back to the Marches with a larger retinue, but he found that the girl was dead. So he sent a message to the king and went to Rome with his clergy, to resign his bishopric. But his resignation was refused, so he set off home. On the way he visited Cîteaux, where he took the monastic habit, and then set off to hurry back to Spain with a few monks. But in the land of the Albigensians he met the legate of Pope Innocent, with a great council of archbishops and bishops and twelve Cistercian abbots; they received him with honour and asked his advice about what ought to be done for the defense of the faith. On his advice, they abandoned all their splendid horses and clothes and accoutrements, and adopted evangelical poverty, so that their deeds would demonstrate the faith of Christ as well as their words; in this way they hoped to bring back to the true faith the souls which had been deluded by the heretics with their false appearance of virtue.[5]

Bishop Diego himself gave the lead in doing this, keeping only brother Dominic and a few other clerics with him; they began energetically to travel round the whole district on foot, preaching in word and deed. The heretics saw this and resented it, and began a counter-offensive of more intense preaching. Amongst other forms of conflict, a debate was held; both heretics and believers compiled tracts against each other, and, on the day appointed, in the presence of the people, a book by St. Dominic, which had found more favour than any of the others, and a book by one of the heretics were read out, and, after a long argument, the judges ordered both books to be thrown into the fire, to be put to the test that way. The heretic's book burned up at once, but the book by St. Dominic emerged unscathed even after being thrown into the fire a second and then a third time. This made it plain on whose side truth and holiness were more surely to be found.[6]

The bishop drew a considerable number of people to the faith, and he also built a monastery to receive the girls who were being entrusted to the heretics to be brought up and educated because of the poverty of their parents. Then, after two years, he decided to return to Spain to raise money for the needs of this monastery of women and, with the Pope's approval, to ordain people who were suitable for the job of preaching. But he died while passing through Castile and, when they heard of his death, the other clerics who had remained in Toulouse to preach returned to their homes, leaving brother Dominic on his own except for a few people who had attached themselves to him by some kind of vow; these few persevered in constant preaching.

The heretics, for their part, mocked the holy man in all kinds of ways, spitting at him and throwing mud at him and fastening straw on his back to make fun of him; but when they threatened to kill him, he was not in the slightest bit afraid. They said to him, "What would you have done if we had ambushed you in such and such a place?". He replied, "I should have asked you not to kill me quickly or easily, but to do it bit by bit, multilating my limbs one by one, then gouging out my eyes, then leaving my truncated body half dead, wallowing in its own blood, or finishing it off in whatever way you liked." This amazed the heretics so much that thereafter they abandoned their pursuit of him.

He was so full of charity and compassion that he wanted to sell himself into slavery to convert a man who had become a heretic because of his poverty; in the same way, in his own country, he had on an earlier occasion offered himself for sale to rescue some woman's brother who had been taken captive by the pagans.

During the whole of Lent he fasted, with his companion, on bread and water; and he took the little sleep he allowed himself on bare wooden boards, and always in a hair shirt.

So St. Dominic remained like this at Toulouse for ten years, and then he went to Rome because of the Council, with the bishop of Toulouse[7] who loved him fondly. There he asked Pope Innocent III to confirm for him, brother Dominic, and his followers, an Order which would be called and which would in fact be an Order of Preachers. The Pope told brother Dominic to go back to his brethren and choose some approved Rule which they could all agree on[8] and then come back to the curia to be granted his petition. At the end of the Council St. Dominic went back and told the brethren what the Pope had said, and at once they all agreed to choose the Rule of St. Augustine, and in addition to adopt certain more strict customs with regard to food and clothing.[9] Meanwhile Pope Innocent III died and Honorius became Pope. St. Dominic went to him and had all that he asked for confirmed in the year 1216.

Six hundred, six again, and yet sixteen,
These were the years since God's own human birth,
When, under Dominic, there first was seen
The Order that should preach to all the earth.[10]

In the following year Count Simon de Montfort[11] died, as St. Dominic had foreseen; and the holy man, knowing that seed bears fruit when it is scattered but goes bad when it is hoarded, no longer wanted all his brethren to remain in one place. So he called them together and said that he wanted to scatter them all to different places, even though they were still only a very small number. He selected brother Matthew[12] to be their abbot, whose judgment was to rule the others, while he himself was going away to preach to the pagans.[13] This brother Matthew was the first and last abbot in the Order, because the brethren preferred that the man who was in charge of the whole Order should, for humility's sake, be called "Master of the Order" rather than abbot,[14] while lower superiors should be known as priors and subpriors. Some of the brethren at that time went to Spain, others went to Paris, and others went to Bologna, and in extreme poverty they grew in numbers, by the power of God.

Brother Dominic himself went to Rome, and while he was there Master Reginald, the dean of St. Aignan in Orléans,[15] arrived in Rome, intending to cross the sea with the bishop of Orléans. He was a man of great learning and virtue, and he had taught canon law in Paris for five years. By the Lord's inspiration he was already intending to abandon everything and devote himself to preaching, but he did not know how best to do it. One day while he was talking about this privately with one of the cardinals, he mentioned this intention of his; and the cardinal said, "A new Order of Preachers has just emerged, whose profession is just what you want, consisting of the job of preaching and voluntary poverty. And the Master of this Order is actually here in Rome now, preaching." At once Master Reginald sent for brother Dominic, and revealed his mind to him. He was attracted by the words and by the appearance of St. Dominic, and from that time he began to think about entering his Order. But shortly after this he fell seriously ill; there seemed to be nothing more that could be done for him in the natural way, and the doctors despaired of his life. But St. Dominic prayed urgently for him to the

Lord, and the blessed Virgin appeared visibly to Master Reginald, with two beautiful girls, while he was lying awake in a high fever. She said to him, "Ask me for anything you like and I will give it to you." While he was wondering what to ask for, one of the two girls suggested that he should not ask for anything except for whatever she wanted to give him. So he left it to the blessed Virgin to give him whatever she liked. Then she stretched out her hand and touched the sick man's eyes and ears and nose, then his mouth and his hands, his loins and his feet, anointing them all with a healing ointment she had brought with her. While she anointed his loins she said, "May your loins be girt with a belt of chastity," and at his feet she said, "I anoint your feet in readiness for the gospel of peace."[16] Then she said, "Three days from now I will send you a bottle which will completely restore you to health," and at the same time she showed him the habit of the Order of Preachers, saying, "Look, this is the habit of your Order." Next morning St. Dominic came to see him and asked how he was. "I am well," he replied. The man of God thought he was referring to his soul's health, but he insisted that he meant the health of his body, and told him all about the vision he had had. So they both gave thanks to God. The doctors were amazed at his sudden recovery, because they had quite despaired of his life.

On the third day after this, while St. Dominic was sitting with Master Reginald, a religious from the Order of the Hospitallers who was with them saw the blessed Virgin coming in near where he was and anointing the whole of Master Reginald's body with her own hand. And that heavenly anointing not only entirely freed the flesh of Master Reginald from fever, it also rid it of the fire of lust, so effectively that, as he later confessed, he never afterwards felt in it even the first stirrings of lust. Immediately he made profession to St. Dominic. Then, at the urgent request of the bishop of Orléans, he went overseas, with St. Dominic's permission. When he came back, he went to Bologna and made many converts by his preaching. From there he went to Paris, and shortly afterwards died.

While St. Dominic was in Rome, he raised from the dead a young relation of Cardinal Stephen's,[17] who had fallen from his horse and been killed. Also, while he was travelling, he protected a whole number of people who were travelling with him from the rain, by interposing the sign of the cross. And when he was in Spain, he had a vision in which he saw a huge dragon with its mouth open, swallowing up the brethren who were with him; the holy man understood that some grave temptation from the devil was threatening the brethren.

While St. Dominic still only had a few brethren, and they were not very well educated, he used to send them out to preach, shielding them with his prayers. One day a priest saw him with his brethren and conceived a holy jealousy of them, and wanted to put everything else behind him and join them and devote himself wholeheartedly to preaching; all he wanted first was to get a copy of the New Testament. All at once a young man came along and offered to sell him just such a book. He bought it without any hesitation, but then began to have doubts about whether it would be best for him to do what he had been planning to do. So he thought he ought to ask for an answer from the Lord. So he prayed and made the sign of the cross on the book and then opened it, and his eye fell immediately on the text from Acts where the Holy Spirit says to St. Peter, with reference to Cornelius' messenger, "Get up, go down and go with them without any anxiety, because I have sent them."[18] Immediately the priest abandoned the world and followed them.

On another occasion, a papal legate, the bishop of Porto, a Cistercian monk,[19] went to Bologna and was received with honour by the brethren; he began to wonder what this new and unheard-of kind of religious Order signified and whether it was from men or from God. So he sat down at the altar, and when he was brought a Missal he made the sign of the cross and opened it in the name of the Lord, and at the top of the first page he read, "To praise, to bless and to preach."[20] Taking this gladly as an answer from heaven, he was reassured and began to love the Order with all his heart, and commended himself to the prayers of the brethren.

We do not mean by these stories to imply any approval of diviners and soothsayers; presuming to have certain knowledge of the future through the diabolical art of divining is quite different from trustingly looking for an oracle from God in prayer, when human counsel is insufficient to resolve a dilemma. The saints and the fathers often used to consult the Lord when the need arose. This is why the Jews were always looking for a sign.

At last St. Dominic, after a lifetime of virtues in which he was more easily admired than imitated, fell seriously ill at Bologna. Calling the brethren together, he referred to his own virginity, which God had preserved in him, and offered himself as an example to them, bidding them especially avoid keeping any doubtful company or holding any doubtful conversations with women, and particularly with young women. He also left the brethren an inheritance, not of earthly money but of heavenly grace; his last will was that they should have charity, preserve humility and possess voluntary poverty.[21] He gave strict orders that no one was to introduce the possession of worldly properties into the Order, terrifyingly laying God's curse and his own on anyone who should dirty the Order's practice of poverty with the dust of riches.[22]

His funeral was attended by the venerable bishop of Ostia, who was then the legate of the Roman see in Lombardy and subsequently became Pope Gregory. He knew and loved his sanctity. He buried with due honour in the church of the friars preachers at Bologna the holy body of him who had been their first father, in the year of our Lord 1221.

On the same day and at the same time that he died, brother Guala, the prior of Brescia, of the same Order, later the bishop of Brescia,[23] having dozed off while resting under the brethren's bell tower there, saw heaven opened and two brilliantly white ladders being let down to earth. The top of the one was being held by the Lord, the top of the other was held by the Lord's Mother, and angels of light were going up and down on them.[24] Between them, down below, there was a chair with someone sitting in it, and the person sitting in it was like a friar with his face hidden in his capuce, which is the normal way in the Order for dead brethren to be buried. As the Lord and his Mother gradually pulled the two ladders up, the chair was drawn up too, with the person still sitting in it, until it reached heaven; the angels were singing the whole time. Brother Guala then woke up and went at once to Bologna, where he discovered that the holy soul of St. Dominic had left his body on the same day at the very time of his vision.

After the death of St. Dominic, God worked many miracles through him, many of which are not widely known because they have been concealed out of humility, and some of which have been forgotten entirely through carelessness, but many of them were written down and they were carefully evaluated and approved as reliable by Pope Gregory.[25]

When the number of his virtues and miracles made it impossible for the sanctity of the blessed Dominic to be hidden any longer, the devotion of the people wanted his body, which was still buried in the ground, to be moved with reverence to a more exalted place. So the cement, which was very hard, was broken with iron tools and the stone was removed; when the tomb was opened, suddenly there came out a fragrance so sweet and strong that it surpassed all perfumes. And this fragrance was not confined to the dust of the holy body or the coffin, it also clung to the hands of the brethren who had touched these things. This enables us to guess what immense delights his spirit enjoys in heaven, if his body while still lying in the dust is as fragrant as this. St. Dominic was translated in the year of our Lord 1233.[26]

# A Sermon on St. Dominic
## by Thomas Agni of Lentini

"He who practises and teaches, he is the one who will be called great in the kingdom of heaven" *(Mt. 5:19)*.

In praise of our blessed father, there are three things indicated in this text which recommend someone to us as a saint: his life, his teaching and his glorification. Our father is to be accounted happy in that he did not lack the merit of perfection of life, because he practised, or the ministry of teaching, because he taught, or the reward of great glory, because, as it says, "he is the one who will be called great."

Take first the merit of his life. He was a doer of the work referred to in 2 Timothy 4:5, "Keep vigil, toil in everything, do the work of an evangelist, fulfill your ministry, and be sober." There are five things laid down here which constitute the perfection of his life and that of every preacher: keeping vigil, toil, work, ministry and sobriety. Keeping vigil concerns study,[27] toil concerns service,[28] work concerns the proclamation of the gospel, ministry concerns responsibility, sobriety concerns a man's way of life.

First, then, St. Dominic kept vigil when he was a student. And he directed his study to three things: wisdom, abstinence and compassion. On the first it says in Proverbs 8:17, "Those who keep vigil for me from early morning will find me." The second is mentioned in Ecclesiasticus 31:1, "Keeping vigil for an honourable life will reduce your flesh." And on the third it says in Psalm 40:2, "Blessed is the man who shows understanding towards the poor." Look all this up in the Life of St. Dominic. This is why it says, "Keep vigil."

Notice here three people who can be blamed for going to sleep. Peter went to sleep when he was threatened with death *(Acts 12:6)*. Jonah went to sleep when he was in danger of drowning *(Jonah 1:5)*. And Abner went to sleep when he was supposed to be guarding his lord: "Why did you not guard the lord your king?" *(1 Sam. 26:15)*. Similarly the apostles went to sleep just when their Lord's passion was about to begin. "Could you not keep vigil even for one hour?" *(Mt. 26:40)*.

Secondly, St. Dominic toiled in service or in labour; this was when he was a canon regular. And this involved three kinds of toil: he laboured to increase his merits, to follow the example of the saints, and to serve his brethren. Look this up in his Life. This is why it says, "Toil in everything."

And notice here three possible faults which may occur in this regard. There is the risk of not toiling sensibly, so Ecclesiastes 10:15 refers to "the toil of fools," and Ecclesiastes 5:15 asks, "What use is it to have toiled for the wind?". Then there is the risk of toiling lazily. "You shall eat the labour of your hands" *(Ps. 127:2)*. "Do whatever your hand can do" *(Eccles. 9:10)*. Finally there is the risk of not seeing your labour through to the end. "Do not let anyone else have the honour which is yours . . . in case outsiders fatten themselves on your resources and your toil goes to benefit another man's house" *(Prov. 5:9–10)*.

Thirdly, St. Dominic worked at proclaiming the gospel, when he became a preacher, and then he "did the work of an evangelist," renouncing everything, refuting the claims of heretics, and preaching the gospel. "Do the work of an evangelist." Or mention here the work of an evangelist, as it was revealed to the Cardinal of Porto: "To praise, to bless and to preach";[29] to praise, that is, in the Divine Office, to bless in all one's conversations, and to preach among the people and the clergy.

But now praise has lapsed into silence. "Where were you when the morning stars praised me?" *(Job 38:7)*. And blessing has turned into insult. "Bless, and do not curse" *(Rom. 12:14)*. And preaching has made way for fighting. "Ruben is divided against himself, and great-hearted men are found to be quarreling" *(Judges 5:15–16)*.

Fourthly, he fulfilled a ministry of leadership, after he had become the founder of the Order of Preachers, and so it says, "Fulfil your ministry." The Gloss says: "Fulfil it by your life, learning and teaching."[30] Or he fulfilled it by humility: "Whoever wants to be great among you shall be your servant" *(Mt. 20:26)*. "It is fitting for us in this way to fulfil all righteousness" *(Mt. 3:15)*. Also by his dedication: "See, you have served us earnestly in all things" *(4 Kings 4:13)*. "He who presides, let him do so carefully" *(Rom. 12:8)*. Also by his purity: "He who walks a blameless way shall be my minister" *(Ps. 100:6)*.

Finally, he was sober in his living, and this has to do with the blessedness of his life. This is why this virtue is mentioned last of all, because it governs all the others. Sobriety is particularly necessary in matters of wisdom: "Do not be wiser than you ought, but only within the limits of sobriety" *(Rom. 12:13)*. It is also necessary with regard to behavior: "Let us live in sobriety and justice and loyalty" *(Titus 2:12)* It is also necessary with regard to the practice of abstinence, and this is how the Gloss interprets it here: "Be sober, do not practise excessive abstinence."[31] This is the "reasonable service" mentioned in Romans 12:1.

This shows us how meritorious our father's life was. You can develop this any way you like.

"He who practises and teaches."

Merely to live well is not enough, and so teaching is brought in as well. So, after dealing with the meritoriousness of St. Dominic's life, take up next his role as a teacher. The teacher of the world says, "He who practises and teaches." Practice is mentioned first, then teaching. "Jesus began to do and to teach" *(Acts 1:1)*. Mere doing is not much, mere teaching is futile, but doing and teaching together constitute perfection.

Not only, then, did St. Dominic possess the life of the gospel, as one who did the work of an evangelist, he also possessed the teaching of the apostles, which is commended to us in the gospel. And there are five things which give this teaching its special quality. It should be savoury, and so it is compared to salt: "You," he says, "are the salt of the earth." It should also be radiant, and so it is compared to light: "You are the light of the world." Also solid, so it is compared to a mountain or to a city set on a mountain: "A city set on a mountain cannot be hidden." Also it should be on fire, so it is compared to a lamp: "Nor do men light a lamp. . . ." Finally, it should be complete, and so the Lord goes on: "Do not think I have come to undo the Law . . ." *(Mt. 5:13–7)*.

Now this is how our father taught. First of all, his teaching was useful, because it was salt. "Let your word be always seasoned with salt by grace" *(Col. 4:6)*. Happy is the man whose teaching is salt. The Gloss points out: "Salt is used to dry meat, to season food and to keep away maggots."[32] But notice how weighty the three things are which the Lord says here: "You are the salt of the earth"; that refers to the job, and this is serious. "But if the salt loses its savour"; this is the risk, and that is more serious. "It is worth nothing"; this is the penalty, and that is the most serious of all.

Secondly, his teaching was radiant, because it was light. "The lips of many will bless the man who is radiant in the bread he bestows" *(Ecclus. 31:28).* Happy is the man whose teaching is light. The light shines to enlighten the world, and this is why it says, "You are the light of the world." And it shines to bring edification to a man's neighbour: "Let your light so shine before men." And it shines to bring honour to God: "That they may see your good works and give glory to the Father."

Next, St. Dominic's teaching was constant, because it was a mountain. "A city set on a mountain cannot be hidden." The Gloss interprets this as "The solidity of the apostolic teaching."[33] And truly it is a high mountain: "Rise up on a high mountain" *(Isaiah 40:9).* And it is a luminous mountain: "You shine wonderfully from the everlasting mountains" *(Ps. 75:5).* And it is an unshakeable mountain: "The floods came and the winds blew . . ." *(Mt. 7:25).*

Next, his teaching was on fire, because he was a lamp that had been lit. "His words burned like a torch"[34] because he "came in the spirit and power of Elijah."[35] This is the meaning of "Nor do men light a lamp." So he was a lamp, a lamp that was lit, and a lamp that had been placed on a lamp-stand.

Also his teaching was effective and complete, because it fulfilled the law and the prophets. This is the meaning of, "Do not think I have come to undo the law, but to fulfil it."[36] The Gloss comments: "Undoing the law means not putting into practice what you understand correctly, or distorting your understanding, or whittling away the wholeness of the law of Christ."[37] The first of these is aimed at men who are educated but immoral, the second at heretics, and the third at people who fall short of perfect completeness. After this, the penalty is indicated for undoing the law: "Anyone who undoes the law and teaches men to undo it will be called least." The saints interpret this in three ways: being least means being unworthy of the kingdom of heaven, or not being anybody, or loving and pursuing things which are of least value, namely temporal things.[38]

This is sufficient to show the quality of our father's teaching.

The meritoriousness of his life and his job as a teacher led to the reward of glorification. Only great men have entry to the court of heaven, so it says: "He will be called great in the kingdom of heaven." In the spirit of what our Lord says, we may go on: "He who acted and taught is great, but even greater is he who made others into teachers." "You anoint kings for penance and make people into prophets to follow after you" *(Ecclus. 48:8).* Greatest of all, then, is a man who has founded an order of teachers. On this look up the Gloss on Luke

14:17, "He sent his servant at the time for the dinner": "His servant, that is, the Order of Preachers."[39]

So "He shall be called great" means more than it says, because there is also "greater" and "greatest."

There are likewise five different elements which make up his greatness. He is great in his mind: "He will be great in the sight of the Lord and will be filled with the Holy Spirit" *(Lk. 1:15)*, because he preserved his baptismal innocence. Also he is great in his working of miracles. "By the word of the Lord he closed up the heavens; thus was Elijah made great in his wonderful works" *(Ecclus.48:3–4)*.[40] Also he is great in his kindness to others. If there is anyone who has not known his kindness, he may refrain from praising him.[41] Who has ever called on Dominic and been let down, whether in sickness or in time of need or in distress? He has done great things for everyone, because he is mighty and holy is his name.[42] He is also great in his reward, and this is what is said here: "He will be called great in the kingdom of heaven." And this is because he is ranked with the virgins because of his integrity, with the confessors because that is what he was, with the martyrs because he was a martyr by desire, with the apostles because of his descent from them (he was their successor), and with the angels because he consorted with them. Truly he is great indeed in the kingdom of heaven.

# The Canonization Process of St. Dominic
*1233*

(2) Brother Ventura of Verona,[43] prior of the convent of the Order of Preachers in Bologna, said on oath that it was thirteen years and more since he entered the Order of Preachers on the advice and encouragement of the blessed father[44] Dominic, the founder of the Order of Preachers and its first Master, and made profession in his hand and received the habit from him.[45] At that time the blessed father Dominic had, after the Pope, full authority over the whole Order of Friars Preachers, to shape and organise and correct it. "In the same year," he said, "the first General Chapter of the Order was held at Bologna, and I was present at it."

He also said that he was with the blessed father Dominic and enjoyed great intimacy with him in his comings and goings throughout the province of Lombardy, being associated with him in his travelling and when he was staying somewhere, and in eating, drinking, sleeping and praying.

(3) He also said that on a journey or wherever he was, he wanted to be always preaching or talking or arguing about God, either in person or through his companions. He was also persistent in prayer, and said Mass every day[46] if he could find a church, though he never did so without weeping. When he arrived at a hostel, if there was a church there he would go there first. When he was staying somewhere other than one of the convents, when he heard others saying Matins he would get up at once and recite Matins devoutly with his companions. After Compline, when he was on a journey, wherever he was, he observed silence with his companions and with everybody else, and did not want it to be broken until the hour of Terce the next day. When he was travelling, he would lie down at night on some straw, fully clothed, barely even taking his shoes off.

(4) He also said that when he was travelling he observed to the full the Order's fasts, from the feast of Holy Cross until Easter, that is, and every Friday in summer. He was content to eat whatever food was set before him, except that he would not eat any meat whatsoever. It made him very happy if the provision of food was coarse and

poor, as the witness testifies he had often observed. As soon as he arrived at any convent of his Order, he called the brethren together and preached to them, bringing them all no little consolation.

(5) He also said that when he was stopping[47] in any convent, he conformed to the common usage of the others in what he ate and in everything else, and he wanted them all to do likewise. He never saw him doing or saying anything different from this.

He never saw him speaking ill of anyone, or ever saw him utter an idle word.

He said that the blessed Dominic was wise, sensible, patient, kind and very compassionate; he thinks he never saw any mortal man so endowed with virtues, although he has seen many religious people in different parts of the world.

He also said that he heard his general confession at the time of his death in Bologna, and he reckoned from this that he had never sinned mortally, and that he had kept his virginity all his life, because the blessed father accused himself to him in confession of once revealing to some people that he was a virgin, though he did so to be useful to them.[48]

(6) When he came to any place where there were any religious houses, he visited them all, preaching and encouraging them to regular observance. There was no one so troubled that he would not go away comforted if he came and listened to his words. He did this particularly in parts of Lombardy like Milan and the Cistercian monastery of Colomba.[49] He also said that he preached nearly every day unless he was prevented, or gave the brethren a conference, during which he would weep a lot and make others weep too. He was strict in punishing the faults of the brethren, and was a great enthusiast for the Rule,[50] but at the same time his words were so pleasant that the brethren endured the penances imposed by their loving father with the utmost patience and eagerness. He was constant in his attendance at the Divine Office, and used to spend the night in prayer, weeping a lot. When the witness was asked how he knew this, he said the he often found him in church praying and weeping, and sometimes overcome by sleep. Sometimes when he was tired because of his vigils, he would go to sleep at table.

(7) He also said that when the blessed Dominic had been visiting the lord Ugolino, Cardinal of Ostia and papal legate,[51] in Venice, he returned to Bologna in very hot weather, late at night, and then spent a long time talking with the witness and with brother Rudolph[52]

about the affairs of the Order, and these fathers urged him to go and rest, but he refused and went into the church and prayed, and then said Matins with the brethren at the proper time. It was from his staying up that night that he got the pain in his head and the sickness which resulted in his going to the Lord. When he was ill, he refused to lie in a bed, but lay on some sacking instead. He had the novices called to him and gave them advice about their salvation. He appeared to be, and indeed he really was, cheerful and happy in his sickness.

(8) When his illness got worse, the blessed father had himself carried to Santa Maria del Monte,[53] which was said to be a healthier place. There he sent for the prior, who came with twenty brethren from the community; he gave them a long talk. When he had received the holy oil there, the prior of Santa Maria said, "I shall bury him in this church, and I will not allow him to be taken away." When the blessed Dominic realised this, he said to those of his brethren who were standing by, "Quick, take me away from here. God forbid that I should be buried anywhere except under the feet of my brethren." So he was taken back to the church of St. Nicholas,[54] and the brethren were actually afraid he was going to die on the way.

An hour later, he called the witness and said to him, "Make yourselves ready." When he, the prior, and the other brethren had got ready in the proper way for the commendation of his soul and had gathered round him, the holy father said to the prior and the brethren, "Wait a little longer." While this was going on, the prior said to him, "Father, you know that you are leaving us desolate and sad. Remember to pray for us to the Lord." And brother Dominic lifted his hands to heaven and said, "Holy Father, you know that I have gladly persevered in your will, and I have watched over and kept those whom you gave me. Now I commend them back to you. Watch over them and keep them."[55] He said that the brethren had told him that when they asked about themselves, he replied, "I shall be more useful to you and more fruitful after my death than I was in my life."[56] After this, saint Dominic said to the prior and the brethren, "Begin." And during the office of the commendation of his soul, the blessed father was saying the words with the brethren, because his lips were moving. While the brethren were saying, "Come to help him, you saints of God, and receive his soul," he breathed his last.

His funeral was attended by lord Ugolino, Cardinal of Ostia, who is now the Pope, and by the lord patriarch of Aquileia and by many venerable bishops and abbots. The Mass was sung at the funeral by the lord Ugolino.

(9) That year everybody noticed an extraordinary fragrance in the whole church, especially near the tomb, and the witness in particular says that he noticed it himself. There were also a lot of miracles worked that year and in the following years for people who came to the tomb of the blessed Dominic, bringing wax images and all kinds of things. When several people tried to present silk cloths to cover the tomb of the blessed Dominic, the brethren would not allow them to, for fear they would be accused of greed.

(10) When the body of the blessed Dominic was due to be moved, for several days the *podestà* of Bologna[57] and many noble citizens guarded it to prevent it being stolen. When the tomb was opened, in the presence of the *podestà* and many citizens of Bologna and other noble men, including religious, bishops and laymen, the brethren found a wooden coffin, shut with iron nails; and such a fragrance came out that they were all amazed, saying that they had never smelled anything like it. So the body was moved by the archbishop and other prelates to the new tomb, and the extraordinary fragrance remained the whole time. Master Jordan held the holy body in his hands and gave it to the three hundred or so brethren who had came to the General Chapter to kiss. When the witness was asked how he knew all this, he said that he was present at all of it.

(11) He also said that the blessed Dominic had such charity that he wanted to extend it to everybody, even the damned, and he used sometimes to weep for them.

## TESTIMONY OF BROTHER WILLIAM OF MONFERRATO (AUGUST 7).

(12) The second sworn witness was brother William of Monferrato, of the Order of Preachers,[58] whose disposition was as follows.

"Going to Rome once," he said, "when I was still in the world, I went to stay in the house of the bishop of Ostia, who is now the Pope, to spend Lent there, and there I consorted with brother Dominic who used to come and see the cardinal frequently, and I recognised him as a holy man and I liked his way of life. I began to love him and I often spoke with him about the salvation of others, and, though I have lived with many people, I never met anyone more holy.

"I went to Paris to study theology for two years, and there I received the habit of the Preachers from the blessed Dominic, although we had previously agreed to go and convert unbelievers.

"I accompanied him when he was going to Rome and elsewhere. Whether he was ill or well, I always found him remarkably strict in his observance. He gave dispensations to the other brethren, but not to himself. Even when he was ill, he kept the Order's fasts. When he had an attack of dysentery on his way to Rome, he would not break the Order's fasts or eat meat or take anything extra with his food except some herbs or a bit of turnip." When the witness was asked how he knew this, he replied that he was with him and saw it all, especially at Viterbo where he had been very ill.

(13) "When he was badly treated in any place where he was staying, in the way of food and drink and bedding and such things, I never saw him complaining, but only his extraordinary patience. When he settled down to rest, he prayed for a long time and wept so much that he used to wake his companions up. He spent more time in prayer than asleep. He slept in his tunic and cappa, with his stockings and belt on. He always slept without a mattress, and more often on a plank than on bedding.

"He always observed silence at the times laid down in the Order, and he avoided idle words and spoke always with God or about God." Asked how he knew this, the witness said that, as one of the blessed Dominic's principal companions, he lived with him by day and by night, whether he was travelling or staying somewhere, and he saw and heard all this.

(14) "I must also say, and I believe it to be true, because of his holy way of life, that the blessed father always preserved his virginity; another reason why I believe it is that I have heard it from many reliable people, especially the bishop of Osma, with whom he had been for a long time,[59] and from some of the bishop's canons, with whom he had also lived; I do not remember their names."

(15) He also says that he was present at the translation of the blessed Dominic, when his body was moved from its previous burial place into the church, to the place where it is now. The brethren, including the Provincial, did not want any seculars to be present, because they were afraid it would stink, since water had already seeped into that tomb; but they could not prevent the *podestà* of

Bologna and twenty four noble citizens from being there, and some
of them guarded the tomb for several days before it was opened.
When the stone was taken away, a wooden coffin was revealed, in
which the body of the saint was lying, and then a pleasant, sweet
smell came out and none of them could decide what it smelled like.

(16) After the translation, many people of various states of life
said that they had received graces of healing. "But I do not remember
their names, because I was a diffinitor at the Chapter and was too
caught up in other things to pay attention to them."


## TESTIMONY OF BROTHER AMIZO OF MILAN
## (AUGUST 8).

(17) The third sworn witness was brother Amizo of Milan, the
prior of Padua,[60] whose deposition was as follows.

Master Dominic, he said, was a humble man, gentle, patient,
kind, quiet, peaceful, modest and very balanced[61] in everything he
did and said. He was a loyal comforter of other people, particularly
his own brethren. He was an outstanding enthusiast for regular
observance, a great lover of poverty, both in the food and in the
clothing of the brethren of his Order, and also in their buildings and
churches and in the style and ornamentation of their church vestments. During his lifetime he was very keen on this and took great
pains to see that the brethren did not use purple or silk vestments in
their churches on themselves or on the altars, and that they did not
have vessels of gold or silver, except chalices.

(18) He also said that he was persistent in prayer, by day and by
night. He followed the Order's observance fully in choir and in the
refectory and elsewhere. He was very fervent in prayer and in
preaching, and, because he was zealous for souls, he encouraged his
brethren most insistently to be the same. He loved other religious and
spoke most highly of them.

(19) He preserved his virginity up to the time of his death, as
nearly everybody said. He also said that he was present when the
podestà of Bologna, with the Master of the Order of Preachers and
many others, had the new tomb and the coffin of the blessed Dominic's body opened,[62] and how they all smelled a wonderful fragrance,
such as they had never smelled before.

# EARLY DOMINICANS

## TESTIMONY OF BROTHER BUONVISO (AUGUST 9).

(20) The fourth sworn witness was brother Buonviso of the Order of Preachers.[63] He was with the blessed Dominic, as he says, at Bologna, in the cloister of St. Nicholas, and at Rome and at Milan, and he looked after him when he was ill. So he said that when the brethren left the church in the evening to go and rest, the blessed Dominic used to remain secretly in the church to pray, and the witness used to watch him sometimes and heard him praying with shouts and groans. He had no place of his own to lie down; if drowsiness ever overcame him, he would go to sleep on a board or a bench or on the bier they used for the dead. He used to lie down at night exactly as he was, as he had been walking about during the day.

(21) When the blessed Dominic went to Rome with the witness, whenever he left a city or village he always took his shoes off and carried them under his arm, though his companion was quite willing to carry them for him, and when he approached a town or village he would put them on again. When they came to a particular path which was full of stones, the blessed father said to his companion, "Here, poor wretch that I am, I was once forced to put my shoes on when I was coming along this path." When his companion asked him why, he said, "Because the rain had made these stones so sharp that I could not bear it." Also on one occasion when it rained very heavily while they were travelling and St. Dominic was caught in it, he quite happily began to sing a hymn; the witness saw this and heard it, because he was travelling with him. When he came to rivers that were swollen because of the heavy rain, he beat them down with the sign of the cross and went over, encouraging his nervous companions to cross too.

During the celebration of Mass and during the psalmody, tears used to flow in great abundance from his eyes.

(22) When they were in a hostel, he never asked for provision to be made to suit his own taste, but always that of the others. And when he was badly treated, he showed all the signs of being particularly pleased. When the blessed Dominic was ill at Milan with a fever, the witness says that when the fever came on, he became quite lifted up to God, and afterwards he had someone read to him.

"When I, brother Buonviso, was procurator at Bologna, once when there was no bread for the brethren at lunch time, St. Dominic sat down at table with them and lifted up his hands in prayer, looking towards heaven, and then two extremely handsome young men came into the refectory with two baskets, with the purest white bread in one, and some figs in the other, and they distributed the bread and the figs to each one of the brethren. I write this[64] and I know this because I was there when it happened and saw it."

He also said that the blessed father was very humble, loving, kind, compassionate, patient, sober, zealous for poverty and for the salvation of souls, and a lover of all religious and religious orders. In himself he kept the Rule strictly. He never returned curse for curse, but blessed those who cursed.[65]

(23) When the *podestà* of Bologna and a great number of the citizens of Bologna together with the Master of the Order and the Provincial of Lombardy opened the new tomb and the coffin where the bones of the blessed Dominic were, a wonderful fragrance came out, such that they all said that nobody had ever smelled anything like it. "I smelled it myself and was present when this happened."

(24) The witness said that when he was a novice and had no skill in preaching, because he had not yet studied scripture, the holy father told him to go to Piacenza to preach. He excused himself, but he spoke so charmingly that he induced him to go, saying that the Lord would be with him and would put words in his mouth. God did in fact give him such grace in his preaching that many people were converted and three entered the Order.

## TESTIMONY OF JOHN OF SPAIN (AUGUST 10).

(25) The fifth sworn witness was brother John of Spain of the Order of Preachers,[66] who was received into the Order by the blessed Dominic in Toulouse, at the church of St. Romain,[67] at the time of the council of Innocent III.[68] He lived with brother Dominic on his journeys and in various places, by day and by night.

He also said that he prayed more persistently than all the other brethren. He used to take the discipline with a triple chain, particularly at night, either giving it to himself or getting someone else to give it to him, and there are many brethren who can attest this, who beat him at his request.[69] He punished people who broke the Rule severely yet mercifully. He was very upset whenever he punished anyone for any fault.

(26) He was zealous for souls and used to send his brethren out

to preach, bidding them look to the salvation of others. He had such confidence in God's goodness that he even sent unlearned men out to preach, saying to them, "Do not be afraid; the Lord will be with you and will put power in your mouths." And it turned out as he said.

When the blessed Dominic was at Toulouse, in the church already referred to, he sent the witness to Paris with five other clerical brethren and one lay brother, to study and preach there and to establish a convent. This was contrary to the wishes of Count Simon de Montfort and the archbishop of Narbonne and the bishop of Toulouse[70] and several other prelates, but he told the prelates, the Count and the brethren, "Do not contradict me; I know quite well what I am doing." He told the witness and the others not to have any fear, because everything would work out well. He also sent some others to Spain with similar instructions.

While the witness and his companions were studying in Paris and applying themselves to the salvation of souls, they were given the church of St. Jacques,[71] situated in the gate of Orléans, by Master John, the dean of St. Quentin, who was at that time a Regent Master in theology in Paris,[72] and by the masters and students of the whole University of Paris. There they established a convent. Many brethren were received into the Order, and they were given a great many properties and revenues and some estates, particularly in the regions of Toulouse and Albi. The witness said that in the days when the Order of Preachers owned estates and many properties in these places and used to carry money with them when they travelled and ride on horseback and wear surplices, brother Dominic worked hard to get the brethren of the Order to abandon and make light of all such temporal things and to devote themselves to poverty and to give up riding on horseback and take nothing with them when they travelled. So their properties in the kingdom of France were given to some nuns belonging to the Cistercian Order,[73] and other properties were given to other people.

To allow the brethren to devote themselves more energetically to study and preaching, brother Dominic wanted them to have uneducated laybrothers, who would be in charge of the educated brethren in the administration and provision of all worldly goods; but the clerical brethren refused to have laybrothers in charge of them, in case what happened to the brethren of Grandmont at the hands of their laybrothers should happen to them too.[74]

(27) St. Dominic was loved by everybody, rich and[75] poor, Jew

and pagan (there were many of these in Spain), in fact by everybody except for the heretics and the enemies of the church whom he pursued[76] and refuted in debate and in preaching.

He lay down at night just as he was during the day, except that he took his shoes off. When he was travelling from one land to another, he took his shoes off, and when he arrived anywhere he put them on again, and he did this in all the towns and villages he came to. He refused to have anyone help him carry his shoes. He used to get great delight from anything untoward that happened to him on the way. For example, if he tripped over a stone his face would light up as he said, "This is doing penance!".

He had a great love of poverty, and he encouraged the brethren to love it too. He exulted in cheap clothes, though he liked them to be clean.

(28) He was most sparing in what he ate and drank. He hardly ever took anything extra, if he was offered it, and he observed the Rule strictly himself, though he gave dispensations to others.

When he was walking about in a city or town, he barely lifted his eyes from the ground.

He did not have any place of his own to lie down in, as the other brethren did. (Asked how he knew this, he said that if he had had a place of his own, he would have discovered it, because he had been most persistent in trying to find out.)[77]

He was elected bishop two or three times, but always refused, preferring to live in poverty with his brethren to having any bishopric. The sees he refused were those of Béziers and Comminges.[78]

(29) He rarely spoke except about God or with God in prayer, and he encouraged the brethren to do likewise. He was happy when he was with other people, but in prayer he sobbed and wept.

He remained a virgin all his life, and this was what everybody said.

He often said that it was his desire to be whipped and cut up for the name of Christ, and finally to die.

In letters and in his spoken words he encouraged the brethren to apply themselves to the study of the New and Old Testaments more than to any other reading. He always carried round with him the gospel of Matthew and the letters of Paul, and he read them so often that he knew them by heart.

The canons with whom he had lived before the Order was founded related that when the blessed Dominic was still in the world, as a student at Palencia, he sold his books and furniture to feed the poor during a time of famine.[79] At his example many other people began to do the same kind of thing.

## TESTIMONY OF BROTHER RUDOLPH OF FAENZA (AUGUST 11).

(30) The sixth sworn witness was brother Rudolph of Faenza of the Order of Preachers, who was the priest in charge of the church of St. Nicholas of the Vines in Bologna, and who gave this church to the brethren, with the permission of the bishop of Bologna, at the request of the lord Ugolino, bishop of Ostia, who was papal legate at the time and is now the Pope.

The witness says that he was with the blessed Dominic in Bologna, in church, at the office, in the dormitory, in the refectory, by day and by night, because he, the witness, was procurator for the brethren and had entered the Order many years before and had made profession before the blessed Dominic came to Bologna, and so he knew him well.

(31) "The blessed father Dominic," the witness says, "nearly always spent the night in church, praying and weeping there, as I saw by the light of the lamp which is in the church, and sometimes I saw him standing on the tip of his toes with his hands stretched up. Because of the intimacy I had with him I sometimes went and prayed beside him, and I saw in him a fervour in prayer such as I have never seen the like of.

"The blessed father wore an iron chain next to the skin. When I stripped him after his death, I took this chain as a great treasure, but eventually I gave it to Master Jordan at his urgent request.

"At night he used to lie down dressed just as he was for walking about during the day. He would lie down on some planks or on the ground or sometimes on a trellis, and he did not take anything off except his shoes. Because of his long vigils in church, he sometimes used to go to sleep at table. He was regularly there with the brethren in choir and in the refectory, and he took the same food as the others.

"When I was procurator for the brethren in Bologna," the witness says, "I once prepared an extra dish for the brethren, and he came to me after lunch and said, 'Why are you killing the brethren by giving them extra dishes?'. When we were short of bread or other food, I often went to him to tell him what we needed. He used to say, 'Go to church and pray'. He would do the same, and I always found that God provided whatever we were short of. Even a little supply of bread put out at his command for a whole lot of brethren was abundantly sufficient for them all. He kept the Rule completely in every respect, with regard to food and fasting and everything else, and he took care to see that it was observed by the others.

(32) "Finally, I never saw a man whose service of God pleased me more than did that of the blessed Dominic. He longed for the salvation of all men, including Christians and Saracens, and especially the Cumans, to whom he wanted to go.

"He was happy, kind, patient, cheerful, compassionate and a comforter of the brethren. If he saw any of the brethren offending in any point, he walked past as if he had not seen it, but later, looking perfectly calm, he would address him with soothing words and say to him, 'Brother, you have done wrong; do penance.' In this kind way he led them all to do penance and make amends; and though his words were humble when he spoke to offenders, he still punished their offenses severely.

"He had a supreme love of poverty and encouraged the others to practise poverty too. For instance, Signor Oderico Galliciani once gave the brethren in Bologna a certain piece of property worth five hundred Bolognese pounds; when the blessed Dominic arrived, he tore up the title deeds and returned the property, saying, 'Preachers ought to live by alms.' If ever they had enough in the house to support the brethren for the day, he would not let them beg on that day, and if anyone gave them any alms, he ordered them to return it.[80] He wanted them to have small houses and cheap clothes and even cheap vestments in church. He did not want the brethren to concern themselves with temporal affairs, except those who had been made responsible for them. When he saw that anyone was suitable to be a preacher, he did not want him to be given any other job.

"Whether he was travelling or at home, he always wanted to talk about God or the salvation of souls. I never heard an idle or harmful word from his mouth, or anything derogatory.

(33) "He was very fervent in his preaching and often used to weep while preaching, which made the people weep too.

"At the first General Chapter in Bologna, in the presence of the brethren, he said that he deserved to be deposed and that they ought to depose him. But the fathers refused to do this, so he appointed diffinitors who were to have the authority to do this[81] for the duration of the Chapter. 'I am slack,' he said, 'and useless, so put me out of office.'

"When he was sick at Bologna, the time he died, the brethren stood round him, in tears. Then the blessed Dominic exhorted them to keep the observances of their religious life, and told them not to be afraid, because he would be more useful to them after his death. 'I was holding his head with a towel,' the witness says, 'wiping away the sweat from his face. One of the brethren came to the blessed Dominic and said, "Father, where do you want your body to be buried?" He said, "Under the feet of my brethren." ' While the brethren were saying the commendation of his soul, the blessed father said the words with them. But when they got to 'Come to help him, you saints of God, come to meet him, you angels of the Lord, and receive his soul and present it before the Most High,' he breathed his last. All this took place in one of the cells at St. Nicholas.[82] I never saw him sleeping in a bed with a feather mattress, or even on sacking except when he died, because he was on sacking then. When he breathed his last, he lifted his hands toward heaven."

(34) He also said that he prepared his tomb and the wooden coffin, since he was procurator. His body was shut in with iron nails and he guarded it carefully until it was put in the tomb. Nor did anyone put any perfumes there, because the witness was present the whole time. He also said that he was one of those who opened the tomb in which the blessed father had been buried first, when his body was moved to the place where it is now. It was he who broke the wall of the tomb with iron hammers; the wall was very strong and was sealed with strong, hard cement. He also raised the stone which was on top, with an iron bar, because the tomb was protected by large stones and sealed with cement. He had had all this done most carefully at the outset, to make sure that people did not steal the body. And when the witness raised the stone that was on top with the iron bar, and the tomb was opened, a great fragrance came out, an overwhelming fragrance, very pleasant and sweet; he did not recognise it. All those who smelled it agreed that there had never been any fragrance like it. It still remains in the bones of the blessed Dominic.

# ST. DOMINIC

## TESTIMONY OF BROTHER STEPHEN OF SPAIN
## (AUGUST 13).

(35) The seventh sworn witness was brother Stephen of the Order of Preachers, the Provincial of Lombardy.[83] He said that "it is fifteen years since I first knew Master Dominic, the founder of the Order of Preachers and its first Master; before I knew him personally I heard from reliable people that while he was still a student he sold his books and fed the poor during a time of famine. He said, 'I refuse to study dead skins while men are dying of hunger.' At his example, other men of great authority did the same sort of thing."[84]

Round about this time, he began to preach in the district of Toulouse against the heretics there, with the bishop of Osma, and he started the Order of Preachers.

(36) He also said that when he, the witness, was a student at Bologna, the blessed Dominic came to Bologna and preached there. "After I had confessed my sins to him, one evening when I was at dinner with some friends in the house where we were staying, the blessed Dominic sent two of the brethren to me to say, 'Brother Dominic says you are to come to him.' I told them to go away and said I would come when I had finished my dinner, but they said, 'He says you are to come now.' So I left everything and went to him. I found him with many of the brethren at the church of St. Nicholas." He said to the brethren who were standing by, "Quick, show him how to do a *venia*."[85] When he had done a *venia*, he put himself in his hands.[86] Then the blessed Dominic received him into the Order, saying, "I am giving you arms with which you will be able to fight the devil all the days of your life." The witness was surprised at the time and afterwards, wondering what had prompted brother Dominic to summon him and clothe him in the habit of the Friars Preachers, because he had not discussed his conversion with him beforehand. He thought that it must have been because of some divine revelation and inspiration that he did it.

(37) He also said that the blessed Dominic was a great comforter of the brethren and of other people who were in distress. "For instance," the witness says, "When I was a novice, I suffered a great many trials, but I endured them all at the encouragement of the holy man. The same thing happened to many of the novices, as they told me."

The witness was with the blessed Dominic at Bologna for a whole year, in the cloister of St. Nicholas, and became very intimate with him there, and he never heard him speak a single malicious or idle word. When he preached, his words were so moving that they made both him and his hearers weep with compunction. Whether he was at home or on a journey, he always spoke about God or other profitable subjects, and he urged the others to do the same.

After Compline, when the common prayer was finished, he made the brethren go to the dormitory, while he remained in the church to pray. And while he prayed, he used to reach such a pitch of groaning and lamenting that the brethren who were nearby were woken up by it. He often used to spend the whole night in church, up to the time of Matins. At Matins he would go round both sides of choir, urging and encouraging the brethren to sing loudly[87] and with devotion. The holy man was so devoted to his vigils of prayer "that I never saw him leave the church and go to any place of his own to sleep, only to the bier."

(38) When he was celebrating Mass, particularly during the words of the Canon, he used to weep and show all the signs of a most intensely fervent love. He was enthusiastic for regular life and was a great observer of the Rule of the Order. He had a supreme love of poverty, and encouraged the brethren to imitate him in this, so he would not accept any properties he was offered nor did he want the brethren to accept them. He had cheap clothes made out of coarse, though clean, material, and he wore a very cheap, short scapular, and would never hide it with his cappa, even in the presence of important people. When brother Rudolph raised the cells by an arm's length, because the brethren used to have poor, mean, low cells, and this was in the absence of the blessed Dominic, when the holy father came back, he said, "Do you so quickly want to abandon poverty and build great palaces?". So he ordered them to abandon the work, and it duly remained unfinished as long as he was alive. He put it in his Rule that the brethren were to use cheap clothes and buildings and that they were not to take money with them when they travelled, but were to live off alms.[88] He was most sparing in food and drink, to such an extent that when the brethren had two dishes, he contented himself with one. While the brethren went on eating after he had finished, he used to go to sleep, because of the long vigils he kept in church.

(39) It was generally said that he preserved his virginity until the end of his life. "I heard his confession several times and could never

discover that he had committed a mortal sin." He was patient and happy in all trials. When he was in need, or the brethren lacked anything, in food or in clothing, he showed every sign of happiness.

Since brother John of Vicenza[89] announced to the people in a sermon a revelation he had received about the blessed Dominic, and since he, the witness, began to think about moving his body, great graces in increasing abundance have been seen plainly both in the brethren and in the people who listened to the life and miracles of the blessed Dominic. In the cities of Lombardy a huge number of heretics has been burned,[90] and more than a hundred thousand people who did not know whether they ought to belong to the Roman church or to the heretics have been sincerely converted to the Catholic faith of the Roman church by the preaching of the Friars Preachers. Their sincerity is shown by the fact that these converts, who had previously been defending the heretics, are now pursuing them and detest them, and in almost all the cities of Lombardy and the Marches the statutes which were opposed to the church have been handed over to the Friars Preachers to correct and emend and bring into line with Catholic truth. They have eradicated feuds and established peace between many cities, they have subdued usury and arranged for repayments, ever since the life and miracles of the blessed Dominic began to be famous.

(40) The witness also said that he was present when the body of the blessed Dominic was moved from the tomb under the ground to the marble tomb, and he says that they broke the limestone and the very hard cement with picks and other iron instruments, and then opened the tomb, on which there was a thick, strong stone; inside they found a wooden coffin, from which a marvellous fragrance was coming. The Master of the Order took the bones and put them in a new coffin, in the presence of many of the brethren and the archbishop of Ravenna[91] and many other bishops and prelates and the *podestà* of Bologna with many noble citizens, and they put the new coffin in a stone monument, where it is now. The fragrance lasted for many days afterwards in the hands of those who had touched the relics.

# EARLY DOMINICANS

## TESTIMONY OF BROTHER PAUL OF VENICE
## (AUGUST 16).

(41) The eighth sworn witness was brother Paul of Venice of the Order of Preachers,[92] who received the habit at Bologna fourteen years ago and made profession in the hands of Master Reginald. After his profession, when the blessed Dominic came to Bologna, the witness was very intimate with him and walked with him round the Marches of Treviso and was with him in eating and drinking, when he was staying anywhere and when he was travelling, in the Divine Office, by day and by night, for about two years. "In all this time, I never heard from him an idle word or a derogatory or flattering word or any damaging word." On the contrary, when he was travelling, he saw him either praying or preaching or giving his time to prayer or meditation. When he was travelling, he would tell his companions to go on ahead, saying, "Let us think about our Saviour." Wherever he was, he always spoke either about God or to God, and he encouraged the brethren to do the same, and put it in his Rule.[93] He was never seen to be angry or upset or worried by the toil of travelling, but was patient and happy in all adversities.

(42) He had a supreme love of poverty for himself and for his Order. When some of the people of Bologna wanted to give the brethren certain properties, he refused them, saying that he wanted his brethren to live off alms. And he put it in the Constitutions that properties should not be accepted in the Order.[94]

When he left any town he used to take his shoes off and walk barefoot. He wore the cheapest of habits. "I sometimes saw the blessed Dominic seeking alms from door to door and receiving bread like any pauper. For example, at Dugliolo one day when he was begging for alms, someone offered him a whole loaf of bread, and the father knelt down and took it with great humility and devotion.

"When he was travelling, I never saw him lie in a bed, though he did sometimes lie on some bedding. Once when I visited the church of Porto Legnago[95] with him, the father had a place prepared for his companions to lie down, but he went into the church and spent the night there until Matins, and then he said Matins with the clergy. When he was travelling, he kept the Order's fasts, though he made his companions eat because of the labour of the journey. In the convent of St. Nicholas in Bologna I looked for a long time to see if he had any place of his own to lie down in, and I found that he had not; he slept either on the ground or on a wicker trellis or on a wooden board, and very often he spent the night in church. When he prayed he wept a great deal, because sometimes when I went to fetch him from prayer I saw his face wet with tears. Every day, even when he was travelling, he wanted to sing Mass, if he could find a convenient church for it.

(43) "He longed jealously for the salvation of believers and unbelievers alike. He sometimes said to me, 'When we have established our Order, we shall go to the Cumans and preach the faith of Christ to them and win them for the Lord.'

He wanted the Rule to be observed strictly by himself and by the others. He reprimanded offenders justly and so affectionately that no one was ever upset by his correction and punishment. He conformed to the community in his food and in the Office. When he spent the night in church, he was still always there with the rest to celebrate Matins. He used to encourage the brethren in choir, now on one side, now on the other, to sing well and excellently and to recite the psalms with devotion.

"He was patient, kind, compassionate, sober, loving, humble and chaste, and he was always a virgin. I never knew anyone to compare with him in holiness of life.

"When he was travelling, he preached to the people who joined his party and urged them on to follow the good.

(44) "I was present at Bologna when his body was moved, when such a delightful fragrance came from it that everyone prostrated themselves on the ground and gave thanks to God. The whole church was filled with the fragrance.

(45) "When I was coming to Bologna from Venice to give evidence about the life of the blessed Dominic, my usual kidney pains attacked me so severely that I thought I would not be able to give evidence at the time appointed. I went to the tomb of the blessed Dominic and when I had prayed about this, I was completely freed from the pain."


## TESTIMONY OF BROTHER FRUGERIO OF PENNABILLI (AUGUST 17).

(46) The ninth sworn witness was brother Frugerio of Pennabilli of the Order of Preachers,[96] who had been in the Order for fourteen years and had made profession in the hands of Master Reginald and

received the habit from him in the church of Mascarella, which was the first place in Bologna where the Order of Preachers was established. After his profession, with permission from Master Reginald, the witness went to visit his family, and when he returned to Bologna he found the blessed Dominic at the church of St. Nicholas, where the brethren had moved. He lived with him there for more than four months. He was also with him in the convent in Florence and in the convent in Rome, and also travelling to Rome and through various other towns, being with him in the Office, in eating and in talking, hearing his confession, in prayer and in discussing God with him, by day and by night.

The blessed Dominic was very devoted in his prayer, both when he was travelling and when he was in a convent, so much so that he, the witness, could not see that he ever slept in a bed, although one was sometimes prepared for him. But sometimes when he was tired, as a result of keeping vigil too long at night, he would go to sleep on the ground or on a piece of wood. When he was celebrating Mass he wept a good deal.

(47) When he was talking to the brethren he used to weep and he made them weep too.

"I never heard an idle or harmful word from him, whether of flattery or of detraction." He always spoke about God or with God, and he used to preach to anyone he met on the way when he was travelling, and he urged the brethren to do the same. This was why he wanted to put this in his Rule.[97] He was zealous for souls, not only those of Christians, but also Saracens and other unbelievers. As evidence of this, he proposed to go to the pagans and die there for the faith, once he had organised his brethren.

He treated himself roughly and observed the Order's fasts very strictly when he was travelling, and would not eat before the set time, even though he made his companions eat. He used a single tunic in winter and in summer. He exhorted the brethren to practise the poverty which he himself loved so much. He used a cheap tunic. He was quick to rebuke and correct any of the brethren who were wearing clothes that were at fault. This was why he directed that they should not accept properties, but should live off alms, and he put this in the Rule. He wanted the brethren to have cheap houses and cheap reading desks, so that they would display poverty in everything.

(48) He himself observed the Rule strictly and wanted it to be

observed by the others. He convicted and corrected offenders with gentleness and kindness in such a way that no one was upset, even though the penances were sometimes very severe.

"He was never defiled by any mortal sin, as far as I could tell from his confession, which I heard. He was kind and patient in all trials, rejoicing in adversities, loving, compassionate, a comforter of the brethren and of others. He was adorned with all the virtues to such a degree that I never saw anyone like him."

(49) *I, Aldrovando, son of the late Tebaldo, notary by imperial authority, received these witnesses, on the instructions of Master Tancred, archdeacon of Bologna, Dom Thomas, prior of Santa Maria di Reno, and brother Palmiero of Campagnola, the judges appointed by the lord Pope, and I put them in official form and wrote them out in the year of our Lord 1233 in the sixth indiction, in the earlier part of August.*

# Miscellaneous Texts
## on St. Dominic

### ST. DOMINIC AT OSMA

It was his very frequent practice to spend the night at his prayers, praying to his Father with his door shut.[98] During these prayers he sometimes felt such groaning in his heart that he began to bellow and make noises outwardly, unable to stop himself bursting out like this audibly. And he had a special prayer which he often made to God, that God would grant him true charity which would be effective in caring for and winning the salvation of men; he thought he would only really be a member of Christ's Body when he could spend himself utterly with all his strength in the winning of souls, just as the Saviour of us all, the Lord Jesus, gave himself up entirely for our salvation. *(Jordan of Saxony)*[99]

### THE BEGINNING OF THE PREACHING

In the year of the Incarnation 1206, the bishop of Osma, Diego by name, a great man deserving of high praise, went to the Roman curia with an intense desire to resign his see so that he could be free to go and preach the gospel of Christ to the pagans; but Pope Innocent refused the holy man's request and told him to return to his diocese instead. Now it so happened that when he was at Montpellier on his way home from the curia, he met there the venerable Arnaud, the abbot of Cîteaux, and brother Peter of Castelnau and brother Raoul, both of them Cistercian monks; these were the Pope's legates, but, depressed by their inability to make any significant headway in their preaching to the heretics, they were thinking of abandoning their mission.[100] Whenever they wanted to preach to the heretics, the heretics raised against them the objection of the appalling lives of the clergy.[101] But if they were to try to reform the lives of the clergy, they would have to give up their preaching. In face of this dilemma, Bishop Diego gave them the sound advice that they should forget about everything else and devote themselves even more earnestly to preaching; and, to enable them to shut the mouths of their malicious enemies, they should proceed in humility, like their loving Master, "doing and teaching,"[102] travelling on foot, without gold and silver, imitating in every way the pattern of the apostles. The legates were reluctant on their own authority to adopt such a novel policy, but said that if someone of suitable authority were to give them a lead in pursuing this way, they would gladly follow. Without hesitating, the God-filled bishop offered himself, and at once sent his retinue and his carriages back to his own town of Osma, and set off from Montpellier with only one companion,[103] together with two of the Cistercians, Peter and Raoul. The abbot of Cîteaux went back to Cîteaux because the General Chapter of their Order was soon to be held there, and because he intended, after the Chapter, to bring some of the abbots of the Order to help him in carrying out the job of preaching which had been laid upon him. *(Pierre de Vaux Cernai)*[104]

When Diego, the bishop of Osma, arrived in the territory of the Albigeois with his episcopal horses and baggage-train, he was told that the district was infected with heresy; so he preached in one of the towns there against heresy. The heretics rose up to oppose him, and the strongest argument they could find to support their false beliefs was the pomp of the bishop's équipe. "How can you believe this man and his like?", they said to their followers; "They turn up with all this pomp and wealth, with their pack-animals and their riding-horses, and then they preach to you a Christ who was humble and poor. We, by contrast, preach in poverty and lowliness and austerity, we display in our deeds what we have told you about in our words." This embarrassed the bishop, so he sent away his horses and his équipe and abandoned his provisions and began to go round the district with the blessed Dominic in poverty and on foot, preaching. This was the reason why our Order was founded. I was told about this by the first brethren who were with the blessed Dominic in that country. *(Stephen of Bourbon)*[105]

On one occasion a public debate was organised against the heretics. The local bishop proposed to go to it with an imposing entourage, but St. Dominic said to him, "No, my lord and father, that is not the way to go to meet such people. The heretics are to be convinced by an example of humility and other virtues far more readily than by any external display or verbal battles. So let us arm ourselves with devout prayers and set off showing signs of genuine humility and barefooted to combat Goliath." The bishop accepted what the man of God said, and he sent his equipage away and they set off barefooted.

The place they were going to was many miles away. On the way there they began to be uncertain of their route, so they asked the way of someone they thought was a Catholic, but in fact he was a heretic. "Certainly," he said, "Not only will I show you the way, I shall be delighted to escort you there myself." While he was taking them through a wood somewhere, he led them astray so viciously, through thorns and thistles, that their feet and legs became quite covered in blood. The man of God endured all this with the utmost patience; breaking out into a hymn of praise to God, he encouraged the others to praise God too and to be patient. "My friends," he said, "hope in the Lord. Victory will be ours, because even now our sins are being washed away in blood." The heretic saw their extraordinary and blissful patience, and he was pricked with compunction at the good words spoken by the man of God, so he admitted the poisonous way he had deceived them, and renounced his heresy.

When they reached the place of the debate, everything came to a satisfactory conclusion. *(Gerald de Frachet)*[106]

## TOULOUSE

In the name of our Lord Jesus Christ. Let all men know, now and in the time to come, that we, Fulk, humble servant, by the grace of God, of the see of Toulouse, hereby appoint as preachers in our diocese brother Dominic and his companions, to root out the evil of heresy, to drive away vice, to teach the rule of faith and to instruct men in sound morals. These men have made a religious commitment to travel on foot in evangelical poverty, preaching the word of gospel truth.

Now the labourer deserves his food[107] and it is not right to muzzle the treading ox,[108] and the preacher of the gospel ought to live by the gospel;[109] accordingly, since these men have come to preach, we desire that they should receive from the diocese their food and all else that is necessary for their support. With the consent of the Chapter of the church of St. Stephen[110] and of the clergy of the diocese of Toulouse, we assign in perpetuity to these preachers and to any others who are moved by zeal for the Lord and a longing for the salvation of souls to attach themselves to this task of preaching in this manner, one half of the third of the tithes which is devoted to the furnishing and maintenance of the fabric of all the parish churches under our jurisdiction. This is to provide for their clothing and whatever else they may need when they are sick and when they want to rest for a time. We decree that whatever is left over at the end of the year is to revert to the parish churches for their furnishing, or is to be used for the poor, as the bishop sees fit. The law requires that a certain portion of all tithes ought always to be devoted to the poor, and it is evident that we are under a special obligation to devote part of the tithes to those who freely choose evangelical poverty for the sake of Christ, and who strive and labour to enrich everyone with the gifts of heaven by their example and teaching. In this way we can appropriately repay those from whom we reap temporal profit by sowing spiritual seed for them, by our own endeavour[111] and by that of others.[112] *(Fulk, Bishop of Toulouse)*[113]

It occurs to me incidentally to mention something about brother John of Navarre[114] which I heard him relate himself. When the holy father Dominic was sending him to Paris, as has already been mentioned, with brother Laurence,[115] John asked to be given some provisions or some money for the journey. The saint refused to give him any, urging them to go like disciples of Christ, not carrying gold or silver. "Trust in the Lord," he said, "for those who fear God lack nothing." John would not accept this; he absolutely refused to obey the saint's word. When the holy and loving father saw the wretched man's disobedience, he fell at his feet, weeping and howling for the miserable man who would not weep for himself. He told them to give him twelve *deniers* for the whole journey to Paris. *(Stephen Salagnac)*[116]

After the death of that renowned prince, Count Simon de Montfort, who died at Toulouse in the Lord's army the day after the Nativity of St. John the Baptist, 1217, when the blessed father Dominic dispersed the brethren, he sent Peter Selhan[117] to Limoges, as I have often heard him relate—it was in his hands that I made my profession. He pleaded ignorance and lack of books, having only a few pages of homilies by St. Gregory. But St. Dominic said, "Go, my son, and go confidently. I will hold you before God twice every day.

Do not doubt, you will win many for God and bring forth much fruit." A short time after that he arrived at Limoges and was received with kindness by the bishop[118] and Chapter of Limoges, and was given a place to live; like one of the prophets of old, he was held in great honour in the land among the clergy and people and grew old there in great esteem. He was the first brother of the Order after St. Dominic. *(Stephen Salagnac)*[119]

Afterwards he often used to say to his friends that whenever he felt oppressed, in the convent or outside, he would invoke dom Dominic[120] and remind him of his promise, and then everything always turned out successfully. *(Bernard Gui)*[121]

## ROME

I was told by Bartholomew de la Cluse, archdeacon of Mâcon and a canon of Chartres, that when St. Dominic was in Rome, almost every day, after attending his Office, he went round the walls of the city and other places where there were recluses[122] and gave them advice for their salvation, like Tobias, who "visited all who were in captivity and gave them advice for their salvation."[123] Incidentally, he also told me that he had gone to confession to St. Dominic in Rome, and he had foretold many things that would happen to him because of his unwillingness to enter the Order; they did happen to him, he said. *(Stephen of Bourbon)*[124]

## BOLOGNA

One of the brethren told me this story about St. Dominic at Bologna. After spending the greater part of the night in prayer, he used to climb onto some wicker hurdles which were by this brother's bed. The brother heard him repeatedly groaning and roaring, and wondered what on earth it could be. However late he went to bed, he never found anyone there, and however early he got up he never found anyone there. So he asked another brother about it, and he told him that it was St. Dominic, who used to go there to rest a little, when it was nearly time for Matins. *(Stephen of Bourbon)*[125]

# ST. DOMINIC

## VARIOUS STORIES

Once when he was at prayer, after the brethren had already gone to bed, the devil came in the form of a friar and pretended to be praying at one of the altars. The saint was surprised that any brother should have stayed behind after the bell had gone, and signalled to him to go to bed. He bowed his head and went away. After Matins he warned the brethren that they were not to stay in church after the last bell. But that pretended brother did the same thing again a second and then a third time. So on the third night, while he was pretending to be praying, the saint came up to him and rebuked him. "What disobedience is this?", he said; "I have already told you repeatedly that no one is to stay behind, and this is the third time I have found you here." The devil laughed. "Now I have made you break the silence!" he cackled. The saint, perceiving his cunning, retorted, nothing abashed, "Wretch, don't let that make you too happy. It won't do you any good. I am above silence and can speak whenever I see fit." The devil retired in confusion. *(Gerald de Frachet)*[126]

St. Dominic once told brother Bertrand,[127] his companion, not to weep for his own sins, but for those of others; this was because he noticed that he was tormenting himself excessively for his sins. His words had such a powerful effect that thereafter Bertrand wept profusely for others, but was unable to weep for himself, even when he wanted to. *(Gerald de Frachet)*[128]

Truly the holy father was a Jacob in his preaching and an Israel in his contemplation, so that neither Leah nor Rachel was lacking to him in this way of life.[129] He used to travel round and send out his first brethren, even though he had only a few and they were indifferently educated and mostly young. Some religious of the Cistercian Order were amazed at this, and particularly at the confident way he sent such young friars out to preach. They set themselves to watch these young men, to see if they could find fault with anything they did or said. He put up with this for some time, but one day, filled with a holy boldness, he asked them, "Why do you spy on my disciples, you disciples of the Pharisees? I know, I know for certain, that my young men will go out and come back, will be sent out and will return; but your young men will be kept locked up and will still go out."[130] *(Stephen Salagnac)*[131]

91

# EARLY DOMINICANS

## ST. DOMINIC'S DEATH

Meanwhile at Bologna, Master Dominic began to be seriously ill, as the end of his earthly pilgrimage drew near. He summoned twelve of the more sensible brethren to his sickbed and exhorted them to be fervent and to foster the religious life of the Order and to persevere in the way of holiness, and he advised them to avoid keeping dubious company with women, particularly young women, because they are a real temptation, all too liable to ensnare souls which are not yet completely purified. "Look at me," he said, "God's mercy has preserved me to this day in bodily virginity, but I confess that I have not escaped from the imperfection of being more excited by the conversation of young women than by being talked at by old women." *(Jordan of Saxony)*[132]

It was in brother Moneta's[133] bed that St. Dominic was lying when he died, because he had no bed of his own; and he was wearing his tunic, because he had no second one of his own to give him a change from the one he had long been wearing. It was brother Moneta himself who told me this. *(Stephen Salagnac)*[134]

## THE TRANSLATION OF ST. DOMINIC

I want to give a faithful account of the translation of St. Dominic, the founder of the Order of Preachers, at which I was myself present.

In the year of Christ 1233, many of the brethren of the Order met at Bologna for the General Chapter, together with Master Jordan of fond memory, St. Dominic's successor. At that time miracles were becoming more and more common in the church where his holy body was buried ingloriously enough, and there was a flourishing devotion among the people. The archbishop of Ravenna and several other bishops were asked to come, including the lord William who was at that time bishop of Modena, but is now Cardinal Bishop of Sabina,[135] who was a doubting Thomas with regard to these miracles, but who afterwards, as I have been told, gave evidence that they were genuine.

These men were entrusted by Pope Gregory with the job of putting the remains of the holy body in a more fitting resting place; it had lain for about twelve years buried low in the ground, and the tomb had several times been exposed to the rain and the snow. So on the 23rd of May, which was the Tuesday after Pentecost,[136] to avoid having too many people present, the bishops and some of the brethren and some other devout people assembled at night to perform their appointed task. With iron tools they just managed to raise the huge stone which lay on top of the grave, and they found underneath it a very hard cement, which they could only remove with difficulty. They then found the wooden coffin, and when they opened the lid of it, they all smelled such a sweet scent that it was like an exhalation from a spice cabinet of paradise. This fragrance was unlike any other scent. It seemed to be "the smell of a good field which the Lord has blessed,"[137] to make it plain that Dominic, the preacher of the Lord's praise, had been the "good odour of Christ"[138] in the field of the church. And not without reason, because he excelled in the violet of humility, he was white with the lily of virginity, and patience blossomed in him like a rose in spring. He had trodden the grape of cheerful preaching in the saving chalice of his King. He had indeed been a chest of spices and had preserved untainted the balm of a good reputation and the purity of his conscience. And there was another remarkable thing too: this scent not only clung to the body itself and the things that were near it, but if the bones were touched by anybody's hand or by any cloths, the same scent clung to them too for quite a long time. In the morning people came thronging with great devotion, and the choir intoned, "Receive the joy of your glory"[139] with loud voices, and the liturgy was celebrated very happily. *(Bartholomew of Trent)*[140]

# The Nine Ways of Prayer
*of St. Dominic*

The holy teachers Augustine, Leo, Ambrose, Gregory, Hilary, Isidore, John Chrysostom and John Damascene and Bernard[141] and other devout teachers, both Greeks and Latins, have spoken extensively about prayer, recommending it and describing it, telling us how necessary and useful it is, how to do it and how to prepare for it, as well as indicating the obstacles that may arise. In addition to these, the renowned and glorious teacher, brother Thomas Aquinas[142] and brother Albert[143] of the Order of Preachers in their books, and brother William in his treatise on the Virtues,[144] have expounded the subject nobly and systematically, devoutly and attractively.

However, what we must say something about here is the way of praying in which the soul uses the members of the body in order to rise more devotedly to God, so that the soul, as it causes the body to move, is in turn moved by the body, until sometimes it comes to be in ecstasy like Paul,[145] sometimes in agony like our Saviour,[146] and sometimes in rapture like the prophet David.[147] The blessed Dominic used often to pray like this.

We find, in fact, that the holy men of the Old and New Testaments sometimes prayed like this. This manner of praying stirs up devotion, the soul stirring the body and the body stirring the soul. Praying this way used to make St. Dominic dissolve utterly into weeping, and it so kindled the fervour of his good will that his mind could not prevent his bodily members from showing unmistakeable signs of his devotion. So, by the sheer force of his mind at prayer, he sometimes rose up in petitions and entreaties and thanksgiving.

Apart from the common ways of prayer in the celebration of the Mass and in the prayer of psalmody in the canonical Hours, which he practised very devoutly both in choir and when he was travelling, and during which he often seemed suddenly to be caught up above himself to speak with God and the angels, his ways of praying were as follows.

# ST. DOMINIC

## THE FIRST WAY OF PRAYER

First of all, bowing humbly before the altar as if Christ, whom the altar signifies, were really and personally present and not just symbolically.[148] As it says, "The prayer of the man who humbles himself pierces the clouds."[149] He used sometimes to say to the brethren the text from Judith, "The prayer of the humble and meek has always been pleasing to you."[150] It was by humility that the Canaanite woman obtained what she wanted,[151] and so did the prodigal son.[152] Also, "I am not worthy to have you come under my roof."[153] "Lord, humble my spirit deeply because, Lord, I am utterly humbled before you."[154] So the holy father, standing with his body erect, would bow his head and his heart humbly before Christ his Head, considering his own servile condition and the outstanding nobility of Christ, and giving himself up entirely to venerating Him.

He taught the brethren to do this whenever they passed before a crucifix showing the humiliation of Christ, so that Christ, who was so greatly humbled for us, should see us humbled before his greatness.[155] Similarly he told the brethren to humble themselves like this[156] before the whole Trinity whenever the *Glory be to the Father* was recited solemnly. This way of prayer, as illustrated in the picture, was the beginning of his devotion: bowing deeply.

## THE SECOND WAY OF PRAYER

St. Dominic also often used to pray by throwing himself down on the ground, flat on his face, and then his heart would be pricked with compunction, and he would blush at himself and say, sometimes loudly enough for it actually to be heard, the words from the gospel, "Lord, be merciful to me, a sinner."[157] And with great devotion and reverence he would recite the words of David, "It is I who have sinned and done unjustly."[158] He would weep and groan passionately, and then say, "I am not worthy to look upon the height of heaven, because of the greatness of my sin; I have provoked your anger and done evil in your sight."[159] He would also say, emphatically and devoutly, the verse from Psalm 43:25, "My soul is laid low in the dust, my belly is stuck to the earth."[160] And again, "My soul is stuck to the floor, make me come alive according to your word."[161]

Sometimes, wanting to teach the brethren with what reverence they ought to pray, he would say to them, "The Magi, those devout kings, entered the house and found the child with Mary his mother.[162] Now it is certain that we have found him too, God and man, with Mary his handmaid, so come, let us fall down and worship before God, let us weep before the Lord who made us."[163]

He exhorted the young men too, saying to them, "If you cannot weep for your own sins, because you have none, still there are many sinners to be directed towards mercy and love, for whose sake the prophets and apostles groaned in distress, and for their sake too Jesus wept bitterly when he saw them, and similarly the holy David wept and said, 'I saw the half-hearted and I pined away.' "[164]

## THE THIRD WAY OF PRAYER

For this reason, rising up from the ground, he used to take the discipline with an iron chain, saying, "Your discipline has set me straight towards my goal."[165] This is why the whole Order determined that all the brethren, out of respect for the memory of St. Dominic's example, should take the discipline on their bare backs with sticks of wood every ferial day after Compline,[166] saying the *Miserere* or the *De Profundis*. They were to do this either for their own sins or for those of others whose gifts supported them. So no one, however innocent, should withdraw himself from following this holy example.

## THE FOURTH WAY OF PRAYER

After this, St. Dominic, standing before the altar or in the Chapter Room, would fix his gaze on the Crucifix, looking intently at Christ on the cross and kneeling down over and over again, a hundred times perhaps; sometimes he would even spend the whole time from after Compline till midnight getting up and kneeling down again, like the apostle James,[167] and like the leper in the gospel who knelt down and said, "Lord, if you will, you can make me clean,"[168] and like Stephen who knelt down and cried out with a loud voice, "Lord, do not hold this sin against them."[169] And a great confidence would grow in our holy father Dominic, confidence in God's mercy for himself and for all sinners, and for the protection of the novices whom he used to send out all over the place to preach to souls. And sometimes he could not contain his voice, but the brethren would hear him saying, "To you, Lord, I will cry, do not turn away from me in silence, lest in your silence I become like those who go down into the pit,"[170] and other such words from sacred scripture.

At other times, however, he spoke in his heart and his voice was not heard at all, and he would remain quietly on his knees, his mind caught up in wonder, and this sometimes lasted a long time. Sometimes it seemed from the very way he looked that he had penetrated heaven in his mind, and then he would suddenly appear radiant with joy, wiping away the abundant tears running down his face. At such times he would come to be in an intensity of desire, like a thirsty man coming to a spring of water, or a traveller at last approaching his homeland. Then he would grow more forceful and insistent, and his movements would display great composure and agility as he stood up and kneeled down.

He was so accustomed to genuflecting that, when he was on a journey, both in a hostel, after the toils of the road, and on the road itself, while the others were sleeping or resting, he would return to his genuflexions as to his own special art and his own personal service. This way of prayer he taught more by the example of his practice than by what he said.

## THE FIFTH WAY OF PRAYER

Sometimes, when he was in a convent, our holy father Dominic would stand upright before the altar, not leaning on anything or supported by anything, but with his whole body standing straight up on his feet. Sometimes he would hold his hands out, open, before his breast, like an open book, and then he would stand with great reverence and devotion, as if he were reading in the presence of God. Then in his prayer he would appear to be pondering the words of God and, as it were, enjoying reciting them to himself. He had made his own the Lord's practice which we read about in Luke 4:16, "Jesus went into the synagogue on the sabbath day, as he was accustomed to do, and stood up to read." And it says in Psalm 105:30, "Phineas stood and prayed and the pestilence stopped."

At other times, he joined his hands and held them tightly fastened together in front of his eyes, hunching himself up. At other times he raised his hands to his shoulders, in the manner of a priest saying Mass, as if he wanted to fix his ears more attentively on something that was being said to him by somebody else. If you had seen his devotion as he stood there erect in prayer, you would have thought you were looking at a prophet conversing with an angel or with God, now talking, now listening, now thinking quietly about what had been revealed to him.

When he was travelling, he would steal sudden moments of prayer, unobtrusively, and would stand with his whole mind instantaneously concentrated on heaven, and soon you would have heard him pronouncing, with the utmost enjoyment and relish, some lovely text from the very heart of sacred scripture, which he would seem to have drawn fresh from the Saviour's wells.[171]

The brethren used to be greatly moved by this example, when they saw their father and master praying in this way, and the more devout among them found it the best possible instruction in how to pray continuously and reverently, "as the eyes of a handmaid are on the hands of her mistress and as the eyes of servants are on the hands of their masters."[172]

## THE SIXTH WAY OF PRAYER

Sometimes, as I was told personally by someone who had seen it, our holy father Dominic was also seen praying with his hands and arms spread out like a cross, stretching himself to the limit and standing as upright as he possibly could. This was how he prayed when God restored the boy Napoleon to life at his prayer at San Sisto in Rome, both in the sacristy and in the church during the Mass in which he rose from the ground, as we were told by that devout and holy sister, Cecilia, who was present, with a great crowd of others, and saw it all.[173] Like Elijah when he raised the widow's son, he stretched himself out over the boy's body.[174]

He also prayed in the same way when he rescued the English pilgrims near Toulouse when they nearly drowned in the river, as has been related elsewhere.[175]

And this was how the Lord prayed when he hung on the cross, his hands and arms stretched out, when, with great cries and weeping, his prayer was heard because of his reverence.[176]

The holy man of God, Dominic, did not use this kind of prayer regularly, but only when, by God's inspiration, he knew that some great wonder was going to occur by virtue of his prayer. He neither forbade the brethren to pray like this nor did he encourage it.

When he raised the boy from the dead, praying standing with his arms and hands stretched out like a cross, we do not know what he said. Perhaps he used the words of Elijah, "Lord my God, I beseech you, let the soul of this boy return within him,"[177] just as he followed his manner of praying. But the brethren and the sisters and the cardinals and the rest who were there were paying attention to his manner of praying, which was unfamiliar and remarkable to them, and so they did not take in the words he spoke. And afterwards they could not ask the holy and extraordinary man, Dominic, about it, because in this deed he had shown himself to be an object of awe and reverence to them all.

However, he did sometimes recite, seriously, deliberately and carefully, the texts from the Psalms which refer to this manner of praying: "I cried to you, Lord, all day long I have stretched out my hands to you" *(Ps. 87:10)* and "I have stretched out my hands to you, my soul is like soil without water before you, speedily hear me, Lord" *(Ps. 142:6–7)*.

This makes it possible for any devout man of prayer to understand the teaching of this father, praying in this way when he desired to be extraordinarily moved towards God by the power of his prayer, or rather, when he felt himself being moved by God in a particularly expansive way, through some hidden inspiration, in view of some special grace for himself or for somebody else. He can base himself on the teaching of David, the symbolic expression of Elijah, the love of Christ and the devotion of Dominic.

## THE SEVENTH WAY OF PRAYER

He was also often found stretching his whole body up towards heaven in prayer, like a choice arrow shot straight up from a bow. He had his hands stretched right up above his head, joined together or slightly open as if to catch something from heaven. And it is believed that at such times he received an increase of grace and was caught up in rapture, and that his prayer won from God for the Order he had founded the gifts of the Holy Spirit, and, for himself and his brethren, such delight and enjoyment in putting the Beatitudes into practice, that each one would consider himself blessed in the most profound poverty, in bitter grief, in severe persecution, in great hunger and thirst for righteousness, in all the cares and worries of mercy, and that they would all consider it a pleasure to observe the commandments with devotion and to follow the evangelical counsels. At such times the holy father seemed suddenly to enter the Holy of Holies and the third heaven. And so after this kind of prayer, he bore himself like a prophet, as has been related in the *Miracles*,[178] whether he was rebuking or dispensing or preaching.

To give just one example, briefly, for edification's sake,[179] once at Bologna, after praying like this, the holy master Dominic asked the advice of some of the senior brethren about some decision that had to be made. This was his normal practice because, as he said, something may be shown to one good man which is not shown to another, as can be seen in the prophets. The sacristan then came and called one of the people taking part in this council to go to the women's church to hear a confession, I think, and stupidly added, though not loudly enough to be heard by the holy master Dominic, "A beautiful lady is asking for you! Come at once." The Spirit came upon St. Dominic then and he began to be disturbed in himself, and the councillors looked at him with fear. Then he told the sacristan to come to him, and he asked him, "What did you say?". He replied, "I was asking for a priest to come to the church." And the father said, "Reproach yourself and confess the sin which came to your lips. The God who made all things made me aware of what you thought were your secret words." And he disciplined him there severely and long, so that those who were present were moved to compassion because of his bruises. Then he said, "Now, my son, go your way. Now you have learned how to gaze at a woman in the future: make sure you don't judge of her appearance. And you too should pray that God will give you chaste eyes." In this way he knew what was hidden, rebuked the brother's folly, and punished him and taught him, as he had foreseen it all in prayer. And the brethren were amazed that this was what he said had to be done. And the holy master said, "Our judgments, by comparison with those of God, are nothing better than filth."[180]

So the holy father did not remain long in this kind of prayer, but returned to himself as if he were coming from far away, and at such times he seemed to be a stranger in the world, as could easily be seen from his appearance and his behaviour. While he was praying he was sometimes clearly heard by the brethren saying, as the prophet did,

"Hear the voice of my supplication while I pray to you, and while I lift up my hands to your holy temple."[181]

And the holy master taught the brethren to pray like this both by his words and by his example. He quoted the verses from Psalm 133:2, "At night lift up your hands to the holy place," and Psalm 140:2, "The raising of my hands like an evening sacrifice."

## THE EIGHTH WAY OF PRAYER

The holy father Dominic also had another beautiful way of praying, full of devotion and grace. After the canonical Hours and the grace which is said in common after meals, the father would go off quickly on his own to a cell or somewhere, sober and alert and anointed with a spirit of devotion which he had drawn from the divine words which had been sung in choir or during the meal; there he would sit down to read or pray, recollecting himself in himself and fixing himself in the presence of God. Sitting there quietly he would open some book before him, arming himself first with the sign of the cross, and then he would read. And he would be moved in his mind as delightfully as if he heard the Lord speaking to him. As the Psalm says, "I will hear what the Lord God is saying in me."[182] It was as if he were arguing with a friend; at one moment he would appear to be feeling impatient, nodding his head energetically, then he would seem to be listening quietly, then you would see him disputing and struggling, and laughing and weeping all at once, fixing his gaze, submitting, then again speaking quietly and beating his breast. If anyone was inquisitive enough to want to spy on him secretly, he would find that the holy father Dominic was like Moses, who went into the innermost desert and saw the burning bush and the Lord speaking and calling to him to humble himself.[183] The man of God had a prophetic way of passing quickly from reading to prayer and from meditation to contemplation.[184]

When he was reading like this on his own, he used to venerate the book and bow to it and sometimes kiss it, particularly if it was a book of the gospels or if he was reading the words which Christ had spoken with his own lips. And sometimes he used to hide his face and turn it aside, or he would bury his face in his hands and hide it a little in his scapular.[185] And then he would also become anxious and full of yearning, and he would also rise a little, respectfully, and bow as if he were thanking some very special person for favours he has bestowed. Then, quite refreshed and at peace in himself, he would continue reading his book.

## THE NINTH WAY OF PRAYER

This way of prayer he used to observe when he was going from one country to another, especially when he was in a lonely place. He disported himself with his meditations in his contemplation. And sometimes he would say to his travelling companions, "It is written in Hosea, 'I will lead her into the wilderness and speak to her heart.' "[186] So sometimes he went aside from his companion or went on ahead or, more often, lingered far behind; going on on his own he would pray as he walked, and a fire was kindled in his meditation.[187] And a curious thing about this kind of prayer was that he seemed to be brushing away ashes or flies from before his face; and because of this he often defended himself with the sign of the cross. The brethren thought that in this kind of prayer the saint acquired the fulness of sacred scripture and the very heart of the understanding of God's words, and also a power and boldness to preach fervently, and a hidden intimacy with the Holy Spirit to know hidden things.

And so it happened once, to mention just one story out of many which we leave out,[188] that the devil came to the church of the Friars Preachers in Bologna, in the form of a young man of frivolous, licentious character, and asked for someone to hear his confession. Five priests were brought to him, one after the other. This was because the first confessor was so viciously disturbed and enflamed by his words that he got up from listening to his confession and refused to hear such dreadful things through to the end. The second did the same, and so did the third, the fourth and the fifth. But they went away without saying anything, and they were not prepared to reveal this confession because, as far as they were concerned, the confession they had heard was a sacramental confession, even though this was not how the devil saw it. Then the sacristan approached St. Dominic, who was in the convent at the time, complaining about these priests, because five of them had not been able to hear one sinner's confession. "It's scandalous!" he added; "the priests preach penance and then they refuse to give penance to sinners." Then the holy father Dominic got up from his reading and prayer and contemplation, not, I think, unaware of what was afoot, and went to hear the devil's confession. When he entered the church, the devil came to him and at once the holy father recognised him and said to him, "You evil spirit, why do you tempt the servants of God under this veil of piety?". And he rebuked him severely. The devil disappeared at once, leaving the church reeking of sulphur. And the sacristan was appeased and stopped being angry with the priests.

# St. Dominic
## Notes

1. Mt. 24:12.

2. Prophetic visions like these are too much part of the stock-in-trade of hagiography, Christian and pagan alike, for us to be very confident of their reliability here. "Setting the world on fire" goes back to Hecuba, the mother of Hector of Troy (Apollodorus III 12:5). St. Bernard's mother is supposed to have had a dream about a dog (signifying a preacher) before Bernard was born (PL 185:470). See F. Lanzoni, *Il Sogno Presago della Madre Incinta, Analecta Bollandiana* 45 (1927) pp. 225–61.

3. Bl. Diego of Azevedo, prior of Osma, then bishop from 1201 until his death on December 30, 1207. He was an eager supporter of his predecessor, Martin Bazán, in his attempts to reform the clergy of his diocese, and was instrumental in turning the Cathedral Chapter back into a Chapter of Canons Regular. See Vicaire, *SDHT* pp. 35–6.

4. I.e., Denmark or Northern Germany. Koudelka, AFP 43 (1973) p. 9.

5. For a truer account, see Cernai, above, pp. 86–7. For an evaluation of the different accounts of the beginnings of the preaching in Languedoc, see Vicaire, *Dominique et ses Prêcheurs*, pp. 133–6. For the dating of the meeting at Montpellier, see J. Gallén, *Les Voyages*. Jean de Mailly's account is derived from Jordan, *Libellus* 19, which telescopes three distinct historical realities into one. The twelve abbots were in fact recruited afterwards by Amalric (Vicaire, *SDHT* p. 106); the large gathering of prelates with one papal legate occurred at Montpellier in 1215, not 1206 (Cernai, 543). This telescoping in the Dominican tradition may be due to an unconscious desire to highlight the importance and originality of the Dominicans by ignoring the real contribution made to the preaching in Languedoc by the legates and other preachers. Cf. Stephen of Bourbon, 251, where a Provençal Dominican tradition is reported, according to which the twelve abbots (curiously become 13, not an apostolic number!), when faced with the heretics' criticism of their horses and wealth, simply abandoned their mission and went home, in evident contrast to Diego, who responded by sending his retinue away (see above, p. 87). This tradition is quite false to the facts, as we learn them from good contemporary evidence (Vicaire, *SDHT* pp. 106–114), but is in accordance with the feeling, endorsed by successive popes, that the Order of Preachers was a God-sent provision for a desperate situation (cf. Honorius III's Bull, *Quoniam abundavit* [MOPH XXV p. 124] and Gregory IX's Bull of Canonization of St. Dominic [MOPH XVI pp. 190–4]).

6. For this dispute, which took place at Montréal, see Vicaire, *SDHT*

pp. 101–5; Griffe, II pp. 255–7. In spite of the miraculous element in the dénouement, the role of doctrinal argument in the dispute should not be minimised. If we may trust Puylaurens, 9, about 150 heretics were converted by the *arguments* of the Catholics.

7. Bl. Fulk of Marseilles (c. 1155–1231). At first a poet and business-man, he and his family all became Cistercians c. 1195; c. 1201 he became abbot of Le Thoronet. In 1205 he became bishop of Toulouse. See Vicaire, *SDHT* p. 119; SCH 12 pp. 83–93.

8. This was in accordance with the ruling laid down at the Council (Lateran IV, canon 13).

9. It was normal for houses of canons to adopt Constitutions of their own, as well as the Rule of St. Augustine. Cf. Thomas, *Constituties*, pp. 8–29. The Dominicans made use of those of the strict Order of Praemonstratensian canons, though their borrowing was very selective. See below, Appendix, pp. 456–65.

10. These doggerel verses are not original to Jean de Mailly. They are also found in the autograph of the Praemonstratensian chronicler, Robert of Auxerre. See A. Dondaine, *Jean de Mailly*, p. 308.

11. Simon de Montfort (c. 1165–1218): commander in chief of the Albigensian Crusade until he was killed during the siege of Toulouse in 1218. For a sensitive account of the man, see Y. Dossat, CF 4 pp. 281–302. He was a friend and supporter of St. Dominic, and got the saint to baptize one of his daughters (who subsequently became a Cistercian nun at St. Anthony's, Paris) and to solemnize the wedding of his eldest son, Amaury; another daughter, Amicie de Joigny, both persuaded her son to join the Order and herself founded a monastery of Dominican nuns, of which she became the prioress, at Montargis (MOPH I p. 322). Simon's younger son was the Simon de Montfort who is famous in English history.

12. Matthew of France, who had come to the *Midi* with the Crusaders, became prior of the canons at Castres, where he met St. Dominic when the saint visited the church there; he shortly afterwards joined the Order (MOPH XXII p. 12); the church itself was later given to the Order, in 1258 (MOPH XXIV p. 135). Whether the title "abbot" was meant to indicate that Matthew was to be superior of the whole Order (as Jean suggests, following Jordan, *Libellus* 48), or just superior of the brethren in Paris, is controverted. See Vicaire, *SDHT* p. 234; Koudelka, AFP 33 (1963) pp. 92–4. In any case, he never functioned as more than the superior of the brethren in Paris. As prior of Paris he accepted the gift of the hospice of St. Jacques in 1221 (MOPH XXV pp. 160–2).

13. It was St. Dominic's constant ambition to go off and preach to the pagans, an ambition first fired, it seems, during his journey to Denmark with Diego. See Vicaire, *SDHT* pp. 56–7; Koudelka, AFP 43 (1973) pp. 5–11. He did not realise this ambition himself, but before his death he was able to send

Dominican missions to Scandinavia and to Hungary (Vicaire, *SDHT* pp. 363–4).

14. "Master" had less grandiose associations than "abbot" in the church of this period, and involved less canonical separation of the superior from his community. It was a title often used for the head of a band of itinerant preachers, or the head of a pious confraternity. See Koudelka, AFP 33 (1963) pp. 90–5; Thomas, *Constituties* p. 74[300]; CF 2 p. 66; Meersseman, *Ordo Fraternitatis*, p. 161. In particular, it had been used of the head of the preaching in the Midi (Cernai, 51, 67), and of Dominic after the establishment of his preaching there (Vicaire, *SDHT* p. 474[124]).

15. Bl. Reginald, canon of St. Aignan, joined the Dominicans in 1218, and was immediately put in charge at Bologna, as St. Dominic's vicar. While there he recruited energetically, with marked success. In 1219 he was sent to Paris, where, amongst others, he attracted Jordan of Saxony to the Order (Jordan, *Libellus* 58, 61–3). Both Reginald and his bishop were involved in the Albigensian Crusade (Vicaire, *SDHT* p. 248). † 1220.

16. Cf. Eph. 6:15.

17. Cardinal Stefano di Fossanova: appointed papal chamberlain in 1206, he became a cardinal in 1212. He was an important benefactor of the Cistercian abbey of S. Galgano near Siena, one of whose monks, James, features in several early Dominican stories. The cardinal became a good friend and supporter of St. Dominic and of the nuns at S. Sisto, for whom he secured various revenues, including some from England, a country with which he had been connected for some time. He died c. 1227. See Koudelka, AFP 35 (1965) pp. 5–15.

18. Acts 10:20.

19. Conrad of Urach, former abbot of Villers in Belgium, had been present at the siege of Toulouse in 1217 and may have known of Dominic since then. See Vicaire, *SDHT* p. 344. According to Ferrandus, *Legenda S. Dominici* 43, he told the Dominicans, "Although I wear the habit of a different religious profession, inwardly my mind is yours. I belong to your Order."

20. Text from the Preface of the Mass of our Lady. It became one of the mottos of the Dominican Order.

21. On the so-called Testament of St. Dominic, see R. Creytens, AFP 43 (1973) pp. 29–72. It is a literary invention, not an accurate report of anything St. Dominic actually said on his deathbed. This does not, of course, mean that it does not reflect his teaching fairly.

22. On the "curse" of St. Dominic, see Creytens in the article cited in the previous note. Once again, it is a literary device, not a historical record.

23. Bl. Guala entered the Order in 1219; he founded the convent in Brescia, and was made bishop of Brescia in 1229. †1244. See AFP 10 (1940) p. 345; MOPH XXII p. 75.

24. Cf. Gen. 28:12.

25. Cf. Vicaire, *SDHT* p. 387. This refers to part of the ceremony of Canonization.

26. The details of the Translation of St. Dominic are unusually well attested. Apart from the evidence in the Canonization Process, and that of Bartholomew of Trent, both contained in this book, we have two other eye-witness accounts: one ascribed, falsely, to Jordan (MOPH XVI pp. 82–8) and one from Pelagius of Portugal († 1240) (Kaeppeli, *Scriptores* III p. 210).

27. It is interesting that the traditional ascetic practice of keeping vigil in thus re-interpreted to apply to study. Thomas of Cantimpré claims that one reason why the friars were better lecturers in the University of Paris was that they "kept vigil and studied" at night, while the secular Masters ate and drank so much in the evening that they were unable to do this (*De Apibus* II x 31). That there was a conflict between some of the less intellectual brethren from the very early years of the Order (who were more enthusiastic about their prayers and devotions, and not very sensitive to the need for study) and the more educated friars who joined later is suggested by such stories as we find in MOPH I pp. 160–1 and Humbert II 91–2 (about a brother who "turned silly because of his excessive devotion"). In 1260, when Gerald de Frachet completed the *Lives of the Brethren*, people looked back with a certain nostalgia, as well as a certain amusement (not to mention a certain exaggeration), to the days when the brethren were habitually to be found in church (MOPH I p. 148). But it was Dominic himself who initiated the policy of looking for recruits especially in University circles, and the emphasis on study in the Constitutions goes back at least to 1220, if not to 1216 (Prim. Const. I 13: the novices are to be told that they ought to be "intent on study, always reading something or thinking about something, by day and by night, at home and abroad"; II 29 specifies that students can stay up at night, if they want to, to study). Ideally, in fact, study and prayer merged to form a whole life of attentiveness to God and his words and works (cf. William of Tocco, *Life of St. Thomas Aquinas* 30).

28. It is interesting to notice in Pecham's reply to Kilwardby's letter to Dominican novices how the Franciscan instinctively takes "toil" (*laborare*) to refer to the hardships and austerities of life, whereas the Dominican instinctively applies it (as here) to working at something useful. See Pecham, *Tractatus Tres*, pp. 128–9.

29. Cf. above, note 19.

30. Interlinear Gloss to 2 Tim. 4:5.

31. Cf. Marginal Gloss to 2 Tim. 4:5, though the printed text and the MSS I have seen all have "To prevent him from tormenting himself too much," not the text given in Thomas Agni.

32. Marginal Gloss to Matt. 5:13.

33. Interlinear Gloss to Matt. 5:14.

34. Ecclus. 48:1.

35. Luke 1:17.

36. Matt. 5:17. The marginal Gloss includes the interpretation of these words to mean that Christ completed the Law by adding to it. Cf. next note.

37. Marginal Gloss to Matt. 5:19. The actual text of the Gloss reads: "Undoing the Law means not putting into practice what you understand correctly, or failing to understand what you have distorted, or whittling away the integrity of what the Lord added to the Law" (this is the text as it is found in the *Catena Aurea*, and, judging from the MSS I have looked at, it is a better text than that printed in Lyranus). I am not confident that the text of Thomas Agni ought not to be emended accordingly.

38. Cf., for example, Hilary (PL 9:937A), Chrysostom, *Homilies on Matthew* 16:4, Bede (PL 92:26D), Augustine, *On the Sermon on the Mount* I 8:20.

39. Interlinear Gloss to Luke 14:17.

40. This is presumably a rather inflated way of referring to St. Dominic's stopping the rain miraculously (cf. Jordan, *Libellus* 101).

41. This echoes what St. Bernard says about our Lady in *Sermons on the Assumption* IV 8 (V p. 249:17–18).

42. Cf. Luke 1:49.

43. Ventura entered the Order either in 1219 or in 1220 (Vicaire, *SDHT* p. 514[9]), became prior of Bologna in 1221, and was at some time provincial of Lombardy, but we do not know when (AFP 10 [1940] p. 373).

44. There is no consistency in the MSS in the way in which St. Dominic is designated. Koudelka (AFP 42 [1972] p. 60) suggests that C's fairly consistent use of *frater* or *magister* is likely to be original; but even C allows the occasional *beatus* and gives evidence that in his lifetime St. Dominic was addressed as *pater*. Even *sanctus* must be regarded as possible; Margaret of Hungary is frequently so designated in the seemingly reliable text of her Canonization Process. I have therefore simply followed B the whole way through.

45. In spite of the arguments of A. H. Thomas (AFP 39 [1969] pp. 5–52), it seems to me that we can and should take seriously the evidence that at least some early Dominicans were professed as Dominicans *before* receiving the habit. The earliest form of profession seems to have been a very simple gesture of a man putting himself "in the hands of" Dominic (or his representative). The subsequent clothing would indicate that this self-giving had been accepted and that the consequence of it was incorporation into St. Dominic's brotherhood of preachers. The mood is well caught in *Lives of the Brethren* IV 10 iv (see below, p. 131).

46. CV read "almost every day."

47. *Firmus* B, if correct, must be being used in a sense pointing to the development of Italian *fermato*. *Infirmus* T is out of the question. CV omit the word.

48. This probably refers to St. Dominic's deathbed conversation reported in Jordan, *Libellus* 92. It is a typically Dominican touch that St. Dominic should have ventured on this, to him, rather dubious self-revelation in order to be *useful*. The basic orientation of the Order towards usefulness is affirmed in many texts, especially and most authoritatively in the Prologue of the Constitutions (see below, p. 457).

49. The Cistercian abbey of Chiaravalle della Colomba, between Parma and Piacenza, was founded by St. Bernard in 1137 (Lippini p. 251[22]).

50. There are several references to St. Dominic's "Rule," which possibly hark back to an early formulation of the friars' principles of life, before the formal Constitutions were drawn up. Cf. Thomas, *Constituties*, pp. 58–60 for different views that have been propounded on this question. For a different interpretation, see Koudelka, AFP 33 (1963) p. 93.[13]

51. Ugolino (c. 1148–1241): nephew of Innocent III, who made him a Cardinal in 1198, and Cardinal Bishop of Ostia in 1206. In 1227 he became Pope as Gregory IX. He was a friend and supporter of both Dominic and Francis. In 1221 he was mandated by the Pope and the Emperor to raise troops in Northern Italy for a new Crusade and also to support their campaign to enforce the decrees of Lateran IV (cf. below, note 90). He was in Venice on June 13, and Dominic joined him there. According to CV Dominic arrived back in Bologna towards the end of July.

52. Rudolph of Faenza. See his own testimony, pp. 76–78. He entered the Order in 1219, on the occasion of the church of which he was parish priest being given to the Order. He was almost immediately made procurator of the convent. He died not long after 1250 (MOPH I p. 275; Quétif-Echard I p. 127).

53. Santa Maria del Monte was a Benedictine priory on St. Benedict's Hill, just south of Bologna. There was a popular shrine of our Lady there (Lippini, p. 252[25]).

54. On the history and archaeology of the great Dominican church and convent in Bologna, see Venturino Alce, *Il Convento di S. Domenico in Bologna nel secolo XIII* (Bologna, 1973).

55. Cf. John 17:12.

56. St. Dominic's promise is recalled in a much-loved responsory, *O Spem Miram*, composed some time before 1256.

57. The podestà in 1233 was Uberto Visconti (Sorbelli, p. 101).

58. William of Monferrato received the habit from St. Dominic in 1219. If, as seems probable, he is the "William" referred to in the most affectionate terms by Honorius III (MOPH XXV p. 137), he must have been left at the papal curia in 1220, and then decided to return to Paris for further study in December of that year. In 1235 he was at last given the satisfaction of being sent to the missions; he died in the East some time after 1237 (Quétif-Échard I pp. 48, 104–5).

59. It is out of the question that William should have known Diego personally. Possibly he had heard of Diego's comments through Ugolino (Gregory IX), or through former canons of Osma who had become Dominicans (Vicaire, *SDHT* p. 502[136]).

60. Amizo of Milan: a lawyer and notary of the Sacred Palace until he received the habit from St. Dominic in Milan in 1219. As prior of Padua, he would have been at the Provincial Chapter at Bologna in 1233, following immediately after the General Chapter. He acted as notary in 1252 for the commission investigating the murder of Peter of Verona (AFP 10 [1940] p. 320; AFP 23 [1953] p. 111[6]; Lippini, p. 266[44]).

61. *Maturus* CV, *modestus* BT.

62. This refers to the re-opening of the tomb for devotional purposes a week after the Translation.

63. Buonviso entered the Order in 1219. The same year he was sent to preach in his home town of Piacenza, and later, probably in 1221, he founded a convent there (Vicaire, *SDHT* p. 511[134]).

64. CV omit the curious detail that Buonviso apparently submitted this part of his evidence in writing. The procedure is certainly unusual, but this makes it all the less likely that it is a later falsification. Written testimonies from people not called to give evidence in person are not unknown; cf. Raymund of Peñafort, MOPH IV ii p. 54.

65. 1 Peter 3:9.

66. John of Spain, also known as John of Navarre, entered the Order in 1215; in 1217 he was, reluctantly, sent to Paris, but in 1218 he turns up in Rome, and from there is sent to Bologna, and is back again in Paris by August. We hear of him again in Languedoc in 1236 (Jordan, *Libellus* 51, 55; Vicaire, *SDHT* p. 249; Balme-Lelaidier I p. 128).

67. The church of St. Romain was given to the Dominicans in July 1216 (MOPH XXV pp. 68–9), though, if John's dates are correct, they must have had the use of it since at least August 1215. They stayed there until 1230, when they took possession of their new and definitive site, where they built the magnificent church and cloister of the Jacobins, recently restored to something of its former glory (CF 9 pp. 185–6).

68. I.e., Lateran IV (1215).

69. However repugnant it may seem to the modern mind, the use of the discipline was widespread in this period. The intense desire of many christians of the time to suffer with Christ and to do penance for their sins led them to seek out ways of afflicting themselves. But, as we can see from the Letters of Jordan of Saxony, for instance, the friars were not prepared to let this desire for self-punishment go entirely unchecked, nor did they lose sight of the fact that feats of bodily mortification are no substitute for the development of essential christian virtues.

70. The archbishop of Narbonne was Arnaud Amalric (see below, note 100); the bishop of Toulouse was Fulk (see above, note 7).

71. The house of St. Jacques, which was to become one of the main centres of Dominican life, and which gave the friars their French nickname of *Jacobins*, was put at their disposal in 1218 (Jordan, *Libellus* 53) and was given to them definitively in 1221 (MOPH XXV pp. 160–2). Before that it had been, since its establishment in 1209, a student hostel. After the Dominicans had moved in there, it became a University college as well as a convent, since lectures in theology were given there (Vicaire, *SDHT* pp. 260–1; Hinnebusch, *History* I pp. 58–9). In due course the Dominicans themselves began to provide Masters in theology, the first being Roland of Cremona, who graduated as a Master in theology and began to lecture in 1229 (Glorieux, *Répertoire* n. 1).

72. This was John of St. Albans, a lecturer in theology who had founded the hostel of St. Jacques; on him see Hinnebusch, *History* I p. 73.[112] After giving the hostel to the Dominicans, he lectured there at the request of the Pope (MOPH XXV p. 162). Later John of St. Giles, who entered the Order in 1230, established the second chair of theology there (Glorieux, *Répertoire* n. 3).

73. In March 1220, the Dominicans in Paris handed over control of their property at la Ferté-Alais to one of the chaplains of the Cistercian nuns at St. Anthony's, Paris (a monastery connected with the de Montfort family, as we learn from Stephen of Bourbon, 288; Simon de Montfort's daughter, Petronille, who was baptised by St. Dominic, became a nun there [MOPH I p. 322]); in May 1220 the archbishop of Sens authorised the foundation of a new monastery of Cistercian nuns at Villiers on the strength of this property (MOPH XXV pp. 122–6).

74. CV specify that the reason for this proposal was to secure the freedom of the clerics to devote themselves to study and preaching (cf. Acts 6:2–4). The Order of Grandmont grew out of the eremitical foundation of St. Stephen Muretus at Muret in the late eleventh century. It was from him that St. Dominic culled his famous principle of speaking always with God or about God (SOG p. 21). The laybrothers in the Order had abused their privileged position so cruelly that the Pope and the King of France had had to intervene, and it was only in 1216 that some kind of settlement was reached. See J. Becquet, "La première Crise de l'Ordre de Grandmont," *Bulletin de la Société Archéologique et Historique du Limousin* 87 (1960) pp. 283–324; Vicaire, *SDHT* p. 311.

75. I have added "rich and" from CV.

76. On the meaning of St. Dominic's "pursuit" of heretics, see Vicaire, *Dominique et ses Prêcheurs*, pp. 36–57, 143–8. There is no evidence that he ever deviated from his peaceful methods of preaching and debate. To call him

"Inquisitor" is, at the very least, anachronistic, as the office did not exist until ten years after his death.

77. I have added this sentence from CV.

78. Comminges is probably a mistake; it should be Couserans (Vicaire, *SDHT* p. 485[125-6]). Two witnesses in the Languedoc Canonization process say that they heard Dominic declare that he would "run away by night with his stick rather than accept a bishopric or any other such honour" (MOPH XVI p. 186). As Vicaire brings out well (*SDHT* pp. 152–3), the reason for Dominic's refusal is not just humility, but a concern to protect his freedom as a preacher and, above all, to maintain the clear distinction between the apostolic preaching of God's word and any exercise of power or authority.

79. It is interesting to notice that, as we learn from Jordan, *Libellus* 10, he did not just offer *ad hoc* assistance to the poor, he "founded an almonry" (cf. Vicaire, *SDHT* p. 451[70]).

80. The practice of begging only for one day at a time is primitive. It is found, for instance, in the *Life of Alexander Akoimetes* III 27, and cf. Didache 11:6. St. Dominic could have learned it from Grandmont (*Rule* 9 and 13), or from the Poor Catholics (G. Gonnet, *Enchiridion Fontium Valdensium* [Torre Pellice, 1958] p. 133). St. Francis seems to have adopted it too: see K. Esser, *Anfänge*, pp. 247–252. The Dominicans later abandoned it, to avoid wasting time that could have been given to study and preaching: see AGC 1240; Thomas of Cantimpré, below, p. 134; St. Thomas, IIa IIae q. 188 a.7.

81. *Potestatem haec faciendi* BT must mean "the authority to depose him." CV have a significantly different text: "Since the brethren refused to depose him, brother Dominic decided to have diffinitors appointed who would have authority, for the duration of the Chapter, over him and all the others, and over the whole Chapter, to make decrees and decisions and ordinations." There is a similar text in §2 in CV, similarly missing in BT. It is hard to choose between the two readings. In 2 and 33 the extra words in CV seem out of place; BT has all that is needed in 2, and in 33 it seems decidedly odd that St. Dominic should give such far-reaching powers to a limited group just because the whole group refused to depose him. Furthermore, in Dominican law going back, probably, to 1221 (Prim. Const. II 7-9), the whole Chapter is treated as constituting the diffinitory, and it is difficult to believe that this differs radically from the practice followed in 1220; even though, as Thomas points out, the Cistercian practice of entrusting certain decisions to a restricted group of diffinitors has left some traces in the Dominican legislation of 1221 (Prim. Const. II 20-1; *Constituties*, pp. 192-5), this surely refers only to matters of administrative detail, not to crucial matters of legislation. It is far more credible that, having failed to get the whole Chapter to depose him, St. Dominic instituted a procedure by which they could change their minds without making them all discuss the whole thing all over again. On the other hand, if we accept the reading of BT, it is very hard to imagine what could

have prompted the subsequent addition in CV.

82. On the archaeological and historical evidence for our knowledge of the precise place where St. Dominic died, and on the recent discovery of part of the original floor, see Venturino Alce, *La Cella dove morì S.Domenico* (Bologna, 1978). The site is now a chapel and is a favoured place of Dominican pilgrimage.

83. Stephen of Spain entered the Order in 1219; he was provincial of Lombardy from 1229–1238. In 1249 he became archbishop of Torres in Sardinia. He died before 1261 (AFP 10 [1940] p. 373; MOPH XXII p. 93; Eubel I p. 532).

84. CV, supported by Flaminius, give the detail that the books which Dominic sold were annotated in his own hand, and also add: "and they began to preach with him from that time onwards." From this, several scholars have inferred that Dominic lectured for a time at Palencia, as well as being a student there, and that he began his career as a preacher while still in Spain, either at Palencia or at Osma. See, for instance, Quétif-Échard I pp. 4, 52; Mamachi, p. 124; V. D. Carro, *Domingo de Guzman* (Madrid, 1973), pp. 289–298 (giving references to the highly fanciful development of Dominic's Spanish apostolate in some earlier writers); J. M. de Garganta, *Santa Domingo de Guzmán* (Biblioteca de Autores Christianos, Madrid, 1966) pp. 59–60. However, Stephen is plainly confused in his chronology, and other dependable sources, such as Jordan and Rodrigo of Cerrata (who was specially interested in the early Spanish background of Dominic) do not mention any teaching activity of Dominic at Palencia or any apostolate in Spain before the founding of the Order. It is quite possible, though, that some of the Spaniards who later joined Dominic had already known and admired him in Palencia (cf. Vicaire, *SDHT* p. 30).

85. The *venia* was a ritual prostration, used in many situations, including the rites of clothing and profession. For an illustration, see Vicaire and von Matt, *St. Dominic* no. 132.

86. The essential nucleus was (and is) the feudal gesture of putting one's hands in those of the superior and putting oneself at his disposal.

87. The Dominicans evidently liked loud singing in choir. Cf. Humbert, II p. 105.

88. Cf. Primitive Constitutions I 19, II 31, II 35.

89. John of Vicenza was a flamboyant and controversial figure, who made fierce enemies, like the Franciscan chronicler Salimbene, but was regarded by others as a saint. Thomas of Cantimpré gives him a hagiographical write-up (*De Apibus* II i 3ff). He played an important part in the devotional uprising of 1233 known as the "great Alleluia" (see Vicaire, *SDHT* pp. 377–9). For a rather negative assessment, see Tugwell, pp. 36–7. Cf. also pp. 128–9 below.

90. The evident satisfaction with which the gruesome fate of heretics is

greeted is a reminder that it was popular demand, as often as not, that called for the burning of heretics. It was only in 1224 that Frederick II decreed that this should be the penalty for convicted heretics (text in BOP I 126); before that, the burning of heretics was due to lynching rather than to the verdict of any court of law. During the thirteenth century popular opinion wavered considerably, but at least in some places at some times it was fiercely against the heretics. See Yves Dossat, CF 6 pp. 236–7, 370–4; Meersseman, AFP 21 (1951) p. 58; R. Manselli, *Studi sulle Eresie del secolo XII* (2nd ed., Rome, 1975) pp. 19–38; Vicaire, *SDHT* pp. 94, 469.[95] On the concerted campaign of Frederick II and the Pope to root out heresy and enforce the decrees of Lateran IV, see C. Thouzellier, RHE 45 (1950) pp. 508–42. This campaign should not be confused with the work of the Inquisition, which was only just beginning to come into existence in 1233. In view of the popular image of the Inquisition, it is worth recording the judgment of the most recent book on the subject, that the Inquisition "was set up in order to moderate popular zeal against heretics" and that "It substituted the rule of law for mob violence. . . . Once the Inquisition was established, except for isolated instances . . . the pyromania which had characterised lay attempts to suppress heresy came to an end" (Bernard Hamilton, *The Medieval Inquisition* [London, 1981] pp. 57, 98).

91. Theodoric (archbishop of Ravenna 1228–1249).

92. Paul of Venice entered the Order in 1219. It is possible, but not certain, that he is the same as the Paul mentioned in *Lives of the Brethren* I vi 4 (see below, p. 137). He died later in Venice, after a sickness that may be connected with the kidney trouble referred to in §45 here (MOPH I p. 270). We do not know the date of his death.

93. Cf. Primitive Constitutions II 31.

94. Cf. Primitive Constitutions II 26.

95. The Humiliati had a little church at Porto Legnago; in the early fifteenth century it passed to the Dominicans (Lippini, p. 301[91]).

96. Frugerio of Pennabilli. I follow Lippini in opting for Pennabilli, rather than the various other places that could earn a man the designation *Pennensis*. Nothing more seems to be known of him, unless he is the same as the Frugerius who was rebuked by the Provincial Chapter of the Roman Province in 1254 for totally neglecting his responsibilities as a visitator (MOPH XX p. 18).

97. If this refers to preaching to all comers, rather than to speaking about God or to God, it failed to get into the Constitutions.

98. Matt. 6:6.

99. *Libellus* 13.

100. On these three monks and their missions, see Vicaire, *SDHT* pp. 80–93. Arnaud Amalric was abbot of Poblet (1196–8), then of Grandselve (1198–1202), before becoming abbot of Cîteaux. In 1204 he was sent by the

Pope to combat heresy in the *Midi*. In 1212 he became archbishop of Narbonne. He died in 1225. For a balanced assessment of his character, see Griffe, II pp. 231–6. Less favourable, Vicaire, CF 4 pp. 265–8. Peter of Castelnau was archdeacon of Maguelonne from 1197; he became a Cistercian at Fontfroide in 1203, in which year he also became the Pope's legate in the *Midi* to counteract the heretics. In 1208 he was murdered by the heretics; his death, and the suspicion of implication in it that fell upon Count Raymond of Toulouse, led Innocent III to call the Crusade against the Albigensians. Raoul was also a monk of Fontfroide, also papal legate since 1203. He died in 1207. He seems to have been more of a preacher and less of a campaigner than his two colleagues.

101. From at least the time of the Council of Lombers in 1176, the attempt to discredit the Catholic clergy had been a major part of the heretics' strategy (Mansi XXII 159–60). But it was not only the heretics who complained about the clergy. In a letter from about July 1, 1200, Innocent III makes a swinging attack on the state of the clergy in the South of France, and particularly Berenger, the archbishop of Narbonne, "Whose God," he says, "is money" (PL 214:905; cf. Griffe, II pp. 210–2). A similarly savage attack is made in a letter of May 28, 1204 (PL 215:355–7). Jacques de Vitry, *Hist. Occid.* I–V, gives a very gloomy account of the state of civic and ecclesiastical life in Europe in the early thirteenth century, and lays the blame squarely on the clergy. Cf. Mandonnet-Vicaire II pp. 17–22; Renard, pp. 175–6.[16,17] In 1204 Innocent III instructs his legates in the South of France to make sure that their conduct and speech are such that "not even a heretic will be able to find fault with them" (PL 215:360B).

102. Acts 1:1.

103. I.e., Dominic, at this time still subprior of Osma.

104. *Historia Albigensis* 20–1.

105. Stephen of Bourbon, 83.

106. *Lives of the Brethren* II 2.

107. Matt. 10:10.

108. Cf. 1 Cor. 9:9.

109. 1 Cor. 9:14.

110. This was the Cathedral of Toulouse.

111. Koudelka (MOPH XXV p. 57) proposes to emend *nos* to *hos*, but this does not seem necessary.

112. I take this rather contorted sentence to mean that the bishop proposes to make this his spiritual return for the tithes and other dues paid by the laity to the church. Fulk's experimental employment of diocesan preachers may have influenced Lateran IV's canon 10 on preachers. Cf. R. H. Rouse and M. A. Rouse, *Preachers, Florilegia and Sermons*, p. 57.

113. 1215. MOPH XXV n. 63.

114. The same man as John of Spain. Cf. note 66 above.

115. Laurence the Englishman: apart from a vision he is said to have had in connexion with the friars' establishment in Paris, nothing more seems to be known of him (Jordan, *Libellus* 51).

116. *De Quatuor* III 7:8.

117. Peter Selhan: one of the very first to make profession to St. Dominic, he not only gave himself to the Order in 1215, he also gave his house in Toulouse, and there the Order began to take its institutional shape. He used to say, "The Order did not receive me, I received the Order" (Gui, *Libellus de Magistris*, p. 400). Probably in 1218 he was sent to Paris, from where, in 1219, he was sent to Limoges to establish a priory there; he was prior there until 1232. He died in 1257 (Jordan, *Libellus* 38; MOPH I p. 324; MOPH XXIV pp. 57–9).

118. Bernard de Savène (Eubel I p. 313, Gallia Christiana II 527–8).

119. *De Quatuor* I 8.

120. "Dom Dominic": this unexpected appellation of St. Dominic presumably echoes what Peter called Dominic in the early days, when Dominic was still technically a canon of Osma. The title "dom" was still given by some people to Dominic and other Dominicans for some years (e.g., MOPH XXV nos. 70, 74, 95, 139).

121. MOPH XXIV p. 59 (immediately after an almost exact citation of the paragraph given above from Salagnac).

122. *Immurati* here means "recluses," not, as is sometimes supposed, "prisoners." Cf. Koudelka, AFP 35 (1965) p. 17.

123. Tob. 1:15.

124. §158.

125. §199.

126. *Lives of the Brethren* II 15.

127. Bl. Bertrand of Garrigues is called "Prior of St. Romain" in October 1216 (MOPH XXV pp. 69–71); he was one of the party sent to Paris in 1217. In 1221 he became the first provincial of Provence. His family made over to the Order the original nucleus of the site in Toulouse where the Jacobins was to be built (MOPH XXII p. 151).

128. *Lives of the Brethren* II 19.

129. The Old Testament symbolism is classic. Augustine (PL 42:432–7) uses Leah and Rachel as types of the active and contemplative lives, and Jacob as the type of the would-be contemplative engaged in active apostolic work. Israel was normally taken to mean "seeing God," in spite of the fact that the Marginal Gloss on Gen. 32:28 refers to St. Jerome's refutation of this etymology.

130. In fact there is reason to believe that quite a few monks were leaving their monasteries in this period, often to join newer apostolic movements like the friars. Cf. Selge, pp. 267–8; Grundmann, *Religiöse Bewegungen*, pp. 391–2; PL 172:1411; PL 181:1722; Thomas, *Constituties*, p. 168.[182] For

Cistercians who became Dominicans, see below, pp. 257, 479; also ASOP I pp. 370–2; Vicaire, *SDHT* pp. 247, 364.

131. *De Quatuor* I 7.

132. *Libellus* 92.

133. Moneta of Cremona: a well-known Master of Arts lecturing in Bologna; when Bl. Reginald began his spectacular recruiting mission there in 1218, Moneta at first tried to resist, but was soon won over, and made profession to Reginald at the end of the year, though it was over twelve months before he was free actually to join the Order (MOPH I pp. 169–70). He was co-founder with Roland of Cremona of the convent in Cremona (1228). C. 1241 he composed a *Summa against the Catharists and Waldensians.* †c. 1250. See Kaeppeli, *Scriptores* III p. 137–9.

134. *De Quatuor* III 2:5.

135. William first became friendly with Dominic when he was still employed in the papal chancery (MOPH I p. 334); in 1222 he became bishop of Modena, then Cardinal Bishop of Sabina in 1244. †1251 (Eubel I pp. 7, 370). Bartholomew of Trent, who knew him personally (AFP 45 [1975] p. 100) tells us that he asked St. Dominic to receive him into the Order (ASOP XXII p. 42). Though he never became a friar, he seems to have had some affiliation to the Order (cf. Vicaire, *SDHT* p. 462[108]).

136. May 23 was the Monday, but the night was regarded as belonging liturgically to the following day.

137. Gen. 27:27.

138. 2 Cor. 2:15.

139. Introit for the Mass of the Tuesday after Pentecost.

140. *Translation of St. Dominic.*

141. It is unlikely that the author has specific works of these writers in mind; more probably he is going by some anthology of texts. All the fathers listed here, except Leo and Hilary, are quoted in the section on Prayer in the mid-thirteenth century florilegium, *Pharetra*, ascribed, falsely, to Bonaventure and printed in all the older editions of his works. Most of them feature also in slightly later *Manipulus Florum* of Thomas of Ireland.

142. Cf. *Commentary on the Sentences* IV d.15 q.4; *Summa Theologiae* IIa IIae q.83.

143. I do not know what works of Albert the author had in mind, but prayer is discussed several times in his commentaries on the works of the pseudo-Denys. See especially vol. XXXVII of the Cologne edition, s.v. *oratio* in the Index. The *De Forma Orandi* ascribed to him by its editor, A. Wimmer (Regensburg, 1902), also ascribed to Vincent of Beauvais (Quétif-Échard I p. 238), is almost certainly by Peraldus, in view of the close similarity to certain works of his.

144. William Peraldus (c. 1200–1271) treats of prayer in his *Summa de Virtutibus* III v 7.

145. 2 Cor. 12:2ff.

146. Luke 22:44.

147. Psalms 30:23, 115:11.

148. It is the altar itself which was regarded as a symbol of Christ; there does not seem to be any question yet of a tabernacle on the altar. However, Humbert already assumes that there would generally be a tabernacle on the main altar (I 175; cf. *Ordinarium* 290), though he does not seem to know of any particular devotion of praying before the Blessed Sacrament.

149. Ecclus. 35:21.

150. Judith 9:16.

151. Matt. 15:25.

152. Luke 15:21.

153. Matt. 8:8.

154. Cf. Psalm 118:107.

155. It is perhaps relevant that *maiestas* was used to designate a figure of Christ in glory (cf. mid-twelfth century Praemonstratensian constitutions, I 4).

156. It is revealing that *humiliari*, for all practical purposes, it taken as equivalent to "bow." Cf. Humbert, Sermons III 24:12 (see below, p. 354).

157. Luke 18:13.

158. 2 Sam. 24:17.

159. Prayer of Manasseh 9–10.

160. Cf. Marginal Gloss to Ps. 43:25: "If you kneel on the ground, you can still humble yourself further; if you do humble yourself further, so that your stomach sticks to the ground, then you can go no further. So this verse expresses extreme self-abasement."

161. Psalm 118:25.

162. Matt. 2:11.

163. Psalm 94:6.

164. Psalm 118:158.

165. Psalm 17:36.

166. Cf. Humbert II p. 145. He points out that this is a universal custom, even though it is not written into the Constitutions.

167. The apostle James the Less was famous for kneeling so much that he had knees like those of a camel (Eusebius, *History of the Church* II 23).

168. Mark 1:40.

169. Acts 7:60.

170. Psalm 27:1.

171. Isaiah 12:3.

172. Psalm 122:2.

173. There is a serious problem about exactly what happened, as we have a rather different account also emanating from Cecilia, in her *Miracula*

2, not to mention a somewhat more sober account in Jordan, *Libellus* 100, which comes from another eye-witness, Tancred, the prior of Rome.

174. 3 Kings 17:21.

175. *Lives of the Brethren* II 3. M has *en otra manera,* which must represent *aliter;* this must either be taken to mean "elsewhere" (cf. Humbert, Sermons I ii), or be emended to *alibi.* R omits the word, CV¹V²D adjust the text to make it refer back to an earlier passage in Dietrich.

176. Hebr. 5:7.

177. 3 Kings 17:21.

178. *Miracula* does not necessarily refer to any particular published collection of miracle stories. Account of miracles of St. Dominic were officially being collected at Bologna at least from 1255 (ACG 1255).

179. R omits this section.

180. Cf. Isaiah 64:6.

181. Psalm 27:2

182. Psalm 84:9.

183. Exodus 3.1ff.

184. The classic progression was *reading–meditation–prayer–contemplation.* Cf. Hugh of St. Victor, *De Meditatione* 1; St. Thomas, *Sent.* IV d.15 q.4 a.1; Guigo II, *Ladder of Monks* 2ff. The implication here is that St. Dominic misses out the middle term, going directly from 1 to 3, and from 2 to 4.

185. *Caputium:* although the dictionaries do not seem to notice this usage, *caputium* often means "scapular" as well as "hood" (in the earlier form of the Dominican habit these were not two separate garments, as they are now). Humbert II p. 6, at least in Berthier's text, treats *scapulare* and *caputium* as interchangeable; novices are told to fold their *caputium* on their knees when they sit down (II p. 220). At profession it is the *caputium* that is blessed (II p. 215; but *scapulare* in Primitive Constitutions I 16). The habit can be said to consist of the tunic, *caputium* and cappa (Humbert I p. 237; *Directorium* 11:10 [AFP 26 (1956) p. 118]). A capitular admonition about *scapularia* in ACG 1260 is repeated with the word *caputia* in ACG 1261. Cecilia, *Miracula* 1, reports that Dominic's *caputium* was so short that it only came down to his knees.

186. Hosea 2:14.

187. Psalm 38:4.

188. R omits this final story.

# B. Blessed Jordan of Saxony & Other Thirteenth-Century Dominicans

When St. Dominic died in 1221, the Order was already well established, and existed in many different countries. The essential structures of its life and government had taken shape, and it was no longer a small band of relatively unimpressive but enthusiastic men. Some of the leading figures in church life had been attracted to join or at least to support the Preachers, and in subsequent decades a great many more were to follow suit.

The second Master of the Order was Blessed Jordan of Saxony, who, although he had been in the Order only about two years, proved his worth admirably; under his rule the Order continued to win many of the best men available, particularly in the Universities, and became more fully conscious of its purpose and identity. He perished tragically in a shipwreck during a visit to the Holy Land in 1237, and his place was taken by the distinguished lawyer St. Raymond of Peñafort. He resigned in 1240, and John of Wildeshausen became Master. He was succeeded in 1254 by Humbert of Romans, a great and wise organiser, under whose leadership the Order acquired the liturgy and academic structure that remained characteristic of it until our own day. He also formulated many of the principles governing the Order's life and spirituality. When he resigned in 1263, his place was taken by Blessed John of Vercelli, who remained Master until his death in 1283.

During this period two of the greatest of all medieval theologians were at work in the Order: St. Albert the Great and St. Thomas Aquinas. But it was not only in the Universities that Dominicans prospered. There was a great deal of missionary work, and special *study houses were set up for the study of Arabic and Hebrew. Up and down Europe Dominican preachers were proclaiming the word of God to all kinds of people. One such preacher was William Peraldus, whose* Summa on the Vices and Virtues *enjoyed enormous popularity.*

*In this section we begin with an Encyclical Letter of Jordan of Saxony, followed by a selection of anecdotes about him, which reveal the sort of man he was and the kind of spirituality he exemplified. We then look at the rather polemical celebration of the mendicants that Thomas of Cantimpré included in a book he dedicated to Humbert of Romans in about 1260. Then, after more stories about a variety of Dominicans, well known or less well known, we take a fascinating extract from Humbert of Romans, which reveals the reluctance of the Order to let itself be bound by an excess of regulations (a reluctance Humbert only half shares). We then look at a sermon preached to the brethren by Peter of Rheims, either when he was prior of Paris or when he was provincial of the Paris province (before 1245, then, in which year he became bishop of Agen, in which position he is last heard of two years later). We conclude with a letter written to encourage Dominican novices to persevere in their vocation by Robert Kilwardby, probably in 1270, while he was provincial of England; in 1273 he became archbishop of Canterbury, and died in 1279.*

# Encyclical Letter of May 1233
## *Blessed Jordan of Saxony*

To all my beloved sons in Christ Jesus, the brothers in the province of Lombardy,[1] salvation and a fervent spirit!

Since I cannot come to you in person, as I should like to, my love for you prompts me and my concern to be useful to you urges me not to neglect this opportunity to pay you a kind of visit in writing. So long as we are still in this place of pilgrimage,[2] so long as men's hearts are crooked[3] and prone to sin, lazy and feeble in virtue, we need to be encouraged and roused, so that brother may be helped by brother, and the eagerness of heavenly love rekindle the flame in our spirit which our everyday carelessness and tepidity tend to extinguish. This is why, my dearest sons, I beg you, with all the force I have, not to forget your holy purpose and your profession. By the precious Blood which redeemed you, by that loving death which restored you to life, I urge you to think of those "ancient paths"[4] by which our predecessors hastened to their rest[5] with all the intensity of their spirit,[6] and now reign with the Lord, for ever comforted in bliss and repose; all the days of pain with which God humbled them[7] have now been turned to joy. When they lived on earth, it was for spiritual gifts that they were jealous[8]; they thought little of themselves and scorned the world. It was the kingdom they longed for, and so they were strong to endure hardship, enthusiastic for poverty, on fire with love.

Surely our father Dominic, of holy memory, was one of these. When he was living with us in the flesh, he walked by the Spirit, not only not fulfilling the desires of the flesh,[9] but actually quenching them at the source. He displayed a true spirit of poverty in his clothing, his food and his behaviour. He prayed constantly, was outstandingly compassionate, used to intercede for his sons with abundant tears, because of the fervour of his zeal for souls. Difficulties did not daunt him, obstacles did not worry him. We could see from the works he accomplished, from his virtues and miracles, what a great man he was on earth. Now that he is with God, his greatness has been made known to us in these last days, when we were moving his holy body from its previous burial place to a more noble tomb. I hope to tell you more fully another time of the signs and wonders that we saw.[10]

Praise to our Redeemer! Praise to Jesus Christ, the Son of God, for choosing such a man as this to be his servant and for setting such a man over us as our father, to form us by his religious training and inspire us by the example of his resplendent holiness. How precious in the eyes of him who judges men's spirits[11] is true humility of heart together with freely chosen poverty. How beautiful in the sight of God it is to give birth chastely and with radiance.[12] God's servant, Dominic, was mighty in all these virtues: he was humble in himself, not at all self-indulgent, jealous with a divine jealousy for all men,[13] and a virgin throughout his life.

Not so are those who glorify themselves. Greedy for their own private reputation, the more grace they receive for their neighbours, the more conceited they become in themselves. Not so are those who seek their own comfort and profess poverty without the reality of it. Instead of being detached from everything as they should be, they fuss spinelessly over small things which are not worth the trouble, and cannot endure to be without anything which their disordered will desires. Then there are those living among us who hide under a bushel[14] whatever grace of preaching or counsel they receive from the Lord, wrapping up the Master's talent in a napkin.[15] They too are not following their father's rule of charity. They are evidently at fault who hide the people's corn—may it not bring a curse on them![16]— and who do not give Christ's household their measure of wheat when it is due.[17] And there is another kind of carelessness which has become all too evident and widespread in these days: many superiors are not concerned about study, and frequently send out people who have got talent and intellectual ability, or employ them in all kinds of jobs, so that they are prevented from studying. Even the lectors themselves in some places are so half-hearted about their job and give lectures so reluctantly and infrequently that it is no wonder the students become even more unenthusiastic than their unenthusiastic teachers.

And even if the lectors are doing their work properly, there is a third problem they run into in the brethren: they are uninterested in their study, they hardly ever stay in their cells, they are lazy about their exercises and stupid in debates. In some cases this is because they do not want to be distracted from their unintelligent devotions; in other cases it comes from a dangerous and wretched appetite for a life of leisure. But the result is the same: apart from neglecting their own benefit and depressing their teachers, they deprive many people of a chance of salvation, when they could have helped them on their way to eternal life if only they had studied properly, instead of being careless about it. This is why so many among us have become enfeebled and why so many of our superiors and teachers have more or less gone to sleep,[18] and why there are even people perishing through their own carelessness.

In such circumstances, happy is the man who keeps to the golden mean, giving everything its proper measure; who avoids both cowardice and impetuousness[19] so that he can help plenty of other people without losing his own most useful practice of self-knowledge and constant, watchful, self-criticism; who does whatever he does, not because he is driven by the wind of human approval, but because charity urges him on[20] and the Spirit of God constrains him; who lets nothing of what he does or says fall fruitless to the ground, and whose path is not aimless:[21] in everything he looks purely and simply to the glory of God, the spiritual benefit of his neighbour, or his own salvation.

My brethren, this is a saying which not all can take.[22] How often do the sordid, aimless meanderings of our affections lead us along crooked paths, not directed in the way of truth[23] and with no eye on our proper goal. We say a lot, we do a lot, we endure a tremendous lot, which would make us so much richer in virtue, so much more fruitful in merit, if only charity abounded in our hearts, directing and ordering everything towards our proper goal, which is God. But as it is, our minds are too often occupied with futile thoughts, our feelings drawn by futile desires; we do not carry through to its end the sifting and purging of our hearts' purposes, so it is hardly surprising that we are so slow to accomplish anything, so sluggish is our ascent towards perfection.

Not that I would want to deny that there are some among you, by the mercy of God, for me to rejoice over and thank God for; there are some whose aim is beauty,[24] who do cultivate their consciences, who do seek perfection and who do work hard at their preaching, who are zealous in study, whose hearts catch fire in their prayers and meditations,[25] who keep the Lord always before them,[26] looking to him as the one who will reward and judge their souls.

My dearest brethren, rejoice, if you are such as these, and seek to abound still more. But if you are not yet like this, work at it, devote energy and attention to it, so that you may grow towards salvation in him who called you to this state of grace in which you find yourself, not to make you lukewarm, but to make you perfect. He it is who is our Saviour, loving and good, the Son of God, Jesus Christ, to whom be honour and dominion now and for ever and ever. Amen.

# Miscellaneous Texts
## on Blessed Jordan of Saxony

### FROM THE LIVES OF THE BRETHREN

One time when he went to Bologna, the brethren told him about one of the novices who was unsettled to the point of leaving the Order. In the world he had lived such an unusually comfortable life, with all that he wanted in the way of clothes and beds and furniture, food, games and other bodily pleasures, that he did not know the meaning of hardship or distress of spirit, except insofar as he had applied himself to study, and had in fact made such good progress in that that in a year's time he would have been qualified to begin lecturing on law. He had never been ill, had rarely lost his temper, had never fasted except on Good Friday, had hardly ever abstained from meat except on Fridays, had never been to confession and knew nothing of the prayers which are said in church except for the Lord's Prayer.

He had visited the brethren one day out of mere idle curiosity, and, not knowing how to say no, he had entered the Order.[27] But he soon regretted it. Everything that he saw and felt seemed like the second death to him. He could not eat or sleep, and even though he had hardly ever been angry at all while he was in the world, he had been so sorely tried since he entered the Order that he once picked up a psalter[28] and attempted to hit the subprior, who had made him join the Order, with it. It was in this state of distress, then, that Master Jordan found him. Learning that he was called Tedalto, he tried to encourage him by means of his name: "Tedalto," he said, "Your name means 'Tending upwards.' "[29] After talking to him for a while, he took him to the altar of St. Nicholas and made him kneel down and say the Our Father, since this was the only prayer he knew. He then laid his hands on his head and began to pray with all the warmth of his heart, entreating the Lord to free him from temptation. He prayed and prayed, and meanwhile the novice felt a certain consolation gradually penetrating his mind; he felt his heart change and become peaceful. When Master Jordan at last took his hands off his head, it felt, as he afterwards told several of the brethren, as if two hands which had been squeezing his heart were suddenly taken away from his mind, leaving his soul in great tranquility and consolation. After this he remained strengthened and fervent enough to endure many labours in the Order; he achieved a lot very usefully in the Order. *(III 6)*

It was his custom, when he was travelling, to give the whole time to prayers and meditations, except when he was reciting the Divine Office or discussing something useful with his companions, and he would only do this at a fixed time. He encouraged his companions to do likewise. Because of this he often walked apart from the brethren. And sometimes he used to sing *Iesu nostra redemptio* or *Salve Regina* at the top of his voice, weeping as he went. Sometimes he was so thoroughly absorbed in his meditations and in the consolation he felt in his heart that he would wander off from his brethren in the wrong direction, but no one ever saw him at all put out when he went astray like this, nor did he ever blame his companions. It was rather they who were put out, and he used to cheer them up, saying, "Never mind! It is all on the way to heaven." *(III 7)*

The father was so full of grace and so fervent in the word of God and in the job of preaching, that there was hardly another to be found his equal. The Lord had given him a certain privilege and a special grace, not only in preaching but also in conversation, so that wherever he was, whoever he was talking to, he overflowed with enthusiastic talk, brilliant with apt and powerful illustrations, so that he spoke to the precise condition of all those he addressed, giving satisfaction and encouragement to all alike. Everyone longed to hear him. *(III 11)*

Once he set off from Lausanne to go and see the bishop, who was in the neighbourhood, because they had been good friends for a long time. Several of the brethren were going on ahead of him and he was following on behind, talking to the sacristan of Lausanne about Jesus. Suddenly a stoat ran out in front of the brethren and disappeared into a hole. They stopped by the hole. When the Master came up and asked, "Why are you standing here?" they said, "Because a beautiful little white animal has gone into that hole." Then the Master bent down and said, "Come out, beautiful little animal, so that we can look at you." It came out at once into the mouth of the hole, and fixed its eye on him. Then the Master put one hand under its front paws and stroked its head and back with the other hand. The stoat did not resist at all. Then the Master said to it, "Go back now to your place, and blessed be the Lord who created you." At once the little animal went back into its hole. The sacristan of Lausanne told this story.[30] *(III 17)*

Once, when the father was going with a crowd of friars to the General Chapter in Paris, he sent the brethren out one day in a certain town to beg bread for their meal, telling them to re-assemble at a certain spring nearby. They brought back a small quantity of coarse bread, which would hardly be enough for four people. The saint broke out into a song of joy and praise, and encouraged the brethren by his word and by his example to do likewise. A woman in the neighbourhood saw them and was scandalised. She said to them, "If you are religious, why are you making merry like this so early in the day?". But when she learned that it was because they were short of bread that they were exulting in the Lord, for whose sake they had chosen to be poor, she ran home and fetched them bread and wine and cheese in abundance, recommending herself to their prayers. *(III 34)*

At the time when brother John of Vicenza was achieving such remarkable results from his preaching in Bologna and rousing almost the whole of Lombardy with his grace of working miracles and of preaching, so that they were all eager to see and hear him, the people of Bologna sent some distinguished and cultured men as their "ambassadors," as they called them,[31] with a message to the Master while he was at the Chapter with the diffinitors and the other brethren who had come to the General Chapter.[32] On behalf of the whole Commune they petitioned them not to move brother John from their city. Among many other arguments, the one they put forward most powerfully and attached most weight to was that he had sown the word of God in their city with much grace, and they were afraid that the results which they expected from his preaching might be lost if he were not there. The Master, thanking them for their devotion and good will to the Order, replied, "Good sirs, the reason you allege why brother John ought to remain here, that he has sown the word of God and that the results might be lost if he were to go away, does not move us very much. When people seed their fields, it is not normal for them, when they have sown in one field, to take their beds there and lie down to wait until they can see what kind of harvest they are going to get from their seed. They are more likely to entrust the seed and the field to God and to move on to sow in another field. So maybe it would be better for brother John to go and sow the word of God somewhere else. It is written of our Saviour himself, 'There are other cities too to which I must preach the word of God.'[33] But because of the love we have for your city, we will deliberate about your petition with our diffinitors, and we will, with God's grace, do enough for you to make you satisfied." *(III 42 v)*

Once, when Master Jordan was in a Cistercian abbey somewhere, many of the monks gathered round him. They said, "Master, how will your Order be able to survive? You have nothing to live off except alms, and you know well enough that, though the world is very devoted to you now, the gospel says that the charity of many will grow cold,[34] and then you will not get alms and will collapse." The Master replied, with all gentleness, "I can demonstrate to you logically from your own words that your Order will fail sooner than ours. Look in the gospel and you will find that the text, 'The charity of many will grow cold,' refers to that time when iniquity will abound and there will be unbearable persecutions. Now you are well aware that at such a time persecutors and tyrants in the full flood of their wickedness will deprive you of your worldly goods, and then you will of necessity collapse, because you have not been in the habit of going from place to place seeking alms. But our brethren will then disperse and bring forth even more fruit, as the apostles did when they were scattered in the time of persecution.[35] Nor will they be too alarmed; they will go from place to place, in pairs, begging for their food, just as they have always done. And, what is more, I assure you that the very men who have robbed you will gladly support them, should they be willing to accept anything from them. We have already found frequently that thieves and bandits are often only too happy to give us alms from what they have stolen from others, if we were willing to accept them." *(III 42 vi)*

Pope Gregory commissioned some of the brethren to investigate certain monasteries[36] and they deposed several abbots without going through the proper legal processes, because they found that they were bad men. The Pope and the cardinals were so upset at this that they were going to rescind what the brethren had done, but Master Jordan arrived and, to soothe them, said, "Holy Father, I was once trying to get to a certain Cistercian monastery, and I found the ordinary road leading up to the door awfully long and twisting. The abbey was just close by, we could see it easily, and I and my companions thought it was a dreadful bore to have to go all that long way round, so I went straight to the door across the fields and got there much more quickly. Now if the porter had said to me, 'You cannot come in, because you did not come along the proper road; go back and come the usual way, otherwise I shall not let you in,' wouldn't you think that unreasonably severe? So, Holy Father, perhaps these brethren found the way of law too drawn out. If you care to look into the affair, you will easily discover that these abbots were well deserving of deposition. So, even though it was not done by way of the law, please accept what was done, however it was done." *(III 42 viii)*

He was asked once why arts men came thronging to join the Order, while theologians and canon lawyers held back. He answered, "Country people, who are used to drinking water, get drunk on good wine much more easily than noblemen and townspeople, who do not find wine very strong because they are used to it. Arts men drink the plain water of Aristotle and other philosophers all week, so when they are offered the words of Christ or his disciples in a Sunday sermon or on a feast day, they fall victim at once to the intoxication of the Holy Spirit's wine, and hand over to God not only their goods but themselves. But these theologians are always listening to the words of God, and they go the same way as a country sacristan who passes the altar so often that he loses his reverence for it and frequently turns his back on it, while outsiders bow reverently towards it." *(III 42 ix)*

Once, when the Master was overseas,[37] he was invited by the Templars to give them a conference. Now they were all French and he spoke hardly any French, but all the same he gladly offered to speak to them. When they were all assembled in a certain courtyard, with the Templars in front of him, he noticed that he could see a wall there, about as high as a man. Wanting to make them understand at the outset that, even though he only knew a very little French, he was confident that one little word of French would enable them to understand a whole long sentence, he said, "If there were an ass behind that wall and it raised its head so that we could see its ear, then we should all realise that there was a whole ass there, grasping the whole from one little part. So it can happen that there may be one

130

little word by which a whole long sentence can be understood, even if all the rest is in German." *(III 42 xvi)*

The Master was once preaching in Paris about people who linger in sin, when it occurred to him that sin is called in scripture "the door of Hell."[38] So he said, "If you were coming to this house today and saw a student sitting in the doorway, and then saw him there again tomorrow and again the next day and day after day, would you not naturally suppose that the student was going to enter the Order? Are we then to believe that those who sit day after day in the doorway of Hell will not eventually enter there?". *(III 42 xviii)*

One of the brethren asked Master Jordan whether it would be more useful for him to devote himself to his prayers or to apply himself to studying the bible. He replied, "Which is better, to spend your whole time drinking, or to spend your whole time eating? Surely it is best for them to take their turn, and so it is too in the other case." *(III 42 xxvi)*

One of the brethren asked him to teach him which would be the best way for him to pray. He replied, "Good brother, do not fail to apply yourself to whatever inspires the most devotion in you. The most beneficial prayer will be the one which moves your heart in the the most beneficial way." *(III 42 xxvii)*

There was also, in Vercelli,[39] a great cleric, a lawyer, and when he heard of the entry of some students who were friends of his into the Order, he forgot the books he had open before him and did not even stop to close them, he forgot everything he had in the house, and rushed off alone to the brethren, like a madman. Meeting an acquaintance of his on the way, who asked him why he was running like this all alone, he did not stop, but simply said, "I am going to God." So he reached the place where the brethren were lodged—they did not yet have a house of their own there. There he found Master Jordan and the brethren assembled together, and he threw off his silk cloak and prostrated himself in their midst as if he were drunk, and all he could say was, "I belong to God." Master Jordan then, without asking any questions first or getting any response[40] out of him except this, said, "Since you belong to God, in his name we make you over to him." And with that he got up and clothed him. *(IV 10 iv)*

# EARLY DOMINICANS

## FROM THOMAS OF CANTIMPRÉ

I remember the time and the place when brother Jordan of blessed memory, the second Master of the Order of Preachers, received into the Order in Paris sixty young men at one time, who were so uneducated that most of them, as I was told, could scarcely manage even to read a single lesson at Matins, even after they had been taken over it repeatedly.[41] They say that the brethren challenged him fiercely about this at the General Chapter, but he was filled with the Holy Spirit and said, "Let them be! Do not despise one of these little ones.[42] I tell you that you will see many of them, nearly all of them, in fact, turn out to be splendid preachers, through whom the Lord will work more for the salvation of souls than he does through many more intelligent and educated men." And we have seen how truly he spoke, and we see it still in our own day. *(De Apibus II xix 2)*

# Defense of the Mendicants
*Thomas of Cantimpré*

I had often heard of the ways in which the friars had to do without things, sometimes in considerable hardship, but I wanted to try it for myself,[43] and will tell you simply what happened to me with the friars in my own native land. I arrived on foot in some town which I did not know, so tired from the journey that I thought my heart would soon fail from my excessive weakness. The friars went to the priest's house, but could not get even a crust of the very black bread which the servants of his household were using. From there they went far and wide through the town and got nothing, except a piece of bran bread from a poor little lady who lived on the edge of the town—a large gift indeed, in fact a huge benefaction! So we sat down in the open air and ate the bread. And though the husks in the bread pricked our mouths as we ate, I never in my life enjoyed such a delicious meal. This made me reflect, not without a certain depression of spirit, on what those blessed men had been enduring all over the place, often in much worse situations than this, while I could not sustain such discomfort for even a single day. So I shall keep quiet about this kind of thing, which is constantly happening to them.

But there is just one thing which I do want to mention here. It is possible to distinguish three different kinds of way of life followed by our clergy. The secular clergy work at their studies, the canons, whether secular or regular, devote themselves to the celebration of the Divine Office, and the monks and other religious apply all their energy to the careful practice of their regular observances. But the friars, both the Preachers and the Minors, in accordance with the requirements of their Orders, seem to follow all three ways of life at one and the same time. They study with the clerics, they devote themselves to the Divine Office with the canons, and, in common with the monks and other religious, they practise community life with its accusations and beatings and fasting, and, in part, they also practise silence, and almost every day they all take the discipline after Compline; in addition to all that, they have certain observances of their own, so that, for instance, the Preachers wear a rough rope next to the skin round their loins, and wear woollen clothes which get prickly with all their sweat as they travel round on foot.[44] And apart from all that, they have chosen to live without owning any properties at all. What a labour it is for the Friars Minor to beg their bread every day! And what a labour it is for all the Preachers who go out generally to beg after August, to collect enough bread for the rest of the year, so that their study will not be hindered or prevented![45]

You most faithful and long-suffering men, do not be ashamed to beg your bread; Christ the Lord begged for a drink of water from a Samaritan woman.[46] Do not be afraid to be called and to be beggars; Christ himself, who is the Truth,[47] declared that the poor are blessed.[48] This is attested by both the New and the Old Testaments.

Christ is my witness that in saying all of this I am not seeking any special glory for these two Orders. They have their judge and it is he who seeks glory for them.[49] I am simply constrained to reply to their critics, who consider these new religious Orders to be superstitious and silly, and reckon their travelling round to be frivolous; to use their own word, they call the friars "gyrovagues."[50] Well, my brethren, you need not be ashamed to be called or to be gyrovagues. You are in the company of Paul, the teacher of the nations,[51] who completed the preaching of the gospel all the way from Spain to Illyria.[52] While they sit at home in their monasteries—and let us hope that it is with Mary[53]—you go touring round with Paul, doing the job[54] you have been given to do. And I am hopeful that if you suffer oppression in the world, you will still have peace in Christ,[55] perhaps even as much peace or more than they have who sit grumbling in their place of quiet, stirring up quarrels among themselves or with their superiors. And if they are free from quarrels, as they will perhaps claim, let them sit there if they want to, with all their warm clothes on, enjoying their peace, but then they should allow the friars, whom they call gyrovagues, to travel round the world in their meagre tunics and in rags, rescuing from the jaws of the demons souls that were redeemed by the life-giving death of Christ, while they, in their peaceful and carefree existence, turn a blind eye while such souls go down to Hell. If they were real religious and real lovers of Christ, these people who malign and criticize and ridicule the friars like this, what a welcome they would give them, how glad they would be to rejoice with the friars, who apply themselves to rescuing and saving the souls Christ thought it worthwhile to ransom with his own precious Blood, valuing them so much that he made nothing of doing whatever he could for the sake of their salvation.

While we are on the subject, let me record a vision seen by a Cistercian monk who was so holy that it would appear wicked and impious not to believe him. Caught up in spirit, he saw the patroness of the Cistercian Order, the loving Mother of Jesus Christ. The blessed Virgin said to him, "I commend to your charity my brethren and my sons, so that you will love them truly and pray for them all the more earnestly." He agreed to this happily, confident that she meant the brethren of his own Order. But she said, "I have other brethren too whom I take to myself, to be cherished and protected by my patronage." With these words, she drew back her cloak and revealed the brethren of the Order of Preachers gathered safely there, and she said to him, "These are men whose life's work it is to make sure that my beloved Son's blood was not shed in vain."

Brother Walter of Trier,[56] of the Order of Preachers, told me a similar story.[57] There was a lady in Saxony, a recluse with a high reputation for sanctity. When she heard of the Order of Preachers, in its early days, she was very excited by its name and passionately wanted to see some of the friars. Eventually, when the opportunity offered, she did see two young friars. She was amazed and said to the Lord, "What is this, Lord? Has the preaching of your word been usurped by such unskilled babies as these?". Soon after she had said this, the Mother of Christ appeared to her and drew back her cloak and showed her the brethren of the Order, saying, "Do not despise any such as these, because I am the one who guides and protects them, and I direct their feet into the way of peace."[58]

Now, reader, see how truly the Mother of Truth said this. Particularly in the beginning of the Order, but also in our own day, we have seen young men with no experience, delicately brought up, only recently converted from the world, touring round the world in pairs, not overthrown even though they are among wicked people, innocent among the harmful,[59] simple as doves among the cunningly malicious, but at the same time prudent as serpents in their care of themselves.[60] Who would not be amazed at boys like this, now even more than before, not being burned through they are in the thick of the blazing furnace,[61] while religious who belong to other Orders which are very strictly kept away from the turmoil of the world can hardly win through without tremendous difficulty, as we have, alas, seen and heard all too often? The friars are tormented by work, distracted by all kinds of different business, and yet they survive unbroken; but these others have nothing else to attend to except their own mental and bodily health, and yet they still wobble. To what are we to ascribe this? To their own strength? Surely not. Rather to the Mother of Christ. If there are some who fall, because they are flesh as well as spirit, it is because they have idly tried to support themselves on a broken reed of Egypt[62] instead of on Mary, the pillar of heaven.

So let our evil-mouthed and impious detractors beware of going against the patronage of the Mother of Christ by persecuting her children; if they do, they are liable to incur her anger, because she supports and defends her children. A certain Pope in our days, whose name we pass over in silence, out of respect for the Holy See,[63] issued letters against the privileges which had been granted by himself and the four previous Popes to these two Orders, one of which is called by the Creator from all eternity "Beauty," through the prophet Zechariah, and that is the Order of Preachers, the other of which is called "Rope,"[64] by which we may obviously understand the Minors. We have it from people who were in the Roman court at the time, and there can be no doubt about it, that on the very same day that he wrote these letters he was struck down by paralysis and lost his ability to talk; nor did he ever again regain his health or leave his bed.[65] What is more, he was seen after his death by a certain holy man living outside the walls of Rome, being handed over to the two saints of God, Francis and Dominic, to be judged.[66]

# Miscellaneous Stories

There was in Lombardy a woman leading a solitary life, who was very devoted to our Lady. When she heard that a new Order of Preachers had arisen, she longed with all her heart to see some of them. Now it happened that brother Paul[67] and his companion were passing through that part of the world, preaching. They visited her and, in the usual manner of the brethren, they addressed her with the words of God. She then asked them who they were and what Order they belonged to. They said they belonged to the Order of Preachers. But when she noticed how young and good looking they were, and how fine their habit was, she despised them, reckoning that people like that touring round the world could not last long in chastity. So the next night the blessed Virgin appeared to come and stand over her, looking annoyed. "Yesterday," she said, "you offended me seriously. Do you not think that I am able to look after my young men who are my servants, even while they run around the world for the salvation of souls? But to make you quite certain that I have undertaken a special responsibility for them, look, I will show you the men you despised yesterday." Lifting up her cloak, she showed her a great crowd of the friars, including those whom the anchoress had previously despised. So the anchoress was duly contrite and ever after loved the friars with all her heart, and published this story throughout the Order. *(Gerald de Frachet)*[68]

A certain brother Bene of Lombardy[69] was once fiercely tempted to leave the Order. So he cried out to the blessed Virgin with tears, "O Lady, when I was in the world, you helped me; do you now forsake your servant?". At once it seemed to him that the blessed Mother appeared to him, smiling gently and encouraging him.

Another night, he imagined that he was being carried out of the cloister by two men, and he cried out in fear, "Lady, keep me in your presence. Give me the grace to preach, for my own salvation and that of others." At once the blessed Virgin answered him, "Gladly." He wrote and told the Master of the Order about this. *(Gerald de Frachet)*[70]

One of the brethren once prepared a sermon carefully, but, at the last minute, when the time came for him to preach, he changed his topic and preached on something he had never intended to talk about at all, and, with the help of the blessed Virgin who gave him the words to say, he preached much better than if he had planned it beforehand. Dom James, a Cistercian from the monastery of San Galgano near Siena,[71] was present and saw the blessed Virgin standing in front of the preacher, holding an open book before him the whole time he was speaking. Those who heard the sermon and the preacher himself felt that it was a better sermon, more fervent and helpful, than any he had preached for a long time. *(Gerald de Frachet)*[72]

Brother Peter of Aubenas,[73] who served as prior and as lector in Provence and who ran his course in the Order happily to its end, has described how he came to join the Order. When he was practising medicine in Genoa and had already made a promise to join the Order,[74] the Poor Men of Lyons, also called the Waldensians, had such a disturbing effect on him that he was in great doubt which of the two he ought to follow. He was rather more drawn to the Waldensians he found there, because he saw in them more outward signs of humility and of the virtues of piety, while he considered the friars too cheerful and showy. So one evening, when he was brooding unhappily about this, not knowing what to do, he knelt down and asked God with all his heart, weeping profusely, to reveal to him, in his mercy, what he ought to do in this dilemma. After his prayer he went to sleep, and shortly afterwards he imagined that he was walking along a road with a dark wood on the left hand side of it, in which he saw the Waldensians all going their separate ways, with sad, solemn faces. On the right side of the road was a very long, high wall, which was extremely beautiful. He walked along it for some time and at last came to a gate. Looking in, he saw an exquisite meadow, planted with trees and colourful with flowers. In it he saw a crowd of Friars Preachers in a ring, with joyful faces raised towards heaven. One of them was holding the Body of Christ in his upraised hands. This sight delighted him and made him want to join them; but an angel who was guarding the gate blocked his way and said, "You will not enter in here now." He started to weep bitterly. Then he woke up and found himself bathed in tears and his heart joyful instead of his previous distress. After some days, when he had despatched some business he was obliged to do, he entered the Order. I heard this and a great deal more from his own lips. He was a very contemplative[75] man, and the Lord revealed many things to him in the Order and about the Order. *(Gerald de Frachet)*[76]

When Peter of Verona[77] was conducting the diffinitors of Spain, Provence, France and England from Vercelli to Bologna for the General Chapter in 1236, in the time of the war,[78] which he was able to do because he was well known and liked in that land, even by the enemy, almost every day he ran ahead into some village or town and rang its main bell and preached to the people. We often heard him crying out loudly, "What I am proclaiming to you is the Catholic faith which the church of Rome preaches, and in that faith and for that faith I am ready to die; indeed, I trust, in Christ, that I shall yet die for it."[79]

There was a novice who had entered the Order of Preachers, and some monks wanted to make him leave the Order he had entered and join their own Order. They said a lot against the Order he had entered, and spoke in glowing terms of their own Order. He then asked them whether the Lord Jesus Christ had given us a pattern of right living which excelled all others, and whether his own conduct was to be our rule. They said, "Yes." "So," he replied, "when I read that the Lord Jesus Christ was not a white monk or a black monk, but a poor preacher, I want rather to follow in his footsteps than in those of anyone else." *(Stephen of Bourbon)*[80]

Brother Gerald de Frachet was a highly favoured preacher to clergy and laity alike, eloquent and productive, and fully instructed in everything that concerns religion, and brought up in it from his earliest years; he was outstanding in his reputation, and in grace, eloquence, birth and esteem, always and everywhere overflowing with edifying words, carrying in his heart a great store of deeds of the saints and famous men and of remarkable and memorable historical facts, and knowing how to use these at the right time. He was a veritable treasure chest of stories. *(Bernard Gui)*[81]

There was in the convent at Castres, in the diocese of Albi, where the body of St. Vincent, martyr and deacon, lies, a brother whose name was John Descalars,[82] who came from Gascony. He was a devoted and good man, a fervent preacher and very religious. Brother Bernard,[83] who was his prior, praised him especially for his prompt and generous obedience in all things. He was a hard worker, very eager to be of service. He kept such a careful and loving watch over the purity of his conscience that he liked to receive the cleansing of sacramental confession, in which all sin is washed away, every day. He would not observe or wait for the usual times of confession, like anyone else, but would often hunt down a confessor after lunch or before or after Compline or at absolutely any hour of the day. In this way he cleansed his conscience, accusing himself of the most minute and trivial faults, for he had no others. Good and pious soul that he was, he saw faults where an experienced confessor could see none. Brother Bernard, who was the prior at the time of his death, has often told me that, listening to his daily confessions, several times a day sometimes, very often he could not help laughing affectionately at the good man's purity and innocence. Sometimes he laughed so much that he could not even manage to pronounce the usual words of absolution, in spite of brother John encouraging him and prompting him, "Say it, father, say, 'I absolve you,' " and sometimes even poking him with his hand. *(Bernard Gui)*[84]

Once, when I was in a large city in Brabant called Brussels, a girl came to me, who was not very well off, but was good looking. She was crying and asked me to help her. I encouraged her to tell me what the matter was. With a lot of sobbing and sighing, she said, "I'm in a dreadful state. A priest tried to take me by force and kissed me against my will, and I slapped him in the face and made his nose bleed. Now the clergy all tell me there is no alternative but for me to go to Rome about it." I could hardly stop myself from bursting out laughing, but I spoke to her very seriously, putting the fear of God into her as if she had committed a grave offence. Eventually I made her swear that she would do exactly what I told her. Then I said, "By the oath you have sworn, I command you: if he or any other priest tries to force his kisses on you or to pet you, clench your first tight and knock his eye out if you can. Whatever his rank may be, do not let him get away with it. It is quite lawful to hit anyone to preserve your chastity, as it is to defend your bodily life." Then I encouraged the girl herself and everybody else who was there to have a good laugh and to cheer up. *(Thomas of Cantimpré)*[85]

# Commentary on the Prologue
# to the Constitutions (Extract)
## by Humbert of Romans


Our Rule commands us to have one heart and soul in the Lord,[86] so it is right that we who live under a single Rule and by a single profession should be found uniform in the observances[87] of our canonical religion, so that the unity we are to maintain inwardly in our hearts will be fostered and expressed by the uniformity we observe outwardly in our conduct.[88]

We who are under obedience to a single Master are said to live by a single profession. And it is right that we who are united in this way should be found uniform in the observances of our canonical, that is, regular, religious life. It is the general practice among approved religious orders which live by a common profession that they should display the highest degree of uniformity in external things, not only in their observances, but also in their habit, their buildings, and in various other things too. It is with a certain sadness that we must realise how far we differ from the rest on this point. They have their churches and monastic buildings all conforming to the same pattern and arranged in the same way, but we have almost as many different patterns and arrangements of our churches and buildings as we have houses.

They are uniform in the colour, shape, size and cost of their clothes; but we are not like that. One man has a black cappa, another a red one, and yet another a grey one. Some people's cappas have a wide opening, some have a very narrow one; some are very expensive, some are cheap and some are in between. One man has a narrow scapular, another a broad one; some of them have pointed hoods at the back, others do not. Some of them have a long neck opening, some have a short one, and some have folds at the cheeks and some do not. Some people have cappas which cover their whole tunic, while others have cappas improperly shorter than their tunics; some of them are so short that they attract attention, while others are so long that they attract attention. Similarly with scapulars: some are very long, some are very short. And it is the same with the laybrothers: one has one kind of scapular, while another has one totally different in colour and in all the other ways mentioned above.

Other orders also observe uniformity in their shoes. But with us one man has black shoes and another has red shoes; some wear coarse, religious shoes, while others wear worldly, open shoes. Some are fastened one way, some are fastened in quite another way. Some of us have got into the way of wearing shoes so large that they almost come up to the knee, whereas others are very short, and some are in between.

Not only in our buildings and in our habit, but also in some of the customs we follow in the Divine Office and in many other things, there is tremendous diversity between our different provinces and even between different houses in a single province.

The reason for this diversity is the difference between different countries, the equal status of all the provinces and houses, and the excellent minds some people have. Different countries all have different customs, and out of this diversity different people have brought different things to the Order, even though it is only one Order. And since the houses and provinces are all equal, one province or house is not obliged to follow the customs of any other or to conform itself to any other. And since intelligent brethren are of the opinion that their own customs are as good as anyone else's, they are reluctant to abandon them unless an ordination of a General Chapter defines what practice is to be preferred.

If you ask why General Chapters have not taken counsel about this, to give us the same kind of written norms for the maintenance of uniformity in all things that other venerable religious orders have, there are many reasons for it.

One is that there are few brethren who travel around many different provinces and houses, and this means that there are only a few who have observed the amount of diversity there is; people think that whatever goes on in their own house is done everywhere. And so, because they are unaware of all this diversity, they have not made any move or sent petitions to the Chapter to give attention to it.

Secondly there are many people who do know about the diversity, but consider it superstitious to make constitutions about all this kind of thing; though it is rash to call men of approved religious orders "superstitious" or the men of old who established such constitutions in their religious orders.

The third reason is that the poverty of the Order is considered to make it more or less impossible to observe uniformity in many things. For example, because of poverty we do not always have uniformity in our clothes: one has better clothes to wear, another has cheaper clothes to wear and yet another has middling clothes, depending on what they are given in alms by people outside the Order. And the same thing applies to many of the things mentioned above.

Fourthly, it is not always helpful to have uniformity. Since we live among men, it is useful for us to conform ourselves to them in some things rather than to maintain our own unity. For example, in some places the brethren follow the local custom of giving a blessing at the end of a private Mass, while they do not do this in other places, where the custom is different. And the same kind of thing applies in other matters too. Religious who do not live among men can far more easily observe uniformity in such things.

Fifthly, the diffinitors have always been anxious not to burden the brethren with a multitude of constitutions.[89]

Sixthly, the diffinitors have been so busy settling matters which are more important and more necessary for the Order that they have not yet been able conveniently to find time for these things. But they will, God willing, in the future. After all, other Orders too did not legislate for all these things right away at the beginning, but they settled them progressively over a period of time.[90]

It would certainly be beneficial if this were to be done. All this variety has two unfortunate consequences. First of all, it disturbs the hearts of the brethren. The brethren are often disturbed when they are travelling round different places and see things being done differently from the way they are done elsewhere. And secondly it causes confusion among people outside the Order. Our diversity makes them think that we do not belong to a single brotherhood or make a single profession. So the text is quite right to say, "May we be found uniform in the observances of our canonical religious life," and then to add, "so that this external uniformity in our manners may cherish the unity which we ought to preserve in our hearts"—unity of a single brotherhood and a single profession, that is: this is directed against the first problem. "And that it may display our unity": this is directed against the second problem. Those who are careless about this kind of uniformity and trouble the unity of charity among the brethren make it obvious that they have no sense of unity with the rest internally in their hearts.[91]

Therefore, to provide for the unity and peace of the whole Order, we intend and declare that our constitutions do not bind on pain of sin, but only on pain of a penance, except in the case of contempt or of a formal precept.

In the Praemonstratensian text and in our own original constitutions, before this constitution was made, it said, "Therefore, to provide for the peace and unity of the whole Order, we have written this book etc," and anybody who compares this text with the present one can see that the older text runs more smoothly. But when this present constitution was made, they did not care where it should be inserted, provided simply that it was inserted—a common enough occurrence. By inserting it here they interrupted the smooth flow of the text. Even so, sense can be made of this constitution; we may say that "therefore" can be taken to mean simply "and," giving the sense, "And to provide etc." And then it makes good sense. By this constitution provision is made for the unity of the Order against the disagreement there had been before among the brethren, with some of them saying that the constitutions did bind on pain of sin and others saying that they did not.

Provision is also made for peace, with reference to people whose consciences were greatly troubled before by innumerable scruples which arose from a fear of sinning, which was due to the thought that the constitutions were binding in conscience.[92]

Or we may say that "therefore" refers back to what was said earlier about the unity we ought to have, giving the sense: According to what has already been said, we ought to have unity, but unity is disturbed if some people say that the constitutions bind on pain of sin and others say that they do not. "So, therefore, to provide for the unity and peace of the Order, we will etc."

Now you may ask why the text says "We declare" after saying "We will."

The reason is this. Before this constitution was written, I remember hearing from my seniors that this was always the intention of the Order, that the constitutions should not bind on pain of sin. So St. Dominic, at the Chapter at Bologna, said, to console the more timid brethren, that even Rules do not always bind on pain of sin. And if this was what people believed, then he would undertake to spend all his time going round convents destroying all Rules with his knife. I was told this by a brother who heard it. So the two things are said in the text: "We will," meaning that if the constitutions did previously bind in this way, they do so no longer; and "We declare," meaning that if they did not bind before, this constitution is to make this quite plain to everyone.[93]

# Sermon on Evangelists
## by Peter of Rheims

"The first living creature was like a lion, the second like an ox, the third like a man, and the fourth was like a flying eagle" *(Apoc. 4:7).*[94]

These four living creatures suit the four evangelists, because they are, in their own kinds, the most noble. The lion is the king of the beasts, the ox is the leader of all cattle, the eagle is the king of the birds and man is the most noble of all creatures.

A moral interpretation can take these four living creatures to mean the four kinds of people there are in our Order: priors, who are responsible for correcting the brethren, preachers and confessors, laybrothers who look after our temporal affairs, and those who are contemplatives and students.[95]

The lion signifies a superior. Lions carefully guard and protect the animals which are subject to them,[96] and so does a good superior. "Do not seek to become a judge unless you are strong enough to break up injustice" *(Ecclus. 7:6).* "The shepherds were watching over their flock" *(Luke 2:8).* "The lion is the bravest of beasts and is not scared by anybody's attack" *(Prov. 30:30).* Also lions are kind to those who humble themselves and cruel to those who rebel against them; similarly it belongs to a superior's position that he should "spare those who acknowledge his sovereignty and fight down those who are proud."[97] "Convince, rebuke, entreat" *(2 Tim. 4:2).* "Admonish troublemakers, encourage the faint-hearted" *(1 Thess. 5:14).* "The wrath of a king is like the roaring of a lion" *(Prov. 19:12)* 1 Macc. 3:4 says of Judas, "He was like a lion in his deeds." "The ox and the lion will dwell together" *(Isaiah 11:6),* when a superior is kind to those who are good and just to the wicked, so that honey will be found in the lion's mouth *(Judges 14:8).* Also lions rouse their dead cubs by roaring, and similarly a superior brings his subjects back to life by his exhortations, when they are dead through sin or carelessness or depression. Thus Christ brought the dead Lazarus back to life with shouts and groans *(Jn. 11:33ff),* and the apostle roared to the Galatians, "My little children, I am in travail again until Christ is formed in you" *(Gal. 4:19),* and Elisha shouted over the boy he was to raise

146

from the dead.[98] Also lions wipe out their tracks with their tails to avoid being caught by hunters; similarly a superior, in view of his final goal on high, ought to hide his good works beyond the reach of vainglory, and reduce them to nothing, because superiors are particularly exposed to the risk of vanity. But when we have done all manner of good things, we ought to say, "We are useless servants" *(Luke 17:10)*. "I am the least of the apostles" *(1 Cor. 15:9)*. Also, to hold lions' courage in check, nature has given them a quartan fever; similarly the Lord always leaves some defect in superiors to humble them, like Paul's sting in the flesh *(2 Cor. 12:7)*. "These are the nations which the Lord has left to train Israel by means of them" *(Judges 3:1)*. Was not Peter's denial a kind of fever? Or Thomas' doubting?

The man signifies preachers and confessors. Man is by definition a rational, mortal animal that is gentle by nature; similarly it is extremely necessary for a man who is a preacher and confessor to be rational, that is, intelligent,[99] and gentle. He needs to be intelligent in order to conduct himself well in the midst of a crooked and perverse people[100] and to distinguish different kinds of leprosy.[101] He needs to be gentle and approachable to extract the twisting snake from the hearts of sinners by the midwifely assistance of the hand of God *(Job 26:13)*. On both of these, "Be prudent as serpents and simple as doves" *(Mt. 10:16)*. Intelligence is well represented by a human form, because, just as man is the most noble of all creatures, so intelligence is the chief of the virtues. "Intelligence is not so much a virtue, as the controller of virtues," as Bernard says.[102]

The ox, being an animal which works the soil, signifies those who administer temporal affairs, and so it is appropriate that its face is said to be "on the left,"[103] because the left hand side signifies temporal things. "Where there are no oxen, the manger is empty" *(Prov. 14:4)*. Notice that the ox submits its neck to the yoke and offers up its body for sacrifice, and similarly these men, in spite of being engaged in worldly business, ought to be found perfect in obedience and voluntary penance.

The eagle, which is "above the four,"[104] refers to the contemplatives, whose position is higher and more peaceful. "Is it at your command that the eagle will rise up and make its nest on high?" *(Job 39:27)*. "From there it will contemplate its food" *(Job 39:29)*. "I saw an eagle flying through the middle of the sky" *(Apoc. 8:13)*. These are the eagles, who look straight in the face of the sun without flinching.[105] Eagles do not come down for mere flies, and similarly these men should not think about or look at things which are not their responsibility, but should always zealously contemplate the sun.

It is by these four living creatures that religious life is pulled along. If these living creatures were to "go" by making progress in the virtues, and "stand" by being solidly established in righteousness, and "rise up" in contemplation, then the wheels, that is, men in the world, would follow, provided that "the spirit of life was in the wheels." And notice that it is right to say, "They went with them as they *went*," not as they spoke.[106]

Notice in connexion with the progress of these living creatures that is says that they went "in the likeness of flashing lightning."[107] Lightning is characterised by speed, heat and brightness, and these three are very necessary attributes of preachers. They should be quick to go when they are sent out on the job of preaching. "If you have pledged yourself for your friend, run, hasten, rouse your friend" *(Prov. 6:1–3)*. This is why their speed is compared to the flight of clouds and doves in Isaiah 60:8, "Who are these who fly like clouds, like doves?". It was to indicate the importance of speed that the Lord commanded them to greet no one on the way *(Luke 10:4)*. "Go quickly, angels, to a torn and shattered people" *(Isaiah 18:2)*. This is why preaching is called "running," as when John is said to have been "running his course" in connexion with his preaching *(Acts 13:25)*.

They ought also to be hot with the fervour of their charity and zeal. This is why the Holy Spirit was sent to the apostles in the form of fire, to make them hot so that they could set others on fire *(Acts 2:3)*. Anyone who is not burning will not be able to set anyone else on fire.

Also they should be radiant with their doctrine, their example and their good reputation. "You are the light of the world" *(Mt. 5:14)*.

# Letter to Dominican Novices
## by Robert Kilwardby

Brother Robert, to the novices of the Order of Preachers, beloved in Christ: May you be enlightened by the grace of the sevenfold Spirit through your pursuit of holiness.

Consider your calling[108] and notice its characteristics, so that you may magnify the Lord and exult in God our Saviour.[109]

First of all, you should know that, before our Order arose, certain holy people were vouchsafed revelations from God, which we now have in writing,[110] showing that the prayer of the glorious Virgin obtained this Order from her Son, when he was angry at the sins of the world, for the reconciliation of sinners. And it is not unreasonable to believe that it is from her too that the Order's progress and advancement and its guidance and preservation come. This has often been revealed from on high. So let us embrace our state of life all the more carefully, seeing how devotedly we ought to love such a patron, guardian and guide as we have in her, and how keenly we ought to honour her and how humbly we ought to reverence her.

Then you should know that this Order resembles the state of life of the apostles, and that which our Saviour deigned to display in his earthly life.[111] Of him it is written, "Jesus began to preach and to teach, 'Do penance, for the kingdom of heaven has come close.' "[112] And again: "Jesus went about all the towns round about, teaching."[113] Then he also laid this job upon his disciples, saying, "Go into the world and preach the gospel."[114] And the apostle says, "He has put in us the word of reconciliation," beseeching people for the sake of Christ, "Be reconciled to God."[115] Now what else, I ask you, does the Order of Preachers do, as it goes round so solicitously preaching the gospel and reconciling sinners?

So those who are called by a divine prompting to such a state of life ought rightly to boast in Christ, seeing that they desire to apply themselves to carrying out the very job of Christ himself and his apostles.

But some, who profess other states of life, say, "We too are likewise preachers, just as much as the members of the Order of

Preachers."[116] To them we reply, in accordance with the truth, that there are indeed people in other states of life who preach, but they do not do it in the same way. For the friars of the Order of Preachers do it by virtue of the very institution of their Order, by virtue of their job which gives them their name; others do it, certainly, but in imitation of them, because they cannot find anything better or more useful that they could do.[117] So what our Order does essentially by virtue of its original institution, others try to do in imitation, incidentally and beside their formal profession. So we, who have been chosen precisely for this purpose, should rejoice that we are an occasion of so much good to other people; we possess by right, in virtue of our foundation, what others imitate out of devotion.

Then you should notice the usefulness of our state of life, my beloved novices. In this, unless I am mistaken, our state of life ought, on any true calculation, to be preferred to all others. For all our Chapters and discussions and debates and all the Order's study aim at nothing else than to prepare people and make them fit for the salvation of souls, and, when they are prepared and equipped in their way of life and in knowledge, to direct them to the task of converting sinners. So I reckon that no other Order works as hard in its concern for this as ours does, or achieves so much by its work.

Therefore those who have such a vocation ought rightly to rejoice, since it is well known that at the last judgment the reward is to be meted out in accordance with what a man merits by his useful labour.[118]

In addition to this, please look thoroughly at the special arrangements made in this Order about penance and austerity.[119] The brethren of this Order are not prevented from edifying their neighbours in the fierce cold by the torment of having to go barefooted, nor, on the other hand, do they receive the comfort of going barefooted in the heat of summer.[120] Also when they go out they do not enjoy the luxuries and delicacies of worldly cuisine.[121] We believe that the reason for the first point, in God's plan, is to avoid being prevented in any way from teaching the people. The second and third points are to give an example of the austerity involved in salutary penance and of perseverance in it. The one is necessary if truth is to be made known, the other is to give an example of how to live.

Who would not cleave to such a state of life, once he had tasted its savour in his spirit?

If a question arises about poverty, on which many people vaunt themselves,[122] I consider that our state is the one which is truly to be praised. Who would dare deny that the poverty of Christ and his disciples was more perfect than that of any other? Well, we read that that most perfectly holy company of Christ and his disciples had purses and carried in them what they were given for their livelihood and bought food from them.[123] We know that the Order of Preachers lives in just the same way, with the addition that they own houses and gardens and schools to hold their teaching in.

At this point some people claim that they possess nothing at all, either in common or individually, they hold no cash or money either in their own persons or through intermediaries, which is a far higher degree of poverty than the one I have been describing, which I said belonged to the company of the apostles. To this we reply that we do not wish nor should we wish to engage in quarrels, so we readily grant that their profession is as they say it is; may they do well in keeping it thoroughly![124] But it is enough for us in this regard not to go beyond the perfection of that apostolic poverty which Christ taught in the gospel.

In addition, I would point out that nobody ought to regard himself as superior to the rest because of his material poverty,[125] unless he is conscious of being more poor in spirit than the rest. It does not say, "Blessed are the poor in things," but "Blessed are the poor in spirit."[126] If there are any who regard themselves as better than the rest because of their state of poverty and because of this make less of others or reduce them in the eyes of men, then they ought to ask themselves whether they can reasonably be said to possess that poverty of spirit, in which humility resides, without seeking to make itself public, and in which charity too principally resides, which seeks always to commend other people.

And, finally, since neither receiving nor possessing is a vice, nor is non-possession or non-receiving a virtue—it is the use of things which matters: if it is intemperate it is vicious, if it is temperate it is virtuous—what good is it boastfully to regard yourself as better than anyone else just on the strength of not receiving or not possessing anything, as if this constituted a more excellent state, when it is in fact indifferent, as far as vice and virtue are concerned?[127]

So, if anyone is to boast, it should be people who reckon that they excel in poverty because of their more sparing and temperate use of things, always provided that they attribute this to Christ and do not wish to be known in order to be praised, nor to be preferred to others in such a way that the others are despised; for if that is the case, not only have they not won their reward, but because they have jettisoned humility and charity, they will actually be in a state of sin.

So let Christ's poor receive and possess what is necessary for this mortal life, saving always the apostolic principle, which the Saviour and his disciples observed, "Having food and enough clothing to cover them, with this let them be content."[128]

Maybe some wag will say, "Why, then, do you possess books and church furnishings, which are neither food nor clothing?"[129] To this the answer is that the text of the apostle, "Having food etc," refers to people's bodily life, but this objection raises a matter of a person's own spiritual benefit and that of his neighbour. The apostle did not neglect his books.[130] And the primitive church established the principle of the faithful living together and having things in common, the first of which is necessary if truth is to preached, the second to give form to charity; for the first, there is no doubt that books are needed, and for the second, where men live together in a common life, church furnishings are needed.

Having said all this, to foster love of our state of life, we must go on to say that we should despise nobody and no state of life; it is profitless to fuss over human statutes and neglect the command of God which bids us love our neighbour as ourselves—on which St. Augustine teaches that "neighbour" must be taken to mean everybody.[131] So let no individual person or state of life be found to be debarred from our love, which we have in God, because in commanding us to love even our enemies,[132] he plainly showed that he wanted no one at all to be excluded from love. So, far from us be all detraction, criticism, insult, gossip or cursing, whether of people or of any state of life, far from us be all comparisons at the expense of others. If we hear anyone telling stories of this kind or insinuating criticisms, we should rebuke him and deny him our attention, turning our faces sadly away from him.[133] For, though we are bound by charity to commend our own state in accordance with truth, we cannot justly detract from any other state.

## A Dominican Blessing[134]

May God the Father bless us,
May God the Son heal us,
May the Holy Spirit enlighten us and give us eyes to see with,
  ears to hear with,
  and hands to do the work of God with,
  feet to walk with,
  and a mouth to preach the word of salvation with,
  and the angel of peace to watch over us and lead us at last,
  by our Lord's gift, to the kingdom.

     Amen.

# Blessed Jordan of Saxony
# & Other Thirteenth-Century
# Dominicans
## *Notes*

1. Thus the MS, but Kaeppeli is right to say that a similar letter must have gone to all the other provinces too.
2. Ps. 118:54.
3. Jer. 17:9.
4. Jer. 6:16.
5. Cf. Hebr. 4:11.
6. Ps. 47:8.
7. Ps. 89:15.
8. 1 Cor. 14:12.
9. Gal. 5:16.
10. No such account survives. The text in MOPH XVI pp. 82–8 is not by Jordan, as I hope to prove in a forthcoming article.
11. Prov. 16:2.
12. Wisdom 4:1.
13. 2 Cor. 11:2.
14. Matt. 5:15.
15. Luke 19:20.
16. Prov. 11:26.
17. Luke 12:42.
18. Cf. 1 Cor. 11:30.
19. Ps. 54:9, a *pusillanimitate spiritus et tempestate.*
20. 2 Cor. 5:14.
21. 1 Cor. 9:26.
22. Matt. 19:11
23. Ps. 24:5.
24. Ecclus. 44:6.
25. Ps. 38:4.
26. Ps. 15:8.
27. This is a revealing hint about the recruiting methods of the friars! A letter of Innocent IV in 1244 (*Registrum* no. 529) indicates that a group of Dominicans were at least suspected of getting a schoolmaster from Asti drunk and then forcing a habit on him.
28. This would, of course, be a substantial tome, quite unlike a modern psalter.

29. *Tendens ad alta*, a specious etymology of *Tedalto* (Ferrua, p. 145).

30. Scheeben dates this to the spring of 1232 (QF 35 p. 65). The bishop in question is St. Boniface (c. 1182–c. 1260), who was born in Brussels, but spent 1199–1229 in Paris, as student and then lecturer in Arts and in Theology. This was presumably where he became friendly with Jordan. In 1229 he went to teach in Cologne, but in 1231 he was made bishop of Lausanne. In 1234 he supported the new Dominican foundation there against his Cathedral clergy (with whom he does not seem to have got on very well). In 1239 he resigned his see and retired to the Cistercian monastery of Cambre, near Brussels, where he got to know Thomas of Cantimpré. See *Gallia Christiana* XV 357–8; Glorieux, *Répertoire* n.126.

31. *Ambaziatores*. I am not quite sure what point is being made here, but it is probably, judging from the references given in the *Mittellateinisches Wörterbuch* (Munich, 1959ff), that the word first gained currency in Lombardy, so presumably it struck Jordan (or Gerald de Frachet) as peculiar.

32. Scheeben dates this to 1233 (QF 35 p. 71). John of Vicenza had conducted a spectacularly successful mission in Bologna in the early months of that year (Sorbelli p. 102), and when the Pope tried to get him to move on to Florence and Siena, the people of Bologna tried to prevent it, prompting the Pope to send a Bull to the podestà on April 29, and, since they evidently did not take any notice, he sent another on June 27, complaining that their stupid devotion to John was preventing him from doing useful work elsewhere, and threatening to excommunicate them all unless they let him go (BOP I 48–9, 56).

33. Luke 4:43.

34. Matt. 24:12.

35. Acts 8:1ff.

36. In 1227 Gregory IX appointed a group of three Dominicans to visit and correct nearly all the monasteries in three Italian dioceses (BOP I pp. 23–4), and this is presumably the occasion for this story (Ferrua, p. 211).

37. This must have occurred during Jordan's visit to the Holy Land in 1236–7; it was while he was returning from this trip that he perished in a shipwreck.

38. Matt. 16:18, as interpreted by the Marginal Gloss.

39. In 1228 a "University" was effectively established in Vercelli, by people from the University of Padua. Jordan preached there in 1229 with impressive results. Amongst others, he recruited a "good student of canon law, a German, canon of Speyer, rector of the German college at Vercelli" (Jordan, Letter 49; Scheeben, QF 35 p. 60). M. Aron (*St. Dominic's Successor* [London, 1955] pp. 139–40) and Altaner (QF 20 p. 94) identify him with the hero of the present story.

40. The normal rite of clothing involved a series of formal questions, in

which the candidate's intentions were probed. Jordan missed all these questions on this occasion.

41. This must refer to Jordan's visit to Paris in the winter of 1235; he stayed there until the General Chapter in 1236 (Scheeben QF 35 pp. 79–80). There is some uncertainty about the date of Thomas of Cantimpré's move to Paris; Ballester (in his Introduction to the splendid facsimile edition of Thomas' *De Natura Rerum* [Granada, 1974]) and LThK give 1237, but that would not allow for any time when he and Jordan would have been there together. It is at any rate highly unlikely that he was there earlier than 1235. Jordan himself says that during this period 72 novices entered the Order in Paris (Letter 42), but he says nothing of receiving them all himself, let alone 60 at a time, nor does he comment on their lack of education. It is probable that Thomas is exaggerating the number, but otherwise there is no reason to disbelieve his story (cf. Scheeben, QF 35 p. 27).

42. Matt. 18:10.

43. This was presumably before Thomas joined the Dominicans.

44. I have not been able to arrive at any great certainty about the text, but the general sense seems to be clear enough.

45. Cf. above, p. 112[80].

46. John 4:7.

47. John 14:6.

48. Matt. 5:3. I follow the printed edition of 1605 here, against the MSS which I have looked at, but without much confidence. The MSS have: "Christ declared these to be the blessed poor," and it is hard to see what Old Testament or New Testament passages Thomas could have in mind to support such a contention.

49. Cf. John 8:50.

50. This was about the worst insult in the vocabulary of medieval monks. See *Rule of St. Benedict* 1:10–12.

51. 1 Tim. 2:7.

52. Rom. 15:19.

53. John 11:20.

54. *Obedientiam*: this was the monastic term for jobs within a monastery; by extension it applies also to jobs, such as preaching, within the Order of Preachers.

55. John 16:33.

56. John Meyer, *Liber de Viris Illustribus Ordinis Praedicatorum* (QF 12, p. 30), does not seem to know anything more about Walter of Trier than we can learn from Thomas of Cantimpré (*De Apibus* II xxix 29). His name was Walter of Meysenburg, and in his teens he renounced his fortune and a prebend at Trier to become a Dominican; in due course he filled the posts of conventual lector and prior in various communities. At some time he was Thomas' travelling companion. He is presumably related to the monk of

Trier, William of Meysenburg, who was illegally appointed abbot of St. Eucharius' monastery and forcibly installed with the armed support of his noble relative, Walter of Meysenburg, in 1263, as we learn from the *Chronicle of Trier* (MGH SS XXIV p. 426).

57. This is plainly the same story that Gerald de Frachet reports (above, p. 137), and which is also reported by Bartholomew of Trent in his *Epilogus* on St. Dominic. Humbert says that he heard it or a very similar story during his noviciate (II p. 136).

58. Luke 1:79.

59. *Inter nocentes innocentes.*

60. Matt. 10:16.

61. Cf. Daniel 3:51.

62. Isaiah 36:6.

63. Innocent IV, whose Bull of November 21, 1254, rescinded all the privileges granted to the mendicants.

64. Zech. 11:7.

65. Innocent IV did indeed die on December 7, less than three weeks after the infamous Bull, and he was a very sick man. But there is no reason to believe the fanciful account given by Thomas.

66. *De Apibus* II x 9–21.

67. This is possibly Paul of Venice. See above p. 114[92].

68. *Lives of the Brethren* I 6 iv. Cf. above, note 57.

69. Only some MSS identify this friar as Bene; he was one of St. Dominic's earliest associates, and was co-founder with Frugerio of the convent in Siena, in 1221 (MOPH XXV pp. 147–50).

70. *Lives of the Brethren* I 6 vi.

71. Dom James features in several early Dominican stories, and is credited with the inspired authorship of the prayers for preachers that were contained in the Dominican Missal. His monastery, San Galgano, may have been connected with the Dominicans through their common benefactor, Cardinal Stefano di Fossanova. See above, p. 106[17].

72. *Lives of the Brethren* I 6 xiv, following Reichert's MS C.

73. Little seems to be known of Peter of Aubenas beyond what Gerald de Frachet tells us here. He died c. 1250.

74. It was a common practice for both the Franciscans and the Dominicans to encourage men to make a promise to join the Order if, for some reason, they were not in a position to enter immediately. The Dominicans' use of this ploy was sufficiently successful to annoy the Franciscans, who secured a papal Bull in 1244 to clarify the legitimacy of transferring to another Order after making such a promise (Cf. Hinnebusch, *EEFP* pp. 268–70).

75. It is interesting to notice the different connotations of the word *contemplativus* in medieval texts. Here it refers primarily to prophetic visions.

Needless to say, it would only confuse the issue to try to read into these earlier texts the kind of distinctions made by the later Carmelite doctors.

76. *Lives of the Brethren* IV 13 v.

77. St. Peter of Verona (Peter Martyr) (c. 1200–1252). He received the habit from St. Dominic in 1221. Although later hagiographers celebrate him chiefly as an Inquisitor, this was a position he held only for a very short time before his assassination in 1252. He was primarily an energetic and successful preacher. The fullest account of his career and personality is that by A. Dondaine, AFP 23 (1953) pp. 66–162.

78. I.e., the war between Frederick II and the Lombard alliance.

79. Marginal addition to the text of the *Lives of the Brethren* in MS Vatican Reg. lat. 584 f.86ʳ. See A. Dondaine, AFP 23 (1953) p. 74.

80. §74.

81. *De Quatuor* III 8:29.

82. John Descalars seems to be otherwise unknown. †1272.

83. Bernard de Bociacis entered the Order in 1248, and filled several responsible positions in the Order in the South of France. †1297.

84. *De Quatuor* III 8:30.

85. *De Apibus* II xxx 51.

86. *Rule of St. Augustine.*

87. Humbert's text has *observantiis*, which is the same as the Praemonstratensian text. But all the other evidence for the Dominican text has *observantia*.

88. For the whole text, see below, Appendix.

89. Cf. Primitive Constitutions II vi (transferred to the Prologue in Raymond's edition).

90. The Dominicans never did get round to it. Humbert's text shows that his view was not, in fact, the only view held in the Order, and maybe it was not the majority view.

91. II pp. 5–8.

92. It is suggestive that the Dominicans chose to insert this text into this particular sentence in the Prologue. In the original text, there can be no doubt that "peace" belongs inseparably with "unity": peace is to be assured by the establishment of rule for uniformity. But the Dominicans are clearly only interested in "peace" in the quite different sense of "peace of mind."

93. II pp. 45–6.

94. The text here, like many of the others quoted in these sermon notes, is more of a paraphrase than an exact citation. The application of these symbols to the evangelists is classic, and goes back to Jerome (PL 23:248), Augustine (PL 35:1665–6) and Gregory (PL 76:625).

95. *Contemplativus* is given a more academic twist here; cf. St. Thomas, IIa IIae q.82 a.3, *in Jo.*, Prol.

96. Most of the bizarre "information" about animals contained in this

sermon probably derives from some bestiary. The reference to the lion raising his dead cubs by roaring refers to the curious belief that lion cubs were born dead and only came alive on the third day, when their father roared (cf. Thomas of Cantimpré, *De Natura Rerum* IV 54). For the lion and the eagle, cf. McCulloch pp. 137–40, 113–5.

97. Vergil, *Aeneid* VI 853.

98. 4 Kings 4:33–5. Although this is the reference given in the text, the author must be thinking of Elijah, not Elisha: it is Elijah who "shouts" while raising the dead child in 3 Kings 17:20.

99. *Discretio* has no obvious exact equivalent in English. It has few of the associations of "discretion" and is not quite the same as "discernment." In Greek monasticism διάκρισις is the essential virtue that enables a monk to see through to the heart of the matter and so to make a right decision about the proper thing to do. Latin *discretio* inherits this sense, at least in monastic circles. "Good judgment" covers much of the same ground, but I have finally favoured "intelligence" here, at the risk of being slightly misleading.

100. Phil. 2·15

101. Deut. 17:8.

102. *Sermons on the Canticle* 49:5 (II p. 76:9–10).

103. Ezek. 1:10.

104. Ezek. 1:10.

105. Literally, "look at the sun in the round" (*in rota*), which Eudes of Châteauroux, in his sermon 37 on St. John the Evangelist (Pitra, p. 306), interprets to mean looking at the sun (i.e., Christ) "in the round, that is, in his eternity, having neither beginning nor end."

106. Cf. Ezek. 1:19–21.

107. Ezek. 1:14.

108. 1 Cor. 1:26.

109. Cf. Luke 1:46–47.

110. *Lives of the Brethren* I 1 and 6.

111. As we can see, for instance, from Pecham's response to this letter, there was considerable controversy between the Dominicans and the Franciscans about what counts as "apostolic" and "Christ-like." The Franciscans claimed that only their absolute refusal to possess anything could claim to be modelled on the example of Christ and the apostles; the common ownership practised by the monks and the Dominicans (on the authority of Acts 4) was regarded by the Franciscans as a lower form of life devised by the apostles for those who were incapable of anything better.

112. Matt. 4:17.

113. Mark 6:6.

114. Mark 16:15.

115. 2 Cor. 5:19–20.

116. I.e., the Franciscans. The purpose of this letter is clearly to encour-

age young Dominicans to resist the propaganda of the Franciscans, who regarded the Dominicans as a legitimate recruiting ground (cf. Introduction, note 85).

117. Although Pecham repudiates this suggestion, it does seem likely in fact that the Franciscans were to some extent influenced by the Dominicans. Cf. Eccleston, *De Adventu* IX; Meersseman, AFP 19 (1949) pp. 134–5; J. Moorman, *History of the Franciscan Order* (Oxford, 1968) p. 106.

118. Pecham very properly retorts that merit is acquired on the strength of charity, not usefulness. But for the Dominicans usefulness is simply assumed to be the way in which charity is practised. Unlike the Franciscans, who were concerned to purify men's motives before letting them loose on a job, the Dominicans regarded the job as too urgent to wait for men's motives. In doing the job, their motives would sort themselves out.

119. Matthew Paris (*Chron. Mai.* IV 279) reports a major quarrel between the Dominicans and the Franciscans about which Order is the more austere. The Franciscans habitually claimed that their way of life was the highest precisely because it was the most austere (e.g. Hugh of Digne, *Expositio Regulae* 108:12ff; Pecham, *Tractatus Pauperis* [ed. A. G. Little in *Tractatus Tres*, Aberdeen, 1910] p. 31). The Dominicans generally took the view that this was a stupid criterion: what matters is that your way of life should be adapted to what you are trying to do. But they did sometimes put forward the claim that they were more austere then the Franciscans, and, indeed, they had to make this claim, as one reason for the argument was the church's policy of letting people transfer from one religious Order to another only when the new Order was more austere. The Franciscans were maintaining, as Matthew Paris informs us, that Dominicans could lawfully become Franciscans on this principle. For further evidence on this quarrel, see AFP 3 (1933) pp. 57–80; AFP 6 (1936) pp. 139–160.

120. One of the silliest parts of the quarrel between the Dominicans and the Franciscans was about shoes (the Dominicans earning in the process the sobriquet of "shod friars"). The argument was rather unnecessary, because in fact the Franciscans were permitted to wear shoes if it was necessary, but we do hear of one Franciscan whose health was totally undermined by his foolishly going barefooted in an English winter: Eccleston, *De Adventu* III.

121. The Franciscans, desiring not to go beyond the law of the gospel, did not have the dietary laws customary among religious, and acquired rather a reputation for being *bons viveurs* (cf. Hugh of Digne, *Expositio Regulae* 165). It is only fair to point out that the Dominicans had acquired a similar reputation for themselves in Toulouse as early as 1229, judging from Peire Cardenal's *Sirventès* 28.

122. I.e., the Franciscans again.

123. Cf. St. Thomas, IIa IIae q.188 a.7. It is unfortunate that the only

reference to Christ having purses in the gospel indicates that it was Judas who carried the purse, which Pecham is quick to point out.

124. Franciscans again. In 1269 there had been a huge quarrel between the two Orders in Oxford on this very point, and Kilwardby, as Provincial, had been drawn into it, evidently rather bemused by the whole thing. He here echoes the ironic policy which he advocated in 1269, and the rather superficial peace-formula worked out by some University secular masters. See A. G. Little, *The Grey Friars in Oxford*, Appendix III, for the text of the quarrel.

125. Thomas of York OFM had in fact advocated precisely this, that the decisive factor in perfection is material poverty. See his *Manus quae contra Omnipotentem* (ed. Max Bierbaum) p. 43.

126. Matt. 5:3.

127. Pecham accuses Kilwardby of simply not understanding what is meant by "state of perfection," and it is noticeable that the concept of states of perfection developed by St. Thomas in his *De Perfectione* is significantly more functional than that being used by the Franciscan theologians, who tended rather to absolutise certain practices as, in themselves, constituting a state of perfection.

128. 1 Tim. 6:8.

129. The Dominicans had, in fact, received a papal Bull in 1261, allowing them full proprietorial rights over their ecclesiastical furnishings and books (BOP I p. 408).

130. Cf. 2 Tim. 4:13.

131. PL 38:563 and in many other passages.

132. Matt. 5:44.

133. There had been a regular succession of instructions from Dominican General and Provincial Chapters about being courteous to Franciscans. In 1236 the General Chapter bids the brethren "make sure that they do not speak rudely about the Franciscans amongst themselves or with other people, however intimately they know them. And if anyone, on the pretext of friendship and familiarity, passes on nasty gossip about them, the Dominicans are to be slow to believe it and are rather to defend them."

134. Cambridge, Trinity Coll. MS 323 f.73$^r$. Printed in Carleton Brown, *English Lyrics of the Thirteenth Century* (Oxford, 1932), p. xxi.

# WILLIAM PERALDUS' SERMON ON PRAYER

*So far we have only looked at what Dominicans had to say to each other, or what they had to say about St. Dominic and his Order. But an Order of Preachers obviously spends most of its time talking to other people. One of the most influential of the early Dominicans was the Frenchman William Peraldus (Peyraut), who, as well as being an extremely energetic travelling preacher, wrote a* Summa on the Virtues and Vices *that rapidly established itself as a standard textbook on Christian ethics. He also published a substantial collection of his sermons. The one presented here antedates 1250, and anticipates the fuller treatment of prayer in the* Summa on Virtues.

"All be of one mind in prayer" *(1 Pet. 3:8).*

As the Gloss says on Psalm 41:9, "The righteousness of man in this life means fasting, almsgiving and prayer. Prayer uses the other two as its wings and so flies to God."[1] That these three things are indeed what human goodness consists of is clear from the fact that man is related to what is above him, namely God and the angels and saints, to what is on the same level as himself, namely his neighbour, and also to what is beneath him, namely his own body. Prayer is necessary because by it he begs help from those above him. Almsgiving is necessary because by it he helps his neighbour in his time of need. Fasting is necessary because by it he chastises his body and brings it into subjection.[2] And it is almost impossible that anyone who practises these three things properly should not triumph over the enemy. Fasting weakens the enemy, namely man's body, and, as a result, it weakens the devil too, who relies chiefly on the flesh. As one of the saints says, "The devil relies more on the help of the flesh because an enemy within the walls does more harm than any other."[3] Prayer wins us the assistance of heaven. And almsgiving wins us the help of earth, because it hires the poor for our service. How shall a man not triumph, when his enemy is weakened, and when he has support from both heaven and earth?

Of these three, prayer seems to enjoy a certain pre-eminence, since it concerns itself with what is above us, and because fasting and

165

almsgiving are in its service as a kind of wings. Prayer is a dove, the bird of the Holy Spirit,[4] which brings the olive branch[5] and wins peace for men. And we call it the bird of the Holy Spirit because devout prayer comes from the Holy Spirit. As the apostle says, the Holy Spirit "prays for us with unutterable groanings"[6]; that is to say, he makes us pray.

Commenting on the text "Let my prayer come before you,"[7] St. Augustine says about prayer, "The power of pure prayer is remarkable; it goes in to God as if it were a living person and fulfils its mission where flesh is unable to come."[8] And Gregory says, "The power of prayer is enormous: when it is poured out on earth, it achieves results in heaven."[9] And though it is more blessed to give than to receive,[10] nevertheless it is more appropriate to the state we are in now to ask than to give, because we have nothing here except what we have received from elsewhere. As it says in 1 Cor. 4:7, "What have you got that you have not received?". Accordingly, we shall concentrate on that prayer which wins for us what we need, demonstrating first of all why everyone ought to be glad to learn how to do this job, and then showing how our supreme Teacher taught us how to pray.

Notice, then, that there are six reasons we can give why everyone ought to be glad to learn how to pray. The first is that our great Teacher, whose chair is in heaven,[11] wanted to teach it to us with particular care. It is unlikely that he would be content for us to learn carelessly what he taught so carefully. It is a disgrace if Christ's disciples have no knowledge of something which their master taught with exceptional diligence. He taught it, first of all, by his example. In Matthew 14:23, "After he had dismissed the crowds, he went up into the mountain to pray alone, and when it was evening he was there on his own." And in Luke 22:44 we read that "being in agony, he prayed all the longer." And sometimes he spent the whole night in prayer.[12] It was not that he needed prayer for his own sake, because he could do whatever he wanted with just a word. He did it to give us an example of how willing we should be to pray.

He also taught in words, showing what we should pray, in Matt. 6:9ff where he gave his disciples the Lord's Prayer, and also, in the same place, showing them where they should pray. "When you pray, go into your chamber and shut the door, and there pray to your Father in secret."[13] He also showed when we should pray, namely always. "Keep vigil at all times, praying, so that you may be found worthy to escape from all these things which are to come" *(Luke 21:36)*. He also showed how we should pray: devoutly, concisely, humbly and with perseverance. For the first point, see John 4:24, "God is spirit, and those who worship him must pray in spirit and in truth." For the second, Matt. 6:7, "When you pray, do not talk a lot, as the gentiles do." For the third point, Matt. 6:5, "When you pray, do not be like the hypocrites etc," and also Luke 18:10ff, where the point is touched on in the parable about the publican and the Pharisee. For the fourth point, Luke 18:1ff, where he talks about the unjust judge who did not fear God or respect man, but who all the same gave judgment for the widow because she bothered him so much. Similarly in Luke 11:8, "If he goes on knocking, I tell you, even if the man will not give him what he wants because he is his friend, he will still get up and give it to him because of his persistence."

The second reason is that if prayer is properly made, it is a present which God particularly welcomes, and which deserves the service of angels. In Tobit 12:12 the angel says, "When you were praying with tears and burying the dead, I presented your prayer to the Lord." No man ought to find it a nuisance to give God a gift which an angel finds it no nuisance to present. And this is not all. Christ himself presents it to God the Father, being High Priest in his humanity. This is symbolised in the way the deacon hands the thurible to the priest, and the priest then offers incense to God. In a similar way Christ presents the prayers of the church to God the Father, and this makes them extremely powerful, for how could God make light of something which is presented by so great a mediator?

The third reason is that prayer is such an easy job. If you tell someone to give alms, he can excuse himself, because people do not always have any money in their bag. It is the same if you tell someone to fast, because many people cannot fast, because their heads are too weak. But no one can excuse himself from praying. Anybody can pray, at least in his mind, even if he is dumb.[14] So David says, "In me there is a prayer,"[15] and on "The righteous man has pity and will lend" *(Psalm 36:21)* the Gloss says, "The righteous man always has something to give; at least he has prayer."[16]

The fourth reason is that this is an honourable job. There are many jobs which it would disgrace some people to do, such as ploughing and digging, but prayer will not disgrace anyone, however aristocratic he is, because, as Gregory says, "When we pray we talk to God."[17] And that is undoubtedly a great honour for anyone.

167

The fifth reason is that prayer is a very profitable occupation. The first proof of this is that there is nothing which prayer cannot accomplish. So 2 Chron. 20:12 says, "When we do not know what we should do, the only remedy left to us is to turn our eyes towards you." This is a task in which a man can make profit the whole time, in winter and in summer, in fine weather and in bad, by night and by day, on holidays and on working days, in sickness and in health, in youth and in old age, whether he is staying or going, at home or abroad. And he sometimes wins more by one hour's prayer than a whole city could earn, because by a little prayer, if only it is devout, a man wins an everlasting kingdom. Sometimes a man is in a state of damnation before he begins his prayer, and before he is finished he is in a state of salvation. Sometimes one little old lady wins more from heaven by one hour of prayer than a thousand armed soldiers could win from the earth in a very long time. As the Gloss on Numbers says, "One saint at his prayers is stronger than any number of sinners at their fighting. The prayer of a saint pierces heaven; how could it fail to defeat his enemies on earth?"[18] The saints win the greatest consolations in this world by praying. For example in Luke 3:21, "When Jesus had been baptised and was praying, the heavens opened." And in Luke 9:29, while Christ was praying, "The appearance of his face was altered and his clothing became white." And in Luke 22:41–3 we read that Christ "knelt down and prayed," and then we are told that "an angel appeared to him from heaven, comforting him."

The sixth reason is the great need we have to pray in this present time. There are three things, in general, which force people to cry out: fire, flood and enemies. And almost every day these three things oblige us to cry out to God in prayer.[19] There is scarcely a day in which the house of our conscience is not set ablaze by the fire of Hell, or, in other words, disordered desire. So we have to clamour for the water of divine grace and have recourse to the water of tears. And this fire is like Greek fire[20]: when it is extinguished in one place, it breaks out in another. Sometimes the very fact that a man is weeping over his carnal lusts brings vainglory to birth in him. And there is scarcely a day in which a man does not feel a flood of bad thoughts coming up over his head, obliging him to cry out, "Lord, save us, we are perishing" *(Matt. 8:25).* And there is scarcely a day in which a man does not see his enemies at the door of his castle, feeling slanderous words, for example, or some other kind of foul speech at his mouth. And it is the same with all the other doors of his castle, or, in other words, his body.[21]

Next we must see how Christ taught us to pray, and we find this in Luke 11:1ff. "When Jesus was in a certain place, praying, when he finished, one of his disciples said to him, 'Lord, teach us to pray, as John taught his disciples.' And he said to them, 'When you pray, say, *Our Father.*' "

Now there are five things which particularly recommend this prayer to us. First, the rank of its author: God composed it, and so we can apply to it the words of Ecclus. 24:5, "I came forth from the mouth of the Most High."

Secondly, its brevity. So Bede's Gloss says, "He composed the prayer in a few brief words, to give us confidence that he will quickly grant what he wanted us to ask for so briefly."[22]

Thirdly, its richness. As the Gloss says, "There is nothing missing: everything is contained in the seven petitions."[23]

Fourthly, its spirituality. As the Gloss says, "There is no prayer more spiritual than the one which came forth from the mouth of the Son of God, who is Truth in Person."[24]

Fifthly, its power. It has great power, because it is most unlikely that Christ would have formulated the petitions it contains unless he meant to grant them. Augustine says of its power, "The daily prayer of the faithful makes amends for the daily, small, quick sins which are inseparable from this life. It belongs to them to say, 'Our Father who art in heaven.' This kind of prayer cancels out entirely the trivial sins of every day, and it cancels out the ways in which the life of the faithful is spoiled by sin, but then gets rectified by penance, provided that we can say 'As we forgive those who trespass against us' as truly as we have to say 'Forgive us our trespasses.' "[25] After the eucharist, the Lord's Prayer is the greatest remedy for venial sin, or one of the greatest.

Now the Lord's Prayer falls into two parts, of which the first prepares people who want to pray to do so devoutly, and the second contains the seven petitions.

It is very necessary that there should be some preparation for prayer. As it says in Psalm 9:39, "Your ear heard the preparation of their heart." God sometimes pays more attention to the preparation than to the spoken prayer. So it says in Ecclus. 18:23, "Before you pray, prepare your soul."

There are two kinds of preparation, one remote, the other more immediate. Remote preparation means observing God's commandments. Anyone who wants God to listen to his petitions must first listen to what God asks of him. So Augustine says, "Anyone who turns away from God's commandments does not deserve to obtain what he asks for in prayer."[26] In Proverbs 28:9 it says, "If a man turns his ear from hearing the law, his prayer will be an abomination." And in Proverbs 21:13, "If a man shuts his ears to the cry of the poor, he too will cry out and not be heard."

There are two things involved in immediate preparation: tears, and confidence that our prayer will be granted. And we are prepared for prayer in both these ways by the first part of the Lord's Prayer, "Our Father, who art in heaven."

It moves us to tears in two ways. First of all by recalling what a great Father they have to people who have been living basely in sin. And secondly by insinuating our absence from our loving Father by saying, "Who art in heaven," and by reminding us of our pleasant homeland from which we are banished here below. The first point is taken up in what Bernard says: "As I reflect on how I have sinned against my Father, there is plenty there to make me blush, if not actually to terrify me. With what nerve can such a bad son as I lift up my eyes to the face of such a loyal Father? I am ashamed that I have lived so unworthily of my descent from such a Father."[27] And the Gloss on our text says, "Everyone must be careful not to defile himself, in case he becomes unworthy of such a Father."[28]

The second point seems to be made in the text from Psalm 41:4, "My tears became my bread by day and by night, while every day I heard them say, 'Where is your God?' ".

The first weeping, weeping because of our sins, is the water that irrigates from beneath; the second, weeping because of our absence from our Father and our distance from our homeland, is the water that irrigates from above.[29]

There are also two ways in which the words "Our Father who art in heaven" inspire confidence that our prayer will be granted. First of all, in giving the name "Father" to the person we are praying to. This Father's love surpasses even the love of a mother. "Shall a woman be able to forget her baby and not have pity on the child of her womb? Even if she forgets, I shall not forget you" *(Isaiah 49:15)*. And secondly by saying that he is in heaven, where there is an abundant supply of all good things. If he is the Father of mercies[30] and has an abundant supply of all good things, how can he fail to have pity on his son who is in the valley of wretchedness where he lacks all good? What Bernard says is relevant here: "Where now is that thundering cry which used to sound so frequently and so alarmingly in the days of old, 'I am the Lord, I am the Lord'? Now I am given a prayer whose very beginning charms me with the name of 'Father,' which fills me with confidence that I shall obtain what I ask for."[31] The Gloss says, on this name 'Father,' "We are given confidence by this name. What will he refuse his children, when he has already given them the right to call him 'Father'?"[32] "If you who are evil know how to give good gifts to your children, how much more will your heavenly Father give his good Spirit to those who ask him!" *(Luke 11:13).*

That tears are a powerful factor in winning what we pray for is shown by what Augustine says in his comment on Psalm 38:13, "Turn your ear to my weeping": "These tears," he says, "do violence when we pray."[33]

That confidence is also an important factor is shown by what it says in James 1:5–7: "If anyone lacks wisdom, let him ask for it from God. . . . But let him ask in faith, not doubting at all. Anyone who doubts is like a wave in the sea, moved and tossed around by the wind. A man like that should not think he is going to receive anything from the Lord."

The second part of the prayer again falls into two parts. Since the spiritual life is twofold, consisting of the life of grace and the life of glory, first there are three petitions concerning the life of glory, and then there are four petitions concerning the life of grace. And the petitions which concern the life of glory come first, because they rank higher, as Matt. 6:33 indicates, "Seek first the kingdom of God and its righteousness." The kingdom of God is what we seek in the first three petitions, while the other four ask for the righteousness which leads to the kingdom.

Notice that a man who has been found guilty of some crime deserving death before some earthly judge, and who is not sure that the judge has yet been won over to have mercy on him, begins by pleading for his life, or by begging to be let off the death he has deserved. In the same way anyone who has committed mortal sin cannot be sure in this life that he has been forgiven, and so must first of all beg to be spared death. This is the significance of the petition, "Deliver us from evil." "Evil" there means mortal sin, which is the first death, and its consequence, namely everlasting death. And this petition ought to be made with intense desire, in just the same way that a bandit begs for his life with much weeping, when he considers what he has done and what torment is waiting for him. This is how a sinner ought to consider the sin he has committed and the torment he deserves for it, and then say, with much weeping, "Deliver us from evil." Someone once said that he was taught to pray by bandits and tramps. Tramps taught him by their shameless way of displaying all that is most wretched in them and hiding anything that is healthy, in the hope that the immensity of their wretchedness will prompt people to have pity on them. Bandits taught him in the way we have already explained.

If we are granted our life, spiritually, we then have to fight for it continuously. As it says in Job 7:1, "The life of man on earth is warfare," or temptation, and this makes it necessary for us to pray the petition in which we ask not to be allowed to fall into temptation. And this petition too ought to be made with intense desire. Just as a man who is about to fight a duel prays to the Lord with great desire before he goes into the field, and gets other people to pray for him too, that the Lord will grant him victory, and gives thanks to God after he has won his victory, so every believer ought to ask God each morning to give him victory that day over the devil. As soon as he gets up in the morning he goes into the field where he must fight a highly perilous battle. As Bernard says, "We are placed in this world as in the arena of battle, in which Christ died. Anyone who is not bruised or wounded here will come before the future judgment as a soldier without honour."[34] Then in the evening, if he has avoided falling, he ought to pass on to thanksgiving. As Augustine says, "The God to whom we must pray that he will do it, must also be thanked when he has done it."[35] Many people fail in this regard. When they have received some benefit from the Lord, they never give it another thought, when they should go on thanking God every day for a long time to come.

Now notice that the soul's foot, by which it enters into, or is led into, temptation, is its consent. "Watch and pray that you do not enter into temptation" *(Matt. 26:41).* Enter, that is, by consenting. The Lord leads a man into temptation by permitting it; the devil leads him into it by as it were driving him.

Even if our spiritual life does not fall under the blows of temptation, it is still tied up with debts. Even when he is freed from guilt and eternal death, a man still remains bound to temporal punishment.

And so he needs the petition, "Forgive us our debts." And this petition ought to be made with intense desire. As people often say, there is no burden like the burden of debt. If a man was tied up in a lot of debts which had to be repaid within a certain time, and if he knew that he would be imprisoned dreadfully if he did not repay them within the time and reckoned that he would probably not be able to repay them within the time, then he would plead with intense desire to be let off his debt, if he thought there was any chance of his plea being granted, and he would be immensely grateful to anyone who would remove his name from his creditor's books and put his own in instead. In the same way anyone who reckons that he cannot pay off his debt before his time is up at death ought to plead with intense desire to have his debts remitted, knowing that he will be placed in the fire of purgatory for any outstanding debts. Of this fire Augustine says, "That fire is extraordinarily severe. It surpasses any pain that anyone has ever suffered in this life."[36]

This petition has a rider attached to it: "As we forgive our debtors." Our own prayer to be forgiven gains particular force if we forgive our neighbour. "Forgive your neighbour who harms you, and then when you pray your own sins will be forgiven" *(Ecclus. 28:2)*. If it is true that every animal loves its own kind, as it says in Ecclus. 13:19, and that, as Seneca says, a wolf does not harm a wolf nor does a lion hurt another lion,[37] then it is more than likely that God's mercy loves nothing in a man so much as mercy, its own sister, and that God will be glad to spare and to pardon anyone who readily pardons his neighbour. On the other hand, a man who does not forgive is forgiven nothing by God *(Matt. 18:35)*. "A man is tormented precisely in accordance with the way he sins" *(Wisdom 11:17)*. "Anyone who wants vengeance from the Lord will indeed find vengeance" *(Ecclus. 28:1)*.

Furthermore, our spiritual life, left to itself, grows faint and needs to be sustained by spiritual food, just as the life of the body is sustained by food. And it ought to be sustained with food before it falls. So in the fourth petition we ask for the sustenance of our spiritual life, when we say, "Give us this day our daily bread." This does not appear to refer to material bread in the first place, since the Lord says that that is one of the things which is to be "added," not something to be "sought": "All these things will be added for you" *(Matt. 6:33)*. And this petition ought to be made with intense desire, because the bread is necessary for us every day and we cannot have it by our own resources. We must be like a man who knows he is going to die unless he can get alms by begging. He begs with great desire.

And notice that this bread is of four kinds: teaching, example, the church's sacraments, particularly confession and the eucharist, and the practice of the virtues. The bread of teaching is referred to in Deut. 8:3, "Man does not live by bread alone, but by every word which comes from the mouth of God." The bread of example is touched on in the Gloss on John 21:18, "Feed my sheep."[38] On good works, it says in Isaiah 4:1, in the person of the virtues, "We shall eat our bread." The virtues fail unless we exercise them in doing good, just as a man's bodily vision fails if he spends a long time in a prison where he cannot see. The sacraments of confession and the eucharist are called "bread" because they are a powerful nourishment for the spiritual life; whenever anyone approaches them worthily, he receives grace or an increase of grace. Approaching them worthily means approaching them humbly, believing that we need the effect of the sacrament, and faithfully, believing that the sacrament has the effect which the church declares it to have, and with the desire to receive that effect. Anyone who comes without desire comes, as it were, with his mouth shut, and so he comes with nothing and goes away again with nothing. The fourth thing that makes a man worthy to approach the sacraments is gratitude to God for establishing these fountains of grace in the church for us to have recourse to when we need grace.

All of this makes it clear enough how much this present life of ours is in need of God. It is so poor that it is obliged to beg, and, as Augustine says, "A man who begs his daily bread is poor, not rich."[39] He is worse than poor, in fact, since he is burdened with many debts. He is also in great danger, surrounded as he is by snares and threats of death.

Let us move on now to the other three petitions. Notice that as man was made for the service of God, so the world was made for the service of man. In return for the service offered by man to God, man was made to have authority over the world in this present life and then, finally, after he had been taken from the earthly paradise into heaven, he was to possess God himself. But because he refused to offer due service to God, by God's just judgment he lost his authority over the world and fell into a condition of such dire slavery that he could not even defend himself from flies and other such minute creatures. As Augustine says, "A man is rude to you and you puff

174

yourself up and get angry. Rather fight off the fleas so that you can get some sleep."[40] But in the time to come man will be put in his proper place, where he will be totally subject to God and all other creatures will be subject to man, and there he will also possess God himself, provided that he was first possessed by God, because, as Augustine says, God will be possessed by no one whom he has not himself possessed.[41]

The petition: "Thy will be done on earth as it is in heaven" concerns the first of these things. It means, "May we come to that state in which we shall conform our wills utterly to your will, as the angels do now."

The petition "Thy kingdom come" takes up the second point. It means, "May that state come in which we shall reign with you, free from all slavery."

The third point is dealt with in the petition "Hallowed be thy name," which means, "May that name be established by which we are called children of God," and this will come about when we enjoy that divine delight which is referred to in Ecclus. 15:6, "He will heap gladness and exultation upon him and will give him the inheritance of an everlasting name." When we feel that unutterable gladness, then we shall be established as firmly as God's angels.

Notice that these three petitions ought to be made with intense desire. It is appalling that we so often offend the Father of mercies from whom we have already received all that is good and from whom we hope for so much greater blessings; it is dreadful that so often we do the will of the devil. That state is much to be desired in which we shall do the will of God in everything and in which we shall be freed from the debasing slavery in which we find ourselves now. It is a crushing burden for one who should be reigning as a king to have to endure slavery. It is deplorable that the children of God so easily become children of the devil. So our final establishment is much to be desired. And notice that the word "Hallowed" refers to the manifestation of this honour, so that it means "Hallowed, that is, may it be seen to be holy." A thing is said to come into being when its existence becomes known. We are already children of God, "but it does not yet appear what we shall be, but when he appears, we shall be like him" (1 John 3:2). Seeing people in their present poverty, it would be almost impossible to believe that they were children of God, if scripture did not say that they were. They go about on foot, while the devil's servants travel on horseback. As it says in Ecclesiastes 10:7, "I have seen slaves on horseback and princes walking like slaves upon the ground." But one day it will, as it were, be plainly written on them that they are children of God. As it says in Apoc. 3:12, "On him who conquers I shall write the name of my God," which the Gloss interprets as meaning, "He will be, in a sense, God."[42] When iron is heated enough in the fire, it becomes fire in a certain sense, and similarly the elect will be God in a certain sense when they come to be very much like him. On their glorified bodies it will be written that they are children of God, in four gifts,[43] like four letters— writing means unambiguous designation. And then it will be unambiguous because of their glorified bodies that they are God's children, in the same way that we can see from someone's valuable clothes that he is a prince. It is in the same sense that it says that it is written on the thigh, that is, the flesh, of Christ, that he is king of kings and lord of lords *(Apoc. 19:16)*.

## Notes

1. Lombard's Gloss, PL 191:421B.

2. 1 Cor. 9:27.

3. I have not been able to identify this reference.

4. Cf. Matt. 3:16.

5. Gen. 8:10–11.

6. Rom. 8:26.

7. Psalm 87:3.

8. Lombard's Gloss on Ps. 87:2 (PL 191:811D). The text comes from Cassiodorus (PL 70:623A), not from Augustine.

9. In Peraldus' *Summa* the same text is attributed to Augustine. I do not know where it comes from.

10. Acts 20:35

11. Cf. Augustine, PL 38:1237, 1320.

12. Luke 6:12.

13. Matt. 6:6.

14. *Oratio mentalis:* in this period "mental prayer" meant nothing more complicated than this. The modern sense only comes into vogue in the sixteenth century.

15. Psalm 41:9.

16. Lombard's Gloss, PL 191:373A.

17. This is part of a longer text quoted in Peraldus' *Summa* under the name of Isidore. It is indeed found in Isidore (PL 83:679).

18. Marginal Gloss on Numbers 31:4–7.

19. In his *Summa* Peraldus presents this as a citation from Bernard.

20. "Greek fire" referred to a variety of incendiary concoctions, of which one variety famously actually caught fire when brought into contact with water. Cf. J. R. Partington, *A History of Greek Fire and Gunpowder* (Cambridge, 1960).

21. The "doors" of the body are the senses; this is a very common image in medieval literature.

22. Marginal Gloss to Matt. 6:9. The same text is ascribed to "Bede's Gloss" in the *Catena Aurea*, but it is not in fact from Bede.

23. Marginal Gloss to Matt. 6:13.

24. Marginal Gloss to Matt. 6:9.

25. Augustine, *Enchiridion* 71.

26. In his *Summa* Peraldus attributes this text to Isidore. It is found in Isidore (PL 83:675).

27. *Sermons on the Canticle* 16:4 (I p. 92:2–9).

28. Marginal Gloss to Matt. 6:9.

29. Cf. Joshua 15:19, Judges 1:15.

30. 2 Cor. 1:3.

31. Bernard, *Sermons on the Canticle* 15:2 (I 83:11–14).

32. Marginal Gloss to Matt 6:9.

33. Lombard's Gloss (PL 191:395D). The text is from Cassiodorus (PL 70:285D), not Augustine.

34. I have not been able to identify this reference.

35. Augustine, PL 33:989.

36. Augustine, PL 40:1128.

37. This is not from the genuine works of Seneca.

38. Marginal Gloss.

39. Augustine, PL 38:686.

40. Augustine, *On St. John's Gospel* 1:15.

41. Augustine, PL 40:1050.

42. Interlinear Gloss.

43. The four gifts with which the body is to be endowed at the Resurrection, i.e., impassibility, agility, subtlety and radiance. Cf. St. Thomas, *Summa Theologiae* III q.45 a.1 obi.3; *Compendium Theol.* 168.

# Section III

## HUMBERT OF ROMANS' TREATISE ON THE FORMATION OF PREACHERS

During his time as Master of the Order, and after his retirement, Humbert of Romans devoted a great deal of his time to writing; and his major concern was to help his brethren to understand the nature of their vocation as preachers, and to clarify the nature of Dominican law and Dominican conventual life. He embarked on a massive commentary on the Constitutions, which he did not manage to complete; he wrote a lengthy treatise on the various officials in Dominican communities; he wrote a short comment on the ways in which the brethren were or were not bound in conscience by the Constitutions and by the decrees of General Chapters. He also composed the huge work On the Formation of Preachers, in which he intended to display, first of all, what it means for a man to be a preacher, and, secondly, to offer some practical advice about preaching. The first part of the treatise, which offers an account of the spirituality of the preacher, is of supreme importance for our understanding of the Dominican way of life. If the Dominican vocation makes sense at all, it must be possible to view preaching as a legitimate nucleus for a whole way of life, a whole way of sanctity, and it is this that Humbert proposes to exhibit. The result was something so unfamiliar to most of his contemporaries that, frankly, the work was not a great success. Only four manuscripts of it survive. It fitted neither into the current model of "spiritual literature" nor into the proliferating "Arts of Preaching," which were concerned simply with the technicalities of preparing and delivering sermons. The enormous bulk of the model sermons that he put into the final section of the book distracted attention from the true nature of the work as a whole: people could appreciate these more easily, because they offered the same kind of assistance to a preacher as other contemporary books. It is not surprising, then, that the work effectively fell to pieces, so that there are far more manuscripts of the model sermons than there are of the more theoretical discussion of what it means to be a preacher (not just to give sermons). Not a single surviving manuscript contains the whole work.

To appreciate what Humbert has to say about being a preacher, it is necessary to realise just how novel his message was. The notion that a man might make preaching the very centre and focus of his whole religious life was exceedingly strange, and people were instinctively suspicious of a religious Order calling itself "The Order of Preachers." The rather fulsome language in which Humbert demonstrates the excellence of the vocation of the preacher is polemical in its intention: its purpose is to re-assure his brethren that, whatever people may say, their vocation is, precisely, to be preachers, and that it is a singularly sublime vocation, well worth undertaking, and that it is, in spite of all the evident hazards, a possible means of salvation for the preacher himself.

But this need to affirm in the strongest possible language the viability of preaching as a way of life had to be balanced by another equally important concern: Humbert realises that there might be seriously inadequate reasons for wanting to be a preacher. In the annals of the early history of the Order we run into several people who were apparently unbalanced in their desire to preach or in their practice of their apostolate. This is why Humbert has also to stress the importance of not rushing precipitately into the job, and the need to be obedient to the decisions of the whole community of the preachers. If Humbert does not, perhaps, succeed always in balancing these two requirements, he reflects a tension that is intrinsic to the nature of the Order, and it is to his credit that he reflects both sides of it so fairly.

At the heart of his teaching, there is his awareness that, strictly speaking, it is only God who makes a man a preacher; his references to "the grace of preaching," though few, are extremely important. It is not enough that a man is eager to preach; nor is it enough that he should have received the best possible training. What has to be discerned is "what grace of preaching" he has, as the early Constitutions direct. It is this that must be seen as the crucial factor, round which both enthusiasm and discipline fall into place.

# Prologue

(I 1) "Consider the ministry you have received from the Lord, so that you may fulfil it" *(Col. 4:17)*.

It often happens, when someone has received a job and does not know what it involves, that he does it less well because of this ignorance, like a cantor who is ignorant of the rubrics for the Divine Office.

In 1 Samuel 2:12–3 we are told why the sons of Eli were bad priests: they did not know what the priests' job was. So Paul, in his desire that the archbishop who had undertaken the job of preaching for the people of Colossae should do the job well, made sure that he was encouraged to think about the job, in the text cited above, so that he would be the better able to do it thoroughly and well as a result of such reflection.

This suggests that it is part of any preacher's job to give the matter careful thought and to see just what this job is and what it involves.

To enable all preachers to understand their job more fully, there are seven[1] topics for us to look at now:

(i)     the characteristics of the job;
(ii)    what a preacher needs if he is to do the job;
(iii)   right and wrong ways of taking on the job;
(iv)   the actual performance of the job;
(v)    ways in which people may come to be without preaching;
(vi)   the results of preaching;
(vii)  things that go with the job of preaching.

# I The Characteristics of the Preacher's Job

(II) In Part One we must consider:

(i)    what a noble job preaching is;
(ii)   how much the world needs it;
(iii)  how acceptable it is in the sight of God;
(iv)  how profitable it is to the preacher himself;
(v)   how useful it is to other people;
(vi)  how difficult it is to do it well.

## THE NOBILITY OF THE PREACHER'S JOB

(2) To see what a noble job preaching is, we must notice that it is an apostolic job: it was for this job that the Lord chose the apostles. "He appointed twelve to be with him and to be sent out to preach" *(Mark 3:14).*

It is also an angelic job. "I saw a mighty angel, preaching with a loud voice" *(Apoc. 5:2).* And was he not preaching who said, "See, I bring you good news of a great joy" *(Luke 2:10)?* And there is nothing surprising in angels being called preachers, since their mission is for the sake of those who are to inherit salvation,[2] just as preachers are sent out for the salvation of men.

Further, it is a divine job. God became man precisely to do this job. "Let us go into the neighbouring villages and towns so that I may preach there too, because it was for this purpose that I came" *(Mark 1:38).*

Now, the apostles are the most outstanding of all the saints, the angels are the most outstanding of all creatures, and in all that exists,

184

nothing is more outstanding than God. So a job which is apostolic, angelic and divine must indeed be outstanding!

(3) Another way of showing the nobility of the preacher's job depends on the privileged status of scripture. Scripture surpasses all other kinds of knowledge in three ways: in its source, in its content and in its purpose.

In its source, because, whereas all other sciences were discovered by the mind of man (though not, of course, without the help of God), the knowledge contained in scripture was directly inspired by God. "The holy men of God spoke under the inspiration of the Holy Spirit" *(2 Pet. 1:21)*.

In its content, because other sciences are concerned either with the things of the mind, or with things of nature, or with things that derive from human free will; but scripture is concerned with the things of God, which infinitely transcend all these other things. This is why divine Wisdom, who bestowed this knowledge on men, says, "Listen, for I am going to speak of great matters" *(Prov. 8:6)*. And indeed she does speak of great matters, such as the Trinity and Unity of God, and the Incarnation of the Son of God, and there is nothing greater than these.

In its purpose, because other sciences are designed to serve the ordering of temporal affairs (law, for example), or the needs of the body (medicine, for example), or to remedy intellectual ignorance (like the theoretical sciences); but scripture aims at the acquisition of eternal life. "Whoever drinks of this water which I shall give him, it will become in him a fountain of living water, welling up to eternal life" *(John 4:14)*. It says this because the water of divine wisdom points to[3] and leads men to eternal life. And eternal life is nothing other than God himself, and so we may say that the purpose of this science is God himself. This is why sacred scripture is referred to as "theology," from θεός (God) and λόγος (word), because its words are from God, about God and directed to God.

Now all proper preaching is woven out of just such words, and not from the words of other sciences. And since the value of a thing is greater if it is made out of more precious material—a golden cup is worth more than one made out of lead—how precious must preaching be, since it is formed from such outstanding material!

(4) Again, the philosophers say that man is the most worthy of all creatures; and of the two kinds of nature that he has, namely body and soul, the soul is the more worthy. And of the many things which

the soul needs, some have little or nothing to do with salvation (learning, for instance), while others are directly relevant for salvation; and these latter are the more worthy. Now preaching is directed at man. "Preach the gospel to the whole creation" *(Mark 16:15)*, which means, "To man," according to Gregory.[4] And it is concerned with the soul, not the body. In response to Peter's preaching, it specifically says that "about three thousand souls were added" *(Acts 2:41)*, because it is souls that are sought by preaching. And what it seeks with regard to them is only what is relevant to salvation, which is why scripture says of an outstanding preacher, "You shall go before the face of the Lord, to prepare his ways before him, to give to his people the knowledge of salvation" *(Luke 1:76–7)*.

Now, the nobility of a job depends on the dignity and worth of its sphere of operation. A job done for a king is more noble than a job done for his horses, and a job done in a temple is more noble than one performed in the stables. So what a noble job it must be, which is concerned with the most worthy of all creatures, and with the more worthy part of that creature, and with the more worthy aspect of that part of the most worthy creature!

(5) So, if we bear in mind the exalted status of those to whom this job is assigned, and the excellence of its material, and the superiority of its sphere of operation, it should be obvious to us that this is a job of quite outstanding value.

## THE NECESSITY OF PREACHING

(III 6) If we want to appreciate how necessary preaching is for the world, we must realise that the souls of the saints who have died are crying out to God, as it says in the Apocalypse 6:10, complaining about those who dwell on the earth. And, according to the commentators, what they are complaining about is that people are so slow to repent and do penance, because this delays the final fulfilment of their joy in heaven, which will be brought about when heaven's loss is made good and when they receive the second robe.[5] Now there is nothing so powerful to speed up the coming of this fulfilment as preaching. This is why it says in Matthew 4:17 that "then Jesus began to preach and to say, 'Repent, for then the kingdom of heaven will soon arrive' ",[6] meaning that its final fulfilment will soon arrive. This shows that the full measure of the glory of heaven will not be reached without preaching.

(7) Again, it says in Isaiah, "The people has been taken captive because it had no knowledge. That is why Hell has enlarged its appetite,[7] opening its mouth wide beyond measure" *(5:13–4)*. So lack of knowledge contributes to the filling up of Hell. But preachers fill the earth with knowledge. "The lips of wise men will disseminate knowledge" *(Prov. 15:7)*. "By preaching," as the Gloss explains.[8] In this way they draw people away from Hell, as it says, "Rescue those who are being dragged off to death" *(Prov. 24:11)*, and this is done "by preaching," as the Gloss says.[9] This shows that preaching slows down the filling up of Hell.

(8) Again, without preaching, which sows the word of God, the whole world would be barren and without fruit. "If the Lord of hosts had not left us a seed (the word of God, that is), we should have been like Sodom" *(Isaiah 1:9)*, a land which is altogether barren and bears no fruit.

(9) Again, the demons have for a long time been applying a lot of care to subjugating the whole world to themselves, and they have subjugated a considerable part of it; and they would have subjugated more of it, had it not been for preachers opposing them with their God-given power, which is referred to in Matthew 10:1, "He gave them power over unclean spirits" and in Matthew 10:8, "He commanded them, 'Cast out demons.' " And this realises what was anticipated symbolically, according to the commentators, in Gideon and his men putting their enemies to flight by blowing trumpets *(Judges 7:19ff)*.

(10) Again, if there were no preaching, the hearts of men would not be stirred to hope for heavenly blessings. "If he holds back the waters, everything will be dried up" *(Job 12:15)*. Gregory comments on this: "If the knowledge of the preachers is withheld, the hearts of people who could have burgeoned with eternal hope will shrivel up instead."[10]

(11) Again, it is supremely necessary for the barbarian peoples of the world to come to faith in Christ, because without it they cannot be saved. It was because of this necessity that a Macdeonian man appeared to Paul by night, saying, "Come over to Macedonia and help us" *(Acts 16:9)*. But people cannot have such faith unless someone preaches to them. "How shall they believe in someone they have

never heard of? And how shall they hear without someone preaching?" *(Rom 10:14)*. It was for this reason that the Lord gave to the preachers of Christ all kinds of tongues, so that they could preach to everybody in a way they would be able to understand, and so bring them all to faith in him. This makes it obvious that without preaching the nations would not have been converted to Christ.

(12) Again, without preaching the church would never have been established. "Where were you, when I laid the foundations of the earth?" *(Job 38:4)*. Gregory says: "When scripture refers to foundations, we understand the preachers, who were the first to be established in the church by the Lord, so that the whole structure which follows rests on them."[11]

Also the church would not have made any progress in the past, nor would she be making progress now, without preaching. "The king commanded them to take large stones, precious stones" *(3 Kings 5:17)*. The Gloss comments: "The layers of stones or wood which come higher up in the building signify the teachers who have come afterwards, whose preaching makes the church grow, and whose virtues adorn her."[12]

Also the church would collapse without preaching. "I will make glorious the place of my feet" *(Isaiah 60:13)*. The Gloss explains: "It is preachers who are called the feet of the Lord, because they support the whole body of the church."[13] So the church stands because of them, just as the human body stands on its feet.

(13) From all of this we can see how necessary the job of preaching is. Without it the fulness of the glory of the kingdom of heaven will not be realised, without it Hell would be filled more quickly and the world would be altogether barren; the demons would prevail in the world, the hearts of men would not rise up to hope for heaven, the peoples of the world would not have received the christian faith, and the church would not have been founded or made progress, nor would she be able to stand.

(14) Furthermore the apostle says to some people, "You were once darkness, but now you are light in the Lord" *(Eph. 5:8)*, because men who lack preaching are like men in the dark. At the beginning of creation, we are told that the abyss was covered with darkness,[14] but once light was created, all that matter was illuminated. In the same way men are illuminated by preaching. "On those who dwell in the region of the shadow of death, light was dawned" *(Matt. 4:16)*, which means, according to the Gloss, the light of preaching.[15] So preaching

is the world's lighting.[16] This is why the first preachers are told, "You are the light of the world."[17]

(15) Again, it says in Hosea 4:2, "There has been a flood of cursing and lying and murder and theft and adultery." This flood would by now almost have wrecked the whole world, like Noah's flood, if it had not been held in check by preaching. An anecdote can illustrate this. Some clerics were talking in the presence of a certain archbishop, who was a man of great authority, and they were saying, "What is the use of all this preaching being done by these modern religious, seeing that there are still so many usurers and fornicators and so many other kinds of evil in the world?." The archbishop said, "If there is still so much wickedness, in spite of the fact that these good men have stopped an untold amount of it by their preaching, what would it have been like if they had never come and preached? Wickedness would surely have grown to such an extent that it would pretty well have choked the whole world."

(16) It is clear, then, that preaching checks the pullulation of wickedness. "The Lord brought a wind over the earth and the waters abated" *(Gen. 8:1)*. It is indeed through the wind of the Spirit who speaks in the preachers that the waters of the flood of wickedness abate.

(17) Again, just as we are told that there used to be frequent famine in the world, so, if preaching fails, there is spiritual famine. "In those days there was a very great famine" *(1 Macc. 9:24)*. The Gloss comments: "When there is a lack of preaching, there is famine, because man does not live by bread alone, but by every word which comes from the mouth of God."[18]

(18) Again, the word of God is the medicine which heals everything *(Wisd. 16:12)*, and preachers are doctors, as Matthew 9:12 shows, "It is not the healthy who need a doctor, but the sick"; and so, when there is a lack of preaching, epidemics of disease rage unchecked. This is why, by contrast, Wisdom 6:26 says, "An abundance of wise men is the health of the world," which the Gloss paraphrases, "The company of preachers is the health of the world."[19]

(19) Again, when there is a lack of wise government, it often comes about that cities are emptied of people; in the same way rational men disappear because of a lack of preaching. "When prophecy is lacking, the people will be scattered" *(Prov. 29:18)*, and almost nobody can be found except men who are no better than animals. But the good sense of preachers brings restoration to cities, and men live

in them once more. "Cities will be inhabited because of the good sense of prudent men" *(Ecclus. 10:3)*, which the Gloss refers to preachers.[20]

(20) Again, just as in a time of serious drought no water can be found, which results in great discomfort and loss for men, the same thing happens when there is a lack of teaching. "The poor and the needy seek water, and there is none. Their tongues are dry from thirst" *(Isaiah 41:17)*. It is the devil who instigates this. "Holofernes commanded the aqueduct which brought water into the city to be broken" *(Judith 7:6)*. The Gloss comments: "The thing the devil is most determined to achieve is the removal of the waters of doctrine."[21] But the Lord on his side sends preachers to pour out such water. "I will open up rivers on the tops of the mountains and springs in the middle of the plains" *(Isaiah 41:18)*. As the Gloss says, that means, "Preachers to peoples who are proud and in the midst of those who are humble."[22]

(21) Again, if there were no preaching, the whole world would be like a trackless waste, in which no path can be discerned. But preaching teaches people the way. So it is said of the outstanding preacher who preached in the desert, "You will go before the face of the Lord to prepare his ways ... to give light to those who are in darkness, sitting in the shadow of death, to direct our feet into the way of peace."[23]

(22) See then how necessary this task is. Without preaching the whole world would be in darkness, everything would be choked by the abundance of wickedness, a most dangerous famine would prevail universally, a plague of diseases would bring countless men to their death, cities would become desolate, the lack of the water of saving wisdom would lead to an unbearable drought, and no one on earth would be able to identify the ways that lead to salvation.

So God, seeing how necessary preaching is in the world, for the reasons we have been considering, has from the beginning never stopped sending preachers, one after the other, nor will he ever stop until the end of time. Gregory says: "The head of the household hires labourers to cultivate his vineyard at the third hour, the sixth hour, the ninth hour and the eleventh hour, because from the beginning of this world until its end, the Lord does not give up assembling preachers to be sent to instruct his faithful people."[24]

# HUMBERT OF ROMANS

## THE ACCEPTABILITY OF PREACHING IN GOD'S SIGHT

(IV 23) To realise how pleasing this job is in the sight of God, we should first of all notice that preaching is a kind of singing. "Singers dwelled in their cities" *(Neh. 7:73)*, on which the Gloss comments: "Singers are those who preach the delightfulness of the heavenly homeland with loving voices."[25] And this singing is so pleasing in God's sight, like minstrels' songs which rulers and princes enjoy in their courts, and he is so charmed by it that he says to the church, "Let your voice sound in my ears, for your voice is charming" *(Cant. 2:14)*. The Gloss interprets this to mean, "I want preaching, because the voice of preaching is delightful to me."[26]

(24) Again, preachers are called hunters. "I will send them hunters, who will hunt them out of every mountain and every hill and out of the caves in the rocks" *(Jer. 16:16)*. Writers who expound the moral sense of this passage explain that the reason for this saying is that preachers hunt wild souls who are in every kind of sin. And just as noblemen enjoy eating game, so God enjoys this kind of venison. As a symbol of this, it says that Isaac enjoyed eating the game caught by his son, Esau *(Gen. 25:28)*. So acceptable to the Lord is this kind of hunting that the desire for it makes him, in figurative language, incite the preacher, "Take up your arms, your quiver and your bow, and go out and catch something, and then make me a dish of it, that I may eat and bless you in the sight of the Lord" *(Gen. 27:3,7)*.

(25) Again, preaching derives properly from zeal for souls. So an outstanding preacher says, "I am jealous for you with the jealousy of God" *(2 Cor. 11:2)*, with holy zeal, that is to say. Gregory says that there is no greater sacrifice we can offer to God than zeal for souls.[27] So if God was once so pleased with the sacrifice of animals that it says of such a sacrifice which Noah offered that "he smelled the smell of its sweetness" *(Gen. 8:21)*, how pleased must we believe him to be with that sacrifice of souls which is offered to him by means of preaching!

(26) Again, preachers are called soliders of Christ. As it says, "Toil like a good soldier of Christ" *(2 Tim. 2:3)*, "by preaching," as the Gloss explains.[28] And it is right that preaching should earn them the title of soldier, because by preaching they do battle against the errors of unbelief and immorality which are the enemies of their king. In 2 Maccabees 12:19 we read of "Dositheus and Sosipater, who were commanders with Maccabaeus," and the Gloss comments on

191

this: "These two commanders signify holy preachers, who are appointed by the true Maccabaeus to do battle against all the errors of those who betray the faith."[29] Also, to enhance the greatness of their divine king, they subjugate foreign peoples to him. "The defeated Arabs asked Judas to give them the right hand of friendship" *(2 Macc. 12:11).* The Gloss interprets this: "As the light of truth dawns on them, they are overcome by the constant perseverance of holy preachers and seek from them the right hand of friendship; abandoning their errors, they seek to enter into the unity of the Catholic faith, and purpose to attach themselves to those who confess Christ."[30] Also, like faithful soldiers, they come and go at his command, totally obedient to him, like the soldiers of the centurion, who go and come on his orders.[31] "I will surround my house with those who are my soldiers, going and coming" *(Zech. 9:8),* "running hither and thither at my command," as the Gloss explains.[32] And this applies to preachers. Such soldiers are indeed dear to their king, and worthy of his love, as they fight down his enemies, subjugate peoples under him and obey him in everything. If the service of good soldiers is generally acceptable to their princes, as it is said of David that he was acceptable in the eyes of Achish *(1 Sam. 29:6ff)* because of his military service, how acceptable in the eyes of the King of glory must we believe the service of his preachers to be, seeing how fruitful it is.

(27) Again, people who want to please great lords often send them gifts of the things they most like, such as a first crop of some harvest, or special[33] fish or that kind of thing. But what the Lord likes most is souls. "O Lord, who love souls" *(Wisd. 11:27),* more than anything else, that is. And it is by preaching that he is sent a gift of souls. Who could tell in words how such an offering pleases him and with what joy he receives it? So it says in Psalm 44:15–16, "Virgins will be led in after her to the king" (the "virgins" being souls restored to innocence by penance); "her neighbours will be carried in to you." The Gloss interprets this: "They will be led in by preaching in season, they will be carried in by preaching out of season."[34] The Psalm goes on: "They will be carried in in gladness and joy," because such an offering will be received with great joy.

(28) Again, any preacher is a kind of envoy sent by God to handle his affairs. "This is my mission," as St. Paul says *(Eph. 6:20, 2 Cor. 5:20).* When an envoy faithfully performs his mission, the person who sent him is delighted; and in the same way God is delighted by a preacher faithfully performing his task. "Like cool snow at harvest

time" (which refreshes the harvesters when they are getting hot), "so is a faithful envoy to the one who sent him; he makes his soul rest content" *(Prov. 25:13)*.

(29) Again, in the Gloss to 3 Kings 5:6ff[35] and Ezra 3:7,[36] preachers are called hewers of wood, stone-cutters, bricklayers and other similar names. They are the workmen who build in the hearts of men a home for God to inhabit in the Holy Spirit,[37] and this home makes him glad, as the Lord himself says: "My delight is to be with the sons of men" *(Prov. 8:31)*. Now if kings are so pleased with the works of the craftsmen who build beautiful palaces that they send far and wide to get such craftsmen (as we find the king of the Indians doing in the legend of the apostle Thomas: he sent his commissioner a long way on just such an errand),[38] who can doubt that the Lord is greatly pleased by the work of preaching, by which such a lovely home is prepared for him to dwell in?

(30) Again, on Job 28:8, "The sons of the pedlars have not trodden it," the Gloss says: "Pedlars are preachers who do spiritual business: they proffer preaching to their hearers, to win from them faith and good works."[39] By this kind of trading souls are won, just as it says in 1 Cor. 9:19, "so that I may win many," "by preaching," as the Gloss indicates.[40] This is the kind of trade which the Lord encourages his preachers to undertake when he says, "Do business until I come" *(Luke 19:13)*. If he is so pleased with the profit that he congratulates the servant who gained five talents and says to him, "Well done, good and faithful servant; because you have been faithful in a few things, I shall set you over many. Enter into the joy of your Lord" *(Matt. 25:21)*, how delighted would he be with the kind of trading which wins for him the souls he values so highly?

(31) Again, preachers are God's servants, as it says in Acts 6:4, "We shall devote ourselves to the service of the word." And of all the different kinds of servant of God, there is none so intelligent as the preachers, as it says in Psalm 63:10, "They declared the works of God, they understood his deeds," which applies to preachers, according to the Gloss.[41] And, of all the factors which make any servant acceptable, the most important is that he should understand well what it is that he has to do. "A king likes an intelligent servant" *(Prov. 14:35)*. This shows us how acceptable this particular service is to God.

(32) From all that we have said, it follows that holy preaching is acceptable to God as a most pleasant kind of singing, as a delightful hunting, as a most pleasing sacrifice, as an arduous military service of

a prince, as the offering of a gift which is most acceptable to a lord, as a faithful execution of a task entrusted to one, as the building of a noble palace for a king, as a trading which is most profitable for the head of the household, as the service of an intelligent servant to his master; and indeed it is not only acceptable to God, but also to those who attend him in his court. "Dweller in the garden, my friends are listening to you. Let me hear your voice" *(Cant. 8:13)*. The "friends," as the Gloss explains, are the angels and the spirits of the just who are with God.[42]

## THE BENEFITS WHICH ACCRUE
## TO THE PREACHER FROM HIS JOB

(V 33) Next we must consider how profitable this job is to the preacher himself.

In the first place we must notice that anyone exercising this function is entitled to all that he needs for this present life, as the apostle proves in many ways, concluding, "Thus the Lord himself told those who preach the gospel to live by the gospel" *(1 Cor. 9:14)*.

And not only is the preacher entitled to the necessities of life, he is entitled to them in a particularly noble way. Other classes of men are obliged to worry about the necessities of life, but to preachers it is said, "Do not be anxious, saying to yourselves, 'What shall we eat?' or 'What shall we drink?' or 'What shall we wear?' Your Father knows that you need all these things" *(Matt. 6:31–2)*. Also other people have to work, eating their bread in the sweat of their brow,[43] but preachers are told, "Consider the birds of the air: they do not sow or reap or gather into barns" and "Consider the lilies of the field, see how they grow! They do not work or spin. But I say to you that not even Solomon in all his glory was clothed like one of them" *(Matt. 6:26–9)*, as if to say, "If the birds have their food and the lilies their clothing from God, without having to work for them, you should not have any doubt that God will do the same for you, because you are worth more in his sight than they are." Further, other people, for all their worrying and working for the necessities of life, are often still very unsure of them. But Gregory, commenting on Luke 10:4, "Do not take a bag or a wallet," says: "The preacher ought to have such confidence in God that, although he himself makes no provision at all for his own support in this present life, he knows for sure that he is not without such support. In this way his mind will not be occupied with temporal affairs, and he will be free to devote himself to making provision for the eternal good of others."[44]

We should notice that the Lord gave experimental proof of this truth, that he provides for preachers without their having to worry and without their having to work (provides what is necessary, that is, of course), which many people would find it difficult to believe: when he was about to depart from this world, he asked his disciples, "When I sent you out (to preach, that is, as the Gloss indicates),[45] without any bag or wallet and without shoes, did you lack anything?" They said, "Nothing" (*Luke 22:35*). This is strong supporting evidence for the truth of what we are saying.

(34) Furthermore, by the merit of their preaching people win many spiritual boons. "He who makes others drunk will himself be made drunk too" (*Prov. 11:25*). The Gloss on this says: "The one who makes his hearers drunk with the words of God will himself be made drunk with a draught of manifold blessing." And it is right to say "manifold," for the merit of preaching wins the gift of an increase of interior grace. The text goes on: "The soul which blesses will be fattened." The Gloss says: "The soul which blesses outwardly, by preaching, will receive inwardly the fatness of increase."[46]

(35) Next, the washing away of any filth that may be contracted by the preacher's active life. "When I washed my feet in butter" (*Job 29:6*). As the Gloss interprets this, "God's feet are preachers, and they are not without fault, but they are washed in butter, because the dust they pick up is washed off by the fatness of their good work."[47]

(36) Next, understanding. "Who gave the cock understanding?" (*Job 38:36*). The Gloss says: "Cocks are the preachers. . . . Who gave the holy preachers understanding except me?"[48] And it is very appropriate that, just as a certain kind of understanding is given to the cock, because he is a cock, understanding should similarly be given to the preacher, even more so, in fact, just because he is a preacher, because understanding is very necessary for his preaching.

(37) Next, eloquence. When Moses tried to excuse himself on the grounds that he was an incompetent speaker, the Lord said, "Who made the mouth of man? Was it not I? Get up then, and I will open your mouth" (*Exod. 4:11–12*).[49] This shows that it belongs to God's grace to open man's mouth.

(38) Next, an abundance of things to say. "Open wide your mouth and I will fill it" (*Psalm 80:11*), by giving you things to say in

abundance. The example of St. Sebastian proves it: when he was preaching, Zoe, the wife of Nicostratus, saw a young man coming down from heaven, holding a book before Sebastian. He read in this book and so delivered his sermon.[50]

(39) Next, powerful results. "The Lord will give a word with great power to the bearers of good news" *(Psalm 67:12)*. The preacher is the mouth of the Lord, so it is appropriate that he who gives a voice of power to his voice[51] should grant power in speech to his preacher, for his own name's sake. And apart from this, there are many other powerful gifts which the Holy Spirit, who is the giver of gifts, distributes to individual preachers as he wishes, giving more to some and less to others; and so, according to a different reading of the Psalm, it says, "The Lord will give many powers to those who proclaim his word."[52] This is why preachers are called "the sky," because they are adorned with various kinds of power, just as the sky is adorned with different stars. "His Spirit decorated the sky" *(Job 26:13)*. Gregory comments: "The sky's ornaments are the different kinds of power possessed by the preachers. St. Paul lists them: 'To one is given a word of wisdom by the Spirit, to another a word of knowledge, by the same Spirit, to another faith, in the same Spirit, to another a gift of healing, in one and the same Spirit, to another the working of powerful deeds, to another prophecy, to another discernment of spirits, to another different kinds of tongues, to another the interpretation of tongues.' "[53] And it is only fair that they should be given more graces than other people, because they undertake a special burden of work for the whole body of the church. But whoever these graces are given to, they are meant for everyone, not just for the recipient himself. "To each one is given a manifestation of the Spirit, in order to be useful" *(1 Cor. 12:7)*. The Gloss comments: "Gifts are not given to an individual in response to his personal merit, but they are given to make people useful for the building up of the church."[54] So if gifts are given to other people for the use of the church, how many more gifts ought to be given to those whose special job it is to be useful to the church? All of this shows that the greatest number of spiritual gifts is acquired by being a preacher.

(40) Moreover preaching tends to inspire devotion in the people and this sometimes makes them burst out in blessing of the preacher. "Anyone who hides corn" (which refers to preaching, according to the Gloss)[55] "will be cursed among the people; but there will be a blessing upon the head of those who sell it" *(Prov. 11:26)*. Take the

woman in Luke 11:27, for instance, who burst out in blessing while the Lord was speaking to the crowds: "Blessed is the womb that bore you," she exclaimed, "and blessed the breasts which you sucked."

(41) Sometimes people burst out in prayer too. There was once a nobleman who was much given to the vain pursuits of a worldly life; he was brought by a preacher one day to the knowledge of himself and God, and began to pay attention to working out his salvation. Later on, when he was ill and in his last agony, he remembered the blessing he had received through that preacher and he lifted up his heart to God and said, "Lord, I pray to you for that man through whom I came to know you."

There is no doubt that many of the people who listen to a preacher pray devoutly for him, especially as preachers themselves usually ask them to do so when they are preaching, both at the beginning and at the end of their sermons. St. Paul frequently made such a request *(Eph. 6:19, Col. 4:3, 2 Thess. 3:1)*. And much may be expected as a result of such prayers, in proportion to the number of people praying. As the authority says, "It is impossible that many should pray and not be heard."[56]

(42) Sometimes this kind of devotion inspires people to follow the preacher in crowds, as we have often seen in our own days and as it says in the gospels about Christ: a huge crowd used to follow him because of his preaching, even in the desert; they came flocking to him from all around.[57]

Further, it inspires them not only to follow, but to wait on the preacher too: "They followed him and served him" *(Mark 15:41)*.

Further, this kind of devotion inspires people to show great honour to preachers. "You received me like an angel of God, like Christ Jesus himself" *(Gal. 4:14)*. No wonder, since priests are held to be worthy of double honour, especially those who toil in word and in teaching *(1 Tim. 5:17)*.

(43) Again, it brings them great renown. "Judas was renowned to the very ends of the earth" *(1 Macc. 3:9)*. Judas stands for preachers. The Gloss comments: "He was renowned to the very ends of the earth, because 'their sound has gone forth into all the world' ";[58] 'sound,' that is, the reputation of their preaching."[59]

(44) Again, all those who have in any way benefited from a preacher's words ought to recognise that they are, to that extent, the preacher's children. "In Christ Jesus I have begotten you through the gospel" *(1 Cor. 4:15)*.

(45) So this devotion on the part of the people is a happy thing, not to be undervalued by the preacher, because it means that he will often be blessed, he will have many people praying for him, it will win him followers and people wanting to serve him, it will bring him honour and wide renown, and it will win him great crowds calling themselves his children in Christ.

(46) This shows that the preacher wins three kinds of benefit from his job as a preacher: the necessities of life, many spiritual gifts and the devotion of the people. And that only covers the benefits he receives in this present life.

(47) But this job is not only profitable to the preacher with regard to this present life. Much more importantly, it is also profitable in many different ways with regard to the future, to the state of glory.

In the first place, the preacher acquires a greater certainty of salvation because of his job. For in any work of kindness, the Lord usually deals with men in the same way that they deal with one another. "Forgive and you will be forgiven, give and you will be given things in return" *(Luke 6:37–8)*. This demonstrates beyond any doubt that the preacher who saves others, even if only as a minister of salvation, will himself be saved. And this is what the Lord says through his prophet: "If you convert (others, that is), I will convert you" *(Jer. 15:19)*.

(48) Secondly, he earns a greater substantial reward. For we may well believe that the charity which makes him work not only for himself but for others too is constantly increasing in him because of his job. And as charity increases, so must his substantial reward increase also. As it says in the Canticle 8:12, "Two hundred pieces of silver to those who guard its fruits," the fruits of the vineyard, that is. The Gloss says: "That means, to the teachers, because a man who keeps himself and wins others earns a double reward."[60]

(49) And thirdly, in addition to his substantial reward, he will have many other incidental joys to increase his glory. On Eph. 1:18–19, "So that you may know how outstandingly great his power is in us," the Gloss comments: "The chief teachers will have a certain increase of glory beyond that which is common to everyone."[61] Theologians interpret this as meaning an extra glory which is given over and above the essential glory. Now if this is true of the chief teachers precisely because they are teachers, the same will be true in varying degrees of all teachers. So any good preacher will receive this

kind of increase, and in many different ways. Proof of this can be derived from the Gloss on the same text: "Those who will shine with the greatest brilliance of all are the apostles." Now it is agreed that this radiance in their state of glory corresponds to the radiance which they had on earth, when they were the light of the world. But any good preacher is a kind of light, as we learn from Psalm 76:19, "Your lightnings flashed over the world," which the Gloss says applies to preachers.[62] So it is only fair that such people should shine with a particular brilliance in heaven. This is why Daniel says, "Those who instruct many others in righteousness will be like stars for ever and ever" *(Dan. 12:3).*

(50) Again, it is a greater thing "to act and to teach"[63] than it is just to act. Since everyone receives a reward in heaven according to his deserts, it seems right that the heavenly reward should be proportionate to this kind of greatness in a man's activity on earth which wins him his reward. So it is not without reason that it says, "Anyone who acts and teaches like this will be called great in the kingdom of heaven" *(Matt. 5:19).* Just as at present, in earthly courts, some are greater and some are less great in their degree of honour, similarly in the court of heaven there will be those who are greater, and it is among them, and not among the less great, that the preachers will be.

(51) Again, in 1 John 3:2 it says, with reference to the glory of the elect, "When he appears, we shall be like him." If this refers to the glory of the elect, it is plain that the greater their likeness to him, the greater will be their glory in consequence. But preachers are like him in putting their rational power to work in its most exalted job, namely preaching. And this is why theologians commonly say that they win a halo, just like virgins and martyrs (in connexion with haloes, see the text and the Gloss at Exod. 25:25[64]); they are like Christ in using, in the one case their faculty of desire, and, in the other case, their faculty of anger and determination, in the highest possible way.[65]

(52) Again, it is the preacher's job to fight our ancient enemy.[66] "Michael and his angels did battle with the dragon" *(Apoc. 12:7).* Michael has his preachers, who are called "angels" because they serve under him to help him against the devil and his host. So if David attained such glory by fighting with Goliath that people made songs about it in his honour when he returned from the fight *(1 Sam. 18:6–7),* what glory awaits the preacher in heaven, when he returns from fighting manfully with such a tremendous foe?

(53) Again, in the courts of princes[67] it redounds to a man's honour and glory if he is given precedence in the seating arrangements or in any other way. But a preacher is given precedence over many other people in the court of heaven: "You are to be set over ten cities" *(Luke 19:17)*.[68] The Gloss interprets this to mean: "The ten cities are souls which come to the grace of the gospel through the words of the law. The preacher who entrusted the 'money' of the word to them in a way worthy of God is there set over them in glory."[69]

(54) Again, it redounds greatly to a man's honour and glory if he enters the king's palace with a large escort. But no good preacher will enter there alone; he will lead with him those whom he converted. In his homily, *Designavit*, Gregory says: "There Peter will appear with Judaea, which he converted and led after him; there Paul will appear bringing almost the whole world with him, since he converted it; there Andrew will bring Achaea with him and John will bring Asia, and Thomas India. There all the rams of the Lord's flock will lead their flocks which they won for God."[70]

(55) Again, it is the highest honour for a man to be crowned or to appear crowned in the presence of a great crowd and a crowd of great men. And there a good preacher will be crowned. "Come and you shall be crowned with the peak of Amana, with the summit of Sanir and Hermon" *(Cant. 4:8)*. The Gloss comments: "When preachers make conversions like this, their crown is enlarged with the princes who have been overcome by their efforts."[71] This is why Paul says, "What is our crown? In the sight of the Lord, is it not you?" *(1 Thess. 2:19)*.

(56) All of this shows what glory there will be for the good preacher, because of his brilliant radiance, his personal greatness, the likeness he had to Christ, the battle he fought with the devil, the precedence he is given over others, the company he brings with him and the glorious crown which will be his.

(57) This makes quite obvious the way in which the job of preaching benefits the preacher, both in this world and in the world to come. And this is confirmed by the Gloss on Ecclesiasticus 31:28, where it says, "The lips of many will bless him who is outstandingly generous with his bread." The Gloss says: "The man who faithfully dispenses the bread which is the word of God will be blessed now and in the world to come."[72] "Blessing" means imparting good gifts.

# HUMBERT OF ROMANS

## THE USEFULNESS OF PREACHING

(VI 58) Next we must consider how useful preaching is to men. In this connexion we must observe that, though preaching is, as has been said, necessary for the whole creation, it is particularly useful to men, and it is useful to them in as many ways as the word of God itself, which is proposed to people through holy preaching.

We must realise, then, that there are many people whose spirits are in their bodies like corpses in their tombs. And, just as God will, at the end of time, raise up dead bodies by his word, so he now gives life to dead spirits by the power of his word. "The hour is coming and is now, when the dead will hear the voice of the Son of God, and those who hear it will live" *(John 5:25)*.

(59) Again, there are many who, spiritually, have nothing to live on. But it is the word of God which sustains man's spiritual life. "Man does not live by bread alone, but by every word which comes from the mouth of God" *(Matt. 4:4)*. Poor people who have nothing with which to keep themselves alive come running for alms; similarly people who are spiritually poor ought to come running to sermons, to receive the word of God in their spirit, to keep themselves alive.

(60) Again, there are many who are always eagerly on the look-out for tasty things to eat. But there is no more delightful food for a healthy palate than the word of God. "How sweet your words are to my taste; they are better than honey in my mouth" *(Psalm 118:103)*.

(61) Again, there are many who go astray on all kinds of points because of their simplicity. And preaching puts them right, with its exposition of the word of God. "The explanation of your words gives light and understanding to little ones" *(Psalm 118:130)*.

(62) Again, there are many who have no perception in spiritual matters and lead an entirely animal life. But the word of God enables them to move on into a spiritual life. So it says, "The words which I have spoken to you are spirit and life" *(John 6:63)*. They are called "spirit and life" because of their effect, which is to instil a spiritual life into people.

(63) Again, there are many who, in the darkness of this world, do not know how to hold to the right path. But the word of God is like a torch by night, showing them the right way. "Your word is a light for my feet, a lamp to show me the way" *(Psalm 118:105)*.

(64) Again, there are some medicines which work against some kinds of sickness, but not against them all. But the word of God

201

works against every kind of spiritual sickness. "Your word is all-powerful, Lord, it cures everything" *(Wisdom 18:15, 16:12)*.

(65) Again, there are people whose hearts are harder than rock. The word of God sometimes breaks this hardness. "Are not my words like a hammer, smashing the rocks?" *(Jer. 23:29)*.

(66) Again, there are people whose piety and compunction and devotion towards God are quite dried up. "My soul is like soil with no water before you" *(Psalm 142:6)*. But the word of the Lord sometimes melts them. "He will send forth his word and it will melt them" *(Psalm 147:18)*.

(67) Again, there are many people in whom charity has grown cold. But the word of the Lord rekindles it. "Are not my words like a fire?" *(Jer. 23:29)*, setting things ablaze, that is.

(68) Again, there are many who are like a barren woman, unable to conceive any good undertaking. But the word of God makes them conceive. So Luke 8:11 says, "The word of God is seed," because, like seed, it is the beginning of conception.

(69) And it not only causes conception, it also makes things bring forth fruit. "As the rain and the snow come down and make the earth drunk and fill it with moisture and make it germinate, so will my word be, which comes from my mouth" *(Isaiah 55:10–1)*.

(70) Again, there are wines so weak that they cannot intoxicate. But the word of God is like a strong wine and it does intoxicate. This can be seen in the saints who were so drunk that they were oblivious of everything around them, and seemed not even to notice it when they were dragged off and beaten. "I became like a man who is drunk, like someone sodden with wine, from my encounter with the words of God" *(Jer. 23:9)*.[73]

(71) Again, there are many people whose spirit is so attached to the flesh that they can scarcely be separated from their carnal desires. But the word of God achieves just such a separation. "The word of God is alive and effective, sharper than any two-edged sword, accomplishing even the dividing of the soul (our animal life, that is)[74] from the spirit" *(Hebr. 4:12)*.

(72) Again, there are many who are in great need of help against the temptations of the devil. But the word of God is a sword with which a man can defend himself against them, as we can see from the Lord, who defended himself against temptation with sacred words *(Matt. 4:4ff)*. "And the sword of the spirit, which is the word of God" *(Eph. 6:17)*.

(73) Again, the word of God is like powerful soap which is strong enough to wash the filth out of dirty linen. "You are clean because of the word which I have spoken to you" *(John 15:3)*. A dirty jar becomes cleaner if it is frequently immersed in water, even if it does not retain any of the water, as it says in the *Lives of the Fathers.*[75]

(74) Again, there are many who are a long way from being saints. But the word of God makes them saints. "Sanctify them in the truth: your word is truth" *(John 17:17)*.

(75) Again, grace is supremely necessary to men in this life. But it is given to men through the power of the word of God, as the early church shows. "Good teaching will give grace" *(Prov. 13:15)*.

(76) Again, there are many who are in danger of their souls dying because of their serious sickness and weakness. But they are set free by the word of the Lord. "He sent his word and it healed them, he rescued them from death" *(Psalm 106:20)*.

(77) Again, just as bodies are healed at the doctor's words, so souls are saved by God's word. "Receive in meekness the word which is implanted in you, which can save your souls" *(James 1:21)*.

(78) And these are not the only useful results with which the word of God benefits men. There are many others too. This is why it says, "The word of God is full of power" *(Ecclesiastes 8:4)*, which refers to the many different kinds of effectiveness that it has, like a precious stone which is good for many different purposes.[76]


## THE DIFFICULTY OF THIS JOB

(VII 79) Now we must turn to the difficulty of this job, and we must notice that it is very difficult to do the job of preaching well, as we can see from three considerations.

First, there are only a few good preachers. In the primitive church there were few preachers, but they were so good that they converted the whole world. Now there are preachers too many to count, but they achieve little. Why should this be, unless the ancients were good preachers and the moderns not? But it is symptomatic of the difficulty of any art, if it has many practitioners, but few of them are good at it.

Secondly, there are many people who try to preach, without ever succeeding. There are, and there were in the past, many very well educated men, who have struggled for all their worth to acquire a grace of preaching, and yet, for all their effort, they have not succeeded. And it is symptomatic of the difficulty of an art, when someone who is otherwise well suited for its practice can nevertheless not master it.

And thirdly, there is the difficulty of the way in which this art is learned. Other arts are mastered by practice and frequent exercise. By building we become builders, by playing the harp we become harpists, as the philosopher says.[77] But a grace of preaching is had only by God's special gift. So it says, "The ability of a man is in the hand of God" *(Ecclus. 10:5)*.[78] "Man" means "preacher," according to the Gloss.[79] The point of this is that it is by God's gift that a man is empowered to preach. And what a man cannot bring about by his own labour, but has to depend on some outside factor for, is particularly difficult for him.

(80) There are also three reasons why the job of preaching is difficult to do well. One concerns the teacher of this art. There are plenty of people to teach other arts, and they are easy to get hold of; but there is only one who can teach this art, and there are few who have access to him: and that is the Holy Spirit. That is why the Lord did not want those pre-eminent preachers to start preaching until the Holy Spirit had come to teach them everything.[80] After he had come and entered into them, then they began to speak "as the Holy Spirit gave it to them to speak" *(Acts 2:4)*.

Another reason concerns the instrument of preaching. Preaching is performed by means of the tongue, and the tongue goes astray extremely easily, unless it is directed by the power of God. As it says, "It belongs to the Lord to govern the tongue" *(Prov. 16:1)*. Now we are much less likely to do something well with our left hand, which easily makes mistakes, than with our right hand, which does not so easily make mistakes. In the same way, it is difficult to do the job of preaching well, because it is done by means of the tongue, which is of all our limbs the most prone to error.

A third reason concerns the things which are necessary if this job is to be done in a commendable fashion. There are a great many of these, as we shall see in Part Two. And the more things you require to practise any art, the harder it is. For example, it is harder to paint a picture which needs a lot of different colours than one which only requires a few. But there are a great many things required for good preaching, so that is an added difficulty.

(81) The next thing to notice is that there is not much credit in

doing any good work unless it is done well, which is why it says, "Learn to do well" *(Isaiah 1:17)*. And preaching is difficult to do well. And when something is difficult, it is necessary to work hard at it. So a preacher must apply himself very carefully to doing all that is in him to practise his job well and with grace.[81]

In this attempt, there are three things which are particularly helpful: the first is meticulous study, the second is to observe how other preachers tackle the job, and the third is prayer to God.

## STUDY

(82) Though a grace of preaching is strictly had by God's gift, a sensible preacher still ought to do what he can to ensure that his preaching is commendable, by carefully studying what he has to preach. "The seven angels who held the seven trumpets prepared themselves to play their trumpets" *(Apoc. 8:6)*. According to the Gloss, this means "all those who preach in imitation of the apostles."[82] Against this, Matthew 10:19 says,[83] "Do not consider what you are going to say." But the apostles were privileged in their preaching; those who are not so privileged are permitted to think out what to say beforehand. So Jerome says, in his comment on Ezekiel 3:1, "Eat the book": "The words of God should be stored up in our hearts and carefully examined, and only then proffered to the people."[84]

(83) Now there are some preachers whose preparatory study is either all devoted to subtleties, with a view to producing an intricate web of subtleties, or, at other times, it is exclusively devoted to looking for novelties, their intention, like that of the Athenians,[85] being always to find something new to say. At other times they occupy themselves entirely with philosophical points, wanting only to win renown for their tongues. But a good preacher's concern is rather to study what is useful. When he goes back over a sermon he has prepared, he will cut out whatever strikes him as less useful and retain only what is really useful, like the apostle, who says, "You know that from the first day I entered Asia, I have not held back from you anything useful, but have declared it all to you" *(Acts 20:18–20)*.

(84) There are others who work hard to find a lot to say, multiplying the sections of their sermons or using too many distinctions or producing long lists of authorities or strings of arguments or illustra-

tions; or they look for lots of different words all meaning the same thing, or they repeat the same ideas over and over again, or they produce interminable prothemes or expound a single word in all kinds of different senses.[86] All of these are serious faults in a sermon. A reasonable amount of rain is good for the fruitfulness of the earth, but too much just swamps it. A moderate amount of food is good for the stomach, but too much revolts it. A short act of worship encourages devotion, but one that is too long just sends people to sleep. So concise preaching is useful, but it becomes useless if it goes on too long. So a good, intelligent preacher ought not to devote his attention to having a lot to say, he should rather study how to contain what he says within a reasonable limit. And if he finds that he has thought of too many things to say, he should cut back what is less useful, so that he will be giving the household a reasonable measure of wheat, like a good steward *(Luke 12:42)*, not the whole crop that he can get hold of.

(85) There are some people who either use nothing but arguments to make what they are saying more convincing, or else nothing but anecdotes or else nothing but authorities. It is much better to use all three, so that someone who does not respond to the one may be moved by one of the others. There are many people who respond more to one than to the others.

When these three all work together, the hook of preaching has a strong triple line attached to it, and that is a line which no fish can easily break.[87]

(86) We can gather from all of this that when a good preacher is working on his sermon, he should first make sure what he proposes to say is useful, like a good host making sure that the food he gets prepared for his guests is good. Then, out of such useful material, he should aim to prepare something which is not immoderately long, just as a good host does not serve up absolutely everything that can be found at the butcher's, however fond he is of his guests, but he takes a moderate amount from what is best there. And thirdly he should consider how to make what he is going to say more persuasive, like a host ensuring that a meal is prepared carefully and tastefully, so that his guests will get more pleasure out of eating it and digest it with less difficulty.

(87) Then there are some people who apply a great deal of ingenuity to finding strange texts for the sermons they are going to preach, like the man who was going to preach on the apostles Peter and Paul, and took Numbers 3:20 as his text, "The sons of Merari

were Moholi and Musi."[88] But such extraneous texts can usually only be adapted to the subject of the sermon with a considerable degree of inappropriate twisting of the sense, and they are more likely to make people laugh at the sermon than they are to edify them.

(88) On the other hand, there are some preachers so intent on finding a text to suit the day that this very concern for appropriateness makes them overlook the criterion of usefulness, so that they take texts which contain little or nothing that is of any use to their audience. People like this should be called church cantors rather than preachers of Christ. It is the job of the church's cantors to chant the texts which are proper to the season or the feast, without regard to whether the sense of what they are singing is useful to those who listen to it or not.

(89) Others again take a text so short that there is only one point contained in it, like people who give their guests a meal of only one dish.

Others take a longer text, containing several points, of which some are not very useful, and then give a long commentary on every little detail, whether or not it contains anything useful. That is rather like wanting to make a meal out of a cow and preparing one dish from the horns, one from the skin, another from the hoofs, and so on till the cow was quite used up. That is not a sensible way to cook. A sensible cook would make a meal out of the best parts of the animal and leave the rest.

Then there are others who take a text which contains many useful points, but spend so long expounding the first one or two points that they cannot deal with any of the others. They are like boorish people who give you such a large helping of the first course of a meal and make it go on so long that you cannot eat anything of the other courses, even though they may actually be better than the first. Hosts who are gentlemen do just the opposite. They give you many different courses, but only give you a little of each one. This style of eating is far more agreeable to the guests.

(90) So a preacher ought to abandon all such abuses and devote his careful attention to finding a text which clearly fits his subject and which contains something useful which is adapted to his audience, and not just one point but several; and if it contains anything which is not so useful, he should give little or no time to developing it.

(91) There are also some preachers who do not have the mental

capacity to produce decent sermons themselves, but who will not stoop to studying what other people have said, insisting on saying only what they can discover for themselves. They are like people who insist on providing only bread that they have made themselves, even though they are not good bakers. This is the opposite of what we find in the gospel, where the Lord ordered bread to be distributed by the disciples: they had not made it themselves, it had already been made by somebody else *(Mark 6:37ff)*.

I have been told that once Pope Innocent (under whom the Lateran Council was held) was to preach on some great feast.[89] Now he was a highly educated man, but even so he had someone stand by him with St. Gregory's homily for that feast, and he preached it word for word, turning it from Latin into the vernacular, and when he could not remember what came next he asked the man with the text there to remind him. When he was asked afterwards why he had done this, when he was quite capable of finding plenty of new things to say for himself, he said that he had done it as a rebuke and lesson for people who thought it was beneath them to use other people's words in their sermons.[90]

(92) Then again there are others who are quite clever and intelligent enough, but who are so confident in their own cleverness that they ignore the saints' comments on Holy Scripture and rely on their own exegesis. As Jerome says, "They disdain to find out what the prophets and the apostles really meant. They fit texts to their own view which do not really fit, forcing reluctant scriptures to serve their own purposes."[91] They are like people who imagine that bells they hear chiming are saying whatever they themselves happen to be thinking of. To quote Jerome again, "They suppose that whatever they may say is the law of God."[92]

(93) There are others who are more interested in their literary style than in the content of what they are saying. That is like being more interested in the beauty of the dishes in which food is served than in the food itself. As Augustine says in the *Confessions,* "I learned that wisdom and foolishness are like useful and useless kinds of food, and that elegant and inelegant words are like elegant and inelegant dishes: you can serve either kind of food in either kind of dish."[93]

(94) So a wise preacher should abandon these three faults, and study what others have said about the bible, and rely more on the saints' interpretations than on his own, and prefer good content in what he says to good style.

## LEARNING FROM OTHERS

(95) Those arts which consist in doing something are learned better by practical example than by teaching in words. No one would ever learn so much about playing the fiddle from mere words as he would from watching someone actually playing. Similarly it is a great help to someone who is trying to learn the art of preaching to observe the methods of good preachers, and of others too, and the differences between different preachers' methods. Then he can avoid what he finds wrong in anybody's preaching, and try to imitate what strikes him as admirable.

This is why Gideon, who is a symbol of a good preacher, says, "Do what you see me doing" (*Judges 7:17*).

## PRAYER

(96) Since human effort can achieve nothing without the help of God, the most important thing of all for a preacher is that he should have recourse to prayer, asking God to grant him speech that will be effective in bringing salvation to his hearers. As Augustine says in his book *On Christian Teaching*, "Queen Esther prayed before going to speak to the king in the hope of winning earthly salvation for her people, and asked the Lord to put the right words in her mouth. How much more ought a man who is labouring in word and teaching for the eternal salvation of men to make the same prayer."[94]

(97) From all of this we can see that there are three things which indicate that preaching is a difficult job, and three reasons for this difficulty, and three things which a preacher ought to do to overcome the difficulty.

(98) All these reflections on the nature of preaching show how different preaching is from other jobs. Others are commonplace, but preaching is outstanding; others are not particularly necessary, but preaching is necessary for the whole world. There are some jobs which are displeasing to God or not very pleasing, but preaching is extremely acceptable to God. There are some jobs which bring little profit to those who do them, but preaching wins the greatest possible benefit for the preacher. Other jobs do not do anybody else much good, but the service given to men by preaching is of the most useful kind possible. And finally some other jobs are easy, but preaching

cannot be done worthily without immense difficulty, and it is no wonder, seeing what a great undertaking it is. Anyone who wants to do it well will find problems in his way.

## *Notes*

1. All the MSS have "six," which is plainly wrong.
2. Cf. Hebr. 1:14.
3. *Tendit* ASL. M's *fodit* is certainly the *lectio difficilior*, but in the case of a writer like Humbert, who habitually avoids using unexpected language, this is, if anything, an argument against it; if accepted, it would presumably have to be translated "goads."
4. PL 76:1214A.
5. "Making good heaven's loss" refers to the belief that the place of the fallen angels in heaven is to be taken by redeemed human beings. Cf. Augustine, *De Civitate Dei* XXII 1. The "second robe" is the resurrected body. The closest parallel to Humbert's interpretation of this Apocalypse text that I can find in the commentators is in Anselm of Laon (PL 162:1524) and Richard of St. Victor (PL 196:768–9).
6. The reading *appropinquabit* (as against *appropinquavit* of modern editions of the Vulgate) is guaranteed, not only by all the MSS of Humbert, but also by the Gloss and by the commentaries of St. Thomas and Hugh of St. Cher.
7. *Animam suam.* Hugh of St. Cher interprets this to mean "appetite."
8. Interlinear Gloss.
9. Marginal Gloss.
10. PL 75:960A.
11. PL 76:455C. All the MSS have "established on the earth" (*terra*). I follow the text of Gregory and read *ecclesia*.
12. Marginal Gloss.
13. Marginal Gloss.
14. Gen. 1:2.
15. Interlinear Gloss to Matt. 4:16. This supports the reference in all the MSS to Matt. 4, but in fact the text is quoted as it is found in Isaiah 9:2.
16. All the MSS have *illuminaria*, against *illuminativa* (B) and *illuminatio* (Max.). *Illuminare* is recorded as a noun, meaning "lamp."
17. Matt. 5:14.
18. Marginal Gloss. Cf. Matt. 4:4.
19. Interlinear Gloss.
20. Interlinear Gloss.

21. Marginal Gloss. I have corrected *suadet* of Humbert's MSS to *studet*, in accordance with the text of the Gloss.

22. Interlinear Gloss.

23. Luke 1:76–9.

24. PL 76:1154C. Cf. Matt. 20:1–6. I have added "and eleventh" from the text of Gregory; it is missing from all the MSS of Humbert.

25. Interlinear Gloss to Neh. 7:1.

26. Interlinear Gloss.

27. PL 76:932C.

28. Interlinear Gloss.

29. Marginal Gloss. There are several textual problems. The MSS all have *nostri Machabei* ("our Maccabaeus"); the printed editions of Humbert all have *veri* (which I have translated). This is supported by MS Bodley 255 of the Gloss, but the printed text in Lyranus and PL 109:1248C have *viri*. The printed editions of Humbert also fill out the quotation: . . . *Machabei dispositione, hoc est fortissimi praeliatoris, de quo in Ps. scriptum est: Dominus fortis et potens in proelio.* This is not found in the MSS of Humbert, but is found in the Gloss (though Berthier and PL 109 read *praeliatores*, which seems less probable).

30. Marginal Gloss.

31. Cf. Luke 7:8.

32. Marginal Gloss.

33. *Notabilibus* L seems preferable to *nobilibus* MAS.

34. Lombard's Gloss (PL 191:445–6). Cf. 2 Tim. 4:2.

35. I conjecture this to be the intended reference. The MSS have "Luke 5."

36. Marginal Gloss to 3 Kings 5; Interlinear Gloss to Ezra 3:7.

37. Cf. Eph. 2:22.

38. Cf. Acts of Thomas 2.

39. Marginal Gloss.

40. Interlinear Gloss.

41. Interlinear Gloss.

42. Marginal Gloss.

43. Gen. 3:19.

44. PL 76:1140D.

45. Marginal Gloss.

46. Interlinear Gloss.

47. Marginal Gloss. It is interesting to contrast this with Bonaventure's presentation of St. Francis. He presents Francis too as being aware that preaching involves "getting one's feet dirty" (*Legenda Maior* 12:1); but, far from supposing that the dust is washed off by the very goodness of the act of preaching itself, he shows his hero withdrawing into solitude "to wash off any dust that had stuck to him from being in the company of men" (13:1).

48. Marginal Gloss.

49. This "text" is a conflation of Exod. 4:11 and Ezek. 3:27; a similar conflation is found in the Marginal Gloss to Exod. 4:11–12.

50. PL 17:1032A.

51. Psalm 67:34.

52. This is the text in the *Psalterium Romanum.*

53. PL 76:1224D. Cf. 1 Cor. 12:8–10.

54. Marginal Gloss.

55. Interlinear Gloss.

56. Cf. Marginal Gloss to Rom. 15:30, a text cited in a variety of different forms. St. Thomas quotes it in a very similar form in his commentary on John, 2142; in *in Matt.* 1526 he uses exactly the same words as Humbert, but without giving any reference.

57. Cf. Mark 1:45, 5:24; John 6:2.

58. Marginal Gloss. Cf. Psalm 18:5.

59. Cf. Interlinear Gloss to Psalm 18:5; but, so far as I can discover, the Gloss reads *fama etsi non praesentia eorum.*

60. Interlinear Gloss.

61. Marginal Gloss.

62. Interlinear Gloss.

63. Acts 1:1.

64. Marginal Gloss.

65. Cf. St. Thomas, *IV in Sent.* d.49 q.5 a.5; *in 2 Tim. IV* lect.II. Also an anonymous thirteenth-century treatise reported by J. Leclercq, *Archives d'Histoire Doctrinale et Littéraire* 15 (1946) p. 112.

66. *Hoste* MSL. A reads *serpente,* which may be correct (cf. Apoc. 12:9).

67. *Magnatum* M, *magna cum* ASL. I conjecture *magnatum* < *cum* >.

68. This "text" seems to be a conflation of Luke 19:17 and 19:19.

69. Marginal Gloss. I follow the reading of the Gloss, *verbi Deo digne* (Oxford, Bodleian MS Auct. D 1.6) rather than *verbi Dei digne* of Humbert's MSS.

70. PL 76:1148B.

71. Marginal Gloss. I have added *victis* ("overcome") from the text of the Gloss.

72. Marginal Gloss.

73. This is the text of all the MSS. The printed editions follow the Vulgate text.

74. *Anima* ("soul") is the principle of "animal," bodily, life.

75. Cf. PL 73:929AB.

76. The medievals ascribed all kinds of extraordinary powers to stones, ranging from the medicinal to the magical. Cf. J. M. Riddle and J. A. Mulholland, "Albert on Stones and Minerals," in J. A. Weisheipl, *Albertus*

*Magnus and the Sciences* (Toronto, 1980) pp. 203–234. On medieval lapidaries, see Dorothy Wyckoff, *Albertus Magnus: Book of Minerals* (Oxford, 1967), pp. xxxiv–v and Appendix B. A good example is Book 14 of Thomas of Cantimpré, *De Natura Rerum.*

77. Aristotle, *Eth. Nic.* II 1103a33–4.

78. This is not the text generally printed in modern editions of the Vulgate, but it was a common reading in the thirteenth century.

79. Interlinear Gloss.

80. Cf. Luke 24:48–9; John 14:26; Acts 1:4–8.

81. *Gratiose.* Early Dominican sources are continually exploiting the ambiguity of the words related to *gratia.* It can mean "grace" (as in God's grace), but it also means "graciousness," which in turn wins the "favour" of men.

82. Interlinear Gloss.

83. I do not know what the correct reading is here. Berthier's text cannot be right; Humbert does not intend any reference to the Gloss on Matt. 10:19 or any of the parallel texts. MAL read *alia glossa in evangelio contradicitur,* which runs into the same difficulty. S reads *illa glossa in evangelio contradicitur,* which would be admirable if it could mean "This Gloss is contradicted in the gospel," but transitive use of *contradico* is only very doubtfully attested, and the passive would be even more tricky. But the general sense is clear enough.

84. PL 25:37C.

85. Cf. Acts 17:21.

86. For a study of medieval sermons, cf. Th. M. Charland, *Artes Praedicandi* (Paris and Ottawa, 1936); R. H. Rouse and M. A. Rouse, *Preachers, Florilegia and Sermons* (Toronto, 1979) pp. 65–90. A thirteenth-century sermon would invariably be divided into several *membra;* Humbert warns against having too many of them. A favourite way of dividing a sermon was by exploiting different senses and uses of scriptural words, and this was referred to under the name *distinctiones,* and this is almost certainly what Humbert is referring to here. Each idea would then be developed, and the three basic ways of supporting and filling out such development were quotations from authoritative texts (especially scripture and the fathers), arguments and anecdotes *(exempla).* A rhetorical device favoured by some preachers was the use of different ways of saying the same thing, especially to avoid taking up the elements in the *thema* in its actual words (cf. Charland, p. 157); but Humbert is probably thinking more of the use of synonyms as a way of padding out the development of the ideas in a sermon. Returning to the same ideas over and over again (in different words, presumably) is a similar ploy. The *prothema* showed quite remarkable development during the thirteenth century, amply justifying Humbert's warnings; properly it was a

secondary text, used to introduce the preacher's request to the audience to pray for him and for themselves. Finally Humbert goes back to the *distinctiones* and warns against excessive use of the ambiguities of language.

87. Cf. Ecclesiastes 4:12.

88. I do not know of any other evidence for this particular sermon, but there are some equally strange texts attested. For instance, Eudes of Châteauroux begins one sermon with Numbers 20:28: " 'When Moses had stripped Aaron of his garments, he put them on his son, Eleazar.' In these few words, the Lord shows, in a veiled, figurative way, why Synods were instituted and what the bishops and archdeacons ought to do at them." See M. M. Davy, *Sermons Universitaires* (Paris, 1931) p. 207. (For Eudes of Châteauroux and his devotion to the Dominicans—he refers to St. Dominic as "our father"—see J. J. Berthier, *Le Testament de St. Dominique* [Fribourg, 1892] pp. vii–x; A. M. Walz, ASOP 17 [1925] pp. 174–223.)

89. MA have "Feast of St. Mary Magdalene," in which case the sermon in question is perhaps no. 33 from the sermons on the gospels, which is the Homily appointed for the feast of St. Mary Magdalen in the old Dominican lectionary (British Library, MS Addit. 23935 f.216ᵛ).

90. For a brief comment on Innocent's preaching, and on this passage in particular, see H. Tilmann, *Pope Innocent III* (Amsterdam, 1980) p. 216.[12]

91. PL 22:544.

92. PL 22:544.

93. *Confessions* V 6:10.

94. *De Doctrinia Christiana* IV 30:63. Cf. Esther 4:16.

# II Things That a Preacher Needs

(VIII) In Part Two we must consider the things that are necessary for a preacher. And these fall under six general headings:

(i)    the quality of his life;
(ii)   his knowledge;
(iii)  his speech;
(iv)   his merits;
(v)    his person;
(vi)   things signified symbolically in scripture.

## THE QUALITY OF A PREACHER'S LIFE

(99) Goodness of life is necessary for every preacher. "Anyone who speaks the word of God must first consider his own manner of life," as Gregory says.[1] Now there are many things involved in goodness of life, all of which a preacher must have. One is a holy conscience. The reason for this is that he must be able to speak boldly, and a bad conscience prevents this. "A man whose conscience trips up his tongue will find that his teaching becomes less confident," as Gregory says.[2]

(100) Another thing he needs is that his life should be beyond reproach. How can a man rebuke others when he himself needs rebuking? So it says in Philippians 2:15–6, "You must be without reproach in the midst of a crooked and perverse people, carrying the word of life"; you, that is, who are carriers[3] of the word of life.

(101) Another factor is austerity of life, like that of John, the preacher of penance.[4] "I beat my body and reduce it to servitude, in

case, after preaching to others, I myself might be found reprobate" *(1 Cor. 9:27)*.

(102) Another thing is a certain pre-eminence of life. A preacher stands in a high place to preach, and he ought similarly to be in a high condition of life. "Go up on to a high mountain, you who preach good news to Zion" *(Isaiah 40:9)*.

(103) Another thing is a certain radiance about his life. It is not enough for a preacher to lead a good life in private; his life is meant also to shine before men[5] in such a way that he preaches by his example as well as by word of mouth. "Among whom you shine like lights in the world, carrying the word of life" *(Phil. 2:15–6)*; you, that is, who are carriers of the word of life.

(104) Another thing is that his actions should be in harmony with his words. Jerome says, "Do not let your deeds thwart your words. Otherwise, when you are speaking in church, your hearers will tacitly retort, 'Why do you not put your own words into practice?' "[6]

(105) Another thing is a reputation which spreads like perfume, so that he can join the apostle in being a "good odour of Christ"[7] which attracts others. "Judas was renowned to the very ends of the earth" *(1 Macc. 3:9)*. The Gloss explains that this applies to a preacher.[8]


## THE KNOWLEDGE A PREACHER NEEDS

(IX 106) A preacher ought to be knowledgeable, since he has to teach others. This is why 1 Timothy 1:7 reproaches some people with the words, "Wanting to be teachers of the law, they understand neither what they are saying nor the things which they speak so dogmatically about."

Now there are many kinds of knowledge which are necessary for preachers. One is knowledge of the holy scriptures, because all preaching ought to be taken from them, as it says in Psalm 103:12, "From the middle of the rocks they will give utterance," the rocks meaning the two testaments, and preachers cannot do this unless they have knowledge of the two testaments. So this kind of knowledge is necessary. Even though the Lord called simple, uneducated people to be preachers, he still gave them knowledge of the holy scriptures, as we can see from their writings, in which they often adduce arguments from the Old Testament. As Jerome says, "The benefits which others acquire by training and daily meditation on the law were supplied to them by the Holy Spirit and they were, as scripture says, 'taught by God.' "[9]

(107) Then there is knowledge of creatures. God has poured out his wisdom over all his works,[10] and this is why St. Anthony said that creation is a book.[11] Those who know how to read this book well draw from it many things which are very serviceable for helping people to grow. The Lord made use of this kind of knowledge in his preaching, when he said, "Consider the birds of the air" and "Consider the lilies of the field" *(Matt. 6:26,28).*

(108) Then there is knowledge of historical stories. There are many stories told not only among believers but also among unbelievers, which can sometimes be very useful and edifying in a sermon. The Lord made use of some of them when he said of those who resisted the word of God, "The queen of the south will arise at the judgment with the men of this generation and condemn them, because she came from the ends of the earth to hear the wisdom of Solomon, and see, there is something more than Solomon here now," and when he said against people who would not repent, "The men of Nineveh will rise at the judgment with his generation" *(Luke 11:31–2).*

(109) Then there is knowledge of the church's precepts, which is important because people need to be instructed about many of them. "Paul went round Syria and Cilicia strengthening the church, bidding them observe the precepts of the apostles and elders" *(Acts 15:41).*

(110) Then there is knowledge of the church's mysteries. The apostle is referring to this when he says, "If I knew all mysteries."[12] The church is full of mystical symbols, and it contributes greatly to people's edification to have these expounded to them, and so it is helpful if the preacher understands them. That is why it says, "In the middle of the church he opened his mouth" (the preacher's mouth, that is) "and filled him with the spirit of wisdom and understanding" *(Ecclus. 15:5).*[13] The "spirit of understanding" refers to that spirit which enables a man to understand what is hidden under the symbols, because to "understand" means to take your "stand under" the symbolic surface.[14]

(111) There is also experiential knowledge. People who have had much experience in dealing with the state of man's soul can say much

more about the affairs of the soul. "A man who is experienced in many things will think many things, and a man who has learned much will declare understanding" *(Ecclus. 34:9)*.

(112) There is also the kind of knowledge which is called discretion. This enables a man to know to whom the word of God ought not to be preached—it ought not to be preached to swine or dogs[15]—and to whom it ought to be preached. It also enables him to know when he ought to preach and when not, because "there is a time for keeping silent and a time for speaking."[16] It also enables him to know what to say to whom, in accordance with Gregory's teaching in the *Pastoral Rule*, where he identifies thirty-six different situations.[17] It also enables him to know how to refrain from going on too long and from talking too loudly, from gestures that would not be seemly and from saying things in a disorderly way, and from all the other things of this sort which can go wrong in preaching. So discretion is one of the things that belong to the job of being a preacher. Gregory says, " 'The sole of their feet is the sole of a calf's foot' because every preacher has his 'divided hoof' in the form of discretion."[18]

(113) Finally there is knowledge of the Holy Spirit. This was the kind of knowledge which the first apostles had, and it taught them everything, and they spoke according to the way it taught them. "The apostles spoke in various tongues, as the Holy Spirit gave it to them to speak" *(Acts 2:4)*. Happy would he be who had such knowledge! It is this that makes up for what is lacking in all the other kinds of knowledge.

## THE PREACHER'S SPEECH

(X 114) A preacher must have the appropriate ability to speak, sufficient to ensure that he is not rendered unintelligible by any deficiency in his way of speaking. When Moses excused himself to the Lord because of his defective speech, he was given the help of his brother Aaron, who was an able speaker, to speak for him to the people. "The Lord said to Moses, 'I know that your brother Aaron, the Levite, is a capable speaker. . . . He will speak for you to the people and will be your mouth, but you will be to him in the place of God" *(Exod. 4:14–6)*.

(115) He must also have a good facility with words. The first preachers in the church were given all kinds of tongues for the sake of

their preaching, so that they would have an abundance of words for everyone; so it is very unfortunate when a preacher sometimes runs out of words, whether because he has a bad memory or because he does not know enough Latin or whatever modern language it may be, or for any other reason. Over against this kind of deficiency, it says in Apocalypse 1:15, "His voice" (Christ's that is) "was like the voice of many waters," because the preacher, who is Christ's voice, ought to be overflowing with words.

(116) He must also have a sonorous voice. A great deal of the effectiveness of a sermon is lost if the preacher's voice is so thin and feeble that he cannot be heard clearly. This is why scripture often compares the voice of a preacher to the sound of a trumpet, because it ought to sound powerfully and clearly like a trumpet. "Let there be a trumpet in your throat" *(Hosea 8:1)*. This is said to a preacher.

(117) He must also have a fluent style of speech, so that he is easy to understand. In his book *On Christian Teaching*, Augustine says that men who are difficult to understand should never or hardly ever, and then only if it is absolutely necessary, be sent out to speak before the people.[19] It is to make this point that it says, "The teaching of wise men is easy" *(Prov. 14:6)*.

(118) His enunciation must be balanced too; that is to say, not too fast and not too slow. If he speaks too quickly, it makes it hard for people to understand, but if he speaks too slowly, it makes for boredom. So Seneca says, "The philosopher's enunciation, like his life, ought to be orderly. But where there is precipitate haste, there is always disorder." He also says, "I want him to dribble his words as little as I want him to run. He should neither stretch men's ears nor swamp them."[20] Now if this is required of a philosopher simply for the sake of worldly reputation, how much more is it required of a preacher for the sake of the good of souls?

(119) He must also be able to speak concisely. As Horace says,

Whatever you command, be brief, that what you say
Men's learning minds may quickly grasp and store away.[21]

Accordingly it says in the Canticle 4:3, "Your lips are like a scarlet headband." The Gloss says this refers "to preachers,"[22] who are the lips of the church. And just as a headband restrains overflowing hair, so these lips ought to avoid any overflowing excess of words.

(120) His speech must also be simple, without fancy rhetorical

flourishes, so that, like Shamgar, he can be said to take only a ploughshare as his weapon.[23] As Augustine says, "We must be careful not to detract from the weight of sacred and serious pronouncements by giving them cadences."[24] By "cadences" he means measured rhythms, metres and rhetorical embellishments. It is not surprising that the saints should say this, since the philosophers are of exactly the same mind. Seneca says, "A speech which is concerned with truth ought to be simple and straightforward."[25] Other arts are a matter of ingenuity, but in this art of preaching there is a serious business for the mind to deal with.[26] A sick man does not look for an eloquent doctor. If the doctor who can cure him can also make an elegant speech about what has to be done, that is like having an expert helmsman who is also handsome.

(121) He must also be sensible about saying different things to different people. Gregory says, in his *Register of Letters*, "Our speech should be a consolation to the good and a sting to the wicked, it should deflate the puffed-up and bridle the angry, it should stir up the lazy and set fire to the slack with its encouragement; it should seek to convince those who are running away, soothe those who are rough and comfort those who are in despair."[27] This is the meaning of Isaiah 50:4, "The Lord gave me a learned tongue."

(122) Finally, since all of these will be of little value unless there is a graciousness upon the lips,[28] in accordance with what it says in Ecclesiasticus 20:21, "A man without grace is like an idle tale," above everything else it is necessary for a preacher to have grace in his speaking, grace to season everything.[29] This is what is said of the best preacher of all in Psalm 44:3, "Grace is poured upon your lips."

## THE PREACHER'S MERIT

(XI 123) Provided that he does his job in a praiseworthy fashion, the preacher gains much merit from his preaching over and above the merit of his own good life. "He who acts and teaches will be called great in the kingdom of heaven" *(Matt. 5:19)*.

But there are many ways in which this merit can be cancelled out or diminished. One is if anyone preaches without authority. "How shall they preach unless they are sent?" *(Rom. 10:15)*.

(124) Another is if someone preaches when he is guilty of some notorious sin. "God said to the sinner, 'Why do you declare my

judgments and take up my covenant in your mouth?' " *(Psalm 49:16)*. This refers to notorious sinners.

(125) Another is when somebody departs from the truth in his preaching, for whatever reason, like those who are spoken of in Ezekiel 13:19, "They have violated me" (who am the truth, that is) "before the people, for the sake of a fistful of barley and a piece of bread, to give life to souls which are not alive and to kill souls which are not dying,[30] deceiving a people who give ear to their lies." As Augustine says in his book *On Christian Teaching*, "Maybe people will not understand so much, maybe they will not like it so much, maybe they will not be so moved, but still you should only speak what is true and just."[31]

(126) Another is when the preacher does not practise what he preaches, making his deeds conform to his words. "Bind them round your throat," as it says in Proverbs 3:3, on which the Gloss comments, "In encouraging others to live good lives, the preacher binds himself to live a good life."[32] This is why it says, "You teach others, do you not teach yourself? You preach a ban on thieving; do you then go and thieve?" *(Rom. 2:21)*.

(127) Another is when wordly results are given precedence over spiritual results, contrary to the example of the apostle, who was not looking for gifts, but for results *(Phil. 4:17)*. He was not after the goods of the people he was speaking to, he was after themselves *(2 Cor. 12:14)*. Gregory says in his *Morals on Job*, "Good preachers do not preach in order to receive their livelihood, they accept their livelihood in order to be able to preach. And when their hearers give them the necessities of life, they are not only pleased with the material gift, they are pleased with the generosity of the givers."[33]

(128) Another is when a preacher does not seek what belongs to God, but what belongs to himself, such as reputation or honour, preaching himself and not our Lord Jesus Christ, contrary to the example of the apostle *(2 Cor. 4:5)*. Gregory says, in his *Homilies on Ezekiel*, "To seek only a passing moment of fame from the labour of preaching is to sell a precious treasure for a pittance."[34]

(129) Another is when Christ is preached from a desire to do other people down, instead of with good will. "Some preach Christ out of envy and a spirit of competition, but others from good will" *(Phil. 1:15)*.

(130) Another is when a preacher upsets people by his rough way of speaking. "A mild tongue is a tree of life," because it brings

forth good fruit; "but an unbridled tongue will wear a man's spirit away," the spirit of his hearer, that is *(Prov. 15:4)*.

(131) Another is when an indiscreet preacher inveighs against one fault in such a way as to give occasion to another fault. What Gregory teaches in his *Pastoral Rule* is quite different: "Humility must be preached to the proud in such a way that the timid do not become more fearful; confidence must be imparted to the timid in such a way that the proud do not become even more arrogant. Concern for good works must be preached to the idle without giving the restless any excuse for excessive activity; a limit must be set to the activity of the restless without making the idle complacent in their sloth. The anger of the intolerant must be quenched without encouraging the indifference of the lazy and slack;[35] those who are too slack must be fired with zeal, but without adding fuel to the fury of others. Misers must be urged to be more generous in giving, without allowing full rein to the extravagant; the extravagant must be taught how to save, without fostering the misers' posessiveness about their perishable goods.[36] Marriage should be commended to the promiscuous, without leading those who are chaste into sexual indulgence; bodily virginity must be commended to the chaste without making married people come to despise the fruitfulness of the flesh. Good must be preached in such a way that evil is not preached too by implication. The highest values must be commended in such a way that lower values are not disparaged; lower values must be fostered in such a way as not to give the impression that they are sufficient in themselves or to stop men aspiring to the higher values."[37]

(132) Another way in which the preacher may reduce his merit is by not displaying any signs of penance. Jerome says, "What an embarrassment, what a humiliation, to preach Jesus our Master, who was poor and hungry, with our own bodies stuffed full, and to proclaim the teaching of the fasters with our ruddy cheeks and our mouths full! If we occupy the place of the apostles, let us not only imitate their words, but also their way of life and their abstinence."[38]

(133) Another is when the preaching is not motivated by charity. "If I speak with the tongues of men and of angels, but do not have charity, I have become like a tinkling cymbal or a booming gong" *(1 Cor. 13:1)*. The tinkling cymbal benefits others, but wears itself away.

(134) So if preaching is to be meritorious for the preacher as well as being beneficial to those who listen to it, the preacher must avoid preaching without authority, he must not be a notorious sinner, he

must not deviate from the truth, what he does must accord with what he says, he must be more interested in spiritual gain than in worldly profit, he must seek what belongs to God rather than what belongs to himself, he must not preach with a view to doing other people down, he must not upset his hearers with foolish words, he must not give occasion for any evil, he must not be without some evidence of doing penance, and his motivation must not lack charity.

## THE PREACHER'S PERSON

(XII 135) In connexion with the preacher's person, we should notice that he must be of male sex. "I do not permit a woman to teach" *(1 Tim. 2:12).*[39] There are four reasons for this: first, lack of understanding, because a man is more likely to have understanding than a woman. Secondly, the inferior status imposed on women; a preacher occupies a superior position. Thirdly, if a woman were to preach, her appearance would inspire lustful thoughts, as the Gloss on this text says.[40] And fourthly, as a reminder of the foolishness of the first woman, of whom Bernard says, "She taught once and wrecked the whole world."[41]

(136) Next, he must not have any obvious or remarkable bodily deformity. People whose bodies are disfigured in this way are debarred from the Lord's service in Leviticus 21:17ff, and similarly the church has banned them from public office, for fear of popular scandal and ridicule.[42]

It is also useful to him to be strong in body, so that he can stay up late at night studying, speak loudly when he is preaching, endure the labours of travelling, and the poverty of not having things he needs, and many other such hardships, as the apostles did. "They will be truly patient," that is, truly strong in endurance, "so that they may proclaim" *(Psalm 91:15–6).*

(137) He also ought to be of suitable age. Gregory says, "Our Redeemer reigns in heaven as Creator, and he has always been the teacher of the angels by the display of his power, yet he refused to become the teacher of men until he was thirty. In this way he wanted to instil a healthy timidity into the over-hasty by letting them see that even he who cannot fail did not preach the grace of the fulness of life until he had reached the fulness of maturity in years."[43]

(138) He also ought to have some superiority over the other

people present, in his position or education or religious life or something of the kind, except that occasionally it may be useful for a man to preach in the presence of his superiors, as a kind of exercise. This is why preaching is not the job of a layman, because the laity occupy the lowest rank. "How beautiful on the mountains are the feet of him who proclaims and preaches" *(Isaiah 52:7)*. This implies that a preacher ought to be high up, in some way, as on a mountain.

(139) Finally, he ought not to be in any way contemptible, for fear that his preaching too will be despised. Gregory says, "If a man's life is despised, it will follow that his preaching too is despised."[44]

## THE SCRIPTURAL SYMBOLS OF THE PREACHER

(XIII 140) The scriptural figures which symbolise preachers are almost beyond counting, as we can see from the Gloss. This is in order to make preachers realise what they have to do and so bring forth fruit of all the different kinds indicated by the various symbols.

"If you separate the valuable from the cheap, you will be a kind of mouth for me" *(Jer. 15:19)*. This is glossed, "Separate: with your words, that is."[45] And this is what a preacher does. This shows that he is a kind of mouth of the Lord.

"The light of my face did not fall to the ground" *(Job 29:24)*. This is glossed, "The light of the Lord's face does not fall to the ground, because the church does not preach her radiant mysteries to earthly men."[46] This shows that the preacher is called God's face.

"I will honour the place of my feet" *(Is. 60:13)*. This is glossed, "Preachers are called the Lord's feet."[47]

So, since preachers are called the Lord's mouth, the Lord's face and the Lord's feet, they must make sure that nothing comes from their mouth which is unworthy of the mouth of the Lord, and that nothing can be seen in them which is unworthy of the face of God, and that wherever they go they carry God with them, as feet carry the rest of the body to which they belong.

(141) Preachers are also called angels. "The seven angels prepared themselves to blow the trumpet" *(Apoc. 8:6)*. This is glossed, "The whole company of preachers."[48] So every preacher must ensure that there is nothing demonic or bestial in him; he must rather conduct himself in a way that is suitable for angels, above the common nature of men.

(142) They are also called the eyes and teeth and neck and breasts of the church, and other similar things, as we see from Cant. 4:1–5. This is because of the various functions which belong to them, as the Gloss on Cant. 4:5 says: "Preachers are called eyes, because they are on the watch for hidden things, and teeth because they seize the wicked and drag them into the belly of the church, and neck because they supply the breath of life through preaching the joys of heaven and they also supply the food of doctrine, and breasts because, in Christ, they give milk to the little ones."[49]

(143) They are also called heaven. "His Spirit adorned the heavens" *(Job 26:13)*. This is glossed, "Preachers."[50] So the preacher must take care to shine like the sky with all the different virtues which ought to adorn him.

(144) They are also called stars. "He enclosed the stars" *(Job 9:7)*. This is glossed, "Stars: preachers,"[51] and so they ought to shine on the earth in the darkness of this world, like the stars.

(145) They are also called doors of heaven. "He opened the doors of heaven" *(Psalm 77:23)*. This is glossed, "The doors of heaven are the preachers,"[52] and so they ought to see to it that men enter heaven through them, and that the things of heaven come into the world through them.

(146) They are also called clouds, because, like clouds, they are sent to travel about over the whole world. "Clouds give light to everything throughout their course" *(Job 37:11–12)*. This is glossed, "The clouds of God give light to everything throughout their course because they enlighten the ends of the world with the light of their preaching."[53]

(147) They are also called snow. "He commanded the snow to descend upon the earth" *(Job 37:6)*. This is glossed, "Water is packed together in the sky above to become snow; when the snow falls to the earth it melts again and changes back into water. So snow falls from heaven to earth when the lofty minds of the saints, nourished on a contemplation that is well packed and solid, descend to the lowly words of preaching out of love for their brethren."[54]

(148) Then again, they are called thunder. "When the seven thunders had spoken" *(Apoc. 10:4)*. This is glossed, "Thunders, that is, preachers."[55] They are called thunder because it is their job to instil the fear of God. So Gregory says in his *Morals on Job*, "Thunder refers to the preaching of the fear of heaven; when the hearts of men hear it, they quake."[56]

(149) Again they are called precious stones. "The king commanded them to bring great stones, precious stones, to set in the foundations of the temple" *(3 Kings 5:17)*. This is glossed, "The layers of stones which come higher up are the teachers whose preaching makes the church grow and whose virtues adorn her."[57]

(150) They are also called mountains, because, like mountains, they are the first to receive the bounty of heaven, which they then transmit to the places below. "Let the mountains receive peace for the people, and the hills justice" *(Psalm 71:3)*. This is glossed, "Mountains, that is, preachers."[58]

(151) They are also called fountains, because they gush like fountains. "You made fountains burst forth" *(Psalm 73:15)*. This is glossed, "Fountains, that is, preachers, and you made them burst forth so that they would pour forth their flow of wisdom."[59]

(152) They are also called eagles, because, just as eagles fly to corpses, so they fly to those who are dead in their sins. "Wherever there is a corpse, there will soon be an eagle"[60] *(Job 39:30)*. This is glossed, "A holy preacher flies with eager haste to wherever he considers there are sinners, to show forth the light of new life to those who are lying dead in their sins."[61]

(153) They are also called cocks. "Who gave the cock understanding?" *(Job 38:36)*. This is glossed, "Cocks are the preachers, who, in the darkness of this present life, zealously proclaim the light that is to come, by 'crowing' or, in other words, preaching."[62]

(154) They are also called ravens, because of certain good qualities which they have. "Who prepared his food for the raven, when his little ones cry to God?" *(Job 38:41)*. This is glossed, "The raven is a preacher, from whom the chicks, cheeping in the nest, wait open mouthed to receive their food. Because of this discretion of his, God gives the raven a greater abundance; he receives more, because he receives not only for himself, but also for those whom he feeds."[63]

(155) They are also called dogs. "Dumb dogs which cannot bark" *(Is. 56:10)*. This is glossed, "Bark, that is, preach."[64] So the preacher is called a dog, and therefore he ought to wander round hither and thither like a hungry dog, eager to swallow up souls into the body of the church. "They will feel hunger like dogs and go about the city" *(Psalm 58:7)*.

(156) They are also called horses. "Will you give strength to the horse or put his whinnying in this throat?" *(Job 39:19)*. This is glossed, "In this passage the holy preacher is referred to under the

name of a horse. For the preacher first of all receives strength by extinguishing vice in himself, and then moves on to the utterance of preaching in order to educate others."65

(157) They are also called oxen. "A thousand yoke of oxen" *(Job 42:12)*. This is glossed, "Oxen: preachers."66 So they ought to work the fields energetically to show their strength. "Where there are no oxen, the manger is empty. Where there is an abundant harvest to be seen, it proves the strength of the oxen" *(Prov. 14:4)*.

(158) Also they are the standard-bearers of the army of the king of heaven, carrying his banner. "Lift up a sign for the people" *(Is. 62:10)*. This is glossed, "Lift up, by preaching, a sign, namely the cross, by proclaiming the Passion and the Resurrection."67

(159) They are also the messengers of that Ahasuerus who is our joy, carrying his letters and commands throughout all his provinces. "King Ahasuerus sent letters throughout all the provinces of his realm" *(Esther 1:22)*. This is glossed, "Through his preachers he sent out instructions and rebukes."68

(160) They are also the strong men of David,69 through whom he accomplished mighty deeds in the world. "I have called my strong men in my wrath" *(Is. 13:3)*, on which the Gloss says, "Paul, for example."70 The text goes on: "The Lord of hosts has given the word to the army which fights his war." This is glossed, "He has given the word to the preachers, who are equipped with the armour of the apostle, to kill all those who raise themselves up against the knowledge of God."71

(161) Then again they are the officers of the true Solomon, who carefully see to the food for his table. "The officers, with immense care, supplied what was needed for the table of King Solomon at the appropriate time" *(3 Kings 4:27)*. This is glossed, "To ensure that there is nothing lacking in the king's house, the order of preachers labours, in writing and in speech, to make plentiful provision on the Lord's table for the nourishment of the faithful."72

(162) They are also bricklayers, who work with Ezra to repair the temple of the living God. "They gave money to bricklayers" *(Ezra 3:7)*. This is glossed, "The bricklayers are preachers, who build men up in good works and bind them together with the bond of charity, as if they were cementing together cut and polished stones, to keep them in place in the whole construction."73

(163) They are also the watchmen of the house of Israel, that is, the church, to tell it what they see coming. "Son of man, I have

appointed you watchman to the house of Israel" *(Ezek. 3:17)*. This is glossed, "He calls the preacher a watchman because his way of life should be such as to set him up on high, where he can be useful by being able to see into the distance."[74]

(164) Notice that all these symbols fall into nine sections, with reference, respectively, to: God, angels, the church, heaven, the sky, the earth, things that fly, earth-bound creatures, and human responsibilities. Happy the preacher who realises in himself all the symbols which apply to his office!

## *Notes*

1. PL 76:890C.
2. PL 76:265D.
3. Hugh of St. Cher takes *continentes* to mean "containing" like a jug *(vas)*, which contains something in itself which can then be poured out for others.
4. Cf. Matt. 3:4.
5. Matt. 5:16.
6. PL 22:533.
7. 2 Cor. 2:15.
8. Marginal Gloss to 1 Macc. 3:1ff.
9. PL 22:543. Cf. John 6:45.
10. Cf. Ecclus. 1:10.
11. PL 73:1018C.
12. 1 Cor. 13:2.
13. Quoted in the form used for the Introit in the Mass of a Doctor.
14. *Intelligere est intus legere.*
15. Matt. 7:6.
16. Ecclesiastes 3:7.
17. PL 77:50–1.
18. PL 76:807B. Cf. Ezek. 1:7.
19. Augustine, *De Doctrina Christiana* IV 9:23.
20. Seneca, *Letters* 40:2–3.
21. Horace, *Ars Poetica* 335–6. I do not know why the MSS give *Eunuchus* as the source for these two lines.
22. Marginal Gloss.
23. Cf. Judges 3:31.
24. *De Doctrina Christiana* IV 20:41.
25. Seneca, *Letters* 40:4.
26. *Negotium animi* MA. (SL's *cum*, followed by Max., is presumably a

misreading of the abbreviation for *animi*.) Berthier reads *negotium animarum*, giving the sense, "there is serious business in hand, the business of souls."

27. PL 77:1034B.

28. *Gratia labiorum*: cf. above, p. 213[81].

29. Col. 4:6.

30. This is the reading of all the MSS, contrary to the Vulgate text.

31. *De Doctrina Christiana* IV 14:30.

32. Marginal Gloss.

33. PL 76:111A.

34. PL 76:1052D.

35. *Lenibus*, the reading in Gregory, is supported only by L, against *levibus* MAS. Since there is evidence that the scribe of L, or his source, sometimes corrected the text of Humbert from a text of Gregory, L's evidence is worthless. But nevertheless *lenibus* is probably to be preferred.

36. *Peritura rerum custodia* in the MSS must be corrected to follow Gregory's text, *peritura < rum > rerum custodia*.

37. PL 77:121.

38. PL 25:1172B.

39. To prevent misunderstandings, a few points need to be noticed about the position of women in the thirteenth century and about Humbert's attitude toward them. It was unthinkable at the time that St. Paul's categorical ban on women's teaching in church should be challenged directly, and Humbert here repeats some of the commonplaces that had been used to explain the ban. This did not, however, prevent some women from having a real, if informal, teaching role. Jacques de Vitry, for instance, secured from Honorius III a rescript explicitly permitting free-lance religious women to form communities and to encourage each other "with mutual exhortations" (Letters I p. 74); Jacques himself was particularly impressed by Mary of Oignies, whose life he wrote, and whom he called his "Mother," of whom, after her death, he cherished a relic (ibid., p. 72). By the time Humbert was writing, these women, by now generally called "béguines," had become an important and rather unruly force in the church, and Humbert proposed that the Council of Lyons should take steps to curb them (*Opus Trip*. III 3). But his major concern is to ensure that no communities are allowed to come into existence without adequate means of support, and the main reason for this concern is that he considers it dangerous for such women to go gadding about begging or doing business. Neither in the *Opus Tripartitum* nor in his model sermon to béguines (I liv) does he suggest that they ought to be more strictly controlled by the clergy or restrained from offering each other moral and spiritual instruction. He evidently means it when he says that women are generally less intelligent than men; this is why he is unhappy about letting them roam about too much. Unlike Jacques de Vitry or St. Dominic or Jordan of Saxony, he does not seem to have been a ladies' man, and he

probably had little occasion to question his prejudice about their intelligence. But he does not seem to have been very serious about their "inferior status," which he mentions here. This was another commonplace, derived from Gen. 3:16 and such Pauline texts as Eph. 5:22ff, but, in fact, in the thirteenth century women, as such, patently did not have an inferior status. As has been pointed out often enough, women were at least as well protected by law as men, and some of them were considerably more powerful in law and in fact than their masculine neighbours (cf. F. Heer, *The Medieval World* [New York, 1963] pp. 318–9; J. F. Stephens, *Mediaevalia* I 1 (1975) p. 105; R. Fossier, *Cahiers de Civilization Médiévale* 20 [1977] p. 99). Dominican history runs into several of these women. Throughout the first twenty years of the thirteenth century, seigneurial rights at Fanjeaux were held by Dame Cavaers (a strong supporter of the heretics); the rather autocratic patroness of the Dominicans in Burgundy, Countess Alix de Vergy (see p. 383[28]), was a powerful heiress in her own right; further north, the Dominicans benefited from the generosity of Joanna of Constantinople and her sister and successor, Margaret, who ruled Flanders between them for much of the century (cf. Meersseman, AFP 19 [1949] pp. 122–160). In religious affairs too women often took the initiative and sometimes exercised authority *de iure* and *de facto* over men, clergy included, as well as women. The Cistercian nuns and, to a lesser extent, the Praemonstratensian nuns resulted from the initiative of the women, not the men, and the male Cistercians only intervened in the affairs of the nuns under secular pressure—and their intervention was not very successful. The Praemonstratensian nuns too came to possess considerable autonomy—to such an extent that the canons had to try to prevent them from receiving *men* into the Order without consulting the canons (Grundmann, *Religiöse Bewegungen*, pp. 170–198; R. Southern, *Western Society and the Church in the Middle Ages* [Harmondsworth, 1970] pp. 312–8; A. Erens, *Analecta Praemonstratensia* 5 (1929) pp. 5–26; SCH Subsidia 1 pp. 227–252). Later the mendicants found themselves faced with a similar army of determined women wanting to affiliate themselves to their Orders. Throughout the whole period, the men attached to these nunneries, including the chaplains, were canonically subject to the abbesses of the communities they served. The Dominicans did not supply their nuns with resident chaplains, but the men who looked after the nuns' business affairs and properties were required to promise obedience to the prioress. When Humbert revised the nuns' constitutions, he did nothing to change the status of their menfolk (Creytens, AFP 19 [1949] pp. 5–45). With all of this, Humbert seems to be quite content. In his sermon to noble women (I xcv) he shows no sign of disapproving of their social, economic and political power; in his sermon to the "chaplains, clerics and laymen" attached to nunneries (I liii) he is quite explicit that they have the same kind of status as the servants of noble lay women: they are subject to the nuns. In his sermon for women in general (below, pp. 330–32) he in fact indicates several ways in which women are more privileged than men. Dominican women, as such, were subject to the Master of the Order and to their local provincials, but Humbert made an innovation in their law to ensure that they were no *more* subject to them than any community of friars would be. He reaffirms the principle that it is for them to make their own decisions about people who want to join them (this goes back to St. Dominic, who forbade the brethren to take it upon themselves to accept people as Dominican nuns: MOPH XXV p. 127); and he gives them the right to elect their own superiors, subject only to the same confirmation as priors in the houses of the brethren. To appreciate the equanimity with which Humbert accepts the secular and ecclesiastical rights of women, it is instructive to contrast what he says with some of the ways in which what we may call the medieval "men's lib." supporters expressed themselves. Andreas Capellanus, for instance, towards the end of the twelfth century, responding in a highly ambiguous way to the romantic world of the court of Marie, Countess of Champagne, concludes his *Art of Courtly Love* with a ferocious denunciation of women (J. J. Parry, *Andreas Capellanus: The Art of Courtly Love* [New York, 1941] pp. 200–9). Nearer the time of Humbert, we may listen to the exasperated cry of the abbot and community of Marchtal. This Praemonstratensian double monastery had evidently reached the point where the men could take no more, so in 1273 they solemnly committed themselves to having nothing more to do with nuns for at least fifty years; their declaration is quoted by Erens, l.c. p. 10,[20] and Southern, l.c. p. 314: "We, Conrad, superior of Marchtal, together with the whole community of our canons, seeing that the wickedness of women surpasses all other wickedness in the world, and that there is no anger to compare with the anger of a woman, and that it is easier for a man to heal and to endure the poison of asps and serpents than it is for him to endure the close company of women, and wishing to make provision for the future for the health of our souls and bodies, and also of our goods: decree unanimously that hereafter we shall accept no sisters to increase our ruin, but shall rather avoid accepting them as we should avoid accepting poisonous beasts." That is the voice of anti-feminism, though it comes from the crushed, rather than the dominant, male! And it is utterly different from what we find in Humbert. See, in general, E. Power, *Medieval Women* (Cambridge, 1975); SCH Subsidia 1: *Medieval Women*.

40. Marginal Gloss to 1 Tim. 2:11.

41. This text is quoted in a very similar form by St. Thomas, *in 1 Cor. 14*, lect. VII, and by Hugh of St. Cher on 1 Tim. 2:12, but both of them ascribe it to Chrysostom. It is in fact found in Chrysostom (PG 62:545). Why it is attributed to Bernard here, I do not know.

42. The MSS all have a reference here to the Decretum, I d.55 *Si evangelica* and II c.7 q.1 *Cum percussio*. In Gratian's Decretum I d.55 is about debarring people with maimed or deformed bodies from public exercise of

the priesthood, though c.13, *Si evangelica,* is no more relevant than the other chapters, but II c.7 q.1 c.2, *Cum percussio,* is quite irrelevant. However Gregory IX's Decretals III tit.VI, beginning *Cum percussio,* deals with the point at issue here.

43. PL 77:98C.

44. PL 76:1119A.

45. Interlinear Gloss.

46. Marginal Gloss.

47. Marginal Gloss.

48. Interlinear Gloss.

49. Marginal Gloss.

50. Marginal Gloss.

51. Marginal Gloss.

52. Marginal Gloss: "The doors are the preachers, by means of whom heaven is entered."

53. Marginal Gloss. The curious idea of the clouds giving light derives from the ambiguity of *lustro,* which can mean either "travel round" (its real meaning in Job) or "shine."

54. Marginal Gloss.

55. Interlinear Gloss, not as found in the printed text, but as found in Oxford MS Bodleian Auct. D 1.15.

56. PL 76:503C.

57. Marginal Gloss. I have corrected *suppositi* of the MSS, to bring the text in line with the Gloss and with Humbert's earlier citation of the same passage in §12.

58. At least in the printed text, the Interlinear Gloss has *id est maiores,* not *praedicatores;* but the Marginal Gloss makes it clear that preachers are intended.

59. Interlinear Gloss.

60. The Hebrew *nesher* is ambiguous, meaning either eagle or vulture. The Septuagint and the Vulgate both opt for "eagle," which leads to a certain confusion in later terminology. "Vulture" would have been more appropriate.

61. Marginal Gloss.

62. Marginal Gloss.

63. Marginal Gloss. *Expectant* MSB is supported against *expetant* L and the printed text of the Gloss by the two MSS of the Gloss I have looked at in Oxford, Bodleian MSS Auct. D 1.15 and 1.16. The reference to "discretion" is clarified by the rest of the text in the Gloss: "The preacher does not feed his disciples with all the highest mysteries until they have become like him, displaying the blackness of humility and the appearance of flight. Until then, he lets them feel the pain of hunger so that they will cry out to God and, cheeping in the nest, wait open mouthed to receive their food." This, in turn,

is explained by the curious belief, found in the Bestiaries, that the raven does not feed its young until they are old enough to start producing black feathers. Cf. McCulloch, p. 161; Thomas of Cantimpré, *De Natura Rerum* V 31.

    64. Interlinear Gloss.

    65. Marginal Gloss. *Ante,* in the printed editions, is supported by the Gloss against *animo* in the MSS.

    66. Marginal Gloss.

    67. Interlinear Gloss.

    68. Interlinear Gloss.

    69. Cf. 1 Chron. 11:10.

    70. Interlinear Gloss.

    71. Marginal Gloss.

    72. Marginal Gloss.

    73. Marginal Gloss.

    74. Marginal Gloss.

# III  Right and Wrong Ways
of Becoming a Preacher

(165) Next we must discuss the way in which a man comes to be a preacher. And first we must mention certain abuses, and then we must consider the harm that results from them.

## ABUSES IN THE WAY OF BECOMING A PREACHER

(XIV 166) There are three possible kinds of defect in the way a man comes to the job of preaching. There may be something lacking in the man himself, or he may have an inordinate desire for the job, or he may take it on in an improper and arrogant way.

It should be noticed that there are sometimes people who want to be preachers before they are fully purged of their faults. They appeal to the example of Isaiah, who said to the Lord, "Here am I, send me" *(Isaiah 6:8)*, but they overlook what goes before about his being purged. Gregory says, "He desired to be sent, but only after he saw that he had been purged by the coal from the altar; this is to prevent anyone who has not been purified from daring to approach the holy mysteries."[1]

(167) There are others who have perhaps been purged, but have not yet received in themselves the fulness of those heavenly blessings which they must have before they can pour them out upon others. Bernard says, "These people, through whom the streams of heaven flow, have such an excess of charity that they want to pour them out again before they have even been poured in!"[2] His own advice is quite different: "If you are sensible, make yourself into a bowl, not a pipe. A pipe receives and pours out almost simultaneously, but a bowl waits until it is full."[3]

This fulness which we are talking about is, according to Luke, the fulness of the Holy Spirit: "They were all filled with the Holy Spirit and began to speak" *(Acts 2:4)*. According to Paul, it is the fulness of knowledge and love: "You are full of love, full of all knowledge, so that you can admonish one another" *(Rom. 15:14)*. According to Bernard, it is the fulness of several more particular good things: "What a range of things have to be poured in first, if we are to dare to pour anything out. First compunction, then devotion, then the labour of penance, then fourthly works of piety, fifthly zealous practice of prayer, sixthly the repose of contemplation, and seventhly the fulness of love."[4]

(168) There are others who do indeed have many good qualities, but have not yet been strengthened with power from on high; their virtues are still delicate and weak, and so, if they come to the job of preaching, in their desire to help others they will often lose ground in themselves. In the *Lives of the Fathers* we read that St. Apollonius went into the desert when he was fifteen and spent forty years there in spiritual exercises; then a voice came to him, "Apollonius, through you I shall destroy the wisdom of the wise in Egypt. Go now to the places where men live and you will beget for me a perfect people." He was terrified to hear this and said, "Lord, remove from me the spirit of pride, otherwise I may come to feel myself to be better than my brethren and so fall away from all good." Again the voice of God spoke to him, and said, "Put your hand to your neck and seize whatever you find there and bury it in the sand." He put his hand to his neck and took hold of something like a small black man, and he buried it at once in the sand. As he did this, it kept crying out, "I am the demon of pride." After this the voice said to him, "Go now." Then he set off to preach.[5] Now if a man so mature and so thoroughly tested in every kind of holiness for such a long time was so frightened of the job of preaching, we must reflect how hesitant weak men ought to be about it. So Bernard says to someone who is ambitious to preach, "Brother, your own salvation is not yet secure, and your charity is so delicate and reed-like that it will yield to every puff of wind; or rather you have such abundant charity that it goes beyond the commandment[6] and loves your neighbour more than yourself. Yet at the same time it is so tiny that it cannot resist when it is shown partiality, loses heart before anything frightening,[7] is disturbed by sorrow, cramped by greed, stretched by ambition, tormented by suspicions, shaken by reproaches, worn out by worries, puffed

up by honours, and pines away with envy. You, I say, if this is how you feel yourself to be, by what kind of madness, I ask you, are you so ambitious to undertake responsibility for others?"[8]

(169) This shows that a man who is not yet purged, or who is not too fully gifted, or who is well endowed but not sufficiently well established in his gifts, ought not to undertake the job of preaching.

(170) On the second kind of abuse, we must notice that there are some people who realise that preaching is a particularly splendid kind of job and set their hearts on it because they want to be important, due to a certain kind of ambition. Gregory says, "They want to appear as teachers, they long to be superior to everybody else, they want the seats of honour."[9] Such people do not reflect that the devil put the Lord on the pinnacle of the temple[10] where, as the Gloss explains, the teachers' seats were, from which they spoke to the people, the roof being flat on top. There the devil ensnared a whole lot of people who were puffed up because of the honour of being teachers.[11] Against such people James says, "Do not becomes teachers, most of you, my brethren" *(James 3:1)*. According to the Gloss, he is speaking of the teaching position of preachers.[12]

(171) There are others who twist preaching to make it serve the purposes of their own vanity or their own earthly desires, when properly its purpose is the salvation of others. Bernard attacks such people: "Woe to those who have received from God the gift of a good mind and an ability to speak, and then mistake profit for piety and devote to the purposes of their own foolish glory the gifts God gave them to make profit with for him."[13]

(172) There are others who have an unhealthy desire to rival other preachers, even if they have not received the same grace for the job that others have. They are like Elihu who wanted to be on a par with Job's other friends, who were great men. "I too," he said, "will have my say and show forth my knowledge" *(Job 32:17)*. But the apostle says, "Are all apostles?" *(1 Cor. 12:29)*, which is glossed, "Preaching in place of the Lord."[14] This is tantamount to saying, "This grace is not given to everyone, and so there should be no rivalry about it."

(173) This shows that the desire for this job may be reprehensible either because of ambition, or because of a distorted purpose, or because of a wrong spirit of rivalry. But, of course, the job in itself is highly commendable. So the Gloss on "first seats" in Matt. 23:6 says,

"He is not forbidding the first teachers to sit there, he is rebuking those who have an improper desire for such things, whether they have them or not."[15]

(174) On the third kind of abuse, we should notice that there are some who jump at the opportunity when they are given the job of preaching. Bernard makes such people say, "I have a little knowledge, or, more truly, I appear to have a little knowledge, and I cannot keep quiet, eager as I am to speak, eager to teach."[16] This is quite different from what Gregory writes about Jeremiah: "Jeremiah is sent, but, in his humility, struggles not to be sent, saying, 'Ah, Ah, Ah, Lord God! I cannot speak, I am only a child.' "[17]

(175) There are others who are not only eager to accept the job, but actually intrigue to get it given to them, directly or indirectly, themselves or through other people. This is quite contrary to the example of Moses, who begged to be let off the job himself, and for it to be given to someone else. "I beseech you, Lord, send whoever you are going to send" *(Exod. 4:13)*. He insisted so much that he prevailed upon the Lord to entrust his words to Aaron instead. Here is a remarkable thing! A great man like Moses, chosen by God and given the job of proclaiming his word, gets the job given to someone else, and then a man who is almost worthless tries to get the job given to himself!

(176) There are others who take it as an insult if the job is not given to them, and get upset about it. In them the words of Job 32:18–19 come true, "I am full of words and my spirit within me constrains me. My stomach is like fermenting wine without an outlet, which bursts new bottles." This is fulfilled in them, because they are all agitated internally like wine fermenting in a bottle, when they do not get the job of preaching which they are so eager for. And sometimes the bottle does indeed burst and their agitation overflows into external signs of indignation. But since, as Gregory says, "It is much safer to refuse the job of preaching"[18] than to practise it, holy and humble men are not at all inclined to undertake it, and would rather someone else did it; they are quite ready to endure being without the job themselves, though they are occasionally forced into doing it by someone else, and this is sometimes very commendable. As Gregory says, "Some people are dragged forcibly into the job of preaching, and this is praiseworthy."[19]

(177) From all of this, we can see that a right approach to the

undertaking of this job requires that the preacher should himself be up to it, that his motivation should be good, and that he should take it on only when he is constrained to do so by obedience.

## THE EVIL RESULTS OF UNTIMELY ASSUMPTION OF THE JOB

(XV 178) There are three unfortunate consequences of a man's taking up the job of preaching before the proper time.

First, it prevents his preaching being fruitful in others later, when the right time for it does come, as happens with boys who try to have children too soon, which unmans them[20] so that they are less potent later on when they are of age to beget children. Gregory says, "Those who are driven by undue eagerness to assume the job of preaching, when their lack of maturity indicates that they should not preach or when they are too young, should be rebuked; otherwise, if they take on the burden of such a responsibility too hastily, they will cut off from themselves the possibility of their own subsequent improvement. By taking on too soon a job they are unable to do at the time, they ruin something they might have been capable of doing later on."[21]

(179) Secondly, it is an obstacle to their own development. By trying to exercise some power before they have really got it sufficiently, people always become weaker. So someone in the *Lives of the Fathers* says, "Do not teach before the time is ripe, otherwise your mental powers will be reduced for the rest of your life."[22]

(180) Thirdly, there is a serious risk of disaster. Gregory says, "Those who are driven by undue eagerness to assume the job of preaching must be warned to consider that if young birds try to fly before their wings are fully formed, the only result of their desire to ascend to the heights is that they are swallowed up in the depths, and that if you place a great pile of heavy wood on a recently built structure which has not yet set firm, instead of a house you will only build yourself a ruin, and that pregnancies[23] which bring babies to birth before they are fully formed fill tombs, not homes."[24]

(181) So, because of all the evils which flow from this kind of inordinate haste, the wise man says, "A wise man will keep quiet for a time, but the wanton and foolish man knows no seasons" *(Ecclus. 20:7)*. For the same reason, the prophet threatens, "Unripe is the

growth which has sprouted; its branches will be cut back with sickles and what is left will be cut off and thrown down and abandoned to the mountain birds and the beasts of the earth, and all summer long there will be birds upon it and the beasts of the earth will winter on it" *(Isaiah 18:5–6).* For the same reason the Lord commanded his preachers, "Stay quietly in the city until you are clothed with power from on high" *(Luke 24:49).* Gregory says, "We stay in the city if we shut ourselves within the enclosure of our minds and do not wander outside in speech; then, when we are perfectly clothed with divine power, we shall be able to go, as it were, outside ourselves and give instruction to others."[25]

## Notes

1. PL 77:20C.
2. *Sermons on the Canticle* 18:3 (I p. 104.25–6).
3. *Sermons on the Canticle* 18:3 (I p. 104:19–21).
4. *Sermons on the Canticle* 18:6 (I p. 108:3–6).
5. Cf. PL 21:40D–411B.
6. *Contra mandatum,* taken from the text of Bernard, must be correct, against *qui mandatum* M, *qui mandati* A, *quae mandati* SL.
7. *Pudore* MASL must be corrected to *pavore,* as in the text of Bernard.
8. *Sermons on the Canticle* 18:4 (I p. 105:12–20).
9. PL 77:B.
10. Matt. 4:5.
11. Marginal Gloss to Matt. 4:5.
12. Marginal Gloss.
13. *Sermons on the Canticle* 41:6 (II p. 32:3–5).
14. Marginal Gloss to 1 Cor. 12:28.
15. Interlinear Gloss.
16. *Sermons on the Epiphany* 1:7 (IV p. 299:15–17).
17. PL 77:20B. Jeremiah 1:6.
18. PL 77:20C.
19. PL 77:20A.
20. *Sic enervatur* MA, *sic enumeratur* SL. I read *sic enerva < n > tur.*
21. PL 77:98A.
22. PL 73:967B.
23. *Conceptus soboles* MASL can, at a pinch, be translated, but the printed editions' *conceptas soboles feminae,* which is also Gregory's text, is undoubtedly easier.
24. PL 77:98AB.
25. PL 77:98B.

# IV The Actual Performance of Preaching

There are six topics which we must discuss in connexion with the actual performance of the job of preaching:

(i)   cases in which it is a serious fault not to preach;
(ii)  trivial reasons which deter some people from preaching;
(iii) the undiscriminating way some people carry out the job;
(iv)  the things which make for good performance;
(v)   the things that are actually involved in good performance;
(vi)  the reasons why those who have the grace for it should gladly do this job.

## CASES IN WHICH IT IS A SERIOUS FAULT NOT TO PREACH

(XVI 182) It is a serious fault in a prelate not to preach. By virtue of being a prelate, he is obliged to preach. "Let the sound of Aaron be heard when he goes in and out of the sanctuary in the sight of the Lord; let him not die" *(Exod. 28:35)*. Gregory says, "A priest whose sound is not heard when he goes in and out dies, because he calls forth upon himself the anger of the unseen Judge, if he goes without the sound of preaching."[1] He is speaking of any priest who is responsible for the cure of souls.

(183) The same applies to one who is well endowed. Bernard says, "You are retaining possession of your neighbour's property if you tie up in a useless, indeed, a damnable, silence, the word which you have the gifts of knowledge and eloquence to speak, and which would have brought benefit to many if you had spoken it."[2]

(184) The same applies to anyone who has been told to preach. "If I say to the wicked man, 'You shall die the death,' and you do not declare it to him to make him turn from his wicked ways and live, then he will indeed die in his sin, but I shall require his blood at your hand" *(Ezek. 3:18)*.

(185) It is also wrong not to preach when there are men ready to listen. Chrysostom comments on Matt. 5:1, "Seeing the crowds, Jesus went up into the mountain," that the sight of the people all ready to listen stirred the Lord to do his job, to preach, that is,[3] just like a fisherman moved to start fishing by the sight of a suitable place for it. What kind of a fisherman is he who sees that there is good fishing to be had and ignores it?

(186) Similarly when there are people not only ready to listen, but actually asking to be preached to. In Lamentations 4:4, it complains, "The little ones asked for bread, and there was no one to break it for them." Gregory says, "What punishment is reserved for those who do not distribute the bread of the grace they have received, when there are souls perishing for lack of the bread of the word?"[4]

(187) Similarly when there are not only people asking for a word, but listeners who are in need of a word. Gregory says, "People who withhold the word of preaching from their sinning brethren and hide away the life-giving remedies from minds that are perishing ought to realise how guilty they are."[5]

(188) Similarly when there is good hope that the word will bear fruit. This is why it says, "Do not withhold the word in the time of salvation" *(Ecclus. 4:28)*.

(189) The same applies when a stipend has been given of worldly goods. If it is true that a man who sows spiritual seed is entitled to receive wordly benefits in return, it is even more true that he is obliged to sow the spiritual seed in return for the worldly benefits. So Job says, "I have not eaten the fruit of the earth without payment" *(Job 31:39)*. Gregory comments, "Eating the fruit of the earth without payment means receiving an income from the church without paying it the price of preaching."[6]

(190) The same applies also when there is nobody else to preach. The failure to preach is more serious when there is nobody else to take your place, than when there is somebody else to do it. It is the same as with almsgiving, when there is nobody else to do that. So it says in Isaiah 41:17–18, "The poor and the needy seek water" (the water of instruction, that is[7]) "and there is none; their tongues are

dry with thirst. I, the Lord, will hear them, I will open up rivers on the top of the hills and springs in the middle of the fields," which is tantamount to saying, "Because there is no one else to do it, I will do it myself." And, seeing that God is with preachers, this is what they all ought to do too.

## TRIVIAL REASONS WHICH DETER PEOPLE FROM PREACHING

(XVII 191) There are some people who are deterred from preaching by an unreal lack of confidence; they think that they are inadequate for the job, when they are really quite adequate. Against this it says, "Rescue those who are being dragged off to death, do not hold back from freeing those who are being led off to perdition. And do not say, 'I have not got the power,' because he who searches men's hearts knows what is going on, nothing escapes him who watches over your soul" *(Prov. 24:11–12).* The Gloss says that this is meant of the preacher.[8]

(192) There are others who hold back from preaching because of false humility, considering themselves unworthy of such an important job. But their refusal to obey shows that their humility is false. So Gregory says about this, in his *Pastoral Rule,* "Notice that though he[9] tried to decline the job, he was not completely obstinate about it, to avoid refusing God, under a cloak of humility, when heaven's grace had chosen him for the task."[10]

(193) There are others who hold back because they love the tranquility of contemplation. In opposition to them, Gregory says in his *Pastoral Rule,* "There are some people who are endowed with great gifts, but because their sole passion is for contemplation, they refuse to respond to the summons to be useful to others by preaching. They love the hidden life of quiet, they seek a retired place for contemplation. If they are judged strictly on this, they will without doubt be held responsible for all the good they might have done if they had come out into the open."[11]

(194) There are others who hold back because they are afraid of the kind of sins which will unavoidably occur in the course of the preacher's active life. Against them it says, "Better the iniquity of a man than a woman doing good" *(Ecclus. 42:14).* Commenting on this, Bernard says that "the iniquity of a man" is the kind of unevenness[12]

of life which is attached to being a preacher, while the "woman doing good" is the purity of a soul resting peacefully in the life of contemplation.[13] And the one is rightly declared to be better than the other, because it is more useful. Is it not[14] better that men should work, even if they are going to pick up a certain amount of dust as they work, than that they should always stay quite clean at home?

(195) There are others who are held back from the job because their preparation for it takes too long. They spend a long time assembling material for their preaching, and want to wait until they have attained the perfection they consider appropriate for the job, and which they will perhaps never attain. But meantime their friends are sleeping on and their house is ablaze, and there are enemies at the door; yet they put off waking them up! Against this it says, "Run! Hasten! Wake up your friend" *(Prov. 6:3)*. According to the Gloss, this refers to the preacher.[15]

(196) There are others who hold back because they feel nervous about doing this job. But the Lord encourages them through Isaiah, when he says, "Speak, timid men,[16] be strong and do not fear" *(Isaiah 35:4)*. According to the Gloss, this refers to preachers.[17]

(197) There are others who hold back because they are too lazy to prepare a sermon, which requires attention and often a lot of work too. To rouse his disciple from this kind of laziness, St. Paul says, "You must stay awake and toil always and do the job of an evangelist" *(2 Tim. 4:5)*, as if to say, "Do not hold back from evangelising just because it is a job that involves staying awake and a lot of work; put up with all of this, so that you can do the job."

(198) There are others who are deterred by the poverty which has to be endured in the course of preaching, especially by poor preachers who neither carry provisions with them nor have any entitlement to support. If only they would pay attention to what is said about the poverty which Christ endured when he was preaching. "After looking round the whole crowd, when it was already evening, he went to Bethany" *(Mark 11:11)*. This is glossed, "He looked round to see if anyone would offer him hospitality. He was so poor that, since he never flattered anyone, he could find no lodging in the town, for all its size."[18] I ask you, what modern preacher has had to endure such want that he could not find the necessities of life at least in the more densely populated areas?

(199) There are others who are deterred by the physical labour involved in travelling around on foot. But the apostle, in addition to

the labour of all his travels, was almost always working with his hands too. "You remember, brethren, our toil and weariness; working day and night to avoid being a burden to any of you, we preached to you the gospel of God" *(1 Thess. 2:9).*

(200) Others are put off by the corruption to be found in the rulers of the church, who often put obstacles in the way of preaching, instead of fostering it as they ought to, like the scribes and pharisees among the Jews and the priests of the temples among the pagans, who always did their best to thwart the preaching of Christ, and even persecuted his preachers fiercely, as we can see in the Acts of the Apostles and the legends of the saints. But if this had deterred the first preachers, the faith of Christ would still not have been preached. Now if serious persecution did not stop the first preachers doing their job, how much less should men be put off in our own day by this kind of wickedness.

(201) There are others who are deterred by the lack of devotion among the people. They will preach gladly to devout peoples and congregations, but abandon those who are not devout, even though their need is greater. But the Lord sent prophets not only to the devout, but also to a stiff-necked people. "My children to whom I am sending you set their faces hard and will not yield their hearts" *(Ezek. 2:4).*

(202) There are others who are put off by unfortunate experience of preaching. For instance, maybe they took the risk of preaching some time and the results did not win them much credit. But on this principle, no one would learn any art at all. Who ever[19] learned to speak Latin without often speaking bad Latin? Who ever learned to write without frequently writing incorrectly? And the same applies to every art. It is by frequently making mistakes in this way that we eventually master it. So the philosopher says, "By building we become builders."[20] Similarly with the practice of preaching: though at first a man may often stumble, it eventually makes him into a good preacher.

(203) Others hold back because there are so many preachers already. They say, "What need is there for me to preach, when there are so many other preachers?" But it is foretold that preachers are to increase in a prosperous old age *(Psalm 91:15–16).* If he is outside their number, how is a man to benefit from this prophecy? A man who wants to share in the catch joins the fishermen, and similarly anyone who wants to share in the rewards of preaching must do

likewise, if he can. When Simon Peter said, "I am going fishing," the others said, "We are coming with you" *(John 21:3).*

(204) There are others who will not preach because they find the company they are given unattractive.[21] And since preachers are obliged to go out in pairs, they would rather lose the good result of preaching than travel with certain people. Of course, it does say, "You shall not plough with an ox and an ass,"[22] but even so, a poor man would rather yoke an ox and an ass together sometimes to get his ploughing done, than leave his ground untilled. And preachers are oxen: Job 24:3, "A widow's ox," is glossed, "The widow is the church and any preacher is her ox."[23] So the ploughman who is answerable to the landlord for the fruits of the land surely has a right to complain about an ox which will not plough with a horse or an ass, but only if it is given another ox. He cannot give it another ox, since he does not have one.

(205) So such trivial matters are no reason for not devoting oneself eagerly and fervently to preaching, in according with 2 Tim. 4:2, "Preach the word insistently, in season and out of season."

## UNDISCRIMINATING WAYS OF PREACHING

(XVIII 206) There are some people who do not wish to listen to the word of God, and it is a mistake to preach to them. "Where no one is listening, do not pour out speech" *(Ecclus. 32:6).*

(207) There are others who do listen, but do not take in what they hear, like fools. "The fool does not take in the words of wisdom" *(Prov. 18:2),* that is to say, he does not take them in inwardly in his mind. And it is wrong to preach to them. "Do not speak in the hearing of fools" *(Prov. 23:9).*

(208) There are others who bite and rend preachers, and it is wrong to preach to them. "Do not give what is holy to dogs" *(Matt. 7:6),* which is glossed, " 'dogs' means people who bark and tear to pieces what is whole."[24]

(209) There are others who make light of holy teaching, and it is wrong to preach to them too. "Do not throw your pearls before swine" *(Matt. 7:6),* which is glossed, "The 'swine' are those who make light and trample under foot."[25]

(210) There are others who provoke the Lord by the excess of their wickedness, to such an extent that they do not deserve any grace

of preaching. "I will make your tongue stick to your palate and you will be dumb, like one with no more reproaches to make, because this is an infuriating house" *(Ezek. 3:26)*. This is glossed, "An infuriating house: so bitter are they against God and so contentious that they do not deserve to hear his reproaches."[26] This shows that because of the abundance of their sins, there are sinners unworthy of being corrected by the Lord.

(211) There are others even worse than these, who blaspheme the teaching of the gospel, like some unbelievers. The preacher must be careful not to preach publicly before them. "The Jews blasphemously contradicted what was spoken by Paul. Then Paul and Barnabas said boldly, 'It was necessary to speak the word of God to you first, but since you have rejected it and judged yourselves unworthy of eternal life, look, we are now going to the gentiles' " *(Acts 13:46)*.

(212) We must also notice that, even in situations in which it is right to preach, it is not right to preach the same thing to everybody. Different people should have different things preached to them, according to their condition. Gregory says in his *Pastoral Rule*, "As Gregory Nazianzen of blessed memory taught us long ago,[27] there is no single exhortation which is suitable for everyone, because men are not all held in any necessary equality of moral standards. Often what helps one man harms another, just as many plants nourish one kind of animal and kill some other kind, and a soft whistle soothes a horse and excites a dog, and a medicine which reduces one sickness makes another more virulent, and the bread which nourishes the life of the healthy adult is death to a baby.

(213) "So the teacher must devise a sermon which fits the quality of his congregation. There is one way to address men, another way to address women, one way for the young, another for the elderly, one way for the poor, another for the rich, one way for the cheerful, another for the sad, one way for subjects, another way for superiors, one way for servants, another way for masters, one way for those who are worldly wise, another for those who are dimwitted, one way for the shameless, another for those who are modest, one way for the insolent, another way for cowards, one way for the impatient, another way for those who are patient, one way for generous people, another way for mean people, one way for the innocent, another way for the impure, one way for the healthy, another way for the sick, one way for those who fear punishment and so live blamelessly, another way for those who are so hardened in their sin that they cannot even

be corrected by punishment, one way for those who are taciturn, another way for those who talk too much, one way for the indolent, another way for the precipitate, one way for the gentle, another way for the irascible, one way for the humble, another way for the proud, one way for the grimly determined, another way for those who are always changing their minds, one way for the gluttonous, another way for the abstemious, one way for those who give generously of what belongs to them, another way for those who are always trying to get hold of other people's property, one way for those who neither steal what is not theirs nor give away anything that is theirs, another way for those who are generous with what is theirs, but also constantly stealing what is not theirs, one way for the quarrelsome, another way for the peaceful, one way for those who provoke quarrels, another way for those who make peace, one way for those who misunderstand the words of the holy law, another way for those who understand them rightly, but are not humble in the way they speak them, one way for those who could preach properly but are cowed by their humility, another way for those who are driven to preach by their own impetuousness, when they are really disqualified by immaturity or youthfulness, one way for those who are successful in their wordly ambitions, another way for those who desire the good things of this world, but are wearied by the burden of bad luck, one way for those who are married, another way for those who are not, one way for those who have known carnal intercourse, another way for those who have not, one way for those who weep for actual sins, another way for those who weep for sins committed only in the mind, one way for those who weep for their sins but do not abandon them, another way for those who abandon them but do not weep for them, one way for those who actually approve of the sins they commit,[28] another way for those who condemn wickedness but do not avoid it,[29] one way for those who are overcome by sudden lust, another way for those who deliberately entangle themselves in sin, one way for those who sin frequently, though only in small things, and another way for those who keep clear of minor offences but occasionally fall into serious sin, one way for those who do not even make a beginning of doing good, another way for those who begin but never bring anything to its conclusion, one way for those who sin secretly and do good in public, another for those who hide the good they do and yet allow themselves to acquire a bad reputation for one or two things they have done."[30]

(214) Then there are some people who preach too infrequently, and others who preach too often, and both are at fault. Gregory says, "If preaching is infrequent, it is not enough; if there is too much of it, it is not appreciated."[31] So you should preach in moderation. Rain is useful if it is neither too infrequent nor too continual.

(215) Again, it is important to realise that the same manner of speech is not appropriate on every occasion of preaching. It must be varied, first of all, in accordance with the circumstances of the person who is speaking, and secondly in accordance with the circumstances of the people to whom he is speaking, and thirdly in accordance with the subject matter of the sermon.

With regard to the first point, there is one manner of speaking proper to a man of little authority, and another which is proper to a man of great authority. A man of little authority ought always to speak humbly. "The poor man always speaks with entreaty" (this means the man of little authority). But a man of greater authority can speak more emphatically: "The rich man will speak sternly" *(Prov. 18:23)*. This was how John the Baptist behaved; he was rich with the fulness of his holy life, and did not have to mince his words. "You brood of vipers" and so on *(Matt. 3:7)*. Likewise Stephen, who was rich with the fulness of the Holy Spirit, said, "Uncircumcised in your hearts and ears" *(Acts 7:51)*. Likewise Paul, who was rich in the power he had been given by God, said, "The Holy Spirit spoke well through the prophet Isaiah about our fathers, when he said, 'Go to this people and say to them: You will hear with your ears, and not understand' " *(Acts 28:25–6)*.

(216) With regard to the second point, the Lord spoke in one way to his disciples, and in another way to the scribes and pharisees. To the disciples he spoke kindly, promising them blessings: "Blessed are you poor, for yours is the kingdom of God" *(Luke 6:20)*. But to the scribes and pharisees he spoke with terrifying threats: "Woe to you, scribes and pharisees" *(Matt. 23:13)*.

(217) On the third point, there must be a difference between speaking about men's sins and speaking about the good things given them by God. In the one case it is appropriate to speak with compassion, as the material is sad, like the apostle who says, "There are many people going about, whom I have often mentioned to you and now mention to you again with tears, who are enemies of Christ; their end is destruction, their god is their belly, and they glory in what is really their shame, earthbound in all their attitudes" *(Phil. 3:18–19)*. But

when it comes to God's good gifts, it is right to speak with thankfulness, as the apostle does when he says, "I thank my God for you always, for the grace of God which has been given you, because you have become rich in him in everything, in all knowledge and all speech" *(1 Cor. 1:4–5)*.

(218) Then, it is necessary to speak crudely with uneducated people and more subtly with more clever people, boldly in the presence of tyrants, cautiously and reverently in the presence of truly great and good men; sometimes one should speak with spiritual enthusiasm, sometimes with prudent reserve, now in an encouraging way in the presence of the timid, now in a discouraging way in the presence of the presumptuous. The sound of preaching must have as many different tones and variations as singing does. And since it is difficult always to get the right manner for the occasion, the apostle asks, "Pray for us, that God will open our mouth to speak the mystery of Christ, for whom I am in chains, so that I may be able to declare it properly, speaking in the way that is required" *(Col. 4:3–4)*.

(219) It should also be remarked that there is a right time for preaching, and this should be observed. There is, as it says in Ecclesiastes 3:7, "a time for keeping silent and a time for speaking."

It is not a suitable time to preach when men cannot take time off to listen to the word of God because of their other occupations. Mary was at leisure to hear the word of the Lord *(Luke 10:39)*.

(220) Nor is it suitable when men are so deep in some sorrow that they cannot turn their minds to listening to the word. This is why Job's friends did not speak to him for seven days; they saw that his grief was overwhelming *(Job 2:13)*.

(221) Nor is it a suitable time when men are so tired that they cannot keep awake. There is no point in talking to people who are asleep. As it says, "Speaking wisdom to a fool is like talking to someone who is asleep" *(Ecclus. 22:9)*, which implies that you ought not to talk to people when they are asleep.

(222) Nor is it suitable when there is a row which cannot be quietened down. This is why Paul gestured for silence before beginning to speak *(Acts 13:16, 21:40)*.

(223) Nor is it a suitable time when people are worked up against the preacher. Thus Paul and Barnabas withdrew from the Jews when they were raising persecutions against them *(Acts 13:50–1)*.

(224) As it says, there is a right time, an opportune moment, for every kind of business *(Ecclesiastes 8:6)*, and so the preacher ought to

be careful not to preach at an unsuitable time, or his preaching will be fruitless. As Gregory comments on "Preach in season and out of season," "He says 'in season' before 'out of season,' putting 'opportunely' before 'importunately,' because if his importunity knows no opportuneness, it simply destroys itself in the minds of its hearers by making itself cheap."[32]

(225) It is important also to observe that not every place is suitable for formal preaching. It is wrong to preach in a secret place, as the heretics do: formal preaching ought to be done openly, following the practice of the Lord, who "spoke openly to the world,"[33] saying nothing in secret.

(226) Nor is it appropriate to preach in undignified places, as some people do, preaching in market places and busy streets and at fairs;[34] but men are already busy in such places, and busy with worldly occupations, so it would be liable to undermine their respect for the word of God to preach there. A more dignified place is more suitable. Paul preached in synagogues, the Lord preached in the temple, or sometimes he preached in open countryside, where no worldly business was being transacted.

(227) Nor is it appropriate to preach in places which are dangerous to men, but in places where men can safely gather. This way preaching will not lead to anybody's destruction, which is what happened to the followers of Theudas and Judas the Galilaean *(Acts 5:36–7)*.

(228) From all of this, we can see that with some people we should preach to them, but with others not; and that when it is suitable to preach, different things have to be preached to different people; and that preaching should be done in moderation, neither too often nor too seldom; and that different situations call for different styles of address; and that it is wrong to preach at any time or in any place indiscriminately; and that it implies a lack of judgment on the part of the preacher if he preaches to the wrong people, or if his material is wrong, or if the quantity of it is wrong, or if he preaches in an unsuitable way, at an unsuitable time or in an unsuitable place. So it makes all the difference, if the preacher wants to exercise his function judiciously, that he should always pay attention to the kind of people he is addressing, to what he is to preach, how much of it there should be, how he is going to preach, when and where he is going to preach, and so on.

# HUMBERT OF ROMANS

## THINGS THAT MAKE FOR GOOD PERFORMANCE

(XIX 229) One important factor which makes for good performance in the job of preaching is freedom from all responsibilities. This is why the apostles appointed others to serve tables, so that they would be the more free to devote themselves to preaching. "It is not right," they said, "that we should abandon the word of God and serve tables" *(Acts 6:2)*. The Lord also said to a disciple who wanted to take time to bury his father, "Leave the dead to bury their dead; for your part, go and proclaim the kingdom of God" *(Luke 9:60)*. Paul too, for the same reason, did not consider it his job to baptise; "Christ has not sent me to baptise, but to preach the gospel" *(1 Cor. 1:17)*. If such men as these forsook such holy occupations in order to be more free to preach, how much more ought preachers to abandon all other tasks, so that the true Abraham may have his servants unimpeded in their work.[35]

(230) Another factor is the absence of all disturbance. A disturbed mind is a great obstacle to preaching. Gregory says, "It takes a very peaceful, unoccupied mind to speak of God. It is when a man's mind is tranquil and at rest that his tongue hits the mark when he speaks."[36]

(231) Another factor is a good collection of items of secular knowledge which are useful for edifying people and building them up. Anyone who is engaged in building collects things from all over the place which may be useful for him to build with. "Josaphat and the rest of the people came to remove the spoil from the dead" *(2 Chron. 20:35)*. This is glossed, "Holy doctors together with the crowd of the faithful gather up from the spoils of their enemies whatever has usefully been said about physics, ethics or logic in lectures, in books or in classes, and they turn it to the use of the whole church; what others possessed uselessly, the faithful thus come to possess for the salvation of their souls."[37]

(232) Another factor is that the preacher should be able to confirm everything he says from scripture. Gregory says, "Anyone who is preparing to speak words of true preaching must take all his points ultimately from scripture, so that he can trace everything he says back to the fundamental authority of scripture and build on that the whole structure[38] of his discourse."[39]

(233) Another factor is that the preacher should mix prayer with

his preaching. The power of his prayer will make his preaching more effective. Augustine says in his book *On Christian Teaching*, "A good speaker, when he is saying things which are good and just and holy, should do all that he can to ensure that people listen to him with understanding, gladly and obediently . And if he can achieve this, he should have no doubt that it is thanks to his devout prayers rather than to his well-trained fluency in speech; it is because he prays for himself and for those he is to address. So let him be a pray-er[40] first, and then a teacher."[41]

(234) Another factor is that he should obtain the prayers of others. Paul, who was a great preacher, expresses his confidence in such prayer when he says, "Brethren, pray for us, that the word of God may speed ahead and win renown everywhere, as it did among you" *(2 Thess. 3:1).*

(235) Another factor is periods of quiet and recreation. In worldly activities men take a rest from time to time, so that they can resume their occupation with more energy thereafter; and in the same way a preacher ought sometimes to rest from his work, so that he can carry out his job more powerfully when he has regained his strength. On this principle Solomon's workers who were engaged in cutting down trees in Lebanon (who represent preachers, according to the Gloss)[42] rested for two months and worked in the third.[43]

(236) It is also useful that during such periods of rest the preacher should not cultivate idleness, but should devote himself to such things as reading, study and thought, which will help his preaching later on. Gregory says, "When preachers are resting, they should absorb in contemplation something they can give out later in their sermons, when they are busy again for the good of others."[44]

(237) It is also useful for the preacher to be careful about the kinds of risk of sin which occur in the course of his preaching. We do not think highly of a sea fisherman who is so devoted to fishing that he takes no notice of storms at sea or other such hazards. Similarly it is a foolish way to engage in preaching to go rushing into dangerous occasions of sin in one's eagerness to win the souls of others. As it says, "What does it profit a man if he gains the whole world, but loses and ruins himself?" *(Luke 9:25).*

(238) It is also useful for him to examine himself when he has finished his preaching. A wise preacher ought to return to himself after going out to preach, and carefully examine everything that has happened to him, so that he can wash away any defilement that he

has incurred and repair anything that has got broken. He should be like a traveller who cleans and mends his shoes when he arrives at a hospice, so that he can journey better thereafter. So Ezekiel was told, after he had been in the field, "Go in, shut yourself in your house" *(Ezek. 3:24)*, on which Gregory comments, "The preacher is told to shut himself in, after being out in the field, so that he can return to his own self-knowledge, after serving others with the grace of his teaching, and carefully examine himself."[45]

(239) Another contributory factor is knowing how to be silent. "I went to the exiles and sat where they were sitting, and I remained there for seven days, grieving in their midst; after seven days had passed, the word of the Lord came to me" *(Ezek. 3:15–16)*. Gregory comments, "He had been sent to preach, and yet he kept silence and grieved for seven days, because it is the man who has learned how to be silent who truly knows how to speak. The discipline of silence is a kind of cultivation of speech."[46]

(240) Also holiness in the preacher's soul. "The soul of a holy[47] man sometimes speaks as much truth as seven scouts posted on high to keep watch" *(Ecclus. 37:18)*. Gregory says, "An awareness of holy love is a greater asset for preaching than knowledge of well-trained speaking."[48]

(241) A valuable contribution is also made by reflecting before preaching. Any job is done better by someone who carefully thinks out beforehand what he is to do and how he is to do it. And this applies to preachers too. "I went out through the Valley Gate in the night and gazed at the broken wall of Jerusalem and its gates, burned with fire; and I went across to the Fountain Gate" *(Neh. 2:13–14)*. Bede's comment in the Gloss says, "He wanders round visiting the various places in the ruined city and carefully considers how each one ought to be restored. Similarly spiritual teachers often have to get up in the night and examine carefully the state of the church, while others sleep; they must keep vigil to consider how they can put right and restore whatever has been dirtied or ruined in the war with sin."[49]

## THINGS INVOLVED IN GOOD PERFORMANCE

(XX 242) The first thing involved in the good performance of the job of preaching is a preference for preaching where it is most needed. What value is there in persistently preaching to religious, béguines and such people who do not need it much, if you abandon those who need it more? "It is not the healthy who need the doctor, but the sick," as the Lord says *(Matt. 9:12)*.

(243) Secondly, the preacher should prefer to preach where others have not already done so, rather than going where there is already a lot of preaching. What kind of gardener ignores the part of his garden which is parched, and keeps on watering the part which is always well watered anyway? "I preached the gospel, not in places where Christ was already named, but, as it is written, 'people who have never heard tell of him shall see him, and those who have never heard of him will understand' " *(Rom. 15:20–1)*.

(244) He should also not neglect places which are less well populated, as some people do, who will only preach in the cities and large towns. This is the opposite of what it says about our Saviour: "He went about the villages" (small settlements, that is) "teaching as he went" *(Mark 6:6)*.

(245) Also he ought not to pass by any place without preaching there, following the Lord's example, of whom it is said, "Jesus went about the whole of Galilee teaching in their synagogues and preaching the gospel of the kingdom" *(Matt. 4:23)*.

(246) Also he ought not to miss out any class of men in his preaching. "Preach the gospel to the whole creation" *(Mark 16:15)*.

(247) Further, he ought to give priority to people from whom there is reason to hope for results, and abandon those who are too hardened. This is what the apostles did, when they abandoned the obstinate Jews and went to the gentiles *(Acts 13:46)*. The Lord himself prompts his disciples to do this, when he says to them, "Lift up your eyes and see how the fields are already white for harvesting" *(John 4:35)*, as if to say, "Go and reap, because the fields are ready."

(248) Further, wherever wickedness is on the increase, there ought to be a more intensive response to it in preaching. Gregory says, "When the wickedness of evil men increases, preaching, far from being cut off as a result, ought to be intensified."[50]

(249) These considerations all arise in connexion with the people whom the preacher addresses.

(250) There are other things which concern the preacher himself. He ought not to do anything which will put obstacles in the way of his own preaching, like those who thoughtlessly upset the clergy or

the people, or do other things of the kind, which can sometimes hinder the course of preaching. Against such thoughtlessness, St. Paul says, "We put up with everything to avoid tripping up the gospel of God" *(1 Cor. 9:12)*.

(251) He should also not be easily deterred from preaching, like those who give up preaching just because of some slight upset or difficulty which they run into. What Paul says is, "Before God and before Christ Jesus who is to judge the living and the dead, by his coming and by his kingdom, I adjure you, preach the word insistently, in season and out of season" *(2 Tim. 4:1–2)*.

(252) Again, he should preach not only with his voice, but with all that he is, like John the Baptist, who for this reason is called "Voice,"[51] because he spoke with all of himself. Isidore says, "A teacher in the church is like a coin: just as you test a coin for its metal, its stamp and its weight, so a teacher is tested as to what he follows, what he teaches and how he lives. His teaching corresponds to the metal of the coin, his likeness to the fathers corresponds to the image on the coin, and his humility corresponds to the weight of the coin. Anyone who does not fit this description is not metal but mud,"[52] that is to say, he will not ring true like good metal, but will make no more sound than a lump of clay.

(253) He must also persevere in his preaching. One day's rain is of little use to parched soil; it has to go on raining. Similarly one or two sermons will not achieve much. It is said of the Lord, "And he taught in the temple every day" *(Luke 19:47)*.

(254) Further, he ought to supplement his preaching with individual exhortations in suitable times and places, as Paul did: "I taught you publicly and in your homes. . . . For three years, night and day, I never stopped exhorting and encouraging you individually, with tears" *(Acts 20:20,31)*.

(255) He must also proclaim the commandments of the Lord faithfully, like a faithful messenger, whose job is to say precisely what he was told to say. "Say to them what I command you to say" *(Jer. 1:7)*. It is no wonder that a genuine preacher should do this, when even Balaam says of himself, "Even though Balak should give me his own palace full of silver and gold, I cannot change the word of the Lord my God by adding or subtracting anything" *(Numbers 22:18)*.

(256) Again, he must be enthusiastic in doing his job, like Apollos, of whom it is said, "There was a Jew called Apollos, a capable

speaker, powerful in his knowledge of scripture. He was instructed in the way of the Lord and spoke with a spirit of enthusiasm, eagerly teaching about Jesus" *(Acts 18:24–5).*

(257) He must also declare the truth with confidence, especially among real sinners, like the apostles who spoke the word of God with confidence[53] among the Jews. "I am filled with the might of the Spirit of the Lord, with judgment and power, to declare to Jacob his sin and to Israel his iniquity" *(Micah 3:8).*

(258) He should at the same time moderate his manner of speaking, so that he does not offend people by being too harsh. Ambrose says, "Let your admonitions be without roughness, and your exhortations without offense."[54]

(259) Finally, he must set about his job with proper carefulness, for without such carefulness not much good comes of anything. "Be careful to show yourself to God" (for his honour, that is) "a worker who is not to be put to shame, handling rightly the word of truth" *(2 Tim. 2:15).*

## WHY THOSE WHO HAVE THE GRACE FOR IT SHOULD GLADLY DO IT

(XXI 260) Of all the spiritual exercises commonly practised by spiritual men, those who have the grace for it ought to prefer the practice of preaching. There are three reasons for this.

First of all, this particular exercise has certain advantages over other exercises.

(261) There are, for instance, some people who practise mortification of the flesh, afflicting their bodies with fasting and abstinence, with rough clothing, with vigils and that kind of thing. But this kind of practice, according to the apostle, is useful only to a limited extent *(1 Tim. 4:8).* But preaching is useful in many ways, as we have seen in §§58ff. And in any case, who could ever fully describe the hardships endured by a poor preacher who is zealous for souls? With what anxiety he looks out for things that will be useful, what hard work his constant travelling entails, how much he has to do without, how eager he is to make progress, and so on! He is quite properly compared to a woman in travail, whose pain is beyond reckoning: "My little children, I am in travail with you all over again, until Christ is formed in you" *(Gal. 4:19).*

Someone once said, who transferred from the Cistercians to the Order of Preachers, that he had endured more discomfort during his few days on the road than he had ever had to put up with in his previous Order.

So the exercise of preaching is to be preferred to fasting and other ways of mortifying the flesh, because it too involves heavy mortification but also benefits other people greatly.

(262) Then there are people who gladly devote themselves to corporal works of mercy. But preaching is concerned with pity for souls that are perishing, and so it is as much to be preferred to corporal works of mercy as souls are more important than bodies. This is why the Lord says to the man who wants to bury his father, "Leave the dead to bury their dead; for your part, go and proclaim the kingdom of God" *(Luke 9:60)*. Now if burying your own father, which is one of the most important works of mercy, has to take second place to preaching, in accordance with this precept of the Lord, how much more must preaching take precedence over all other corporal works of mercy? Gregory says, "It is better to strengthen a mind which will live for ever with the food of the word of God than to fill bellies which are flesh and must die with earthly bread."[55]

(263) Then there are others who gladly devote themselves to holy prayers, not only for themselves but also for others. But preaching is better than such prayers, because the prayer of a sinner is not going to benefit other people,[56] whereas the preaching of many people who are thoroughly wicked in the sight of God often does a lot of good to others; the prophecy of Balaam, for instance, has brought people great benefit in the past and it continues to do so and will continue to do so for ever. "If I do not have charity, I have become like a booming gong or a tinkling cymbal" *(1 Cor. 13:1)*, which brings benefit to others, even though it does damage to itself.

(264) There are others again who happily devote themselves to sacred reading; but if all this study is not devoted to teaching and preaching, what good is it? "Wisdom that is hidden, treasure that is not seen, what good is there in either?" *(Ecclus. 20:32)*. Therefore the apostle says, "Be attentive to your reading, to exhortation and to teaching" *(1 Tim. 4:13)*. He puts reading first and then teaching, because teaching ought to be the purpose of the reading. And the end is more important than the means.

(265) There are others who have a certain holy devotion which makes them frequent the sacred mysteries of the Mass; but though

this sacrament is extremely useful to the church as a whole, yet it becomes a great hazard to many individuals because of their unworthiness. For "if anyone eats and drinks unworthily, he eats and drinks condemnation to himself," as it says *(1 Cor. 11:29)*, and this must apply even more to one who celebrates Mass unworthily. But it does not apply to preaching. A sinner can preach without sinning, provided he is not a notorious sinner.

(266) There are others who gladly devote their time to hearing confessions. But preaching has one advantage over hearing confessions: when you are hearing confessions, you can only help one person at a time, but preaching helps many people all at once. When Peter was preaching, there were added to the church about three thousand believers *(Acts 2:41)*, and on another day five thousand *(Acts 4:4)*.

(267) There are others who prefer to concentrate on celebrating baptisms and anointing the sick and confirmations and the consecration of virgins and clerical ordinations and other such ecclesiastical rites. But these do not benefit adults unless they are received with real awareness and with good will. And it is preaching which produces such awareness and good will. "I heard of you with the hearing of my ears" (through preaching, that is), "and now my eyes see you" (this refers to awareness); "therefore I blame myself" (this refers to good will) *(Job 42:5–6)*. Now even without the sacraments, awareness of God and good will are beneficial. This shows that preaching is to be preferred to these other practices.

(268) Then there are others who like being present at divine worship, haunting churches when the Divine Office is being celebrated. But the laity do not understand what is being said during such celebrations, whereas they do understand what is said in a sermon. So God is praised more clearly and openly by means of preaching. And so the title "divine praise" can actually be transferred to preaching. In Psalm 72:28 it says, in the text we use, "To declare all your preachings in the gates of the daughter of Zion," but in another version it says, "All your praises."[57]

This makes it quite obvious what considerable advantages preaching has over other spiritual exercises.

(269) The second reason why preaching should be preferred by those who have the grace for it is that there is exceptionally good precedent for so doing.

When Christ was in this world, he celebrated Mass only once, on

Maundy Thursday; we do not read of him ever hearing confessions, he administered few sacraments and those infrequently, he did not very often assist at any canonical[58] divine worship; you will find that the same thing is true of all the practices mentioned above, except prayer and preaching. And once he started preaching, we find in the gospels that he is presented as having devoted his whole life to preaching, even more than to prayer.

(270) Paul likewise, that outstanding apostle, thanks God that he had baptised only a few, saying that he had not been sent to baptise, but to preach the gospel *(1 Cor. 1:14,17)*. We do not hear of his engaging in any other spiritual exercise as much as he engaged in preaching. But of his preaching we read that he completed the preaching of the gospel of Christ from Jerusalem right round to the Illyrian sea, and then set off for the West *(Rom. 15:19,24)*.

(271) And what else did the apostles and disciples of the Lord do in the whole world, except devote themselves to preaching, far more than to anything else? "But they went out and preached everywhere" *(Mark 16:20)*.

So we have a precedent for this preference in Christ himself, in Paul, and in fact in all the apostles and disciples of Christ.

(272) The third reason for this preference is that it seems to accord with the Lord's special wishes. At his departure from the earth, it was this that he bid his disciples do, as something particularly acceptable to him. "Go into the whole world, and preach the gospel to the whole creation" *(Mark 16:15)*.

(273) He also appointed a special reward for the performance of this job, namely the halo, which is mentioned in the Gloss to Exodus 25:25.[59]

(274) It was also in view of the good performance of this job that he worked his own most important miracles. It was in view of this that he infused the most profound and exalted knowledge in an instant into uneducated men. It was in view of this that he gave them all kinds of tongues. It was in view of this that he granted them the power to work miracles, so that he might thereby validate their words. All of this shows how much more pleasing to him this particular job is than any other.

(275) So, since preaching has so many advantages, such impressive precedents, and since it is such an acceptable exercise in the eyes of the Lord, it is not unreasonable that it should be preferred to all other spiritual exercises by spiritual men who are capable of it.

Indeed, they are constrained to prefer it. "Woe is me if I do not preach the gospel. A necessity to preach lies upon me" *(1 Cor. 9:16).*

## Notes

1. PL 77:31B.
2. *Sermons on the Canticle* 18:2 (I p. 104:9–13).
3. PG 56:679.
4. PL 77:96B
5. PL 77:96B.
6. PL 76:246C.
7. Interlinear Gloss.
8. Marginal Gloss.
9. Jeremiah.
10. PL 77:20C.
11. PL 77:19C.
12. *Inaequalitas.*
13. *Sermons on the Canticle* 12:9 (I p. 66:6ff).
14. *Numquid non est melius* M (*numquid est melius* A). SL's *numquam* would give an even stronger sense: "It is never the case that it is not better. . . ."
15. Marginal Gloss.
16. The vocative, *pusillanimes,* given in all the MSS, is supported by the reading and interpretation of the Gloss.
17. Interlinear Gloss: *dicite, O doctores.*
18. Interlinear Gloss.
19. *Enim numquam* MA, *ergo numquam* S, *numquam* L. The printed editions read *umquam* for *numquam,* which must be correct. I read *enim umquam.*
20. Aristotle, *Eth. Nic.* II 1103a33–4.
21. No preacher was allowed to go without a companion (*socius*); in spite of a tendency before long to treat the *socius* as a way of forcing the friars to behave themselves, the basic idea was simply to follow the example of Christ, who sent his preachers out in pairs *(Mark 6:7).* See Vicaire, CF 2 pp. 186–7.
22. Deut. 22:10.
23. Marginal Gloss.
24. Marginal Gloss.
25. Marginal Gloss.
26. Marginal Gloss.
27. Cf. PG 35:425B, 437.
28. *Illicita quaeque faciunt et laudant* MAS, *illicita quae faciunt laudant* L. L's text is probably due to scribal correction from the text of Gregory, but

*quae* must be right. The omission of *et*, however, is probably not right; Gregory has *etiam*.

29. This phrase is found only in L, which is poor evidence for the text of Humbert; but it is a genuine part of the quotation from Gregory and probably got lost by accident in the other MSS.

30. PL 77:49C.

31. I cannot find this text in Gregory, but it is also found in Thomas of Ireland's *Manipulus Florum* under *Praedicatio*, ascribed to Gregory's Homilies. Fr. A.M. Kenzeler O.P. has drawn my attention to an almost identical text in Peter Lombard, which might be the genuine source (PL 192:444).

32. PL 77:32B.

33. John 18:20.

34. *Triviis* MA, *nundinis* SL. Without too much confidence, I have conflated the two readings. Humbert himself provides model sermons for some unlikely situations, including fairs and tournaments, so he is clearly not totally rejecting St. Dominic's readiness to talk to anybody anywhere about God; in this passage he is only talking about formal preaching.

35. Cf. Gen. 14:14.

36. PL 76:917BC.

37. Marginal Gloss.

38. *Aedificium* in Gregory's text seems preferable to *fundamentum* in Humbert's MSS.

39. PL 76:58AB.

40. *Orator*, which, of course, basically means "speaker"; but here Augustine revives the much rarer sense, "pray-er," by stressing the derivation of the noun from *orare*, whose normal meaning in Latin is "to pray."

41. *De Doctrina Christiana* IV 15:32.

42. Marginal Gloss to 3 Kings 5:15.

43. 3 Kings 5:13–14.

44. PL 75:761A. Notice that Gregory and Humbert are both quite explicit that this contemplative activity is *in view of* preaching, not an end in itself. Cf. below, §264.

45. PL 76:922D. I conjecture <*se*> *subtiliter* from the text of Gregory, though Humbert's text is more of a paraphrase than a direct quotation.

46. PL 76:907A.

47. *Sancti* is missing from all the MSS, but it is part of the Vulgate text and is needed to make sense of the quotation.

48. PL 76:890C.

49. Marginal Gloss. Cf. PL 91:886C.

50. PL 76:1151C.

51. John 1:23.

52. PL 83:708A.

53. Acts 4:31.

54. PL 16:53B.

55. PL 76:1098C.

56. On the whole medieval writers were pessimistic about the efficacy of the prayers of sinners; cf. Jacques de Vitry, *Hist. Occid.* XXXIV (ed. cit., p. 167); Peraldus, *Summa Virt.* III v 7:5 *(De impedimentis orationis).* The outstanding exception is St. Thomas, IIa IIae q.83 a.16.

57. This is the reading of the *Psalterium Romanum.*

58. *Canonicis,* the reading of the printed editions, must be right; *canoris* of the MSS makes nonsense.

59. Marginal Gloss.

# V Various Ways in Which People Come to Be without Preaching

In connexion with the various ways in which people may come to be without preaching, we must consider:

(i)     the possible causes of such a situation;
(ii)    people who withdraw themselves from preaching;
(iii)   the harm that results from lack of preaching.

## REASONS WHY PREACHING MAY BE LACKING

(XXII 276) Sometimes preaching is withheld for reasons known only to God. On Luke 10:13 the Gloss says, "Why there should be preaching for those who were not going to believe, and no preaching for those who would have believed, he alone knows who knows everything."[1]

(277) Sometimes it comes about at the devil's instigation. "After this, I saw four angels standing over the four corners[2] of the earth, holding in the four winds to prevent them blowing upon the earth or the sea or on any tree" *(Apoc. 7:1)*. This is glossed, "The devil tries to hold back preaching everywhere through his minions."[3] And it is quite right to say "through his minions." Surely the scribes and the pharisees were his minions among the Jews, and the priests of the temples among the pagans, and Mahomet among the Saracens.

In all of these cases, it was sometimes for the good of the people concerned that this happened. "They were forbidden by the Holy Spirit to speak the word in Asia" *(Acts 16:6)*—"to prevent the wicked hearts of men incurring a more severe condemnation because of contempt for preaching," as the Gloss comments.[4]

(278) Sometimes it is due to the guilt of the people. "I will make your tongue stick to your mouth, because this is an infuriating house" *(Ezek. 3:26).* This is glossed, "Sometimes the word of preaching is withdrawn because of the sin of the hearer."[5]

(279) Sometimes preaching is lacking because of a deficiency on the part of the church's leaders. "The little ones asked for bread, and there was no one to break bread for them" *(Lam. 4:4),* that is to say, no priest or archdeacon or bishop; and this is either because they are ignorant or because they are engaged in other, less important, tasks and have no time to preach, or because they are devoid of any zeal for souls and so take no interest in preaching.

(280) Sometimes there is no preaching because it is actually prevented by the church's leaders. There are many prelates who not only do not preach, but also stop others from doing so, who would have been able to preach quite satisfactorily. "They kept your holy children shut up, through whom the incorruptible light of your law was beginning to be given to the world" *(Wisdom 18:4).* Preachers are shut up when they are not allowed to preach freely.

(281) Sometimes it is due to men's curiosity, as for example when people come to sermons not because they wish to make any real progress, but simply because they enjoy listening to them. There is an example in the *Lives of the Fathers.* Some brethren came to abba Felix, together with some seculars, seeking a word of edification. When they had waited there a long time, he said to them, "Brethren, there is no word now. When men who are not prepared to put what they hear into practice come to the elders, then God removes grace from the elders and they find nothing to say."[6]

## THOSE WHO WITHDRAW THEMSELVES
## FROM PREACHING

(XXIII 282) Some people keep themselves away from preaching at the devil's instigation. The devil does not want those who belong to him to listen to the preaching of Christ, in case they are drawn to Christ. This was why Mahomet decreed in his law that the Saracens were not to hear any preaching about Christ.[7] "You do not listen, because you are not from God," but "from your father the devil" *(John 8:47,44).*

(283) Some people stay away because of their human laziness, which will not make even a small effort to get to hear a sermon. Against people like this the Queen of the South will rise up in the judgment, because she came from the ends of the earth to listen to the wisdom of Solomon *(Luke 11:31)*.

(284) Some people are too proud to demean themselves by joining the company of vulgar, uneducated people at the feet of those who are preaching. But this contempt for God's messengers reflects on God himself. "Anyone who spurns you, spurns me" *(Luke 10:16)*.

(285) Some people are too embarrassed. They are aware of all the sins which are frequently mentioned in sermons, like usury, fornication and so on, and they are afraid of being branded as guilty of these, and so they do not come. "Everyone who does evil hates the light and does not come to the light, to avoid having his deeds proved against him" *(John 3:20)*.

(286) Others are too busy with wordly affairs. But when Martha was busy, Mary sat at the feet of the Lord and listened to his word, and she was praised by the Lord *(Luke 10:39ff)*.

(287) Others keep away because of a silly piece of sophistry. They tell themselves that it is better not to know what they are supposed to do, than to know it and not do it. But, poor men, they do not appreciate that such cultivated and affected ignorance is no excuse for sin. So Paul says, "Anyone who does not know, will not be known" *(1 Cor. 14:38)*.

(288) Others are afraid of doing good. They are afraid that if they go to the sermon, they may be inspired with some good purpose there. They are like the deaf adder in the Psalm, which "blocks its ears to avoid hearing the voice of the charmers and of the wizard with his cunning song" *(Psalm 57:5–6)*, to make sure that it does not lose the power of its poison.[8]

(289) Others are too fastidious. Their taste is too delicate for them to frequent sermons, which are the food of the soul, though they are not too delicate to take their bodily meals each day. But in Amos 8:11 it says, "Behold the days are coming, says the Lord, when I will send a desperate hunger[9] on the land, not a hunger for bread or a thirst for water, but a hunger for the word of the Lord." Notice how intense this desire for the word of God must be, if it can be referred to as "desperate hunger."

(290) Others are obstinate in their wickedness, like the pharisees

and the lawyers, who hardened themselves against Christ, and resisted becoming his disciples or even his hearers. "They made their hearts like flint rather than listen to the law" *(Zech. 7:12).*

(291) Others keep away because they despair of ever making any progress, after long experience of getting nowhere in spite of sermons. But the word of God can hardly avoid bringing forth some fruit, perceptible or imperceptible, immediately or some time later. "My word will go out from my mouth and will not return to me empty" *(Isaiah 55:11).*

(292) So woe to all these men! They are accursed. As it says, "Accursed is the man who will not hear the words of his covenant" *(Jer. 11:3).*

## THE HARM THAT RESULTS FROM LACK OF PREACHING

(XXIV 293) Where preaching is missing, there people remain in unbelief. This is why many nations are still to be found in their ancestral errors. "How shall they believe in one of whom they have never heard? And how shall they hear without someone to preach to them?" *(Rom. 10:14).*

(294) Similarly people remain in error about morals. Lack of preaching explains why many people make mistakes about what they ought to do, because they do not know what is lawful and what is not. And so they walk a way of evil deeds, because they have not received any enlightenment about such things from preaching. So in Wisdom 5:6 the damned say, "We strayed from the way of truth," and this is because "the light of righteousness never shone upon us." And what is the light of righteousness, if not preaching, which discloses what is right and what is not right?

(295) Another consequence of lack of preaching is that people do not know themselves. The word of preaching is a kind of mirror, as it says in James 1:23, and people see themselves in it. And so many people do not know themselves, and do not realise what state they are in or what danger, or what is wrong with them, and all that kind of thing, because they never listen to any preaching.

(296) Another consequence is that people make foolish assessments of the value of things. The doctrine contained in holy preaching teaches people how much more precious spiritual things are than bodily, eternal than temporal, heavenly than earthly, and so on. Those who lack such instruction often make mistakes about the value

of things. So it says, "Never give up listening to teaching, my son. Do not be ignorant of the words of knowledge" *(Prov. 19:27)*. "Words of knowledge" refers to a man's knowing how to state the value of a thing correctly.

(297) Another consequence is a dearth of goodness. Just as the soil dries up when it does not rain, and so does not bring forth its fruit, so when there is a lack of preaching, men do not produce their crop of good works. "Where there is no knowledge of the soul, there is no good" *(Prov. 19:2)*. Knowledge of the soul is the subject matter of preaching. Its kind of knowledge is concerned with the soul, while other sciences are about other things.

(298) Another consequence is that it leads to a pullulation of evil. When there is not enough rain, not only does the earth fail to produce its good crop, it starts producing more and more thorns and thistles and weeds. Similarly when there is not enough preaching, evil abounds. "There is no knowledge of God in the land"—and knowledge of God derives from preaching; therefore "there has been a flood of cursing and lying and murder and theft and adultery, and bloodshed follows immediately upon bloodshed" *(Hosea 4:1–2)*.

(299) It also leads to our enemies romping in exultantly. Where no warning shout is heard, enemies can invade more easily. So it says in Hosea 8:1, "There should be a trumpet in your throat," which is glossed, "Open preaching."[10] The reason follows: "There is a kind of eagle upon the Lord's house," namely the devil, who is like an eagle, and is close at hand and all set to invade the house of the Lord.

(300) Finally, people go to sleep in their time of danger. Like Jonah, who was fast asleep in the bottom of the boat when they were in great danger, many people would never wake up to take stock of their situation, unless they were roused by preaching, as Jonah was roused by the ship's captain, who asked him, "Why are you sleeping so heavily? Get up and call upon your God."[11]

Gregory says, "By a subtle and hidden judgment of God, holy preaching is withheld from some people's minds, because they do not deserve to be roused by grace."[12]

## Notes

1. Marginal Gloss.
2. I have added *statnes super quatuor angulos* from the Vulgate; these words are missing from all the MSS of Humbert.

3. Marginal Gloss. The printed text of the Gloss does not include *per satellites suos,* but the extra words are found in Oxford, Bodleian MS Auct. D 1.15.

4. Marginal Gloss.

5. Marginal Gloss.

6. Cf. PL 73:863A.

7. This does not seem to be strictly true, but Jacques de Vitry, *Historia Orientalis* I vi (Douai, 1596, p. 16), claims that Mahomet forbade his followers to listen to anyone preaching against him, and in general Islamic states did not allow Christian preachers to attempt to convert Muslims to Christianity.

8. The reason Humbert gives for the snake's wilful deafness, "so that it will not lose the power of its poison," is not the one usually given. Cf. McCulloch, pp. 88–90. But Thomas of Cantimpré, *De Natura Rerum* VIII 2, says that the reason for trying to charm the snake is to "stop it killing you with its poison."

9. *Fames* in the text of Amos means "famine," in the sense of "lack of food," but Humbert takes it to mean primarily "hunger."

10. Interlinear Gloss.

11. Jonah 1:5–6.

12. PL 76:1089D.

# VI The Results of Preaching

Sometimes preaching has no effect at all, sometimes it unintentionally produces bad results, sometimes it produces results which are not altogether bad, but which are not specially good either, and sometimes it produces results which are thoroughly good. Such good results depend on people's hearing the word of God with devotion and then putting it into practice. Accordingly, what we must discuss in Part Six is:

(i)   the possibility of there being no results at all;
(ii)  bad results;
(iii) imperfectly good results;
(iv)  thoroughly good results;
(v)   listening to the word of God;
(vi)  putting it into practice.

## PREACHING WITH NO RESULTS AT ALL

(XXV 301) Many people's preaching sometimes leads to no results at all. And this should not surprise us, since the same thing happened when our Saviour was preaching, as it says in John 8:37, "My word does not catch in you," on which the Gloss says that the word is "like a fish-hook."[1] It fails to catch when it does not succeed in removing from the hearts of the hearers such things as promiscuity and greed, just as a hook is said not to make a catch when it does not pull any fish out of the water.

(302) Sometimes this lack of results is due to the fault of the hearers. There are some people who are like bad soil: however hard you work on it, it never yields any harvest at all. "When you have worked it, it will not yield any fruit" *(Gen. 4:12).*

269

(303) On other occasions it is due to the inadequacy of the preacher. A hard-working farmer can, if he applies himself to it, make even rather poor soil fruitful; but if the farmer is inadequate, even his good soil may not produce anything. Similarly an inadequate preacher may sometimes lose the fruit that there might have been in his hearers. "I passed by the field of the lazy man, and it was all full of nettles" *(Prov. 24:30–1)*, because of his laziness, that is.

(304) Sometimes it is due to the ineffectiveness of the actual sermon. People sometimes put forward arguments or textual authorities or images or anecdotes which are so silly that they have almost no effect, and so they bring nothing good to birth in their hearers, any more than mouldy seed will lead to a good harvest. Seneca's advice is pertinent here: "There is need, not of many words, but of effective words."[2]

(305) Sometimes it comes about because divine grace is lacking. Seed that is sown will not fructify without rain or dew, and in the same way preaching will have no effect in the minds of the hearers unless the grace of the Holy Spirit is there. Gregory says, "Unless the Holy Spirit is present to the heart of the hearer, the teacher's words are a waste of time. . . . No teaching is communicated by the spoken word unless the mind is being anointed by the Spirit."[3]

(306) Sometimes it is due to the enemy's plotting. Just as birds come and eat the seed that has been sown, so that no crop results, so the devil takes away the word that has been sown and the results are lost. "These are the ones who hear, and then the devil comes and takes the word out of their heart, to stop them believing and being saved" *(Luke 8:12)*.

(307) So preaching has no effect sometimes because of the hearers, sometimes because of the preacher, sometimes because of the sermon, sometimes because grace is lacking and sometimes because of the enemy.

(308) In a different way, there are ten other things which can prevent the effectiveness of preaching.

First, there is hardness of heart. There are some people whose hearts are devilish, hard as rocks. They are hinted at in Job 41:15. Preaching to them is as unprofitable as sowing seed on a boulder. Conversely, it says in Psalm 94:8, "Today, if you would hear his voice, do not harden your hearts."

(309) Secondly, there is stupidity. A stupid man does not take in

what is said to him, and so words are wasted on him. It is like planting a seed in soil which cannot hold it. So it says in Ecclesiasticus 22:9, "Telling wisdom to a fool is like talking to a man who is asleep"; he does not take it in, that is, any more than a man who is asleep.

(310) Thirdly, there is wickedness running riot. If there are too many thistles in a field, it cannot yield a proper crop until it has been weeded. So it says, "Cast away the excess of your wickedness, and then in meekness receive the implanted word" *(James 1:21)*, as if to say, "The word will not achieve anything unless this excess is first removed."

(311) Fourthly, there is insensitivity to time and opportunity. Every undertaking has its proper time,[4] and when this is not respected, preaching does not achieve anything, any more than seed could be sown out of season. So it says, "A proverb in the mouth of an idiot does not find favour, because he does not speak it at the proper time" *(Ecclus. 20:22)*.

(312) Fifthly, there is sensuality. Just as some soil is good enough for coarse crops like barley and millet, but not for wheat, so men who are very sensual are unfitted for the spiritual seed which is sown by preaching. "The sensual man cannot take to himself the things of God; they are foolishness to him" *(1 Cor. 2:14)*. If he does not take them to himself at all, how can he make progress in them?

(313) Sixthly, there is forgetfulness. A forgetful man is like a leaky jug which cannot hold water. "The heart of an idiot is like a broken pot. It will not hold any wisdom" *(Ecclus. 21:17)*. If it does not hold it at all, how will it benefit from it?

(314) Seventhly, there is lack of taste for the word of God. Gregory says, "The word of God is the mind's food; if it is not retained in the mind's stomach, which is the memory, it is like food taken into a sick stomach: it is thrown up again. But if a man cannot hold any of his food down, we begin to despair of his life."[5]

(315) Eighthly, there is worldly business. "They are choked by the cares of this life, and yield no fruit" *(Luke 8:14)*.

(316) Ninthly, there is disobedience towards the word.[6] Augustine says, in *On Christian Teaching*, "Men will not listen obediently to a man who does not listen to himself; and so it comes about that they despise the word of God together with the preacher."[7]

(317) Finally, there is estrangement from God, and this is the

state of many people. "My sheep hear my voice and follow me. . . . They do not follow a stranger, because they do not recognise the voice of a stranger" *(John 10:27,5)*.

## BAD RESULTS OF PREACHING

(XXVI 318) Sometimes people hear the word of God, but do not put it into practice. As it says, "My people sit before you and hear your words and do nothing about it" *(Ezek. 33:31)*. They are left, then, only with the guilt of disobedience.

(319) Sometimes people do not really believe what they hear, either about the punishment that is to come or the rewards and that kind of thing. "They did not believe his word, they murmured in their tents" *(Psalm 105:24–5)*, saying, no doubt, "How can this happen?" or "How can that happen?" And so they are left with the evil of disbelief.

(320) Sometimes people do not like what they hear. "The promiscuous man hears a wise word and he will not like it" *(Ecclus. 21:18)*. And so all that comes of it is the evil of disliking the good.

(321) Sometimes people despise what they hear. "They made light of the words of the Lord" *(2 Chron. 36:16)*. "Fools despise wisdom and instruction" *(Prov. 1:7)*. And so the only result is contempt for the word of the Lord.

(322) Sometimes people laugh at what is being said to them. "They mocked the Lord's messengers and ridiculed his prophets" *(2 Chron. 36:16)*. The only result then is the evil of laughing at God's servants.

(323) Sometimes a man who preaches something contrary to what men want to hear comes to be hated by them. "I hate him, because he never prophesies any good for me. Micaiah the son of Imlah always prophesies evil" *(3 Kings 22:8)*. And so the only result is the evil of hating those who ought to be loved.

(324) Sometimes people not only hate preachers like this, but actually persecute them seriously, as we can see from the case of the apostles and the Jews. "See, I send you prophets. . . . You will persecute them from city to city" *(Matt. 23:34)*.

(325) These are the tares which the devil sows after the good seed has been sown, and they are destined to be burned at the end. "Lord, did you not sow good seed in your field? How then does it come to

have tares in it?" He said to them, "An enemy has done this. . . . First of all, collect up the tares and bind them in bundles for burning" *(Matt. 13:24–30)*.

They are also the thistles and thorns which are the disgrace of soil which has drunk in the rain which keeps falling upon it; soil like that is next door to a curse and is destined only to be burned *(Hebr. 6:7–8)*.

People like this are also like that vineyard which the Lord cultivated with loving care, looking forward to its sweet wine, and all that it gave him was bitterness. "Their grape is a poisonous grape, their young grape is very sour; their wine is the venom of snakes, the poison of vipers which cannot be healed." What follows ought to inspire fear: "Is not this what I have prepared in my house, sealed away in my storehouse? Vengeance is mine, and I will pay them back in due course" *(Deut. 32:32–5)*.

## RESULTS OF PREACHING WHICH ARE LESS
## THAN PERFECT

(XXVII 326) Sometimes preaching produces results which are good, but which fall short of being effective for salvation.

One such result is understanding. "The utterance of your words gives light, it gives understanding to little ones" *(Psalm 118:130)*. But of what use is good understanding to a man who does not act on it? "If a man knows how to do good and does not do it, it is a sin" *(James 4:17)*.

(327) Another is enjoyment. There are some people who greatly enjoy listening to the word of God, but they listen to it in the same way that they would listen to pleasant singing. The word of God "is like a musical performance to them, like a sweetly sung song" *(Ezek. 33:32)*. But in Matt. 11:17 people are reproached for not stirring their feet in response to this attractive singing: "We sang to you and you did not dance." The one does not suffice without the other. So it says in Psalm 31:11, "Rejoice" (in your heart, that is) "and jump for joy" (dance externally, that is, by doing something about it) "O you just."

(328) Another is that people are stirred emotionally. Sometimes during a sermon people are moved to compunction, maybe, like the people mentioned in Acts 2:37, "When they heard this, they were cut to the quick," or to fear, like Felix, who was scared when he heard

Paul speak *(Acts 24:25)*. Or they may be moved to feel a good kind of interest and concern, like the people in Athens who said, after listening to Paul preaching, "We will hear you again about this" *(Acts 17:32)*. Or they may be moved to some other pious emotion. "Your lightnings flashed across the earth" (your preaching, that is) "and the earth was moved and trembled" *(Psalm 76:19)*. But this does some people no good, because, as soon as the sermon is over, they freeze up again, like a boiling pot when it is removed from the fire. This kind of emotional response by itself does not suffice for salvation. "The Lord was not in the commotion" *(3 Kings 19:11)*.

(329) Notice that these three results concern the three powers of the soul.[8]

(330) Another result of this kind is that people make critical judgments. Many people are able to comment excellently, saying, "He spoke well" or "He spoke badly" or "The sermon was too long" or "Too short" or "Too subtle" or "Not subtle enough" and so on. "Does the ear not judge words?" *(Job 12:11)*. But what are these words? Are they not the chaff?[9] People who derive nothing else from a sermon are like a field in which no wheat is found, but only empty husks. "What is chaff to wheat, says the Lord" *(Jer. 23:28)*, that is, what is chaff worth by comparison with wheat?

(331) Or people may commend the preacher, like the woman in the gospel who shouted out from the crowd, while Jesus was speaking, "Blessed is the womb which bore you and the breasts which you sucked!" But because this is of little value unless the word of God is put into practice, Jesus replied to her, "Rather, blessed are those who hear the word of God and keep it" *(Luke 11:27–8)*.

(332) Another result is that people learn how to teach. This is one reason why some people gladly listen to sermons: they want to learn how they too can become teachers. But this is not much good to them, unless they begin by teaching themselves. As the apostle says, "You teach others, do you not teach yourself?" *(Rom. 2:21)*

(333) These three effects of preaching involve only the words, and so achieve little, because "the kingdom of God is not in words, but in power," as the apostle says *(1 Cor. 4:20)*.

(334) Another possible effect is that people conceive some good purpose. This is why the word of God is called a seed, because, like a seed, it causes conception. But there are many people who never see it through to the point of bringing anything to birth, and so they are not much the better for their conceiving. This is why Hezekiah[10]

laments, "Children have come to the very point of being born, but the parent has no strength to deliver them" *(4 Kings 19:3).*

(335) Or people may seek advice. A sermon sometimes affects people enough to make them seek advice about their salvation. After Peter's sermon "they were cut to the quick and said to Peter and the other apostles, 'Brethren, what are we to do?' " *(Acts 2:37).* But there are many people who get as far as asking for advice, but then do not act on it, and so it does them little good. As the philosopher remarks in the *Ethics,* it does not do a sick man much good to consult a doctor, if he does not follow the doctor's instructions.[11] "Then they will call upon me and I shall not respond . . . because they did not obey my advice" *(Prov. 1:28–30).*

(336) Or people may make a beginning in some good work. But then they do not all persevere. "The seed which fell on rocky ground is those who believe for a time, and then fall away in time of trial" *(Luke 8:13),* and so they do not reach salvation, because salvation is only won by perseverance.

(337) These last three effects of preaching concern deeds, either their conception or consultation about them or the actual undertaking of them.

## THE THOROUGHLY GOOD RESULTS OF PREACHING

(XXVIII 338) There are ten thoroughly good effects which sometimes result from preaching.

First, the conversion of unbelievers to the faith, which obviously occurred during the preaching of the apostles and disciples of Christ, which converted the whole world to Christ. "Some men from Cyprus and Cyrenaea went into Antioch and began to speak to the gentiles, proclaiming the Lord Jesus to them, and the hand of the Lord was with them, and a great number of believers was converted to the Lord" *(Acts 11:20–1).*

(339) Secondly, the conversion of wicked men to repentance. "The men of Nineveh did penance at the preaching of Jonah" *(Luke 11:32).*

(340) Thirdly, the conversion of worldly men to humility. There have been many men brought from worldly pride to a humble way of life because of their listening to the word of God. "When Ahab heard these words, he tore his clothes and covered his flesh with sackcloth,

he fasted and slept on sacking and walked with his head bowed" *(3 Kings 21:27)*.

(341) Fourthly, sinners going to confession. Many people are stirred by what they hear in sermons to confess sins they have never confessed before. At the preaching of John, "The whole of Jerusalem went out to him, and all Judaea and all the region round the Jordan, confessing their sins" *(Matt. 3:5–6)*.

(342) Fifthly, reception of the Holy Spirit. Many people receive him while listening to sermons. "While Peter was still speaking, the Holy Spirit fell upon all of them who were listening to the word" *(Acts 10:44)*.

(343) Sixthly, the sanctification of men from their sins. The word of God has the power to make men holy, according to the principle, "Sanctify them in the truth; your word is truth"[12]: "You are now clean, because of the word which I have spoken to you" *(John 15:3)*.

(344) Seventhly, the increase of the mystical body of Christ. Many souls are added to it through preaching. "On that day about three thousand souls were added" *(Acts 2:41)* at the preaching of Peter.

(345) Eighthly, the release of the devil's prey.[13] "From his teeth I rescued his prey" *(Job 29:17)*. This is interpreted as referring to the devil's prey, which is rescued by preaching.[14]

(346) Ninthly, joy to the angels. They rejoice when they hear the glory of Christ being proclaimed far and wide in preaching. So Christ says to the Church in Cant. 8:13, "Dweller in the gardens, my friends are listening to you." This is glossed, "That is, the angels."[15] And it is implied that they enjoy what they hear, because this is the significance of the word "listen."

(347) Tenthly, the defeat of the devil's forces. As a result of preaching, the devil, with all his army of sins, has been chased out of many provinces and cities and estates and towns and from the hearts of many individuals. "Three hundred men pressed forward blowing trumpets, and the Lord set a sword in every township, and they slaughtered each other as they fled" *(Judges 7:22)*. This is interpreted to refer to the preachers of the Blessed Trinity.[16]

# HUMBERT OF ROMANS

## LISTENING TO THE WORD OF GOD

(XXIX 348) First, we must consider why it is necessary that people should be glad to listen to the word of God; then how they should listen to it.

We should be drawn to listen to the word of God by the importance of the one whose word it is. The greater a person is, in authority or wisdom or anything else of the kind, the more readily people will listen to him. Now the sacred words of preaching do not come simply from man, like the words of other sciences, they come from the inspiration of God himself. And so the Lord says to the preachers, "Whoever hears you, hears me" *(Luke 10:16)*, because they are his mouth, speaking his words. To make people listen to what they said for this reason, the prophets used to conclude their words with "Thus says the Lord," as if to say, "You ought to listen, because these are not my words, but the Lord's."

(349) We should also be moved by the importance of the subject matter of the word of God. The word of God is not concerned with any trivial or cheap affair, but with one of immense importance. And words of this kind are usually listened to more eagerly. So Wisdom says, "Listen, because I am going to speak about great things" *(Prov. 8:6)*.

(350) We should also be moved by the usefulness of the word. Legal talk is useful in worldly business, medical talk is useful for the health of the body, the talk of philosophers is useful if we want to know the truth about things; but the word of God is useful for salvation. So if we are happy to listen to teaching which contributes to the health of the body, how much more ought we to listen to these words, which are effective for the salvation of our souls. And so James says, "In meekness receive the implanted word which can save your souls" *(James 1:21)*.

(351) Another consideration is the way in which our bodily ears are placed. In human beings, unlike other animals, the ears do not face the earth, they are high up in the head; it is as if nature were declaring that they are placed like this so that they will be ready to hear words spoken on high. So it says, "He who has ears to hear" (that is, made for hearing the word of God), "let him hear" *(Luke 8:8)*.

(352) There is also natural instinct. A lamb or a young partridge or chicken naturally runs towards the sound of its mother's voice, and it is the same with many of the animals. And man ought to react in

the same way when he hears the voice of his Creator. So it says, "He who is born of God hears the words of God" *(John 8:47)*.

(353) Also there are frequent warnings given to us in scripture. Who could list all the times it says in Solomon and David and the prophets and the other holy books, "Listen! Listen!"? So James excuses nobody from this, when he says, "Let everybody be quick to listen" *(James 1:19)*.

(354) We also have the example of the early church, when people came flocking from everywhere to the preaching of John and of Christ, even in the desert, as we see in Matt. 3:5 and John 6:2. If the Jews behaved like this, how much more ought we who are Christians?

(355) We should also remember that preaching is a special grace only given to some. "He declares his word to Jacob. . . . He has not done this for every nation" *(Psalm 147:19–20)*. Woe to anyone who refuses such a grace as this! By so doing he condemns himself as unworthy of eternal life. "Since you have rejected the word, you have judged yourselves unworthy of eternal life" *(Acts 13:46)*.

(356) Finally, there is a point to be made about this kind of teacher's salary. In any other school, the students have to pay the teacher, but here it is the other way round: the teacher pays the students, and he does so lavishly. Who could ever say how many and how great are the blessings that the Lord gives to those who listen to him? So eternal Wisdom says, "Blessed is he who listens to me and keeps vigil at my gate every day, and watches at the posts of my doorway" *(Prov. 8:34)*. Preachers are her gate, and her doorposts are the holy scriptures.

(357) In view of all these reasons why we should listen to the word of the Lord, Jeremiah is right to say, "Earth, earth, earth, listen to the word of the Lord!" *(Jer. 22:29)*.

(358) Now we must turn to the question of how we ought to listen to the word of God.

There are some people who are depressed by the news that they are to get a sermon. They ought to be glad. "I will rejoice over your words, like one who finds great treasure" *(Psalm 118:162)*.

(359) Then there are people who come to the sermon, but arrive late. But in Luke 8:4 we read that "they came hurrying to him" (to hear him, that is) "from the cities," and in Luke 21:38, "The whole people arose early in the morning to come and listen to him in the temple."

(360) There are others who leave before the sermon is finished.

"They would not wait, but turned their backs and went away" *(Zech. 7:11)*. In this way they sometimes lose indulgences or prayers offered at the end of the sermon; sometimes they miss the best part of the sermon, which is sometimes kept for the end; sometimes they lose all the merit that there is in listening to sermons, because this depends more on the end than on the beginning. So people ought to stay right up to the end of a sermon, because "the end of a speech is better than the beginning" *(Ecclesiastes 7:9)*. As with any other good undertaking, its completion is better than its inception.

(361) There are others who keep on sitting down and standing up again, going out and coming back in, so careless about listening to the sermon that they take no trouble about things like getting close to the preacher or finding some other suitable place in which they will be able to hear and understand what is being said. But Augustine says, "A man who is careless in listening to the word of God is no whit less guilty than a man who allows the body of Christ to fall to the ground through his carelessness."[17]

(362) There are others who keep making a noise, when silence is what is required of an audience. "The Levites made the people keep silence, so that they could hear the law" *(Neh. 8:7)*. "Paul stood up and gestured for silence, and said, 'Men of Israel and God-fearers, listen!' " *(Acts 13:16)*.

(363) Then there are people who disturb the others by making their way in and out of the crowd, or by pushing and shoving, or by being a nuisance in other ways. But it says, "Be gentle to listen to the word" *(Ecclus. 5:13)*. A gentle animal does not annoy other animals by biting them or hitting them or anything else of the kind, and that is the way it ought to be with people at a sermon, so that everyone can listen peacefully.

(364) There are other people who are too busy saying their prayers during a sermon, or reading or doing other such things, and so cannot pay attention to what is being said. But the word of God ought to be listened to with full attention: "Pay attention, my people, to my law" *(Psalm 77:1)*, that is, listen attentively. "The crowds attended to what Philip was saying, all being of one mind in listening to him" *(Acts 8:6)*.

(365) There are others who listen disdainfully. But the word of God ought to be listened to greedily and hungrily. "The more noble people who were in Thessalonica received the word of God with all avidity" *(Acts 17:11)*.

(366) There are others who easily get bored if the sermon goes on for any length of time. But it says about the Jews, "Ezra read from morning until mid-day in the presence of the men and women and the wise, and the ears of all the people were pricked up to hear the book" *(Neh. 8:3)*. It is remarkable that no one was bored during such an enormous sermon. This example shows us that we ought to be able to endure for a long time in our listening.

(367) There are other people who easily become impatient during a sermon, if anything is said which they do not find completely to their liking. But they ought to be tolerant in such circumstances. So Paul says to Agrippa, "I beseech you, listen to me patiently" *(Acts 26:3)*.

(368) There are others who show no sign of devotion when they are listening to the word of God. But it is said of Mary that she sat at the Lord's feet, listening to his word. Bernard says, "The word of God has to be received and listened to with devotion."[18]

(369) So, if the word of God is to be heard in the proper way, it must be received with joy, people must hasten to it, they must remain until it is finished, they must listen carefully, in silence, peacefully, attentively, avidly, they must not be in a hurry for it to end, they must be patient and they must listen with devotion.


## PUTTING THE WORD OF GOD INTO PRACTICE

(XXX 370) If people only listen to the word of God without acting on it, we must realise that a great deal of evil results in them.

For instance, it makes good turn into bad. The knowledge of righteousness, which is in itself a good thing, becomes bad in these circumstances. "It would be better if they had never known the way of righteousness, than to turn back, after coming to know it, and forsake the holy precept given to them" *(2 Peter 2:21)*.

(371) It also makes sin worse. A man who knows what he should do and does not do it is more guilty than he would have been if he had not known. "A servant who knows the will of his master and does not make himself ready and does not act according to it will receive many strokes" *(Luke 12:47)*. And this is simply because his offense is the greater.

(372) Another evil consequence is that a man becomes an object of detestation. A man who knows that he is filthy and still does not

wash is far more obnoxious than if he did not know. And that is what a man is like who hears the word of God without acting on it. "If anyone is a hearer of the word and not a doer, he will be like a man who looks at his own natural face in a mirror and then, when he has had a good look, goes away and immediately forgets what he looks like" *(James 1:23–4).*

(373) It also results in people's actions becoming futile. "Everyone who hears my words and does not act on them will be like a foolish man who built his house on sand, and when the rain fell and the floods came and the winds blew, it collapsed with an enormous crash" *(Matt. 7:26–7).*

(374) It also leads to men's lives being despaired of, like people whose stomachs cannot tolerate any food. "Their soul detested every kind of food, they came close to the gates of death" *(Psalm 106:18).* Gregory says, "The mind's food is the word of God. And we despair of the life of anyone who cannot hold down his food."[19]

(375) It also leads to condemnation in the sight of God. "If anyone hears my words and does not keep them, it is not I who judge him. . . . The word I have spoken will judge him on the last day" *(John 12:47–8),* that is to say, it will be the occasion of his damnation. And so it says, "Agree with your adversary" (the word of God, that is, which opposes human wishes) "while you are still on the way, otherwise your adversary will hand you over to the judge, and the judge will hand you over to his officer, and you will be put in prison" *(Matt. 5:25).*

(376) We should also notice that there are many desirable consequences of putting what has been heard into practice.

One such consequence is that people become Christ's disciples. In the case of other teachers, a man becomes their disciple simply by listening to them, but this is not so in the case of Christ. A man becomes his disciple by obeying his word. "If you abide in my word, you will truly be my disciples" *(John 8:31).*

(377) Another consequence is that men become friends of Christ, and this is an even greater boon. "He who has my commandments" (passed on to him through preaching) "and keeps them, he it is who loves me" *(John 14:21).*

(378) It also makes men into his brothers, and this is the greatest thing of all. "My brothers are those who hear the word of God and do it" *(Luke 8:21).*

(379) Another good consequence is God's blessing. "The soil

which drinks in the rain which falls upon it and brings forth a crop which is useful to those who cultivate it, receives blessing from God" *(Hebr. 6:7).*

(380) Another consequence is justification. "It is not the hearers of the law who are righteous; those who do the law will be declared righteous" *(Rom. 2:13).*

(381) And finally, beatitude. "Blessed are those who hear the word of God and keep it" *(Luke 11:28).*

(382) So we can see that a great many evils flow from merely hearing the word of God without acting on it, while a great many blessings flow from hearing it and acting on it; therefore people ought to devote all the energy they have to acting on the word once they have heard it.

## *Notes*

1. Interlinear Gloss: "Like a fish-hook, which catches when it is caught."
2. *Letters* 38:1.
3. PL 76:1222A.
4. Ecclesiastes 8:6.
5. PL 76:1132A.
6. Although most of the hazards listed here seem to occur in the potential hearers, this one and the next plainly concern the preacher himself: it is *his* disobedience and alienation from God that jeopardise the preaching.
7. *De Doctrina Christiana* IV 27:60.
8. In a rough and ready way, the preceding three paragraphs can be allocated to the reasoning power of the soul, the appetitive power and the "irascible" power.
9. It will be recalled that, after the strange experience that brought his teaching and writing career to an end, St. Thomas explained that he could write no more, because "all I have written seems like chaff *(paleae)* to me, by comparison with what I have seen and what has been revealed to me" *(Naples Canonization Process* 79; see Kenelm Foster, *The Life of St. Thomas Aquinas: Biographical Documents* [London/Baltimore, 1959], p. 109).
10. The MSS all have *dicitur Isai. 38,* but the text quoted here is not from Isaiah 38, but from the parallel passage in 4 Kings 19. Very tentatively, I conjecture *dicit Ezechias.*
11. Aristotle, *Eth. Nic.* II 1105b12–18.
12. John 17:17.

13. M adds: *Unde dicuntur praedicatores quasi praedae captatores* ("Hence the word 'preachers,' 'prey-catchers' ").

14. Cf. Gregory, PL 76:127D.

15. Marginal Gloss.

16. Interlinear Gloss.

17. PL 39:2319 §2.

18. *Sermons on Peter and Paul* 2:3.

19. PL 76:1132A.

# VII Things That Go with the Job of Preaching

There are ten[1] things that we must now consider, which go with the job of preaching:

| | |
|---|---|
| (i) | the preacher's travelling round the world; |
| (ii) | his conduct among other people; |
| (iii) | personal conversations; |
| (iv) | staying with strangers; |
| (v) | involvement in human affairs; |
| (vi) | requests for advice; |
| (vii) | hearing confessions; |
| (viii) | *prothemes;* |
| (ix) | material for sermons and conferences; |
| (x) | prayers that the preacher enjoins on people.[2] |

## The Preacher's Travelling round the World

(383) It is to be noticed that there are various scriptural figures which indicate the preacher's travels. But some people are rather lazy about this, and so they need to be roused. Others commit various faults in connexion with it, and they need to be rebuked. Others conduct themselves excellently, and they must be commended. So what we have to deal with now is (a) the scriptural figures, (b) incentives to preachers to travel, (c) various faults and (d) commendation of what is good.

284

# HUMBERT OF ROMANS

## SCRIPTURAL FIGURES OF TRAVELLING ROUND

(XXXI 384) The preacher's travelling round is signified by the movement of the clouds which go east and west and south and north, to show forth the greatness of their creator. "By his greatness the clouds roam round" *(Deut. 33:26)*. This is glossed, "By preaching."[3]

(385) Another figure is the movement of lightning flashing. "The Lord sent lightning racing over the earth" *(Exod. 9:23)*. Gregory says, "The lightning moves when preachers are brilliant with miracles, and transfix the hearts of their hearers with reverence for God."[4]

(386) Another figure is to be found in the movement of the sacred Living Beings which Ezekiel saw coming and going. They signify preachers. "This was a running vision" *(Ezek. 1:13)*, that is to say, a vision of beings running about.

(387) Another figure is the running of powerful horses, mentioned in Zechariah 6:7, "The horses which were most powerful came out, seeking to go and run around the whole world." According to the Gloss on Job 39:19, "horses" refers to preachers.[5]

(388) Another figure is the travelling of the messengers referred to in Esther 8:10, "Letters were sent in the king's name by means of couriers who went round all the provinces to get the new message there before the previous letters." The Gloss applies this to preachers.[6]

(389) Another figure is the travelling of the soldiers mentioned in 2 Macc. 5:2–3, "It came to pass that throughout the whole city of Jerusalem, for a period of forty days, horsemen were seen moving through the air, with golden raiment and spears." This is a mysterious symbol of the fact that preachers like this travel around the church throughout the whole time set for repentance.

## INCENTIVES TO PREACHERS TO TRAVEL

(XXXII 390) In scripture preachers are often referred to as "feet," because it is their business to travel round all over the place for the sake of preaching; but in spite of this, there are some who are reluctant to set out and preach, because they are inclined to be lazy or for some other inadequate reason, like those mentioned above in

§§191ff. So they need to be roused. And there are many incentives to rouse them.

(391) First, there is the instruction given in scripture: "Run about, hasten, wake up your friend" *(Prov. 6:3).*

(392) Then there are excellent examples and precedents. Christ himself, after he began to preach, had no home in which to rest his head;[7] instead, he travelled round through the villages and towns, preaching throughout the whole of Galilee, as the gospels tell us *(Mark 6:6; Matt. 4:23, 9:35).* The apostles too are said not to have had any homes of their own to stay in; they went out into the whole world, preaching everywhere *(Mark 16:15,20).* So what kind of a preacher is he who wants always to stay quietly at home or in his convent?

(393) Then there is the need to rival our opponents. The pharisees traverse land and sea to make a single proselyte *(Matt. 23:15).* The heretics never stop risking their very lives to travel round houses and towns to lead souls astray—they are symbolised by the running round of Samson's foxes in Judges 15:4–5. The devil himself goes about like a roaring lion, looking for someone to eat *(1 Pet. 5:8).* What an embarrassment! All of these are running round to bring souls to damnation, and yet preachers will not stir a foot for their salvation.

(394) Preachers should also consider the job that they have been given. It is not their function to stay put, but to move: "I have appointed you to go" *(John 15:16).*

(395) Also men's need of them. People will always run to help their neighbours if they are in any kind of danger. So the angels are told in Isaiah 18:2 (and they represent preachers), "Go, angels, hurry to a people which is torn to pieces and pulled apart."

(396) Also the great desire of the one who sends them. The Lord was so keen to have his preachers go that he would not release them from it even because of persecution. "Go. See, I am sending you out like lambs among wolves" *(Luke 10:3).*

(397) Finally, preachers ought to be provoked by the example of worldly businessmen. They are so eager in their pursuit of profit that many of them spend their whole lives running around the world without a break to increase their profits. And this is exactly what the apostles did, running round different provinces to win souls. What will these preachers say on the day of judgment, when they are asked to produce their takings? They had been told, "Do business until I come" *(Luke 19:13).* But, like the lazy servant, they wrap up their

master's money and bury it, instead of travelling round to increase it. Gregory comments on this passage, "Look, he is coming, he wants to know about the profit we have made by our transactions. But what profit shall we be able to show him from our trading? There Peter will appear with Judaea, which he converted and led after him; there Paul will appear bringing very nearly the whole world with him; there Andrew will bring Achaea with him as his convert, before his Judge, and John will bring Asia and Thomas India. Heaven help us! What shall we say then, when we come back to the Lord from our trading with empty hands?"[8]

## CERTAIN FAULTS WHICH ARISE IN CONNEXION WITH TRAVELLING

(XXXIII 398) Some preachers are always quite ready to travel, but out of sheer flightiness. On this, "Thus says the Lord to this people which loves moving its feet"—which is reprehensible, so he goes on to say, "With which the Lord was not pleased" *(Jer. 14:10)*. As Seneca says, "It is a sign of a good mind that a man stays put with himself and dwells with himself."[9] The converse of this is just as true.

(399) Others go running around just in order to escape from the discipline of conventual life, like children playing truant from school. Hagar began to flee, when Sarai distressed her (Sarai signifying religious life); but the angel says to her, "Return to your mistress and humble yourself under her" *(Gen. 16:6,9)*.

(400) Others travel for the sake of their stomach, because of the meagre fare they receive in their convents. They are like the dogs in Psalm 58:7. "They will be hungry like dogs and will go prowling round the town." They are like singers[10] who go round from house to house for the same reason. But this is the opposite of what the Lord told his disciples to do. He said, "Do not move round from house to house," looking for food, that is. To make the point quite plain, he had already said, "Stay in the same house, eating and drinking what they have there" *(Luke 10:7)*.

(401) Others travel because of their wordly friendships. They want to go visiting all the time, now one set of friends, now another. This is quite unlike the brother in the *Lives of the Fathers* who refused even to see his own mother, when she came to visit him. He sent her a message that she would have to be content to see him in the next world.[11] Seeing that it says,[12] "Forget your own people and your

father's house" *(Psalm 44:11)*, how can we justify constantly going to visit those whom we are supposed to forget?

(402) Others travel because of worldly affairs, like wills and that kind of thing. But against this it says, "No one who is fighting for God gets himself entangled in wordly affairs; his aim is to please him in whose service he has enrolled" *(2 Tim. 2:4)*.

(403) Others travel out of curiosity, wanting to see different kinds of people, and to peer at things and hear things which are no business of theirs, like the women it speaks of in 1 Tim. 5:13. "Having nothing to do, they pick up the habit of wandering round people's houses. And they are not merely idle, they are garrulous and inquisitive, saying things they ought not to say." People like this belong to that class of monks which St. Benedict calls "gyrovagues," and which he particularly abominates.

(404) Others travel because of their superiors' lack of judgment in sending them out. They make their subjects wander round everywhere too much, and sometimes this does them no little damage. "My people is an abandoned flock. Their shepherds have led them astray, and made them wander in the mountains. They have gone from mountains to hills, and have forgotten their fold" *(Jer. 50:6)*.

(405) Even worse, some people go travelling where they have not been sent, contrary to obedience. "I did not send these prophets, yet they set off at a run" *(Jer. 23:21)*.

(406) Sometimes they also travel on horseback or make people carry money for them on their journey and other such things, which are contrary to the terms of their religious profession.[13] But this is contrary to Mark 6:8, in which Christ "commanded them to take nothing with them on their journeys except a staff; no bag, no bread, no money in their purse."

(407) And sometimes they also travel uselessly, achieving nothing as they go. And this is contrary to John 15:16, "I have appointed you to go and bear fruit."

(408) Finally we must notice that there are three bad things which result from religious preachers wandering round too much.

The first is that men get fed up with them.[14] Excess usually breeds weariness. This is why it says, "Withdraw your foot from your neighbour's house, or he will be surfeited and come to hate you" *(Prov. 25:17)*.

(409) The second is the preacher's own spiritual loss. It is difficult to be among worldly men for very long without deteriorating in

some way. "Whenever I went among men, I came away less of a man."[15]

(410) The third is that their position as preachers is cheapened. If there is a lot of anything around, its value decreases. So it says, "No prophet is accepted in his own country" *(Luke 4:24)*, in the place, that is, in which he has lived for a long time and where he has often been seen.

So this kind of excess is always to be avoided, even when there is good reason to travel.

## THE RIGHT WAY TO TRAVEL

(XXIV 411) There are seven things required to make a preacher's travelling praiseworthy.

First, the preacher himself must be fitted for it, which not everybody is. This is why the disciples were told, "Stay in the city until you are clothed with power from on high" *(Luke 24:29)*.

(412) Secondly, the aim of his travelling must be to produce spiritual results. "I pray that I may at last, in God's will, be able to succeed in visiting you. I long to see you, so that I may impart to you some spiritual grace" *(Rom. 1:10–11)*.

(413) Thirdly, it must be seasoned with obedience. So Isaiah asked to be commanded to go, even though he wanted to go. "Here I am, send me" *(Isaiah 6:8)*.

(414) Fourthly, the travelling preacher must proceed carefully. It is easy for a traveller to lose the goods he has with him through being attacked or because of some accident or in many other ways, unless he is careful. So it says, "See that you walk carefully" *(Eph. 5:15)*.

(415) Fifthly, he must always have his eye on the chance to achieve some good, whether he is on the way or in someone's house, whether he is with few people or many. "As they went, they went sowing their seed" *(Psalm 125:6)*, that is to say, sowing their seed not only when they were staying somewhere, but also when they were on the move.

(416) Sixthly, he must not undertake an undue burden of travelling. Some people cover so much ground in one day that when they arrive at some lodging place, they are unable to say Mass or the Office with reverence, or to preach or to do anything of the kind; they are so tired that they must simply rest and do nothing else at all. But it says

of the holy Living Beings in Ezekiel 1:7 (which are a symbol of preachers), "The soles of their feet were like the soles of the feet of a calf," which moves in a balanced way.[16]

(417) Seventhly, he must see that his journey is shielded by continual prayer, like David, who constantly utters prayers like this: "Lord God, make my way straight in your sight."[17] This is why religious have a custom of reciting special prayers every day for the journey they are engaged in.[18]

### How a Preacher Should Live Among Men

(418) We must now consider (a) why good conduct among men is necessary for a preacher, (b) what this means in practice and (c) what can help him to achieve it.

## WHY A PREACHER'S CONDUCT AMONG MEN MUST BE GOOD

(XXXV 419) It is part of the preacher's job to live in such a way that God is glorified not only by his words but also by his example, in accordance with the commandment given to the first preachers, "Let your light so shine before men, that they may see your good works and glorify your Father in heaven."[19] And it is good conduct that brings this about. "Your conduct among the gentiles should be good, so that, even if they revile you as evildoers, they may yet come to glorify God because of the good works they find in you" *(1 Pet. 2:12).*

(420) Also preachers are concerned to win the salvation of others in any way they can. And sometimes this is achieved better by good conduct than by words. "Wives are to be subject to their husbands, so that even men who do not give credence to the spoken word may be won over by the conduct of their wives" *(1 Pet. 3:1).* If good conduct in a woman is so effective by itself, how much more effective will it be in a preacher when it is added to the spoken word?

(421) It is also their responsibility to assist the sick not only with words and prayers, but also by their merits. And merits are a matter of good conduct. And so it is often the quality of their conduct which actually helps the sick. "They will ask the Lord to prosper their patients' rest and healing because of their own conduct" *(Ecclus.*

*38:14).* This is interpreted as applying to doctors of the soul as well as to doctors of the body.[20]

(422) They ought also to bring credit on their ministry, like the apostle, who says, "As long as I am apostle to the gentiles, I will bring honour to my ministry" *(Rom. 11:13).* And this is done by good conduct. So it says, "Giving offense to no one, so that our ministry will not be reviled" *(2 Cor. 6:3),* on which the Gloss says, "The ministry is that of the apostolate, and it would be reviled if we were to do this,"[21] namely fail to demonstrate by our example the message we teach with our words.

(423) It is also necessary for preachers to confound their enemies to their face. And good conduct makes this possible. "Having a good conscience, in a modest and respectful spirit, so that people who abuse your good conduct in Christ may find that their reproaches turn to their own confusion" *(1 Pet. 3:16).*

And not only do they have to confound them to their face, they also have to stop their mouths; and good conduct makes this possible too. "This is the will of God, that by doing good you should silence the ignorance of foolish men" *(1 Pet. 2:15).*

And not only do they have to stop their mouths, they even have to quell their hearts; and this too comes about by means of holy conduct. "Always show yourself an example of good deeds, in teaching, in integrity, in seriousness, a word which is sound and beyond reproach, so that the enemy may be afraid, having nothing evil to say against you" *(Titus 2:7–8).*

(424) What we have said shows that good conduct enables us to give glory to God, to save souls, to help sick souls, to bring honour to the office of preacher, to withstand enemies. And all of these things are relevant to preachers. And so it is obvious in what way it is necessary that his conduct among men should be good.

## WHAT THIS GOOD CONDUCT CONSISTS OF

(XXXVI 425) We must notice that there are many things involved in the preacher's good conduct among men, but the first thing is that his conduct should be good in the sight of God. Otherwise his whole public presentation of himself would simply be hypocrisy. Paul speaks of this when he says, "I have lived with a completely good conscience in the sight of God" *(Acts 23:1).*

(426) But his conduct must not only be good in the secrecy of his own conscience before God, it must be seen to be good publicly, before men. "Be an example to believers in word and conduct, in love, in faith, in chastity" *(1 Tim. 4:12)*.

(427) And it must not be good just from a particular point of view, it must be thoroughly good in every respect. "Wishing in everything to conduct yourselves well" *(Hebr. 13:18)*. And there is no human company in which this does not apply: "Taking thought for good not only in the sight of God, but in the sight of all men" *(Rom. 12:17)*. And his conduct must be good everywhere: "We lived our life in the grace of God in this world" *(2 Cor. 1:12)*, not just in one part of the world. And it must be good the whole time: "I have lived with a completely good conscience to this day" *(Acts 23:1)*. So it says, "Be holy in all your way of life" *(1 Pet. 1:15)*—*all* your way of life, that is, with regard to everything and everybody, in every place and all the time.

(428) It must be adult too. It is unseemly for a preacher to have anything childish or frivolous in his character. Gregory says, "A preacher will have difficulty in getting his words accepted, if he appears to be frivolous in his character."[22]

(429) It must also be solid. There are some good men who change when they are with wicked men, and adapt themselves to them like a chameleon changing its colour in accordance with whatever it is attached to. "They mingled with the gentiles and learned their works."[23] But Jeremiah says, "They shall be converted to you, not you to them" *(Jer. 15:19)*.

(430) A preacher's way of life ought also to be productive. It is not appropriate that a preacher should ever be idle in the presence of the people he is living with. He should always be devoting himself to some chance of getting results, like Paul, who says, "For three years I have never stopped encouraging and admonishing each one of you, with tears, by day and by night" *(Acts 20:31)*.

(431) He should also live in such a way that people find him acceptable and likeable. "All his family and all his children continued in a good way of life and in holy conduct, so that it was acceptable to God and to men and to all the inhabitants of the land" *(Tobit 14:17)*.

(432) There are many things which make for this kind of likeableness. One is being sensible in what you say. "A man who is wise in his words makes himself likeable" *(Ecclus. 20:13)*.

(433) Another is to be gentle in all you do. "My son, do all your

works with gentleness, and you will be loved beyond human glory"[24] *(Ecclus. 3:19)*.

(434) Another is to avoid behaving in a way which is strange to people. This is why Paul conformed himself to everybody as far as he reasonably could. "Every animal likes its own kind" *(Ecclus. 13:19)*.

(435) Another is to be ready to comply with others in your affairs. The wise man says, "Compliance makes friends."[25] Because of this Paul says, "In everything I try to please everyone, seeking not my own good, but the good of many" *(1 Cor. 10:33)*, as if to say, "Trying to please people by this kind of compliance."

(436) Another is humble comportment. "Pride is revolting to God and man" *(Ecclus. 10:7)*. This must mean conversely that humility wins men's love.

(437) Another is affectionate sympathy. Anyone is pleased to find somebody who will sympathise with him. "Men of mercy find favour in the eyes of all flesh" *(Ecclus. 44:27)*.

(438) Another is manifest virtue. Virtue is so powerful that it wins love wherever it appears openly. It is said of Sebastian, whom God had steeped in his grace, that "nobody could help loving him."[26] Cicero says, in his book *On Friendship*, "Nothing is more likeable than virtue, nothing is more certain to attract people to love you."[27]

## AIDS TO THE ACHIEVEMENT OF GOOD CONDUCT

(XXXVII 439) It is not much use knowing that it is necessary for our conduct to be good and knowing what this consists of, unless our conduct actually is good; so we must consider what will help us to achieve it.

One aid is to have a good model to look at. We see this in painters, who paint better when they follow a good model which they keep before their eyes. "I learned discipline by example" *(Prov. 24:32)*. And what a good model for us the Son of God is! Bernard says of him, "O good Jesus, how attractively you lived among men!"[28] And what a good model the apostle is, who offers himself as an example of good conduct to the assembled senior priests, saying, "You know how, from the first day I entered Asia, I have been with you the whole time, serving God in all humility and gentleness, in tears and in trials arising from the plotting of the Jews; you know that I have not withheld from you anything that was helpful, but have proclaimed it all to you and taught you publicly and in your homes" *(Acts 20:18–20).*

(440) Another aid is instruction, as the case of a novice makes clear: as a result of his master's instruction, he learns how to do everything that is involved in the discipline of regular life, which he did not know beforehand. The apostle gives instruction about this to the preacher, saying in 1 Tim. 3:14–15, "I am writing to you, my son Timothy, though I hope to come to you soon, so that, if I am delayed, you will know how you ought to conduct yourself in the house of God, which is the church of the living God."

(441) Another aid is provided by commandments, as we see in the case of a servant whose master says to him, "Do this," and he does it. The apostle gives a commandment about good conduct to the preacher Titus, "In everything show yourself an example of good works, in teaching, integrity and seriousness" *(Titus 2:7).*

(442) Wisdom is also a help, because it teaches a man how to conduct himself well in the middle of a perverse and crooked race. "Who is the wise and disciplined man among you? Let him show his works by his good conduct, with gentleness" *(James 3:13).*

(443) Also attentive study. A woman who wants to be beautifully dressed devotes a lot of thought and attention to the matter, and holy men should do the same to acquire beautiful conduct. "Studying to be beautiful," as it says in Ecclesiasticus 44:6, with reference to holy men, meaning "beautiful in their conduct."

(444) Also determined effort. It is hard to walk through dirt and keep oneself spotless, and so it calls for a lot of care. So Peter, talking about the virtues involved in good conduct, says, "Taking every precaution, supply virtue in your faith, knowledge in your virtue, abstinence in your knowledge, patience in your abstinence, love of the brotherhood in your patience, and charity in your love of the brotherhood" *(2 Pet. 1:5–7).*

(445) Another aid is giving up bad habits, in the same way that people take off their old clothes when they want to dress themselves finely in new clothes. "Put off the old man with your former way of life . . . and put on the new man, who is created in the likeness of God in justice and in the holiness of truth" *(Eph. 4:22,24).*

(446) Another aid is diligence in keeping a watch on oneself. It is as easy to lose goodness in the company of bad men, unless you guard it jealously, as it is to lose your clothes in a bad hostelry. So it says, "Blessed is he who keeps watch and guards his clothes, to avoid

having to go about naked and let men see his shame" *(Apoc. 16:15)*. The clothes referred to are a man's good external conduct.

(447) It is also helpful frequently to wash off whatever dirt may be picked up, as we do when clothes get dirty: they are washed to make them presentable again. So Leviticus 15:5ff says that if anyone touches one of the things listed, things which are unclean, that is, "He is to wash his clothes." That stands for his external conduct. So holy men frequently examine their lives and ask for the comments of others too, and whenever they find anything bad, they wash it off by contrition, confession and penance.

### Personal Conversations with People

(448) (a) There are some preachers so silent, when they are not preaching, that they hardly ever say anything edifying in private conversation with anybody; and this is a fault.

(b) There are others, and this is a worse fault, who bubble over with words, as if they were not religious at all, not minding what they say.

(c) Finally, there are some who observe the mean, not being unduly silent, but equally not being careless in what they say, overflowing with edifying words. And this is excellent.

## PREACHERS WHO HAVE NOTHING TO SAY WHEN THEY ARE NOT PREACHING

(XXXVIII 449) People like this are certainly not following any example given by our Lord Jesus Christ. He poured out edifying words, not only in his public preaching, but also in private conversation. He did this when he was travelling, for instance. While he was actually on the move, walking, "Beginning with Moses and all the prophets, he expounded to them everything that is said about himself in all the scriptures," so that they said, "Was not our heart ablaze while he spoke to us on the way?" *(Luke 24:27,32)*. Similarly, when he was resting during a journey, "Being tired from his travels, Jesus sat down by a well" *(John 4:6)*, and there ensued a wonderful, long, conversation which he had with a Samaritan woman. He also spoke to his travelling companions: "He said to those who were following him, 'Truly I say to you, I have not found such faith in Israel. I tell you, many will come from the east and from the west and will sit down with Abraham and Isaac and Jacob in the kingdom of heaven' " *(Matt. 8:10–11).* He also spoke to those who met him on the way: He said to some lepers who came to meet him, "Show yourselves to the priests" *(Luke 17:14).*

(450) He did the same thing too when he was staying in someone's house. He spoke to people before a meal, while the food was being prepared, as the case of Mary shows, who sat at his feet and listened to his words, while Martha prepared the meal *(Luke 10:39–40).* He also spoke to people during the meal: "Noticing how they were all choosing the best places, he told the guests a parable, 'When you are invited to a wedding, do not occupy the place of honour' " *(Luke 14:7–8).* He also spoke after the meal, as we can see in John 13:2ff, in the discourse which he spoke to his disciples after the Last Supper.

(451) He spoke to people at night, as we learn from the conversation he had with Nicodemus *(John 3:2ff),* and also during the day, as when he spoke with Nathanael *(John 1:47ff).* He spoke to his disciples, as we can see in many places in the gospels; he also spoke to his opponents: "Jesus replied to the lawyers and pharisees" *(Luke 14:3).* And he did not only speak to people before his Passion—"These words I spoke to you while I was still with you" *(Luke 24:44)*—but also after his Resurrection: "He appeared to them during forty days and spoke to them about the kingdom of God" *(Acts 1:3).*

(452) And we do not have only Christ's example for this. Another outstanding preacher says, "For three years I have never ceased exhorting each one of you, by day and by night, with tears" *(Acts 20:31).*

So we have the example of Christ himself and of the most important preacher to come after him for private edifying conversations of this kind.

(453) And every priest ought to follow this example. So Gregory says to priests in his homily *Designavit,* "Anyone who attaches himself to our company ought to be seasoned with salt from our mouth. If we see anyone loping around from one liaison to the next, we must encourage him to try to restrain his iniquity by getting married,[29] so that he can learn to control his unlawful passions by using what is lawful. If we come across a married man, we ought to encourage him

to make sure that his involvement in worldly responsibilities does not lead him to put the love of God in second place, and that his desire to give his wife pleasure does not make him displease his Creator. If we come across a cleric, we should encourage him to live in such a way that he will be an example for men living in the world, and to make sure that men's opinion of our religion is not diminished because of any fault of his—as it will be, if people can rightly find fault with him in any way. If we meet a monk, we must encourage him to consider always the reverence due to his habit in everything he does or says or thinks, and to leave behind him completely all wordly concerns, and to present before the eyes of God a picture of life and character which accords with the picture presented before the eyes of men by his religious habit. So anyone we meet who is already holy must be encouraged to grow, and anyone who is still a sinner must be encouraged to mend his ways, so that everyone who comes into a priest's company will find himself seasoned with the salt of his conversation and will turn from evil."[30]

(454) The same commandment is given not only to priests, in fact, but to all christians. So the supreme Pope, Peter, says, "If anyone speaks, he should do so as one speaking God's words."[31] And the supreme teacher says, "No evil word should come forth from your mouth, but whatever is good and likely to build up faith, so that it may bring grace to those who hear it" *(Eph. 4:29).*

(455) Now if every priest and, indeed, every christian is obliged to do this, what ought the preacher to do about it, when his very job is to be a teacher?

(456) It is also worth remarking that a private conversation about some good matter is often more effective than a public sermon, and there are two reasons for this. One is that in private conversation you can give a man advice and encouragement about the things that are most necessary for his particular situation. It is the same as with a doctor, who can talk to a sick man in his home about his more personal requirements, in a way which would be impossible in a public lecture in the classroom. We are taught this in Ecclesiasticus 37:12–14, where it says, "With an irreligious man talk about holiness, with an unrighteous man about righteousness, with a woman about her jealousies, with a coward about war, with a merchant about transport, with a buyer about sales, with an envious man about thankfulness, with unkind men about kindness, with a dishonourable

man about honour, with a farm worker about every kind of work, with a salaried worker about the end of the year, with a lazy servant about working hard."

(457) The other reason is that words spoken in private conversation are likely to make a deeper impression. An arrow aimed directly at someone usually goes in further than one shot at random. So Tobit, speaking personally to his son, says, "My son, listen to the words I speak and lay them like a foundation in your heart." They are to be a foundation because they are fixed deeply in place. His son replied, "Father, I will do everything you have commanded me" *(Tobit 4:2, 5:1)*. Who ever said such a thing about everything he heard in a public sermon?

(458) It should also be noticed that talk of this kind enhances the reputation of the speaker. It is a very powerful evidence that a man really has God in his heart if he chooses to speak about him often. So Gregory says, "In the judgment of men, a man's heart is always gauged on the basis of what he says."[32] And Isidore says, "It is a man's tongue that publishes his character; the sort of mind he has is shown by the sort of words he speaks."[33] And so the kind of people who talk about God often and everywhere are generally considered to be good, holy men.

(459) It also serves to increase a man's merit. A manual labourer earns the more, the more often he applies his hands to his job, and similarly a preacher merits more, the more often he uses his tongue to good purpose, not only in public speaking, but also in private exhortation. So it says, "The Lord gave me a tongue for my income" *(Ecclus. 51:30)*.

(460) This means that the preacher himself benefits from such conversations both with regard to his reputation and with regard to his merit.

(461) So we can see that there are four considerations which ought to inspire the preacher to be a ready source of edifying words in his private conversations with other people: the example of great men, the precepts of less great men, fruitfulness in others and benefit to himself.

# HUMBERT OF ROMANS

## PREACHERS WHOSE CONVERSATION IS
## DEVOID OF SERIOUS CONTENT AND WORLDLY

(XXXIX 462) Some preachers forget what they are and overflow with idle chatter in their private conversation. In them is fulfilled what it says in Psalm 40:7–8, "If he came in to see me, he spoke idle words. . . . He went out and did the same," because when they come into their convent for a time of contemplation, they retail idle gossip from outside to the brethren, and when they go out again they do the same thing with men in the world.

(463) This may happen at the devil's prompting. He gladly engineers it so that a mouth which speaks the praises of God and strives for the good of souls becomes cheap because of this kind of idle chatter and gives a bad example to others. Chrysostom says in his *Homilies on Matthew*, "Every idle word which is spoken comes forth at the inspiration of an unclean spirit."[34]

(464) Sometimes it is due to the fatuousness of the preacher's heart. The tongue can bring forth into speech only what is already there in the heart, and so a tongue which speaks fatuous words is evidence of a fatuous heart. As Isidore says, "Empty speech is evidence of an empty conscience."[35]

(465) Sometimes it comes from thoughtlessness. Many people do not think before they speak; whatever comes into their mouth, they utter it without hesitation. This means that they often pour out a stream of idle words. There is an anecdote about this in the *Lives of the Fathers*. Two brothers went to visit St. Anthony, and while they were on their way there they were joined by an old man who wanted to go the same way. While they were in the boat, the two brothers talked a lot of nonsense. When they arrived at St. Anthony's cell, he said to the brothers, "Did you find the old man a good travelling companion?" They said, "Yes." Then he asked the old man, "Did you find these brothers good travelling companions?" He said, "Yes, only their house has no door. Anyone who wants to can go in and untie the ass." By this he meant that they always uttered any word that came into their mouths.[36] This is the opposite of what is said of the just man, that "his mouth ponders wisdom,"[37] which means that he ponders on what he is going to say before he says it. Ambrose says, "A word ought to be tested before it is spoken."[38]

(466) Sometimes it comes from a lack of anything good to say. Many people come out with pointless remarks just because they

299

cannot for the moment think of anything to say. But in that case it would be better to say nothing, because that is how even a fool can come to be thought of as wise. "He is silent because he lacks the intelligence to speak" *(Ecclus. 20:6)*.

(467) Sometimes it is the result of spending a long time with other people who engage in idle chatter. This is, after all, the way in which people learn to speak the language of other men and forget their own, even if their own is a better language. A Frenchman who lives for a long time with people of a different language will to some extent forget his own language and learn theirs. The children of some of the Jews "spoke half in the language of the gentiles" *(Neh. 13:24)*. This was because of their fathers' wives, who spoke foreign languages.

(468) Sometimes it is due to lack of balance and measure. It sometimes happens that people catering in a household do not measure the corn or wine, so that they supply too much, which is then wasted. In the same way a foolish man who does not weigh his words pours out too many unnecessary words. As Gregory says, "People who do not know how to measure their words will inevitably drift towards idle words."[39]

(469) There are many reasons why preachers ought to keep clear of idle words. They are, as it says, God's mouth: "If you distinguish between what is valuable and what is cheap, you will be, as it were my mouth" *(Jer. 15:19)*. This text is taken to refer to preachers.[40] And it is most unseemly that the mouth of God should speak idle words.

(470) Again, the mouth of the preacher is a spring from which the sweet water of wisdom flows. So it is unnatural for it to yield the bitterness of foolish words. "Does a spring produce sweet water and bitter water from the same opening?" *(James 3:11)*.

(471) Again, the preacher's mouth is consecrated to the words of God, and so he ought all the more to avoid the words of the world. Anything which is consecrated to God ought never to be put to worldly use. As Bernard says, "You have consecrated your mouth to the gospel; to open it for trifles is unlawful, and to make a habit of it is sacrilege."[41]

(472) Again, good preachers are not of this world, they are from above, just as Christ was not of this world. So as they travel about through the world, they ought not to abandon the language of heaven in favour of that of the earth, any more than a Frenchman will readily abandon his own language, wherever he may go, in favour of

any other language, because he respects the nobility of his own language and his own country. "He who is of the earth speaks from the earth. . . . But anyone whom God has sent speaks God's words, not those of the world" *(John 3:31,34)*.

(473) Again, children at school are supposed to speak Latin, not the vernacular, and if they accidentally slip into the vernacular they are punished immediately with a cane, to their great embarrassment. How much more ought people to be embarrassed and punished who speak idle words, when they were supposed to be saying something useful. "On the day of judgment men will have to answer for every idle world they have spoken" *(Matt. 12:36)*. This must apply particularly to preachers.

(474) Again, Bernard says, " 'The lips of a priest guard knowledge and men expect to receive the law from his mouth': the law, not trifles or gossip."[42] How much more is this true of someone who is not only a priest, but a preacher too. It is not trifles or gossip that people look for from his mouth.

(475) Again, there is a story in the *Lives of the Fathers* about two sisters, who were the wives of two brothers, who lived in the same house. They contracted with each other that for the rest of their lives no worldly speech should ever be heard from their lips.[43] What an embarrassment! Here are two women, who are not allowed to preach, keeping themselves so carefully from worldly speech, and yet preachers gush out with worldly speech!

(476) Again, Isidore says, in his book *On the Supreme Good*, "There ought to be no idle speech in a christian's mouth. Bad behaviour is undermined by good conversations, and so is good behaviour undermined by bad conversations."[44] Now if every christian has to avoid undermining himself like this, how much more ought a preacher, whose task it is to edify others with his words.

(477) Again, there is some excuse for it when worldly men talk about worldly affairs, because they are ignorant of the scriptures which give us useful things to talk about. But this cannot excuse preachers, because they do know the scriptures. Ambrose says, "You have all these utterances of God and all these deeds of his in Genesis, Exodus, Leviticus, in Numbers and Deuteronomy and Joshua and Judges and the books of Kings and Ezra, and in the gospel and the Acts of the Apostles. You take no small risk if you ignore all this and talk about worldly things instead and listen to worldly talk."[45]

(478) Again, Gregory says in one of his *Dialogues* that when we

talk with worldly men, "We move from what is idle to what is harmful, from what is trivial to what is grave, and the more our mouths are defiled with foolish speech, the less they will be heard by God when we pray."[46] This shows what harm a preacher can do to himself, if he abounds with idle words like this. He travels round for the good of others, but after he has finished his work of preaching, it is to prayer that he has to return, and in this way he makes his prayers useless.

## PREACHERS WHO ARE CONCERNED THAT THEIR CONVERSATION SHOULD BE HELPFUL

(XL 479) Preachers who do intend to edify other people in what they say in their private conversation need to bear several things in mind. Gregory says, "A teacher has to ponder what to say, who to say it to, when to say it and how much to say,"[47] and we may add that he has also to ponder how to say it.

(480) When we are considering what to say, we must realise that in conversations of this kind it is sometimes right to speak holy words,[48] sometimes right to tell some good illustrative stories, and sometimes right even to speak a few words about worldly things.

Holy words ought not to be uttered at random all over the place, but only some which are remarkable for their clarity, so that people will not have any difficulty in understanding them, and for the attractiveness of their subject matter, so that people will like to hear them, and for their usefulness, so that people will be the better for hearing them.

Exemplary stories must be of sufficient authority not to be despised, and they must be credible enough not just to be met with disbelief, and there must be some useful moral in them, so that it is not pointless to refer to them.

If worldly talk is sometimes used, to make people feel at home, it should never be allowed to become too remote from the words of God. As it says, "If anyone speaks, it should be as one who speaks God's words" *(1 Pet. 4:11)*. Worldly talk should not be used too often, and when it is used, there should always be something mixed in with it which is of spiritual value.

(481) When we are considering who to talk to, we should realise

that there are some people to whom we should not talk like this at all, as we have already said in §§206ff. There are others with whom it is proper to converse, but not proper for everybody. It is not appropriate that a man of little authority or with little grace should converse with people more important than himself. "Do not take liberties in the presence of important people, and do not speak much where there are old men present" *(Ecclus. 32:13)*. But there are some people with whom anyone who knows how to converse can properly speak, such as people of less importance, uneducated people and the laity.

(482) When we are thinking about when to speak, we should be careful never to address people except when they are sober, because that is when the mind is alert to understand what is being said; free from other occupations—the Lord did not speak to Martha, who was busy, but to Mary, who was at leisure;[49] and ready to listen, because you ought not to speak when no one is listening.[50] So when the Lord wanted to speak to the pharisee, he attracted his attention first by saying to him, "Simon, I have something to say to you," to which he replied, "Speak, Master."[51]

The most important time to speak in this way is when there is a chance of your words turning the conversation discreetly and unobtrusively away from worldly and wicked talk.

(483) When we are considering how much to say, we must see that we do not speak all the time and do not say too much and do not go on too long, in case people get bored with us. A right balance will be observed if we only make occasional interventions in the conversation, and not too many of them, and keep them brief.

(484) When we are considering how to speak, it all depends on whom we are with. We must do as Paul teaches, "Do not rebuke an old man, but entreat him as if he were your father, address young men as brothers, elderly women as mothers, girls as sisters, in all purity" *(1 Tim. 5:1–2)*.

Again, it is sometimes right to speak secretly, away from other people, and sometimes it is better to speak openly in the presence of others, as our Lord teaches.[52]

Sometimes it is right to say little and to say it concisely, sometimes it is right to speak at greater length, depending on the people and the subject matter.

More can be found on this subject in the section on the judicious practice of preaching in §§206ff.

## The Preacher and His Hosts

(XLI 485) There are some poor preachers who do not have enough confidence in God, and so, when they are travelling, they become too anxious about finding somewhere to stay, where they will be able to get all that they need. They are rebuked by what the Lord says, "When I sent you out without a bag or purse,[53] did you lack anything?" They answered, "Nothing" *(Luke 22:35)*.

(486) Some of them do not just worry too much about where they are going to stay, but because of this they even turn aside from places in which their preaching might have been more fruitful, in their determination to find good lodgings and avoid bad. But this is quite contrary to the example of our Saviour, who very frequently went to preach in Jerusalem, in spite of the fact that, after preaching there all day long, he had to go away again in the evening, owing to the lack of hospitality there, to find lodging at Bethany (see Mark 11:11 and the Gloss there).[54]

(487) Others do even worse than this, because of their lack of confidence, and take some provisions with them, which they are not allowed to do. This is contrary to Luke 9:3, "Take nothing with you on the way, no purse or money or bread."

(488) Others are less careful than they might be about what kind of hosts they stay with, and so they sometimes lodge with people of bad or doubtful repute. This is contrary to Matt. 10:11, which says, "In whatever city or village you enter, find out who is worthy there." This is glossed, "A host should be chosen on the basis of what his neighbours say about him; in this way the preaching will not be harmed by his bad reputation."[55]

(489) Others ask for far more than they need in the way of food and drink, or let it be prepared for them, and this is most unseemly in Christ's poor. In Luke 10:7 it says, "Eat and drink what is there," which is tantamount to saying, "Be content with what is there in the house, so that no extra provision has to be made because of your arrival."

(490) There are others who show few or no signs of holiness in the places where they stay, and so do not leave a good opinion of themselves behind them. This is quite unlike what Elisha's hostess said of him to her husband. She said, "I realise that this man who keeps passing by this way is a holy man of God." And see how this increased her devotion to him: she goes on, "Let us make a little room,

and put a bed in it and a table and a chair and a candle, so that he can stay there when he comes to us" *(4 Kings 4:9–10).*

(491) There are others who wear out devoted hosts by visiting them too often. To avoid this, Paul even worked with his own hands. "Working night and day to avoid being a burden to any of you" *(1 Thess. 2:9).*

(492) There are others who receive many kindnesses from their hosts and yet are too ungrateful to give them anything in return. This is contrary to what we read of holy men who were very grateful to their hosts and laboured on their behalf before God and men. Elijah is an example of this: he cried out to God on behalf of his widowed hostess's son, "Lord my God, have you now afflicted even this widow who looks after me, and killed her son?" *(3 Kings 17:20).* At his prayers, the boy was brought back to life.

Elisha is another example. He said to his hostess, "You have served me zealously in every possible way, what can I do for you? Is there any affair of yours you would like me to mention to the king or to the commander of the army?" She replied that she lacked a son, so he got her a son through his prayers, and later restored him to life when he died *(4 Kings 4:13ff).*

Paul is another example. He says, "I commend our sister Phoebe to you, who is a servant of the church at Cenchreae. Receive her in the Lord in a way which is fitting to the saints, and assist her in any affair in which she may need your help. For she has assisted many people, including me" *(Rom. 16:1–2).* According to the Gloss she was a woman of the highest nobility, who maintained the church at Cenchreae, and she had gone to Rome on some business, and this was why Paul, who was grateful to her, made this request. [56]

(493) There are other people who get angry with those who refuse to put them up, and sometimes burst out in abuse and other foul language. They ought to take note of Luke 9:51ff. "He set his face to go towards Jerusalem, and he sent messengers before him, and they came to a Samaritan city to make preparations for his arrival. But the people would not receive them, because his face was towards Jerusalem. When his disciples James and John saw this, they said, 'Lord, would you like us to tell fire to come down from heaven and destroy them, as Elijah did?' " Notice how the Lord checked them at once: the story goes on, "He turned and rebuked them. 'You do not know what spirit has inspired you. The son of man has not come to destroy men's lives, but to save them.' "

(494) From all of this we can gather that a good, poor, preacher of Christ ought not to be very worried about where he is going to stay, nor should he avoid places because of this, if they are likely to respond fruitfully to his preaching; nor should he take provisions with him. He ought to avoid staying in places of doubtful repute. He ought to be content with simple, meagre fare wherever he goes. He ought to leave behind him, wherever he has been staying, a good impression of himself. He ought to be careful not to be a burden to his hosts. He must be grateful for the hospitality he receives, and not be resentful when hospitality is refused him.

### The Preacher's Involvement in Secular Affairs

(XLII 495) Some preachers are so averse to any kind of worldly business that they refuse to help their hearers even in works of kindness. They are like ostriches which neglect their young,[57] and are not following the example of the Lord, who had such compassion on the crowds which followed his preaching that he fed them miraculously in the desert, so that they would not faint by the wayside[58] *(John 6:5ff)*. He also granted healings and many other boons to his hearers. "He went about doing good and healing those who were oppressed by the devil" *(Acts 10:38)*.

(496) Paul also wrote letters on behalf of his converts to the faith, as we see from the last chapters of his letters to the Romans *(Rom. 16:1–2)* and the Corinthians *(1 Cor. 16:10–11)*. He also organised collections for them *(1 Cor. 16:1, 2 Cor. 9:1–5)*. His compassion made him so anxious about them that he said, "In addition to all these external things, there is my constant anxiety every day for all the churches. Who is weak and I am not weak? Who is upset and I am not set on fire" *(2 Cor. 11:28–9)*.

(497) All the apostles too in the early church cared for their converts to such an extent that they provided them with all their needs, as we see from the Acts of the Apostles *(Acts 4:35)*.

(498) Moreover the *perfecti* among the heretics take such care of their followers that they never stop travelling around collecting alms for them, so that they will be able to support their poor and in this way lure others to subscribe to their belief. How much more does it belong to true preachers[59] to undertake this kind of charitable work.

(499) Again, on John 21:18, "Feed my sheep," the Gloss says, "If need be, provide them with material support."[60] And when it says,

"Feed the Lord's flock that is with you, providing for them" *(1 Pet. 5:2)*, the Gloss comments, "Providing your subjects with all that they need."[61]

(500) This makes it clear that it is not the good preacher's part to keep himself so free of his hearers' concerns that he does not assist them in their needs and in works of kindness, when and where it is appropriate. So Gregory says, in his *Pastoral Rule*, "Some people are so keen to have all their time to themselves for spiritual affairs, that they do not concern themselves at all with any external matters. But their radical neglect of the concerns of the body means that they fail to help their people in their needs. This often leads to their preaching being ignored, because they castigate the activities of those who go astray without providing them with the necessities of this present life, so that there is no joy in listening to them. If a man is in want, no word of teaching will reach his mind, if it is not backed up by the hand of mercy. The seed of the spoken word will germinate most easily when it is watered in the hearer's heart by the kindness of the preacher."[62]

(501) On the other hand, there are some who become too much entangled in human affairs, whether it be in connexion with their friends' affairs or in connexion with taking on responsibility for women or in connexion with all the various people who apply to them. Gregory says of them in his *Pastoral Rule*, "Some pastors forget that they have been given responsibility for the sake of men's souls, and apply all their energy and attention to worldly affairs. They love working on worldly business when there is any to hand, and when there is none, their minds seethe day and night in eager anticipation of more to come. And when they are forced to retire because there is no opportunity to engage in any kind of business, they are more worn out by their enforced leisure than they ever were before. They consider it a pleasure to be weighed down with jobs to do, and a frightful chore to have no earthly work to tackle."[63]

(502) We must notice that this excessive involvement on the part of a poor, religious preacher has three unfortunate consequences.

First, it defiles his position as a preacher. Jeremiah laments this, according to Gregory's interpretation in the *Pastoral Rule:* "How tarnished their gold has become, how changed is its excellent colour! The stones of the sanctuary are scattered at the head of every street" *(Lam. 4:1)*. Gregory comments, "Their gold is tarnished when their life of holiness is polluted by worldly pursuits. Their excellent colour is altered when people come to think less well of those who had been regarded as living a religious life. When a man takes on a religious habit and then proceeds to involve himself in worldly activities, his colour is, so to speak, altered in the eyes of men, and the respect he enjoyed pales into disregard. The stones of the sanctuary are scattered in the city streets when those who ought to be devoting themselves to beautifying the church inwardly by their service, as in the hidden place of the sanctuary, come out to seek the broad paths of secular concerns."[64]

(503) The second ill effect is that it gives the devil a feastday. Secular occupations of this kind are a sort of snare; when the devil finds a preacher caught in them—and preachers are his favourite quarry—he has much less difficulty in effecting his capture, and then he revels cruelly over him, like a hunter who has found an animal in his trap. "He put his foot in a snare and stepped in its meshes. His foot will be held fast in his net, and thirst will burn against him" *(Job 18:8–9)*, "thirst" meaning the devil, as the Gloss explains, the reason for this name being that he is thirsty for the death of man.[65]

(504) The third ill effect is that it gets in the way of preaching. A man who becomes too busy with this kind of business becomes too busy to preach. And a preacher ought to avoid that. So preachers are told, "Carry no purse" *(Luke 10:4)*, on which Gregory comments, "What does he mean by 'purse' except the burdens of the world? So it is only right that anyone who takes on the job of being a preacher should not carry the burden of worldly business, in case it comes to weigh so heavily on his neck that he cannot rise up to preach the things of heaven."[66]

(505) Notice also that the Lord was so determined that nothing should get in the way of the preaching that he forbade his disciple to go and bury his father, saying, "Let the dead bury their dead. For your part, go and proclaim the kingdom of God" *(Luke 9:60)*.

(506) For the same reason he did not want his disciples to greet anyone on the road. "Greet nobody on the way" *(Luke 10:4)*. Gregory comments, "He does not permit the preacher to greet anyone on the way, because he wants to demonstrate with what urgency and speed he should undertake the preaching journey."[67]

(507) For the same reason he did not want them to have to worry about the necessities of life. He said, "Do not carry a bag with you" *(Luke 10:4)*. Gregory comments on this in the Gloss, "This is to prevent the preacher's mind becoming so preoccupied with temporal

things that he is less able to adminster to others the things of eternity."[68]

(508) So, if we have to abandon such things as the burial of a
father, greetings on the way, the provision of our necessities of life,
because they would constitute an obstacle to preaching, how much
more must we abandon other, even more worldly, kinds of business?

(509) So it is plain that the preacher must be careful about
getting too involved in such things, out of regard for the dignity of
his position, because of the enemy's plotting, and for fear of impeding
the preaching.

(510) This is why the pagan Jethro reproaches Moses for being
too much caught up in the people's business *(Exod. 18:14–18)*. Now
this was actually Moses' responsibility, so if he was to blame for his
involvement, how much more to blame is a preacher who does not
have any such responsibility? Gregory says, "The criticism of Jethro
the foreigner declares Moses to be putting a ridiculous amount of
work into serving the people's temporal concerns; then he offers his
advice, that he should appoint others to settle their quarrels,[69] so that
he can be free to study the mysteries of the spiritual realm for the
people's instruction."[70]

(511) For the same reason Paul the apostle is reluctant to have
men who are suited to spiritual things tied up in this kind of affair:
"If you have any secular affairs, appoint people who are of no account
in the church to settle them" *(1 Cor. 6:4)*. Gregory says that the point
of this is that "those who are not adorned with any spiritual gifts
should be entrusted with the task of ordering earthly affairs."[71]

(512) For the same reason our Saviour wanted those first and
greatest of all preachers to be poor, in case involvement in temporal
business darkened their minds about spiritual things. Gregory says,
"Rulers should keep their minds on the highest things, leaving it to
their subjects to deal with lower things, so that no concern for the
dust darkens the eye which guides men's steps from on high."[72]

Notice that if he did not want preachers to be at all concerned
about their own temporal affairs, he will not be too pleased to find
them deeply involved in other people's temporal affairs.

(513) So it is fault in a preacher to avoid men's affairs entirely,
but it is also a fault to immerse himself in them too much. So Gregory
writes in the *Pastoral Rule* about the church's leaders, part of whose
responsibility is to benefit others by their preaching, "A ruler in the
church ought not to lessen his concern for interior things because of

his involvement in external affairs, nor should he give up looking after men's external affairs in his concern for interior things. In this way he will not be so devoted to external affairs that he falls away from more interior things, nor will he be so exclusively occupied with interior things that he fails to give to his neighbours the external care which is their due."[73] So it says, "Priests are not to shave their heads or cultivate long hair; they shall keep their hair properly cut" *(Ezek. 44:20)*. Gregory comments, "Priests are rightly forbidden to shave their heads and to cultivate long hair; they must neither cut off entirely all thought for the material welfare of their people nor let such concern grow to a disproportionate size. They just cut their hair; this means they must both see to temporal concerns, in so far as it is necessary, and see that they are cut back quickly, so that they do not grow beyond due measure."[74]

(514) So we must observe the mean. And, with this in view, the preacher must be careful not to involve himself in business which reeks of the world,[75] such as looking after the worldly business of his worldly friends. The business he undertakes must always savour of the Lord, like works of kindness, negotiations for peace, pleading on behalf of people in distress, giving advice to the uneducated, and things like that. This is the spirit in which Paul forbids Timothy to be involved in secular affairs, but at the same time prompts him to perform works of kindness: "Exercise yourself in kindness" *(1 Tim. 4:7)*.

(515) Further, it is important for a preacher to avoid giving any kind of offense to anybody, so that the fruitfulness of his preaching will not be obstructed. He must be like Paul, who tried to please everyone in every way, as he says *(1 Cor. 10:33)*. Therefore he ought to shun jobs which incur men's dislike, such as arbitrating settlements, official investigations,[76] visitations and other such judicial work, in the course of which it is frequently impossible to avoid offending many people. When the Lord was asked by somebody to tell his brother to divide an inheritance with him, he replied, "Man, who appointed me a judge or arbitrator over you?" *(Luke 12:14)*. So, if the judge of the living and the dead declined this kind of judicial activity, when he had become a preacher, how much more ought other poor preachers to do likewise?

(516) Then there are some kinds of business which are risky and uncertain of success, such as marriage negotiations,[77] canvassing for

people to receive appointments or ecclesiastical benefices, assisting in the councils of rulers, and that kind of thing, and a wise preacher ought to avoid all such tasks, for fear that in his desire to help others, he will simply ruin himself. "What does it profit a man to gain the whole world, if he suffers the loss of his own soul?" *(Matt. 16:26)*.

(517) Again, there are some jobs which take a long time, such as being executor of somebody's will, or guardian to somebody, or contracting to get something done, and so on. The preacher ought to avoid these too, because he has to keep himself free the whole time to do his own job. So the apostle says quite explicitly, "No one who is God's soldier gets himself tangled up in worldly affairs."[78] "Tangling yourself up" means getting involved in such a way that you cannot get out again when you want to.

(518) And all this kind of business, if it is taken up at all, should only be taken up of necessity, not from desire. So Gregory says in his *Pastoral Rule,* "Secular business must sometimes be endured out of compassion, but it should never be sought as a matter of preference."[79]

### Giving Advice

(XLIII 519) It often happens that people come to preachers for advice. Crowds of people, including tax collectors and soldiers, went to John when he was preaching in the desert, asking him, "What shall we do?" *(Luke 3:10)*. And in Matt. 19:16 we are told that a man came up to the Lord Jesus and said, "Good teacher, what good deed must I do to have eternal life?" And in Acts 2:37, when Peter was preaching, the people who heard him were cut to the quick and said to him and the other apostles, "Brethren, what shall we do?"

(520) But it must be observed that some people came to the Lord with insincere questions, intended to catch him out. "Some pharisees came to Jesus to test him, and asked, 'Is it lawful for a man to divorce his wife for any reason?' " *(Matt. 19:3)*. The pharisees also tested him with the question, "Is it lawful for tribute to be paid to Caesar or not?" *(Matt. 22:17)*. On another occasion a lawyer got up and tested him with the question, "Teacher, what shall I do to possess eternal life?" *(Luke 10:25)*. The Lord reacted with caution when he was dealing with such people; he recognised their disingenuousness and

replied to their questions with prudence, as we see in the passages referred to. In this he gives subsequent preachers an example that they ought to follow.

(521) Sometimes people come wanting advice about temporal matters. And this should not be refused, when it would be kind to offer advice, provided the preacher is competent in the matter. For example, Joseph gave Pharaoh advice about gathering in the fruits of the earth for the common good of the land.[80]

(522) Some people want advice about their bodily needs, like the sick. And this too should not be refused by those who have any competence in the matter. Paul advises Timothy to use a little wine for the sake of his stomach and because of his frequent illnesses.[81]

(523) More importantly, there are sometimes people who come to ask advice about things which concern their soul and its salvation. And the preacher should devote himself more carefully to this, because men's salvation or damnation will depend on whether he gives good advice or bad.

(524) And there are some preachers who do sometimes give bad advice about things which concern men's salvation.

Sometimes this is due to ignorance. This is why advice should always be sought from the wise, and not from fools, to avoid being led astray by their ignorance. "Do not take counsel with fools" (Ecclus. 8:20).

(525) Sometimes it is due to cowardice. Some people do not have the courage to speak the truth when they are giving advice to important people, unlike John the Baptist, who boldly told Herod, "It is not lawful for you to have your brother's wife" (Mark 6:18).

(526) Sometimes it is due to flattery. People who want to please give soothing advice on such matters as restitution, which are really very serious. They are like the bad prophets of whom it says, "Woe to those who make cushions for every elbow and put pillows under the head of every generation, to ensnare souls" (Ezek. 13:18). According to the commentator,[82] the moral sense of this passage concerns people who give flattering reassurances to sinners in their wickedness. Sinners rest peacefully in their sins because of such flattery, as comfortably as men rest on cushions and pillows.

(527) Sometimes it is due to false kindness, as in the case of those who feel sorry for some of the poor and assure them that they do not have to sell everything to make restitution, and things of this kind.

But this is contrary to what it says in Exodus 23:3, "Do not spare the poor when you give judgment."

(528) Sometimes it is due to covetousness, as in the case of priests who tell people who ought to be making restitution to use the money to have Masses said instead, and anniversaries celebrated and that kind of thing, so that the money will come to them. "They have violated me before my people for the sake of a handful of barley and a piece of bread, to kill souls that were not dying and give life to souls that were not alive, lying to my people" *(Ezek. 13:19)*.

(529) Sometimes it is due to a desire to curry favour with men. This is the case with priests who claim[83] to offer "cut price" penances, so that more people will come to them. They are like Absalom, who assured all who came to him for judgment that their cause was a good one, to draw people to his side *(2 Sam. 15:2–3)*.

(530) This kind of bad advice leads to a great deal of evil. First of all, it involves deceiving the people to whom it is given. They trust the advice they receive and are led astray by it, because this does not mean that they are excused from blame if they act on it. "If you act on wicked advice, it will fall on your own head" *(Ecclus. 27:30)*. That is why it says, "Preserve your soul from a bad counsellor" *(Ecclus. 37:9)*.

(531) It also involves harm to many other people. For sometimes bad advice given to one man damages many others too, as we can see in the case of Rehoboam, who set about oppressing a whole great nation on the bad advice of his young advisers. And this led to a host of tragic consequences for the whole kingdom of Israel *(3 Kings 12:6ff)*. In the same way bad advice given to any important man about the government of his land has tragic consequences for his subjects.

(532) The adviser too suffers for it. The man who gives bad advice about the salvation of a man's soul, like the doctor who gives bad, ignorant advice about the health of a man's body, will not escape the doom of falling into the ditch with the blind man he blindly led astray by his advice.[84] "Whatever judgment you give will return upon yourselves" *(2 Chron. 19:6)*.

(533) It is also an embarrassment to the position held by the man who gives bad advice. If a ruler has bad counsellors in his court, it brings shame on the whole court; similarly it brings shame on a whole church or chapter or religious house if it has men in it who give bad advice about the salvation of men's souls. So the Lord says, to console a church which is deprived of good advisers, "I shall

restore your counsellors as they were of old" *(Isaiah 1:26)*, in the early church, that is.

(534) It also puts the church's superiors in a dangerous position. Their own souls are at risk, if they appoint men who are not competent to the job of counselling souls. So Mattathias did not give just anybody to his children as their counsellor, but a man who was tested and found competent: "I know that Simon your brother is a man of counsel; always attend to him" *(1 Macc. 2:65)*. "You shall appoint judges and teachers" *(Deut. 16:18)*, that is to say, judges of such a kind that they are also, or can be considered to be, teachers.

(535) And sooner or later a débacle occurs. For a time, maybe, such bad spiritual advisers may escape detection, but at last they are shown up and their lack of wisdom comes to the notice of their higher superiors, and then much scandal and upset results. "He brings counsellors to a foolish end" *(Job 12:17)*. According to the Gloss, this refers to certain wicked preachers.[85]

(536) To avoid this kind of danger to souls, those who have to give advice to others should make a careful study of the teaching given by wise men on restitution, simony, ecclesiastical censures, irregularities and their dispensation, vows, marriage and oaths and contracts;[86] in all of these there are particularly serious and hazardous problems that arise. The first two concern natural law, the next two concern positive law, the fifth is a matter of a man's will with regard to God, the sixth a matter of a man's will with regard to another human being, and the seventh is a matter of a man's will with regard to both God and men.

(537) For the same reason, when difficult cases arise, they should be reserved to a higher and wiser authority. As Moses says, "If anything seems too difficult for you, bring it to me and I will attend to it" *(Deut. 1:17)*.

(538) Also it is sometimes best to put off giving an answer, so that you can think about the problem more thoroughly, and take advice about it, like Job, who says, "A case which I did not understand, I investigated thoroughly" *(Job 29:16)*.

(539) Sometimes it is better to find some pretext for giving no answer at all, for instance by saying that you have no authority in the matter. It is much better to give no advice at all in cases of uncertainty than to give uncertain advice which might turn out wrong. "If you have any insight, reply to your neighbour; otherwise, keep your hand over your mouth" *(Ecclus. 5:14)*.

(540) From all of this we can see how preachers get asked for advice and on what subjects they should give advice; we see why they sometimes give bad advice about the salvation of souls, and what terrible consequences result from such bad advice; and finally we see what steps can be taken to avoid giving bad advice.

## Hearing Confessions

(XLIV 541) Sometimes there are a lot of people who are moved by a sermon and come eagerly to the preacher to make their confessions. But some preachers absolutely refuse to hear confessions, even though they are perfectly capable of doing so. They are like a farmer who is quite happy to sow, but refuses to reap, because preaching is a kind of sowing, and its harvest is gathered in in confession. Against this, it says, "Sow and reap" *(Isaiah 37:30).*

(542) There are other preachers who do sometimes hear confessions, but are only prepared to do so for favoured individuals. But the right to be heard in a public court of law is supposed to belong to everyone, and so it does too in the soul's lawcourt. "There shall be no distinction made between people; you shall listen to the small as to the great" *(Deut. 1:17).*

(543) There are others who hear as many confessions as they have time for, and confessions of all kinds of people, but all the same they give preference to those who are less sinful and need it less, over against those who need it more. This is contrary to Matt. 9:13, "I have not come to call the just, but sinners to repentance."[87]

There is a story told about a certain jester who was in church somewhere one day in Lent, and he was watching people going to confession to a particular priest who was a good man, and he noticed that he always heard the confessions of young girls first, pushing away the old women when they tried to squeeze their way in. When he saw this, the jester went out and began to shout in all the streets and thoroughfares of the town, "Old women have not got souls! Old women have not got souls!" As a result of this, he was reported to the bishop for heresy. He was summoned to come before the bishop, and they asked him if he had been saying this. He replied confidently that he had, and that he was prepared to prove it. He was given leave to speak. "My lord," he said, "You know such and such a priest, and you know that he is a good man and a good scholar?" The bishop said, "Yes." "Well," he went on, "I saw with my own eyes that he refuses to let old women come to confession, when he is hearing confessions, but only young girls. Now it is obvious that if old women had souls, they would need to go to confession more than young girls, who have lived a shorter time and committed fewer sins. Granted then that this priest is a good man and a good scholar, and granted that he refuses to hear the confessions of old women, the only possible conclusion is that old women do not have souls." When he had said this, everyone burst out laughing. But it is not just a laughing matter, it makes a mockery of the whole thing, if children who have done no harm and young girls and béguines and such like who have little need of confession are given precedence over serious sinners, when it is not the healthy who need the doctor, but the sick, as it says *(Matt. 9:12)*.

(544) There are others, by contrast, who plunge recklessly into hearing the confessions of anybody and everybody, in spite of their lack of standing, their weakness in face of temptation or their deficiencies of understanding or learning, regardless of the risk of scandal, oblivious of the temptations that come from some of the things a priest hears in confession, and with no concern for the need to give advice to their penitents. Sometimes they are motivated by curiosity, wanting to know men's secrets; sometimes they are driven by a need to be with people, because they can barely endure their own company; sometimes they have a real zeal for souls, but without knowledge,[88] which means that in striving to bring others to salvation, they may ruin themselves and the others, like someone who throws himself into the sea to help a drowning man and succeeds only in drowning with him. "He who loves danger will perish in it" *(Ecclus. 3:27)*.

(545) Then there are some people who are so jealously attached to their penitents that they cannot endure it calmly if they go to confession to somebody else, in spite of the undoubted fact that a sick man is often much the better for showing his complaint to several doctors. This was not how our Saviour behaved. When some lepers came to him, asking his mercy, he sent them elsewhere: "Go and show yourselves to the priests" *(Luke 17:14)*.

(546) There are others who make confessions an opportunity to beg, paying more attention to the material benefit which may result than to the salvation of souls. This is contrary to the apostle's teaching: "I am not looking for gifts, I am looking for results" *(Phil. 4:17)*, spiritual results, that is. And elsewhere: "We do not seek your goods, but yourselves" *(2 Cor. 12:14)*.

(547) There are others for whom hearing confessions is an occasion for them to form such intimate relationships with particular women that they defile themselves and their religion disgracefully. Just what a serious matter this is is shown by Augustine's remark, that "guilty chastity and celibacy of ill-repute are worse than adultery."[89] People like this get religion a bad name, and all their painful efforts to preserve chastity inwardly are a waste of time if they spoil it and bring it into disrepute through their outward behaviour.

(548) Others often make mistakes as confessors because they have not been adequately instructed in the job, or because they have not paid enough attention to their instruction. They make mistakes in the questions they ask, or in the absolutions they give, or in the advice they offer, or in many other things, which we have discussed fully in the last chapter of our *Treatise on the Jobs in the Order*.[90] But there is no credit in just practising some art or virtue: credit lies in practising it well. As it says, "He has done all things well' *(Mark 7:37)*.

(549) From all of this we may gather that it is part of the preacher's job to hear confessions gladly, provided he is competent enough at it; then he must not be a respecter of persons, and he must give preference to those who need confession most. But it is a bad thing if someone who is not really capable of doing the job properly is too eager to hear confessions, or if he feels aggrieved[91] if his penitents go to somebody else for confession, or if he turns hearing confessions into begging or makes it an occasion for entering into excessive familiarity with women or falls short in any other aspect of the job.

## *Prothemes*[92]

(XLV 550) It is not always necessary to have a protheme at the beginning of a sermon, or to preface the sermon with a prayer; this would be the case, for instance, in a chapter of religious who are accustomed to having sermons frequently just for themselves.

(551) Sometimes all that is needed is a preliminary prayer, asked for by the preacher; this is sufficient in parishes in which sermons are frequently preached.

(552) But on some occasions there ought to be a protheme at the beginning of the sermon. This applies, for example, when a sermon is to be preached for some very formal occasion, or when a large crowd is expected and not everybody has arrived yet, or when the sermon

has not been previously announced, so that people can discover before the sermon begins what the occasion for it is.

(553) The protheme ought to be brief enough not to be tedious, otherwise the whole sermon which follows will become a bore, if the preliminaries have been found boring.

(554) It should also be attractive, to make the listeners attentive and well-disposed and ready to learn. This is what writers usually do in the preamble to their books.

(555) At the end of the protheme, the listeners should always be asked piously for their prayers, that grace may be given during the sermon, following the example of Paul, who says, "Pray for us, brethren, that the word of God may speed on and be glorified" *(2 Thess. 3:1)*.

(556) The protheme is sometimes about the person of the preacher. For instance, if some preacher from the Order of Preachers or the Minors, who is not well known, wishes to preach in some parish in which he is not known personally nor is his Order known, he should explain straight away what he is and what his Order is, so that people will not mistake him for a man who is preaching to collect money. He can use Paul's words, "We are not in pursuit of your goods, but of yourselves" *(2 Cor. 12:14)*. Or he may wish to acknowledge his own inadequacy, and so declares it like Jeremiah, saying, "Ah, Ah, Ah, Lord, I am only a child" and "I do not know how to speak" *(Jer. 1:6)*. Or he may give the reason why he has to preach, whether it be because of some position of responsibility he holds, or because he is acting under obedience, in which case he can use 1 Cor. 9:16, "Woe is me if I do not preach the gospel to you; I am under constraint, an obligation rests upon me."[93] And similarly in other similar situations.

(557) Sometimes the protheme is about the people to whom the sermon is addressed, as when the preacher puts forward a text by which he hopes to make the listeners not only listen to what is said, but also put it into practice, in accordance with what James says, "Be doers of the word and not just hearers" *(James 1:22)*. Or he may quote a text which allows him to draw attention to the different kinds of listener, in many of whom preaching is completely wasted, but in some of whom it achieves something; such is the situation in our Saviour's parable about the sower who went out to sow his seed *(Luke 8:5ff)*. Or he may promise a good reward to those who listen well, and threaten evil consequences to those who listen badly, following He-

brews 6:7, "The earth which drinks in the rain that often falls upon it. . . ." There are many other such possibilities.

(558) Sometimes the protheme is about the topic of the sermon. For instance, when the sermon is about something elevated and mysterious, like the Trinity or the Incarnation or the sacrament of Christ's Body, it can be prefaced with a word in which the preacher asks to be given understanding, so that he may be able to speak fittingly about these things, following the example of Paul, who says, "Pray for us, that God will open our mouth in speech to declare the mystery of Christ" *(Col. 4:3)*. Or when the sermon is to be in praise of something, like a sermon about the saints, who are to be praised to give glory to God and honour to them and help to men, something may be said which relates to their praise, like the text in Ecclus. 44:15, "Let the church declare their praise." Or when the sermon is about something particularly helpful for salvation, such as penance, a word may be spoken to encourage the hearers to listen gladly to this kind of sermon; "In gentleness receive the implanted word, which can save your souls" *(James 1:21)*.

(559) Sometimes the protheme concerns the text chosen for the sermon, as, for example, when it is an obscure text which it is difficult to understand; then a word is spoken to ask for the Holy Spirit to be given, so that the text may be expounded by the same Spirit by whom it was inspired.[94] As it says, "Who will know your mind unless you give wisdom and send your Holy Spirit from on high?" *(Wisdom 9:17)*. Or when the text is about some particularly important subject, a word is spoken about its importance to make the listeners attend more carefully for that reason: "Listen to me, because I am going to speak about important things," as Wisdom says *(Prov. 8:6)*. Or sometimes attention is drawn to the greatness of the author of the text, for in any word of scripture it is not man who speaks, but God. "It was at the inspiration of the Holy Spirit that the holy men of God spoke" *(2 Pet. 1:21)*.[95] This is why the prophets used to say so often, "Listen to the word of the Lord," as if to say, "The reason why you ought to listen is that it is the Lord who speaks." There are many other things like this that might be appropriate.

(560) Sometimes the protheme is about the season during which the sermon is preached. In Advent, for instance, it is pointed out that it is proper to preach about the things that are associated with the Lord's coming, because this is what all the prophets prophesied

about, as it says in Acts 3:24, "All the prophets who have ever spoken, from Samuel onwards, foretold these days." Or during Lent, because it is a season of penance, it may be pointed out that it is right to speak about penance at such a time, since John and the Saviour, even without such a season, made this the first and principal part of their preaching. Or during the time of Easter it may be pointed out that it would be most unfitting for any tongue of flesh to keep silence at such a time, when the flesh of its Maker rose again, as Gregory says.[96] And so on.

(561) Sometimes the protheme may be about the nature and purpose of preaching, pointing out, for instance, that it is meant to lead to results: "We are not like many people, who adulterate the word of God" *(2 Cor. 2:17)*, which is what happens when men look simply for pleasure and not for results. Or it may be pointed out that preaching should be simple. "Wise men's teaching is easy" *(Prov. 14:6)*. Or that it ought to be concise, in accordance with Cant. 4:3, "Your lips are like a scarlet band." And so on.

(562) This shows that there should sometimes be a protheme before a sermon, and sometimes not; it also makes plain what it should be like and what different kinds of material may be used in it.

### Material for Sermons and Conferences

(563) It is sometimes harder for many people to find useful, good material out of which to construct their sermon than it is for them actually to construct it once they have found their material. And so it is helpful for a preacher always to have material in readiness for preaching or giving a conference about God, (a) to suit different kinds of audience, (b) to suit different kinds of occasion, (c) to suit the different seasons of the church's year and (d) to suit the different festivals of the year.

[The rest of the work is devoted to a huge collection of model sermons, arranged under these four headings. A selection is given in the pages that follow.]

# HUMBERT OF ROMANS

## Notes

1. All the MSS have *decem*. *Novem in Max.* and *octo* in B are wanton editorial alterations.

2. It was quite common for preachers to conclude their sermons with a series of bidding prayers (cf. L. J. Bataillon, *Leeds Studies in English* NS 11 [1980] p. 29); for some excellent examples, see N. Bériou, *Recherches Augustiniennes* 13 (1978) pp. 124, 128, 129, 132 etc. After the disporportionate bulk of (ix), which consists of the whole set of 258 model sermons, (x) seems to have got lost. Either Humbert never wrote it, or it dropped out of the manuscript tradition.

3. Interlinear Gloss.

4. PL 76:526A.

5. Marginal Gloss.

6. Interlinear Gloss.

7. Matt. 8:20.

8. PL 76.1148AB.

9. *Letters* 2:1.

10. *Goliardi:* see, for example, Helen Waddell, *The Wandering Scholars* (paperback, London, 1968), esp. pp. 198ff.

11. PL 73:792AB, 869AB.

12. *Sed dixit Ps.* MAL *sed dicit Ps.* S. On the face of it, a subject is required, which B supplies, rather implausibly, by interpreting *Ps.* as *Psaltes.* *Dicit Ps.* is also found in the model sermons, I iv, and it is probably to be accepted here as meaning "It says in the Psalms." Possibly the text should be emended to *dicitur.*

13. By 1220 St. Dominic had persuaded his brethren to renounce the use of horses when they travelled and not to take money with them on their journeys (*Acta Canon.* 26), and this was duly written into the Primitive Constitutions (I 22, II 31). In Raymund's Constitutions (I 17) it was further specified that it was a serious fault to arrange for somebody else to carry money on behalf of a travelling friar, and I take it that this is what Humbert is referring to here; this seems to fit the context better than the other possible rendering of *pecuniam deferri facientes* as "making people give them money," which is how Mosca takes it.

14. In his *Opus Tripartitum* III 3, Humbert says, "Almost the whole world is upset and complaining about the huge rout of poor religious which has invaded the world; many people call them tramps, now, not religious, and this results in a colossal depreciation of the religious state."

15. Cf. Seneca, *Letters* 7:3. This is far from being an exact quotation, but it is found in precisely the same form, ascribed to Seneca, in Thomas à Kempis, *Imitation of Christ* I 20:5. Meersseman, in his study of medieval pseudo-Senecan texts (*Italia Medioevale e Umanistica* 16 [1973] pp. 131–2)

cannot give any further evidence for this text, but suggests that it may derive from some collection of *Proverbia Senecae*, a suggestion considerably strengthened by its appearance in Humbert (of which Meersseman was unaware) as well as à Kempis.

16. Cf. Gregory, PL 76:807B.

17. This is a conflation of Psalms 5:9 and 7:2.

18. Some prayers for travellers are suggested in the Dominican *Ordinarium* (drawn up under Humbert's supervision), 494.

19. Matt. 5:16.

20. Cf. Marginal Gloss and Hugh of St. Cher on this passage. In my translation, I have followed Hugh of St. Cher's interpretation.

21. Interlinear Gloss.

22. PL 76:807B.

23. Psalm 105:35.

24. *Super hominum gloriam diligeris.* I do not know what this is supposed to mean. Hugh of St. Cher, rather unconvincingly, suggests that it means "People will love you more than they love worldly glory—and they love that a lot." Fortunately, all that matters here is "you will be loved."

25. Cicero, *On Friendship* 24:89. It is a quotation from Terence, *Andria* I 41, and in fact Cicero expresses his disapproval of the sentiment. Humbert probably got it from a Florilegium and was unaware of its context in Cicero.

26. PL 17:1021.

27. Cicero, *On Friendship* 8:28.

28. PL 184:771C.

29. I have adopted the reading in Gregory, *coniugio*, in preference to the various readings in the MSS: *coniugi* M *cum coniuge* A *coniugem* S *coniuge* L. B has *cum coniuge*.

30. PL 76:1149A.

31. 1 Peter 4:11.

32. PL 76:357A.

33. PL 83:1248D.

34. PG 56:691.

35. PL 83:1248D.

36. Cf. PL 73:864CD.

37. Psalm 36:30.

38. I have not been able to find this text, but cf. PL 16:25A, 880–1.

39. PL 75:1122B.

40. Cf. above §140.

41. *De Consideratione* II 22 (III p. 430:1–2).

42. *De Consideratione* II 22 (III p. 430:2–3).

43. PL 73:778C.

44. PL 83:629B. Cf. 1 Cor. 15:33 and, lying behind that, Menander,

fragment 218 and Euripides, fragment 1024 (where Nauck indicates an impressive list of patristic texts in which it is cited).

45. PL 15:1517CD.

46. PL 77:256C.

47. PL 76:910D.

48. *Verba sancta:* primarily, words of scripture.

49. Luke 10:39.

50. Ecclus. 32:6.

51. Luke 7:40.

52. Matt. 18:15ff.

53. L, like the Vulgate, adds "or shoes." It is tempting to see the omission in MAS (which is probably to be followed) as a reflection of the heated controversy with the Franciscans about the legitimacy of wearing shoes (cf. above, p. 160[120]). In *De Perfectione* 21 St. Thomas also cites this text without the reference to shoes, though he quotes it in full elsewhere.

54. Interlinear Gloss.

55. Marginal Gloss

56. Marginal Gloss.

57. The believe that the ostrich neglects its eggs goes back to Job 39:14–16, and is found in the Bestiaries (cf. McCulloch p. 146 and Thomas of Cantimpré, *De Natura Rerum* V 110). St. Albert, as we should expect, gives a sensible explanation of the ostrich's apparent neglect of her eggs. He also, incidentally, reveals his own highly empirical approach in a comment on the belief that ostriches eat metal: "I have not found this to be true. I have often offered metal to several ostriches, and they all refused to eat it" (*De Animalibus* [ed. H.Stadler, Münster, 1921] XXIII 139).

58. Cf. Matt. 15:32.

59. *Veros praedicatores* A, *nos praedicatores* MSL.

60. Marginal Gloss.

61. Interlinear Gloss.

62. PL 77:41AB.

63. PL 77:38D.

64. PL 77:40A–C.

65. Interlinear Gloss.

66. PL 76:1141A.

67. PL 76:1140D.

68. Marginal Gloss. Cf. PL 76:1140D.

69. I have followed the text of Gregory here, *iurgia dirimenda*. MA's *negotia dirimenda* seems scarcely possible, and SL's *negotia dirigenda* looks like an attempt to make sense of it.

70. PL 77:39CD.

71. PL 77:39C.

72. PL 77:39D.

73. PL 77:38CD.

74. PL 77:42AB.

75. *Saeculari sapientia* M, *saecularia sapientia* A, *saecularia* SL. I follow B and read *saeculum sapientia*.

76. *Inquisitiones:* this word has much wider reference than what we call the Inquisition, and refers to all kinds of official investigation. W.R. Thomas, *Friars in the Cathedral*, p. 75, says that *inquisitores* were "itinerant ombudsmen." Cf. Y. Dossat, *Inquisiteurs ou Enquêteurs? (Bulletin Philologique et Historique* [1957] pp. 105–113).

77. I have translated the text in B. MA have "There are some kinds of business which are risky, such as marriage negotiations—you never know how such things will work out," linking the doubt with the marriages rather than the kinds of business. SL omit all reference to marriage negotiations, as does Max. B's text involves the transposition of *quae incertos eventus habent* to before *ut procuratio matrimoniorum*.

78. 2 Tim. 2:4

79. PL 77:41A.

80. Gen. 41:33–6.

81. 1 Tim. 5:23.

82. Cf. Gregory, PL 76:42A.

83. *Dicunt* S, *dicimur* M, *dicuntur* AL.

84. Matt. 15:14.

85. Marginal Gloss.

86. Dominicans very quickly realised the need for textbooks to help confessors on these and similar problems; one of the earliest Dominican writings was a *Summa de Poenitentia* composed by Paul of Hungary at Bologna, before 1221; this was followed soon afterwards by the larger and more famous *Summa* by Raymund of Peñafort.

87. This is actually the text of Luke 5:32, but all the MSS give the reference to the parallel text in Matt. 9 (which does not say "to repentance").

88. Cf. Rom. 10:2.

89. This text does not come from Augustine, but from the anonymous *De Singularitate Clericorum* 7 (in vol. III of the CSEL edition of Cyprian, p. 180). It is quoted as being from Augustine in Marbod's letter to Robert of Arbrissel, to support his objection to Robert's practice of cohabiting and even sleeping with women (PL 171:1482). (On Robert and his *mulierum consortium*, see D. Iogna-Prat, "La Femme dans la perspective pénitentielle des ermites du Bas-Maine," *Revue de l'Histoire de la Spiritualité* 53 [1977] pp. 47–64. On celibate cohabitation in general, see also P. de Labriolle, "Le 'Mariage Spirituel' dans l'Antiquité Chrétienne," *Revue Historique* 137 [1921] pp. 204–225. Iogna-Prat needs to be balanced by SCH Subsidia 1 pp. 175–184).

90. II 360ff.

91. All the MSS have: *Quod confitentes sibi, si aliis confiteantur, non graviter ferat, vel confessionum audientiam ad quaestum vertat vel earum occasione nimias mulierum familiaritates contrahat vel in exequendo minus bene in aliis se habeat.* All of this is still clearly dependent on *reprehensibile est*, and the printed editions' insertion of *non* before *vertat* and *contrahat* cannot be right. The problem is what to do with *non graviter ferat.* Without much confidence, I have deleted *non* in my translation.

92. The protheme is "a second text, usually scriptural, allied verbally or logically to the theme itself, and serving as an introduction to remarks upon the necessity of invoking divine aid, which invocation is the purpose and termination of the protheme structure" (R. H. and M. A. Rouse, *Preachers, Florilegia and Sermons*, p. 73). Many of the sermons of Jacques de Vitry provide admirable examples of prothemes: e.g. Pitra, pp. 346–7, 353–4, 365–6, 375 etc; cf. also the sermons of Bonaventure: e.g., *Opera Omnia* IX pp. 23, 27, 30–1, 45, 575–6 etc.

93. Notice that Humbert does not quote Jeremiah or Paul exactly; he is illustrating the way in which a preacher can adapt these texts for his own purposes. There is a slight textual problem in the quotation from 1 Cor. 9:16; *necessitas mihi* has to be inserted, as in B. MAS have *est necessitas enim mihi incumbit* (*contulit* S). L has tried to make sense of the reading of S with *necessitas enim mihi tulit.*

94. *Eodem Spiritu exponatur quo fuit editum:* this is ascribed to an unspecified *auctoritas* in Humbert's sermon for Doctors, IV 16:2 (see below, p. 358). I do not know where it comes from.

95. *Petri 1* is my conjecture. *Pater qui* M, *pater quia* AL, *pater cum* S.

96. PL 76:1170C.

# A. Sermons for Different Kinds of Audience

*XXXII Laybrothers of the Order of Preachers*

(1) Though the Lord gives a great grace to everyone whom he calls to religious life, and an even greater grace to those whom he calls who are not clerics, he seems to give[1] the greatest grace of all to those whom he calls to be laybrothers in the Order of Friars Preachers.

(2) Elsewhere there are many laybrothers who receive very little spiritual teaching, and that only rarely, but these laybrothers receive it more or less the whole time. There are many elsewhere who only rarely attend Mass, but these can attend not only Mass, but also the Divine Office, every day. Also elsewhere they only have Chapter occasionally, and infrequent access to confessors; but here they have both as regularly as the clerics. Also elsewhere there is considerable inequality between the laybrothers and the clerics in the way they are provided with the necessities of life; but here they receive exactly the same treatment with regard to food and clothing, medicine, beds, accommodation and all that kind of thing. Elsewhere the laybrothers are often not treated very respectfully, but here they are treated respectfully, and so, for example, they do not have to go out alone, nor do they have their meals apart from the clerics, and they are served by the clerics, just as they serve the clerics. Elsewhere they have to do all kinds of mean jobs, like looking after the farm animals,[2] cleaning out stables, and that kind of thing; but here they are only given decent jobs to do. Again, elsewhere they are often ordered about like serfs, but here they serve freely, as members of the family.

(3) But they ought to be careful not to abuse a grace like this. There is an abuse with regard to themselves, if they become proud because of their position. There is an abuse with regard to their neighbour, if they want to assimilate themselves[3] too much to the

326

clerics. There is an abuse with regard to God, if they spend too much time in contemplative occupations, like hearing lots of Masses or attending long Offices or staying too long in prayer, to the neglect of their duties.

(4) Not only ought they to avoid this kind of abuse, they should live up to the grace they have been given, and this means that, as they have received a greater grace, so they ought to surpass all other laybrothers, in their bearing outside when they are among men, and in their bearing at home among the brethren, and in the bearing of their inner man before God. Since they often have to be in the company of men, their demeanour ought to be such that they do not stain the Order's reputation by any kind of impropriety. As well as giving a good example, they ought to have a ready flow of good words, so that they will be a help to people on their way to salvation. They ought to conduct the friars' business graciously, making sure that the Order does not become a nuisance to the world, through any tactlessness of theirs. In the cloister, they ought to work faithfully, so that the alms by which they live do not become a danger to their souls because of idleness. They ought to serve all the brethren alike, with no favourites, so that they will share in the benefits of all of them, on the principle that "Anyone who receives a prophet, in the name of a prophet, will receive the reward of a prophet."[4] They should be careful not to offend anyone, so that everyone will welcome their company. And in the sight of God they should avoid hidden sins, wrong intentions and evil desires, so that all the enlightenment they receive from the frequent teaching they are given will achieve in them the good result of purity of conscience, right intention and continual holy desires.

(5) This provides the material for the sermon. For a text: 2 Cor. 6:1, "We exhort you, do not receive the grace of God in vain."

## XLVIII Sisters in the Care of the Order of Preachers[5]

(1) In the flesh we find that some people die without children, while others leave children behind them; and of these, some leave not only sons, but also daughters. In Genesis it is said of the patriarchs, "He begot sons and daughters."[6] And the same thing happens in the realm of the spirit too. Some of the saints did not create orders, in which to leave children behind them; others created orders in which to leave sons, and others again not only left sons behind them like

this, but also daughters, in the orders they created. And in this third category we find St. Dominic, who not only established an Order of brethren, but also an Order of sisters.

(2) Being a man extremely zealous for souls, he was prompted to create this Order of sisters by the holy intention of saving souls. And this purpose was, in fact, twofold. One aim of his was to prevent people being contaminated by heresy. In the region of the Albigeois the impoverished nobility were entrusting their daughters to the heretics to be looked after and educated, and so they were becoming heretics too. So he founded a monastery at Prouille, where these noblemen could place their daughters. His other aim was to remedy impropriety. At that time there were various houses of nuns in Rome which were in a state of spiritual decay, and so, on the authority of the Pope, he gathered the nuns together at San Sisto to live more properly as nuns, and there he enclosed them. Then, on the model of these two houses, many others were formed all over the world, where the sisters serve their heavenly bridegroom inside their enclosures. There would have been many more if the Friars Preachers had been prepared to tolerate it.

(3) Now, in general, people guard their daughters more carefully than they guard their sons, and so we may believe that it was due to God's providing that a way of life was imparted to his daughters by St. Dominic, in which there was a threefold protection. First of all, the enclosure; then the companionship, because no sister ventures to go to the window to talk with any outsider without her appointed companion who hears everything that goes on. And finally, the brethren outside, who look after them.

(4) Notice that there are many kinds of religious women who sometimes go wandering round the world, and this leads to innumerable risks;[7] but these sisters live under perpetual enclosure. And there are many others who, even if they do not go wandering round, make no difficulty about letting people come into them indiscriminately; but no one ever comes into these sisters, except perhaps bishops or kings and queens, and then only with a few, respectable attendants, and even this only happens rarely and never except in the presence of the friars. Then there are many who let outsiders converse with them, when they come inside the monastery, but no outsider can speak to these sisters inside their monastery. Then there are many whose chaplains are insufficiently wise and learned, but nobody is given to these sisters to look after them except choice friars who are

quite capable of doing the job well. Then there are many who have quite capable chaplains, but they hardly ever visit them or give them any instruction; but these sisters are preached to frequently, and their confessions are heard frequently, and they receive many spiritual consolations. Again, there are some[8] whose way of life is not determined on many points, because of a lack of rules; but these sisters have statutes which were drawn up for them with great care, and which make plain to them what they are to do in all matters.[9] Again, there are many religious women living in situations which encourage private property and other kinds of malpractice, because of the inadequacy of the communal provision made for them; but these sisters have everything provided in common, and plentifully too.

(5) What grace has been given to the women who are called to this state of life! And how dreadful it is if they do not recognise it. And how much more dreadful if they do recognise it, but do not give thanks to God for it. And the worst thing of all is if they abuse it. As the apostle says, "We exhort you, do not receive the grace of God in vain."[10] And anyone who does not recognise a grace, or recognises it but does not thank God for it, or, worst of all, abuses a grace, is receiving it in vain. You must not act like that, dear sisters whom God has blessed so much. You must recognise the grace you have been given for the salvation of your souls, and you must give thanks for it, and you must make good use of it, so that it brings credit to St. Dominic and pleasure to the brethren who toil for you, and wins you a constant good reputation in the world.

(6) This provides the material for the sermon. For a text: Ecclesiasticus 26:13,[11] "In the case of a daughter who does not keep aloof, guard her closely." Notice that a daughter is said not to keep aloof when she is guileless, because there are many who do not appreciate[12] the dangers of this life.[13]

Another text is Ecclus. 7:26, "Do you have daughters? Guard their bodies." Notice that no one can guard anyone else's heart, but it is possible to guard someone else's body. And this is useful in many ways in the case of women. Women's feet are prone to useless gadding about, their eyes prone to inquisitive prying, their ears to idle gossip, and so on. Religious life with an enclosure protects women from gadding about outside and from having too many visitors inside, and from seeing and being seen, hearing and being heard, giving and receiving presents, touching and being touched, and the rest of it.

## XCIV For Women in General

(1) Notice that the Lord has given woman many advantages, not only over other living creatures, but even over men too, and that in the time of nature, and the time of grace, and the time of glory.

(2) First of all, at the time of the making of nature, man was made in this dingy world,[14] but woman was made in Paradise. Man was made from the mud of the earth,[15] which is a dingy substance, but woman was made from the man's rib.[16] And she was not made from some part low down in man's body, such as his foot, which would have suggested that man should regard her as his servant; she was made from the middle of his body, namely from a rib in his side, so that he would have her as his companion. As Adam said, "The woman whom you gave me as my companion" *(Gen. 3:12)*. So woman has three privileges: first, the place where she was created, secondly, the material from which she was made, and thirdly, the particular part of the man's body from which she was taken.

(3) In the time of grace, the Lord, who could have taken his flesh from a man, just as he had earlier formed the woman from a man, did not do this, but preferred to take his flesh from a woman. Again, we do not read of any man trying to prevent the suffering of the Lord; it was a woman, Pilate's wife, who wanted to stop her husband from committing this terrible crime, because of all she had suffered in a dream because of Christ *(Matt. 27:19)*. Again, at the time of the Resurrection, he appeared to a woman first, Mary Magdalene.[17] And so woman has three privileges in the time of grace: one concerning the Incarnation, one concerning the Passion and one concerning the Resurrection.

(4) In the state of glory too there is no mere man who will be king in that country, but there is someone who is nothing but a woman who will be queen[18] there. And there is no one who is just a man who will be as much higher than the angels and the whole court of heaven as is that one who is just a woman. Similarly there is no man who will be as powerful in that heavenly court as that mere woman. And so woman's nature is privileged in glory, because of its greater dignity, exaltation and power, all in the person of the blessed Virgin.

(5) All of this ought to encourage women to love the God who gave them all this, and to pursue for love of him all that is good in a woman; it should also deter them from all that is evil.[19]

(6) In connexion with this, note that a woman ought not to be a fortune-teller, which is a kind of unbelief; she ought to be faithful. Women must be "faithful in everything" *(1 Tim. 3:11)*. The Canaannite woman who came to the Lord Jesus is an example *(Matt. 15:22)*. The commentator says in one of his Homilies, "She did not go to diviners, she did not summon magicians, she did not look for women who could cast binding spells, she called for no help from fraudulent women." She did not have recourse to any false assistance; instead "she abandoned all the devil's lies and came to the Lord Jesus, the Saviour of all."[20]

(7) Also women ought not to be ill-disposed and hard-hearted; they should be devoted to God and to his servants, like the women we read about in Matthew 27:55, "There were many women who had followed Jesus from Galilee, serving him."

(8) Also women ought not to be shameless or vain in dressing up; they should be modest and decently apparelled. "Women should dress decently and adorn themselves with modesty and sobriety, not with curled hair or gold or pearls or expensive clothes" *(1 Tim. 2:9)*. "Decently apparelled" is glossed, "Dressing themselves in their religion."[21]

(9) Nor should they be talkative, as St. Paul says some women are *(1 Tim. 5:13)*. They should rather be quiet. "Women in the churches" (when the church meets together, that is) "are to be silent. . . . They are not permitted to speak" *(1 Cor. 14:34)*.

(10) Nor should they be idle; they should always have some work to do. "She does not eat her bread in idleness" *(Prov. 31:27)*.

(11) Again, they should not go gadding about all over the place, like Dinah,[22] as Paul says some women do *(1 Tim. 5:13)*. They should be quiet at home with Mary, who "sat at home," as we find in John 11:20.

(12) Also they should not be cruel, but should be kind to the poor. "She opened her hand to the needy and stretched out her hand to the poor" *(Prov. 31:20)*.

(13) There are many other things which good women ought to do, which you will easily find if you look carefully.

(14) This provides the material for the sermon. For a text: Proverbs 31:31, "Give her the fruit of her hands, and let her works praise her in the gateway." Note that a woman ought to love God because of the advantages he has given her, and for his love do the good works mentioned above, and, if she does do this for the love of him, she will

enjoy the fruit of her hands, that is, she will receive the fruit of her works in the world to come, in glory, and in this present life she will receive praise. This is what our text means.

(15) Another text: Acts 16:13, "On the sabbath day, we went outside the gate by the river, where there seemed to be a praying, and there we sat down and addressed the assembled women." The Gloss explains that a "praying" means a place suitable for speaking.[23] This shows that we should address women when the chance occurs.

(16) Another text: Jeremiah 9:20, "Women, hear the word of the Lord."

# B. Sermons for Different Kinds of Occasion

*V General Chapters or Councils of Religious*

(1) There are some religious who never hold any meeting to discuss their common good, even though they have many members. Against this, 1 Macc. 8:15 says, the Romans "took counsel every day with 320 men about the mass of the people, to make sure that they did what was worthy." But this is absurd! The Romans gather their wise men together regularly every day to discuss the common good, and the same practice is followed by all the Italians; but these religious do not assemble anyone to discuss the good order of their condition, not even once a year or once every two years or once in many years![24]

(2) There are others who do periodically meet for some kind of chapter, but when they get there they do nothing but eat and drink lavishly and entertain each other and hold a great party. This is the kind of meeting referred to in Job 15:34, "The meeting of the hypocrite is barren." A hypocritical religious life, which has nothing but a religious habit and a certain outward appearance of religion, achieves no good in its meetings and so is appropriately called barren.

(3) There are others who do some good at their meetings, in connexion with their temporal affairs, like demanding an account of the debts of priories and that sort of thing; but they give little or no attention to spiritual things. If some little property of theirs is going to ruin, they will discuss carefully how to preserve it. But if their religious life is going to ruin, they take no notice. If some tyrant is plundering any of their goods, a plan will be drawn up for dealing with him, but the devil can plunder the souls of the brethren all over the place without any antidote being applied. If some trivial case has come before a judge, they are most diligent in seeking advice about it; but the day of judgment before the eternal Judge is drawing ever

nearer, when many will speak against us and we shall be obliged to give an account of all we have done,[25] yet no one gives a thought to what answer can be given there. It is people like this that Bernard makes fun of, when he says, "They are fine judges of the value of things! They pay the greatest attention to the smallest things, and the least attention to the greatest."[26] By "smallest" he means temporal things, by "greatest" he means spiritual things.

(4) This is not how holy men behave. They meet together in the name of the Lord, to advance the things that belong to him, in accordance with Isaiah 60:4, "They all met together and came to you," to do the things that belong to you, that is. They take counsel about the things which concern his glory, in accordance with Psalm 88:8, "God, who is glorified in the council of the saints." And we can have much more confidence when we are engaged in this kind of business, inasmuch as we believe that the Lord is with people who meet like this: "Where two or three are gathered together in my name, I am there in the middle of them" *(Matt. 18:20)*.

(5) But though much good is done in these assemblies,[27] nevertheless some things quite often happen which are not good. Some of these concern everybody in general, some concern those who belong to the body of the chapter, some concern the judges who preside at the chapter, and some concern the junior members.

(6) When the brethren meet each other at such gatherings, they ought to engage in holy conversation with each other, but sometimes it happens that they waste their time instead in worldly gossip and trivialities and silly jokes and other such distractions. Bernard says, "When you meet, you do not discuss the holy scriptures at all, but only trifles and jokes, and you cast empty words upon the wind."[28] The apostle, by contrast, says, "When you meet together, every one of you has a psalm or some teaching or a revelation or a tongue or an interpretation." That is to say, "This is the kind of thing you talk about." So he goes on, "Let everything be done with a view to edification" *(1 Cor. 14:26)*.

(7) Then it sometimes happens that at such meetings there is considerable excess in the food and drink and bedding that is provided, and in many other frivolities, and that people are careless in the way they walk about or stand or comport themselves or in their gestures, offending against the holiness that such people should display. And this means that many of the important people who come to witness such meetings, in the expectation of being edified, go away

upset and scandalised, and this brings such religious into disrepute. This is contrary to what it says in 2 Cor. 6:3–4, "Give no offense to anyone, so that our ministry will not be brought into disrepute; rather let everything about us show that we are God's ministers."

(8) Again, it sometimes happens that some of the people at such meetings are not walking in the way of charity, but only trying to arrange things so as to embarrass others or get their own back on them, or in some other way achieve results that are less than good. But in 1 Cor. 16:14 it says, "Let all that you do be done in charity."

(9) To avoid these three faults, all the conversations that people have should be holy; care must be taken not to give a bad example to outsiders; and, in the sight of God, they should make sure that nothing is done from wrong motives.

(10) Furthermore, it sometimes happens that the people who constitute the body of the chapter are not wholly suitable, because they lack discretion or zeal or authority or whatever else it may be. And this is not right, because it is their job to discuss extremely important affairs.[29] In 2 Tim. 2:2 it says, "What you have heard from me, pass on to such believers as are suitable."

(11) Again, there are sometimes people among them who are awkward and a nuisance to the rest; and this sort of thing ought to be entirely absent from the meetings of the saints. "If anyone seems to be quarrelsome, that is not the custom we have, nor is it the custom of God's church" *(1 Cor. 11:16)*. "God's church" refers to the meetings of good men.

(12) Again, there are sometimes people among them who ignore the convenience of everybody else, and devote themselves simply to furthering their own business or that of their community, and this makes them vote for and otherwise support the people they think will be favourable to themselves. But in 1 Cor. 10:24 it says, "No one should seek what is his own, but only the good of the others." So there are three faults, then, arising here.

(13) Turning now to the judges, they are sometimes at fault because they are too halfhearted about correcting and punishing past offenses, like Eli the priest, who was halfhearted in correcting his sons *(1 Sam. 2:22)*. This is a far cry from the example of the Lord in John 2:15–16, who was so zealous to correct the sins that had been committed in the temple that he whipped the offenders with his own hand, indicating thereby that sins committed in the Lord's temple, in religious life, that is, are to be corrected fiercely.

(14) Again, they are sometimes less than prudent in the statutes and ordinances which they make to prevent future ills; for example, sometimes they make too many of them, sometimes too few, and sometimes they make them without sufficient reason. Things like this happen because they act too impetuously and carelessly. In 2 Chron. 19:7 judges are told, "Let the fear of the Lord be with you; do everything carefully".

(15) Again, they are sometimes less favourable than they might be in granting quite feasible petitions made to them by insiders or outsiders,[30] and this puts many people off and scandalises them. In Luke 6:30 it says, "Give to everyone who asks," that is, give him either what he asks or, failing that, a friendly and reasonable answer.

(16) Then sometimes the junior people there judge wrongly in their hearts about their seniors, saying to themselves, "This was done wrong, that was a silly thing to do, and that was a wicked thing to do" and such like. But in Ecclus. 8:17 it says, "Do not judge the judge." And sometimes they grumble openly, as the sons of Israel often did about Moses. But in 1 Cor. 10:10 it says, "Do not grumble as some of them did and perished at the hand of the avenger."

(17) Sometimes they obey in practice with insufficient devotion, not doing what they are told from the heart. But St. Benedict says, "The disciple must offer obedience with a good spirit, because 'God loves a cheerful giver.' For[31] if he is grudging, even if he obeys and does what he is told, he is still not acceptable[32] to God, because God sees the heart."[33]

(18) This provides the material for the sermon. For a text: Psalm 110:1, 'I will praise you, Lord, with all my heart, in the council of the just and in their meeting." Notice that no reason for praising God is found in those religious who never meet for any chapter, or who meet but take no counsel, or who take counsel but not about spiritual things. It is in the meeting of the saints, who take counsel about spiritual things and avoid the faults mentioned above that reason is found for confessing God with praise.

### LXXXV For Tournaments

(1) Provided you can get sufficient hearing, a sermon can be extremely useful at tournaments, because a lot of people attend them who are very much in need of instruction. But if you cannot get a

hearing, you should not preach, because of what it says in Ecclus. 32:6, "Where no one is listening, do not make a speech."

(2) To get material for such a sermon, we should notice that, though tournaments are, as such, forbidden by law because of the frequent danger to body and soul that they involve, nevertheless we may make a distinction: Some of what goes on is entirely to be condemned, but there are some things which can be tolerated, and some things which are positively good.

(3) To illustrate the utterly wrong things, there are some noblemen who spend so much so extravagantly on tournaments that they ruin themselves, their house and their family. Woe to them! If the Lord requires an account of five talents, and even of two talents or one *(Matt. 25:19ff)*, what will he do about so much wealth entrusted to the nobility for them to use in giving alms and acquiring some good profit to show to the Lord on the day of judgment, if they spend it on unlawful, dishonourable pursuits in his despite?[34]

(4) Then there are people whose primary aim in tournaments is nothing more serious than acquiring a vain reputation for themselves for prowess or courage or something. An example of this is Seron, the ruler of the Syrian army, who said, "I will defeat Judas and those who are with him" and "I shall make a name for myself" *(1 Macc. 3:14)*. They are like the wild ass Jeremiah speaks of: "In the desire of his soul, he has sucked in the wind which he loves" *(Jer. 2:24)*. What else is the love of fame, except love of a wind which soon passes?

(5) Then, even worse, there are people who inject real malice into these tournaments. They may, for instance, do serious damage to people they hate, or execute nefarious plots, or take the occasion to acquire things wrongly, contrary to the rules of the game; or they may do all kinds of ridiculous things to make mock of others, or they may expose themselves to the sinfulness of bad women who sometimes come to such occasions, or to many other kinds of sin. In this way the tournaments of christians become pagan games. As it says in 1 Macc. 1:15–16, "They have built a gymnasium in Jerusalem according to the laws of the nations, and they have made foreskins for themselves and abandoned the covenant and united themselves with the gentiles and sold themselves to do evil."

(6) These three things, then, are utterly to be condemned in tournaments: extravagant expenditure, vanity in people's intentions and any injection of malice[35] into the proceedings. People ought to

avoid all of them in a tournament. "Everyone who contends in a competition abstains from everything" *(1 Cor. 9:25)*, which is glossed, "Everything, that is, which would get in the way of winning the prize; so we too ought to abstain from anything which would make us stumble."[36] So in christian tournaments people ought to keep clear of these stumbling blocks[37] which have been mentioned here.

(7) With regard to the second element, those things which are to be tolerated, we should notice that it is lawful to fight for justice. "Struggle to the death for justice" *(Ecclus. 4:33)*. This means fighting to defend the rights of the faith or any other rights, but particularly the rights of the nation. As Cato said, "Fight for your country."[38] And it is most lawful of all to fight when obedience requires it. Gregory says in his *Letters,* "Of all his merits, a soldier's highest praise is that he shows obedience to the sacred cause of the nation,[39] and carries out what he has been usefully told to do."[40] So if a soldier has the intention to fight for God's sake only and in lawful circumstances, and takes part in tournaments in a modest way with a view to making himself better able to fight as a result of such practice, then what he is doing is quite tolerable, because no practical art can be learned without practice. This is supported by Judges 3:1–2, where it says, "These are the peoples whom the Lord has left there, to train Israel by means of them, and all the people who did not take part in the Canaanite wars, and so that afterwards their children will be able to learn how to fight with their enemies and become accustomed to battle."

(8) With regard to the third point, an example of something which is positively good is that sometimes in a tournament the knights encourage each other to do for God's sake in the future what they have been doing for so long for the sake of worldly vanity; this would mean going to fight the Saracens[41] or something like that. "Every man said to his neighbour ... Now, children, be zealous for the law and give your lives for the sake of the covenant of our fathers" *(1 Macc. 2:40, 50)*.

(9) Sometimes people who fear God manage to get prostitutes and hangers-on and other undesirable characters kept away from the tournament, and to prevent any outrages happening or anything else which would be offensive to God. Respectable estates should always see that this is done. "When you go out against your enemies to do battle, guard yourself from all evil ... so that your camp may be holy

and that no defilement may be seen in it" *(Deut. 23:9, 14).* If the Jews did this, how much more ought christians to do it.

(10) Sometimes also people are inspired to lament over themselves, seeing how often men are disgracefully overcome by sin and the lusts which war against the soul.[42] As Augustine says, "Let conjugal modesty adorn your character, and sobriety and frugality.[43] It is a very disgraceful thing that a man who is not defeated by any other man should be defeated by lust, and that he should be overthrown by vice when he is not conquered by any sword."[44]

(11) These three things, then, are all good, and anyone who injects this kind of thing into the levity of a tournament is to be congratulated.

(12) This provides the material for the sermon. For a text: Isaiah 2:4, "They shall no more train for war." Notice that the text indicates that this was still in the future; it refers to the time of Christ, when such military exercises ought not to take place, which is why they are banned with good reason by the church.

# C. Sermons for Different Times and Seasons

*I For Any Day of the Year*

(1) Notice that any single day in this present life is called a "good day." So Ecclesiastes 7:15, "In a good day you will enjoy good things," is glossed, "A good day: that is, this present life."[45] And it is called a "good day" because we can accomplish meritorious works in it, just as in ordinary language people refer to a day in which it is possible to work as "good," and call it a "bad day" if bad weather prevents them from working.

(2) But it must be remarked that on this good day, which is ideal for our work on our salvation, some people remain idle. They are referred to in Matt. 20:6, "Why do you stand here idle all day long?" Such idleness ought to be avoided. According to Ecclesiasticus 18:27, "The wise man will keep himself from inactivity during the period of sinfulness," which is glossed, "The period of sinfulness is the period of this present life,"[46] which is subject to sinfulness.

(3) What is worse, there are others who spend days like this in works of wickedness. "Wickedness will prowl round its walls all day long" *(Psalm 54:11)*. This too must be avoided, because the daytime is unsuitable for works of darkness. "The day has come, so let us cast off the works of darkness" *(Rom. 13:12)*, when they come to tempt us, that is, so that they will not be able to get close to us.

(4) Banishing these mistakes, then, we should above all devote ourselves on a day like this to good works, like the Lord who says, "I must perform the works of him who sent me as long as the day lasts" *(John 9:4)*. "I must perform the works," he says, which is the not the same thing as being idle. And "the works of him who sent me," not those of the devil; and that means good works.

(5) Consider now how well David passed his days in just such

good works. There are some people who sometimes spend much of the day in bad thoughts, but he spent the day rather in good thoughts, turning over the law of God in his heart. "How I have loved your law, Lord; it is my meditation all day long" *(Psalm 118:97)*. Others spend the day in idle words, but he spent the day in useful words. "My mouth will proclaim your justice and your salvation all day long" *(Psalm 70:15)*. Others often mingle in the course of the day with evil people, and a great deal of evil results from this, but he chased such people away as soon as it was day. "In the morning I slaughtered all the sinners in the land" *(Psalm 100:8)*. There are others who hardly ever pray during the day, but he prayed almost the whole time. "All day I have stretched out my hands to you" *(Psalm 87:10)*. Others very rarely attend the praises of God in the church's liturgy, but he says of himself, "Let my mouth be filled with praise, so that I may sing all day long of your glory and your greatness" *(Psalm 70:8)*. There are others again who spend their days in this vale of tragedy revelling in good things, but he says of himself, "All day long I walked in sorrow" *(Psalm 37:7)*, which is a commendable attitude in this world of ours which gives us every reason for sorrow.[47] There are others who do almost no penance during the day, but he says of himself, "I was whipped all day long and took a beating in the morning" *(Psalm 72:14)*. Others again are so entangled in earthly desires that hardly any day in the year sees them sighing towards God, but he sighed and wept every day in his yearning for God. "My tears were my bread day and night, while daily I heard people say, 'Where is your God?' " *(Psalm 41:4)*. And there are others who often get very indignant when trials come upon them, but he remained patient whatever happened. "I waited for you all day" *(Psalm 24:5)*.

(6) Notice next that, though David and other holy people were accustomed to fill their days with a variety of holy occupations, there are some things which happen every day and which everybody ought to do spiritually. First of all, waking up. "God, my God, I wake towards you at dawn" *(Psalm 62:2)*. This happens spiritually when a man shakes off all sleepy laziness and devotes himself energetically during the day to the things of God.[48] Next comes dressing, so that we are not seen naked in the light of day. "Walk decently, as befits the day" *(Rom. 13:13)*. This happens spiritually when a man's conduct displays nothing unseemly. Thirdly, people go about their own proper business. "Man goes out to his work," after the sun has risen, that

is, "to his labour until the evening comes" *(Psalm 103:23)*. This happens spiritually when a man devotes himself to working out his own salvation. There is no business which belongs to a man so properly as this. The fourth thing in the day is eating. A man needs to eat his bread every day to nourish his body, and the soul too needs to be fed daily with good teaching, which is the food of the soul. Seneca says, "When you have read a lot, cull from it something to digest during the day."[49] The fifth thing in the day is going on with a journey. Travellers proceed on their way during the daytime, and similarly we ought every day to cover another lap of our journey to heaven. "Walk while you have the light" *(John 12:35)*. The sixth thing is mutual encouragement in worthwhile pursuits; both travellers and workmen encourage each other like this. "Encourage each other every single day, as long as it is still 'today' " *(Hebr. 3:13)*.

(7) Notice next that good people do not merely perform good works of this kind during the day, they also try to make sure that no part of the day passes them by without yielding some profit. "Do not let the smallest part of the day pass you by" *(Ecclus. 14:14)*. Thus we are told of one holy man who spent half the day saying, "Have mercy on me, God, have mercy on me, God," having regard to his sins, and the other half of the day he spent saying, "Thank you, God, thank you, God," having regard to God's gifts.[50] This is why not only clerics but good lay people too go to church twice a day, once in the morning and once in the evening, as we are told Augustine's mother did, offering to God the morning and evening sacrifice of her prayers.[51] This is also why wise men reflect in the morning on what they are going to do, and in the evening on what they have done. Jerome says, "Pythagoras declared that particular attention should be paid to two times in the day, the morning and the evening; to what we are going to do, that is, and to what we have done."[52] This is also why David says, "In the evening and in the morning and at noon I will declare" (my sins, that is) "and proclaim" (his praise, that is) "and he will hear my voice" (in prayer) *(Psalm 54:18)*. For the same reason he also recited the praise of God seven times a day,[53] and it was his example which taught the church to divide the day into seven Hours, in and for each of which she recites the Divine Office. Good lay people too recite certain prayers in devout remembrance of the Lord's Passion: he was bound at the time of Matins, led before Pilate at Prime, taken to the Cross at Terce, crucified at Sext, and at None

he died, was taken down from the Cross at the time of Vespers and laid in the tomb at Compline at the end of the day.

(8) Notice also that every day in this present life is extremely useful to men, because they can work out their salvation in it. But it passes rapidly, and once it is gone it can never be recovered, and the uncertainty of death means that we can never be sure of having another day. And no one is so rich in goodness that he lacks nothing, and since we lack a great deal, we have to work every day to acquire what we lack. Further, there is a supreme Judge who sees everything and will be strict in demanding an account of how we have spent every day and indeed how we have spent every part of every day. So we must all be careful not to lose any day by letting it pass without doing any good in it.[54]

(9) The preceding paragraphs show why each day of this present life is called a "good day," and that it is to be devoted to good works, and what an excellent example of this David provides, and what the general good works are which everybody ought to devote himself to every day, and how good people fill even each part of the day with good deeds, and why we must be careful not to waste any day.

(10) This provides material for the sermon. For a text: Ecclesiasticus 14:14, "Do not be swindled out of a good day," which is what happens when a day passes without any good deed.

## IV For the Third Day of the Week

(1) In connexion with this day of the week, we must notice what the Lord did on it, what the church does on it, and what it suggests we ought to do.

(2) First of all, then, we must observe that, after arranging the upper part of creation, the Lord arranged the lower part, separating the earth from the water, so that the dry land appeared.[55] He also made the earth produce flourishing vegetation,[56] and not just vegetation, but also various kinds of fruit trees.[57] All of this has a moral value, if it happens also in the microcosm, namely man, who is called "the smaller world."[58] But there are many people in whom just the opposite happens.

(3) There are some people whose earth is mixed with the water of excessive self-indulgence, and so they are swampy and frogs come and live in them, namely the three spirits of avarice, impurity and

pride, which appear in the form of frogs in Apoc. 16:13. This is why the evil spirit is said to sleep "in damp places" in Job 40:16.

(4) There are others whose works are dead, because they are not watered by charity, and so they are not green and flourishing. Gregory says, "The branch of good works cannot be green unless it remains rooted in charity."[59] People like this, then, produce no flourishing vegetation.

(5) There are others who possess the virtues in principle, but do not bring forth their fruit according to each one's nature, and so they are like unfruitful trees, "trees in the autumn," which is the time for them to bear fruit, "that have no fruit on them" (*Jude 12*). They have branches, then, but they do not bear fruit.

(6) So, if the arrangement of the lower part of the microcosm is to correspond to the arrangement of the lower part of the macrocosm, man must shun excessive self-indulgence, so that he will be dry land, not a swamp; and he needs charity, to ensure that his works are verdant; and he must use the good things which God gives him to produce a variety of fruit trees all bearing the appropriate fruit.

(7) Secondly, we must remark that the church gives each day of the week certain peculiarities in the ferial Office; each day has its own nocturns and its own Ambrosian hymns and its own Invitatory and Benedictus and Magnificat antiphons. In addition to this, the church has special practices for every day of the week,[60] except for the third day, which has nothing special except the Office. And so, though it is possible to draw material for a sermon from the liturgy of any day of the week, it is most appropriate to do this on the third day, since it has nothing else which is proper to it.

(8) Notice, then, that on this day the church invites us at the beginning of the night Office to sing the church's song: "Let us sing joyfully to God our Saviour."[61] And there are three reasons why the church militant rejoices vocally like this. First of all, it is to imitate the church triumphant, which is totally taken up with exultant song, as we can see in Apoc. 4:8–11 and 5:9–13. As Bernard says, nothing represents the condition of the church triumphant so precisely as "the eagerness of men praising God."[62] Seeing that we are meant to follow "the pattern revealed on the mountain" in all we do,[63] it is only right that we should follow it by exulting with might and main "in loud song."[64]

The second reason is to alleviate the boredom of our earthly pilgrimage, singing as pilgrims do as they pursue their way. "Your judgments became my song in the place of my pilgrimage" *(Psalm 118:54)*.

The third reason is to draw people away from vain contentment. The heart of man prefers to be happy, and so it is helpful for him to be given a chance to rejoice in the Lord, to stop him drifting away towards worldly happiness; for the same reason the Jews were commanded to sacrifice animals to God to prevent them offering sacrifice to idols.[65] This is why scripture so often says, "Sing to the Lord";[66] it is as if scripture were telling us to concentrate on this and abandon all other singing.

(9) Notice, next, that the church's singing differs in several respects from worldly singing. It differs from it, in the first place, in its content. Worldly singing is about harmful subjects, because the world enjoys and sings about the worst possible things, whereas the church enjoys and sings about the things which make for salvation. This can be seen in the reasons given for singing in the Psalms, like, "Sing a new song to the Lord, because he has done wonderful things" *(Psalm 97:1)*. There are many other reasons like this which can be found in the Psalms.

There is also a difference in the outcome of the two kinds of singing. The world's singing leads to Hell, and this is even suggested in the fact that worldly dances always go from right to left. "They hold a drum and a lyre, they enjoy the sound of the organ . . . and in a moment they go down to Hell" *(Job 21:12–13)*.

There is also a difference in authorship. Worldly songs were composed by mean, vulgar people, but the church's canticles were composed by prophets, apostles and evangelists and other holy men. In Ecclesiasticus 44:5 it says of holy men, "In their skill they sought out musical tunes and composed the songs of the scriptures."

(10) We must notice, thirdly, that the church's singing has a number of splendid results. One concerns God, because he enjoys it as much as any king enjoys the singing of minstrels. And so the Lord says to the church, "Let your voice sound in my ears, because your voice is charming" *(Cant. 2:14)*.

Another concerns the angels, who are attracted to join people who are singing, just as people join in when they see anyone dancing. "The princes went on ahead, having joined themselves to the singers" *(Psalm 67:26)*, which is interpreted to mean the angels.[67]

Another concerns demons, because it frightens them and makes them run away. When David played his harp, the evil spirit withdrew from Saul *(1 Sam. 16:16–23)*.

Another concerns human beings, and this has several facets. One result is that it melts men's hearts, not leading to wrong desires, which is what happens with worldly singing, but leading to a holy emotion. It is written that Augustine "wept copiously at the hymns and canticles, being deeply moved by the voice of the sweetly singing church."[68] Another result is that men's hearts are raised up on high, Bernard says, "The song of praise lifts up the eyes of our hearts."[69] This is why people are sometimes caught up in rapture as a result of this kind of joyful singing: "There" (that is to say, at the blessing of God which takes place in church) "the young man Benjamin's mind was in rapture" *(Psalm 67:28)*. Another result is that it drives away all dangerous sadness. The Gloss on James 5:13 says, "If anyone is sad, he should drive from his heart the harmful plague of sorrow by frequent application of the delights of psalmody."[70] Another result is that the Spirit of God is poured in, as we can see from the example of King Saul, on whom the Spirit of the Lord fell when he attached himself to the chorus of singers *(1 Sam. 10:10)*. As Gregory says, "When the sound of psalmody comes from the heart's own purpose, the way is made ready for almighty God to come into the heart."[71]

(11) The reasons, then, for the establishment of the church's song, and the differences between that and the song of the world, and the glorious effects of the church's song reveal how much at fault people are who lightly keep away from listening to the church's Office. This is why such people are rebuked by the Lord: "Where were you when the morning stars together praised me and when all the sons of God sang for joy?" *(Job 38:7)*.

(12) To move on, now, to our third heading, we should notice that there is a war on between men and demons, as Paul says in Ephesians 6:12. Our battle "is against principalities and powers." And man has to fight bravely in this war. "Resist the devil" *(James 4:7)*. There is also a war between the spirit and the flesh: "The flesh lusts against the spirit and the spirit against the flesh" *(Gal. 5:17)*. Unless the spirit fights manfully in this war, it is faced with imminent death. This is why it says, "If you do to death the deeds of the flesh by the spirit, then you will live" *(Rom. 8:13)*, which suggests that otherwise, if the flesh wins, death will not be far off. There is also a war between the reason and the will, which are often out of

harmony with each other, the will desiring one thing, and the reason another. And in this war we must work hard to see that the reason triumphs. Cicero says, in the first book of the *De Officiis*, "We must make our appetites obey our reason, and not let them go racing ahead of it[72] or desert it through laziness or cowardice."[73]

There is a fourth war too, a war between man and man, and, unfortunately, there are many people who fight manfully in this war and lag behind in the other three. Any mercy they may have had is dried up, and they are hot in pursuit of vengeance[74] and obstinately determined to win, whether on the battlefield or in a lawcourt or in an argument in words. This means that they belong to the household of Mars, which is a dry planet (their first characteristic), and hot (their second characteristic) and Mars is also said to be the lord of the battlefield (their third characteristic).[75]

(13) But this is quite contrary to the teaching of our Lord Jesus Christ. He taught us to forgive our enemies, not to take vengeance on our enemies,[76] and to yield to our enemies, as many texts of scripture make clear.

So the vices of Mars ought to be banished together with his name,[77] and to this end christians ought to abandon the fourth kind of warfare, which belongs to Mars, and devote themselves[78] to the other three, to which they are incited by the scriptures.

(14) Notice that there is a reference to Mars in Acts 17:19, where the Areopagus is mentioned, the *pagus*, that is, meaning the district,[79] of *Arioth*,[80] Mars. You can look this up in the *History*.[81]

(15) This provides the material for the sermon. For a text: Genesis 1:13, "There was evening and there was morning, the third day."

### XVIII The Middle of Lent

(1) Notice that this world is like a road. People who are travelling along a road do not stay very long in the hostel to which they turn aside, and similarly we do not spend long in this world. "We do not have any abiding city here" *(Hebr. 13:14)*, that is to say, a city in which to spend a long time.

Also, when travellers turn aside to a hostel, they are sometimes tucked up in expensive bedclothes, and they eat and drink out of valuable ware, but after they have finished eating they do not take these things away with them, any more than they brought them with them when they came. And it is the same with us in this world. "We brought nothing into the world, and there is no doubt that we cannot take anything away with us either" *(1 Tim. 6:7).*

Again, the owner of the hostel makes good cheer with his guests and is very affable to them, while they are there and he is expecting to make money out of them, but when they are gone he soon consigns them to oblivion. And this is how the world treats us when we are dead. "It is like the memory of a passing visitor of a day" *(Wisdom 5:15).*

On a road, too, some people go in one direction, while others go in the opposite direction. And so it is here. Some people are going towards eternal life, while others are going towards the eternal fire. But those who are going towards perdition are many, because that is a wide road and there are many who travel by it.[82] The others, who are going towards life, are few, because that is a narrow road, and there are few who find it.[83] Those who are travelling that narrow road are the penitents. Just as the people who take up their bag and their staff are on the way to Santiago, and those who receive the cross are going overseas,[84] so the people who adopt true penance are pilgrims on their way to Paradise.

(2) Because at this time there are many people in this position, who have been toiling now since the beginning of Lent, the church offers them some encouragement today, in case they collapse. The Lord "has given penitents the way of righteousness and has strengthened those who were flagging to enable them to bear up" *(Ecclus. 17:20).*

(3) There are four ways in which pilgrims are generally encouraged on their way.

One is by singing, and the church does this in the Introit of today's Mass, singing the song of Isaiah, "Rejoice, Jerusalem," and the response of David in the Introit verse, "I was glad at what they said to me."[85] As the Psalm says, "Your judgments became my song in the place of my pilgrimage" *(Psalm 118:54).*

Another way in which pilgrims are encouraged is by telling stories. So the Lord told the two sad disciples who were going to Emmaus everything about himself, and he entertained them in this way until they reached the village where they were going.[86] This is what the church does in today's Epistle, relating the happy[87] tales which Paul brought back from that heavenly city to which he had been caught up,[88] and which is the goal of the pilgrims. "The Jerusalem which is above, which is our mother, is free."[89] "It is free," the church tells us, and so we ought to yearn for it passionately, because freedom is one of things men long for most. And it is "above," and so we ought to put down all our burdens, so that we can climb to it. And it is "our mother," because that heavenly court waits for our arrival with all the eagerness of a mother looking forward to the arrival of her son. And so we ought to make haste.

Another way in which pilgrims are encouraged is by feeding them. Elijah walked for forty days in the strength of the food he had taken when he was exhausted, until he came to the mountain of God, Horeb.[90] The church does this today by speaking in the Gospel about the meal which the Lord gave his followers from the five loaves and two fish.[91] The five loaves are the five books of Moses, which the church begins to read at the night Office at this time.[92] They are tasty inside, but have a hard crust outside. The two fish are the psalms and the prophecies, which are more immediately attractive. These seven together refresh the minds of the Lord's followers.

Another encouragement is thinking about the pleasant conclusion of the journey, which is encouraging because the goal is something greatly desired. "I was glad at what they said to me: 'We shall go to the house of the Lord' " *(Psalm 121:1)*. That really is something to be desired, because there we shall see the Lord himself and have him as our reward.

(4) This is why the church in Rome has the custom of displaying a rose today,[93] signifying Christ, who is the prize and goal of all our penance. And notice that this rose which is displayed is not a mere flower, which is of little value and does not last long or have a very powerful fragrance; it is a golden rose, made up with balsam and musk. These things are the most valuable of their kind, and so is Christ valuable, so valuable that the apostle reckoned everything else to be dung in comparison with him.[94]

Also this rose lasts, and of Christ is says in Hebrews 13:8, "Christ yesterday and today and the same for ever."

Also this rose has a more powerful[95] fragrance than anything else, because of the balsam and musk. And the fragrance of Christ fills heaven and earth, drawing all things to himself. Thus John the Evangelist said to him, "Your fragrance, Lord Jesus, has roused eternal desires in me."[96] "We will run towards the fragrance of your scent" *(Cant. 1:3)*.

So this rose is an excellent symbol of Christ, because of its value, its durability and its immense fragrance.

(5) And this rose is not produced by nature; it is made by a craftsman out of three substances, gold, balsam and musk. Similarly it is due to the working of the Holy Spirit, not of nature, that three substances came together in Christ, namely the substance of Godhead, signified by the gold, the substance of the human soul, signified by the balsam because balsam is a supreme protection against corruption and Christ's soul was not corrupted by sin, and the substance of the flesh, well represented by the musk, which is an animal product, and excels everything else which comes from animals, just as the flesh of Christ excels all natural animal life.

This precludes three wrong beliefs about Christ. One is the error of those who denied that he was truly God. The second is the error of those who denied that he had a soul, maintaining that his Godhead served instead of a soul.[97] The third is the error of those who denied that he had a real body.[98] Just as the rose really possesses the three ingredients listed, so Christ truly possessed all these three things.

(6) Notice that this rose is shown to everyone in the season of penance, because Christ is the prize stored up for all penitents. But it is given to a prince, who can be expected to appreciate such a flower, to make you realise how superior this golden rose is to other roses, so that our consolation[99] must be in Christ and in the capabilities of his power, not in any worldly flower. And it is presented by the Pope or on his authority, because it is he who has the spiritual power to lead men to Christ.

(7) This provides the material for the sermon. For a text: Ecclesiasticus 24:18, "Like a rose planted in Jericho." This is spoken by eternal Wisdom, the Son of God, about himself. Like a rose growing in Jericho and tempting all passers-by to pick it because it is so attractive, the nature of Christ ought to prompt everyone who thinks about it to try to win him.


### XXIV Rogation Days before the Ascension

(1) Notice that, although it is always a good thing to apply oneself to works of penance, the church has certain times set aside specially for such works: Lent is specially consecrated to fasting, and the Pentecost associations[100] are specially consecrated to almsgiving, which is what they are for, like the practice in the early church of breaking bread from house to house (Acts 2:46). The Rogation days are particularly set aside for solemn public prayers. In this connex-

ion, there are three things to consider: why Rogation days were appointed, why they were appointed for this time of the year and what such prayers achieve.

(2) On the first point, notice that when some people get into any kind of distress, they fall at once into despair and do not dream of any way of improving things. But this is contrary to Ecclesiasticus 38:9, "My son, do not neglect yourself in your weakness."

Others resort to their wealth: in sickness they resort to doctors, in legal problems to lawyers, in war to mercenaries, all of whom can be had for money. But this is contrary to 1 Timothy 6:17, "Tell people who are rich in this world not to put their confidence in the uncertainty of wealth."

Others resort to soothsayers, like Saul going to the sorceress in 1 Samuel 28:7ff. But this is contrary to Leviticus 19:31, "Do not go to magicians or enquire of wizards about anything."

But the Jews of old did not behave like this, they resorted to the Lord in their time of need. "They cried to the Lord when they were in trouble" *(Psalm 106:6)*. Nor did the pagan Ninevites when they were afraid that their city was going to be destroyed, but they fasted and put on sackcloth and cried mightily to the Lord *(Jonah 3:4–9)*. Nor do holy christians, but they have recourse to God when troubles press upon them: "I cried to the Lord when I was troubled" *(Psalm 119:1)*. And this was what the blessed Mamertus, archbishop of Vienne, did. Because of the trials which afflicted his city, he established the Rogation days, and the practice then spread to other churches. Look this up in the Matins reading.[101] This is the reason why we have Rogation days.

(3) On the second point, notice that there are three occasions on which important people are particularly likely to be generous. One is when they are holding court on a large scale. Ahasuerus is an example of this: he gave away gifts "on a princely scale" *(Esther 2:18)* when he was holding court like this. Another such occasion is when they have won a great victory. David is an example of this. In 1 Samuel 30:24, after his victory, he wanted the same share in the booty to be given to the people who had stayed behind with the baggage as was given to the people who had actually been engaged in the battle. The third occasion is when a great friend of theirs pleads with them. Solomon is an example, who told his mother, "Ask whatever you want; it is not right for me to deny you anything" *(3 Kings 2:20).*[102]

Now when the Lord ascended to heaven, bringing with him all

the saints who had been held in Limbo, the greatest possible court was held in heaven with God the Father. And Christ ascended there in great triumph, "leading captivity captive."[103] And he made his entry there, as the apostle says, "to intercede for us" before the face of God.[104] It is therefore a good arrangement that there should be Rogation days each year when the celebration of the feast of the Ascension is imminent on earth, and, we may believe, in heaven too,[105] because the greatness of the court that is held there, the splendour of the triumph and the effectiveness of our intercessor all give us grounds for hoping that we shall obtain what we pray for at such a time.

(4) On the third point, we should remark that one of the reasons why prayers have no effect is that the people praying are at fault. As a general rule, anyone who knows he is in a state of sin and does not repent does not deserve to be heard by the Lord, because he is the Lord's enemy.[106] "If I have observed iniquity in my heart, the Lord will not hear me" *(Psalm 65:18)*.

(5) But, though every kind of sin hinders prayer, there are three which particularly have this effect. The first is disobedience towards God. "If anyone turns his ear aside from hearing the law, his prayer will become detestable" *(Prov. 28:9)*. The second is lack of pity for the poor. "If anyone shuts his ear to the cry of the poor, when he himself cries, he will not be heard" *(Prov. 21:13)*. And the third is bearing a grudge against your neighbour. "Does a man retain his anger against another man and then ask God for help?" *(Ecclus. 28:3)*.

(6) To ensure the effectiveness of prayer, then, everyone who prays ought first to confess his sins. "Confess your sins to one another," it says in James 5:16, and then it goes on, "And pray." He must also obey God's commandments. As Gregory says, "If we do what God tells us, there is no doubt that we shall obtain what we ask him for."[107] He must also be kind to the poor. "Break your bread for the hungry," it says in Isaiah 58:7; "Then you will call to the Lord and he will hear you" *(Is. 58:9)*. He must also forgive other people. "When you stand to pray, forgive whatever it may be that you hold against anyone, so that your Father who is in heaven may forgive you too" *(Mark 11:25)*.

(7) Sometimes our prayer loses its power because of the nature of the thing we are praying for.[108] This is the case when, for example, we ask for vengeance on our enemies or for something sinful, which

would be deadly for us, or for worldly prosperity, which is often harmful to foolish people who ask for it, or for the removal of some scourge or trial, as the apostle prayed for his "thorn in the flesh" to be taken away *(2 Cor. 12:7–9)*; he did not get what he prayed for, because it was useful for him to suffer in this way. It is like the case of a sick man asking for things which would actually kill him or harm him, or clamouring to be relieved from his tiresome sweating: a kind doctor does not listen to him, and it is for the same reason that the Lord rejects this sort of prayer. So it says in James 4:3, "You ask and you do not receive, because you ask badly." Things like this, then, ought not to be prayed for; instead we should pray for things which are useful and which will really count. In John 16:24, the Lord says, "So far you have not asked for anything," anything that will really count, that is; it is like the common idiom, "You are not saying anything," meaning "What you are saying does not really amount to anything." "Ask," he goes on, meaning "Ask for something which will count," "and then you will receive."

(8) Sometimes our prayers have no effect because the person we are praying for is not worthy. "Do not pray for this people, do not take up praise and petition on their behalf, because I shall not hear you" *(Jer. 7:16, 11:14)*. This means that people who ask for our prayers should be warned that they must also help themselves. In the *Lives of the Fathers* one of the old men said to someone who was troubled by a spirit of fornication and was asking for his prayers, "It is out of the question that the spirit of fornication will leave you at the prayers of others, unless you yourself tackle the job, with fasting and prayers and vigils, beseeching God with tears and groans."[109]

(9) Sometimes the inefficacy of our prayer is due to a lack of intercessors. It is sometimes possible to obtain something by the prayers of others, which we could not obtain by our own prayers. This is illustrated by the story of the Canaanite woman who was not heard when she cried out on her own account, but was heard when the apostles interceded for her *(Matt. 15:22–8)*. This is why when Moses is praying he brings in the saints in God's presence, "Remember Abraham, Isaac and Jacob" *(Exod. 32:13)*. And we too should have recourse to the assistance of the saints in our prayers. "Turn to one of the saints" *(Job 5:1)*.

(10) Sometimes what is lacking to our prayer is the support of its assistants, such as fasting and almsgiving, which are the two wings, so

to speak, which enable a prayer to fly to heaven. This is why anyone who wants to pray ought to apply himself to them. "Prayer with fasting and almsgiving is good," as the angel says in Tobit 12:8.

(11) Sometimes the ineffectiveness of our prayer is due to the curses of people complaining about us, as when a poor man who has been rebuffed by a rich man or oppressed by somebody powerful curses them. "One is praying, another is cursing: whose voice will the Lord hear?" *(Ecclus. 34:29).* This is why we should accept the advice of Ecclesiasticus 4:5–6, "Do not leave beggars to curse you behind your back; the imprecation of a man who curses you in the bitterness of his soul will be heard: he who made him will listen to him."

(12) Sometimes it is due to the manner of our prayer, as, for instance, when it lacks the proper features which normally make prayer effective. There are three[110] such features. One is the affection of the heart, which means that a man invokes the Lord with his heart, not just with his voice. This is the psalmist's plea: "I have called with all my heart, hear me, Lord" *(Psalm 118:145).* Another feature is the humility which consists of such things as genuflexions and prostrations. "He looked on the prayer of the humble and did not despise their petitions" *(Psalm 101:18).* The example of the men of Nineveh shows this to be true.[111] The third feature is perseverance. A poor man who will not wait at the door often fails to get the alms that another man gets, who stays there clamouring. "If he perseveres with his knocking. . . ." *(Luke 11:8).*

(13) This provides the material for the sermon. For a text: Luke 11:9, "Ask, and it will be given to you, seek and you will find, knock and it will be opened to you." Augustine says, "He would not encourage us so much to ask, unless he wanted to give. Human laziness should blush: he is more eager to give than we are to receive."[112]

Another text could be Jeremiah 33:3, "Cry to me and I will hear you."

# D. Sermons for
## Saints and Feast Days

*VII The Most Holy Virgin Mary*

(1) Notice that there have been some people who have enjoyed great renown in their lifetime, but their sins made them unworthy of any remembrance after their death. "You rebuked the nations and the impious man perished, you destroyed their name for ever and ever.... Their remembrance has perished with all report of them" *(Psalm 9:6–7)*. There have been others whose memory has lived on for a time, but not for very long. "Like the remembrance of a passing visitor of a day" *(Wisd. 5:15)*. But there are others who have been inscribed in the list of the saints, and their remembrance will last forever. "The just man will be remembered forever" *(Psalm 111:7)*. This is why there are feast days and commemorations and churches and altars and other such things in their honour, to preserve their memory always.

(2) Now among all the men and women saints, there is none who is remembered as much as the blessed Virgin. She has the most images in our churches, she has her own day in every week, she has a special Office which is said every day, and many churches hold a procession in her honour every day and make a remembrance of her; and throughout the world she has more feast days than any other saint.

(3) Now notice that there are three reasons why we celebrate saints' days. The first is to give honour to the saints, and this is the purpose of the church's Office for them. Secondly it is to provide us with an example, and this is why there should be a sermon making known the saint's life. And thirdly it is to win the saint's help, and that is why we make prayers to him.

(4) Now among all the saints, the highest reverence is due to the

blessed Virgin. Reverence is shown to a thing for a variety of reasons. It may be due to its holiness. "Fear my sanctuary" *(Lev. 26:2)*, with reverential fear, that is. But the blessed Virgin is holier than anything else. Or it may be due to rank. This is why we show reverence to a bishop. But the blessed Virgin's rank is higher than any other, which is why it says in Psalm 44:13, "All the richest men of the people will entreat your countenance." Or it may be due to power. But her very name means "Lady" in Syriac,[113] and she is commonly referred to as "Our Lady." So on the grounds of supreme holiness, supreme rank and supreme power, supreme reverence is owed to her. At this point the preacher can mention anything that will inspire people to serve and honour her.

(5) Also there is no better model for us among all the holy men and women. Some among them possessed some good qualities, but they also possessed some bad qualities.[114] But she is not like that. She is a model with no blemishes at all. "You are entirely beautiful, my love, there is no blemish in you" *(Cant. 4:7)*. And indeed there was no blemish in her; as Ambrose says in his book *On Virginity*, "When did she ever hurt her parents, even by so much as a look? When did she have any disagreements with her neighbours? When did she despise the humble? When did she mock the weak? When did she shun the needy? There was no fierceness in her eyes, nothing impertinent in her words, nothing shameless in her deeds, no sudden gestures, nothing dissolute in her gait, no petulance in her voice."[115]

(6) And there have been many holy men who had real virtues, but imperfectly. But her virtues were absolutely perfect.[116] Ambrose says in his book *On Virginity*, "She was a virgin in mind as well as in body, humble of heart, serious in her words, sensible in mind, sparing of speech, studious in reading, putting her hope in the poor man's prayer, not in the uncertainty of wealth, attentive to her work, bashful in conversation, used[117] to making God, not man, the arbiter of her opinions, accustomed to harming nobody, wishing well to everyone, standing up respectfully in the presence of her elders, free from envy of her contemporaries; she always shunned boasting, followed reason, and loved virtue."[118] This is why Ecclesiasticus 24:17–19 several times calls her "Exalted"; it is because of the excellence of her virtues.

(7) Also there are many holy people in whom an example can be found of many virtues; but not of all virtues. But she offers an

example of all virtues. So Ecclesiasticus 24:25 says, "In me is every grace of life and virtue."

This shows what an outstanding model she is for us, because she was pure and perfect and complete.

(8) Also the assistance of the blessed Virgin is better than that of all the other saints. She is extremely powerful in the court of heaven. "My power is in Jerusalem" *(Ecclus. 24:15)*. Bernard says, "She can never be without the means to help, since she is the queen of heaven."[119] And she is energetic in getting help for us; this is why she is appropriately symbolised in Abigail, the sensible woman whose wisdom soothed king David and secured the deliverance of her foolish husband from death *(1 Sam. 25:3,23ff)*. As Bernard says, "As man, you have a sure way to God. To approach the Son, you have his mother, and to approach the Father you have the Son. The mother shows her Son her breasts, the Son shows his Father his side and his wounds. Where so many marks of charity come together, you can never be repulsed."[120]

She is also kind and well-disposed to help, "Like a beautiful olive tree in the fields" *(Ecclus. 24:19)*, from which everyone can take what he wants. Bernard says, "Most blessed Virgin, no one should be silent about your mercy, unless there is anyone who has called upon it in his time of need and felt that it failed him."[121] How happy, how deserving of all praise, is the assistance of her who has the power, the wisdom, the will and the kindness to help us in our distress.

(9) So we ought to venerate so venerable a virgin, being careful not to do anything in her presence which would be unseemly, whether in our hearts or in our mouths or in any movement we make. Then the reverence we show to his mother will win us grace and glory from the Son. And we should look carefully at such an excellent model, and, as Ambrose says, "Anyone who desires her prize should imitate her example."[122] Let us come with confidence to the throne of Christ's grace, the blessed Virgin, that is, so that we may receive mercy and find the timely help of grace *(Hebr. 4:16)*. As Bernard says, "If she is holding you, you will not fall, if she is protecting you, you have nothing to fear, if she is leading you, you will not grow weary, if she is merciful, you will arrive."[123] Here the preacher can mention all the stories of her help found in the *Histories* and *Miracles*.[124]

(10) This provides the material for the sermon. For a text: Ecclesiasticus 24:28, "My remembrance is from age to age."

## XVI  For Doctors of the Church

(1) It is to be noticed that the Lord established in his church first of all apostles, who passed on to us the tradition of christian faith and morals, and then prophets, who taught us about the future, as we can see in the Apocalypse,[125] and thirdly doctors, who expounded the writings of the first two. All three are explicitly mentioned in the text and in the Gloss[126] at 1 Cor. 12:28.

(2) Now these doctors are called "holy," because their teaching was not about fables, like that of the poets, nor was it just concerned to satisfy our curiosity, like that of many of the philosophers, nor was it just about worldly wisdom, like that of the lawyers, nor was it about the wisdom of the flesh, like that of the physicians; their teaching was about the righteousness which brings salvation. This kind of teacher is accordingly called a "teacher of righteousness" *(Joel 2:23)*.

Another reason for calling them holy is that they were holy men, who practised what they taught, unlike the scribes and pharisees, who spoke but did not act.[127]

Also they were taught by the Holy Spirit, because the Holy Spirit, who inspired the scriptures, is also the one who expounds them, as the authority says.[128]

And notice what Daniel 12:3 says in praise of such people, "Those who instruct many people in righteousness will shine forever like stars." And the apostle ranks them before the workers of miracles: "Thirdly doctors, then powers," by which he means people who work miracles *(1 Cor. 12:28)*. And Christ himself said, "Whoever practises and teaches will be called great in the kingdom of heaven" *(Matt. 5:19)*.

(3) Notice also that almost all error has arisen because of some wrong understanding of scripture. Gregory says, "The plain statements of the commentators have now made clear to us the views of the men of old."[129] In this way they have guided us into right belief.

(4) Again, just as Solomon had an armoury in which his weapons were stored,[130] so these holy doctors stored away countless weapons in the armoury of their books, in the form of arguments and authorities, with which the church can defend herself against all her enemies, whether heretics or demons or vices or anything else. This is "the complete armament of the strong" in Cant. 4:4, which is glossed, "That is, thorough training in the works and the doctrine of heaven,

by which the saints overcome the ranks of wickedness."[131]

(5) Again, as Gregory says, just as in the appearance of the sky we notice some stars whose rising is not followed by rain, and others which herald the coming of plenty of rain, so it is in the church too: there have been some saints who have not given us any teaching, and others who have poured into the world an abundance of important doctrine.[132] From this has come a great crop of good results. So Moses says, "May my teaching grow like the rain" *(Deut. 32:2).*

These holy doctors, then, have taught us the authentic interpretation of scripture, they have equipped the church against her enemies, and have made the world fruitful.[133]

(6) But, alas, there are many people whose attitude to them and to their teaching is quite wrong.

There are some who turn away from these great men, who were outstanding in philosophy[134] and in every kind of learning, as well as being instructed by the Holy Spirit, to follow some ignorant, untrained heretic or other, accepting his interpretations rather than theirs. But 1 John 4:1 says, "Beloved, do not trust every spirit, but test the spirits to see if they are from God," which implies that we ought to follow holy men who have the Spirit of God rather than these seducers.

(7) Then there are others who ascribe authority to their own interpretations (or, more often, fantasies) and despise those of the saints. Jerome says that some people "consider that their every word is God's law; they disdain to find out what the apostles and prophets really meant, and use texts which do not fit to bolster up their own views,"[135] despising the interpretations of the saints, that is.

(8) Then there are people who find the teaching of the saints insipid by comparison with the words of the philosophers or law or other sciences, and this is a symptom of spiritual sickness. Augustine says, "Anyone who finds the honey of heaven tasteless has a sick palate."[136] By the "honey of heaven" he means the sweet flavour of the exposition of the scriptures.

Scripture's honeycomb you opened,
Teaching us its hidden meaning.[137]

It is a serious abuse to prefer the opinions of heretics to those of the saints, or to follow one's own views rather than theirs, or to find more taste in the insipidity of other sciences than in the sweetness of this doctrine. It is a symptom of serious disorder when someone loses the taste for what is really tasty and enjoys only what is tasteless.

(9) Then there are others who cannot even be bothered to listen to their teaching. "Fools despise wisdom and teaching" *(Prov. 1:7)*, the teaching, that is, of the wise. Such people are like babies who refuse their milk. The teaching of the saints is milk squeezed out from the breasts of the Old and New Testaments by the church's doctors. To refuse it is the way to death. "The babies' refusal," of the breast, that is, "will kill them" *(Prov. 1:32)*. On the other hand, it says in 1 Peter 2:2, "Like newborn babes, desire milk."[138]

These are also the people who die of thirst because they will not drink the good water drawn from the well of scripture by the ministry of the doctors. "Because they have no knowledge, the whole multitude of them is parched with thirst" *(Isaiah 5:13)*. But Rebecca drew water in a pitcher and said, "Drink, sir."[139]

They are also the people who refuse to eat the bread of scripture which the hands of the doctors have broken for them. If the prophet laments that "the children asked for bread and there was no one to break it for them" *(Lam. 4:4)*, how much more distressing it is if there is no one to eat the bread which has been broken.

(10) Then there are other people who do listen to this kind of teaching, but do not profit by it, like a tree planted by the running streams[140] which never bears fruit. But it says in Ecclesiasticus 39:17, "Bring forth fruit like a rose planted by streams of water."

The holy doctors are like good cooks, too. They prepare a splendid banquet from the words of our Saviour and the prophets and apostles. But these wretches, though they are at the banquet, do not take or digest any of the food. But in Cant. 5:1, it says, "Eat, my friends, get drunk, my beloved companions."

They also provide us with armour so that we can defend ourselves, as has already been said. But these people refuse to put it on, and so they are easily defeated, because they are unarmed. But the apostle says, "Put on the armour of God" *(Eph. 6:11)*.

(11) This provides the material for the sermon. For a text: 1 Cor. 12:28, "Thirdly he established doctors in the church."

### XX For Mary Magdalene and Other Such Saints

(1) Notice that the church celebrates not only holy virgins and widows, but also penitent sinners; but she does not celebrate all such

penitents indiscriminately, but only some who were great sinners at first, and then did great penance, and who are believed finally, on the evidence of definite signs, to have flown to heaven, like the blessed Magdalene and St. Mary of Egypt and St. Pelagia and some others.

(2) Notice that there are three factors which make it difficult for people to abandon their sins. The first is sensual pleasure, which is the devil's birdlime. This is why it is difficult to abandon the sin of fornication, because there is particularly intense sensual pleasure in this sin. "They will not give thought to return to the Lord, because there is a spirit of fornication in their midst" *(Hosea 5:4)*. The second is habit, because, as Augustine says, "A habit which is not resisted becomes a need."[141] "If the Ethiopian can change his skin, then you too will be able to do good after you have learned to do evil" *(Jer. 13:23)*. The third is notoriety. Once his sin has become notorious, a man acquires the "cheek of a harlot"[142] and loses all sense of shame, and so comes to be all the more hardened in his sin. The Gloss on Matt. 18:15, "Take him aside and rebuke him between yourselves" says that this is to avoid making him lose all shame and so remain in his sin.[143] What a grace it was from God, then, that women like these were able to forsake sins in which not only one of these factors was present, but all of them: they were sins of the flesh, they were habitual, and they were well known.

(3) Notice next that some people who turn from their sins to do penance fall short in that they do not grieve sufficiently over their past sins. But it says in Jeremiah 6:26, "Take to yourself grief as for an only son, bitter lamenting." David is a good example. When he was converted after his sin, he said, "I have toiled in my groaning" *(Psalm 6:7)*.

Others fall short in not being careful enough to avoid backsliding in the future, and to flee from the occasions of sin. But in Genesis 19:17, after he had left Sodom, Lot was told, "Do not stay in this neighbourhood." Again David is an example. He said, "See, I have fled far away and remained in solitude" *(Psalm 54:8)*.

Others fall short in undertaking works of penance which are inadequate by comparison with the magnitude of their previous sins. But it says in Luke 3:8, "Bring forth worthy fruits of penance." Manesseh is a good example. It says of him in 2 Chron. 33:12, "He did penance strenuously in the sight of the Lord, the God of his fathers."

(4) There are three things, then, which make for greatness of penance: great grief over the past, great carefulness for the future,

and great works of penance in the present. And all three were found in the kind of penitent sinner the church celebrates.

The first is obvious from the quantity of tears they shed, as anyone can find out by looking at the *Lives* of Mary Magdalene, Mary of Egypt and St. Pelagia.[144] The second is obvious from their *Lives* too. Mary Magdalene, for instance, after her conversion lived her life either with the Lord and his disciples, or in a cave, where she remained for more than thirty years. And Mary of Egypt went into the desert immediately after her conversion, and remained there, unknown to the world, for more than forty years. St. Pelagia, after her conversion, fled secretly and became a recluse in the guise of a monk. The third feature is obvious from all the fasting and austerities and vigils and other such things which we read about in their *Lives*. This shows how great their penance was.

(5) It should also be noticed that the sons of Israel, after they had left Egypt, went through the desert to the Promised Land; in the same way these women left their sins and then made their way through the desert of penance to the kingdom of heaven.[145] The evidence of their arrival there is the number of extraordinary things which occurred in connexion with their deaths. St. Mary Magdalene, at the time of her death, was seen by the hermit who buried her, raised up in front of the altar, surrounded by angels. When St. Mary of Egypt died, Zosimas, who found her in the desert, was too old and weak to dig her grave; a lion came and dug a grave with its claws. When St. Pelagia died, having lived as a recluse under the name of the monk Pelagius, and was found to be a woman, she was buried in an honourable place by the bishop of Jerusalem, and was mourned with incredible devotion by the monks and virgins and others. Then there was also Thais, who had been a famous courtesan and was converted by St. Paphnutius. She lived in remarkable penance for three years as a recluse. When St. Paphnutius went to St. Anthony to enquire whether God had accepted her penance, Paul, Anthony's disciple, was shown a vision of a splendid bed being guarded in heaven by three virgins. Paul remarked that it could only be the bed reserved for his father Anthony, but he was told that it was not for Anthony, it was being reserved for Thais the harlot. He told this to Paphnutius, who went back and brought her out and comforted her. Fifteen days later she died in peace.[146] See what signs there were that these sinful women had passed to everlasting glory, changed from vessels of shame to vessels of glory.

(6) There are three things to consider in all of this. First, the great condescension of the Creator. In the law, the high priest never took a prostitute to wife, as it says in Leviticus 21:14. But now the highest priest of all, Christ himself, is so full of mercy that he takes prostitutes like this to be his bride. "I will betrothe you to myself in mercy and compassion" *(Hosea 2:19)*. And this is not so fully realised in this life as it is in the state of glory, where this kind of marriage is never dissolved.

Secondly, there is the humiliation of many people who are still decaying in their own filth, while prostitutes overtake them and get to the kingdom of heaven first. "Truly I say to you, prostitutes will enter the kingdom of God before you" *(Matt. 21:31)*.

Thirdly, this should inspire great confidence in all sinners, seeing that the Lord accepts a prostitute who had sinned with many people in fornication, and he is not merely reconciled with her when she returns to him, he promotes her to glory like this. "I will give them the valley of Achor to open out their hope" *(Hosea 2:15)*, which the moralising interpreters expound as referring to Magdalene, who was a "valley of Achor" (which means "disturbance") because of the depth of her disturbance and contrition.

(7) This provides the material for the sermon. For a text: Romans 5:20, "Where sin abounded, grace has abounded all the more." There was great grace in their conversion, greater grace in their great penance, but superabundant grace in their glorification. None of these could have happened without grace.

## Notes

1. *Videtur facere* R, *creditur fecisse* ABSL.
2. *Pecorum* RB, *porcorum* ("pigs") AL, *porcarum* ("female pigs") S.
3. *Se parificare* BSL, *de se parificare* A, *parificari* R.
4. Matt. 10:41.
5. *Sorores de cura fratrum praedicatorum*: for several centuries there seems to be a pronounced reluctance, especially, but not exclusively, in non-Dominican sources, to say bluntly "nuns of the Order of Preachers." No doubt this reluctance, at least among the Dominicans, was increased by the controversies surrounding the nuns. The main fear of the brethren is that they would get swamped by the nuns, and so not be able to do their primary work of preaching to the unconverted and the semi-converted. For a concise account of the whole affair, see Hinnebush, *History of the Dominican Order* I

pp. 387–393. C. Casagrande, *Prediche alla Donne del secolo XIII* (Milan, 1978), which contains an Italian translation of this sermon, as well as a study of related material, came into my hands too late for me to use it.

6. Gen. 5:4, 7 etc.

7. Like many of his contemporaries, Humbert was deeply unsympathetic to religious women who wanted to practise the same kind of itinerant religious life as the friars. At the beginning of the century one of the regular conditions laid down for evangelistic groups seeking reconciliation with or recognition by ecclesiastical authority was that they should not have women travelling with them or engaging in any kind of apostolic activity. Humbert himself, in his *Opus Tripartitum* prepared for the Council of Lyons in 1274 (III 3), recommends that no foundation should be authorised for religious women unless they could demonstrate their means of subsistence, so that the "unseemly and dangerous" practice of letting them wander round could be halted entirely.

8. *Quaedam* SL, *multae* B, om. RA.

9. There is perhaps a hint of complacency in this remark, as Humbert himself was probably responsible, as Provincial of France, for the constitutions of the nuns at Montargis (see Creytens, AFP 17 [1947] p. 56), which provided the basis for the constitutions imposed, by Humbert again, this time as Master of the Order, on all Dominican nuns in 1259. For a brief account of the complicated early history of the constitutions of the nuns, see Hinnebusch, *History* I pp. 380–1.

10. 2 Cor. 6:1.

11. There is rather a muddle in the MSS I have looked at here. L cuts the Gordian knot by only giving the second proposed text, with its comment. The others give both texts, but with their references reversed. RBL all omit the comment on the first text.

12. The common confusion between *avertere* and *advertere* seems to have affected the interpretation here. The MSS have *avertit*, but the comment seems to presuppose *advertit* (but (which is found as a variant in the Vulgate). Similarly Hugh of St. Cher clearly reads (and means) *avertit*, but comments in a way that suggests both *avertit* and *advertit*: "Not turning away from suitors, because she does not understand what suitors are."

13. This sentence is found only in AS.

14. This is inferred from Gen. 2:8.

15. Gen. 2:7.

16. Gen. 2:21–2. A adds: "which is nobler"; SL add: "which is better and nobler."

17. Mark 16:9.

18. A reads: "No mere man who will be king of kings ... a woman who will be queen of queens."

19. The MSS I have studied do not give a satisfactory text, though the

general sense is clear: *Haec autem omnia movere debent mulieres ad Dei dilectionem, qui haec contulit eis, et retrahere ab eis quae mala sunt et sectandum (sequendum* R) *quae bona sunt in muliere pro eius amore.*

20. Ps. Chrysostom, PG 52:452–3. For the Latin text, see the edition by Gelenius (Basle, 1547), II 1181–2.

21. *Earum religione ornantes,* the reading in Lyranus, seems preferable to *earum religionem ornantes* of the MSS. Interlinear Gloss.

22. Gen. 34:1ff.

23. Interlinear Gloss.

24. Canon 12 of the Fourth Lateran Council obliged all religious to hold chapters at least every three years, on the model of the Cistercian General Chapter.

25. "Said and done" B.

26. *De Consideratione* IV 20 (III p. 463:26–8).

27. "Holy assemblies" APB.

28. *Apologia* 19 (III p. 97:6–10).

29. APS add "of their religious life."

30. Only AS have "or outsider," but it is required by the syntax.

31. *Nam* is the reading in Benedict; RAPB have *non,* S omits it.

32. *Acceptus* RP, *accepta* ABS, *acceptum* Benedict.

33. *Rule of St. Benedict* 5:16–18. 2 Cor. 9:7.

34. The MSS are in a muddle here. I have followed APB, which seem to have the best reading.

35. *Malitiae in admixtione* APB, *malitia in admixtione* RS. Neither of these will really do. I conjecture either *malitiae inadmixtio* (though I know of no other evidence for there being such a word) or *malitiae admixtio.*

36. The latter part of this text is from the Interlinear Gloss. The first half is not in the printed text of the Gloss or in any MS I have looked at, but it is not an implausible comment to look for in the Gloss.

37. The MSS I have seen all have *offendiculis divinis,* which I find difficult. I have omitted *divinis* in my translation.

38. *Disticha Catonis* 23 (ed. M. Boas [Amsterdam, 1952] p. 19).

39. I read *reipublicae,* with the text of Gregory; RAPBS all have *rei.* Hagenau's *Regi* looks like an ideological misreading!

40. PL 77:565B.

41. Humbert is probably thinking of the episode in late November, 1199, at the beginning of the Fourth Crusade, when a group of knights who had come to a tournament at Écry decided to become crusaders. See K. M. Setton, *A History of the Crusades* II (Philadelphia, 1962) p. 158.

42. 1 Pet. 2:11.

43. RAPBS all have *tranquillitas;* I have imported *frugalitas* from the text of Augustine.

44. PL 33:856 §7.

45. Interlinear Gloss.

46. Interlinear Gloss.

47. P inserts here the text from Job 21:13, which is echoed in the previous lines: "They spend their days in good things."

48. P adds a line from the Lauds hymn, *Aeterne rerum conditor*: "So let us rise energetically" (*surgamus ergo strenue*). This hymn was not used in the Dominican rite.

49. A slightly inaccurate quotation from *Letters* 2:4.

50. This story comes from Jacques de Vitry. See J. Greven, *Die Exempla aus den Sermones Feriales et Communes des Jakob von Vitry* (Heidelberg, 1914), no. 27.

51. Cf. Augustine, *Confessions* V 9:17.

52. PL 23:485B.

53. Psalm 118:164.

54. P adds a line from another Lauds hymn, *Lux ecce surgit aurea*: "The watcher is present on high" (*speculator astat desuper*). This hymn was not used in the Dominican rite.

55. Gen. 1:9.

56. Gen. 1:11.

57. Gen. 1:11.

58. The explanation of "microcosm" is given only in B.

59. PL 76:1205B.

60. Humbert here refers back to his sermon for Mondays, and forward to the sermons for the other days of the week. There we learn that on Mondays, the church thinks specially of the dead, and people go and visit cemeteries; Wednesday is a fast day, Thursday is specially dedicated to the Holy Spirit, Friday to the remembrance of the Cross, and Saturday to our Lady.

61. This is the Invitatory for Matins on ferial Tuesdays.

62. *Sermons on the Canticle* 11:1 (I p. 54:25–55:2).

63. Hebr. 8:5.

64. Psalm 32:3.

65. The belief that Jewish sacrifices were instituted to channel an unconquerable lust for sacrifice is widely attested in the early church, and is found in St. Thomas, *Summa Theologiae* Ia IIae q.102 a.3, and in Peraldus, *Summa de Virtutibus*, Justice VI 3. It is even found in Maimonides, *Guide for the Perplexed* III 32, and this is quoted by another Dominican, Raymund Martin, *Pugio Fidei* III d.3 c.12:13. For earlier texts, see Justin, *Dialogue* 19:6, 22; *Clementine Recognitions* 1:36; Chrysostom, *adv. Iud.* 4:6; Aphrahat, *Dem.* 15:7.

66. E.g. Psalms 95:1, 97:1, 149:1; Isaiah 12:5, 42:10; Jeremiah 20:13.

67. This is mentioned as a possible interpretation by Hugh of St. Cher.

68. Cf. Augustine, *Confessions* IX 6:14. Also the Legenda for Augustine's feast day in the Dominican Lectionary (Regensburg Lectionary, Oxford, Keble MS 49, f.176$^r$; Brit. Libr., MS Addit. 23935 f.229$^r$).

69. I cannot identify this reference.

70. Marginal Gloss. I have emended the text in accordance with the reading in the Gloss: *pestem <de corde> depellat.*

71. PL 76:793A.

72. "Go racing ahead" is omitted by RB, but it is in P and in Cicero.

73. *De Officiis* I 102.

74. *Vindicandum* B, *iudicandum* RP.

75. The pagan name for this day was "Mars' day" (as in French *Mardi*); similarly in English "Tuesday" is derived from the Norse god of war, Tyr. For Mars being hot and dry, cf. Albert, *Metaphysica* XI 2:25, *De Caelo* II 3:2–3.

76. *De inimicis se non vindicandum* is only in P.

77. In his sermon for Mondays, Humbert attacks the prevalent custom of retaining the pagan names for the days of the week.

78. There is a complex play on words here, which I can see no way of reproducing in English: *feria* (by this time little more than ecclestiastical jargon for "day of the week") is connected with *feriare*, "take a holiday from," the fourth kind of warfare, and *feriare*, "give one's time to," the other three kinds.

79. Πάγος really means "rock."

80. A rather uncouth distortion of "Πάγος."

81. Petrus Comestor, PL 198:1702B.

82. Matt. 7:13.

83. Matt. 7:14.

84. The bag and the staff were the typical emblems of the pilgrim, and the pilgrimage to Santiago was one of the most popular in the Middle Ages; the Cross was the emblem of the crusader.

85. Isaiah 66:10 and Psalm 121:1 form the Introit for the Mass of the Fourth Sunday in Lent.

86. Luke 24:13ff.

87. *Beatos* PB, *bonos* R.

84. 2 Cor. 12:4.

89. Gal. 4:26. The Epistle for this Sunday is Gal. 4:22–5:1 (British Library, MS Addit. 23935 f.532$^r$).

90. 3 Kings 19:5–8.

91. The Gospel for the day is John 6:1–14 (Brit. Libr. MS Addit. 23935 f.552$^r$).

92. This is misleading: the readings from the Pentateuch began at Septuagesima. The most likely explanation, as Fr. A. Dirks, O.P., suggests to me, is that on the fourth Sunday in Lent the readings and responsories began

to be taken from Exodus and so to concern Moses in person.

93. On this curious custom, see New Catholic Encyclopaedia, *Golden Rose*.

94. Phil. 3:8.

95. B adds "and better."

96. PG 5:1250 (Pseudo-Melito). This text is used for the fifth Matins lesson for St. John the Evangelist in the Sarum Breviary.

97. This was the heresy of the Apollinarians.

98. This was a common pattern of heresy in the early church, known as "docetism." It re-appeared in the Middle Ages with the Albigensians.

99. *Confortetur* RPB, but I cannot see what the third person can refer to.

100. The Pentecost Confraternities (or Assemblies) seem to have been a kind of "retreat" for lay people during the days before Pentecost, in which the participants engaged in spiritual exercises and charitable works. We get an idea of what they were from Humbert's own sermon for them (II 89—the printed text is simply entitled *De Confratriis*, but the MSS indicate clearly that the proper title is *In Confratriis Pentecostes*): "We can believe that the practice of holding these assemblies at this time was introduced in antiquity because of the example of the early church. The disciples were assembled together then, and so now the faithful gather in these assemblies; the disciples then were shut in, and similarly the participants in these assemblies are enclosed; the disciples devoted themselves to works of holiness, and similarly for the duration of these assemblies the participants conduct themselves in a more intensely holy way. This is why some of them even sleep there, to abstain from the embraces of their spouses. The disciples put all they had into the common fund, and similarly in these assemblies they all contribute something to the common stock. The disciples then had one heart and mind, and similarly in these assemblies people who had any quarrel are reconciled with one another. And there are directors and masters at such assemblies who are responsible for correcting people if it is necessary, just as discipline prevailed in the early church."

101. The Matins reading for Rogation Tuesday, as found in the Dominican Breviary (i.e. the Office book for travellers) (Arch. Gen. OP XIV L 2 f.210ᵛ; Prototype f.107v), though not in the lectionaries intended for use in choir, reports the institution of these Rogation days by St. Mamertus, bishop of Vienne (c. 470). The main source is the Homily by one of Mamertus's successors at Vienne, Alcimus Avitus (PL 59:289–294).

102. This is not an exact quotation.

103. Eph. 4:8.

104. Hebr. 7:25.

105. *Imminente festo ascensionis in coelo (coelum B) sicut et in terra creditur*

*fieri (fieri creditur* B) RPB does not seem to be correct, but the general sense is clear.

106. B adds a quotation from Isaiah 1:15, "When you multiply your prayers, I shall not listen to them."

107. PL 76:42D.

108. B adds "either its sinfulness or its uselessness."

109. PL 73:746A.

110. "Four" according to B.

111. B adds: "Another feature is that the prayer should be sustained and that it should be made with unshakeable confidence. 'Let him ask in faith, not doubting at all' *(James 1:6)*. This is what Susanna did, whose heart was full of confidence in the Lord *(Daniel 13:42–4)*."

112. PL 38:619.

113. This is a standard etymology in the Latin fathers. Cf. Jerome, PL 23:1236, Isidore, *Etymologies* VII 10:1. *Maria* naturally looks like the feminine of *Mari*, Lord.

114. This is the reading of PB; R has "But there were some good qualities which they did not possess."

115. PL 16:209B.

116. P adds a reference to Prov. 31:29, "Many daughters have accumulated riches, but you have surpassed them all."

117. I have added *solita* from Ambrose. It is missing in RPB.

118. PL 16:209A.

119. *Sermons on the Assumption* 1:2 (V p. 229:21–2).

120. This is actually a text from Arnold of Bonneval, PL 189:1726CD. I have put in the fuller text from P, as it makes the sense clearer; but since P concludes by repeating, "The mother shows her Son her breasts," which is all that RB quote, I suspect that this may be all that Humbert originally included from this text.

121. *Sermons on the Assumption* 4:8 (V p. 249:17–18).

122. PL 16:210D.

123. *Homilies on 'Missus est'* 2:17 (IV p. 35:13–14).

124. From the twelfth century onwards there was an incredible pullulation of Lives of our Lady and collections of Miracles of our Lady, in Latin and in the vernacular. For some bibliographical information, see J. Leclercq, F. Vandenbroucke, L. Bouyer, *The Spirituality of the Middle Ages*, pp. 251–2.

125. Cf. Apoc. 4:1.

126. Marginal Gloss; but Humbert does not in fact follow the Gloss's interpretation. The Gloss takes the prophets to be the interpreters of scripture, leaving the Doctors with the job of providing the church with moral teaching and giving elementary instruction to children.

127. Matt. 23:3.

128. Cf. above, p. 325[94].

129. PL 76:71C.

130. 2 Chron. 9:16.

131. Marginal Gloss.

132. PL 76:405B.

133. This is the reading of P. RB have: "They have equipped us against our enemies, and have made the church and the world fruitful."

134. *Philosophia* B *prophetiis* RP.

135. PL 22:544.

136. I cannot identify this reference, but cf. Augustine, *Enarr. in Ps. 18* II 11.

137. From the Matins hymn for the feast of St. Augustine.

138. Quoted in the form used in the Introit of the Mass of Low Sunday.

139. Gen. 24:18.

140. Cf. Psalm 1:3.

141. *Confessions* VIII 5:10.

142. Jer. 3:3.

143. Interlinear Gloss.

144. The legend of Mary Magdalen underwent considerable development in the thirteenth century; Humbert's version of the story is close to that of James of Varagine. His account of Mary of Egypt and Pelagia corresponds to those given in their lives in PL 73:663–690.

145. RPB diverge significantly in this sentence. I have followed R. B omits most of it, while P expands it.

146. For the life of Thais, cf. PL 73:661–2.

# Appendix to Humbert

## A SELECTION FROM "THE GIFT OF FEAR"

# Prologue

*Both Humbert of Romans and Stephen of Bourbon compiled collections of* exempla *(illustrative anecdotes), structured on the basis of the Gifts of the Spirit, for the use of preachers. The demarcation between the two works is far from clear in the surviving manuscripts. It is probable that both writers used a common stock of anecdotes, and it is certain that they swapped anecdotes, since each one refers to the other as a source. We may recognise, behind the work of each individual, a collective enterprise similar to that which produced the great biblical studies in the Dominican house of St. Jacques in Paris.[1] Humbert refers to at least two sections of his own collection of* exempla *in the model sermons that conclude his work* On the Formation of Preachers, *which sufficiently guarantees the authenticity of at least part of the surviving treatise. One of these sections is translated here. There seems no reason to doubt the authenticity of the Prologue either. At what point in his career Humbert composed this work we cannot now tell, but it must antedate at least the completion of* On the Formation of Preachers.

As Gregory says,[2] people find exemplary anecdotes more moving than mere words; they are also easier to grasp and make a deeper impression on the memory, and many people find them more enjoyable to listen to, so that the sheer pleasure of them attracts some people to come to sermons. It is therefore useful that men who have been given the job of preaching should have a ready flow of such anecdotes for use in public sermons and in conferences to people who fear God and in private conversations with all kinds of people, to bring help and salvation to all men.

373

This manner of teaching and preaching certainly ought not to be despised. It evidently has weighty authority behind it. The Most High poured out his wisdom over all perceptible creatures[3] in such a way that even ants can be proposed to us as an example of wisdom.[4] Almost the whole Law was given to Moses under certain symbolic figures which dramatise the truth. Almost everything that the prophets said about spiritual things, under the inspiration of the Holy Spirit, was stated in the guise of bodily ideas. And was not the whole wisdom of Solomon expressed in parables and proverbs, illustrating what he wanted to say? Did not the Saviour himself give most of his teaching by means of comparisons? And finally what else are all the many sacraments and sacramentals of the church, but a kind of bodily representation of spiritual realities? Many considerations like this show how well grounded this manner of teaching is.

This is why many wise and holy men are found making use of it. This was how Gregory preached; as his Homilies show, he included *exempla* of this kind in nearly every sermon he delivered. We are also told that the founder of the Orders of Friars Preachers, St. Dominic, overflowed with *exempla* like this when he was talking to his companions on the road and in his conversations with all kinds of people.[5]

And it is not surprising that such people followed this method, considering how fruitful it is. Bede reports in his *History of the English* that a learned and sophisticated bishop was sent from Ireland by his colleagues to convert the English, and he achieved nothing with his clever preaching; but then another bishop was sent, who was less learned but more circumspect, and he converted almost the whole of England by using anecdotes and parables in his sermons.[6] Master Jacques de Vitry, a holy and educated man, who was a Canon Regular first, then bishop of Acre, and finally Cardinal bishop of Tusculum, set the whole of France on fire with his sermons in that kingdom, by using *exempla*; there is no record of anything like it, before or after.[7] John Damascene relates in his book called *Barlaam* how the hermit, Barlaam, was sent by God to convert Josaphat, the son of a pagan king, who was being kept in seclusion to prevent his being reached by any christian preaching; Barlaam worked for a long time to convert him and instruct him in the catholic faith, and he almost always used parables and exquisite *exempla* in all he said, and in this way Josaphat was not only converted to the catholic faith, but also attained such a peak of perfection that, when he succeeded his father as king, he converted the kingdom to faith in Christ and eventually abandoned his throne and became an outstandingly perfect hermit and so passed away to Christ.[8] Augustine's conversion too was provoked more by what Simplicianus told him about Victorinus and by the example of the extraordinary life of St. Anthony the hermit, which moved him deeply, than by the sermons of St. Ambrose or by his mother's prayers and tears or by the scourge of sickness, as we can see from his *Life*.[9]

Of these instances, the first two show that famous men have made use of this kind of *exemplum* to save souls, the next two show what results can be achieved by this kind of public preaching, and the last two show how profitable the use of *exempla* can be in private conversation.

But we must notice that there are various things which have to be taken into account in this kind of teaching.

The first concerns the person of the teacher. Many people have been given more grace[10] to use authorities or arguments or exegesis in what they say, than they have for the use of *exempla*; maybe they lack the ability to tell stories attractively,[11] and in this case they ought not to abandon the style in which they do have grace,[12] for one in which they do not.

The second point concerns the people being taught. We should hesitate to offer *exempla* like this to highly intelligent, wise men, unless they are particularly good and worth telling; we should offer them rather to people of less intelligence, for whom they are appropriate as milk is for babies.[13]

Thirdly, the preacher must use *exempla* in a balanced way. It is not right to weave a whole sermon out of such material. Moderate use must be made of them, following the example of Gregory, who never put more than one or two into a single sermon. They should be like the entremets served in between courses at an aristocratic banquet to give extra pleasure to the guests.

Fourthly, an *exemplum* should not be left standing on its own. The preacher should try hard to ensure that he always supports it with an effective authority or argument, if not both, to make his point more strongly.

Fifthly, care must be taken in selecting *exempla*. Out of the many possible ones, the most telling and the most obviously useful should be chosen, and they should, if possible, be concise, and if they involve a long story, only what is relevant to the point at issue should be related; less useful elements, or utterly useless elements, should be cut back to a minimum.

The sixth point concerns truthfulness. Implausible stories should never be told, nor should stories which do not contain some probable basis in fact. And if some tale is related, because of some very edifying meaning it is capable of—and this should only be done very infrequently, if at all—the speaker must always make it quite clear that what he is relating is not true, but is only mentioned because of what it signifies.

Seventhly, no *exemplum* should be included which does not have a sufficient weight of authority behind it. In such matters a story can be taken to have sufficient authority if it derives from something that has been said by distinguished people like masters in theology or bishops or cardinals. But it is better to take material which is found in one of the books which the church uses, even if they are not fully authoritative, like the *Lives of the Fathers* or the liturgical lives of the saints. But it is better still to take material from the books of the approved doctors of the church, like Gregory and Isidore and Jerome. The best thing of all is to take material from the Bible. But the books of well-known philosophers can also count as having sufficient authority, as can the book of creation. The *exempla* contained in this treatise are almost all taken from these sources.

But it is important in such things not to ascribe to any story more certainty than it deserves, in case some falsehood gets mixed up with what is really sure. And with a view to this, since all the material used in edifying talk can be subsumed under the seven Gifts of the Holy Spirit or the things that go with these gifts, the present treatise is divided into seven parts, corresponding to the gifts of the sevenfold Spirit, and it is he who must be invoked if the work is to be brought to a useful conclusion.

## SUFFRAGES FOR THE SOULS IN PURGATORY

In connexion with the suffrages which are made for the dead, it is to be noticed that some heretics claim that Masses and offerings and other such suffrages do the dead no good, but are simply an invention of the clergy to get money out of uneducated people.[14] People who are cruel to the dead in this way resemble that cruel beast, the hyena, which savages the tombs and the bodies of the dead.[15] In Jeremiah 12:8, "Is not my inheritance like a lion in the woods?," another version has, "Like a hyena's cave,"[16] because, that is, it rends and savages the dead in their tombs.

And they are not just ordinarily cruel, they are quite outstandingly cruel, because they do not merely not help the dead, they forbid others to help them too. But Ecclus. 7:37 says, "Do not deny grace to the dead."

And the christian faith indeed does not deny grace to the dead. It is aware, as Augustine says, that its suffrages do not help the very good or the very bad, but it believes that they do help those who are in between, in Purgatory.[17] This view is supported by 1 Corinthians 15:29, where, according to the Gloss,[18] we are told that in the early church people had such faith in suffrages for the dead that some of them were even baptised for the sake of the unbaptised dead.

There are many different kinds of suffrage which help them, and the greatest of them all is the celebration of the Mass. Augustine says in the *Enchiridion*, "There should be no doubt that the souls of the dead are given some relief by the kindness of their survivors, when the sacrifice of the Mediator is offered on their behalf."[19]

There is an illustration of this in Peter of Cluny's book, in the story of a bishop who suspended one of his priests for saying Mass for the dead every day. One feast day the bishop was going to Matins, and his way took him through the cemetery, and it seemed to him that all the dead rose up against him, each one bearing the appearance of the job he had had in his lifetime, and they were threatening him, saying, "Here comes the bishop who took away our priest and who does not say Mass for us; unless he mends his ways, he will certainly die." He was terrified and reinstated the priest and starting saying Mass for the dead himself.[20]

The same point is made in the stories in the four books of the *Dialogues* about the two nuns, the little monk, the man found at the baths and the man buried in dung.[21]

There is another relevant story in the *Miracles of the Blessed Virgin* about two brothers in Rome, Peter, who was an archdeacon and a good man, but rather miserly, and Stephen, who was a judge and a bad man. They both died, and when Stephen was hauled off for judgment, St. Laurence came and accused him bitterly of stealing some houses of his. St. Agnes came too, from whom he had taken a garden, and accused him of betraying the truth for money, for which he deserved to have the same fate as Judas. But because he had been generous in giving alms, the poor went to St. Preject, whom he had celebrated each year by entertaining the poor. They entreated St. Preject on his behalf, and he in turn asked St. Laurence and St. Agnes to spare him, because he would make amends yet. Then he sought help from the Blessed Virgin, who secured for him the chance to return to life for thirty days to do penance, telling him, amongst other things, to say Psalm 118 every day. On his way back, he passed through Purgatory, and there he saw his brother, who was in terrible torment because of his miserliness; but he told him that he hoped he would be released if the Pope and the cardinals said Mass for him. Returning to the body, he related all this; and, to prove that it was true, he died when the thirty days were up.[22]

Another kind of suffrage for the dead is to make an offering at the altar. Peter of Cluny tells a story to illustrate this. In the diocese of Grenoble it happened once that somebody was digging in the mines, when an enormous weight of earth collapsed upon him. His wife thought he was dead, and every day for the next year she offered bread and wine and a candle on his behalf. She failed to do this only once. At the end of the year he was dug out, and was found to be alive and well, and he reported that he had been brought bread and wine and light every day except once.[23] Now if such offerings had such a powerful effect for someone who was only supposed to be dead, how much more effective must we take them to be for those who are really dead? Thus it says in 2 Macc. 12:43 that Judas sent twelve thousand silver drachmas to Jerusalem as an offering for the sins of the dead.

Another kind of suffrage is the public prayer of the church. The prayers and the intentions of the living show that the church does have regard for the dead in her public prayer; and it would not be right for the church as a whole to be thwarted in her intentions, so we may conclude safely that such prayers do benefit the dead. So Master William of Auxerre said once that he believed that not a single Mass was properly sung in church without many souls coming out of Purgatory as a result.[24] The freeing of the Canaanite woman's daughter in Matt. 15:21–8 is a symbol of this, as is the raising of the widow's son in Luke 7:12–15.

Another kind of suffrage is the prayers that are offered for the dead by individuals. "It is a holy and saving thought to pray for the dead to be released from their sins" (*2 Macc. 12:46*). Gregory illustrates this in the story of Paschasius in the *Dialogues*. He was a man of remarkable sanctity, who cherished the poor and thought nothing of himself, and he was archdeacon of the church of Rome. When the election was contested between Laurence and Symmachus, he supported Laurence. After his death, a demoniac was freed by touching his dalmatic. Now one day bishop Germanus of Capua went to the Angulan baths, on the advice of his doctors, and there he found Paschasius in attendance on him. He was terrified to see him there, and asked what he was doing there. He replied that the only reason why he had been sent there was that he had supported Laurence's party. "But," he said, "pray for me, and if you do not find me here when you return, you will know that I have been set free." So Germanus prayed for him, and never saw him there again.[25]

We also read in the *Life of Mary of Oignies* by the bishop of Tusculum that when she was praying she saw an immense number of hands stretched out towards her, and when she enquired what this meant, she was told that these were souls in Purgatory seeking her prayers.[26]

These stories show how much the dead are helped by our prayers.

Another kind of suffrage is penance undertaken on behalf of the dead. It is more than likely that people will win freedom in God's kindness if someone else, particularly if it is someone who is pleasing to God, undertakes to make amends on their behalf. Why else should the apostle say, "Bear one another's burdens?" *(Gal. 6:2).* Master Nicholas of Flavigny, archbishop of Besançon, told the story of two students who were faithful friends. One of them sinned gravely, and the other rebuked him and accompanied him to Rome, where he was given a three-year penance. But, after accepting the penance, he fell seriously ill, and was deeply upset at the thought of not being able to complete his penance. So his friend promised that he would complete it for him. So he carried it on after his companion was dead, and at the end of the first year the dead man appeared to him, radiantly white in a third of his body, but foul as pitch in the other two thirds. At the end of the second year, he appeared to him white in two thirds of his body, but black as black can be in the remaining third. At the end of the third year, he appeared entirely white, and thanked his friend for his freedom.[27]

Another kind of suffrage is to make restitution on behalf of the dead. A certain duchess told a story which illustrates this, a very noble lady. A nine-year old grandson of hers who was dying made his confession before he died, but after his death he appeared to her saying that he was in great pain because he had not paid some debts which he had contracted in his father's household to finance his amusements, and he had not thought of them at the time of his death. She looked into it and saw that all his debts were paid. After that he appeared to her again and indicated that he had been freed and was in great happiness.[28]

Another story on the same subject was told to one of the Friars Preachers by a cavalry officer. He was a dependable man, and wanted his advice. He told him that another officer, a relation of his, who was dead, had appeared to him when he was alone in church, and when he asked how he was, he replied that he was being gravely tormented because of some borrowed property that he had, which he had forgotten at the time of his death. He told him what it was and who it belonged to, and asked him to see that it was returned. He told him that he was hopeful that he would be released from the dreadful punishment he had been suffering for the past seven years once this was done.[29]

The reason why this kind of restitution helps the dead is that it is an act of kindness, and it is only fair that God should deal kindly with those on whose behalf kind deeds are performed by others.

Another sort of suffrage is to carry out some good plan which the dead man had. It is likely that they are the more helped when some good intention of theirs is put into effect. There is a story about this in the *History of Charlemagne:* a cavalry officer in Charlemagne's army was dying at Bayonne, and asked that his horse should be sold and the money be given to the poor. His relative, to whom he had entrusted this commission, sold the horse but then used the money for his own purposes. Thirty days later the dead man appeared to the survivor and said, "My sins have now been forgiven, but you should know that because you failed to carry out my commission, I had to spend thirty days in Purgatory. Now I am going to my rest, but you will have to pay for what you have done." This terrified the man, and in the morning he told his companions what he had seen. And on that very day there came a sound like the roaring of lions and other wild beasts, and he was taken up into the air and disappeared. They looked for him for four days and could not find him. Twelve days later, when the army was going through Navarre, they found him a long way from the place where he had vanished; he had been thrown down from a mountain[30] and was pitifully mangled.[31]

# HUMBERT APPENDIX

Another form of suffrage is almsgiving. Augustine says in a sermon on some words from the apostle, "There is no doubt that the dead are helped by almsgiving undertaken for the benefit of their spirits."[32] To illustrate this, a story is told of a student in Paris who, when he was dying. left his companion a certain bed to be made over to the poor. But his companion kept it instead. And one night, while he was asleep in it, the dead man appeared to him in great distress, lying on a bed with nothing but bare ropes. He was terrified, and went to confession and then sold the bed and gave the money to the poor. Then the dead man appeared to him again, resting comfortably in a well-made bed.[33]

Another form of suffrage is the intercession of the saints. It is more than likely that souls are sometimes released from Purgatory because of their intercession, when we have recourse to them on behalf of the dead, since we hear stories of the Lord's doing greater things than this for them, like calling the damned back to life, as we know happened to Trajan and many others.[34] If human pity can be stirred to free a man rightly condemned to perpetual imprisonment at the request of good men, we may surely believe that God's pity is all the more likely to be stirred to free a man who has only been condemned to prison for a limited time. This is why, in the prayer for the dead, the church says, "At the intercession of the blessed Virgin Mary and all the saints, grant that they may come to share eternal bliss."[35]

## Notes

1. Cf. Y. Congar, *In Dulcedine Societatis quaerere Veritatem*, in G. Meyer and A. Zimmerman, *Albertus Magnus—Doctor Universalis* (Mainz, 1980) pp. 47–57.

2. Cf. PL 76:1290D, 77:153A.

3. Ecclus. 1:10.

4. Prov. 6:6.

5. Jordan, *Libellus* 104; Constantine, 60; Stephen of Bourbon, 4.

6. This seems to be a garbled version of Bede, *Ecclesiastical History* III 3 about the missionaries from Iona.

7. Jacques de Vitry (c. 1170–1240), bishop of Acre (1216–1228), then cardinal bishop of Tusculum (c. 1228–1240), was an acute observer of his times and, on the whole, a supporter of the new religious movements like those of the béguines and the Franciscans. He was indeed famous for his use

of *exempla*, and his sermons became one of the major sources for collections of *exempla*. See T. F. Crane, *The Exempla of Jacques de Vitry* (London, 1890). He himself recommends their use in the Prologue to his collection of sermons (Pitra, p. 192). The occasion when he "set France on fire" was presumably his preaching of the Albigensian Crusade in 1213 and of the Fifth Crusade in 1214. On this and on his life and works in general, see the Introduction to J. F. Hinnebusch, *The Historia Occidentalis of Jacques de Vitry*.

8. The romance *Barlaam and Josaphat*, ascribed to St. John Damascene, derives ultimately from the life of the Buddha. See D. M. Lang, *The Balavariani* (London, 1966).

9. Victorinus was a prominent philosopher who became a christian. The *Life of Anthony* by St. Athanasius, rapidly translated from Greek into Latin, became one of the major classics of monasticism in both the East and the West. The story of Augustine's reaction is derived from *Confessions* VIII 3 and 6, and from there it found its way into the lectionaries. Cf. the Dominican Regensburg lectionary, Oxford, Keble MS 49 ff.172$^v$–173$^v$, Brit. Libr. MS Addit. 23935 f.228$^v$.

10. Humbert interestingly here subdivides the "grace of preaching," which was such an important concept among the early Dominicans. Not only must the preacher have the grace to preach, he must also try to discover precisely what kind of grace of preaching he has. Cf. Jacques de Vitry's Prologue, Pitra, p. 193.

11. *Gratiosam narrationem:* cf. p. 213[81].

12. *Gratia*: both "grace" and "attractiveness."

13. Cf. 1 Cor. 3:2.

14. It was a common element in many medieval heresies to deny the value of suffrages for the dead. For the Petrobrusians, see R. Manselli, *Studi sulle Eresie del secolo XII* (Rome, 1953) pp. 39–40; for the Catharists, see A. Borst, p. 220. For the more ambiguous position of the Waldensians, see K. V. Selge, *Die ersten Waldenser*, Index s.v. *Suffragia mortuorum*. For the accusation that suffrages were instituted by the clergy simply as a way of making money, cf. Geoffrey of Auxerre (J. Leclercq, *Studia Anselmiana* 31 [1953] p. 197; G. Gonnet, *Enchiridion Fontium Valdensium*, p. 48) for the Albigensians, and the Passau Anonymous (in J. Gretser, *Opera Omnia* XII 2:30C [Regensburg, 1738]; E. Peters, *Heresy and Authority in Medieval Europe* [London, 1980] p. 163) for the Waldensians.

15. On the habits of the hyena, see McCulloch, p. 131.

16. In fact the reference is to the Vetus Latina of Jer. 12:9, not 12:8.

17. Augustine, *Enchiridion* 110.

18. Marginal Gloss.

19. *Enchiridion* 110. The MSS I have seen all have *Mediatori* which I have corrected to *Mediatoris* in line with Augustine's text.

20. This story is widely attributed to Peter of Cluny, though it does not

in fact feature in his *De Miraculis*. See J. A. Herbert, *Catalogue of Romances in the British Museum* III (London, 1910) p. 383; G. Constable, *Manuscripts of Works by Peter the Venerable, Studia Anselmiana* 40 (1956) pp. 229–30.

21. The references given in the MSS are somewhat erratic, but it is clear which stories are intended: Gregory, *Dialogues* II 23, 24; IV 55 (PL 66:178–9, 66:179, 77:417, 77:420–1).

22. This story, taken from Gregory, *Dialogues* IV 36 (PL 77:381–3), was used in a great many medieval collections of *Miracles of our Lady*, including that of Bartholomew of Trent (see *Salesianum* 12 [1950] p. 381). James of Varagine refers to it as coming from *The Miracles of the Blessed Virgin* in his account of St. Laurence in the *Golden Legend*, §6.

23. PL 189:911–2.

24. William of Auxerre (c. 1150–1231) was an extremely influential Parisian theologian.

25. PL 77:396–7. Symmachus was elected Pope in 498, but the election was challenged by a party that supported Laurence. Violent dissension went on for several years as a result.

26. Jacques de Vitry, *Life of Mary of Oignies* 27. This *Life* was composed at the request of bishop Fulk of Toulouse (*Acta Sanctorum* June V [Paris, Rome, 1867] 547D). Bl. Mary of Oignies (1177–1213) is an interesting figure in the history of lay spirituality. Her mystical piety and her miracles attracted attention to her in her own lifetime. She was one of several people credited, in the Dominican tradition, with having foretold the founding of the Order (MOPH I p. 12). Cf. SCH Subsidia 1 pp. 253–273.

27. Nicholas of Flavigny, dean of Langres and Master in Theology in the University of Paris, then archbishop of Besançon (1229–1235) (Glorieux, *Répertoire* n. 123). Stephen of Bourbon says that he heard this story from Nicholas himself (28).

28. Stephen of Bourbon, 33, says that he heard this from the duchess herself, and identifies her as Alix de Vergy, Duchess of Burgundy, the effective instigator and founding benefactress of the Dominican priory at Dijon, who also persuaded Innocent IV in 1245 to allow any secular clergy who wished to study at the Dominican studium there to do so with the same financial privileges as were given to students at the University of Paris (M. D. Chapotin, *Histoire des Dominicains de la Province de France* [Rouen, 1898] pp. 263–8). At that time her son, Hugh IV, was the reigning Duke, so Alix was known as "the Duke's mother," and this is what Stephen calls her here, misleadingly in this case, since this particular story relates to the time when her husband, Eudes III, was still alive, and the dead child is her son, not her grandson. Humbert, not surprisingly, misunderstood this. Eudes III had been one of the most distinguished participants in the Albigensian Crusade (Griffe III, pp. 17–20); it was in fact he who persuaded Simon de Montfort to join the Crusade (Cernai, 103).

29. Stephen of Bourbon, 34, is the source of this story too. Indeed, he was the preacher to whom the officer went for advice. The officer, he tells us, was William de Contres, who was with Simon de Montfort during the Albigensian Crusade, and who was celebrated for his valour (*Chanson de la Croisade Albigeoise* 130).

30. *De monte* S²M; S¹ omits it, and the printed edition reads *daemonibus*. The text of the *Historia Caroli* says that he was found *on* the mountain.

31. Pseudo-Turpin, *Historia Caroli* 7 (ed. H. M. Smyser [Cambridge, Mass., 1937] pp. 61–2).

32. PL 38:936.

33. This comes from Jacques de Vitry, who says that he "heard it in Paris." T. F. Crane, *The Exempla of Jacques de Vitry* (London, 1890) p. 53.

34. It was widely believed in the Middle Ages that the prayers of Gregory I had won the emperor Trajan a postponement of divine judgment. Cf. F. C. Tubach, *Index Exemplorum* n. 2368.

35. This comes from the prayer *Deus veniae largitor*, used in the Dominican rite for all the dead who had any connexion with the Order.

# Section IV

# THE DOMINICAN FAMILY

# A. The Nuns

The "Dominican family" is a modern term, but from the outset the work of St. Dominic involved women as well as men. The first institution he founded was a convent for women. Apart from the urgent problem of providing a Catholic refuge for young women who were being driven by sheer poverty into the hands of the Albigensians, there is little doubt that St. Dominic saw the usefulness of having a domestic base for the preaching, on the model of, in fact, the Albigensians and other itinerant preaching movements, like that of St. Robert of Arbrissel, and the cloistered women provided just such a base, with their stability and their chance of a more regular liturgical and contemplative life. For the same reason, when he was looking for a base in Rome, St. Dominic saw the possibilities for his purposes in the proposed new monastery for nuns at San Sisto, which had been in abeyance since the Gilbertines abandoned it. St. Dominic therefore seems to have asked to take over the site and the project, and eventually he saw it through to fruition, and so founded another convent. In fact, the brethren themselves did not live there long, but the convent remained, with a small staff of friars to help them. He also founded a convent in Madrid, which he entrusted to his brother, Bl. Mames. He also founded some sort of convent in Toulouse, but this does not seem to have lasted long. In Bologna he encouraged the aristocratic Diana d'Andalò in her desire to be associated with the Order, and this led to the founding of the convent of St. Agnes there under Dominic's successor, Bl. Jordan of Saxony. After this an enormous number of communities of religious women began to seek association with the Order, especially in Germany; in spite of considerable opposition and anxiety on the part of the brethren, the Order valued its connexion with such women, and what came to be known as the Second Order took shape and prospered.

# EARLY DOMINICANS

*As we shall see in this section, St. Dominic himself and his successors and associates developed a warm friendship with the nuns; Bl. Jordan's friendship with Bl. Diana is particularly striking, and led to the series of letters that constitute perhaps the most moving spiritual document from our period.*

*The role of these convents was no longer to provide the domestic base for the preachers, but this did not mean that they lost their involvement in the apostolate of the friars. We can see that Dominic and Jordan expected the sisters to be deeply concerned with the work of the Order, and many prominent friars expressed their appreciation of the importance of the nuns' prayers, as well as the support of their affection.*

*From the early period, we look at documents concerned with Prouille, founded in 1206, San Sisto, founded in 1221, Madrid, founded in 1220, Bologna, founded in 1223. It is to the convent at Madrid that we owe the only surviving personal document from the founder himself, a letter to the prioress.*

*We then look at a small sample of documents concerning some of the monasteries founded by or taken into the Order. St. Peter's in Milan was founded in 1247 or 1248. In Hungary we catch some glimpses of the life of the nuns in the royal monastery founded by King Bela IV for his daughter, Margaret (later to be canonized), who made her profession in the hands of Humbert of Romans in 1254, on the occasion of the General Chapter at which Humbert became the Master of the Order. From Germany, where the Dominican nuns played an immense role in the development of a new kind of mysticism, in which famous friars like Eckhart, Suso and Tauler also played a part, we look at two of the Lives of the Sisters of Unterlinden (founded in 1232 and incorporated into the Order in 1245). In these last documents we are faced with the extraordinary taste for bodily mortification, which Jordan and others tried to restrain in the nuns, and which is liable to be offensive to a modern reader. But it was part of the piety of the age, and to omit it would leave a distorted picture. But we also find the recognisably Dominican passion for the salvation of souls, and the typical love of the liturgy, celebrated loudly and enthusiastically.*

# Prouille

In the year 1206, when St. Dominic had been in the district of Toulouse about two years, he founded a monastery called Prouille, between Fanjeaux and Montréal, in the diocese of Toulouse, with the assistance of the man of God, Diego, bishop of Osma, under the patronage of Fulk, the bishop of Toulouse, a man in every way worthy to be remembered; his help and support were very necessary, especially in his own diocese. St. Dominic established this monastery to house some noble women, whose parents, because of their poverty, could see no alternative to entrusting them to the heretics to be educated and brought up by them, or rather to be deceived with their lies and to have their souls ruined. At that time there were a great many heretics living in and around that region. The date and purpose of this foundation can be discovered in the little book by the venerable father Jordan, Master of the Order, entitled *On the Beginnings of the Order of Preachers*[1]; further evidence is to found in some ancient letters and documents and in the many privileges granted to the monastery by the Holy See.

To support himself and his companions, St. Dominic held the church of Fanjeaux and St. Martin's in Limoux and several other endowments, including an important estate called Casseneuil in the diocese of Agen, which was given him by Count Simon de Montfort, who was particularly fond of him. The Order of Preachers had not yet been founded at this time. Whatever they could spare from these revenues, they gave to the monastery at Prouille, because at first their income and revenues there were meagre, and their buildings few and unimpressive. But God granted them increase.[2] They were helped the whole time by the merits and prayers of St. Dominic, their founder, and also by the hard work and loyal management and administration of the friars who served them, as well as by the grace and merits of the sisters who lived there, praising God by night and by day. To this present day these handmaids of Christ offer acceptable service to their Creator with robust holiness. Their observance is remarkable; they keep strict silence and perpetual enclosure, they work with their hands to avoid laziness and idleness, and so they work out their salvation.[3] The excellence of their lives and the purity of their consciences gain salvation for themselves and give an example to others, bring joy to the angels and win favour with God. Both in numbers and in merit they have increased beyond telling, so that the fragrance of their sanctity has spread far and wide, inspiring many other devout women to follow their holy example, and establish similiar communities elsewhere.

The sixth prior was brother Raymund Cathala,[4] who was prior in 1229, in 1230 and again in 1233, as appears from ancient documents at Prouille. I reckon that he became prior in about 1228. He enclosed the sisters more fully and strictly, though they were enclosed before. He ruled and helped the monastery for about thirty-two years, and was relieved of office by the provincial, Gerald de Frachet, shortly after the General Chapter in Toulouse in 1258, on account of his old age. *(Bernard Gui)*[5]

# Rome

## *[From The Miracles of St. Dominic by Bl. Cecilia]*

(6) It was our revered father's constant practice to devote the whole day to the good of souls, either preaching assiduously or hearing confessions or engaging in other works of charity. But in the evening he would visit the sisters and give them a conference or a sermon, in the presence of the brethren, instructing them in their religious life, because they had no other master to do this for them.

One day he came rather later than usual, so late that the sisters had already given up waiting for him and finished their prayers and retired to the dormitory. All at once the brethren rang the bell, which was the signal for the sisters to assemble whenever the blessed father came to them. When they heard it, all the sisters hurried to the church, and when they opened the window, they found him already sitting there with the brethren, waiting for them. He said to them, "My daughters, I have been fishing, and the Lord has given me a big fish." He was referring to brother Gaudio,[6] whom he had received into the Order; he was the only son of a certain Alexander, who was a man of good family and a citizen of Rome. After that, he gave them a long conference, which brought them great consolation.

When he had finished speaking, he said, "It would be good, my daughters, to have something to drink." He called brother Roger, the cellarer,[7] and told him to bring some wine and a cup. When the brother had brought them, St. Dominic told him to fill the cup right up to the brim. Then he blessed it and drank from it himself, and then all the brethren who were there drank from it. There were twenty-five of them there altogether, clerical and lay, and they all drank as much as they wanted, but the cup remained as full as it was to start with. After the brethren had all had a drink, St. Dominic said, "I want all my daughters to have a drink." Then he called sister Nubia[8] and said to her, "Come to the turn and take the cup and give all the sisters a drink." She went with one of the other sisters and took the cup, which was full to the brim. In spite of its being so full, not a single drop was spilled. Then all the sisters drank from it, starting with the prioress, and then the others, and they all drank as much as they wanted, encouraged by St. Dominic, who kept on saying, "Drink up, my daughters!" At that time there were 104 sisters there,[9] and they all drank as much wine as they wanted, but, far from emptying, the cup remained as full as ever, just as if someone had been continually pouring more wine into it. After that, he had the cup brought back as full as it was when he had given it to us. What became of it, we still do not know.

Then St. Dominic said, "The Lord wants me to go to Santa Sabina."[10] Then brother Tancred, the prior of the brethren, and brother Odo, the prior of the sisters,[11] and the other brethren, as well as the prioress and the sisters, tried to restrain him, saying, "Holy father, it is too late now. It is nearly midnight, you cannot leave now." But he was adamant, and said, "The Lord absolutely wants me to go. And he will send his angel with us."[12] Since they could not persuade him to stay, he took brother Tancred, the prior of the brethren, and brother Odo, the prior of the sisters, with him, and set off.

When they reached the door of the church to go out, there, just as St. Dominic had promised, standing by the door, was a most beautiful young man with a staff in his hand, ready for walking. St. Dominic put his companions between himself and the young man and walked behind them in third place. When they reached the door of the church, they found it carefully bolted. But the young man who had led them on their way applied himself to one part of the door, and it opened for them immediately. He went in first, then the brethren, and finally St. Dominic. When they were all inside, the young man went out again and immediately the door shut tight as it was before. Then brother Tancred asked St. Dominic, "Holy father, who was that young man who came with us?" He answered, "My son, it was the angel of the Lord, whom the Lord appointed to watch over us."

When the bell for Matins went, the brethren came into choir and were amazed to see St. Dominic and his companions there in choir; they wondered how they had got in when the doors were locked.

(10) One time when St. Dominic came back from Spain, he brought the sisters a little present of some spoons made out of cypress wood, one spoon for each sister.

(15) St. Dominic's appearance was like this. He was of medium height, of slight build, with a beautiful face, slightly ruddy complexion, and slightly red hair and beard; his eyes were beautiful. There was a kind of radiance about his forehead and between his eyebrows,

which attracted everyone to respect and love him. He was always cheerful and happy, except when he was moved to compassion by any kind of suffering on the part of his neighbour. He had long, beautiful hands, and a powerful, beautiful, resonant voice. He never went bald, but had a complete ring of hair round his tonsure, with just a sprinkling of grey.

# Madrid

## [*Letter of St. Dominic to the sisters May 1220*]

Brother Dominic, Master of the Preachers, to the dear prioress of Madrid and all the nuns in the community, greetings. May you make progress every day!

I am delighted at the fervour with which you follow your holy way of life, and thank God for it. He has indeed freed you from the squalor of this world.

Fight the good fight, my daughters, against our ancient foe, fight him insistently with fasting, because no one will win the crown of victory without engaging in the contest in the proper way.[13]

Until now you had no place where you could practise your religious life, but now you can no longer offer that excuse. By the grace of God, you have buildings that are quite suitable enough for religious observance. From now on I want you to keep the silence in the prescribed places, namely, the refectory, the dormitory and the oratory, and to observe your Rule fully in everything else too. Let none of the sisters go outside the gate, and let nobody come in, except for the bishop or any other ecclesiastical superior, who comes to preach to you or to visitate. Do not be shy of using the discipline or keeping vigil. Be obedient to your prioress. Do not chatter with each other, or waste your time gossiping.

Because we can offer you no help in temporal affairs, we do not want to burden you by allowing any of the brethren any authority to receive women or make them members of your community; only the prioress shall have such authority, on the advice of the community.

Furthermore, I instruct my dear brother,[14] who has worked so hard to bring you to this holy state of life, to organise you and make whatever arrangements he considers useful, to enable you to conduct yourselves in the most religious and holy way. I also give him power to visitate you and correct you, and, if necessary, to remove the prioress from office, provided that a majority of the nuns agree. I also authorise him to grant you any dispensations he thinks appropriate.

Farewell in Christ.

# Bologna
## [*From the Chronicle of St. Agnes' Monastery*]

In the course of the year 1218, some Friars Preachers were sent to Bologna from Rome by St. Dominic. When they arrived there, they asked for the church of St. Nicholas from brother Rudolph, who was the priest of that church. The church was situated in a place called "At the Vines," which belonged to Signor Andalò, the father of that most illustrious woman, Donna Diana. This Signor Andalò was unwilling to give the place to the friars, but at the pleading of Donna Diana, who later founded the house of St. Agnes, he gave his consent and granted them the place. The friars built there a house and a cloister, and, by the grace of Christ, they began to increase in numbers.

Meanwhile Master Reginald came to Bologna and began to preach the word of God there with great zeal, and Donna Diana, the daughter of Signor Andalò, the gentleman we have mentioned, drawn by the Spirit of God, began to spurn the glamour and vanities of the world and to spend more time in the company of the Friars Preachers and in conversation with them. So when St. Dominic came to Bologna, she began to love him with all the affection of her heart, and to discuss with him the salvation of her soul. Not very long afterwards she put herself in his hands, and made profession, in the presence of Master Reginald and some other brethren, namely brother Guala of Brescia and brother Rudolph, and some ladies who are still alive today; this took place at the altar of St. Nicholas. Many other noble ladies and illustrious women of Bologna followed her example and began to spend time with the Friars Preachers, conversing with them about the salvation of their souls. As a result of this, great devotion was aroused among many of the nobility who were related to these ladies, and they began to help and respect the friars.

Meantime Donna Diana did not forget her vow; she began to discuss with St. Dominic how she could put it into effect. So one day St. Dominic gathered his brethren and asked them what they thought about building a house of nuns which would be called and which would be a part of the Order. The brethren answered as they thought fit, and then St. Dominic said to them, "I do not want to give you my decision today; I want to consult the Lord. I will tell you what I think tomorrow." In his usual way, he turned his attention to prayer.

The next day, when he had finished praying, he sat down with the brethren in Chapter and said, "It is absolutely necessary, brethren, that a house of nuns should be built, even if it means leaving off for a time the work on our own house." Since he was about to leave Bologna, he entrusted the whole business to four of the brethren, Master Paul of Hungary,[15] brother Guala, who was later bishop of Brescia, brother Ventura of Verona, who later became Provincial, and brother Rudolph of Faenza, of whom mention has already been made. So, during the lifetime of St. Dominic, these four brethren found a site where the house of nuns was to be built, but the bishop of Bologna refused permission for a church to be built there, because it was too close to the city.[16]

Meanwhile Donna Diana was living in her father's house, at least she was living there in the flesh, but not in her mind. She wore a hair shirt next to the skin, and an iron chain round her waist, but above them she wore purple and silk and precious stones and gold and silver. She stayed in her room from early morning until the time of Terce, in prayer and silence. Seeing that her fear of her parents was preventing her from fulfilling her desire and her promise to St. Dominic, which was that she would build a house of nuns which would belong to the Order of Preachers and be so called, one day, on the feast of St. Mary Magdalene, she announced that she wanted to visit the monastery called Ronzano.[17] So she went to the house there with immense pomp and honour, with a great throng of ladies attending her. When she arrived there, she went alone into the sisters' dormitory, and suddenly asked for the habit, and was given it.

When all the ladies who had come with her realised what she had done, they sent a messenger to the city. At once a huge crowd formed of men and women who were friends and relations of hers. They came to the monastery and dragged her out with such violence that they broke one of her ribs, and she carried the mark of the fracture until the day she died. Because of this injury which they did her that day, she lay sick for about a year in her father's house.

The blessed father Dominic was in Bologna at that time, and when he heard of her entry he was immensely pleased, but when he then heard of the injuries she had sustained, he was very sorry for her. While she was lying sick in her father's house, he sent her letters secretly, because her parents would not allow her to speak with anybody unless one of the family was present.

During this period, St. Dominic passed happily on into eternal joys. Sister Diana remained like this in her father's house, and she was very distressed at the death of such a father as Dominic. But almighty God, who had chosen her before the foundation of the world,[18] did not abandon her. Bit by bit he mercifully removed the obstacles from her path, and she began to recover from her great infirmity. When she was a little better, she fled one night, on the feast of All Saints; she left her father's house and went back to the same monastery as before. Her parents then despaired of her, and left her there. So she stayed in that monastery from All Saints up to the week after the Ascension.

· In the middle of that week, Master Jordan, of blessed memory, who was at that time Provincial of Lombardy, came faithfully to her assistance, together with the other brethren to whom St. Dominic had entrusted the business. They began to take steps to bring the project to the fulfilment which had been for so long desired. As we have said, the bishop would not allow a church to be built in the place mentioned above, because it was too near the city; so the brethren, supported by Diana's family, asked for another place, Valsampero— as the place was called then; later it was called Mount St. Agnes. They obtained the bishop's permission, and began to build there a tiny little house. When it was built, Master Jordan and other friars of the same Order, brother Guala, brother Ventura of Verona, brother Rudolph of Faenza, brother Bernard the German[19] and some others, went to fetch her and installed her in the little house, with four other ladies from Bologna, in the year 1223, in the Octave of the Ascension. On the feast of the apostles Peter and Paul, they received the habit of the Order from Master Jordan.

Then, at the preaching and exhortation of brother Bernard the German, two noble ladies from Ferrara shortly afterwards joined their community.

Master Jordan, of happy memory, wanted four sisters to be fetched from San Sisto, with the Pope's permission, to instruct them in the religious life. So he sent two of the four brethren to whom St. Dominic had entrusted the business to the Curia; these were brother Guala of Brescia and brother Rudolph of Faenza. They went to the Pope and explained why they had come, but for all their pleading they could not make him grant their request. But at last he was prevailed upon by the lord Ugolino, bishop of Ostia, and gave his consent. This lord Ugolino, bishop of Ostia, had heard of the lady Diana when he was papal legate in Lombardy, and had taken pains, with St. Dominic, to visit her while she was still in her father's house.

So Pope Honorius went to the monastery of San Sisto and spoke to the sisters, in the presence of the lord Ugolino and brother Claro,[20] who was the Provincial of Tuscany, and of the prior of the sisters of San Sisto and also the prior of the community of the brethren. Amongst other things, the Pope said that he found it painful to drag any of them away from their monastery, but all the same it would be unfitting and improper to refuse to grant a petition made by such men as these, so he intended to send four of the sisters to the monastery of St. Agnes. So he commanded them, in virtue of the Holy Spirit and their vow of obedience, to choose four sisters who would be the most suitable to undertake this task, not forgetting that the eyes of God's majesty were upon them. So four sisters, who had made profession in the hands of St. Dominic and received the habit from him, came to the monastery of St. Agnes and remained in the community there until they died, mighty in the vigour of their holiness. One of these sisters was sister Cecilia, who is alive to this day, and who was present when St. Dominic raised Cardinal Stephen's relative from the dead at San Sisto.

The brethren also converted other ladies, as they went about preaching in Lombardy and in the Marches, and they did all they could to make them join the community. As a result, women from some of the noblest families in Lombardy and the Marches did soon join them.

When Master Jordan became Master of the Order, brother Guala, at the Master's desire, went to Pope Honorius and obtained letters obliging the Master of the Order to take responsibility for the house of St. Agnes as for any house of the friars in the Order. So Master Jordan, of blessed memory, when the letters were presented to him, accepted the house under his jurisdiction, with the approval of all the diffinitors, at the General Chapter which was being held at that time in Bologna. Then he received sister Diana and the whole community to profession in his hands. Since then the Provincial who is in office at any given time has received sisters who have come to join the community to profession in the name of the Master of the Order.

We can see how much the venerable father, Master Jordan, loved our community and how kind he was to it in every trial and difficulty, from the letters he sent to sister Diana and the other sisters in the same house. The venerable father also gave the sisters some brethren to say Mass in their house every day, as in a house of the Order. At first he had appointed some lay brothers to live in the house and look after their temporal affairs, but as time went by, the sisters thought it would be better if neither lay brothers nor clerics were obliged to live in the house, so the blessed father gave the ruling already mentioned, that they should say Mass for them every day, but not be bound to live in the nuns' house.

As time went on, some of the brethren began to raise questions about this house, and to make difficulties for the sisters. So Master Jordan, together with the diffinitors at the General Chapter in Paris, held urgent consultations with some masters of Paris University, and their unanimous verdict was that they could not separate the nuns' house from their charge without mortal sin. Then the blessed father severely reprimanded the friars who had complained or raised questions about this house, and he encouraged them, both in his presence and in his absence, to love and support the house, as being a house of the Order.

When Pope Honorius had gone the way of all flesh and Pope Gregory had been raised to the dignity of the papacy, sister Diana, the foundress of the house of St. Agnes, took steps to get fresh letters from the Pope obliging the Master of the Order to take responsibility for the house of St. Agnes as for any house of the friars of the Order, and the Lord granted her desire. She obtained what she wanted from the Pope, and so, before she died, the house had been entrusted to the Master of the Order by two popes.

After thirteen years in the Order, the venerable sister Diana, worthy of God, went happily to the Lord. The whole community of Friars Preachers in Bologna, with their prior, came to the funeral, and they buried her venerable body, with all due honour, enclosed in a wooden coffin, near the altar of St. Agnes. How men grieved at her death! In particular, how the sisters and the brethren lamented! But we pass over this in silence, to avoid making our tale too long. This happy woman was extremely sensible and well spoken, and she had a beautiful face and an attractive appearance; in the eyes of all she was charming and lovable. She was upright, devoted to the worship of God, intent on prayer, and so given to devotion that she often moved her sisters to floods of tears. She was a great lover of the brethren and of the Order. She was deeply humble in her own mind, and wore a cheaper habit than anyone; she was remarkably enthusiastic for rigorous religious observance in herself and in others. These and other similar gifts adorned this sister of ours, this sister who was worthy of God. And she was a wonderful asset to the monastery she had founded, both by her words and by her example.

## [*A Selection from the Letters of Bl. Jordan*]

### LETTER 5 (1233)

Brother Jordan, useless servant, of the Order of Preachers, health and joy in the Holy Spirit[21] to his dearest daughter in Christ Jesus, Diana.

As I want myself to prosper, so I want you to, my dearest daughter, because my heart is one with yours in the Lord. But so much is the better part in me yours, that I would rather bear any burden in myself than have it happen to you. So, beloved, strive always to advance and to love God and to cleave to him with all your heart, because it is good to cleave to him and to put your hope in him.[22] So say to him, "My soul cleaved to you."[23]

Meantime, be comforted, because I shall soon see you in the flesh, by the grace of God; I never stop seeing you in the spirit. Greet the sisters for me, who are all my dearest daughters. Farewell.

Your son, Gerard,[24] also greets you and them warmly. Ask them to pray for us. May the Spirit of Jesus be with your spirit. Amen.[25]

If you think fit to receive the daughter of Lambertina, you have my authority to do so. I am content with whatever you do in the matter.

I, brother Gerard, your unworthy son, greet you, dearest mother, and all my dear sisters in Jesus Christ. Greet them all for me; I love them and they love me. Give my special regards to those whom you know to be my special friends. Among all the cities of Lombardy, Tuscany, France, England, Provence and, I can almost even add, Germany, Bologna holds a unique and particularly tender place in my heart. May the grace of Jesus Christ dwell in your heart. Amen.

### LETTER 9 (DATE UNCERTAIN)

Brother Jordan, useless servant, of the Order of Preachers, eternal health to his dearest daughter in Christ, sister Diana, of the monastery of St. Agnes in Bologna.

Dearest, you are quite sensible enough to know that as long as we are held in exile in this world, we all suffer from far too many defects, and cannot come to that stability which will be given us in the time to come. This is why we do not conduct ourselves with equanimity in all the circumstances of our lives. Sometimes we are unduly excited when things go well, and at other times we are too alarmed when things go badly. But all the same, we ought to conform ourselves to some extent, even now, to that future life, if we really want to arrive at the unfailing constancy of the world to come. And that means that we ought to establish our hearts firmly in God's strength,[26] and struggle, as best we can, to place all our hope and confidence and stability in the Lord, so that we shall be like him, as far as it is possible for us, even in his unchanging rest and stability. He is our safe refuge which never fails and is always there, and the more we fly to him, the more we shall all become stable ourselves. This is how the saints, who had such tremendous hope in the Lord, were easily able to make light of any trials that came upon them in this life.

So, dearest, always fly to the Lord, more and more. If anything burdensome or painful happens to you, still the foundation of your heart will not slip, provided that it is solidly established. Impress this deeply and repeatedly on your heart, and encourage the sisters to do likewise.

As a little encouragement to you, I will just mention briefly something which I dreamed about you recently. I thought I saw you speaking to me, in an honest, balanced way, which it still cheers me to think of. And you said, "The Lord spoke to me like this: 'I and Diana, I and Diana, I and Diana.' In the same way he then repeated: 'I am good, I am good, I am good.'" You can imagine that I find this most consoling.

## LETTER 12 (DATE UNCERTAIN)

Brother Jordan, useless servant, of the Order of Preachers, eternal health in Jesus Christ our Saviour, to his dear daughter, or rather his dearest sister in Christ, Diana, in Bologna.

Dearest, though I have had to rush to get something written, I wanted to try and get something off to you, even if only a few words, to give your fondness a little encouragment. You are so deeply imprinted on my heart, that I could never forget you; indeed, I remember you all the more often, the more I have come to realise that you love me genuinely with all your heart. The affection you have for me inspires a more ardent affection in me, and stirs my mind all the more powerfully. Now I must conclude, but may the supreme comforter, the Spirit of truth, possess your heart and comfort you and grant that we may be together in that heavenly Jerusalem for ever, by the gift of our Lord Jesus Christ, who is blessed above all else for ever. Amen.[27]

Farewell, dearest; pray for me often and faithfully to the Lord, because I need it, because of my many failings. I hardly every pray, and so ask the sisters to make up for my deficiency in this regard.


### LETTER 13 (AFTER 1236)

Brother Jordan, useless servant, of the Order of Preachers, health and the constant friendship of Jesus Christ, to his dearest daughter, Diana, in Bologna.

Since I cannot see you in the flesh, my dearest, and comfort you and receive comfort from you as often as either of us would like, my heart's desire has to find some little refreshment from time to time and some little appeasement whenever I can visit you by letter and tell you how I am doing. I wish I could know how you are too, because your progress and your happiness are my spirit's choicest food. But you can never be certain what part of the world I shall turn out to be in, and even if you did know where I was, you would not have any messengers handy, by whom you could send anything to me. But after all, my dear, it is only a small thing that we write to each other; there is a fire of love in our hearts, in the Lord, and there you speak to me and I speak to you the whole time, in feelings of affection which no tongue could adequately express and which no letter could adequately contain.

O Diana, what a wretched state of affairs this is, which we have to endure! Our love for each other here is never free from pain and anxiety. You are upset and hurt because you are not permitted to see me the whole time. And I am upset because your presence is so rarely granted me. I wish we could be brought into the fortified city,[28] the city of the Lord of Hosts,[29] which the Most High himself established,[30] where we shall no longer be stranded from him or from each other. Here we are tormented every day and our hearts are cruelly torn. Our very wretchedness makes us cry out every day, "Who will free us from the body of this death?"[31] All the same, we must bear this kind of thing with patience, and gather our minds together totally into him alone, insofar as our daily needs permit, because he alone can rescue us from our wants, and true repose is found in him alone, and apart from him whatever we look at only gives us trouble and matter for distress. So for the time being let us accept with joy whatever may happen to sadden us, because whatever measure of tribulation we accept for his sake now, we shall receive the same measure of joy in return[32] from the Son of God, Jesus Christ, to whom be honour and glory, power and authority for ever and ever. Amen.

Pray for me, as I know you do. Greet Galiana, the prioress,[33] for me. And greet all our friends outside, and particularly those who are in your own house,[34] when they come to see you, and commend me to their prayers. Farewell, dear daughter, in Jesus Christ, the Son of God.

## LETTER 14 (1229)

Brother Jordan, useless servant, of the Order of Preachers, health and complete contentment in the embrace of Jesus Christ, to his dearest sister in Jesus Christ the Son of God, Diana, in Bologna.

I know you are anxious about how I am, as I am anxious about you in Christ, and so I thought I would briefly tell you how things are going. When I came to Vercelli, the Lord gave us several very good men, with an excellent education; three very fine Germans, who were in the city, four outstanding men from Provence, and three or four good men from Lombardy, who all entered within a short space of time.[35] Give thanks to God with your sisters, because he never forgets his mercy towards us, or not for long.

I am in good bodily health, by God's gift. Do not take it too badly, dearest, that you do not have me there in the flesh the whole time, because my spirit is always with you in the most earnest love. But I am not surprised that you should be upset by my absence, because I too cannot manage not to be upset at your absence. But I comfort myself with the thought that this separation will not last forever. It will soon be over, soon we shall see each other always, in the presence of Jesus Christ, the Son of God, who is blessed forever and ever. Amen.

Greet the prioress and all the sisters, who are all my very dear daughters, and especially Galiana the novice. Pray for me, all of you.

## LETTER 15 (AFTER 1230)

Brother Jordan, useless servant, of the Order of Preachers, health to his dearest daughter in Jesus Christ, sister Diana, of St. Agnes' in Bologna, wishing her the blessings of the enjoyment of the Spirit of knowledge.

What do I think I am doing, my dear daughter, writing you these little letters of mine to give comfort to your heart, when you can derive much better and more enjoyable comfort from taking and reading that book of life, that scroll of the perfect law which converts our souls,[36] which you have daily before your mind's eye? That law which is perfect, because it takes away all imperfections, is charity, and you find it written with strange beauty when you gaze at Jesus your Saviour stretched out like a sheet of parchment on the Cross, inscribed with wounds, illustrated in his own loving Blood. Where else, I ask you, my dearest, is there a comparable book of love to read from? You know better than I do, that no letter could inspire love more passionately. So fix your mind's attention there. Hide in the clefts of this rock,[37] hide yourself away from the clamour of those who speak wickedness. Turn this book over, open it, read it; you will find in it what the prophet found: lamentations, song and woe.[38] Lamentations, because of the pains which he endured; a song of gladness, which he won for you by his pains; and the woe of unending death, from which he redeemed you by his death. In his lamentations, learn to have patience in yourself, learn love in his song of joy, because surely he has the first claim on your love, seeing that he wanted you to be a sharer in such great joys. And when you realise that you have been rescued from that woe, what else should result but thanksgiving and the sound of praise? These are short words, but to a loving heart they are long and deep enough. I want you, my daughter, to accustom yourself to dwelling in these words, and to learn the wisdom of the saints, as you are taught and stirred and guided by the Son of God, Jesus Christ, to whom be honour and glory forever. Amen.[39]

Farewell in Christ Jesus. Greet everybody for me whom you know I should want to greet.

Your son, brother Gerard, greets you. Pray for us now, until we come.

## FROM LETTER 16 (OXFORD, FEBRUARY 2nd, 1230)

I hope that, by the grace of Jesus Christ, you are walking in a holy way in all things, devoted to prayer, taking time for meditation, quick to obey, eager to work, slow to speak, constant in silence, clothing yourselves in compassionate pity, in kindness, in humility, in patience, in modesty[40] and in charity.

## LETTER 17 (AFTER JUNE 29th, 1223)

Brother Jordan, useless servant, of the Order of Preachers, health and the comfort of the Spirit, the Paraclete, to his dear sister in Christ, born of the same spiritual father as himself, his dearest daughter Diana, left to him by that same father.

For the love of Jesus Christ, your dear spouse, you have spurned earth's kingdom and all worldly splendour,[41] and have chosen to adopt his poverty instead, and so you will live in his courts and be filled with the blessings of his house.[42] But what am I saying? You have adopted poverty? Nothing of the kind! You have cast poverty from you and chosen to be rich. Christ's poverty is a freely chosen poverty, and that means poverty of spirit, and having that, the kingdom of heaven is yours. And I do not say that it *will* be yours, because your spouse says, "Blessed are the poor in spirit, for theirs *is* the kingdom of heaven."[43] So anyone who possesses Christ's poverty disregards all the world's riches. Is not this a greater treasure than any, in comparison with which and because of which all other treasures are regarded as worthless and reckoned as nothing better than beggary? You are no pauper; you are abundantly endowed with the glory and wealth of his house, seeing that you possess the kingdom of heaven. You are no beggar girl, you are a queen; you must be, if you possess a kingdom.

So take up your position at your spouse's right hand, clothed in gold,[44] in a charity which is not feigned,[45] but pure and ruddy with the fire and fervour of Christ. But where will you get your gold from, to gild your clothes with? From the land of Havilah,[46] which means "Suffering." This means Christ, who says, "Look and see if there is any suffering like mine."[47] There you will find gold, and the gold of that land is the best there is. There he displays love at its greatest, because no one has greater love than to lay down his life for his friends.[48] This is as good as saying, "This is the greatest love, this is the very best of gold." And there are mines there, dug out and open. "They have dug," he says, "in my hands and my feet."[49] Others have worked in digging these mines, you can go in and benefit from their work, and dwell like a dove, and like his friend, in the clefts of the rock;[50] and the rock is Christ.[51] There you will find plenty of gold, plenty of charity. And when you find it, what then? Will you not gather it up and keep it? The abundance of gold there is proved by the streams which flow red from the Saviour's wells[52] and clefts; indeed, the streams themselves are gold.

So, if you take up your position at his right hand,[53] you will be gilt by the stream which flows out from his right side.[54] Draw near and stand closer, so that you may be plunged more deeply into it, so that your garments may become red from him who treads the wine-press.[55] That is where the saints stood, at his right, with the queen,[56] mother church, and there they washed their robes in the blood of the Lamb.[57] This is what you should be thinking, this should be your concern, this should be your work. This is where the gold of the Arabs is to be found, gold, that is, of the humble; this is where you will be given gold of Araby,[58] that is, of humility. And it is called gold of the Arabs, that is, the humble, because it is only the humble who find it, who seek it out and gather it up. It is the humble who are able to go into those deep and narrow mines. So be small and humble in your own eyes, because he gives understanding to little ones[59] and grace to the humble.[60] So let him give you understanding, let him instruct you in the way you should go, let him keep his eyes on you,[61] because his eyes look upon the poor.[62]

I have briefly recommended poverty, charity and humility to you, because I want you to come by means of these three things to the true wealth and delight and honour, by the help of him who is a strong helper,[63] our Lord Jesus Christ, who is blessed forever and ever. Amen.

# EARLY DOMINICANS

## LETTER 36 (1231–3)

Brother Jordan, useless servant, of the Order of Preachers, to his beloved daughter, Diana, and to his other daughters at St. Agnes', health and eternal salvation.

I stayed at Modena till the ninth and sowed much, but, because of my sins, I reaped little. So I left there and went to Reggio, and from there I planned to go gradually from house to house until I had to cross the mountains. And reckoning that I had to cross the mountains before winter, it was difficult for me to return to Bologna. So I beg of your charity, put up with my moves patiently and forgive me for not taking leave of you in person, as I usually do. I did this to spare myself and you, because I could not have faced your flood of tears without becoming upset myself, and also I was still uncertain what I was going to do and was reluctant to tell you, in case I distressed you.

I ask you now, then, as you love me, not to be sad, so that I too can be cheerful; instead, rejoice in your spouse, Jesus Christ, who is in you and who comforts you with his own Holy Spirit who is also called the Paraclete, that is, the Comforter, so that his consolations may gladden your souls, in proportion to all the many different pains which you must expect to have to bear sometimes in your hearts[64] in this present life, as a result of all the different kinds of trials and tribulations. And as you are strengthened by these consolations and drawn on by them as by the scent of perfumes,[65] you can continue on your way until you come to our Saviour, in whom we shall win joy and happiness, and in whom every pain and distress will flee away,[66] and we shall be filled with the blessings of his house.[67] Dwelling there with his saints and chosen ones, we shall praise him forever.[68] Amen. Farewell in Christ Jesus.

# [Letter from St. Raymund of Peñafort to the prioress of Bologna]

## (BETWEEN 1231 AND 1236)

Brother Raymund, of the Order of Preachers, penitentiary of the Pope, to his dear sister in Christ, the prioress of the sisters of St. Agnes in Bologna: greetings and prayers.

Living, as I do, in the whirlwind of the court, I am hardly ever able to reach, or, to be quite honest, even to see from afar, the tranquillity of contemplation. I am so busy with Leah's morning shortsightedness and fruitfulness that in my present position I cannot reach the beauty of Rachel[69] to which I have aspired, however feebly, since I was quite young. So it is a great joy and an enormous comfort to me to feel how I am helped by your prayers. I often think of this service which you and your sisters do for me, sitting as you do at the Lord's feet with Mary,[70] enjoying the delights of your spouse, our Lord Jesus Christ, contemplating the face of him whom the angels desire to look upon.[71] So when all is going well for you with your spouse in the secrecy of your chamber, do not forget, in your mutual uninterrupted love, to pray for me and beg alms for me in my poverty and need. Though it is but a small return, indeed hardly a return at all, I never stop praying for you. May the grace of our Lord Jesus Christ and the love of God and the fellowship of the Holy Spirit be with you all forever. Amen.[72]

# Milan

## [*Letter of St. Peter Martyr to the prioress of St. Peter's in Campo Santo, Milan*]

Brother Peter, servant of the brethren at Asti,[73] to his dearest sister T., prioress of St. Peter's in Campo Santo: may you reign with Peter and receive with him the gift of the perfect, spotless, kingdom.

It made me very happy to receive your welcome letter, from which I could easily gather that your daily progress from strength to strength[74] has enabled you to win the prize of your monastic struggle. You have gone up into the mountain of sacrifice, while I still dwell in the valley of care, and have spent almost all my life for others. You take the wings of contemplation and soar above all this, but I am so stuck in the glue of concern for other people that I cannot fly. Woe is me, for my exile is prolonged.[75] Who will give me wings like a dove, so that I can fly away and find rest?[76] In everything I sought rest,[77] in everything I have found toil and grief.[78] There is no rest except in the inheritance of the saints, of which it is written, "This is my place of rest for ever."[79] But I cannot see the freedom of the children of God as I should like to, as I long to, I cannot come in to breathe that air of freedom. Help me in your prayers, dearest sister; my days are passing, as Job says.[80] The way I am going, there is no returning. I am not far from that limit which is set for all flesh. Already my grey hairs herald my last hour. So, dearest sister, please pray; in your most intimate tears, make a remembrance of me, offering it in the sight of the Son of God. I know that the persistent prayer of a righteous man is very powerful,[81] and that the intercession of someone else achieves what our own prayers do not.

Dearest sister, you have been chosen by Christ to serve, to serve him in prayer and to make your sisters pleasing to the Lord, followers of good works, forming them by your words and by your example of prayer. Abandon all that is vain and strive to fulfil your ministry by your way of life, and clothe yourself in holiness, so that you can pay your due service to him who is the Holy of Holies. Be upright in your riches, I beg you, modest in your speech, discerning in what you command, eager to help others, reliable in your advice, circumspect in the answers you give people, and inclined always towards patience.

410

Show devotion to the older sisters, gentleness to the younger ones, and kindness to your equals; show yourself stern to the proud, kind to the humble, merciful to the penitent, unyielding to the obstinate. Be a John the Baptist to the incestuous,[82] a Phineas to those who apostatise and go whoring,[83] a Peter to liars,[84] a Paul to blasphemers,[85] a Christ to traders.[86] The course of this mortal life is soon run, and its end is terrifying. The higher the title you bear because of your job, the more glorious it will be for you if you can surpass others in holiness.

Most dear sister, I have thought fit to encourage you like this, not because you need any encouragement from me, but to help you run even more eagerly towards the prize and reward, and hasten to enter the house of God and the house of St. Peter, with all your and my dear sisters, so that, when I come to you after the Chapter, I may receive full consolation from seeing your habit and your religious life. I was going to come to you, but certain recent events meant that I could not come after all. I am going to the Chapter with brother Ulrich,[87] and I commend you all to God until I come. And I will come soon.

Brother Ulrich greets you in the Lord and commends himself to your prayers. Give my good wishes to brother Peter and to Donna Petra,[88] and also those of brother Ulrich.

Farewell. We are all well.

# St. Mary of the Isle, Buda
## [*From the Canonization Process of St. Margaret of Hungary*]

### TESTIMONY OF DAME BENEDICTA (JULY 27, 1276)

Asked about the life and behaviour of the said virgin, Margaret, she replied on oath, "I know well that the virgin Margaret was humble and simple in the Lord, and that she led a good and holy life." Asked how she knew this, she replied, "I know it well, because I knew her the whole time since she was ten years old, and I was with her in this monastery."

She also said that the virgin Margaret used to stay at her prayers continually from dawn until lunch time, and she would not leave off her prayer for any message from her father or mother or anybody else who was asking for her, unless she was sent for by the prioress. Asked how she knew this, she replied, "Because I saw her, and I lived with her in the monastery." Asked in what part of the monastery she used to be at her prayers like this, she replied, "Sometimes in a private place of her own in choir, and sometimes before the Crucifix, and sometimes before the Holy Cross altar; and she was always present at all community Masses with the other nuns." Asked how she knew this, she replied, "Because I saw it."

She also said that after Compline, the virgin Margaret used to remain in prayer until cockcrow. Asked how she knew this, she replied, "Because I saw it." Asked where this took place, she replied, "In the Chapter Room of the monastery, before the Crucifix; there she used to say the seven penitential psalms. After that, she went and stood in front of her bed until the cocks began to crow." Asked how she knew this, she replied, "Because I saw it several times and I heard the other sisters talk about it too."

She also said that when the prioress gave any orders to all the sisters in general, the virgin Margaret, if she was there, was quicker than any of the others to carry them out. Asked how she knew this, she replied, "Because I saw it."

She also said that she used to wear clothes in which there were a lot of lice, and when she took these clothes off, she did not want the lice to be removed. For a time she wore on her back a fur with more lice in it than you could possibly tell, and she did not want the lice removed from it. Asked how she knew this, she replied, "Because I saw it, and I often ran away from her because of the lice." Asked why she wore clothes with so many lice in and did not want them removed, she replied, "So that it would be a greater penance." Asked how she knew this, she replied, "I know it because I once said to her, 'Why do you wear clothes with so many lice in?', and she answered, 'Let me do it if I want to; it is not your body that is wearing them.'"

She also said that one day in winter, when it was very cold, the virgin Margaret, who was doing her week in the refectory then, called sister Kinga to help her carry out and empty a big bowl of water in which the sisters had been washing their hands. Sister Kinga refused to come, so she called her again; she became a bit angry,[89] and while they were emptying the bowl, sister Kinga spilled the water over sister Margaret's breast. And she began to laugh, and said, "My good sister, why did you do that?" And then sister Kinga walked away from her. Asked how she knew this, she replied, "Because I was there when it happened."

She also said that she wore a hair shirt next to the skin. Asked how she knew this, she replied, "Because I was told so."

She also said that when it was her week, she did the kitchen and washed the dishes and swept the house and did all the other things the sisters did when it was their week. Asked how she knew this, she replied, "Because I saw it."

She also said that she asked the prioress if she could be given the job of serving the sick, and the prioress gave her this job, so she served the sick after that, doing the cooking for them and washing the dishes and pots and serving them in every other way she could; and she often did their week for them, when any of them were sick. Asked how she knew this, she replied, "Because I saw it, and others told me about it."

She also said that she fasted the whole time in accordance with the Rule, and fasted a whole lot more in addition, and if the prioress told her not to fast so much, because she was afraid that she was too weak to bear it, then she got upset and cried, and then the prioress gave her permission to go on fasting. Asked how she knew this, she replied, "Because I saw it and heard about it."

She also said that she enjoyed giving alms to the poor sick people she sometimes saw from the window in choir, when they were in church, giving them some of her own clothes, with the prioress' permission. Asked how she knew this, she replied, "Because I saw it."

She also said that from the fifth Sunday in Lent until Easter she used to remain in prayer, with a lot of weeping and moaning, very humbly and devoutly, even more than she did at other times. Asked how she knew this, she replied, "Because I saw it."

She also said that one time the Danube overflowed into the yard where the nuns' servants are, and then subsided again. And brother Marcellus,[90] who was the Provincial of Hungary at the time, came to the monastery some time afterwards, and Margaret began to tell him what a flood there had been, and he said, "How can I believe that? It isn't possible." Then sister Margaret prayed to God and to the blessed Virgin to make brother Marcellus see that what she had said was true; and at once the Danube became so swollen that the water came into the servants' yard and into the nuns' cloister, and brother Marcellus climbed onto a piece of wood and went into the nuns' Chapter Room. Asked which of the nuns was present then, she replied, "Margaret who was the daughter of Lord William, and Judith the subprioress and many others, but I do not remember exactly who they were." Asked where they were when this happened, she replied, "In front of the parlour."[91] Asked how long ago it was, she replied, "It happened three years before the death of the virgin Margaret." Asked about the month, she replied, "I do not remember, but it was between Epiphany and Shrove Tuesday." Asked about the day, she replied, "I do not remember." Asked what time of day it was, she replied, "I do not recall."

Asked how old the witness herself was, she replied, "I think I am thirty-eight; and I have been a sister in this monastery for twenty-four years."

Asked how long it was since the virgin Margaret died, she replied, "Seven years."

## TESTIMONY OF DAME CATHERINE (AUGUST 5, 1276)

Asked about the life and conduct of this virgin, she said on oath that there was nothing but goodness and humility in her; she was a nun of good life and great holiness, and used to stay for a long time at her prayers, "and I saw this, because I often accompanied her as her companion."

She also said that "it is the custom of the nuns here always to go to confession and to receive the Body of Christ on the feast of All Saints, and when St. Margaret was due to go to confession and make her communion on this day, she thought of a certain sister who had not spoken to her for three days and wondered whether she had done something to upset her. So she prostrated herself at her feet. I saw this and asked her, 'Dame, why did you do that?' She answered, 'I was asking her pardon, if I had done anything to upset her; otherwise I could not bring myself to go to confession and communion.'"

She also said that she remained at her prayers for a very long time by her bed, while the other sisters were asleep, "and when I woke up, sometimes I saw her standing there praying, and sometimes I saw her going quietly round the dormitory listening to see if any of the sisters was in distress, and if she heard anyone complaining she went and asked if they wanted anything, and if they asked for a drink or something, she went to the cupboard at once, or to the kitchen, and brought them whatsoever they asked for, and she did all this very quietly, so as not to wake up the sisters."

She also said that in this monastery, which had been presented with many generous benefactions by her father and mother, she refused to accept or to have anything more than any of the other sisters in the way of clothes or food or anything else; in fact, she took much less than any of the others. Asked how she knew all this, she replied, "I saw it."

She also said that she used to wear terrible clothes, all torn and patched. Asked how she knew this, replied, "Because I saw it, and sometimes I patched her clothes for her."

She also said that she did not opt out of serving the sick sisters, "and one day, when I went with her to collect some meat for the sick, and we could not immediately find anything to carry the meat in, I saw her take her scapular off at once and put it on the ground, and she wrapped the meat in that and carried it to the kitchen." And she said that "when I went into the kitchen with St. Margaret with this meat, my scapular was all greasy and dirty from the meat I had carried, but her scapular was none the worse for it. I got very upset and annoyed at her, and she began to laugh and said to me, 'Why are you angry? I know perfectly well what you are thinking,' and then she told me exactly what I was thinking."

She also said, "Because of all the jobs she did, I noticed that in winter the skin on her hands was very broken and cracked. And when she listened to the sermons which were preached to the sisters, I sometimes sat next to her and saw that she wept a lot."

Asked if she wanted to say anything more, she replied, "I have said all I know."

Asked how old she was, she replied, "I do not know." Asked how many years she had been in religion, she replied, "I have been in this monastery for twenty years, and I was in the monastery at Alba for three years."

Asked if she had been told or asked to give this evidence, she replied, "No."

## FROM THE TESTIMONY OF DAME JUDITH
### (AUGUST 6, 1276)

Asked about the life and conduct of this virgin Margaret, she said on oath, "I noticed that St. Margaret made a lot of prostrations and that she prayed a lot and wept."

She also said, "I saw her fetching water for the sick and carrying it through the mud, and she was carrying such a big tub that we wondered how she could carry it."

She also said, "I saw her washing the wool even when the weather was at its coldest, and she made compote with her own hands and trampled it with her feet in a tub, even when it was extremely cold, so that her clothes were all frozen with the water from it, and her hands were all cracked and bloody because of the cold."

She also said that sister Olimpiades, her novice mistress, once rebuked her, when Margaret was praying prostrate on the ground, and said to her "You are like a pig, grubbing for God with your nose and face in the mud! Why do you do it? Why are you ruining yourself?" And she took it all quite peacefully. Asked how she knew this, she replied, "Because I saw it."

# Unterlinden
## [*From the Lives of the Sisters*]

### SISTER AGNES OF OCHSENSTEIN, OF HAPPY MEMORY

Sister Agnes of Ochsenstein, one of the first sisters of this holy community, led a pure and innocent life from childhood, and kept the flower of her virginity untainted all her life. From the time when she was young up to the time of her death, she lived most religiously in our community's monastery at Unterlinden resplendent like a beacon of holiness. She was a model of holiness, a pattern of religious life, the very image of monastic purity, and exceptionally faithful to regular observance. So fine was her character, so fervently was she inspired by divine zeal, that we may with confidence call her a vessel of honour and of grace.

In addition to this, she was a very gentle and effective comforter of all the sisters, so that anyone who went to her because of any kind of upset always came away consoled; she also often helped them with the support of her prayers. Her heart was full of the most holy affections, and she was loyally responsive to all the ups and downs of her neighbours. She always overflowed with pleasing and comforting words. Her heart was fired with an incredible yearning to win all men for Christ, so she never rested from holy and persistent exhortations, speaking most warmly about God to her sisters and also to outsiders at the window, for she held for many years the job of attending at the window,[92] and she did it in such a spirit of holiness and religion that all who came there, religious and seculars alike, went away greatly edified.

When she was given the job of subprioress and many other different responsibilities in the monastery, she worked at them humbly, devotedly and energetically, and out of regard for her holiness the whole community of sisters took her to their hearts with special love.

She was beyond all comparison in her practice of abstinence. She practised the utmost moderation in food and drink, mortifying herself most severely for the sake of the Lord; almost all her life she abstained, in things great and small, from any food which might possibly appeal to her appetite, and, when the other sisters were eating two dishes at table, she always did without one of them for herself, and she would eat dry barley bread, refusing white wheat bread if she was offered it. She always refused to take even a taste of apples or nuts or other such fruits.

Her way of life was very strict and tightly disciplined. She wore down and punished her innocent body most aggressively with vigils and fasts, constant prayers, and with no end of other such good works. In summer and winter alike she used always to get up early enough before Matins to have time to recite the whole psalter. She kept this practice up throughout her life, whether she was in good health or bad. Then she always took part in the celebration of Matins with a devout and attentive mind, and she never or hardly ever returned to bed afterwards. Any devout sister who reads this can calculate what a tiny amount of time this left for her poor body to rest at night.

But this was not nearly enough to satisfy the fervour of her spirit, which was always seething with the fire of divine love; she added yet another way of grievously afflicting herself. For many years she tied three different kinds of girdle tightly round herself next to the the skin: one was entirely made of iron, with broad iron plates just slightly separated from each other with iron rings inserted between them, carrying very sharp nails which pricked savagely; she wore this round her breast. She wore another one round her waist, which was like a chain and was also entirely made of iron. The third was a great rope, which she wore tied around her loins. After her death, the skin and flesh under these girdles was found to be as black as if it had been stained with coal, and we saw that it was all decayed.[93]

To make her torments even worse, she wore her stockings night and day, and I suspect that this was because the Constitutions say that the sisters must wear stockings even in bed in places where it is the custom for women to wear stockings, and that she was eager to observe the Constitutions of the Order to the full, perfectly, in this as in every other point.[94]

While she was in this way making vast progress in the virtues, the Lord permitted her to be for a long time in a kind of thick mental fog about the sacrament of the Body and Blood of our Lord Jesus Christ, so that she had no clarity about the reality of this sacrament and no sense of it in her soul. She had every intention of holding on to the faith as presented in the tradition of the church, so she constantly resisted the repugnance of her feelings and most carefully avoided talking about this divine sacrament or listening to others talking about it, for fear of falling even more dangerously from the certainty of faith into the doubtfulness of human opinion.[95] When the time came for her to receive mercy, the loving Lord, who comforts the humble, came to her, enlightening the darkness of her mind in this way: one day, during the celebration of the Mass, at the time when the sacrifice was being offered on the altar, she was watching with her mind devoutly attentive to what was going on; suddenly the most brilliant light from heaven shone round the most holy eucharist in the hands of the priest. As soon as she saw this, she was completely freed from all her previous darkness. Thereafter she used to feed with extraordinary sweetness on the contemplation of this heavenly manna of the Lord's sacrament, finding great pleasure and enjoyment in constantly thinking about it or talking about it or listening to others talk about it.

After this, the holy sister was afflicted for a time with a persistent and burdensome doubt and uncertainty, not, I believe, without a kindly purpose of God, by whose benevolent providence all things work together for good for those who love him.[96] Her uncertainty was whether the enigmatic words of the prophets were uttered under the inspiration of the Holy Spirit or rather from a merely human spirit. The latter view attracted her, because she found their words very obscure and silly. But the merciful Lord, who does not abandon those who hope in him, took pity on this lover of his, and, scattering the darkness of her ignorance, flooded her with the light of his saving grace. One time when she was praying with great devotion, she was suddenly carried right outside herself in ecstasy and raised up on high to the knowledge of the supreme Truth; God took the veil from her eyes and granted her a most pure contemplation in the very light of eternity, so that she could know and understand everything that the holy prophets wrote and said, word by word from the beginning, concerning the incomprehensible essence of the Most High Godhead, and about the Incarnation of our Lord and Saviour, and at the same time it was given to her to see clearly that these holy prophets were inspired solely by the grace of the Holy Spirit to utter all their prophetic sayings. The greatness of this heavenly vision and of her consequent progress in celestial illuminations, with which she was at this time marvellously enlightened, which shone into her powerfully from the everlasting mountains,[97] was known only to her and to the Father of lights, from whom all good things come in abundance.[98]

It only remains now to say how the Lord God, who is so good to those whose heart is right,[99] and whose delight it is to be with the sons of men,[100] marked with an even more special gift of his generosity this beloved servant of his, whom he had established quite specially in hope with such an abundance of particular graces. After receiving with her usual purity of mind the most holy sacrament of the altar, at the time appointed by the customs of the monastery, she was immediately caught up above herself, and all her bodily senses were entirely put to sleep through the ecstasy of her mind. Then she saw, with the mind's spiritual vision, a luminous crowd of angels surrounding her. They escorted her with great honour to the Lord of highest majesty. He looked at her with the kind and peaceful face of his divine compassion, and took her to himself to be his everlasting bride, in the presence of the whole glorious crowd of angels. As it seemed to her, she was pledged and engaged to the Lord Jesus Christ in this heavenly vision with visible tokens to bear witness to this union and secure their eternal bond and love. The blessed vision was soon finished, but in the heart of her who saw it, the intimate devotion which it produced could never finish. Ever after she had a remarkable confidence in God. Frequently thereafter in her prayer she used to say to God with loving trust, "O Lord God, good Jesus, remember the pledge and betrothal with which you graciously engaged me to yourself forever in the presence of your noble angels." So eager ever after was her devotion to the love of her beloved Spouse, that she completely lost all interest in herself; this passing life with all its pleasures seemed as nothing to one whose whole desire was to be dissolved and to be with Christ.[101] And no wonder! After a taste of the Spirit, everything carnal loses its savour. This godly vision, together with all the other heavenly revelations we have mentioned above, she related to a very spiritual and devout sister, on condition that they should not be spoken about at all until after her death. She insisted that these heavenly visions were shown her far more clearly and wonderfully than could ever be expressed in words, and we hold her account to be unquestionably true, especially as her holy way of life was such that we should consider it wicked not to believe what she said.

Fortified with this constant faith and virtue, beloved of God and man,[102] she put off the material body of corruptible flesh and went in to the heavenly wedding of the Lamb, for which she had been made ready, and there she will be forever, as well off as well can be. To God the king of the ages be praise and honour for ever and ever. Amen.

After her death, a certain good sister of our monastery had a vision in the night, in which she seemed to see her tomb apparently open. She looked into it with some curiosity, and saw that it was completely empty except for a very large crystal, excellently conformed in length and size to the measure of the dead sister's body. This crystal was flanked by three gold and silver rings, shining more brilliantly than the sun, slightly separated from each other. When she woke up, she realised that the Lord had wanted to show the outstanding merits of this blessed sister by means of this dream.

## SISTER GERTRUDE OF COLMAR, OF WORTHY MEMORY

Sister Gertrude of Colmar, of fond memory, a sister of our monastery, was very religious and worthy of imitation in everything. This holy sister, of pure and innocent life, began to do battle for the Lord energetically in her thirteenth year, and she carried the Lord's pleasant yoke[103] with unwearying enthusiasm until her death. All the days of her life she strove to follow her Rule wholly and perfectly, making no concessions to herself. She always followed the common life in all its rigour, in choir, in refectory, in food and drink, in watching and fasting and in everything else, aiming to keep the Rule with the utmost strictness. She always observed the regular fasts of the Order, whether she was in good health or in bad. For thirty years she wore down and afflicted her flesh with unbelievable abstinence. She did not eat meat at all, and hardly ever took any dripping,[104] in spite of the fact that she suffered sometimes from serious bouts of fever and other bodily pains and discomforts. What is more, throughout these thirty years she spent the whole of every Thursday night in prayer up to the time of Matins, and still attended Matins, singing enthusiastically and making her voice carry even to heaven. In executing the Divine Office she was most efficient and devout, not giving herself any rest by day or by night. For many years she did the job of chantress and so had to intone things in choir, and she did this energetically and well. She brought such fidelity and mental concentration to this job, and to everything else she was obliged to under obedience, that all could admire her with incredulous amazement, but few could hope to imitate her. She made sure that she was the first to come into choir, and devoted a great deal of care to ensuring that all the sisters sang their psalms to God harmoniously, loudly and solemnly, in whatever way was fitting to each solemnity and season. She herself would never abandon the singing, never sparing her voice; she considered it no small stain on her conscience if ever she was prevented by any hoarseness or sickness from giving of her best to the solemn singing of the psalms.

Every day she used to beat herself with very sharp disciplines, and her prayer was so assiduous and constant that if I were to report it, it would probably seem to go beyond the bounds of humanity and the credulity of the reader. Since she abounded in so many good works and virtuous practices, our Lord Jesus Christ was pleased to give his beloved servant the consolation of a wonderful heavenly vision. On the day of Pentecost, when the sisters in choir were singing the hymn *Veni Creator Spiritus*, with devout urgency and great solemnity, suddenly he who came to cast fire upon the earth[105] and who had already kindled a mighty fire of devotion in this blessed sister showed her his wonders. She suddenly saw a divine fire coming down visibly, with a terrific noise, from heaven upon the holy community of sisters while they were praising God in their psalmody. It filled the whole choir where the sisters were gathered together to praise God,[106] making them so radiant with divine light that they all appeared to be on fire. A ray of heavenly light shone visibly round each one of them, remaining visible until the whole of that divine hymn was finished. At that time the Lord our God, who is a consuming fire,[107] without any doubt burned up any filth of sin that was in the sisters by the presence of his goodness in them, making their hearts clean vessels, passionately ablaze with love of him. Eventually the happiness of this celestial vision was withdrawn from the eyes of the sister who was watching, but the immense joy of the devotion that her heart had conceived remained with her, so that ever after she was always wonderfully moved to devotion by the remembrance of this sacred vision, and it always restored her to complete contentment.

Another time this holy sister of whom we are speaking had another vision in which she saw in choir a young sister of this monastery who had died a few days before. She had had the job of chantress while she was alive, being richly gifted with a most noble voice. She it was that sister Gertrude now heard with her bodily ears and saw in choir, in the holy place where she had sinned, being tormented by God's just judgment and beaten for a long time so fiercely and cruelly that she looked as if she was going to pass out and expire forthwith at every single blow. The sister who was watching all this felt deeply sorry for the agony of this soul and broke out into bitter lament. But then she learned from the voice of God what the reason was for this dreadful punishment. She was divinely taught that this dead sister was undergoing these appalling torments because she had several times failed to use the God-given beauty of her pleasant voice to sing with the others in the Divine Office, preferring to spare her voice; she had also sometimes sought human glory from her singing rather than the glory of God, and finally, she had been lazy about coming into choir and too quick to go out of choir.[108] So we must be very vigilant and attentive in our endeavour to serve the Lord with a faithful and sincere intention in our mind, to avoid falling through carelessness into the dreadful curse we find in the text that says, "Cursed is the man who performs the work of God negligently,"[109] and to make sure that we do not lose our heavenly reward because of our appetite for vainglory. As the Lord thunders in the gospel, "I tell you, they have their reward."[110]

This blessed sister, of whom we have been speaking so far, before she died, uttered a good remark, worth remembering, about herself: "There are three things in whose execution I have never in my life, even slightly, lost interest: constant attendance at the Divine Office in choir, constant devotion to prayer, and regular participation in the work of the community." And this was quite true. It was proved beyond any doubt by her life and conduct. Right into her extreme old age she worked usefully and well at several jobs in the monastery. Last of all, she was given the job of *circatrix*,[111] which she carried out religiously and energetically, correcting and admonishing, in season and out of season,[112] manfully rising up with the zeal of God against all the sisters' negligences and transgressions of the Rule and Constitutions, not hesitating to set herself up as a wall[113] to defend God's house. Neither fear nor love made her spare the sisters even in the slightest transgressions; without fail she would accuse them in Chapter. On one occasion she accused twenty sisters in one Chapter, harshly enough too. And so the practices of the Order and the Rule were excellently kept in those days.

423

At last this happy, holy sister, of blessed memory, released into welcome death, gave back her spirit to God and received a crown of righteousness from the Lord Jesus Christ, who lives and reigns, God, forever and ever. Amen.

# The Nuns
## Notes

1. *Libellus* 27.
2. 1 Cor. 3:6.
3. Phil. 2:12.
4. Raymund Cathala is included in Bernard Gui's supplement to Salagnac's list of "Famous and *gratiosi* preachers," and he is said to have worked a few miracles after his death (MOPH XXII pp. 161–2). Vicaire argues that he must have been prior of Prouille from as early as 1225 (*SDHT* p. 476[59]).
5. MOPH XXIV pp. 7–8, 24.
6. Cecilia seems to have got a bit confused; Gaudio is mentioned as being already in the Order in *Miracula* 3, which refers to an episode which took place earlier than that recorded here. Vicaire identifies him with a brother Gaudius of whom we hear in Siena in 1227 (*SDHT* p. 523[121]).
7. Roger was cellarer for the brethren when they were still living at San Sisto (*Miracula* 3; AFP 31 [1961] p. 39[80]), and was one of the friars left behind when the brethren moved to Santa Sabina. According to Benedetto da Montefiascone (AFP 31 [1961] p. 70), his job there was to attend to the "turn" (the place where things were passed in and out of the enclosure); Benedetto says that he was a Spanish laybrother.
8. Nothing more seems to be known of sister Nubia. The glowing account of her virtues in the seventeenth-century Chronicle of Domenica Salomoni (*Chroniques de S. Sisto* I p. 49) seems to be due only to pious supposition.
9. Koudelka (AFP 31 [1961] pp. 59–60), Lippini (op. cit. p. 199[22]) and Walz (AFP 37 [1967] p. 31[3]) point out that this figure is far too high. Even in the late 1250s there do not seem to have been more than fifty nuns there (Koudelka). Similarly Cecilia's figure of twenty-five brethren is unrealistic; there cannot have been many more than six friars living there, and there would not have been visitors at this time of night, except for those who came with St. Dominic.
10. Santa Sabina, with its exquisite fifth-century basilica, was given to the Order in 1222, but they had already been granted effective possession of it in 1221, and the friars moved in in February of that year (BOP I 15; Cecilia, *Miracula* 14). It is still the central house of the Order and the residence of the Master of the Order.
11. Tancred entered the Order in Bologna as the result of a vision, probably in 1218, before Reginald's arrival there (MOPH I pp. 190–1; Quétif-Échard I 91a). Jordan speaks highly of him as a "good and fervent man"

(*Libellus* 100). He presumably went to Rome with St. Dominic at the end of 1220. He is generally referred to as having been "prior of Rome," which surely means prior of Santa Sabina. Benedetto da Montefiascone says that he was left at San Sisto as prior there (AFP 31 [1961] p. 70), but he ignores Odo, and it is not clear why there should be two priors in one house. Berthier asserts that he died in 1230 (*Jordanis de Saxonia Opera*, p. xi), but I do not know that there is any evidence for this. Odo seems to be otherwise unknown.

12. Cf. Gen. 24:40.

13. 2 Tim. 2:5.

14. St. Dominic's half-brother, Bl. Mames, was one of the friars sent to Paris in 1217. In 1219 he was evidently sent to Madrid, where he was shortly afterwards put in charge of the monastery of nuns. He was regarded as a "holy, contemplative" man (MOPH I p. 67). After his brother's canonization, he encouraged the people of Caleruega, his birthplace, to build a church in his honour; he died some time later at the Cistercian monastery of St. Peter's, Gumiel, only a few miles from Caleruega, where both St. Dominic's parents were buried, and where, in all probability, his other brother had also retired and died (MOPH XXII pp. 152–3; Mamachi, *Annales*, Appendix 331–2; Vicaire, *SDHT* pp. 9, 19–20).

15. Paul of Hungary was a lecturer in canon law in Bologna, who entered the Order there and was prior of Bologna by January 1221. Later that year he was sent to establish a missionary province of the Order in Hungary, where he died, probably in 1223 (Vicaire, *SDHT* p. 363). When he left for Hungary, he had just completed a manual for confessors, on which he had been working with the help of St. Dominic and the other brethren (Mandonnet-Vicaire, I pp. 249–269).

16. Enrico della Fratta, bishop of Bologna since 1213 (Sorbelli p. 77) does not seem to have taken much notice of the Dominicans there (Vicaire, *SDHT* p. 270), but it may be surmised that his opposition to the establishment of their monastery of nuns was prompted more by the hostility of Diana's family than by the reason officially alleged here. Once their objections had been silenced, the bishop made no further difficulties. Cf. Hinnebusch, *History* I p. 102. (Grundmann's suggestion [*Religiöse Bewegungen*, pp. 214–5] that Dominic himself had turned against the idea of making the foundation seems quite gratuitous.) In 1227 he seems to have tried to interfere with the brethren's election of a prior, and was duly rebuked by the Pope (BOP I 24). He resigned he see in 1240 and died a year later (Sorbelli pp. 113–5).

17. This was a hermitage belonging to the Canonesses of St. Mark of Mantua (Cambria p. 52[15]).

18. Eph. 1:4.

19. On Bernard the German, see Scheeben, QF 35 pp. 154–5. He is

surely to be identified with the German Bernard who features in several of Jordan's Letters, and who became the first provincial of Germany, though the dates of his provincialate cannot be established, except that he was provincial in 1224. He died in 1236.

20. On Claro, see AFP 4 (1934) p. 126. After lecturing both in the Arts faculty and in Law at Bologna, he entered the Order in 1219. He became the second provincial of the Roman province, probably about 1224. At some time he was papal penitentiary and chaplain.

21. Rom. 14:17.

22. Psalm 72:28.

23. Psalm 62:9.

24. Gerard seems to have become Jordan's secretary and constant companion in the summer of 1229 (Altaner, QF 20 pp. 97–8. He perished with Jordan in the shipwreck of February 12, 1237 (MOPH I p. 130).

25. 2 Tim. 4:22.

26. Psalm 47:14.

27. Rom. 9:5.

28. Psalm 59:11.

29. Psalm 47:9.

30. Psalm 86:5.

31. Rom. 7:24.

32. Cf. Matt. 7:2.

33. *Saluta mihi priorissam Galianam.* M. Aron (*St. Dominic's Successor*, p. 179), K. Pond and G. Vann all translate this, "The prioress and Galiana," following the doctrine of Altaner and Scheeben, who tacitly refuse to identify Galiana as prioress. But the Latin text cannot naturally be made to give any other sense than "Galiana, the prioress." If the dating of this letter to 1236 is correct, there is nothing in the Letters to contradict this suggestion. There is documentary evidence for Cecilia's being prioress in January 1237 (Cambria, p. 246). There is evidence in Jordan's Letters that Galiana was not prioress in 1233 (Letters 7 and 4). But this allows time for her to be prioress in between. The chief problem is that in Letter 14, written in 1229, Galiana is described as a novice. But there is nothing impossible in the notion that she entered the Order as a mature woman, who might be a suitable prioress. It is generally supposed that the first prioresses were all chosen from the nuns who came from S. Sisto (for the view that Agnesia, the first prioress came from there, see Scheeben, QF 35 p. 88; Walz, AFP 37 [1967] p. 8; the next certainly known prioress is Cecilia, who is definitely one of the Roman nuns). However, Cambria raises difficulties about the suggestion that Agnesia came from Rome (op. cit., p. 54[22]); there is an Agnes who is known to have been at S. Sisto, but no Agnesia, and there is no reason to suppose that Agnes ever left S. Sisto.

34. These "outsiders" living in the house are evidently pious ladies who attached themselves to the nuns, living as some kind of oblates or tertiaries.

35. Cf. p. 155[39].

36. Psalm 18:8.

37. Cant. 2:14.

38. Ezek. 2:9.

39. Rom. 16:27.

40. Col. 3:12.

41. This echoes the responsory, *Regnum mundi*, which was evidently already used in the rite for clothing new nuns in the habit of the Order.

42. Psalm 64:5.

43. Matt. 5:3.

44. Psalm 44:10.

45. 2 Cor. 6:6.

46. Gen. 2:11.

47. Lam. 1:12.

48. John 15:13.

49. Psalm 21:17.

50. Cant. 2:14.

51. 1 Cor. 10:4.

52. Isaiah 12:3.

53. Psalm 44:10.

54. Ezek. 47:2; cf. John 19:34.

55. Isaiah 63:2.

56. Psalm 44:10.

57. Apoc. 22:14.

58. Psalm 71:15.

59. Psalm 118:130.

60. James 4:6.

61. Psalm 31:8.

62. Psalm 10:5.

63. Psalm 70:7.

64. Psalm 93:19.

65. Cant. 1:3.

66. Isaiah 35:10.

67. Psalm 64:5.

68. Psalm 83:5.

69. Cf. Gen. 29:17. Leah traditionally stood for the active life and Rachel for the contemplative life. Cf. p. 116[129].

70. Luke 10:39.

71. 1 Pet. 1:12.

72. 2 Cor. 13:13.

73. St. Peter was prior of Asti from 1248–9 (AFP 23 [1953] p. 86).

74. Psalm 83:8.

75. Psalm 119:5.

76. Psalm 54:7.

77. Ecclus. 24:11.

78. Cf. Psalm 114:3.

79. Psalm 131:14.

80. Job 7:6.

81. James 5:16.

82. Cf. Matt. 14:4.

83. Cf. Numbers 25:6–8.

84. Acts 5:1–11.

85. 1 Tim. 1:19–20.

86. Matt. 21:12–13.

87. Ulrich appears not to be known otherwise. See AFP 23 (1953) p. 93[83].

88. On Peter and Lady Petra see Dondaine, AFP 23 (1953) pp. 94–5. Lady Petra is almost certainly the mother of the prioress to whom St. Peter is writing, the benefactress who made possible the foundation of the monastery from which St. Peter's in Campo Santo was shortly afterwards founded. Peter is probably her husband, the prioress' father.

89. The Latin leaves it ambiguous as to which of the nuns was angry, but it was presumably sister Kinga.

90. S. Ferrarius (*De Rebus Ungaricae Provinciae Ordinis Praedicatorum* [Vienna, 1637] pp. 108–9 gives a singularly uninformative eulogy of Marcellus. He had, at any rate, stopped being provincial by the time of St. Margaret's death in 1270.

91. *In lebio ante locutorium*. I do not know what *in lebio* means.

92. The "window" was the place where people could come and talk to the nuns. There was evidently quite an "apostolate of the window" at Unterlinden, though this does not seem to be a traditional element in the life of Dominican nuns. The Rule of San Sisto provides for three sisters to be put in charge of the window, but their job is to ensure that no frivolous conversations go on there, not to talk to visitors (ASOP III pp. 632–3). Four sisters are given a similar job in the Constitutions of Montargis (ch. 12; AFP 17 [1947] p. 73), and in the definitive constitutions of the nuns (ch. 13; ASOP III p. 342).

93. The rather alarming bodily mortifications described here would have seemed much less extraordinary in the thirteenth century (cf. *SCH* Subsidia 1 pp. 263–4); even so, one might wish that Bl. Jordan's insistence to the nuns at Bologna that there are more important things in life than ruining one's flesh had been heeded more universally.

94. See chapter 9 of the nuns' constitutions (ASOP III p. 341; AFP 17 [1947] p. 72). The nuns' stockings must have been singularly uncomfortable to

compete with the iron belts mentioned above! But it is worth remarking that complete fidelity to the Constitutions was enough to attract attention. The implication is fairly obvious that on the whole the nuns did not expect to keep the Constitutions fully to the letter.

95. One cannot help feeling that it would have been better if the nuns had been encouraged to study more, instead of treating such problems as "temptations." But study was not regarded as part of their life. Unfortunately the "evidence" sometimes alleged for study as part of the nuns' life at San Sisto is due to Berthier's misunderstanding of *eruditio literarum* in the Rule (*Chroniques* I p. xxvii). It really only means "learning to read," as was seen by J. M. Veselý, *Il Secondo Ordine di S. Domenico* (Bologna, 1943) p. 150, and M. Gelabert and J. M. Milagro, *S. Domingo de Guzmán* (Madrid, 1966) p. 806.

96. Rom. 8:28.

97. Psalm 75:5.

98. James 1:17.

99. Psalm 72:1.

100. Prov. 8:31.

101. Phil. 1:23.

102. Ecclus. 45:1.

103. Matt. 11:30.

104. Dripping was sometimes allowed even to religious whose Rules prescribed total abstinence from meat (see Du Cange, *Glossarium Mediae et Infimae Latinitatis*, s.v. *Sagimen*). Stricter Orders therefore specifically forbid it: e.g., Praemonstratensians (mid-twelfth-century Constitutions, IV 12), Oigny (Consuetudines 25, ed. Pl. F. Lefèvre and A. H. Thomas, *Le Coutumier de l'Abbaye d'Oigny* [Louvain, 1976]). No such prohibition is mentioned in the Dominican constitutions.

105. Luke 12:49.

106. Cf. Acts 2:1–2, whose language is echoed here.

107. Hebr. 12:29.

108. Heaven help us! But the medievals had a stringent view of God's justice, which made it seem proper to them that even small sins for which due penance had not been done in this life should have to be expiated in purgatory.

109. Jer. 48:10, with the variant mentioned in the Interlinear Gloss.

110. Matt. 6:2.

111. It was the job of the *circator* or *circatrix* to tour round the monastic buildings, looking out for any infringements of the Rule or Constitutions. By the thirteenth century this was a well-established role in religious life, and it is significant that the earliest Dominican constitutions know nothing of such a character. But Humbert inserted a *circatrix* in his Rule for the nuns at Montargis (ch. 22, AFP 17 [1947] p. 79), and this remained in the Rule for all

the nuns (ch. 25, ASOP III p. 346). At his first General Chapter as Master of the Order, he saw to it that the brethren too acquired a *circator* in every priory (ACG 1254).

    112. 2 Tim. 4:2.

    113. Cf. Jer. 1:18.

# B. Dominican Laity

The thirteenth century saw an enormous increase in the demand for ways in which lay people could express their piety, and two ways in which this demand was met were the Order of Penance, which took shape during this century, and the development of new kinds of lay confraternity. The Dominicans were the first actually to set up an Order of Penance that would formally be part of the Order, under the jurisdiction of the Master of the Order; this was done in 1285. The most famous member of the Dominican Order of Penance was St. Catherine of Siena († 1380), who developed its apostolic possibilities in an unprecedented way. In addition to this, the Dominicans also contributed to the formation of a variety of confraternities, and stamped something of their spirituality on their way of life. Here we shall only take two such confraternities, whose statutes show particularly clearly the temper of their Dominican guidance, especially in the great concern that the members should be encouraged to give themselves with unforced generosity to works of devotion and compassion, rather than be bullied by laws and sanctions.

# Statute of the Congregation of St. Dominic, Bologna
## *1244*

To all the faithful christians who belong to the confraternity of St. Dominic at Bologna, brother John,[1] by the grace of God bishop and Master of the Order of Preachers: may you walk worthily in the works of saving grace, in the sight of God and man.

The grace of God's regard has shone in your hearts; inspired by the example of St. Dominic and confident of his help and support, you have joined together to devote yourselves to works of kindness, by which the wretchedness of the poor will be relieved and a service provided for the salvation of souls.

We see how wonderful the Lord is in his saints.[2] The example of only one man has been like a tiny seed sown in the ground, from which the Lord has raised up an abundant harvest of faithful souls. Congratulating you, then, on your devotion and the spiritual zeal you have conceived in the Lord, we judge your way of life and your organization, which are contained in the chapters written here, to be holy, fruitful and useful, pleasing and acceptable to God. The details are as follows:

This is the brotherhood or congregation of St. Dominic, confessor, established for his honour and for the salvation of souls.

(1) Whoever wishes to become a member of this brotherhood is to be accepted unless he has been denounced for or suspected of any error of faith, in which case he is certainly not to be admitted until his name has been cleared by his good conduct.

(2) On the last Sunday of every month, all the members of the congregation are to assemble, if they conveniently can, in the church of St. Dominic, to hear Mass in his honour and to listen to the word of God, if it is to be preached to them; and there each member of the brotherhood is to offer one *denaro* to the treasurers of the brotherhood, or, if he is unable to attend in person, he is to get somebody else to bring his offering.

(3) There are to be four treasurers for the brotherhood; it shall be their responsibility: to encourage those who are at enmity to make peace, to visit the fatherless and widows and orphans and the sick and

prisoners and the poor and any others who are afflicted in any way, offering them brotherly and loving service of help and advice. They are to use the money raised by the monthly collection faithfully for these people or for others; so that they can do this in the best possible way, the treasurers are to meet after None on the Sunday mentioned above, in the church of St. Dominic, to discuss these and other similar good works, as the Lord Jesus Christ, in his mercy, chooses to inspire and guide them.

(4) Every year, on the solemnity of St. Dominic, all those who belong to the brotherhood are to come to the church of St. Dominic with reverent and devout minds, to hear Mass and to offer one candle each, according to each one's position, in honour and praise of our Lord Jesus Christ and of St. Dominic. We say that they are to do this unless they are prevented by some legitimate difficulty.

(5) Each member of the brotherhood is to say the Our Father seven times a day in remission of his sins.

(6) Each member of the congregation is also to say the Our Father seven times for any member of the congregation who has died, and they are to do the same for any Friar Preacher who dies at the church of St. Dominic in Bologna.

(7) If they have been notified, all the members of the brotherhood who can conveniently manage it are to attend the funeral of a dead brother or sister, and if the dead person was poor, the cost of the funeral is to be supplied from the money raised by the collection already mentioned.

(8) They are always to keep one lamp burning before the altar of St. Dominic.

(9) The brotherhood as a whole is to keep two large candles in the sacristy of St. Dominic's, which are to be carried at the funerals of dead members of the brotherhood.

(10) Because we believe that God is more pleased with services performed freely than with those performed under constraint, and because our purpose is rather to remove snares from the necks of men than to place snares, we do not want to bind anyone in the sight of God to incur either guilt or a penance[3] in the case of transgression of any chapter or activity contained in this Rule; if they do anything good in these or any other ways, under the inspiration of the Holy Spirit, we desire and pray for them, through the power of our Lord Jesus Christ and the merits and prayers of the most blessed ever-

virgin Mary his Mother and of St. Dominic and the other saints of God, that such good deeds will bring them happily to everlasting life.

So it is our desire to advance with fitting approbation the special devotion which you have, by the gift of the Holy Spirit, towards our holy father, St. Dominic, and therefore, granting your loyal desire and your fair request, on behalf of all the brethren, we receive you and all those who will later join your brotherhood in honour of God and St. Dominic, giving you a share in the benefit of all the Masses, prayers, preaching, and other spiritual undertakings which our Order will, by God's inspiration, perform throughout the whole world, granting you also the privilege that, when any of you, brother or sister, is called by God's will to move from the light of this world to a better world, he or she shall receive the same prayers as are normally said for the dead brethren of our Order.

To authenticate this, we have seen fit to validate this document with our seal.

Given in Bologna on the 12th of June, 1244.

# New Statutes of the Congregation of Our Lady, Arezzo
## 1262

In the name of eternal God, Amen. In the year of the Annunciation of the Lord Jesus Christ, 1262.[4] The customs and ordinances of the fraternity of St. Mary of Mercy, drawn up and approved by wise, sensible men belonging to the fraternity, which they started in the month of June. They run as follows:

## (1) THE FOUNDATION AND APPROVAL OF THE FRATERNITY

The Lord, who is compassionate and merciful,[5] whose compassion is on all that he has made[6] and whose mercy fills the earth,[7] wanting no one to perish, but to bring everyone back to the way of truth, decreed lovingly in the law of his gospel and established it as an inviolable precept forever, that anyone who wants to obtain his marvellous mercy in this world and in the world to come must follow his most sacred example with regard to mercy, in this time which he has granted for the salvation of men, and must love mercy and devote himself zealously to the works of mercy. He exhorts us in the gospel to practise mercy, following the example of the Father: "Be merciful as your Father in heaven is merciful."[8] He also entices us to be merciful, by indicating the precious fruit of mercy, when he says, "Blessed are the merciful for they will obtain mercy."[9] So in the Last Judgment he will give unutterable happiness to the merciful, giving them a generous reward, when he says to them, "Come, you who are blessed by my Father, receive the kingdom which has been prepared for you from the beginning of the world. For I was hungry, and you gave me something to eat."[10] On the other hand, those who despise mercy or are careless about it he threatens with a dreadful warning, through his apostle James: "There is judgment without mercy for those who have not shown mercy."[11] And he will himself blast them appallingly in the Last Judgment, when he says to them, "Depart from me, you cursed, into the everlasting fire which has been pre-

436

pared for the devil and his angels. For I was hungry, and you gave me nothing to eat."[12] In consideration, therefore, of the splendid example we have to follow of mercy, and the immense profit which results from practising mercy, and the dreadful danger and harm that there is in despising it or being careless about it, we, certain citizens of Arezzo, came together in the church of St. Dominic, of the Friars Preachers, on the inspiration of God's grace and on the advice and encouragement of certain sensible friars of the same Order, with the permission and good will of our venerable father, the Lord William, Bishop of Arezzo,[13] and decided to found a fraternity, to be made up of ourselves, albeit unworthy, and any others whose hearts God may touch in the future and who offer themselves freely to the fraternity, to win God's mercy for themselves by performing works of mercy, and to relieve the various needs especially of the embarrassed poor, and of widows and orphans and also, in times of urgent distress, to help religious houses, poor monasteries, hospices and recluses,[14] to foster mutual charity and love and harmony, to strengthen the bond of peace and to encourage everything that is good, with the help of our Saviour's grace and with the support of the glorious intercession of his most merciful Mother, of our valued martyr bishop Donatus, and the blessed confessor Dominic and all the saints.

## (2) THE APPROPRIATE NAME FOR THE FRATERNITY

So this association of ours, which we founded for the undertaking of works of mercy, so that by means of it we might obtain God's mercy in this present world and in the world to come, we thought it appropriate to call the Fraternity of Saint Mary of Mercy, both because its aim is works of mercy, and because it is under the patronage of the Queen of Mercy, by whose merciful ruling and guiding we believe and hope that the fraternity is supported and advanced and led into all success and all that makes for salvation.

## (3) COMMENDATION OF THIS FRATERNITY

That fraternity, whether this means the spiritual assembly of the faithful or, sometimes, their actual bodily assembly to honour God and to be useful to other people, would be pleasing to God, the

Saviour himself proclaims in the gospel, when he says, "Where two or three are gathered together in my name, there am I in the midst of them."[15] People may surely claim to be gathered together in the Saviour's name when they come together at set times to carry out his will and commandment concerning mercy, and when they oblige themselves freely and unanimously to abide by certain common salutary laws for this purpose. This brotherhood of mercy, I say, derives the origin and vigour of its laws from our patriarch, the teacher of the gentiles, the apostle Paul, particularly with regard to collecting alms on one day in every week; he declares in his letter to the Corinthians, "With regard to the collections which are made among the saints on the first day of the week, you too are to follow the practice I established in the churches of Galatia" *(1 Cor. 16:1)*. This brotherhood is also eagerly recommended by the prince of the apostles, when he says to us in his letter, "Be compassionate and lovers of the brotherhood" *(1 Pet. 3:8)*. Solomon too praises it splendidly in Proverbs 18:19, "A brother who is helped by his brother is like a strong city." The merciful works of this brotherhood are expressed and commanded by the Lord through Moses in the Old Law, when he says, "If one of your brothers is reduced to poverty, you shall not harden your heart or withdraw your hand," and he adds, "I command you to open your hand to the poor and needy" *(Deut. 15:7,11)*. How glorious and pleasing such brotherhood is, which is enlightened by such teaching and adorned with such examples! And how impressive and how free from any suspicion of covetousness it is made by the edifying humility of respectable people, who are well enough off, begging in person for money or for bread, for the common good; for that is what the four directors of this fraternity do each week, taking it in turns for three months at a time. Apart from their humility in doing this, it is a burdensome responsibility for them, so they must often abandon their own business for it and freely take on the embarrassment and the unwonted labour of begging to do the business of fraternal charity.

## (4) THE ELECTION OF A PRIOR

It is well known that any congregation needs to be directed and led by some good and understanding man, if it is to survive and grow, and so, by our common will and good pleasure, and with the grace of

God going before us, we elected brother D., of the Order of Friars Preachers, from the chapter of the friars of St. Dominic's, to be the prior of our fraternity, and we promised obedience, or observance, to him and to his successors, in everything pertaining to this fraternity, in accordance with what is contained in the following chapters and with whatever may be decreed in the future by him or one of his successors at any given time, in conjunction with the directors and councillors of the fraternity. But we did not intend thereby to put ourselves in the position of incurring any risk for our souls, should we fail to observe or should we neglect any of the rules contained in these chapters, out of human fraility or out of carelessness, nor did we intend ourselves to be bound by them in conscience, as the prior mentioned above explained to us at the outset and over and over again afterwards. We also decided that the practice was to be maintained in the future of having some sensible priest who is a lover of our fraternity to rule it as prior, taken from the chapter of the friars of St. Dominic's, or from any other chapter, church or religious house. It shall be at the discretion of all the directors and councillors who hold office during the priorship of the present prior or of any prior who comes after at any given time, to choose the priest they consider suitable, in the church of St. Dominic where the fraternity began. He is to be chosen within fifteen days before the departure from office of the present prior or any who comes after, and he is to present himself before the altar at a time fixed by the four directors, and there the priest who has been chosen to be the new prior of the fraternity is to be invested, by the outgoing prior, with the book of these present chapters, and, when he has accepted his office, he is to kiss the altar reverently.

## (5) THE OFFICE OF THE PRIOR OF THE FRATERNITY

It shall be the responsibility of the prior of the fraternity to see carefully to everything that he regards as helpful for the good condition and for the progress of the fraternity, and to take counsel about it and discuss it with the directors and councillors of the fraternity who hold office at any time, and particularly with regard to receiving people into the fellowship of this fraternity, whether they are clerical or lay, men or women, from the city and diocese of Arezzo or from anywhere else, with the appropriate ceremony, described below, once a month on the day on which the fraternity meets, or on some other day, either together or one by one, as people come, wanting to keep the practices and decrees of this fraternity, for their own salvation or as a saving intercession for a dead father or mother or any other dead person who is dear to them. Also with regard to convening the fraternity once in each month, or at other times, whenever it is necessary, to preach to it and offer it exhortations and reprimands, if he sees it to be required that anything should be put right with regard to the fraternity. Also with regard to making the arrangements, together with the directors and councillors, for collecting and distributing alms, through the directors, and for the accounts which the directors are to submit to the councillors, whether or not the prior himself is present, once a month, or whatever other arrangement they decide to make. Also with regard to dispensing people from the rule of the fraternity or pardoning them for failing in or neglecting any of its observances, and generally with regard to dealing with everything which he considers useful for the fraternity, with the help of the Saviour's grace.

## (6) THE OFFICE OF THE DIRECTORS OF THE FRATERNITY

We also elect four men from the four districts or gates of the city, who are suitable by reason of their integrity and fidelity, to be directors of our fraternity, to be the workers and pillars of the fraternity, supporting its burdens; they are to receive the gifts and bequests generously made to the fraternity, and to beg in support of the work of the fraternity, namely, the relief of some part of the wretchedness of the poor, and they are to do this every week, begging once for bread, either themselves or through some deputy, and once for money. They are to dispense alms, providently and generously, either by themselves or through suitable intermediaries, to people who are genuinely in distress, and also, in time of critical need, when they have the resources, they are to help religious houses, such as poor monasteries and people who are serving God shut up as recluses, and, in sum, to practise any holy concern for the relief of the poor to which they are inspired by the grace of the Holy Spirit.

# DOMINICAN LAITY

## (7) THE OFFICE OF THE COUNCILLORS
## OF THE FRATERNITY

To provide a strong foundation for our fraternity, we decided to elect four other men from the four gates or districts of the city, to be councillors of the fraternity, to audit the accounts rendered once a month by the four directors, and we want these accounts to be rendered to safeguard the good name of the afore-mentioned officials and of the whole fraternity, and to protect it from any rash suspicions. It shall be the concern of the councillors to deal with and discuss whatever is useful and beneficial for the fraternity, together with the directors and the prior.

## (8) THE TERM OF OFFICE OF THE PRIOR,
## THE DIRECTORS AND THE COUNCILLORS

Because the burdens of the fraternity are to be shared out among many, we ordain that whoever is chosen in the way indicated above to be the prior of the fraternity is to exercise the office of prior for a period of six months, either in person, when he is in the city and can conveniently do so, or through some other suitable person, if he is away or legitimately prevented. The offices of director and councillor we want to be held for a period of three months, and the directors and councillors of any period are to meet in the church of St. Dominic or somewhere else decided by the directors and councillors, fifteen days before they come out of office, and are to choose four other suitable men to be directors and four more to be councillors, and when the prior of the fraternity has approved them, he is to call them and encourage them to take up these jobs, in remission of their sins and in view of God's mercy and brotherly love and for the sake of the reward of eternal salvation; he is to encourage them, but in no way to force them or oblige them to take up these jobs, because that would only be a stumbling block to them. And each of them, when they take up the job that is given them for their salvation, for the redemption of their souls, shall take office at the altar of the blessed Mary, the Mother of God, and shall kiss the altar and the book, in her honour.

## (9) IN WHAT WAY THE DIRECTORS ARE TO RENDER ACCOUNTS

Because, as the apostle says, "Everything ought to be done honestly and in good order among us,"[16] we want and, in this present chapter, ordain, that within eight days of the entry of the new directors upon their office of directing the fraternity, the previous directors are to submit their accounts to the new directors, in the presence of the councillors of the previous period and the new councillors; the prior of the fraternity should also be present. At least in outline, they are to give an account of all goods received, whether as a result of begging or from legacies or from any other kind of gift made to our fraternity, and of all expenses or distributions or concessions of alms made during each month of their term of office. We also want the directors to be obliged to give an account each month to their councillors, as it says in the chapter on choosing councillors, of goods received and distributed, and this should be a fuller account, and the prior shall be there if he wants, otherwise these accounts shall be submitted in his absence. We also want the outgoing directors to be obliged to pass on peaceably to the new directors, within eight days, all moneys and documents and title deeds and everything else there may be, and also to explain to them any debts they may have, and we want their successors, by virtue of being their successors, to be obliged to pay these debts. But we want the directors of the fraternity not to contract debts, except perhaps small ones, without the knowledge and advice of the councillors and the prior of the fraternity, so that through such due caution the good name of the fraternity may be safeguarded.

## (10) HOW SOMEONE ENTERS THIS FRATERNITY

We direct that if anyone wants to enter the society of this fraternity of Saint Mary of Mercy, he is to be exhorted by the prior of the fraternity to fear God, to honour the church and all clerics, to organise and govern his household well, to love, foster and maintain the peace and harmony of his city and its good condition in every way. If it is necessary, the rules of the fraternity are to be explained to him. And if he offers himself, wishing to observe them for his own salvation and that of those who belong to him, both living and dead, the prior is to say, "May the Lord who has granted you the will to do good, give it to you also to accomplish it, by the merits of the most blessed Virgin, who is the leader of this fraternity; and may the author of all good things, Jesus Christ, the Son of God, make you a sharer in all the good things which are brought to pass because of this fraternity, whether through its members or through those who bene-fit from it." And before he says, "Amen," the new member is to kiss the book, which should be open, with devotion and reverence.

However, we wish it to be stated clearly to everyone, by this present chapter, in accordance with the original terms of the founda-tion of this fraternity, and in accordance with our own intention, and the express will of the first prior of the fraternity, and with the agreement and approval of the venerable Lord William our Bishop, that the laws and ordinances of this fraternity do not bind us on pain of sin or put our souls at risk, if it should happen that we fail to comply with them in any point or points, whether through forgetful-ess or inability or some legitimate difficulty or simply out of careless-ness. If something can be done, which is similar to the duty which has been omitted, to make it up, then let it be done and let it automatical-ly count as satisfaction for the fault. But if it is impossible for someone to do anything like this, or if it is possible but he thinks that it would be difficult, then he can be mercifully dispensed by the prior of the fraternity, who may either give him something else to do to make up for it or simply release him from the obligation; he can do this for individuals separately or for everyone together, provided only that at least once a year every member of the fraternity, whether clerical or lay, man or woman, must tell the prior of the fraternity about all his or her transgressions of these rules, and humbly ask his absolution, and the prior will then kindly grant absolution, imposing something on him or her for his salvation, as a kind of symbol of making up for his failures, rather like a penance.

## (11) CLERICS WHO WISH TO JOIN THE FRATERNITY, AND THE HONOUR DUE TO THEM

Since it is God's command that we should particularly honour ecclesiastical or clerical persons, out of respect for the Lord whom they serve, we want any clerics who desire to join the fellowship of our fraternity to be accepted as fathers, according to their rank, and held in respect, and inscribed in the register with the others, and obliged only to the prayers and the monthly meetings, unless they are freed from this obligation too at the prior's will, because of their rank or for some other reasonable cause; they are not to be burdened, against their will, with the other jobs of the fraternity.

### (12) WOMEN WHO WISH TO JOIN THE FRATERNITY

Because there is no difference in the sight of God between men and women in the performance of the works of salvation, we want both men and women to be received into the saving company of this fraternity, and the women are to be obliged in just the same way as the men are to the daily prayers for the living and the dead, whether they are to be said in church or at home, and to offering the fixed suffrages for the dead members of the fraternity, which are indicated in the chapter on suffrages for the dead; also, unless they are prevented by their personal condition or by their domestic duties, they are obliged to attend the meetings held on one Sunday each month and on the four feasts of the glorious Virgin, the Mother of God, Mary, and on the feast of All Saints, at a time and place fixed and announced publicly or in some other way at the discretion of the prior and the directors. But they are not in any way obliged to give alms of bread or money, unless they freely want to, nor are they at all obliged to any of the other rules and ordinances of the fraternity, whether those already made or those which will come to be made in the future, unless they are specifically mentioned in them.

### (13) MEMBERS WHO LIVE IN OTHER PARTS OF THE DIOCESE OF AREZZO

Moreover, we have ordained that anyone, clerical or lay, man or woman, from our diocese, living outside the city, whether nearby or far away, who wants to become part of the community of our fraternity, and to share in all the benefits accruing to it either through its members or through those who receive alms from it, is to be received into the fraternity, even though he may not be able to come to its meetings and observe all its rules; he is to be inscribed in the register with the others, if he is willing to observe the rules about the prayers to be said in church or elsewhere, and about giving alms to the directors of the fraternity for the poor, either all at once or at different times, and about suffrages for the dead who come to his notice, and provided that he must, if he conveniently can, attend our meeting at least once in the year, on one of the four feasts of the most blessed Virgin Mary or on the feast of All Saints, to satisfy the directors that he has given the required alms. And he is to ask the prior of the fraternity about the news of the fraternity, and in particular about how many of its members have died during the year, and he is also to seek pardon for any omissions and negligences of his with regard to the laws of the fraternity, and he is to do something to make up for it, at the prior's discretion. In fact, to secure the basis of our fraternity, we want the same to be done at least once a year by every member of it, even those who live in the city, whether clerical or lay, man or woman, to prevent the observance of our laws disappearing through carelessness.

## (14) MEMBERS WHO LIVE IN OTHER DIOCESES

The gift of God is not limited to any one place or country, and, according to the text of the apostle, anyone who fears God, whatever his race, is acceptable to him;[17] so it is right that the establishment of a fraternity which offers service by the grace of God should not be limited by any geographical boundaries. So we wish that anybody, whatever his condition, even if he lives far away outside the diocese of Arezzo, may be enrolled in our fraternity if he asks to join our fellowship out of devotion, and is to receive the prayers of the brotherhood in life and in death like all its other members. And we do not want such people to be bound to anything except the daily prayers and almsgiving at the rate fixed for each year, and the suffrages for the dead in the form of prayers and money, as stated below,[18] after the death of any member has come to his notice, either by word of mouth or by letter; he should be informed of such deaths at least once a year. Also we desire that the prior or the directors of the fraternity should be informed of the death of any such member by his surviving relatives or friends, so that they can put his name in the register of anniversaries and that the proper suffrages may be offered on his behalf.

## (15) THE DAILY OBSERVANCES IN CHURCH, AND PRAYERS FOR THE LIVING AND DEAD

We have ordained that every member of the fraternity, in honour of God and of his glorious Mother, our advocate, should go to his own church or any other which he finds more convenient for his business, at some time every day, thinking, if he cares to, how our Saviour once came into this world for us and for our redemption, and also that he is to come again to judge the world and repay each man according to his works; thinking also of the kindness of our advocate, the most blessed Virgin Mary, the Mother of God, who intercedes for us with her Son and who promotes and protects the good condition of our city in all that is good. Also every day, whether he is in the city or in some other province, in some church or elsewhere, he is to offer at least two prayers, one for himself and for all living christians, saying one Our Father and one Hail Mary and also "Into your hands, Lord, I commend my spirit," either in Latin or in the vernacular, and then one other prayer for his dead dear ones and all the other dead, saying in the same way one Our Father and one Hail Mary and "Eternal rest grant to them, O Lord."

## (16) THE WEEKLY ALMSGIVING

We have ordained that every member of the fraternity is to give to one of the directors one *denaro* for the support of the poor once every week, on Thursday or on some other day, whether he is asked for it or not; if he does not give it in one week, he is to make up for it in another. And we decree that this principle of making up is to be observed by everybody, in the city or anywhere else, both in the daily prayers and in the weekly almsgiving.

## (17) THE MONTHLY MEETING

We have ordained that on one Sunday each month all the members of the fraternity are to come together after the time of Terce in winter or after the time of None in summer, in the church of St. Dominic, where our fraternity began and from where it has grown, or in some other church or religious house, which may from time to time seem suitable to the prior of the fraternity and its directors and councillors, to listen to the word of salvation and to the admonitions of the prior of the fraternity, or of someone else, at the discretion of the prior and the directors, to promote the well-being of the fraternity, and there the names of the dead are to be announced, if any member or members of the fraternity have died in the past month. They are also to be repeated every year in the month of their death, just as in other churches the anniversaries of the dead are announced every week to ask for prayers for them. At the same time, everyone is to give the directors one *denaro* for the soul of everyone who has died in the past month, and the directors are to give this money to have Masses said for the dead, in whatever way they think best. Also, at the same time, after the names of the dead have been announced, there is to be a common prayer made by everyone present, consisting of one Our Father and one Hail Mary and "Eternal rest." Finally the church's prayer for the dead is to be recited by the prior of the fraternity for the dead member of the fraternity in particular and for all the souls of the departed; he is to recite it without singing it, and to say it clearly: "The Lord be with you. Let us pray. O God, Lord of all pardon, grant to the souls of your servants, the anniversary of whose burial we keep today, a place of rest and refreshment, the blessedness of peace and the glory of light, through Christ our Lord. Amen."

## (18) THE MEETING ON THE FOUR FEASTS OF THE GLORIOUS VIRGIN MARY

We have ordained that, in honour of the glorious Virgin Mary, our advocate, all the members of the fraternity, after Terce or None according to the time of year, are to come together on her four feasts, wherever the prior and the directors decide: that is to say, the feast of the Annunciation, the Assumption, the Nativity of our Lady and the feast of the Purification, commonly known as Candlemas; this is to commend to her our fraternity and the good state of our city. And in honour of her every member of the fraternity is to give the directors two *denari*, with which candles are to be bought and money given for

Masses of the blessed Virgin to be said for our fraternity and for the good state of our city; the directors can decide where they want such Masses said.

## (19) THE MEETING ON THE FEAST OF ALL SAINTS

We have ordained that on the feast of All Saints all the members of the fraternity are to come together after Terce or None in some church or religious house which is announced beforehand, at the discretion of the prior and the directors; and in honour of all these great advocates and in supplication of their help, and for the health and salvation of the souls of the living and dead, every member of the fraternity is to give whatever God inspires him or her to give to the directors, for clothes for the poor, at least twelve *denari*, or eight or six or whatever he can and will give, so that, at the prayers of the saints, he may merit to be clothed in the glory of immortality by God.

## (20) SUFFRAGES FOR THE SOUL OF ANY MEMBER OF THE FRATERNITY WHO DIES

We have ordained that every member of the fraternity shall say three Our Fathers with Hail Marys and "Eternal rest grant to them, O Lord," for each member of the fraternity who dies, when he hears of the death. He is also to give one *denaro* to the directors, as has already been said, to have Masses said for his soul and for the souls of all the faithful departed.

## (21) THE ANNIVERSARIES OF PEOPLE WHO BELONGED TO THE FRATERNITY

We have ordained that, when any member of the fraternity dies, the director in whose district the dead man lived is to go to the prior of the fraternity the same day, or as soon as he can, and tell him the name and day of his death, so that the prior can write his name and the day of his death in the register which contains the calendar of anniversaries of the dead. The prior is to announce the dead man's name at the next meeting of the fraternity, so that everyone can do what he has to, to fulfil the suffrages specified above. Also every year the anniversaries of the dead members of our fraternity are to be read out, by name, a month at a time, in the first meeting after the day of their death, just as the anniversaries of the dead are generally read out each week in churches, so that everybody may humbly pray to God's mercy for their repose.

## (22) THE PERPETUITY OF THIS FRATERNITY

Seeing that we ought to have an effective concern to promote and preserve whatever is praiseworthy, with the utmost zeal and good will that we are capable of, we decree, in accordance with our unanimous desire, on the advice of the aforesaid friar, our prior, and with the consent and approval of the venerable father, Lord William our Bishop, that this fraternity, with its ordinances or laws contained here, and with whatever ordinances may subsequently be made by God's grace, as being something pleasing to God and as something he has inspired us to form, and as something entrusted to his glorious Mother, and as something beneficial to us and to the common welfare of our city, is to continue forever, with no limit in time, by God's merciful favour, in us and in those who come after us and will be received into its fellowship; may the kindness of our Redeemer preserve this will in us and in those who come after us until the end, by the merits and prayers of his most blessed Mother. Amen.

## (23) THESE ORDINANCES DO NOT BIND US IN SUCH A WAY AS TO PUT OUR SOULS AT RISK

Because it would be inappropriate if the provisions we have made in the simplicity and trust of our hearts for the common good and for our individual salvation were to militate against our safety, and because it would be wrong for arrangements which were made for showing mercy to our neighbours to become an occasion of God's wrath being stirred up against us, we, the directors, together with our prior who drew up these laws, having sought and received the wishes and opinions of all the members of our fraternity, and with the consent and approval of our venerable father, the Lord William, Bishop of Arezzo, will and declare that the ordinances we have made and any ordinances which may be made in the future do not bind us on pain of sin, if we fail to observe any of them through forgetfulness or frailty or any legitimate difficulty or even through carelessness; all we are bound to is that we should make it up by doing some good deed specifically for this purpose, or that we should seek pardon from the prior of the fraternity, whether individually and privately, or publicly and all together, seeking the pardon which will be given by him or his vicar.

## (24) THE ORDINANCES OF THE FRATERNITY ARE NOT TO BE CHANGED EXCEPT AFTER MUCH DELIBERATION

Because thoughtless alterations usually block even things which were established for our salvation, we will and ordain that no prior, no individual director or councillor and no group of directors or councillors in our fraternity, or any other individual or group, shall have the right to add any new laws to those contained in these chapters, or to change or cancel any of the laws in these chapters, in whole or in part, without the approval of the prior of the fraternity and all the directors and councillors of the whole year, meeting in the church of St. Dominic where our fraternity began. We want it to be understood in general that this approval means that the proposed change seems good to the majority of the people mentioned. After such approval, the alteration or addition can be made public to all the members at the next meeting of the fraternity.

## (25) ON MEETING WORTHILY IN THIS WORLD, AND GLORIOUSLY IN HEAVEN

May the Holy Spirit impress on our minds these ordinances which have been made for our salvation and for the comfort of the poor, particularly the embarrassed poor, and for the good and peaceful state of our city; may he also long preserve our fraternity and make it grow, at the prayers of the most glorious Virgin Mary, who is the leader and head of our fraternity, so that we may deserve to come to the meeting on high of the citizens of heaven, by his kind mercy, to whom alone be honour and glory and authority forever and ever. Amen.

# Dominican Laity
## Notes

1. John of Wildeshausen, Master of the Order from 1241–1252. He was provincial of Hungary from 1231–3, then bishop of Bosnia from 1233–7. After he resigned his see, he became provincial of Lombardy in 1239 and Master in 1241, in which office he remained until his death (Kaeppeli, *Scriptores* III pp. 47–8).

2. Psalm 67:36.

3. Meersseman (*Ordo Fraternitatis*, p. 1306) interprets this to mean that there is no "penance" in the strict sense of "penance *for sin*"; but there is no mention of any kind of penalty for infringement of the statute, and we should probably take this phrase at its face value as meaning that there is not any kind of penance at all.

4. In the Middle Ages some people reckoned the year as beginning at the Annunciation, whereas others calculated from Christmas ("Year of the Incarnation)."

5. Psalm 110:4.

6. Psalm 144:9.

7. Psalm 32:5.

8. Luke 6:36.

9. Matt. 5:7.

10. Matt. 25:34–35.

11. James 2:13.

12. Matt. 25:41–42.

13. William de Pazzi, bishop of Arezzo from 1248–89 (Eubel I p. 105).

14. *Incarcerati*: in view of chapter 6, this almost certainly means "recluses," not "prisoners."

15. Matt. 18:20.

16. 1 Cor. 14:40.

17. Acts 10:35.

18. *Supradictum* must be a mistake, as the reference is to chapters 17 and 20.

# Appendix

# THE EARLY DOMINICAN CONSTITUTIONS

As early as 1215, when St. Dominic went to Rome to seek approval for his new Order, we may presume that the brethren had some form of written guidelines for their life and work, but it is in 1216 that they first set themselves to draw up their formal laws. In addition to the Rule of St. Augustine, we are told that they "adopted certain strict customs with regard to food and fasting and bedding and woollen clothes. They also established the rule of not owning properties" (Jordan, Libellus 42). Their legislative work was rounded off in succeeding chapters, particularly those of 1220, 1221 and 1228. The material was re-arranged in a more orderly fashion by Raymond of Peñafort in 1241.

Close verbal similarities indicate that, in drawing up the Constitutions in 1216, the Dominicans made extensive use of the Constitutions of the Praemonstratensian canons, which has led some people to assert that the Dominicans saw themselves as belonging essentially within the same movement of reformed Canons as the Praemonstratensians; however a closer comparison of the two texts shows that the Dominicans were creating a very different kind of legislation, in view of a very different kind of Order. They abandon almost all the fussy details regulating the way of life of the religious.

To help the reader appreciate this, I have included here, not only a selection from the Dominican primitive Constitutions, but also some of the corresponding texts from the Praemonstratensians.


## FOREWORD TO THE DOMINICAN CONSTITUTIONS
### (1228)

In the year of our Lord's Incarnation 1228, the eight priors provincial met in Paris, in the house of St. Jacques, together with Jordan, the Master of our Order, each one accompanied by two diffinitors appointed by their Provincial Chapters. All the brethren had unanimously made over their votes to them, giving them full authority, so that whatever was done by them in the making or suppressing of constitutions, in making alterations, additions or subtractions, was to be regarded as established and valid, and no subsequent Chapter, whatever its authority, was to have the right to change anything which they decreed to be in force forever. So these provincials with their diffinitors unanimously issued several constitutions for the benefit and good name and preservation of the Order, after invoking the grace of the Holy Spirit and after careful discussion, and they saw that these constitutions were inserted into their proper places in the Constitutions.

They declared their will that some of the constitutions should be observed inviolably and unchangeably in perpetuity: namely, the constitution absolutely forbidding the Order to hold properties and revenues,[1] the constitution disallowing appeals,[2] and the constitution requiring that provincials and diffinitors must make their capitular decisions without prejudicing each others' Chapters.[3]

Other constitutions they desired to remain unalterable in the sense that only an equivalent chapter could make any alterations to them, should the need arise because of new controversies, crises, circumstances or problems. These were the constitution about not making new constitutions unless they are approved by three General Chapters, and the constitutions about not travelling on horseback, not carrying travelling money, and not eating meat except because of sickness. But all of these can be dispensed by the superior if time and place require it.

## FROM THE PROLOGUE

### Praemonstratensian

Our Rule commands us to have one heart and one soul in the Lord, so it is right that we who live under a single Rule and by a single profession should be found uniform in the observances of our canonical religion, so that the unity we are to maintain inwardly in our hearts will be fostered and expressed by the uniformity we observe outwardly in our behaviour. And we shall be able to observe this more adequately and fully, and retain it in our memories, if what we have to do is stated in writing, if we all have the evidence of the written text

### Dominican

Our Rule commands us to have one heart and one soul in the Lord, so it is right that we who live under a single Rule and by a single profession should be found uniform in the observance of our canonical religion, so that the unity we are to maintain inwardly in our hearts will be fostered and expressed by the uniformity we observe outwardly in our behaviour. And we shall be able to observe this more adequately and fully, and retain it in our memories, if what we have to do is stated in writing, if we all have the evidence of the written text to tell us how we ought to live, and if no one has the right to change anything or to add or remove anything at his own pleasure, and if we avoid carelessness even in the smallest details, to prevent us from gradually going astray.

Therefore, to provide for the peace and unity of the whole Order, we have carefully compiled this book, which we call the Book of Customs.

to tell us how we ought to live, and if[4] no one has the right to change anything or to add or remove anything at his own pleasure, to prevent us from gradually going astray by being careless about even the smallest details.

However, the superior is to have the right to dispense the brethren in his own community whenever it seems useful to him, particularly in things which seem likely to obstruct study or preaching or the good of souls, since our Order is known to have been founded initially precisely for the sake of preaching and the salvation of souls, and all our concern should be primarily and passionately directed to this all-important goal, that we should be able to be useful to the souls of our neighbours. Priors are to use dispensations just like all the other brethren.[5]

Therefore, to provide for the unity and peace of the whole Order, we intend and declare that our Constitutions do not bind us on pain of sin, but only on pain of a penance, except in the case of contempt or of a formal precept.[6] And we have carefully compiled this book, which we name the Book of Customs.

## FROM THE FIRST DISTINCTION

### 1. Matins

When the first signal is heard for Matins, the brethren are to be quick to get up. The prior meanwhile is to ring the dormitory bell. When they have attended to their bodily needs, they are to sit on their beds waiting for each other.

When the prior gives the signal, they are to go out in order, one after the other,

### 1. Matins

When the first signal is heard, the brethren are to get up, saying Matins of the blessed Virgin according to the time of year. When they have finished this, the brethren are to come into choir and bow deeply before the altar.

into the church. When they come into choir, they are to bow deeply before[7] the altar, gathering their capes with both hands, above the knee. They are to do this whenever they bow. When they have reached their seats, they are to stand facing the altar; then, when the prior gives the signal, they are to say the Creed and the Our Father once, leaning back on their misericords or prostrating over the desk, according to the time of year.

When they have reached their seats, at a sign from the prior, they are to kneel down or bow deeply, depending on the time of year, and say the Our Father and the Creed.

*[A lot of detailed rubrics follow, for the celebration of the Divine Office.]*

*[A lot of detailed rubrics follow.]*

*[Chapter 2 gives details about Prime and specifies that priests who wish to say Mass must do so after Prime.]*

*[Chapter 3 details when and where people may go to Confession.]*

### 4. The daily Chapter.

When confessions and Masses are finished, the sacristan is to ring the bell for Chapter. When they hear it, those who are not already there are to go into the cloister, and, when the bell stops ringing, they are to go into the Chapter Room in order. Writers and people who are occupied outside the monastery should hurry so that they come into the Chapter Room with the community. When the community enters the Chapter Room, they are all to bow, in order, to the Crucifix; when they have all reached their places, while they are still standing, the reader is to say *Iube domne* and the hebdomadary, or the abbot, if it

Chapter is held after the end of Matins, or after Prime, or sometimes it may even be omitted entirely, to avoid hindering study, as the superior sees fit.

### 2. The daily Chapter.

When the community enters the Chapter Room, the reader announces the lunar day and the other details from the calendar.

is a feast, is to say the blessing, *Divinum auxilium*. Then the reader announces the lunar day and the other details from the calendar.

*[Rubrical details follow.]*

*[Rubrical details follow.]*

*[Chapter 3 rules that women are never to be allowed to enter the cloister.]*

*[Chapter 4 gives a few more liturgical details.]*

## 5. How the brethren are to live in summer.

From Easter until the feast of Holy Cross, the brethren are to eat twice a day, except on the Greater Litany and on Rogation days, the vigils of Pentecost, the Ember day fasts, and the vigils of John the Baptist, Peter and Paul, James, Laurence, the Assumption, Bartholomew. So during this period the brethren will work, on ferial days, from the end of Chapter until Terce. Terce is followed by the High Mass, which is followed immediately by Sext. After Sext they are to devote themselves to reading, while the servers and the readers have their meal. Then the community is to have its meal, and everyone who is in the house is to be present at it. If anyone has some evident reason for not being able to be present, he is to eat with the servers.

If the refectory servers are unable to serve the community by themselves, they can be assisted by the servers of the Low Mass. All those who eat apart from

## 5. Meals.

From Easter until the feast of Holy Cross, the brethren are to eat twice a day, except on Rogation days, Fridays, the vigil of Pentecost and the Ember day fasts, and the vigils of John the Baptist, Peter and Paul, James and Laurence, the Assumption of our Lady, and Bartholomew.

the community must sit in the places
they would have occupied if they had
eaten with the community. They are not
to occupy each other's places. After the
meal and grace, they are all to go up to
the dormitory to sleep until None. At
the bell for None they are to go into
church in the same way as for Prime.
After None they are all to wash their
hands and drink together in the refectory. Then, when the signal is given,
they are to go out and work until Vespers. After Vespers, the community has
supper first, then the servers. While the
servers have their supper, the brethren
are to read, in community, each one
reading his own book, until the bell for
the collation. On Sundays and on feast
days on which we do not work, no
change is made in this timetable, except
that the brethren read at the times appointed for work, and the servers go out
to have their meal after the gospel at the
High Mass. On any fast days which fall
within this period, the Mass is said after
Sext, and then the brethren read until
None. None is followed by the meal.
After the meal they can go to sleep until
the prior gives the signal in the dormitory for them to get up. In the time of
reaping and harvesting, the Mass is to be
sung first thing in the morning, if this is
required by the needs of the job, and
then anyone who can do so is to go out
and work, even on feasts with nine readings which are not celebrated in the diocese. The community will generally
work at such times from Prime until
Sext, and, if need be, eat and sleep outside the monastery. If they are far from
the Oratory, they can go on working
even after the bell has been rung for
Vespers, something which should hardly
ever be done at any other time. They are
to sing Vespers where they are, before
returning to the monastery. And, if it is
necessary, the prior can leave some of
them there. Since it is not possible to

follow the same arrangements for this time of the year everywhere, each church must make its own suitable arrangements in these and other matters, depending on where things are, according to the will of the abbot or prior.

## 6. How the brethren are to live in winter.

From the feast of the Holy Cross until Easter we shall observe a fast continuously, with the meal coming after None, except on Sundays and Christmas day. So during this period Terce is followed immediately by Chapter. After Terce the children and anybody who has been given permission because of sickness are to take a little food. Then, when the signal is given, the brethren are to work until Sext. After Sext the Mass is said, and then they are to devote themselves to reading until None. After None the community has its meal first, then the servers. After the community meal, the brethren are to read or work, depending on what is needed and how much time there is, until Vespers. After Vespers they are to read until the bell for the collation. During this period, on feasts with nine readings and on Saturdays when our Lady's Mass is sung, Terce is to be postponed and the Mass is sung after it, followed at once by Sext. Otherwise the timetable is the same as usual. On Sundays everything is the same as in summer, except that None is said immediately after the meal, because we do not sleep before None. On all feast days on which we do not work, the brethren read at all the times at which they work on ferial days. In Lent the only change is that the seven penitential psalms are said after Chapter, followed immediately by Terce, and the Mass is sung after None, and the meal is after Vespers. After that we read, and do not work.

## 6. Fasting.

From the feast of Holy Cross until Easter we shall observe a fast continuously, with the meal coming after None, except on Sundays. Throughout the whole of Advent and Lent and on the Ember day fasts, the vigils of the Ascension, Pentecost and saints John, Peter and Paul, Matthew, Simon and Jude, and All Saints, the apostle Andrew, and on all Fridays, unless Christmas falls on a Friday, we eat lenten fare, unless anyone is dispensed because of his work; we do not do this, though, in places where the normal practice is different, or on special feast days. Those who are travelling can eat twice, except in Advent and Lent and the principal fasts laid down by the church.

# APPENDIX

[*Chapter 7: When the servers for the High Mass ought to vest.*]

[*Chapter 8: Details about the canons' manual labour.*]

### 9. How the brethren are to behave during the time for reading.

All the brethren are to settle down to read, except those who are too busy with their official jobs to have time to read. They too, when they have finished, are to go back to their reading. While the Work of God is being celebrated in church, they are not to read, except for those who do not know the psalms by heart, and those who need to look something up in connexion with the particular Office, or who have to read or sing something during it. When they are sitting in the cloister, they should behave as good religious, each one reading his own book, except for those who are singing something from the antiphonars, graduals or hymnbooks, and those who are preparing readings. The person who has been deputed for this task is to fix and listen to the readings. They are not to disturb each other by asking questions. If anyone has his hood up when he is in the cloister or in choir, he must hold himself in such a way that it can be gauged whether he has gone to sleep. If anyone needs to go out, he should put his book back in the cupboard, or, if he prefers to leave it in his place, he is to signal to the brother who is sitting next to him to keep an eye on it. If anyone wants to take a book which someone else is reading or singing from, because he needs to consult something in it, he is to give him another book in its place, and the other brother is to surrender his book peacefully. But if the brother refuses to let him have his book, the one who wanted it is to accept this peacefully until he can accuse him of it in Chapter. . . .

## 10. Meals.

At the appropriate time, before lunch or supper, the sacristan is to ring the large bell a few times, so that those who are outside can hurry in for the meal without delay. Then the prior is to ring the internal bell. If it should happen, through carelessness, that the food is not yet ready, he is not to ring it until the food is ready, nor are the brethren to wash their hands, but they are to read until the bell goes. When they have washed and dried their hands, they are to sit down outside the refectory until the prior rings the refectory bell once, then they are to go in in order and stand in front of the tables, one side facing the other. While this is going on, the prior keeps on ringing the refectory bell. When he has rung the bell for long enough, the cantor begins *Benedicite* etc. and the community take it up with the rest that is meant to be said. When the priest has said, "And lead us not etc.," he is to stand up and give the blessing, facing the high table; he is to make the sign of the cross once only. The abbot, if he is present, gives the reader the blessing. When they have all said, "Amen," they go to their places at table. The cellarer and the servers should try to put out as many of the plates as they can before the blessing, to avoid having to go in front of or behind the tables while the brethren are bowing. When the brethren have taken their places, they can finish the job. Once the reader has begun to read, they should not delay to bring in the second dish. Once the common food has been put out, if the cellarer wishes to provide something extra as a kindness to people whom the abbot or the prior has indicated, he is to take it

## 7. Lunch.

At the appropriate time before lunch or supper, the sacristan is to ring the large bell a few times, so that the brethren will not be late in coming for the meal. Then the internal bell is to be rung, if the food is ready, otherwise it is not to be rung until it is ready. When they have washed their hands, the prior is to ring the refectory bell, and then the brethren go in. When they have gone in, the versicularian says *Benedicite*. The community continue with the blessing, and then they begin to eat. The servers are to begin with the juniors and make their way up to the prior's table.

to them in person and distribute it as he pleases. When the reading begins, the brethren are to uncover their bread.... Anyone who has something sent down to him by the abbot or the prior should first bow his head to the person who brings it to him, and then stand up and bow deeply to the person who sent it. No one is to pass on to anyone else any of the food which is provided for them all, but if anyone has anything extra, unless he has been given it because of bloodletting or sickness, he can share it out with the person on his right or the person on his left, but they are not to pass it on any further.

No brother is to pass any special dish to any other brother, with the exception of the prior; but anyone who receives a special dish may give it to the people on either side of him.

*[Yet more details follow about the meal and the final grace.]*

*[Chapter 8 takes up further the regulations for what the brethren are to have to eat.]*

*11. How the brethren are to conduct themselves after Vespers.*

After Vespers throughout the year, the brethren are to sit in the cloister, except during Lent, and they are not to read or sing loudly, nor are they to sit in groups, nor are they to beat their clothes with sticks.

*[Chapter 12 gives the rules for people who want something to drink apart from the set times.]*

*[Cf. Chapter 8.]*

*[Chapter 13 gives the rules for the collation and Compline]*

*[Chapter 9 mentions the collation without giving details, and then gives the rubrics for Compline.]*

*14. How the brethren are to conduct themselves after Compline.*

*10. Bedding.*

No one should dare to go to bed without his tunic and stockings and belt, except for those who are very sick, and they are allowed linen shirts according to their needs. No one is to get into bed standing up; sitting on the edge of the bed, they are to put their feet into the bed from there. They are allowed to have bedding and blankets to lie on, and pillows for their heads, and the sick may have mattresses, if there are any.

Our brethren are not to sleep on mattresses, unless perhaps they cannot get any straw or anything else of the kind to sleep on. They are to sleep in their tunic and stockings, with their belt fastened. They will be allowed to sleep on straw bedding or wool or sacking.

Outside our houses they can sleep on anything that is provided for them, to avoid being a nuisance to their hosts. But if anyone asks for a mattress, he is to fast for one day on bread and water.[8]

[*The Praemonstratensian Constitutions continue in similar vein; the point should be clear by now, so here we abandon them, and confine ourselves to the Dominicans.*]

*13. The Novice master.*

The prior is to appoint a master to be in charge of the novices. He should be conscientious in training them, and it is his job to instruct them about the life of the Order, to encourage them in church, and to strive to correct them to the best of his ability, by word or gesture, whenever they are behaving carelessly. He must also provide for their needs, as best he can. He can impose a penance on them for any obvious negligences, after they have done a *venia* before him, or he can accuse them in his Chapter. He is to teach them to practise humility of heart and body, and he should strive to form them in this virtue. As it says, "Learn from me, for I am meek and humble of heart."[9] He should also teach them to go to confession frequently, straightforwardly and sensibly, to live without private property, to abandon their own will in favour of that of their superiors, to practise voluntary obedience in all things. He should also teach them how they are to behave everywhere and at all times. He should teach them always to keep to the place they have been given. He should teach them how to bow to everyone who gives them anything or takes anything from them, and to everyone who speaks to them whether in cursing or in blessing. He should teach them how they are to remain in their rooms, to keep their eyes lowered, how and what they are to pray and how quietly they should pray, so that they do not disturb others with their roaring. He should teach them to do a *venia* immediately if they are rebuked by a superior, and never to take it upon themselves to argue with anyone, but to obey their master in all matters. He should teach them to wait in the cloister for the companion who is to go at their side in processions, and not to talk in places and at times when it is forbidden, and to bow deeply and say, "Blessed be God in all his gifts," when they are given any piece of clothing, and never to judge anyone, but always to surmise that people are doing or intending some good whenever they see anyone doing something which looks bad, because human judgment is often mistaken. He should teach them how the *venia* is to be made in Chapter or wherever they are rebuked, and how they should take the discipline frequently, and how they must never talk about people who are absent except to speak well of them. He should teach them that they must use two hands to drink and should only drink sitting down, and how careful they must be with books and clothes and other things belonging to the monastery. He should teach them how earnest they must be in their study, always reading or thinking about something by day and by night, in the house and when they are on a journey, and striving to retain as much as they can in their minds. He should teach them how enthusiastic they ought to be in preaching, at suitable times.[10]

## FROM THE SECOND DISTINCTION

### 20. *Those who are capable of preaching.*

Those who are considered by some of the brethren to be suitable as preachers are to be presented to the [Provincial] Chapter or to the diffinitors, as well as those who have been given the job of preaching on the authority of their priors or of some higher superior or Chapter. They are all to be examined individually by suitable people appointed by the Chapter to deal with this and other questions arising at the Chapter, and the brethren with whom they have been living are to be questioned carefully about what grace of preaching they have from God, and about their study and religious life and the eagerness of their charity, and about their commitment and purpose.

After such brethren have given their evidence on these points, they are to make whatever decision seems most useful, on the advice and with the consent of the major superior; that is to say, they must decide whether these candidates ought to remain longer in study, or whether they should practise preaching under the supervision of brethren who have had more experience at it, or whether they are ready to exercise the office of preacher usefully by themselves.

### 31. Preachers.

We decree that no one is to become a preacher general until he has studied theology for three years.

After they have studied theology for a year,[11] people may be admitted to the practice of preaching, if they are the kind of people from whose preaching there is no risk of scandal. And when those who are suitable for it are to go out to preach, they shall be given a *socius* by the prior, selected in view of what will, in his judgment, be most beneficial for their manners and good name. After receiving a blessing, they are to go out, behaving everywhere like upright, religious men, who desire to win their own salvation and that of others, like men of the gospel, following in the footsteps of their Saviour, talking either to God or about God, within themselves or with others; they shall avoid being intimate with any dubious companions.

When they set off on a journey to exercise the job of preaching, or when they are going anywhere else, they are neither to accept nor to carry gold, silver, money or gifts of any kind, except for food, clothing, necessary equipment and books.

Those who are appointed to preach or to study are to have no concern or responsibility for temporal affairs, so that they will be free to fulfil their spiritual ministry better, unless there is no one else to provide for the needs of the brethren, because it is sometimes necessary to give time to the particular needs of the day.

### 32. Where our brethren should not venture to preach.

No one should dare to preach in any diocese where the bishop has forbidden him to preach, unless he has letters and a general mandate from the Pope.

When our brethren enter any diocese to preach, they should first visit the bishop of the diocese, if they can, and take his advice about the results they hope to obtain among the people. As long as they are in his diocese, they should be ready to obey him in anything which is not contrary to our Order.

### 33. *Preaching and scandal.*

Our brethren should be careful not to upset religious or the clergy when they preach, by "setting their mouths against heaven."[12] If they see anything in them which needs correcting, they should try to put it right by taking them aside and pleading with them as with fathers.

### 34. *Travellers.*

When preachers or any other brethren are travelling, they are to say their Office to the best of their knowledge and ability while they are on the way, and they are to be content to attend the Office in whatever church they go to, and, when they are with bishops or parish priests or anybody else, they are to celebrate or attend the Office in the way that is customary among those they are with.

In bowing, we are to conform to the practice of the people we are staying with.

Brethren who are on a journey should carry testimonial letters with them, and their faults should be corrected in any convent they visit.

The prior of any house is to show due honour to any visiting prior. The guest ought not to go wandering round the town nor should he make a long stay without consulting him.

One who is senior in the Order is to be senior when they are travelling, except when he is *socius* to a preacher, unless the superior makes a different arrangement when they set off.

The *socius* who is given to a preacher should obey him in everything, as he would obey his own prior.

Friars Minor are to be welcomed lovingly and cheerfully, just like our own brethren, and they are to be looked after as generously and politely as the house can afford.

## *Notes*

1. In fact the General Chapter of 1474 asked the Pope to abrogate this constitution, which he did on July 1, 1475 (BOP III pp. 528–9).

2. Appeals to any authority outside the Order, that is.

3. The Dominicans have, almost from the outset, had a "two house" system of government, in which two different kinds of General Chapter meet in different years. Originally there was a General Chapter every year; over a period of three years, there would be one Chapter of provincials, and two in which elected representatives from the provinces, known as "diffinitors," met. In the late 1360s a move was initiated to reduce the frequency of General Chapters, and since 1553 they have been held only every three years, but the alternation of Provincials' and Diffinitors' Chapters has remained in force.

4. *Si* is the reading of all the Praemonstratensian MSS and of Raymund's Constitutions. MS Rodez has *sed*, but, contrary to the information given in Thomas' apparatus, this is not supported by the Constitutions of the Sack Friars, which in fact have *nec*. *Sed* can therefore be dismissed as being no more than a mistake.

5. This paragraph was added in 1220.

6. This declaration was inserted in 1236.

7. The earlier Praemonstratensian MSS have *ante*, which is also what the Dominican text has; but before the end of the twelfth century, the Praemonstratensian text had been reworded to say *tantum versus* (Martène's text and that of MS Glasgow). This further complicates the problem of exactly what Praemonstratensian text the Dominicans had before them in 1216.

8. The second paragraph was added in 1236.

9. Matt. 11:29.

10. *Tempore opportuno.* Vicaire translates "when the time comes" (*La Vie Apostolique*, p. 170), which is linguistically quite possible (cf. Humbert II 340); but sessentially it means "at the right time," and in 1216, when this chapter was probably written, there was evidently no incompatibility between being a novice and being sent out to preach (e.g. *Acta Canon.* 24). It is also likely, in my view, which I hope to develop shortly in an article on the subject, that in the early years recruits were professed immediately and did a "noviciate" afterwards (cf. *Acta Canon.* 25–6 in the CV text). Prim. Const. I 15 (added in 1220 at the earliest) *institutes* a "time of probation," implying that previously the Dominicans, like the Franciscans, did not allow for such a time before profession. I 13 is then dealing with the early formation of already professed brethren, and even during this period they were liable to be called upon to "preach at suitable times." In Raymund's Constitutions the position is quite different: novices are not allowed to preach (II 12), and there is accordingly no mention of preaching in the chapter on the novice

master (I 14). The chapter on the Novice Master in Prim. Const. goes back as a whole to 1216, but some scholars believe that the last two sentences were added in 1220 (cf. Vicaire, *SDHT* p. 417; Renard, p. 224[44]), but Thomas, *Constituties* ad loc., believes that the whole chapter goes back to 1216.

11. The restrictions on who may be a preacher were added some time before 1236, but the rest of the chapter goes back either to 1216 (Thomas) or to 1220 (cf. Renard, p. 218[23]).

12. *Ponendo os in coelum*: this phrase from Psalm 72:9 is also used by Humbert (*Op. Trip.* III 2) to mean "make rude remarks about the clergy." For other references, see Vicaire, *SDHT* p. 516[79].

# Bibliography

## NOTES ON TEXTS
## AND AUTHORS

*Bartholomew of Trent (c. 1195–1251)*

He seems to have spent a significant part of his active life as a papal diplomat, and enjoyed the independence this gave him; he was called to heel in 1248 and made to subject himself more fully to his Order. He wrote several hagiographical compilations, containing a fair amount of incidental autobiography, which shows him to be a genial, sympathetic person. See A. Dondaine, AFP 45 (1975) pp. 79–93.

I have basically used the text of the *Translation of St. Dominic* printed by Dondaine, loc. cit. pp. 101–2, but I have also made use of British Library MS Addit. 18360.

*Cecilia, Bl. (c. 1202–1290)*

As a young nun in Santa Maria in Tempulo, she was attracted by the reforming programme of St. Dominic, and was the very first to enter the new monastery at San Sisto, and make profession to the founder. Later, she was one of the nuns sent to help the foundation in Bologna, where she became prioress c. 1237. She was evidently valued as a source of anecdotes about St. Dominic and, probably in her old age, she dictated some of these to Sr. Angelica; this is the text known as *The Miracles of St. Dominic*.

I have used the edition by A. Walz, AFP 37 (1967) pp. 21–44.

*Cernai, Pierre de Vaux († c. 1219)*

A Cistercian chronicler, with firsthand experience of the anti-Albigensian campaign.

I have used the edition of the *Historia Albigensis* by P. Guébin and E. Lyon (Paris, 1926–39).

*Chronicle of St. Agnes, Bologna*

Compiled by the nuns some time before 1264. I have used the text printed in M. G. Cambria, *Il Monastero Dominicano di S. Agnese in Bologna* (Bologna, 1973). The text is also printed in ASOP I pp. 181–4.

# BIBLIOGRAPHY

*Congregation of Our Lady, Arezzo*

I have used the text of the Statute printed in G. G. Meersseman, *Ordo Fraternitatis* (Rome, 1977), pp. 1015–1027.

*Congregation of St. Dominic, Bologna*

I have used the text of the Statute printed in G. G. Meersseman, op. cit., pp. 628–30.

*Constitutions of the Friars Preachers*

I have used the edition by A. H. Thomas, *De oudste Constituties van de Dominicanen* (Louvain, 1965) (= Prim. Const.). Raymund's edition of the constitutions can be found in R. Creytens, AFP 18 (1948) pp. 5–68.

*Constitutions of the Praemonstratensians*

In view of the impossibility of identifying any known text with that used by the Dominicans, several editions of these need to be used. A mid-twelfth-century text was edited by Pl. F. Lefèvre and W. M. Grauwen, *Les Statuts de Prémontré au milieu du XII*<sup>e</sup> *siècle* (Averbode, 1978). A slightly later text is contained in E. Martène, *De Antiquis Ecclesiae Ritibus* III (Antwerp, 1764), pp. 323–336. From the thirteenth century, later than the first Dominican Constitutions, there is a text in Glasgow, Mitchell Library MS 308892, and then a drastically revised text edited by Pl. F. Lefèvre, *Les Statuts de Prémontré réformés* (Louvain, 1946).

*Dominic, St. (c. 1170–1221)*

*Letter to the Prioress of Madrid*: I have used the edition in V. J. Koudelka, *Monumenta Diplomatica S. Dominici* (MOPH XXV, Rome, 1966), pp. 126–7.

*Bologna Canonization Process (= Acta Canon.)*: Unfortunately the text of this precious document is in a hopeless muddle. Koudelka has pointed out some of the problems (AFP 42 [1972] pp. 47–61), but in fact the position is even worse than he realised. There are three different traditions, characterised most obviously by the fact that one reports the proceedings entirely in the third person ("The witness said that he ..."), another reports the whole proceedings in the first person ("The witness said, 'I ...' "), while the third has a mixture of both. The third-person tradition is represented by a lost MS from Carcassonne, known to us through the edition in Quétif-Échard, *Scriptores Ordinis Praedicatorum* I (Paris, 1719) pp. 44–56, and a MS in Venice; the edition published by A. Walz in MOPH XVI pp. 123–67 is based on these two witnesses. The first-person tradition is found in a very meagre abridgement contained in Dietrich of Apolda's Life of St. Dominic, printed in the Bollandists' *Acta Sanctorum*, August I 558–628, and a version in "humanist" Latin by J. A. Flaminius, *Vitae Patrum Ordinis Preadicatorum* (Bologna, 1529), ff. LXVI–LXXVIII. The "mixed" tradition is contained in two Chronicles: that of Borselli (1432–97), found in Bologna, Bibl. Univ. cod. lat. 1999, ff. 21–6, and that of Taegio (compiled c. 1518) in Rome, Arch. Gen. OP XIV 53 ff. 131–5. It is not clear whether Taegio is simply a copy of Borselli or whether it is an independent witness. The most vexing problem is that the text of the third-person version and that of the first-person version regularly agree, against the mixed version. The mixed version is almost certainly abridged, but nevertheless it probably preserves the original form (there is a similar wild oscillation between first person and third in the Canonization Process of St. Margaret, and it is far more likely that a muddle like this was subsequently sorted out by well-meaning editors, than that a consistent text was subsequently muddled). Very hesitantly, I have elected to trust the mixed version, so my translation is based on the text in Borselli. The dates are added on the basis of Dietrich's epitome and the Venice MS. The paragraph numbers are those given in Quétif-Échard and Walz. (Section 1 is an ancient editorial introduction, not part of the document.)

In the notes, the following abbreviations are used:

B   Bologna, Bibl. Univ. cod. lat. 1999
T   Rome, Arch. Gen. OP XIV 53
C   The lost MS from Carcassonne, in Quétif-Échard
V   Venice, Bibl. Marciana IX 61 (3287)

*The Nine Ways of Prayer of St. Dominic:* It is uncertain when or where this attractive little document was composed, but it evidently derives its material from Bologna, and it antedates Cecilia's *Miracula;*

on the other hand, it is presumably later than the *Lives of the Brethren* (1260).

The manuscript tradition is divided into two halves: the text is found in some, but not all, of the MSS of Dietrich of Apolda; it is also found independently in one Latin MS and one Spanish MS. It is clear that it was not originally part of Dietrich's work.

Research into the MS tradition has made me radically change my mind about the text. The translation printed here is significantly different from that contained in the translation published by me in 1978 (Dominican Publications, Dublin).

I have made use of the following MSS:

R   Vatican, Cod. Rossianus 3
C   Rome, Casanatense, Cod. lat. 168 (Dietrich)
V¹  Vatican, Cod. lat. 1218 (Dietrich)
V²  Vatican, Cod. lat. 10152 (Dietrich)
D   Modena, Bibl. Estense, Campori γ 0.3.25 (Dietrich)
M   Monastery of Santo Domingo el Real, Madrid

It is clear from the text that the work was originally intended to be illustrated; the famous and charming pictures from R have recently been reproduced in a series of postcards.

### Gerald de Frachet (1205–1271)

Entered the Order in 1225 in Paris; he was prior several times, and is described by Bernard Gui as an attractive and eloquent preacher (MOPH XXII p. 163). He was provincial of Provence from 1251–9. His most obvious claim to fame, however, is his *Lives of the Brethren*.

I have used the edition by B. M. Reichert (MOPH I).

### Gui, Bernard (c. 1261–1331)

The most important early Dominican historian, though he also filled many responsible positions in the Order and in the church, and ended his days as a bishop, first of Tuy (1318), then of Lodève (1324).

*De Quatuor in Quibus:* For his continuation of this work, I have used the edition by T. Kaeppeli (MOPH XXII).

# BIBLIOGRAPHY

*De Fundatione et Prioribus Conventuum Prov. Tolosanae et Provinciae:* I have used the edition by P. A. Amargier (MOPH XXIV).

*Libellus de Magistris:* I have used the text in Martène-Durand, *Amplissima Collectio* VI (Paris, 1729) 397–417.


*Hugh of St. Cher († 1264)*
Doctor of Canon Law and Bachelor of Theology in Paris. Entered the Order in Paris in 1225. Provincial of France, 1227–30. Lectured in Theology in Paris c. 1229–33. Prior of Paris, 1233–6. Provincial again, 1236–44. Made a Cardinal in 1244. His most famous work was on the bible: he at least supervised the production of a Concordance, notes on the correct biblical text, and a commentary on the whole bible; but he also composed a commentary on the Sentences of Peter Lombard and some other theological works.

*Postillae in Bibliam:* I have used the edition printed at Venice, 1703.


*Humbert of Romans (c. 1200–1277)*
See Introduction, pp. 31–35.
Apart from the works listed below, references are given, by volume and page number, to J. J. Berthier, *B. Humberti de Romanis Opera de Vita Regulari* (Rome, 1888; repr. Turin, 1956).


*On the Formation of Preachers:* There are four known manuscripts of the first major section of this work (I–XLV), all of which I have used:


A   Avignon, Musée Calvet 327 (fifteenth century)
L   Salamanca, Bibl. Univ. 773 (sixteenth century)
M   Madrid, Bibl. Nac. 19423 (fifteenth century)
S   Segovia, Catedral, Vetr. 28 (fifteenth century).

# BIBLIOGRAPHY

The first printed edition was prepared by Simon Bauça and published in Barcelona in 1607. I have not been able to make use of this, but Bauça's text was reproduced in *Maxima Bibliotheca Veterum Patrum* XXV (Lyons, 1677) pp. 420–456, which I have used (= Max.). This text was taken from a MS found in Portugal, and, though it is close to SL, it lacks some of their distinctive readings and it must be supposed that the Portuguese MS is now lost. Bauça's text therefore has independent value.

The edition by J. Catalani (Rome, 1739) essentially reproduces the text of Max. and is of no independent value.

Berthier also bases his text on Max., but makes occasional, and rather eccentric, use of A.

Of the second part of the work, the series of model sermons, there are far more MSS, of which I have only used six, and only two of these contain all four sections:

A   (sections 1 and 2)
B   Bologna, Bibl. Univ. 2323 (fifteen century ) (complete)
L   (section 1)
P   Paris, B.N. nouv. acq. lat. 1742 (fourteenth century) (sections 2, 3, 4)
R   Rheims 612 (fourteenth century) (complete)
S   (sections 1 and 2).

Only sections 1 and 2 have been printed. The first printed edition (Hagenau, 1508), which I have used, is the basis of all subsequent editions, including Max. XXV pp. 456–567. I have not so far been able to determine the relationship between Hagenau and the surviving MSS.

*On the Gift of Fear:* This work is very erratically represented in a considerable number of MSS. I have used:

M   Munich, Staatsbibl., Clm 14817 (thirteenth century)
$S^1$   London, British Library, Sloane 3102 (fourteenth century)
$S^2$   London, British Library, Sloane 1613 (fourteenth century).

# BIBLIOGRAPHY

I have also used the only printed edition, which ascribes the work to St. Albert and entitles it *De Abundantia Exemplorum* (Ulm. 1478–81).

*Opus Tripartitum:* This work survives complete only in the text printed in E. Brown, *Appendix ad Fasciculum Rerum Expetendarum et Fugiendarum* (London, 1690) pp. 185–229.

### Jean de Mailly († c. 1260)
Author of a collection of short lives of the saints (c. 1230), he then joined the Order and c. 1243 compiled a second edition including, this time, a life of St. Dominic. He seems to have been a member of the community in Metz, where he compiled a Chronicle, whose autograph survives. Little seems to be known of him otherwise. See A. Dondaine, *Jean de Mailly O.P.: Gestes et Miracles des Saints* (Paris, 1947).

*Life of Saint Dominic:* I have used the edition by M. D. Chapotin, *Les Dominicains d'Auxerre* (Paris, 1892), pp. 317–24. I have also used the translation by A. Dondaine, op cit.

### Jordan of Saxony († 1237)
*Encyclical Letter (1233):* This letter is known from a *Golden Rule for Writing* by Albertinus Dertonensis, a Cistercian who became a Dominican c. 1228 (on whom see T. Kaeppeli, AFP 22 [1952], pp. 177–181). I have used the edition of this letter by Kaeppeli, art. cit. pp. 182–5.

*Libellus on the Beginnings of the Order of Preachers:* I have used the edition by H. C. Scheeben (MOPH XVI, Rome, 1935), pp. 25–88.

# BIBLIOGRAPHY

*Letters:* I have used the edition by A. Walz (MOPH XXIII, Rome, 1951).

## Kilwardby, Robert († 1279)

After a career as a philosopher in Paris, he entered the Order, c. 1245; he was provincial of England, 1261–72, then archbishop of Canterbury; in 1278 he was made Cardinal Bishop of Porto.

*Letter to Novices:* This Letter survives only insofar as it is quoted by John Pecham O.F.M. in his pamphlet attacking it; but it is likely that most, if not all, of the Letter is in fact quoted there. I have used the edition by F. Tocco in C. L. Kingsford, A. G. Little and F. Tocco, *Fr. J. Pecham Tractatus Tres de Paupertate* (Aberdeen, 1910) pp. 121–147.

## Lives of the Sisters of Unterlinden

This collection was compiled certainly later than 1282, probably at the end of the thirteenth or the beginning of the fourteenth century. I have used the edition by J. Ancelet-Hustache, *Archives d'Histoire Doctrinale et Littéraire du Moyen Age* 5 (1930) pp. 335–509. For the early story of the monastery see, in addition to the editor's introduction to the Lives, QF 24 pp. 49–50. Their church was consecrated by St. Albert.

## Margaret of Hungary, St. (c. 1242–1270)

Daughter of King Bela IV of Hungary. Like many girls of the period, she entered religious life as a child. She refused several offers of royal marriage, preferring her life of self-abasement as a nun.

*Canonization Process of 1276:* I have used the edition by G. Frank-noj, *Monumenta Romana Episcopatus Vesprimensis* I (Budapest, 1896) pp. 165–296.

# BIBLIOGRAPHY

*Peraldus, William († after 1261)*

An energetic preacher and writer, whose *Summa on the Vices and Virtues* (written before 1250) enjoyed an enormous and lasting success in the Middle Ages. He was prior of Lyons, at least in 1261. See A. Dondaine, AFP 18 (1948) pp. 162–236.

*Sermons:* I have not attempted a critical edition. Out of the many surviving MSS, I have used only those that are available in Oxford:

Trinity College 79; Bodleian, MS lat. th. e.16; Bodleian, Rawlinson A 373; Bodleian, Ashmole 1290; Magdalen College MSS 33, 91, 179; University College 75.

I have also used the edition printed in 1494 (Paris). The 1576 edition (Lyons) gives a very inadequate, abridged, text. (On such abridged versions of sermons, see L. J. Bataillon, *Leeds Studies in English* NS 11 [1980] p. 22.)

*Summa de Vitiis, Summa de Virtutibus:* There are innumerable MSS and editions. I have not made any study of the text for myself.

*Peter of Rheims († later than 1247)*

Prior of Paris and one of the contributors to the scriptural work being done there; provincial of Paris (1224–33, 1244–5). He was made bishop of Agen in 1245.

*Sermons:* I have made use of a text kindly sent me by Fr. Louis Bataillon O.P., based on his collation of MSS Soissons, Bibl. Municipale 125, Paris, B.N. lat. 16503, Paris, B.N. nouv. acq. lat. 366, and my collation of Oxford, Bodleian Libr., Canon. misc. 272 and Laud misc. 506.

481

# BIBLIOGRAPHY

*Peter of Verona, St. (c. 1200–1252)*

An able and ardent preacher, he was martyred by some heretics in 1252, and was promptly canonized. See A. Dondaine, AFP 23 (1953), pp. 66–162. For the text of his *Letter to the Prioress of Milan* I have used the edition given there, pp. 91–3.

*Raymund of Peñafort, St. († 1275)*

A distinguished canon lawyer; he entered the Order in 1222, was papal penitentiary and chaplain (1230–8), Master of the Order (1238–40), and author of a *Summa on Penance* and a *Summa on Marriage*.

*Letter to the Prioress of Bologna*

I have used the edition by F. Balme, C. Paban and J. Collomb (MOPH IV 2, Rome, 1901), pp. 48–9.

*Stephen of Bourbon (c. 1185–1261)*

He entered the Order c. 1223, and was engaged in the work of the Inquisition from 1235. His main claim to fame is his collection of *exempla*, many of them drawn from his own pastoral and inquisitorial experience. I have used the (incomplete) edition by A. Lecoy de la Marche, *Anecdotes Historiques tirés d'Étienne de Bourbon* (Paris, 1877).

*Stephen Salagnac († 1291)*

He was received into the Order by Peter Selhan, one of St. Dominic's first two friars. He was prior several times. He began a compilation of lists of Dominicans who had distinguished themselves in various fields; this was continued by Bernard Gui.

I have used the edition by T. Kaeppeli (MOPH XXII).

*Thomas Agni of Lentini († 1277)*

He founded the Dominican priory in Naples in 1231, where he received Thomas Aquinas into the Order. He was provincial of Rome in 1255–6, and was then made bishop of Bethlehem. After a variety of episcopal jobs, he became Patriarch of Jerusalem in 1277. He composed sermons on the saints, and a Life of St. Peter Martyr.

For the Sermon on St. Dominic, I have used a text kindly sent me by Fr. Louis Bataillon, O.P., taken from MS Vatican, Vat. lat. 4691.

### Thomas of Cantimpré (c. 1201–c. 1276)

Canon of Cantimpré, he became a Dominican c. 1230, and was sent to Cologne, where he worked with St. Albert; later he spent some time in Paris and in Louvain. His chatty *Bonum Universale de Apibus*, structured on a symbolic interpretation of the habits of bees, contains a great deal of interesting historical material, though Thomas is somewhat too inclined to be credulous. He also wrote an encyclopaedic book *On the Nature of Things*.

*Bonum Universale de Apibus:* In addition to the printed edition (Douais, 1605), I have used three MSS from the British Library: Egerton 839; Harleian 3832; Arundel 141.

*Liber de Natura Rerum:* I have used the edition by H. Boese (Berlin and New York, 1973).

## TRANSLATIONS OF SOURCES

### English

F. C. Lehner, *St. Dominic: Biographical Documents* (Washington, 1964).

P. Conway, *Lives of the Brethren* [including Cecilia, *Miracula*] (repr. London, 1955).

K. Pond, *Love among the Saints* [Jordan's Letters] (London, 1958).

G. Vann. *To Heaven with Diana!* [Jordan's letters] (London, 1960).

W. M. Conlon (ed.), *Humbert of Romans: Treatise on Preaching* (London, 1955).

[This is in fact translated from the French translation of 1910]

# BIBLIOGRAPHY

*French*

M. H. Vicaire, *St. Dominique: La Vie Apostolique* (Paris, 1965).
M. H. Vicaire, *Les Premiers Dominicains* (Paris, 1967).
Humbert of Romans, *Traité de l'Instruction des Prédicateurs* (Rome, 1910).


*Italian*

A. Ferrua, *Le "Vitae Fratrum"* (Bologna, 1963).
P. Lippini, *S. Domenico visto dai suoi Contemporanei* (Bologna, 1966).
G. Mosca, *Umberto de Romans: Istruzioni per i Predicatori* (Ed. Paoline, 1969).


*Spanish*

M. Gelabert, J. M. Milagro and J. M. de Garganta, *Santo Domingo de Guzmán visto pro sus contemporaneos* (Madrid, 1966).


## BIBLIOGRAPHY AND ABBREVIATIONS

ACG: *Acta Capitulorum Generalium OP*, ed. B. M. Reichert (MOPH IIIff).
*Acta Canon.*: see NOTES ON TEXTS AND AUTHORS, St. Dominic.
AFP: *Archivum Fratrum Praedicatorum* (Rome, 1931ff).
Altaner, B., *Die Briefe Jordans von Sachsen* (QF 20, Leipzig, 1925).
Aron, M., *St. Dominic's Successor* (London, 1955).
ASOP: *Analecta Sacri Ordinis Praedicatorum* (Rome, 1893ff).
Balme-Lelaidier: Balme and Lelaidier, *Cartulaire de S. Dominique* (Paris, 1893–1901).
Bernard, St.: references are to the edition by J. Leclercq and others, *Sancti Bernardi Opera* (Rome, 1957ff).
Berthier, J. J., *Opera B. Jordanis de Saxonia* (Fribourg, 1891).
Bonaventure, St., *Legenda Maior S. Francisci*: in Analecta Franciscana X (Quaracchi, 1941). See also Introduction, note 4.
BOP: *Bullarium Ordinis Praedicatorum*, ed. T. Ripoll and A. Bremond (Rome, 1729ff).

# BIBLIOGRAPHY

Borst, A., *Die Katharer* (Stuttgart, 1953).

Cambria, M. G., *Il Monastero Domenicano di S. Agnese in Bologna* (Bologna, 1973).

Cardenal, Peire: R. Lavaud, *Poésies complètes du Troubadour Peire Cardenal* (Toulouse, 1957).

Catena Aurea: in most editions of St. Thomas Aquinas.

1 Celano: Thomas de Celano, *Vita prima S. Francisci* (Analecta Franciscana X).

2 Celano: Thomas de Celano, *Vita secunda S. Francisci* (Analecta Franciscana X).

Cernai: Pierre de Vaux Cernai, *Historia Albigensis*, ed. P. Guébin and E. Lyon (Paris, 1926–39).

CF: *Cahiers de Fanjeaux* (Toulouse, 1966ff).

*Chroniques de San Sisto*, ed. J. J. Berthier (Levanto, 1919–20).

Constantine of Orvieto, *Legenda S. Dominici*, ed. H. C. Scheeben (MOPH XVI).

Dondaine, A., *Jean de Mailly* (Paris, 1947).

Eccleston, Thomas, *De Adventu Fratrum Minorum in Angliam*, ed. A. G. Little (Paris, 1909). English trans. in E. G. Salter, *The Coming of the Friars to England and Germany* (London, 1926).

Esser, Kajetan, *Anfänge und ursprüngliche Zielsetzungen des Ordens der Minderbrüder* (Leiden, 1966).

Eubel, C., *Hierarchia Catholica Medii Aevi* (Münster, 1898ff).

Ferrandus, *Legenda S. Dominici*, ed. M. H. Laurent (MOPH XVI).

Ferrua, A., *Le "Vitae Fratrum"* (Bologna, 1963).

Francis, St., *Opuscula* (including *Regula Bullata, Regula non Bullata, Testamentum*), ed. K. Esser (Grottaferrata, 1978).

Gallén, J., *Les Voyages de S. Dominique au Danemark*, in R. Creytens and P. Künzle, *Xenia Medii Aevi Historiam Illustrantia oblata Thomae Kaeppeli OP* (Rome, 1978), I pp. 73–84.

Gallia Christiana (Paris, 1715ff).

Glorieux, P., *Répertoire des Maîtres en Théologie de Paris au XIII^e siècle* (Paris, 1933–4).

Gratian, *Decretum*, ed. E. Friedberg, *Corpus Iuris Canonici* I (Leipzig, 1879).

Gregory IX, *Decretals*, ed. E. Friedberg, *Corpus Iuris Canonici* II (Leipzig, 1881).

Griffe, É., I: *Les Débuts de l'Aventure Cathare en Languedoc* (Paris, 1969); II: *Le Languedoc Cathare de 1190 à 1210* (Paris, 1971); III: *Le Languedoc Cathare au temps de la Croisade* (Paris, 1973).

# BIBLIOGRAPHY

Grundmann, H., *Religiöse Bewegungen im Mittelalter* (Darmstadt, 1970).

Guigo II, *The Ladder of Monks*, ed. E. Colledge and J. Walsh (Sources Chrétiennes 163, Paris, 1970); English trans. by Colledge and Walsh (London, 1978).

Heintke, F., *Humbert von Romans* (Berlin, 1933).

Hinnebusch, W. A., *The Early English Friars Preachers (=EEFP)* (Rome, 1951).

Hinnebusch, W. A., *History of the Dominican Order* (New York, 1966, 1973).

Hugh of Digne, *Expositio Regulae OFM*, ed. David Flood, *Hugh of Digne's Rule Commentary* (Grottaferrata, 1979).

Hugh of St. Cher, *Postillae in Bibliam* (Venice, 1703).

Innocent IV, *Les Régistres d'Innocent IV*, ed. E. Berger, vol. I (Paris, 1884).

Interlinear Gloss: printed in N. Lyranus, *Biblia Sacra* (Venice, 1588).

Jacques de Vitry, *Hist. Occid.*: J. F. Hinnebusch, *The Historia Occidentalis of Jacques de Vitry* (Fribourg, 1972).

Jacques de Vitry, Letters: R. B. C. Huygens, *Lettres de Jacques de Vitry* (Leiden, 1960).

James of Voragine, *Legenda Aurea*, ed. T. Graesse (Leipzig, 1846).

Kaeppeli, T., *Scriptores Ordinis Praedicatorum* (Rome, 1970ff).

Leclercq, J., F. Vandenbroucke and L. Bouyer, *The Spirituality of the Middle Ages* (London, 1968).

*Legenda Trium Sociorum*, ed. T. Desbonnets, *Archivum Franciscanum Historicum* 67 (1974) pp. 38–144.

Little, A. G., *The Grey Friars in Oxford* (Oxford, 1892).

LThK: *Lexikon für Theologie und Kirche* (Freiburg, 1957ff).

Lyranus, N., *Sacra Biblia* (Venice, 1588).

Mamachi, T. M., *Annales Ordinis Praedicatorum* I (Rome, 1756).

Mandonnet-Vicaire: P. Mandonnet and M. H. Vicaire, *St. Dominique* (Paris, 1938).

Mansi: J. D. Mansi, *Sacrorum Conciliorum Nova et Amplissima Collectio* (Florence 1759ff).

Marginal Gloss: printed in N. Lyranus, *Biblia Sacra* (Venice, 1588) and PL 113 and 114.

Martin, Raymund, *Pugio Fidei* (Leipzig, 1687).

McCulloch, F., *Medieval Latin and French Bestiaries* (Chapel Hill, North Carolina, 1960).

Meersseman, G. G., *Dossier de l'Ordre de la Pénitence au XIIIᵉ siècle* (Fribourg, 1961).

# BIBLIOGRAPHY

Meersseman, G. G., *Ordo Fraternitatis* (Rome, 1977).

MGH SS: Monumenta Germaniae Historica, Scriptores (Hannover, Berlin, 1826ff).

Moorman, J., *A History of the Franciscan Order* (Oxford, 1968).

MOPH: Monumenta Ordinis Praedicatorum Historica (Louvain, Rome, 1896ff).

*Ordinarium: Ordinarium iuxta Ritum Sacri Ordinis Praedicatorum* (from Humbert's Prototype), ed. F. M. Guerrini (Rome, 1921).

Paris, Matthew, *Chronica Maiora* (London, Rolls Series, 1872ff).

Pecham, *Tractatus Tres de Paupertate*, ed. A. Kingsford, A. G. Little and F. Tocco (Aberdeen, 1910).

Pecham, *Canticum Pauperis* (Quaracchi, 1949).

PG: Migne, *Patrologia Graeca*.

Pitra, J. B., *Analecta Novissima Spicilegii Solesmensis, altera continuatio, II: Tusculana* (Paris, 1888).

PL: Migne, *Patrologia Latina*.

Pond, K., *Love among the Saints* (London, 1958).

Prim. Const.: see NOTES ON TEXTS AND AUTHORS, Constitutions of the Friars Preachers.

Prototype: the Prototype of the Dominican liturgy, as established under the supervision of Humbert. Rome, Archiv. Gen. OP XIV L 1.

Provincial Chapters of Provence, ed. C. Douais (Toulouse, 1894).

Psalterium Romanum: ed. R. Weber, *Le Psautier Romain* (Rome, 1953).

Puylaurens: Guillaume de Puylaurens, *Chronique*, ed. J. Duvernoy (Paris, 1976).

QF: Quellen und Forschungen zur Geschichte des Dominikanerordens in Deutschland (Leipzig, Vechta, Cologne, 1907ff).

Quétif-Échard: J. Quétif and J. Échard, *Scriptores Ordinis Praedicatorum* (Paris, 1719–1721).

Raymund of Capua, *Life of St. Catherine of Siena*, trans. Conleth Kearns (Wilmington, 1980).

Renard, J. P., *La Formation et la Désignation des Prêcheurs au début de l'Ordre des Prêcheurs* (Fribourg, 1977).

RHE: *Revue d'Histoire Ecclésiastique* (Louvain, 1900ff).

Rouse, R. H. and M. A., *Preachers, Florilegia and Sermons* (Toronto, 1979).

*Rule of the Master*, ed. A. de Vogüé (*Sources Chrétiennes* 105–7, Paris, 1964–5); English trans. by Luke Eberle (Kalamazoo, 1977).

SCH: Studies in Church History. The vols. cited are: 8 (ed. G. J.

Cuming & D. Baker; Cambridge, 1972); 10 (ed. D. Baker; New York, 1973); 12 (ed. D. Baker; Oxford, 1975); and Subsidia 1 (ed. D. Baker; Oxford, 1978).

Scheeben, H. C., *Beiträge zur Geschichte Jordans von Sachsen* (QF 35, Vechta, 1938).

*Scripta Leonis*, ed. R. B. Brooke (Oxford, 1970).

Selge, K. V., *Die ersten Waldenser* (Berlin, 1967).

SOG: *Scriptores Ordinis Grandimontensis*, ed. J. Becquet (Turnhout, 1968).

Sorbelli, A., *Corpus Chronicorum Bononiensium* (Città di Castello, 1911ff) (all references are to vol. II).

Thomas Aquinas, St.: unless specified otherwise, all references are to the *Summa Theologiae* (ed. with English trans., London, New York, 1964ff). Other works cited are: *Scriptum super Libros Sententiarum* (ed. P. Mandonnet, Paris 1929–47); *Compendium Theologiae* (Marietti edition); *De Perfectione* (Leonine edition); *Contra Impugnantes* (Leonine edition); *De Veritate* (Marietti edition); *Super Evang. Matthaei* (Marietti edition); *Super Evang. Iohannis* (Marietti edition); *Super Epistolas Pauli* (Marietti edition); *Catena Aurea* (Marietti edition). For details of editions and translations, see J. A. Weisheipl, *Friar Thomas d'Aquino* (Oxford, 1975).

Thomas of York, *Manus quae contra Omnipotentem*, ed. in M. Bierbaum, *Bettelorden und Weltgeistlichkeit an der Universität Paris* (Münster, 1920).

Thomas, A. H., *Die oudste Constituties van de Dominicanen* (Louvain, 1965).

Thomson, W. R., *Friars in the Cathedral* (Toronto, 1975).

Tubach, F. C., *Index Exemplorum* (Helsinki, 1969).

Tugwell, Simon, *The Way of the Preacher* London, Springfield, Ill., 1979).

Vann, G., *To Heaven with Diana!* (London, 1960).

Vicaire M. H., *Saint Dominic and His Times* (= *SDHT*) (London, 1964).

Vicaire, M. H., *Saint Dominique: La Vie Apostolique* (Paris, 1965).

Vicaire, M. H., *Dominique et ses Prêcheurs* (Fribourg, Paris, 1977).

Vicaire, M. H. and L. von Matt, *St. Dominic, a Pictorial Biography* (London, 1957).

William of Tocco, *Life of St. Thomas Aquinas*, ed. D. Prümmer, *Fontes Vitae S. Thomae* (Toulouse, 1924).

# Index to Preface, Foreword and Introduction

# INDEX

# INDEX

# INDEX

# Index to Texts

# INDEX

*Barlaam* (John Damascene), 374
Bartholomew of Trent, 92–93, 473
Bede, Venerable, 253, 374
Begging, 77, 112, n80, 133, 134;
  confessions as excuse for, 317;
  confraternities, 438
*Beginnings of the Order of Preachers, On
  the* (Jordan of Saxony), 389
Béguines, 229 n39
Bela IV of Hungary, 388
Bene of Lombardy, 137
Benedict of Nursia, St., 336
Benedicta, Dame, 412–14
Benjamin, 346
Bernard of Clairvaux, St., Eve, on, 223;
  good conduct, on, 293; idle words, on,
  300, 301; Mary, on, 357; prayer, on, 94,
  170, 171, 172, 293; preaching, on, 234,
  235–36, 237, 240, 242–43; scripture, on,
  280, 293; singing, on, 344, 346;
  temporal affairs, on preoccupation
  with, 334
Bernardone, Francesco, *See* Francis of
  Assisi, St.
Bernard the German, 397, 426 n19
Bertrand of Garrigues, 91, 116 n127
Béziers, 75
Bishops, preaching as obligatory for, 240
Blessed Virgin Mary, *See* Mary, Mother
  of Jesus
Blessings, 143; Dominican, 153
Body; prayer postures, 94, 95, 96, 97,
  98–101; punishment, *See* Discipline,
  physical: Fasting; soul and, 185
Bologna, 56, 57; Dominic's death in,
  58–59, 78; General Chapter held in,
  66, 77–78, 128, 398; Podestà of, 9,
  70–71, 73, 81, 109 n57; St. Agnes
  Convent, 387, 388, 395–400, 401–9, 473;
  St. Nicholas of the Vines, 76, 78, 79,
  80, 82–83, 84, 395
Bonaventure, St., 211 n47
Boniface, St., 127, 155 n30
Book burning, 54
Book of Customs, Dominican, 457–65
Book of Customs, Praemonstratensian,
  457–65

Boredom, 280
Bread, daily, 173–74; begging for, *See*
  Begging
Bricklayers, *See* Builders
Brothers, *See* Laybrothers
Builders, 193, 194, 227
Buonvisa, 72–73, 110 ns63, 64
Burgundy, ducal family of, 383 n28
Busyness of hearers, 265, 271, 303

Caleruega, Spain, 53, 426 n14
Campo Santo, Milan, 410–11
Cantors, 207
Canon lawyers, 130
Canaanite woman, 95
Capellanus, Andreas, 231 n39
Captives, Dominic and, 55
Casseneuil, 389
Castile, King of, 53
Cathala, Raymund, 390, 425 n4
Catharists, *See* Albigensians
Catherine, Dame, 414–16
Catherine of Siena, St., 432
Cato, 338
Cavaers, Dame, 230 n39
Cecilia, Bl., 98, 119 n173, 391–93, 398,
  473
Censures, ecclesiastical, 314
Cernai, Pierre de Vaux, 104 n5, 473
Chaperonage of women religious, 328
Chaplains for women religious, 328–29
Charitable works, 340–43; Congregation
  of St. Dominic, 433–34; corporal and
  spiritual compared, 257; necessity of,
  306–7; women and, 331
Charity; Humbert of Romans on, 198,
  222, 235, 235, 335, 344; Jordan of
  Saxony on, 124, 407; Kilwardy on, 150,
  151, 160 n118, 161 n133
Chastity; Augustine on, 317; Dominic's
  example, 59; Reginald, Bl., 57
Chatter, 299–301
Chiaravalle della Columba, Cistercian
  abbey of, 67, 109 n49
Children of God, 175–76
*Christian Teaching, On*, 252, 271
Chrysostom, *See* John Chrysostom, St.

495

# INDEX

# INDEX

Fire, 63, 64; symbolic, 148
Flattery, 312
Food, spiritual, 173–74, 349
Forgiveness, 347
*Forma Orandi, De*, 117 n143
*Formation of Preachers, On the*, 181–82;
   sermon outlines, 326–63; text, 183–325
Fornication, 353, 361
Fortune telling, 331
Fourth Lateran Council, 55, 73, 109 n 51
Francis of Assisi, St., 211 n47
Franciscans, 133, 134, 136; austerity, 150,
   323 n53; Dominicans and, 133, 149–52,
   159 n116, 160 na 117–22, 161 ns
   124–29, 468; shoes, 323 n53
Fraternity of St. Mary of Mercy, 436–50;
   accounting, 442; admission procedure,
   442–43; clerical members, 443–44;
   councillors, 439, 441; directors, 438,
   439, 440; meetings, 440, 444, 445,
   446–47, 448; membership, 437, 439–40,
   442–43, 444–46; name, 437; ordinances,
   change in, 450; prior, 438–39; terms of
   office, 441; women, 444
Frederick II, 114 n90
Free will, knowledge and, 185
Friars, *See* Dominicans; Franciscans
Friars Minor, *See* Franciscans
Frivolity, 292
Frogs, symbolism of, 343–44
Frugierio of Pennabilli, 83–85, 114 n96
Funerals of confraternity members, 434
Fulk of Marseilles, Bl., 74, 88–89, 105 n7,
   111 n70, 115 n 112, 389

Galiana the Prioress, 404, 405, 427 n33
Galliciani, Oderico, 77
Gaudio, Bro., 391, 425 n6
General Chapters, Cistercian, 87
General Chapters, Dominican; Bologna,
   66, 77–78, 128, 398; Paris, 399; sermon
   outline for, 333–36
General Councils of the Church, 55, 73,
   109 n51
Gentleness, 292–93
Genuflections, 96, 97
Gerald de Frachet, *See* de Frachet, Gerald

Gerard, Bro., 401, 406
Germanus, Bishop of Capua, 379
Germany, nuns in, 387, 388
Gertrude of Colmar, 421–24
*Gift of Fear, The*, 373–81
Gilbertines, 387
Gluttony, 333, 334
God, *See* individual Persons of Trinity
*Golden Legend*, 51
Golden rose, 349–50
Good works, *See* Charitable works
Gospel, preaching of, *See* Evangelism
Gossip, 299, 301
Grace of preaching, 182, 195, 203–4, 205,
   256; lack of, 270; types of, 375, 382 n10
Grandmont, Order of, 74, 111 n74
Gratitude, women religious and, 329
Great Alleluia, 113 n89
Gregory I (Pope), St., 208; anecdotes and,
   373, 374, 375, 376; charitable works,
   on, 344; conversation of preacher, on,
   298, 300; *Designavit*, 200, 296–97;
   *Dialogues*, 301–2, 377, 378–79; failure
   to preach, 240, 241; faults of preachers,
   on, 215, 234, 236, 237, 287, 292;
   frequency of preaching, on, 248, 250;
   lack of preaching, on, 270, 296–97;
   *Letters*, 220, 338; *Morals on Job*, 225;
   nature of preaching, on, 186, 191, 196,
   220, 225, 239, 251, 253, 257, 285;
   necessity of preaching, on, 187, 190,
   287; *Pastoral Rule*, 218, 222, 242, 246,
   307–8, 309–10, 311; prayer, on, 94, 166,
   352; premature preaching, on, 223,
   238, 239; results of preaching, on, 270,
   296–97; scripture, on, 271, 358, 359;
   temporal affairs and preaching, on,
   194–95, 221
Gregory IX (Pope), 109 n51, 129–30, 155
   n36; Diana d'Andalò and, 398, 399;
   Dominic and, 59, 67, 68–69, 76, 85
Gregory Nazianzen, St., 246
Guala of Brescia, Bl., 59, 106 n23, 395,
   396, 397, 398
Guardianships, 311
Gui, Bernard, Bishop of Lodève, 90,
   139–40, 390, 476

# INDEX

Guzman, Domingo, *See* Dominic, St.
Guzman, Felix, 53
Guzman, Joan, 53
Gyrovagues, 134, 156 n50

Habits, sin and, 361
Habits, religious, 141; Dominican,
reception of, 108 n45, 131, 155 n40
Hardness of heart, ineffective preaching
and, 270–71
Harlots, *See* Prostitutes
Hebrew studies, 121
Hell, 187, 188
Heretics; Albigensians, *See* Albigensians;
burning of, 81, 114 n90; charitable
works of, 306; Dominic and, 54, 55, 75,
104 n6; educational facilities, 389;
Inquisition and, 114 n90; Law of God
and, 64, 359; *perfecti*, 306; Saracens,
263, 264, 268 n7, 338; travel by, 286;
worldliness of clergy and, 86, 87–88
Hilary, St., 94
History, knowledge of, 217
*History of Charlemagne,* 380
*History of the English* (Bede), 374
Holy Spirit; apostles and, 148; preaching
and, 196, 204, 217, 218, 235, 270, 276,
277; scripture and, 185, 319
*Homilies on Matthew* (Chrysostom), 299
Honorius III (Pope), 55, 398; women and,
229 n39
Honors given to preachers, 197–98
Hope, preaching and, 187, 188, 348–49
Horace, 219
Horseback travel, 288, 321 n13
Hospitallers, Order of, 57
Hosts, preachers and their, 304–6
Hugh of St. Cher, 477
Humans, nature of, 185
Humbert of Romans, 120; anecdotes,
373–76; *Commentary on the Prologue to
the Constitutions,* 141–45; *Formation of
Preachers, On the,* 181–82, 183–325;
Margaret of Hungary and, 388;
sermon outlines, 181, 326–63; suffrages
for dead, on, 376–81; women and,
229–31 n39, 388

Humiliati, 114 n95
Humility; false, 242; Jordan of Saxony
on, 407; novices and, 465; poverty and,
151–52; prayer and, 95, 354; preaching
and, 275
Hungary, 106 n13, 388
Hunters, preachers as, 191, 193

Idleness, 340–43
Ignorance; advice resulting from, 312;
culpable, 265
Incense, symbolism of, 166
Individual exhortation, *See* Advice
Infidels, *See* Pagans; Saracens
Ingratitude toward hosts, 305
Innocent III (Pope), 55, 73, 109 n51, 208;
Albigensians and, 115 n100; Diego of
Osma and, 86
Innocent IV (Pope), 136, 157 ns 63, 65
Inquisition, medieval, 114 n90
Instruction, *See* Advice; Preaching
Intercession for others, 353; dead, 376–81,
434, 443, 444, 445, 447, 448
Investigations, 310
Isaiah, 187, 243
Isidore, St., 94, 255, 298, 299, 301, 376
Islam, *See* Saracens

Jacques de Vitry, *See* de Vitry, Jacques
James, St., 236, 278, 318
James of San Galgano, 106 n7, 138, 157
n71
James of Voragine, 51
Jeremiah, 278, 292, 307, 318, 337, 377
Jerome, St., 205, 208, 216, 217, 222, 342,
359, 376
Jesus; advice and, 295–96, 311–12;
charitable works, 306; errors
concerning, 350; exemplar, as, 149,
293; golden rose symbolizing, 349–50;
hosts of, 304, 305; Institution of
Eucharist, 258–59; Mary and, 357;
moneychangers and, 335; Mystical
body of 276; passion, 342–43; prayer
of, 94, 96, 99, 166, 259; preaching by,
184, 258–59; scripture and, 319;
travels, 286; women and, 330, 357

# INDEX

# INDEX

# INDEX

Ostia, Ugolino Cardinal Bishop of, *See* Gregory IX (Pope)

Our Father, 166, 169, 170–74

Ox, symbolism of, 146, 147

Pagans, 84, 105 n13, 187–88, 275

Palmiero of Campagnola, 85

Papal bulls; Dominican property, on, 161 n129; mendicants, on, 136, 157 n65

Papal legates, 104 n5, 115 n100

Paphnutius, St., 362

Parables, 349, 374

Paris, Reginald in, 56, 57

Paschasius, 378–79

*Pastoral Rule* (Gregory), 218, 222, 242, 246, 307–8, 309–10, 311

Patriotism, 338

Paul, St.; charitable works, 306; conduct as model, 293–94, 305, 306, 334, 438; prayer, 94, 252, 318; preaching and, 134, 183, 192, 196, 197, 200, 248, 252, 259; private instruction, 296, 312; secular affairs and, 309, 310; warfare, spiritual, 346, 360

Paul (disciple of Anthony), 362

Paul of Hungary, 396, 426 n15

Paul of Venice, 82–83, 114 n92, 137, 157 n67

Peace of mind, preaching and, 251

Peddlers, 193, 194

Pelagia St., 361, 362

Pelagias, *See* Pelagia, St., 362

Penance, 341, 348; lenient, 313; souls in purgatory for, 379

Penance, Order of, 432

Pentecost associations, 350, 368 n100

Pentateuch, 367 n92

Peraldus, William, 118 n143, 121, 481; prayer, on, 94, 165–76

*Perfecti*, 306

Permission to preach, 467–68

Perseverance, prayer and, 354

Peter, Bro., 411

Peter, 186, 200, 287, 294, 297; advice and, 311

Peter Martyr, St., *See* Peter of Verona, St.

Peter of Aubenas, 138–39

Peter of Castelnau, 86, 115 n100

Peter of Cluny, 377, 378

Peter of Rheims, Bishop of Agen, 146–48, 481

Peter of Verona, St. (Peter Martyr), 139, 158 n77, 410–11

Petra, Donna, 411

Peyraut, *See* Peraldus, William

Pharetra, 117 n141

Physical discipline, *See* Discipline, physical

Pierre de Vaux Cernai, 87

Pilgrims, 98, 367 n84

Podestà of Bologna, *See* Visconti, Uberto

Political activities, 311

Poor men of Lyon (Waldensians), 138

Popes: Gregory I, *See* Gregory I (Pope), St.; Gregory IX, *See* Gregory IX (Pope); Honorius III, 55, 229 n39, 398; Innocent III, *See* Innocent III (Pope); Innocent IV, 136, 157 ns63, 65; Peter, *See* Peter

Porto, Bishop of, 58

Porto, Cardinal of (Conrad of Urach), 62

Porto Legnano Church, 82

Positive law, *See* Law

Postures of prayer, 94–103

Poverty; Dominic and, 71, 74, 80, 81, 112 n80; Dominican and Franciscan compared, 150–51, 160 ns122–25; heretics attracted by, 54; Jordan of Saxony on, 128, 406; preachers and, 215–16, 220, 222, 243, 256; primitive, 112 n80; Thomas of Cantimpré on, 133–36; uniformity and, 143

Praemonstratensians; Constitutions, 105 n9, 430 n104; Rule, 455, 456–65; women, 229–31 n39

Prayer; Augustine on, 94, 166, 170, 171, 172, 173, 174–75, 252, 354; Bernard of Clairvaux on, 94, 170, 171, 172, 293; Congregation of St. Dominic, 434; dead, for, 376–81, 434, 443, 444, 445, 447, 448; Dominic and, 66, 67, 68, 70, 71, 72, 73, 76, 78, 80, 82, 84, 86–91,

# INDEX

Theodoric, Archbishop of Ravenna, 81, 92, 114 n91

Theologians, 130

Theology, scripture as, 185

Theudas, 250

Thomas Agni of Lentini, *See* Agni of Lentini, Thomas

Thomas (prior of Santa Maria di Reno), 85

Thomas Aquinas, St., 51, 120, 282 n9, 482; prayer, on, 94; resurrection gifts, on, 177

Thomas of Cantimpré, 107 n27, 140, 268 n8, 483; Boniface and, 155 n30; Jordan of Saxony and, 132; Defense of the Mendicants, 133–36

Thomas of Ireland, 117 n141

Thomas of York, 161 n125

Thomas the Apostle, St., 287

Timothy, St., 310, 312

Tobit, 298

Toil; concept of, 61, 62; dangers of, 62; work distinguished from, 61

Tongues, gift of, 196

Toulouse, 53, 55; Fulk of Marseilles as bishop of, 55, 74; Proville convent, 328, 388, 389–90

Tournaments, sermons at, 336–39

Travel; excessive, 288–90; faults connected with, 287–89; hardship, as, 256; preaching and, 256–57, 284–90; regulations for, 467; requirements, 289–90

*Treatise on Jobs in the Order* (Humbert), 317

Try (Norse war god), 367n75

Tuesdays, sermon outline for, 343–47

Ugolino, Cardinal Bishop of Ostia, *See* Gregory IX (Pope)

Ulrich, Bro., 411

Understanding, necessity for preaching, 273

Uniformity of Observance, 141

Unity of heart, uniformity and, 144

Universities, Dominicans teaching in, 56, 120

Unterlinden, Sisters of, 388, 417–24

Usefulness as Dominican goal, 150, 160 n18

Usury, 81

Vengeance, 347, 352

*Venia* (ritual prostration), 79, 113 n85, 465, 466

Ventura of Verona, Bro., 66–69, 108 n43, 396, 397

Vercelli, University of, 131

Vestments, quality of, 71, 77

Victorinus, 375, 382 n9

Vigils, 60, 256, 394; Agnes of Ochsenstein, 418; Gertrude of Colmar, 421; Margaret of Hungary, 412, 415; study, 107 n27

Vincent, St., 139

Vincent of Beauvais, 117 n143

*Virginity, On* (Ambrose), 356

Virtue; practice as bread, 174; preaching, for, 215

Visconti, Uberto (Podestà of Bologna), 69, 70–71, 73, 81, 109 n57

Visions; Agnes of Ochsenstein, 419–20; Gertrude of Colmar, 422–23

Visitations, 310

Voice required for preaching, 219

Vows, 314

Waldensians, 138

Walter of Meysenburg, 156–57 n56

Walter of Trier, 135

Weeping in prayer, 170–71

Wickedness, *See* Evil

Will, reason and, 346–47

Will executors, 311

William, Cardinal Bishop of Sabina, 92, 117 n135

William of Auxerre, 378

William of Monferrato, 69–71, 109 n58, 110 n59

Window, apostolate of the, 417

Women; behavior appropriate to, 330–32; cloister of male Dominicans, exclusion from, 459; confessions of,

# Other Volumes in this Series